The subject of rural development, as distinct from agricultural development, is explored in this book by an international and distinguished group of professionals in various fields. It is the first time that the many specific aspects of contemporary rural development have been brought together in one volume. Moreover, each subject is discussed in two contexts: that of the advanced countries and that of the developing ones, an arrangement which may shed some light on the questions of how and to what extent the experience of one can influence the other.

The importance of rural development for developing countries cannot be underestimated. The fact that the majority of the labor force in these countries is engaged in food production on a subsistence level leaves little doubt that rural development is the cornerstone of national growth. Not only does this book elucidate the many problems facing agricultural countries, but it hopes to provide guidelines for their possible solutions.

Chapters in the first part of the book are organized under the headings: Rural Development — Policies and Planning; Agriculture and Industry; Rural-Urban Relationship; The Farm Unit; Agrarian Reform and Cooperative Institutions; Extension Services; and Implementation of Rural Development. The remainder of the book consists of eight case studies of agricultural and urban development in the United States, The Netherlands, Italy, Israel, Greece, Mexico, the Sudan, and Ceylon.

Raanan Weitz is a member of the World Zionist Organization and Head of the Settlement Study Centre, Rehovot, Israel.

Rural
Development
in a Changing
World

The MIT Press

Cambridge,
Massachusetts, and
London, England

Rural Development in a Changing World

edited by
Raanan Weitz

with the assistance of
Yehuda H. Landau

The MIT Press wishes to acknowledge with thanks the collaboration of the Settlement Study Centre, Rehovot, Israel, in the publication of this volume.

Rural
Development
in a Changing
World

Toward a New Approach: Introduction and Conclusions

Raanan Weitz

Rural development has recently become a subject of major concern in the search for a general theory of economic growth and human development. This, despite the fact that the agricultural sector had been relegated to the sidelines and the rural areas had been disregarded in the face of the spectacular expansion of the big cities. The principles of rural development are now being investigated with a new interest, especially by those seeking a strategy capable of expediting the process of development in the undeveloped countries. This has resulted from a recognition of certain specific factors. It seems that the developing nations are not developing as fast as they should, and the gap between them and the wealthy nations is growing instead of diminishing. The last report, in 1969, of the Organization for Economic Cooperation and Development (OECD) in Paris includes a table showing the growth of the per capita product for all the developing nations (apart from those within the Communist bloc), that is, for about two-thirds of mankind. It is clear from this table that for the years 1960-1965, the growth was 2.4 percent; for 1966, 2.3 percent; for 1967, 2.8 percent; for 1968, 2.6 percent; and for the whole period from 1960 to 1968 it averaged 2.5 percent. If we bear in mind the fact that the level of the per capita product in most of these countries is approximately $100 per year, it is clear that such a rate of increase affords no likelihood of any reduction in the gap in the foreseeable future.

One of the reasons for this phenomenon is the rapid rate of population growth. According to the same report, between 1960 and 1965 the average annual population growth in these countries was 2.5 percent, a rate of increase which is being maintained to this day. Yet this reason is not sufficient to explain the phenomenon. The main reason lies in the failure of the system of production in such countries to achieve the accelerated growth which was anticipated when a considerable proportion of the colonial peoples were granted independence. At that time the wealthy nations of the world began to provide technical and financial assistance to ensure the growth of the production system at an ever increasing rate. These hopes have not been realized.

The gap is evident not only in the general standard of living, but particularly in the level of nutrition. According to the calculations of

Thorkil Kristensen, the Secretary-General of OECD, the per capita production of food in 1960 in the developing countries reached $35 as compared with $120 in the developed countries. He predicts that if the level of food production continues at its present rate there will not only be no change in the situation in the 1980s, but possibly not even by the end of the present century. According to his forecast, with the growth of population in the developing nations, the number of hungry people will increase to a degree beyond anything we have imagined.

Despite encouraging signs, which have become evident recently, of improvements due to the spread of better quality varieties of wheat, maize, and rice, leading to the beginnings of the so-called "Green Revolution," it is inconceivable that this factor alone can change the general trend of development which has prevailed thus far.

It is also becoming increasingly apparent that the development strategy adopted by most of the developing countries in the last twenty years does not lead to any solution of these problems. Gone is the faith, the almost blind faith, in a rapid industrialization capable of absorbing the unemployed or underemployed surplus population of the rural areas and of thus creating the possibility of a more effective distribution and exploitation of the means of agricultural production. The unquestioning imitation of methods of development practiced today in the developed countries, the uncritical transfer of techniques created for the technological, cultural, and organizational conditions of the industrialized countries to the situation prevailing in the backward countries, has not produced the desired results. In fact, it is these very methods which have led to the rapid growth of a few big cities or even just one city where the main effort toward industrial development has been concentrated, without any appreciable influence beyond the city limits. The result has been the birth in the world of that cancerous condition known as "dualism," with two separate social and economic systems developing within a single nation, one in the big city and the other in the rest of the country. There can be no salvation as long as these two totally unintegrated systems fail to interact.

However, it is clear that the developing nations need not follow precisely the same path of historical development taken by the developed countries. Technological developments and scientific discoveries—particularly in the field of biology—made since the beginning of the first Industrial Revolution can provide the developing nations with powerful tools and offer them short cuts which the developed nations were unable to take.

If, then, it is agreed that imitation of the methods and processes of development found today in the wealthy countries is ineffective, and that we cannot infer from the history of those countries what may be possible today, then we are forced into the inescapable conclusion that new methods and a completely new strategy must be sought for the process of economic growth and the development of society.

A further factor underlying the present interest in research of the problems of rural development is the assumption, heard lately with increasing frequency, that a prior condition for any development is an accelerated development of the agricultural sector, that is, an increase in scope and efficiency of agricultural production. This assumption has led many to reconsider the hierarchy of priorities in development programs and to place an ever increasing emphasis on the development of agriculture and the rural regions. Economic growth in the early stages of the process of development apparently depends far more than we realized in the past on the possibilities latent in the agricultural sector. The development of other sectors must be more closely integrated, more directly linked with what takes place in agriculture.

These, then, are the reasons which have brought about an increase in the importance ascribed to the development of agriculture and the rural areas.

The facts described have far-reaching implications not only for the fate of the majority of mankind, which is struggling for subsistence, but also for the future of the developed nations. Opinions have recently been voiced to the effect that extending technical and financial assistance to poor nations is like pouring water into a bottomless pit. "Better let them find their own way out of the morass." Such opinions have begun to affect the scope of technical and financial assistance, which shows signs of a tendency to decrease. If this tendency continues, it is likely to have an adverse influence on international relations toward the end of the century. And these may be decisive factors in the development of human history at the beginning of the next century. The problem under discussion has far-reaching implications and is of justifiable concern to policy-makers and experts involved in the problems of development in the world today.

Aim and Structure of the Present Volume

The collection of studies presented in this book is designed to throw light on a number of central problems in rural development. It does not claim to cover them all. The editor has chosen a number of topics which he believes to be of central importance in the study of rural development and about which there exist differences of opinion and some uncertainty among those concerned with the implementation of development plans. All the studies included in this volume have been specially written for it in accordance with a preconceived plan prepared by the editor. The topics discussed have been analyzed with reference both to the developed and to the developing countries, so that the reader may make the comparison and draw his own conclusions. This introduction is intended merely to draw attention to the problems and to give anyone interested in them food for thought.

The problems of rural development included in this book have been described and analyzed by the contributors in two ways, reflected in the two parts of the book. In the first part have been included those studies which deal with a single topic from various points of view. The first part has therefore been called Concepts and Approaches. The studies have been arranged in groups which are ordered progressively from the general to the particular, from macroproblems to micro-problems, from problems of national policy and planning to problems of application and implementation.

In the second part actual case studies of rural development in general and agricultural development in particular have been described and analyzed. These case studies relate to various countries, representing all the stages of development, from an urban, industrialized economy in a "modern" society with a high degree of occupational, geographic, and social mobility to an agricultural subsistence economy with a tradi-tional society based upon a way of life and a set of values which have been handed on from generation to generation since time immemorial.

The examples have also been chosen with another criterion in view. We wished to include examples of rural development at both the national and the regional level, so that both macroproblems and micro-problems would be represented. Accordingly, this book contains ex-amples describing the process of development in an entire country (the United States, Italy, Mexico, Ceylon) as well as descriptions of the pro-cess of development in a specific region (Holland, Israel, Greece, Sudan). In this latter group, we have included descriptions of develop-ment projects in rural areas which were planned and carried out from the start with the deliberate aim of accelerating the process of rural development. The intention throughout has been to bring the light of experience to bear on developments, trends, concepts, and approaches within the entire sphere of policy-making, planning, and implementation.

The editor hopes that this volume will be a contribution to the development of a comprehensive approach to the growth of agriculture and the development of rural areas. His thanks are due to all the contributors for their readiness to further this aim; special thanks must go to Yehuda H. Landau for his assistance in the drafting and editing of the book. As he has already pointed out, the editor intended in this introduction only to clarify a number of central points, without analyzing or drawing any conclusions from the rich variety of material which the writers have contributed from their experience and their learning. He leaves this task to the reader, or more precisely, to the investigator and the student engaged in this most fascinating field of study.

Agricultural Development Has Its Own Special Characteristics

The development of agriculture has its own unique characteristics which differentiate it from the development of other sectors of the economy.

The first and in several important respects the most significant characteristic derives from the organization of the basic unit of production. The traditional unit of production in agriculture—in both the developed and the developing countries—has been and remains the family farm. The large managed farm is a comparatively recent phenomenon. As regards the organization of agricultural production, therefore, two basic patterns can be discerned. In the family farm, the roles of entrepreneur, of manager of production, of farm technologist responsible for methods of work and efficiency, and of farm worker are all united in a single individual or a single family. The large managed farm takes a number of different forms. There are the large commercial farms, or plantations, which employ hired labor; and there are the large farms based on varying degrees of collective ownership of workers, such as the Soviet kolkhoz, the collective ejido in Mexico, and the Israeli kibbutz.

One of the central problems for all those concerned with rural development is the extent to which each of these two patterns is appropriate for the main aim of development—the increase of agricultural production. Since the family farm undoubtedly satisfies the almost instinctive desires of both the modern farmer and the traditional peasant, the question is frequently asked in another way: Can the family farm compete with the large managed farm, especially in the light of the needs of accelerated agricultural development under the conditions prevailing in the developing countries? Section IV, containing four studies by Hermann Priebe, A. K. Constandse, Henri Mendras, and Michel Cépède (Chapters 12, 13, 14, and 15), deals especially with this central-problem. In addition to these studies, which are directly concerned with the problem, interesting applications can be found in other studies, such as those by Shlomo Eckstein (Chapter 19) and Jack M. Potter (Chapter 22); and almost all the case studies in Part Two have some relevance to the topic.

In most countries, developed or backward, the major part of agricultural production comes from family farms. Agricultural production depends on a tremendous number of individual producers; therein lies the uniqueness of agriculture. And it is this uniqueness which must be taken into consideration in any development plan.

The second distinguishing characteristic of agriculture derives from the first. The process of agricultural production is intimately bound up with the way of life of the many producers and with the organization of the rural communities. For these millions, agriculture is not merely an occupation or a source of income, but a way of life. This characteristic of agriculture becomes even more pronounced as we travel a greater "developmental distance" from modern society, urban in spirit and preoccupied with commerce, and as we approach nearer to the traditional society composed mainly of farmers and peasants who spend long hours tilling the soil to which they are inextricably tied. Any change in methods of work, any change in methods of production must involve a change in the peasants' way of life. And any change—biological or technological, administrative or organizational—must be adapted not only to the natural and economic conditions prevailing, but also to the patterns of life and the system of values of the mass of producers. In order to accept the change, these producers must not only understand it but also desire it and be capable of carrying it out.

It is this feature which dictates several aspects of the way rural development should be planned and implemented. A number of studies are concerned with this most important problem, not merely drawing attention to it but offering specific approaches. We would particularly mention the studies of Rainer Schickele, Erich H. Jacoby, Jack M. Potter, and Solon Barraclough (Chapters 3, 17, 22, and 23) and also the descriptions by Yehuda H. Landau and Avshalom Rokach, Arthur Gaitskell, and Asoka B. Andarawewa (Chapters 28, 31, and 32). There are some interesting conclusions to be drawn from their work.

The Unit of Agricultural Production and the National Economy

An examination of the case studies presented in this volume suggests a number of principles concerning the relationship between the structure of the unit of agricultural production and the structure of the national economy. Changes in the individual farm are closely correlated with changes in the national economic system. In the early stages of development it is difficult to determine which of these two variables has more influence upon the other, but there certainly seems to be a mutual relationship between the structure of the individual farm and that of the national economy. These relationships described principally in the studies of Peter Dorner, Charles A. P. Takes, Giuseppe Barbero, and Yehuda H. Landau and Avshalom Rokach, (Chapters 25-28) are also discussed indirectly in the works of Marion Clawson and Mario Bandini (Chapters 1 and 2).

The structure of the individual farm takes on different forms in a continuous process of change, with the growth and development of the national economy. Although these changes are gradual and the transitions slight and drawn out, it is nonetheless possible to distinguish two main stages during the process. The first stage is the emergence from subsistence farming, as described in the work of Gaitskell and of Andarawewa, and the transition to mixed farming as described by Landau and Rokach, and by Abraham Rozenman and G. N. Sykianakis (Chapter 29). The second stage comes with the transition to specialized farming as described by Hermann Priebe, A. K. Constandse (Chapters 12 and 13), Dorner, and Takes.

Of these two stages, the first is especially interesting and clearly the most important. It may be defined as the transition from subsistence farming to commercial farming, and it is the indication of the beginning of the growth process. Perhaps for this reason it also constitutes the toughest obstacle in the long path of the development of the agricultural unit. This transition involves a radical change in a number of basic concepts and is linked to the development of the supporting system, without which no such change can possibly be implemented.

Subsistence farming is characterized by one staple crop designed to meet the needs of the farmer's family, and a number of auxiliary crops which serve mainly to vary the diet. The staple crop varies from country to country—wheat and barley in the Middle East, rice in the Far East, maize in South America, and cassava and other crops in Africa—but the character of subsistence farming is invariable. The produce is meant mainly for home consumption. The technology used by the farmer is traditional, a product of the wisdom of the ages, and he knows exactly how to use it. In the nature of things, the work schedule is unbalanced since it is determined mainly by the needs of the staple crop, with seasons of overemployment, especially during sowing and harvesting, alternating with seasons of underemployment. Cash expenses for running the farm are extremely small; this circumstance leads to an almost complete identity between the total value of farm produce and the income of the farmer. Income is largely identified with consumption, and only small surpluses are available for marketing.

The transition to mixed farming is gradual and begins with the introduction of crops which are primarily intended for marketing, and with the increase of livestock production beyond the consumptive capacity of the farmer's family. The fundamental change which begins with this transition is the balancing of the work schedule. As a result of the changes in the work schedule, seasonal unemployment, or concealed unemployment, disappears; and human labor, the most important production factor at this stage of development, serves as the principal stimulus to increased output.

Those studies dealing with the problems of the family farm describe these transitions indirectly, and show that certain laws are, in fact, operative in the changes which the individual farm undergoes as it climbs the ladder of development from subsistence farm to specialized farming. Some of the studies, such as those of Priebe and Constandse, describe the structure of the family farm when it has reached the stage of specialization, and even try to penetrate the mists of the future and predict a period of "superspecialization." Here there is a division of opinion. Whereas Constandse is not convinced that the family farm can cope with the changes which this period may bring, Priebe is sure that it can. This is one of the most interesting questions that still have no clear answer. Undoubtedly it is worth further study, especially by the planners whose imagination, based on experience, can serve as an analytical tool in any attempt to describe the future. This, of course, is a problem of interest mainly to the developed countries.

Are the stages of development we have described essential? Is the individual subsistence farm obliged to pass through the intermediate stage of mixed farming? It would seem for several reasons that the answer to this question must be in the affirmative. First, this is so because of the relationship between labor and capital. The individual farm cannot make the leap from a labor-intensive to a capital-intensive economy without passing through the intermediate stages during which the basis for this transition is laid. Second, the level of technological, organizational, and administrative know-how required involves putting into operation research and training facilities. There are no short cuts to such services, which must be built up gradually, tier upon tier. Third, the supporting system and the infrastructure can come into existence only gradually, both because of the capital investment that they require and because of the need for training those engaged in supplying services and in the related processes of industrialization. Whereas subsistence farming hardly needs a supporting system at all, specialized farming is quite impossible without a highly developed system rich in capital and know-how. Finally, the structure and absorptive capacity of the local market must also be taken into consideration. This, too, changes gradually, only slowly becoming capable of absorbing more expensive agricultural products, thus enabling the farmer to introduce into his farm crops which will yield a higher price, from vegetables and fruit to animal protein such as eggs, milk, and meat.

The pattern of transformations which the individual farm must undergo is linked to the structure of the national economy; and for every stage in the development of the national economy, there is a corresponding stage in the structure of the individual farm. No quantitative correlation has so far been established between these two variables. This is an important problem which demands further study and which could serve as an important guide and indication to all those practically engaged in planning the development of rural areas in various countries whose national economies are at different stages of development. The work of Barbero, which analyzes the part played by agriculture in the national economic system of Italy at different stages of development, may be particularly helpful to anyone in search of a solution to this key problem.

The Development of Agriculture Depends on a Complex Institutional System

The development of agriculture—that is, an increase in agricultural production—depends primarily on the establishment of a most complex system of institutional structures which influence and even determine the process. This volume discusses a number of problems connected with changes in these institutional structures which we shall survey briefly.

Let us begin with the system of institutions which determines the relationship between man and his land. This system is important under all conditions, both in the developed and in the developing countries. But in the latter its importance is infinitely greater. A precondition for the kind of relations between man and his land that can further development is the implementation of land reform in such a way that a system of institutional relationships can be established suitable for the needs of economic growth and rural development. Land reform is a central and most painful problem in the history of rural development, as described, for example, in the studies of V. M. Dandekar, Erich H. Jacoby, Shlomo Eckstein, and Edmundo Flores (Chapters 16, 17, 19, and 30). Let us not forget that in many countries land ownership bestows a certain status as well as a means of existence. In such cases most of the land, amounting at times to 70 percent and even more of all land in the country, is in the hands of a small number of landowners, who have a decisive influence on government. The first obstacle in the way of development is thus the problem of handing the land over to those who work it. This obstacle is also a political and governmental problem of first importance. It is no wonder that different regimes, differing in many ways, are alike primarily in their attitude to this problem.

At any event, the generally accepted opinion—represented by a number of studies included in this volume—declares that land reform is a precondition for any rural development. It should be pointed out that the concept of land reform refers not only to the division of large areas of land into smaller units, but also to the consolidation of land, that is, to the reparcellation of existing holdings where these consist of a large number of tiny plots, split up and widely dispersed. This is necessary not only in the developing but frequently in the most highly developed nations. These problems are discussed in several places, particularly in the work of Mario Bandini, Jac. P. Thijsse, Charles A. P. Takes, and Abraham Rozenman and G. N. Sykianakis (Chapters 2, 10, 26, and 29).

Although land reform is a precondition of all rural development, it is by no means enough in itself. Land reform must be accompanied by coordinated treatment of the whole institutional system of rural development, especially by the establishment and operation of an appropriate supporting system. Land reform, which does not at the same time take account of the need to build and maintain systems of credit, marketing, and supply, as well as training, educational, medical, and entertainment facilities, will not lead to the desired results. Several studies deal with this topic, such as those of Jacoby, Eckstein, and Francis C. and Kerry J. Byrnes (Chapter 21).

Land reform takes on a new dimension and greater depth of meaning when it becomes an inseparable part of the struggle for an equitable distribution of land and thus for an equitable distribution of income. Reform must be comprehensive; it must concern itself with building those institutions which accompany agricultural development and expedite it. The experience of the past in this respect is of enormous importance for all those concerned with the problems of rural development. This point of view finds expression in the case studies of Israel presented by Yehuda H. Landau and Avshalom Rokach (Chapter 28), of Crete by Rozenman and Sykianakis, of Mexico by Flores, and—a particularly clear example—of the development of the Gezira in the Sudan as revealed in the work of Arthur Gaitskell (Chapter 31).

The second stage in building an institutional framework is the organization of the rural community. This organization must be capable of responding to all the demands which may arise during the course of development. The family farm can be competitive only if it is one link in a communal and supercommunal organization capable of providing the individual with the services of a supporting system appropriate to each stage. This system can work effectively only if each single unit of agricultural production is ready and able to utilize such services. Hence the special importance of the different forms of organization which the rural community, in other words the village, must be able to call upon in order to absorb the transformations brought about by changes in the process of production.

The organization of the various parts of the supporting system can be based either on cooperative organization or on private enterprise. As far as the efficiency of the services is concerned, both forms are satisfactory. The basic characteristic of the supporting system in the developed countries is its operation through vertical organizations. In the studies of Hermann Priebe, Peter Dorner (Chapters 12 and 25), Takes, and others, the supporting system in these countries is described as being operated partly by private enterprise and partly by farmers' cooperatives.

This is not the case in the developing countries. Apparently the peasant at the beginning of the road to development is incapable of coping alone with the traditional system of services—expecially marketing, supply, and credit—as organized today in the rural regions of these countries. These services are concentrated in private hands both within the village and outside it; and instead of serving as a spur to development they usually act as a hindrance. Those who should be serving production become instead the masters of production, and certainly the lords over the producers. Thus instead of being able to get help from those who should serve him, the peasant becomes their slave. Instead of urging him forward they keep him down. A solution must therefore be found which will join the peasants together in an organization capable of coping with the traditional system of services and even causing it to change.

Traditional society is characterized by the stability of the value system upon which the way of life is based. This way of life is laid down in an unwritten code of rules of behavior which can be called "common wisdom." This wisdom has grown up over countless generations and today is accepted almost unconsciously, without any need of proof, by every member of the society. And this wisdom, these rules of behavior determine the conduct of the individual in the face of anything to which he is not accustomed. The trouble is that this "common wisdom" contains no rules for the organization of the rural community in a way appropriate to the demands of technological change and administrative transformation necessary for the development of agriculture. In this connection, opinion is united that the most efficient solution is the multipurpose communal cooperative. Such cooperation has a decisive role to play, especially in the initial stages of development, as described in the studies of Otto M. Schiller (Chapter 18), Eckstein, Jack M. Potter, and Solon Barraclough (Chapters 22 and 23), and as can be inferred from the descriptions included in a number of case studies in Part Two, especially those of Israel, Mexico, and Ceylon.

The third element in the institutional structure of rural development is the pattern of relations between agriculture and industry. It appears that industrialization of the rural areas is a necessary condition of agricultural development, a fact which emerges quite clearly from the studies of Gabriele Pescatore and Joseph Klatzmann (Chapters 6 and 7). However, it also appears as though the process of industrialization as practiced today in the developed countries is not suitable for the developing countries. Their needs are not served by industrialization at a technological level so high that it requires a relatively large investment to create employment and a complex and expensive infrastructure and service system. One wonders occasionally whether such industrialization is not more likely to lead to a loss rather than a profit. This problem is described in the light of Indian experience by P. D. Malgavkar (Chapter 8).

From the studies dealing with this topic it becomes clear that the system of priorities customary in industrial development must be changed. Instead of large industries concentrated in the big towns, industries must be created which can operate in smaller units, using a less advanced technology and being less capital intensive than those prevailing in the developed countries. Such industries can be located within the rural areas themselves. The work of Malgavkar and others describe the types of industry suitable for such a purpose and their main characteristics.

The analysis of the problem of the relationship between agriculture and industry as depicted in this volume points to the need for a considerable change in the strategy of development hitherto employed by most of the developing nations during the past two decades. Further confirmation of this conclusion can be drawn from the case studies of Giuseppe Barbero (Chapter 27) with respect to the experience of Italy, and of Landau and Rokach with respect to development in Israel. The example of Ceylon in the work of Asoka B. Andarawewa (Chapter 32) can also throw light on the subject under discussion. Apparently a thoughtful reappraisal is needed in order to find practical solutions, different from those which are accepted today by a considerable number of policy-makers and development planners. Such a reappraisal will undoubtedly have its effect on the nature of technical and financial assistance given to the developing countries and also on the direction and content of professional training, at the intermediate and advanced levels.

The fourth element in the pattern is the relationship between town and country, which also has an enormous effect upon rural development. The process of urbanization as it is taking place today in the developed countries is quite unsuitable in many respects to the needs of development in the backward countries. This problem is specifically considered by Bert F. Hoselitz (Chapter 11), and analogies can be drawn with the trends which emerge from the analysis of Demetrius S. Iatridis (Chapter 9) concerning the megalopolis on the northeast coast of the United States. The process of urbanization, which is one of the clearest indicators of geographical and occupational mobility and hence of economic growth in the developed nations, cannot serve the same purpose in the developing countries. There are developing countries where the process of urbanization is proceeding at a similar rate as in developed countries, but unaccompanied by economic development. This gives rise to the concept of "overurbanization," the result not of attraction to the big city but of rejection of the backward village by the peasant. The growth of the large cities in the developing countries has led to an intensification of "dualism" and the creation of slums. These slums have sprung up like mushrooms, without even minimal services and without sufficient opportunities for employment.

From our point of view, the essential disadvantage of the trend of urbanization concentrated in a few large urban centers lies in the fact that rural development is deprived of a factor vital to its implementation. A country town, a small town situated in the heart of the agricultural region, is the base for a number of activities without which agriculture cannot develop. Such a town serves as the base for the operation of the supporting system with all that it entails. Such a town should, and under the proper conditions certainly can, provide the framework for the professional workers needed to operate the system. Similarly, in line with what we have already seen, it must serve as a center for industrial installations and as a focal point for social mobility in the whole region.

A new approach must be sought to the relations between town and country which will be suitable to the conditions existing today in the developing countries and which can provide an impetus to the process of development. Hoselitz in his article indicates possible solutions, analyzes them, and suggests one such new approach. Another possible approach can be found in the description by Landau and Rokach of the Lachish region in Israel, where the central town, Kiryat Gat, has been an important factor in the development of the whole area. This town is an example of the small country towns which should serve as the first level in the urban hierarchy, linking the rural hinterland to the complex of big cities. Some interesting thoughts on this topic are included in the work of Thijsse. This problem is one of the most interesting and important in the whole field of rural development and undoubtedly requires further study and research.

Policy and Planning of Rural Development

A great deal can be learned, relevant to many and various areas, from a study of policies for the development of agriculture in the developed countries. This can be seen in the work of Marion Clawson and Mario Bandini (Chapters 1 and 2) and in the case studies by Peter Dorner, Charles A. P. Takes, and Giuseppe Barbero (Chapters 25-27). Also relevant here are the description and analysis of the developing countries, as revealed in the study of Rainer Schickele (Chapter 3) and in the case studies of Mexico in the work of Edmundo Flores, of the Sudan in the work of Arthur Gaitskell, and of Ceylon in the work of Asoka Andarawewa (Chapters 30-32) as well as in certain sections of other case studies. The editor of this volume has chosen here to touch only on certain general aspects of relevance mainly to the developing countries, that is, to the initial stages of development, when agriculture plays a vital role in the whole developmental process. He has not dealt at all with the problems of agriculture in the advanced stages, which, though of great interest and importance, are quite different from those which precede them.

Let us begin with the central theme: Planning policy must take into consideration the entire range of problems simultaneously, from the level of the individual holding and the village to the national level. The success of development depends first and foremost on the extent to which policy is designed to overcome not just one obstacle, however important it may be—as for example land reform—but rather to deal comprehensively with the whole range of problems.

A special importance is attached to the comprehensive planning of those institutional structures which provide the main impetus to rural development at all stages, but particularly at the first stages of transition to a commerical farm economy. An analogy may be made to a cart without wheels which must move up the slope of a hill. The force required to move the cart without wheels is tremendous and in practice unobtainable. It is necessary, therefore, to put wheels on the cart. A wheel is constructed of an outer rim, a hub, and spokes connecting them. For the wheels to fulfill their function and make it possible to push the cart up the hill, they must be complete, with all their parts, with all their separate components. It is not enough to devote loving care and attention to building only a part, half a wheel or even three-quarters of a wheel. The cart will not move properly unless it is equipped with proper wheels. The success of the process of development depends on the simultaneous operation of all the working parts of which it is composed. This view is quite well known, quite routine. It finds expression in several of the studies included in this volume. Nevertheless there have in practice been few cases where development policy has been deliberately planned along these lines.

A second important principle determines that development policy must concentrate in the early stages of development primarily on the creation of a system of supply, that is, on the development of the system of production. This emphasis will of course change fundamentally in the more advanced stages of development.

It should be remembered that the policy designed to accelerate economic growth and the methods of development planning used in the developed countries have been based largely on analysis of the trends of the past and the significance of these trends for the future. This is possible because they are provided with a system of production of long standing, capable of meeting any change which may take place in the pattern of demand. In fact, the whole economic system operates in a situation of surplus production. This kind of policy makes use primarily of methods and techniques available at the national level, and these are by their nature monetary and fiscal, such as taxes, subsidies, price control, fixed interest rates, and so on. Such an approach is unsuitable for the conditions prevailing in the developing nations. The problem here is not to create and direct demand but to build a suitable expanding system of supply. This is particularly true with respect to the development of agriculture.

Calculating the demand for agricultural produce is a comparatively simple matter, especially in the initial stages of development. Fixing norms and estimating quantities at the national level is also fairly simple. But this is not the problem. The main problem for the policy-maker and the development planner is the creation of conditions which will provide the mass of agricultural producers with an incentive and which will enable them to meet the demands arising from a given policy so that the policy-makers' objectives can be realized. Hence the fundamental difference between a rural agricultural development policy suitable for the developing countries and the kind usual in the developed countries. This difference, which finds expression in most of the studies which deal with this topic, is concisely formulated in the essay by Raanan Weitz included in this collection (Chapter 5).

The rural development policy depicted in the studies in this collection and formulated in these paragraphs cannot be translated into practical reality at the national level alone. This is primarily due to the conditions prevailing in the developing nations. Development plans at the national level can lay down only a general framework for action, but the work which is actually to be carried out throughout the rural regions can be planned only at the intermediate level, between the national level and the level of the individual unit of production. This intermediate level is the level of regional planning.

In this volume regional planning for the developed countries is described in the work of S. Herweijer (Chapter 4), and for conditions prevailing in the developing nations in the study by Weitz. Moreover, the collection includes comprehensive descriptions of a number of regional plans in the studies by Charles A. P. Takes, Yehuda H. Landau and Avshalom Rokach, Abraham Rozenman and G. N. Sykianakis, and Edmundo Flores (Chapters 26, 28-30). These studies describe various approaches to regional planning and various methods which have been used. There are, however, two factors which are common to all these approaches.

First, the regional planner must be the link between the decisions formulated at the level of national development planning and the events that actually take place—or should take place—at the level of the unit of production. It is the task of regional planning to maintain a dialogue between these two end points. Only such a dialogue can turn national planning into a practical instrument for the implementation of development policy and at the same time allow regional planning to carry out its role throughout the rural areas.

Second, regional planning must give practical expression to the patterns of overall planning. It has the complicated, diversified task of integrating the various sectors in a particular region and converting the results of this integration into a physical plan with a set of defined projects ready for implementation. Only in this way can planning become an instrument for implementation, suitable to conditions prevailing in any given place. This is absolutely essential in the rural regions of the developing countries.

This concept of rural development planning in the developing countries acknowledges the fact that institutional structure is of primary importance, and that it is the character, the inclinations, and the way of life of human beings which must serve as a basis for any kind of planning. Therefore the administrative body in charge of planning must be flexible enough to take into account the human factor, with all its twists and turns, and harness it to the development effort.

To summarize, the developing nations need a form of planning policy which is different from that in use today among the developed nations. They need a system which we may call *motivating*, capable of impelling the production process forward and getting it to work in the natural and human conditions which prevail among the developing nations. Adjusting this kind of planning to particular local conditions is especially important for the development of agriculture, in view of the welter of problems of which we have been able to touch on only a few. This is, of course, based on the assumption that the government understands the importance of these matters and gives its backing to the implementation of development plans.

Implementation of Rural Development

Many of the studies deal with various aspects of the implementation of rural planning such as those of Raanan Weitz, Erich H. Jacoby, J. M. A. Penders, Francis and Kerry J. Byrnes, Jack M. Potter, Solon Barraclough, and Yitzchak Abt (Chapters 5, 17, 20-24). There are also case studies which treat this subject, directly or indirectly, such as those of Charles A. P. Takes, Yehuda H. Landau and Avshalom Rokach, Abraham Rozenman and G. N. Sykianakis, Arthur Gaitskell, and Asoka B. Andarawewa (Chapters 26, 28, 29, 31, 32). Of the host of problems involved in this subject there are a few upon which there is a general agreement. We shall try to summarize them briefly.

In the final analysis any development plan of the type we are discussing is designed to improve the lot of the population. The most reliable criterion for judging success of a development plan is the condition of the "little man." This is why the task of government does not end with organizing the implementation of the plan. It must know how to make the local population regard itself as an active partner in the development effort. It must rouse and encourage the private initiative dormant in the population. The administration in charge of development must strike a suitable balance between government intervention in the process of development and the sphere of activity of private initiative. The "right" balance will vary from place to place at a given time, and from time to time at a given place. The higher we climb the ladder of development, the greater the part which private enterprise can and must play in the total development effort of a particular region.

However, there may be two regions at a similar stage of development and yet in one, the authorities are compelled to intervene on a far wider scale and far more energetically. It all depends on the human resources. A region where there are active elements among the population will require relatively little intervention by the government. These active elements may be found among the middle classes, among the ranks of the intelligentsia, among the local village leadership, in the local political parties, and in other places. The government administrators must be able to handle this human problem through direct knowledge of the population, with feeling and intuition even more than by calculation and analysis. In getting the population to cooperate in the development effort, particular importance is attached to the various farmers' movements. The support and cooperation of these movements can sometimes weight the scales and determine the success or failure of development plans, especially when they come in the wake of land reform.

Barraclough, in his study, describes these relationships and also draws concrete conclusions concerning the need to foster but not to over-protect and pamper such settlers' movements. Although his work is largely derived from experience in South America, there are lessons to be learned from it of universal reference.

Many and various and sometimes strange are the social factors moti-vating a population. The systems adopted, the character of the tech-niques, and the ways that are used ought therefore to spring from local conditions, and only after close acquaintance with the particular society in question. This aspect of implementation techniques is the subject in particular of Potter but is also dealt with from various points of view in the works of Otto M. Schiller (Chapter 18), Abt, Gaitskell, and others.

In this connection, mention should be made of the existence of opposition among the rural population to the introduction of agro-technical changes and improvements. The most widely accepted ex-planation of this opposition is that the peasant is stubbornly faithful to the tradition and ways of life which have the support of the local leadership. In the light of much experience, as shown particularly in the work of the Byrneses and as illustrated in several other case studies, it is clear that the source of this opposition lies generally in an inappropriate and faulty organization of the pattern of instruction, and especially in the inadequate and ineffective training of the instructors. It is neces-sary, therefore, to pay particular attention to this problem, and to learn the lessons to be inferred from the experience of the developed coun-tries, as depicted in the work of Penders, though within the conceptual framework and the pattern of conditions prevailing in the developing nations.

The main job of anyone practically engaged in the implementation of rural development is to establish and maintain the various institutions which make up and activate the system. Rural development in general, and the increase of agricultural production in particular, are the result of continuous institutional changes which are interdependent and inter-acting. The interaction of the institutional structures operating in a rural area has its own laws. They tend to work in certain directions, as shown in a considerable number of the studies included in this volume.

The structure of the individual farm and its level of development depend on the stage of development of the economic and overall organ-izational system, and these affect the physical planning of the farm and of the village. It is the latter which to a large extent determines the

form of the institution known as the multipurpose communal cooperative. The establishment and development of this cooperative is greatly
affected by the structure of the supporting system with its various
"institutions." And the latter is directly connected with the complex
and ramified "institution" known as rural reform. The success of rural
reform is also a function of the relations between agriculture and industry and the territorial deployment of town and village. All these are
constantly changing as the development plan progresses, and these
changes themselves affect the process of development. The body in
charge of implementing rural reform must be capable of carrying out
these institutional changes in accordance with the special conditions
prevailing in each area.

The above factors should determine the characteristics of the institutions in charge of implementing rural development, and the principles
of their organization. Several studies deal with this topic, directly or
indirectly. We would mention here only those of Rainer Schickele
(Chapter 3), Jacoby, Potter, and Abt, and the case studies in Part Two
from Greece, Mexico, Sudan, Israel, and Ceylon. From all this material
we will summarize here three main problems only.

The first is the organization of the planning body so that implementation of the regional plan can be carried out within the framework of the
principles of the national development plan. Regional planning of this
kind can be carried out by means of an interdisciplinary team containing experts in the various professions which play a part in the
composition of the plan. As far as defining objectives and realizing
limitations is concerned, this team is guided by the policy-makers at the
level of national planning. Within this pattern—generally established by
a dialogue between the regional team and the authority in charge of
national planning—a comprehensive regional plan is formulated which
takes into consideration the establishment and development of institutional structures, the integration of the different sectors, and the translation of the development plan into concrete projects worked out in
detail, to the point where they can be implemented.

Second, care should be taken to see that there is feedback between
those in charge of implementation and the team engaged in planning.
Experience shows that during implementation various factors, some of
them of major importance, come to the surface which were not taken
into consideration during planning, and which sometimes could not
have been considered before implementation. Thus planning must not
only guide and direct those who carry out the plan; the planners must

follow the implementation of the plan at all stages, and be ready to be influenced by the changing conditions that are revealed as the work is done. In this way planning and implementation become an integrated functional system, dynamic and flexible, able to adjust to the local conditions in each different region, and, moreover, able to modify details to fit the changing conditions that are revealed as the plan is carried out. This principle of the need for permanent mutual interaction will remain theoretical unless given concrete expression in the organizational framework of the institution or institutions in charge of development. A number of studies discuss this important and practical topic in greater detail, such as those of Herweijer, Weitz, and Landau and Rokach.

Third, special emphasis must be laid on the need for constant coordination between the various organizations in charge of the different aspects of implementation. The organizational structure of government departments is vertical, and the implementation of comprehensive development plans is entrusted to various ministries, depending on the different sectors involved. Hence the need for constant coordination at the local and regional level between the activities of the various government departments. It is this need which led to the establishment of regional authorities in their various forms. Some of these authorities, especially where new settlement is involved, do most of the work of implementation, while other authorities coordinate the activities of the various ministries, especially in the development of settled areas. The following studies in this volume discuss the problem of the development authority and describe it in action: Herweijer, Weitz, Landau and Rokach, Rozenman and Sykianakis.

Finally, we must emphasize that this introduction touches only briefly on a few of the problems with which the studies in this volume deal. The choice is, naturally, arbitrary, and has been made by the editor alone, with the help of detailed summaries prepared by Yehuda H. Landau. These summaries were of considerable assistance to the editor in selecting from the host of problems involved in rural development, and particular gratitude is due to Mr. Landau for his help.

Rural development in a changing world undoubtedly holds the key to economic growth in the developing countries. It is a precondition for advance. Without it there is no escape from the abyss formed by the growing gap between those whose material well-being is assured and those threatened by starvation. Rural development is the key to the whole process of development. And the key to rural development lies in the hands of millions of peasants toiling in the fields, bending over the soil that keeps them and their dependents alive. In the final analysis, it is an understanding of their feelings and aspirations which will solve the riddles of economic growth and development. It is my hope that this collection of studies will contribute to a solution.

**Part One
Concepts and
Approaches**

I. Rural
Development—
Policies and
Planning

II. Agriculture
and Industry

III. The Rural-
Urban
Relationship

IV. The Farm
Unit

V. Agrarian Reform
and Cooperative
Institutions

VI. Extension
Services

VII. Implementation
of Rural
Development

Part One   **1. Agriculture**   Marion Clawson

                      in an Advanced

I. Rural   **Economy**

Development—

Policies and

Planning

The role which agriculture can play, and should play, in an economically advanced country has many similarities with the role which agriculture should play in developing countries, as well as some important differences.

Objectives for Agriculture

To summarize very briefly what is developed in the remainder of this article, agriculture in any developed country should (1) provide an ample supply of most agricultural commodities, at reasonable prices; (2) exhibit a high and growing efficiency in the use of inputs of land, labor, and capital; (3) speedily release labor force not required in agriculture, so that it may be productively employed otherwise; and (4) provide an attractive "back country" for recreation and other uses of the urban dwellers.

In a developing country, the first of these objectives, for the ample supply of agricultural commodities, is equally applicable. As to the second objective, a growing efficiency in use of inputs is highly desirable, although a high present efficiency may not exist. In developing countries, agriculture often must provide a major part of the export earnings of the country, whereas in a developed country agricultural exports, while often desirable, may not be as critical for national economic growth. In a developing country, agriculture often must generate much of the capital formation required for economic growth, whereas in a developed country agriculture may provide only a minor part of new capital. In a developing country, agriculture often contains an immense reservoir of labor, often poorly trained; developing agricultural technology can release agricultural labor rapidly if economic growth of other sectors demands it.

For the purposes of this article, it is not necessary to define "developed" and "developing" with precision. In addition to criteria of average income per capita, relative industrialization, and the like which

Marion Clawson—United States. Ph.D., Harvard University; agricultural economist; director, Land Use and Management Program, Resources for the Future, Inc., Washington, D.C.; professional assignments in Israel, Pakistan, India, Chile, and Venezuela.

are often used to make this distinction, economically developed countries invariably have an agriculture which is shrinking in terms of relative employment and often in terms of absolute employment also.

Historical Development of Agriculture Differs among Countries

The historical development of agriculture, in those countries which today have an advanced agriculture, has varied among the countries. In Europe, including Britain, agriculture has been known for many centuries. The area of cropland has expanded modestly in some of these countries in the past few hundred years, as new power sources or new agricultural technology have made arable some lands that previously could not be farmed, but much present-day cropland has been farmed for a very long time. These countries are, by and large, in the midst of an agricultural technological revolution today. Crop yields are increasing, output from livestock is rising somewhat, labor input is declining sharply, and various kinds of new inputs are increasing.

The agriculturally advanced countries in the Western hemisphere—the United States, Canada, Argentina, and perhaps others—and those in Oceania such as Australia and New Zealand, have had a very different history. They have been colonized within the past 400 years, some within a much shorter period than that. Settlers spread to all arable lands within the country, from modest beginnings at some initial points of colonization. The area of land in crops in such countries expanded throughout the eighteenth and nineteenth centuries, and sometimes later. Although much progress had been made in agricultural technology in earlier periods, it has only been in the twentieth century, and more particularly since World War II, that the rate of agricultural progress has been so rapid as reasonably to be called a revolution.

In the United States, agriculture expanded, in terms of area of land used, in numbers of farms, and in output, throughout its rather long colonial history and its first century and more of national history. Agricultural settlement was pushed across the nation throughout the nineteenth century. A number of indicators reached a peak about the time of World War I. Acreage of land in crops, numbers of farms, numbers of persons employed in farming, amount of animal draft power, and other factors reached more or less a peak by then. The interwar years were a period of modest changes (in retrospect, although some did not seem so modest at the time) and sometimes of contradictory changes.

Japan, almost alone of the Asiatic world, has also experienced an agricultural revolution similar to that of Europe. Although agriculture was intensive for many decades, in the past two decades output has increased greatly. Land area suitable for crops is strictly limited, and large expansion of crop acreage has been impossible. But yields, already high, have been increased greatly. Mechanical power has been introduced, and hand labor requirements of many crops cut drastically.

In the United States, agricultural output has roughly doubled since the end of World War I; labor used in agriculture has shrunk by more than half; somewhat less cropland is used today than was used two decades or more ago; and capital inputs, while changed greatly in form, have not increased greatly in total. Moreover, except for brief periods during each World War, American agriculture has not produced up to its potential capacity. Were national policy to require it, a simple guarantee of favorable prices (parity or higher) for a decade ahead would encourage American farmers greatly to increase their output—perhaps to double it within a decade.

One result of this technological and economic development of American agriculture is that today the average American spends less than 25 percent of his income for food—a relationship vastly different from that in the typical developing country, where food may account for half or more of the typical family budget. Moreover, about half of what the American housewife spends for food is for services connected with its transportation, processing, and sale; food at the farm absorbs a much smaller proportion of consumer outlays.

Agricultural Research and Education as Public Programs
In every country with an advanced agriculture, public research and education have been vital factors. Generally speaking, in each country there is a specialized agricultural research establishment; the U.S. Department of Agriculture and the Agricultural Experiment Stations of the Land-Grant Colleges in the United States have their counterparts in most countries. Some countries initiated and developed their own systems; others more or less consciously imitated the American experience. The research may be relatively basic, or it may be more directly applied. The early work in the specialized agricultural research organizations in some countries was rather limited in scope, not always professionally sophisticated, and sometimes of limited practical usefulness. But, over the decades, it has improved greatly in all these directions.

A private research effort, by fertilizer companies, suppliers of chemicals, seed producers, agricultural machinery manufacturers, and others has supplemented the public research effort in most countries, increasingly so in recent decades. Provision of agricultural inputs to farmers is a big business, in which competition is often keen. Firms, especially the larger ones, are constantly seeking to develop new products which will increase their sales while at the same time enabling farmers to produce more. In the type of research to develop immediately practical results, the private companies are now able to provide a large share of what is needed by farmers. In the early stages of its growth, agriculture in a developing country may have to rely more largely upon public research agencies.

In order to take advantage of existing agricultural knowledge and of new research results, specialized forms of agricultural education are also necessary. These may take the form of agricultural colleges, of vocational agricultural training in secondary schools, and of various forms of adult education or extension agencies. The results of research have been carried from the laboratory or the experimental field to the farmer; and the successful practices of one farmer have been called to the attention of his neighbors. This educational process has not been perfect, and has in fact at times been criticized; nevertheless, no small part of the credit for the agricultural revolution must go to the specialized agricultural educational manpower and organization. The county extension agent in the United States had a difficult time, fifty years or so ago, persuading the practical farmer that he had anything to contribute to better farming. But county agents did establish their competence, and farmers came to call upon them increasingly. In very recent times, the most advanced farmers, who have a college education as advanced as that of county agents, seek to confer directly with research personnel, rather than to have research results relayed to them by an agricultural generalist. In other countries, similar education specialists, under various names, have performed similar functions, with equally notable results.

Economically advanced countries have found that it pays very well to have such publicly supported research and educational programs for agriculture. Their costs are moderate, and their results are large over a period of time. In many economically advanced countries, it has taken some years—a generation, in some cases—for farmers to utilize these specialized institutions fully and to take complete advantage of the information which was available. Nevertheless, in the end a large proportion of all farmers have come to use such specialized agricultural knowledge. The increases in agricultural output have benefited the nations concerned; sometimes farmers have benefited less, because increased output can mean lower prices.

Managerial Requirements of Advanced Agriculture

A major characteristic of an advanced agriculture in an economically developed country is the heavy burden it places upon the farmer as a manager. The new agricultural technology is only modestly productive, if each item or aspect is considered separately; it is the combination of practices, techniques, methods, and technologies which is highly productive. A new plant variety may produce little more than an old one, if all cropping practices remain unchanged, for instance; or additional fertilizer may produce only modest increases in output from the old crop varieties; or new varieties and more fertilizer will have limited increases in output unless weeds are brought under better control; and so on. It is the close articulation of many improved practices or methods, and their close timing, which is highly productive. This requires a well-educated, highly alert farmer, able and interested to apply the very best combination of methods at exactly the right time, if the full potential of new agricultural technology is to be achieved.

Farmers in advanced agriculture tend to become much more specialized than farmers in technically less advanced agriculture. The farmer no longer grows his own seeds, for instance; production of pure strains of seed, especially of hybridized lines, is in itself a highly specialized business. The farmer in an economically advanced country no longer produces his own fertilizer (animal manures, usually, in the less developed countries); instead, he buys fertilizer made in a specialized factory. Technologically advanced agriculture depends almost universally upon mechanical power—tractors, with fuel from fossil energy sources such as petroleum; for mechanical power not only saves labor, but far more important, it permits a vastly better and more timely performance of farm operations. Farmers in economically advanced countries rarely market their own products, or make the specialized containers in which such products are shipped. In all these, and in numerous other specific ways, the farmer in an economically advanced country becomes a specialist.

This increased specialization in farm production in economically advanced countries has two major consequences. First of all, the value added by the farmer shrinks as a proportion of the value of his gross output. In the United States, for instance, the value added by farmers does not average above 30 percent of the total value of agricultural output for the whole nation; this proportion has shrunk from about half at the end of the war. Farmers are increasingly specialized business-men, buying a major part of their total inputs, processing those inputs, and selling the output; their net income is highly sensitive to the price relationship between inputs and outputs. A small favorable shift in price relationships greatly increases net farm income, a small unfavor-able shift in prices decreases it.

Second, this specialization of farmers greatly increases the economic interdependence between agriculture and the rest of the national econ-omy. The inputs which the farmer buys are the output of many special-ized businesses—fertilizer, machinery, manufacture, and the like. The output of the farm becomes the raw material for many other special-ized businesses—meat packing plants, grain storage and milling, fruit and vegetable canning and preserving, and many others. A highly developed "agribusiness" links agriculture to the rest of the whole national economy.

Generally speaking, these trends toward greater demands upon the farmer as a manager, toward more specialization of production among farmers, and toward greater economic interdependence of agriculture and the rest of the national economy are likely to arise in presently developing countries as they become more advanced economically and as their agricultures change accordingly.

Agricultural Surpluses and Their Control

In several economically developed countries, the agricultural revolution has had some less happy results than those discussed earlier. Increases in output, or increases in potential productive capacity, have come more rapidly than demand for agricultural commodities has increased. As a result, actual surpluses, or potential surpluses, have arisen, or prices of commodities have been reduced, or some combination of these results has occurred. Farmers have understandably been aroused at declining incomes resulting from their increased output. A basic difficulty is that the demand for most agricultural commodities is inelastic; a relatively small increase in supply often results in a substantial decline in price, so that national farm income is less for a large output than for a smaller one. For many industrial products, demand is relatively elastic, and often a producer can increase output greatly, taking advantage of pro-duction economies associated with greater output, while at the same time suffering only modest declines in price, so that net income can actually be higher even though prices are lower. This adjustment of increased volume at lower prices is not available to agriculture as a whole, because of the inelastic demand curve, although the individual farmer may be able to follow a similar route.

As a result of increased output and lower prices, many countries have embarked upon various programs to limit agricultural output, to restrict trade in agricultural commodities, to support prices of such commodities, to store surpluses in the hope they will be in greater demand later, or to undertake other programs, or to undertake some combination of such programs. It is ironic, and to a degree tragic, that a developed country should stimulate agricultural output by research, education, and other programs, and then seek to interfere with the economic adjustment processes by production control or other devices. Such programs, which would have softened the shock of adjustment and helped bring about efficient economic adjustments, might well have been highly desirable, from a broad social viewpoint. However, in all too many cases, agricultural adjustment programs, once begun, are never abandoned or even greatly modified.

Governmental programs for adjustment of agricultural supply and demand have had other, and in some ways more pernicious, effects than those just mentioned. For one thing, such programs have more often than not interfered greatly with the foreign economic policy of the country concerned. The European Common Market, for example, has had more difficulty applying the principles of freer trade to agriculture than to any other aspect of the economy. In the United States, agricultural interests have often affected foreign policy in a major way. The foreign policy of agricultural exporting nations such as Canada, Argentina, Australia, and New Zealand has sometimes been dominated by agricultural export considerations. Farm groups have often exercised political power within a country, to make difficult or impossible the kind of foreign policy which the country would otherwise adopt.

The kinds of production control or other programs undertaken to minimize the economic shock of increased output and inelastic demand have often had the effect of reducing or delaying the adjustment to changed technological or economic conditions. While some softening of the shock of adjustment might be desirable, as we have noted, yet in the end the adjustments should be made. The government programs may, in the long run, impede the economic development of the country.

Manpower Adjustment Problems
Most countries with an advanced agriculture have experienced serious problems of manpower adjustment. Most of the new agricultural tech-

nology means a greater output of agricultural commodities from the same labor input. If the demand for such commodities were highly elastic, then output could expand greatly, with a relatively small decline in prices, and the same labor force could continue to be employed. However, as we have noted, the demand for most agricultural commodities is inelastic; the farmers are faced with severe declines in prices, or with a redundant labor supply, or both. A reduction in agricultural labor force, especially quickly, is often difficult to achieve. A man past 40 years of age, who has farmed all his productive years and whose formal education may be rather limited, may have no real prospects of employment elsewhere. Indeed, the very processes of technological change which have displaced him on the farm have made unskilled labor less necessary in the cities.

The middle-aged and older farmer has hence found it very difficult to move out of agriculture and into new employment. His income might be low, but he would remain in farming—"locked in" by his lack of skills for urban employment, as well as often by various barriers to such employment. His son, however, is likely to have been better educated, is not equally committed to agriculture or to living in the rural area, and is likely to be more acceptable to urban employers; as a result, he leaves the farm for the city. There has long been a farm-to-city migration of youth in most countries, since birthrates among farm people have produced a surplus of young people.

Although this manpower adjustment problem has been particularly severe in agriculture in the United States, it has been marked in Canada also, and it is common in several other countries. In the United States, total numbers of farms reach a peak of about 6½ million in the mid-1930s; since then, they have declined to about half of this level. The reduction in hired labor on farms has been about proportionate; the hired man of a generation ago, who lived with the farm family, is about extinct. Hired labor in American agriculture today is usually short term, often migratory, and often of a different racial or ethnic group than that of the employer. Almost all the reduction in number of farms to date has been the result of young men refusing to enter farming; actual withdrawals of older farmers have been normal for the age of the farmers concerned.

In spite of the rapid decline in farm numbers, and the heavy migration of farm youth responsible for this decline, American agriculture has been seriously overmanned since the war. A number of calculations have suggested that the total agricultural output could have been produced with many fewer farmers—perhaps with no more than a fourth of the larger and abler farmers. Had the technological and economic revolution in agriculture proceeded more slowly, the adjustment in manpower could more easily have kept pace, primarily by fewer young men entering farming. One of the least satisfactory aspects of American agriculture in the postwar years has been its failure to adjust labor employment rapidly and without undue hardship to those concerned. Perhaps it would be more accurate to say that this has been a failure of the whole American economy and society, rather than a failure of agriculture primarily.

History may well show that serious overmanning of agriculture during its period of most rapid change was a one-generation phenomenon. That is, by far the greater part of the adjustment or of the maladjustment may exist during one generation alone. However, a continued high birthrate among farm families and a steady or shrinking demand for labor in agricultural production will necessitate a continuing migration of farm youth to the city.

Farmer Investment in Natural Resources

In a technologically advanced agriculture, farmers both must and can invest in the development and conservation of natural resources. In many less advanced countries, farmers are under considerable pressure to wring as much from their land as they can, even when this means a destruction of the soil and other resources. Most of the newer technologically advanced countries went through a similar cycle. As land becomes more valuable, as the supply of capital increases, and as farmers learn better how to take full advantage of resources, the economic possibilities of natural resource investment and development rise.

The nature of the natural resource investment program varies from country to country, or from one part of a large country to another, depending primarily upon climatic factors. In one country, drainage of lands naturally poorly drained may be the chief form of resource development. In arid and semiarid countries, on the other hand, it may be irrigation which is most important. Measures to conserve the soil itself, by protecting it against soil erosion, may be needed under a very wide variety of natural conditions. In some situations, where the land is naturally wooded, management and improvement of the wooded area within the farm may be a chief form of natural resource investment. The need for natural resource investment, especially soil conservation, varies greatly from one country to another, also depending in large part upon climate. Where rainfall is gentle, as in much of Europe, soil erosion is less likely to be a serious problem than where rainfall is torrential, as in parts of the United States and in many other countries.

A highly productive agriculture, producing an ample supply or a surplus of farm commodities, can well afford to make an investment in its basic resources such as soil and forests. The nation does not need every bushel of grain or every blade of grass that might be produced by an exploitative system of agriculture. Some of the agricultural output can be plowed back into the resources themselves; one problem is to find ways in which this can be made profitable to the farmers concerned, as well as to the whole society. In some of the developing countries, the pressures on land are so great that exploitative systems of farming are followed. In the end, this is usually self-defeating, because yields decline so much that the land exploitation has not really produced any more, if as much, as a more conservating system of farming. But conservation may seem a luxury to a farmer, or to a nation, striving desperately to achieve the maximum output of food to meet immediate needs.

Social and Community Problems

A series of social relationships and a community structure develop in every agricultural area. Farmers buy needed supplies from certain merchants in certain locations, and sell their surplus products to others, in the same or different locations. Many forms of social services, such as schools, churches, hospitals, and the like, develop to serve the rural and small-town people. A web of human relationships grows up, among relatives, friends, and others not so friendly. This whole social side of farming and rural living has been the subject of several studies in every country; while the details may vary greatly, the existence of such relationships and structure is found everywhere.

A changing technology puts the established rural community and social structure under strain. Developments in transportation are particularly disruptive. The farmer need no longer buy and sell at the old places; he can now travel to more distant ones. Competition among suppliers, buyers, and service establishments arises, among towns or other places which previously had been largely isolated from such competition. There is not only a question of price competition, but also one of quality. There are often important economies of scale, in quality as well as in price, as illustrated not only by the large supermarket compared with the small grocery store, but also between the larger and the smaller church. As agriculture advances technologically in an economically developed country, the farm people come to have higher standards of personal consumption.

In many countries with an advanced agriculture, the pattern of small-town service centers of a generation ago is now outmoded. Farmers can travel to larger centers, to buy their needs and for their social services. Many of the smaller towns are decaying; the process is a vicious circle, for every decline in local towns leads more people to go elsewhere, and this in turn leads to a further decline.

Although this situation exists, to a degee, in every country with a technologically advanced agriculture, it is perhaps most serious in the United States. Farmers in rural areas depended upon animal transport a generation or two ago, and roads and towns were located in light of animal-drawn speeds. In the United States, roads are typically found on each mile "section" line, dividing the landscape into square-mile blocks; and rural towns, serving farmers, were often located only a few miles apart. The automobile and the truck today travel at ten times the speed of the horse-drawn wagon; the farmer increasingly bypasses the small town which served his father, to go to a larger but more distant town where all manner of commercial and social services are better. The great reduction in numbers of farms, previously noted, has further complicated the situation.

In a large country, such as the United States, substantial regional differences exist. Where farms have always been rather small and farm towns or cities small but economically viable, and where small-scale industries have come in, abandonment or consolidation of the farming operations has still left a large population in the open country and in the small cities, working in the local industries. This has been the situation in the Piedmont districts of the Southeast, for instance. Although half of the land in crops in 1920 has since been abandoned, and although a great many farms have been consolidated, there are few empty farmhouses. The people who live in the open country and those who live in the small cities work in furniture factories and textile mills. Something of this same sort of adjustment has taken place in many parts of west European countries.

In contrast, in grain-growing or other agricultural regions, where farms were always larger and towns more widely scattered and usually smaller, the reduction in numbers of farms has led to many idle farm homes and to some empty homes in towns. These regions are perhaps not as well suited to any kind of industrialization, and there is often not an adequate labor force within a reasonable commuting distance to support an industrial plant. In these towns, not only the business establishments but such social institutions as church, school, hospital, and entertainment have suffered greatly. As part of its adjustment to changing technological and economic conditions, American agriculture has to face a changing geographical structure on the land.

Recreation and Amenities

Urban dwellers in high-income countries usually like to make trips into the rural or agricultural hinterlands, for outdoor recreation of some kind or merely for sightseeing. With a growth in income, increasing proportions of the city population can afford such travel. The poorest people usually cannot, but even this situation may change with time. In most economically advanced countries, workers get paid vacations of varying length. A considerable proportion of the people who get such vacations want to enjoy them by a trip into or through a rural area, perhaps with such specialized activities as camping or hunting. One of the functions of agriculture in an economically advanced country is to provide an attractive "back country" for the urban dweller; one of the serious problems is to devise means whereby farmers may be rewarded for their efforts to produce such attractive back country.

Selected Bibliography on U.S. Agriculture

Benedict, Murray R., *Farm Policies of the United States, 1790-1950: A Study of Their Origins and Development*. New York: Twentieth Century Fund, 1953.

Clawson, Marion, *Policy Directions for U.S. Agriculture—Long-Range Choices in Farming and Rural Living*. Baltimore: Johns Hopkins Press, 1968.

Cochrane, Willard W., *The City Man's Guide to the Farm Problem*. Minneapolis: University of Minnesota Press, 1965.

Copp, James H., *Our Changing Rural Society: Perspectives and Trends*. Ames: Iowa State University Press, 1964.

Hathaway, Dale E., *Government and Agriculture: Public Policy in a Democratic Society*. New York: Macmillan, 1963.

Heady, Earl O., *Agricultural Policy under Economic Development*. Ames: Iowa State University Press, 1959.

————, and Luther G. Tweeten, *Resource Demand and Structure of the Agricultural Industry*. Ames: Iowa State University Press, 1963.

Higbee, Edward, *Farms and Farmers in an Urban Age*. New York: Twentieth Century Fund, 1963.

Iowa State University Center for Agriculture and Economic Adjustment, *Labor Mobility and Population in Agriculture*. Ames: Iowa State University Press, 1961.

———, *Farm Goals in Conflict—Family Farm, Income, Freedom, Security*. Ames: Iowa State University Press, 1963.

Rasmussen, Wayne D., *Readings in the History of American Agriculture*. Urbana: University of Illinois Press, 1960.

Schickele, Rainer, *Agricultural Policy: Farm Programs and National Welfare*. New York: McGraw-Hill, 1954 (reissued by University of Nebraska Press, Lincoln, 1965).

Shepherd, Geoffrey S., *Farm Policy—New Directions*. Ames: Iowa State University Press, 1964.

Waugh, Frederick V., *Managing Farm Surpluses*. Washington, D.C.: Planning Pamphlet No. 117, National Planning Association, April 1962.

Wilcox, Walter W., and Willard W. Cochrane, *Economics of Agriculture*. Englewood Cliffs, N.J.: Prentice-Hall, 1960, 2nd ed.

Part One

| I. Rural Development— Policies and Planning | 2. National Policies for Rural Development in Advanced Countries | Mario Bandini |

Our task, as we see it, will be best fulfilled not merely by enumerating, in greater or lesser detail, the laws and bylaws governing the agricultural policies pursued in the advanced countries.[1] While giving some instances from Western Europe and North America, our fundamental aim will be to define the nature and logic of those policies.

We have always maintained that agricultural policy should proceed along the lines of overall economic development. Once its guidelines have been laid down, development should be rapid and unhampered, without economic setbacks or social unrest. We do not deal in abstract ideological theories, nor have we any universal panacea for agricultural problems. We shall be content, as already indicated, to seek an understanding of present-day trends in agricultural policies, and to try to help orientate such policies in line with those trends.

Agricultural Structures in Advanced Countries

The following facts seem to emerge more or less clearly from present-day agricultural trends in the advanced countries. Agriculture accounts for a relatively low proportion of the gross national product: 3 percent in Britain, 6 percent in the United States, 8 percent in Germany, 10 percent in France and Holland, reaching 12 percent in Italy. The size of the labor force in agriculture, expressed as percentages of total working populations, is also relatively low, though higher than those just shown: 4 percent in the United Kingdom, 8 percent in the United States, 15 percent in France, and 22 percent in Italy. Generally speaking, agriculture in the countries under review is efficient and set on relatively sound economic bases. Unit production levels are high, technical facilities and machinery are widely used, the prices of produce are relatively high, and the living standards of agricultural workers are far higher than in underdeveloped countries.

Farms are run like industrial or business enterprises, i.e., on com-

Mario Bandini—Italy. Professor of Agricultural Economics and Dean of the Faculty of Economic Sciences, the University of Rome; president of the National Institute of Agrarian Economy; former counselor of the European Economic Community, Brussels.
[1] A renowned scholar has asserted that it is useless to waste time defining a giraffe, since everyone knows what a giraffe is. By the same token, we shall not attempt to define what is meant by "advanced countries."

merical principles. The former "gentleman-farmer" type of land tenure has practically disappeared, and with it the agricultural labor agreements that characterized it, and this has produced a change in the social status of the agricultural community. In other words, systems such as big estates and very small holdings which were strictly interdependent have disappeared or are very rare. Direct farming, whether family based or not, tends to predominate. The social differences have largely been eliminated; the wealth produced is distributed more evenly among the various groups of the agricultural community.

The population engaged in agriculture usually consists of that section of the rural population that was not caught up in the extensive migration phenomenon from agriculture to industry and the tertiary sectors of the economy. This amounts to saying that agriculture does not select its work force, but is subject to the effects of general population movements. It therefore follows that those who remain are, as a rule, older, and that the exodus from agriculture does not occur because of local agricultural unemployment, but rather because of the demand for industrial labor. The rate of abandonment of agriculture is faster in areas near to industrial centers and relatively slower in those areas, often overpopulated, that are located far from industrial concentrations. For some time the imbalance between available labor and land requiring cultivation has tended to increase.

The improvement of communications and of techniques for the conservation or processing of agricultural produce has the effect of expanding the marketing systems for it. As regards individual farms, cultivation systems tend to become specialized, or at least reduced in number, according to the district concerned. Much work formerly done on the farm is now being performed away from the farm and almost always by large independent organizations, whether cooperatives or not, e.g., wine cellars, dairies, edible-oil mills. Many of the facilities that the farm once provided for itself are now supplied from outside: hired machinery, selected seeds and saplings, pest control, technical know-how, finance. A system of division of labor is being developed that enables even the small family farms to take advantage of the services provided by large-scale organizations.

Farm management continues to be based predominantly on individual initiative. Even if in all advanced countries there exist projects for joint enterprises (sometimes limited purely to the commercial sector, sometimes extended to the management of one or more farms), we maintain that it is premature and unrealistic to consider such forms of organization as the future trend in agriculture. (The case of Israel is a story of its own.)

As regards the relation between agricultural production and national requirements, existing situations differ considerably according to the economies of the different countries, as shown by the following three instances:

1. Countries with extensive farmlands. The United States, and to a lesser degree, France, are the clearest examples. Here, agriculture fills most of the nation's requirements; exports of produce are increasing.

2. Countries with an inadequate cultivable area, such as the United Kingdom, Germany, and Italy. Here agriculture, despite its efficiency, cannot meet the full internal demand. Admittedly some of these countries export certain produce, but in value such exports are markedly lower than imports.

3. Countries which have limited land resources under intensive cultivation (Holland, Denmark), and which consistently export a large proportion of their agricultural output, generally obtained from livestock breeding. They therefore have to import large quantities of raw materials, especially of concentrated fodder for livestock. In such cases, agriculture becomes a transformation industry, and in practice there is always a certain amount of this type of farming in all countries.

Gaps between Agricultural and Industrial Development and Their Political Aspects

In advanced countries, agriculture undergoes a process of adaptation to a predominantly industrial economy. This process is relatively slow, usually over periods measurable in decades. Industrial development is much more rapid, as shown by the cases of Japan and Italy, and more recently Spain. The growth rate in agriculture is 1 to 3 percent per annum, in industry 6 to 8 percent and higher. This produces a constant disparity between the growth rates of agriculture and industry. Rapid industrial progress absorbs not only labor in growing numbers but also technicians, entrepreneurs, and capital.

Investment tends to be concentrated in industry, frequently causing an imbalance, with the risk of a decline—both relative and absolute—in agriculture. The rural areas stagnate, a situation worsened by the concentration of industry in favorable areas.

Objective appraisal of the dangers inherent in sharp agricultural decline; the knowledge that a depressed agriculture would have to be reconstructed at a far higher cost to subsequent generations; consideration of factors such as the nation's food supplies, soil protection, conditions of life in the countryside in general—all these factors of necessity lead the governments of advanced countries to assist and subsidize agriculture. A further potent factor is the political pressure of rural communities and organizations.

The great difference as compared with the past, largely as a result of modern communications and relationships, is that the rural community of today is aware of, and able to evaluate, its comparative situation and does not resign itself to the idea that agriculture is a perennially depressed world of its own and that the agricultural worker is condemned to a state of perpetual inferiority. Government intervention is therefore the constant rule. It is obviously more easily implemented in the industrially stronger countries in which agriculture, although important, represents only a modest part of the economy. Thus state support of agriculture is particularly extensive in countries such as the United States, the United Kingdom, and Switzerland.

Government intervention usually occurs either in the field of prices or in the basic economic structure or infrastructures. Despite their obvious interdependence, it is appropriate to consider separately these two principal elements of agricultural policy. Price and cost interventions are aimed at raising the earnings of those engaged in agriculture, in order to reduce social imbalances. Though these differences may never be completely eliminated, such intervention is undoubtedly beneficial.

Let us briefly recall a few well-known facts. In the United States, price subsidies were and continue to be a major factor in agricultural policy. In the United Kingdom, measures have been in force for a considerable time for subsidization of prices of agricultural produce tied to the world market, through deficiency payments. In Switzerland most agricultural prices are heavily supported. In the countries of the European Economic Community prices are not only kept at the "indicative" level, considered necessary to ensure further development, but they are also guaranteed at the level of the intervention price and protected from world markets by means of a sliding-scale tariff mechanism, which in practice results in internal markets functioning quite separately from the world market.

Other measures relate to costs. In an advanced economy the cost of the means of production tends to decrease: industry supplies them on more favorable terms and the state provides grants or low-interest credit for the purchase of such necessities as machinery and fertilizers. Fuel for farm work is often provided at a very low price, tax-free. These measures help agricultural development, both in countries which have been in an advanced state for some while and in those which have more recently progressed, such as Italy, Japan, and Spain.

Social costs deserve special mention. The example of Italy will suffice: social security contributions paid by farms total 70 billion lire, whereas benefits disbursed amount to 700 billion lire. The difference is borne by the state and (to a much larger extent) by the other sectors of the economy. Normally, working capital is also provided for agriculture at reduced rates of interest. All these factors exert a far-reaching influence on agricultural development; but whenever supply increases to the point of exceeding demand, they may also lead to economic "distortions" causing a buildup of surpluses.

Intervention is not always properly controlled or sufficiently flexible. In the United States an attempt was made to reduce the areas under cultivation, in order to prevent the relatively high prices from further aggravating the already serious stock situation. The farmers found it worthwhile to intensify cultivation (e.g., through increased use of fertilizers); thus the problem reemerged in a different form. The policy of disposal of surplus stocks in world markets (Public Law No. 480 and other measures) was only partially successful. In the United Kingdom provision is made for flexibility of intervention in relation to "dangerous" trends of output.

The most recent example, however, is that of the EEC. The criterion for price support was based on the situation in countries where prices were at the highest level: Germany, Belgium, and Italy. Thus the greater price increases occurred in France, where the levels were originally very low. France being a country with extensive land resources, there resulted a sharp rise in production. Those sectors of agriculture which are more easily mechanized reacted quickly to the favorable price. Stocks mounted at an enormous rate, especially in the cereals and dairy produce sectors. Price subsidies and the sale of surpluses in world markets costs the European Economic Community more than $2 billion a year.

Price policies have also influenced agricultural structures, benefiting those based on cereals, and considered unsuitable for a "high quality" agriculture, such as that of Europe. The high cost of fodder cereals (maize, barley, rye, etc.) compared with world prices creates difficulties for production sectors such as beef, pork, and poultry. The matter of structures requires fuller consideration, since they are essential for sound agricultural development and for the integration of a modern agriculture into the overall economies of advanced countries. Actually the agricultural policy that we are reviewing is seen to be largely devoted to that very problem. The EEC, which to a large extent is concerned with the repercussions of intervention on prices and markets, is now turning its attention to structural modifications.

Such action obviously also influences market conditions. More efficient structures, other things being equal, lead to higher productivity. This fact may enable farmers to earn more at lower costs, and therefore to improve their living standards, without increasing production beyond the "dangerous" limits. The proposition that agricultural policy should aim to create more efficient productive structures operating as freely as possible in a market economy, without intervention, has many convinced supporters—including ourselves.

Failure to implement this concept is often associated with concern regarding the time factor. Price interventions take effect quickly; those relating to structures require years and decades. In the former instance, however, it is often a case of building on sand, whereas in the latter the foundations of a lasting development process are created. An honest politician should, however, think in terms of generations and not of elections.

Agricultural and Rural: Two Different Points of View
No analysis, however brief, can afford to omit a preliminary clarification, required by the title of this study. It bears on the terms "agricultural" and "rural"; these not only imply different problems but also a completely different angle of approach to economic policy. The term "agricultural community" refers to persons who engage in farming; the term "rural community" to that section of the population that resides outside cities, towns, or large villages. Thus the rural community obviously includes the agricultural community but also other people, engaged in other occupations, which are sometimes, but not always or predominantly, connected with agriculture. Rural occupations are pursued in the countryside, i.e., in the smaller villages and hamlets. In the case of advanced countries whose economic structure is not over-concentrated, it is not far from the truth to contend that the agricultural community represents only 50 to 60 percent of the overall rural community.

The distinction is important also in matters of economic policy. In support of this, we would recall a very simple concept, almost a watchword, that affects a whole series of derived considerations. In the advanced countries a steady process of agricultural exodus is viewed with favor, whereas a process of rural exodus is discouraged. "Agricultural exodus, yes, rural exodus, no"—thus goes the word. Indeed, one of the major problems in formulating the economic policies of advanced countries is that of the influences of industrial development in areas of industrial concentration and in rural areas, respectively. These influences are of the utmost importance for agriculture itself.

Industrial development in Europe and North America is steadily aggravating zoning problems. The drawbacks of industrial concentration are becoming increasingly evident, especially in their impact on modern community life. Well-known instances include concentrations and conurbations such as those on the Atlantic coast of the United States, those of London, Birmingham, and Coventry in England, the vast Franco-German-Dutch Rhineland, or the Italian industrial triangle of Genoa-Turin-Milan—all these show how the initial economic advantages of concentration are turning into disadvantages, due to excessive concentration.

That is not all, however. Overconcentrated industrial development leads to a shift in the labor force—the rural exodus just referred to—which is extremely costly in view of the expenses of moving, of new housing, and of the adaptation of the individual to the environment. Commuting is only a partial remedy, limited to short distances. In addition to the cost devolving on the individual, there is the public expenditure arising from the need to expand the various services to meet the needs of more concentrated residential areas: roads, power, drainage, schools, hospitals, etc. This public cost is estimated at between $500 and $1,000 per migrant worker. Moreover, former residential areas remain either entirely or partially vacant. If, therefore, beyond a certain limit of concentration or distance, industry moves to the worker instead of the worker to industry, the resulting individual and social costs would be lower, even taking into account the possible increased costs to industry.

Obviously, what has been said does not apply in all cases and in all situations; local conditions must be taken into account. We maintain, however, that in general terms, when a certain level of progress has been reached in advanced countries, a wider territorial distribution of industry should be a matter of economic policy, as is already the case in the more advanced countries; this requires state planning and intervention, aimed at discouraging concentration and facilitating wider dispersion. The United States, Germany, France, the United Kingdom, Sweden, Switzerland, and now Italy, with its policy for the South, provide typical examples of such action, of which available space does not permit consideration. But we might remark that similar problems exist also in developing countries, e.g., in the Sao Paulo, Mexico City, and Caracas areas. We further mention Soviet policy, aimed at spreading industry southward and beyond the Urals.

This trend is of fundamental importance for agricultural development.[2] It facilitates the shift of the work force from agriculture; in addition, a wider territorial distribution of industry favors the launching of projects connected with agriculture and the processing of agricultural produce, in proximity to the cultivation areas. A policy of this kind also acts as an effective deterrent to the rural exodus. Finally, agricultural development is greatly assisted by this process through intensified economic exchanges within rural areas, while considerable advantages accrue to suppliers of services to agriculture.

Modern Agricultural Structures: A Moving Target

Taking agricultural development within the strict meaning of the term, we find that the economic policy of advanced countries is aimed, almost without exception, at facilitating the creation of economically efficient structures. We now propose to examine some general aspects of this policy; later we shall give some concrete examples from various countries.

The primary question is that of the type, size, and organization of a farm. Here again, we shall adopt a realistic approach and not one of theoretical abstraction. Many people air the idea that scientific research involving mathematical models and computers can lead to the determination of the optimum type and size of a farm. But this kind of a priori determination is valid only in certain specific cases: for example, rural settlement on government initiative, in cases of land reform or intervention uninhibited by any restriction. In most cases farms are created and modified as a result of the efforts of those engaged in agriculture. As we have said earlier, in the advanced countries the composition of the labor force available to agriculture is conditioned by external factors. If a relatively small number of farming families remains on the land, the size of the farm tends to increase. If, conversely, the exodus from agriculture is restricted to certain family members, leaving older people and women on the land, the farms will probably

[2]See also Chapter 6, "The Role of Industry in the Development of Rural Areas," by Gabriele Pescatore, and Chapter 8, "Industrialization of Rural Areas in Developing Countries," by P. D. Malgavkar.

not get bigger, or at least only if conditions favor the use of machinery. If executive entrepreneurs in agriculture (not manual workers) can find the incentives to devote themselves to farming instead of applying their capabilities and capital to the management of a factory producing shoes or medical drugs, it is probable that, alongside family farms, large commercial farms with a permanent work force will appear. In our view, the human factor plays a predominant role: an oft-repeated proposition but one not always carried to its logical conclusions.

Agricultural policy in advanced countries generally protects or aims to develop family farms[3] : other types of farms protect themselves. For so-called sociopolitical reasons that are often vaguely expressed but that are nonetheless adequate to influence those in authority, in all the countries that we are discussing, development policy favors the family farm. However, the present concept of the family farm is very different from an earlier one. The agricultural exodus leads to bigger farms run on a commerical basis, technically advanced and highly mechanized, such as to assure a reasonable level of income to those who remain in agriculture. Government policy has been and is directed at consolidating these structures. All legislation in North America, as far back as the homestead laws of more than a century ago, and most of that of Western Europe is based on this principle.

The consolidation of modern family farms calls for consideration of some specific aspects, among which that of size is important. To some extent, the idea is losing ground that the size of a farm should be assessed in relation to land ownership. A farm is often enlarged by leasing, thus making increased use of production facilities, livestock, machinery, and working capital. Farms often consist of land partly owned and partly leased: farm expansion frequently occurs by means of this first transition.

The reasons are obvious. The agricultural exodus does not induce the former farmers to sell their land immediately. The change in occupation involves hazards: they therefore try to hold on to their land as long as possible, even if they do not farm it, since in unforeseen circumstances it would be something to fall back on. The land is therefore often leased to those who remain, and the latter in turn are attracted to the idea of a gradual form of farm expansion. This process of full ownership only after some decades has been very widespread in the United States. Thus, the resulting increase in land ownership is not identical

[3] See also Chapter 12, "The Future of the Family Farm in Developed Countries," by Hermann Priebe.

with the increase in the size of the farm. Cases of partial leasehold are still very common. Similar developments occur with growing frequency in Germany, northern France, Holland, central and northern Italy, and elsewhere. Agricultural policy seeks to encourage such trends in various ways, for example, by drawing up the contract in such manner as to guarantee the tenant a reasonable term of leasehold and the refunding of improvement outlay.

Again in the field of farm structures, another form of state intervention consists in the consolidation of land in cases, very common in Western Europe, where large farmlands have been divided into small holdings. At various times, many countries, as a result of radical reorganization policies, implemented in specific areas schemes for exchanges of farmland, obligatory if the majority of farmers so decide. This has produced outstanding results in France, Germany, Switzerland, and Holland; nevertheless, the results have not always fulfilled overoptimistic expectations. The task of consolidation has also proved much more difficult and costly than expected, because reorganization of land ownership is not limited to exchanging holdings but also involves the adaptation of road and canal systems, buildings, agricultural centers, etc. The cost of exchanging holdings is multiplied many times.

The creation of new farming areas as well as land improvement works are the constant concern of the advanced countries, which willingly devote efforts to zoning, since the results are lasting and contribute increasingly to economic, agricultural, and overall development. Land reclamation and irrigation schemes, for example, are conceived as a preliminary requirement for further agricultural development. Densely populated countries with modest land resources (e.g., Holland, Italy) have made a special effort in this sector, with gradual but appreciable results.

Agricultural reform schemes[4] are also of interest to the advanced countries, though in a special sense very different from the meaning of the term in India, Japan, or Egypt. In certain advanced countries, for various reasons often associated with the slowness of agriculture in adapting itself to the conditions of a modern economy, there exist backward structures, often due to the persistence of outdated land ownership systems. Such situations were formerly widespread in the Iberian peninsula, Greece, central and northern Italy, and the United Kingdom. The problem was tackled in various ways: in Greece, for

[4]See Chapter 17, "Agrarian Reform—Planning, Implementation, and Evaluation," by Erich H. Jacoby.

example, by restricting land ownership; in Italy, by the partial expropriation of large estates and subsequent intensive settlement projects; in the United Kingdom, by indirect means—heavy taxation or death duties on large estates; in Spain, by dividing expropriated land into holdings, often in areas suitable for irrigation.

Space does not permit further discussion of the problem; we must also omit other topics of great interest, such as agricultural credit, vocational training, and rural living conditions. However, the importance of these facets of the problem is clearly apparent in relation to what has already been said.

Policies for Agricultural Development
The foregoing remarks should facilitate an evaluation of the agricultural development policies adopted by various countries. In the limited space at our disposal we shall confine ourselves to the member countries of the EEC.[5]

Germany The 1965 agricultural law is still the conceptual basis of German agricultural policy, and lays down certain general objectives: support of agricultural development and the creation of social conditions for farm workers equal with those of other categories of workers. The federal government is required to present an annual report on the situation of agriculture (*Grüne Berichte*) together with an agricultural development program showing the measures taken and those envisaged. The development plan and the relevant financing are adjusted annually as the situation requires. Thus the drive to improve farm structures has gradually assumed preponderence over price support policies. Interventions at the national level are backed up by regional interventions. In regions where economic development is slow, the scale of intervention is being increased, especially in matters of hydraulic and road projects.

The role of land consolidation is of special importance. With time it has been oriented toward the principle of land improvement, hydraulic schemes, and the creation of adequate road systems. It was estimated that about 15 million hectares of land required consolidation; by the end of 1966 about one-half had been consolidated. It now appears, however, that 3.4 million hectares of consolidated land already require further consolidation. In certain districts accelerated consolidation is under way without provision for reorganization of the water supply and

[5] The author's sources include various EEC documents and the periodical publications of the OECD.

road systems; this scheme affects an area of some 360,000 hectares. A prominent feature of the programs are hydraulic works, carried out largely according to the traditional principles of drainage, irrigation, and protection of land against water. Under the agricultural development plan, financial provision is also made for hydraulic schemes and road building that do not apply to agriculture only but to the entire rural environment.

In Germany the coordination of action between the federal government and the *Länder* (states) is worth mentioning because a real effort has been made to avoid two very serious planning errors: not allowing for special situations in decision-making; and an exclusively regional approach to intervention, which leads to particularist solutions and dispersion of financing. This does not mean that certain projects cannot be planned at an exclusively regional level, e.g., in Germany, the hydraulic improvement schemes for two particularly difficult regions—the North Sea coastal area and the southern Alpine districts.

Particular attention is given to the type and size of farms. To begin with, there is a great deal of part-time farming in Germany, more than in the other countries, and this applies specially in areas nearer to industrial centers, where some members of the farming families work, and where commuting is widespread. We refer to the cases of many newly created industrial centers, especially in central Germany, where more than one-half of the industrial workers are members of farmer families and continue to live on the family farm. In Germany the continuation of this characteristic type of farm is encouraged.

In the far more important field of full-time farming, German agricultural policy, following long-established traditions, aims to ensure that farms are the right size to provide a fair level of income for a family with two labor units. Financial assistance is provided on condition that the applicant submits a farm management plan and demonstrates that it is applicable to a farm of that type.

Political action also is aimed at preventing or hindering the division of farms into units of economically inadequate size. The farm settlement agencies may have the right of preemption in case of sale. A joint heir is given the opportunity of becoming the sole inheritor of the farm. These, too, are instances of long-standing German institutions relating to the inviolability of inherited property (*Anerbenrecht*). Farmers over the age of 65 are encouraged to retire on pensions.

Considerable importance is attached to the scheme for the creation of new farmsteads away from the original village (*Aussiedlung*). This is an obvious consequence of the agricultural exodus. In such cases the farmer receives appreciable financial aid and may obtain long-term loans at low interest rates. About one-half of the newly created farms are over 20 hectares in size.

Special encouragement is provided for investment associated with technical improvements such as the introduction of fodder drying and storage plants, heated greenhouses, and multiple-use machinery. Special facilities are granted for developing cooperative structures that can be utilized by at least five member farmers. Farmers' associations are also considerably assisted, both in matters of processing and marketing (cellars, storage facilities, and dairies) and in the provision of services (supply of high-quality seeds, livestock health control, etc.). Since 1963 considerable attention has been devoted to improving marketing facilities. Farm incomes can be sizably improved in this way. The creation of larger dairies, preparation and sales centers for horticultural products, and also silos, especially in association form, is extensively financed.

Appropriations for agricultural development have doubled during the last eight years. Subsidies and similar aid involve annual expenditure of $413 million, or 9 percent of the value of the gross agricultural product. Loans total $188 million. The financial cost is divided between county (*Bund*) and state (*Land*) the last-named bearing about one-quarter of the total. Most of the subsidies and almost all the loans are granted for structural improvements.

On the whole, German agricultural policy is in classical vein, though with a substantial degree of modernization. State intervention has become organic and continuous, but it provides for considerable flexibility according to developments and results. The creation of sound family farms is still at the core of this policy, but joint initiatives are gaining in importance.

Belgium Belgian agricultural policy also shows a modern trend away from well-nigh exclusive protection of prices and markets and toward structural improvement. The "parity" law of 1963 aims at agricultural development and social advancement of the farming community, stating its aims and methods. Land consolidation, hydraulic schemes, and roads play a role of primary importance here also. It is estimated that about 500,000 hectares of land require consolidation: the period initially contemplated was about twenty years, but the rate of progress to date suggests that it will take considerably longer, providing further proof of the difficulties involved. State grants of up to 60 percent are provided for hydraulic and road schemes.

Joint initiatives by farmers are encouraged. Annual grants up to $50 may be provided for groups of livestock breeders who together own from 7 to 15 head of cattle. The Agricultural Investment Fund grants interest contributions of up to 3 percent. Special attention is paid to technical assistance and vocational training.

A 1965 law grants severance payments at the age of 40 to owners or tenants of farms that are not considered "viable." The land thus freed is utilized for the enlargement of nearby farms that are too small. The scheme has had little success: just over 1,000 farmers, owning 2,875 hectares, have availed themselves of this provision. Better results have been achieved by the Property Development Association, which builds farm dwellings for sale on favorable terms. The activity of this association is not, however, limited to agriculture but includes providing housing for workers and miners.

The leasehold system is of special importance in Belgium, for it applies to more than two-thirds of the area under crops. Political action is afoot in favor of sufficiently long-term contracts, compensation for improvement works by tenants, and preemptive rights in case of sale. Little is done in the field of marketing structures.

It would appear from the foregoing paragraphs that in Belgium state assistance for agriculture does not go very far. The traditional free-trade approach still has a strong influence.

France French agricultural policy, though less fundamental and sometimes more variable than German policy, nevertheless provides for a schedule of vitally important initiatives and assistance measures. First and foremost it seeks new solutions, including long-term ones, which may prove beneficial or not. The role of the state, however, is considered determinant; France is far advanced in this respect.

Agricultural structures are considered not separately, but within the framework of the General Economic Plan, which aims at ensuring coherent growth. Higher productivity is the fundamental objective, and this applies also to the problems raised by Common Market membership. "Parity" of prices is another top-priority objective here. The achievement of an "optimum density of farmers in each agricultural region" is a fundamental principle that entails special state intervention in the less-developed regions.

The fundamental aim of French agricultural policy is to have efficient family farms that are big enough to meet modern requirements. It is also aimed at helping farmers to form associations not only for buying materials and equipment and for selling and processing produce, but also for cultivation. In this respect, France is more advanced than the other countries, since French policy seeks to regulate the type and volume of production, encouraging the growing of produce which is in short supply, and discouraging the cultivation of surplus crops.

As regards actual cultivation, a top-priority item is the development of common facilities: irrigation, cultivation of virgin land, buildings, machinery. This policy continues despite concern regarding surpluses. In 1960, however, there was a distinct shift in policy, aimed at facilitating the diminution of the agricultural population, concurrently with enlarging the farms. Today this principle constitutes the focal point of policy directives. Aged farmers are granted a retirement indemnity, so that the land so freed should be taken over by other farms, on condition that a minimum size is thereby attained that does not differ more than 50 percent from the average size of farms in the relevant territory. The land may also be taken over by other and younger farmers. The indemnity is increased (it may even be more than doubled) if the retiring farmer's holding is three times as large as a reference area. This policy is obviously aimed at creating larger farms cultivated by younger farmers.

The Aménagement Foncier et d'Equipement Rural companies (SAFER) are empowered, with preemption rights, to purchase available land, a move aimed at preventing increases in the price of land. Subsidies for technical improvements are granted only to farms above a minimum size, but they are withheld if the farm is considered too large.

French policy also aims at constituting agricultural enterprises by merging separate farms. The Groupements Agricoles d'Exploitation en Commun, which have a special juridical status, were created for this purpose. In addition, small cooperatives—even of only four members— may operate jointly owned agricultural machinery (CUMA). Other measures are directed at replacing poor quality vineyards or at developing livestock breeding. There are important provisions for improving marketing through the development of cooperatives, the construction of delivery centers, and cultivation under contract.

A sound cooperative credit system has been developed. France appropriates $269 million annually for subsidies and interest contributions (3.7 percent of the gross agricultural product) and grants more than $35 million in loans.

Italy The physical features of Italy and of its land have always called for a policy of regional improvement, land drainage, and reclamation on an extensive scale, preparing the land for agricultural development. In recent times the need for rural settlement brought about the elimination of outdated systems of land tenure. Moreover, with the object of reducing regional imbalances, Italy devotes special attention to problems of economic underdevelopment in the south and in the mountain areas. The extremely rapid decrease in the agricultural labor force (from 8.8 million to 4.2 million in fifteen years) is a favorable factor in solving the problem of increasing the size of farms and raising farm incomes—a problem which once seemed insolvable.

The 1933 land reclamation law aimed at creating new areas of agricultural development; today it is predominantly directed toward the extension of irrigation. With 3 million hectares of land already under irrigation, the target is now 4 million, 450,000 hectares more in southern Italy alone.

Land reform, which involved the expropriation of 750,000 hectares of mainly large landed estates, created a dense network of farm settlements involving the investment of more than $1 billion for land improvement works (roads, machinery, housing, villages, etc.).

With the achievement of a more balanced land structure, agricultural policy was then directed toward improvement of farms and rural services. This policy was implemented by the two five-year agricultural development plans (1961-1965 and 1966-1970). The first plan was aimed at improving infrastructures and farms, at creating vocational training facilities for farmers, and at better marketing. The second development plan follows up the general guidelines of the first but with a shift in emphasis to the structural improvements demanded by the integration of Italian agriculture in the Common Market. Extensive support is given to the development of cooperation in agriculture, to stock breeding, and to mechanization. Legislation provides for capital grants or low-interest agricultural credit. This latter type of incentive is of greater relative weight in the second development program.

Special provisions favor the purchase of land for direct farming; for this purpose 40-year loans are granted at a rate of 1 percent. Since the fundamental aim is still the constitution of large family farms, loans are preferentially granted for the creation of this type of farm or to prevent family farms from being broken up through inheritance. Italy is also studying the problem of land consolidation.

State assistance for agriculture is coordinated within the framework of the National Economic Development Plan. Subsidies granted in 1965 totaled $223 million, or 3.54 percent of the total value of agricultural production; loans totaled $98 million.

Luxembourg This small country firmly supports agricultural prices. The 1965 orientation law defined a structural improvement policy based on the creation of modern, efficient family farms. Land consolidation is under way on a nationwide basis, and considerable effort is devoted to improving rural roads. The vitally important vineyards are being oriented toward quality production.

Holland The outstanding feature of Dutch agriculture has long been the rational breeding of cattle and pigs, involving utilization of large quantities of cereal fodder. Today the emphasis is on raising agricultural labor productivity by every possible means, rather than on increasing production. Another basic concept of Dutch agricultural policy is the creation of favorable conditions for individual and group initiatives. No measures are adopted that would distort free competition among the various producers. The fundamental objectives of this policy are thus to improve agricultural infrastructures, eliminate marginal farms, increase the size of farms, and promote scientific research and extension.

The 1954 law regulates land reform, aiming at the creation of well-structured farms, without limitations on ownership. Land reform includes carrying out all the necessary works and is therefore of an integral nature. Works linked with land reform are being carried out on about 20 percent of the land. The Farmland Management Fund makes land available as farmers move to the polders. Experience gained during the development of the extensive, universally acclaimed schemes for winning new coastal land for the creation of polders has led to certain modifications of criteria.[6] When the works are completed, 220,000 hectares of land will have been won from the sea, and already there are indications that this is leading to a more favorable distribution of the nation's agricultural labor force. By contrast, state intervention in the field of marketing is on a relatively modest scale but cooperation is well developed, marketing being handled by voluntary organizations such as the Farmers' Produce Associations (Produkschappen).

Dutch agricultural policy does not favor a subsidy system likely to exert an undue influence on free competition. Neither do cooperatives enjoy any special facilities, and the process of vertical integration is developing without special assistance, either from the state or from the Produkschappen. The last-named exert a very effective influence on markets, justifying the liberalist approach of Dutch agricultural policy.

[6]See Chapter 26, "New Settlement and Land Consolidation in The Netherlands," by Charles A. P. Takes.

State subsidies amount to $40 million a year (3 percent of the value of production, the lowest percentage within the EEC), while loans total $20 million.

It is first and foremost from the comparative angle that our brief review is of interest. The trends in agricultural policy in the six economically advanced EEC countries have much in common, especially as regards aims and prospects. There are marked differences, however, in methods and criteria; these differences, of course, depend on the diverse nature and understanding of the problems. They provide some good examples of application of the principles of development policy which we have discussed in general terms in our study.

Part One

3. National Policies
for Rural
Development
in Developing
Countries

Rainer Schickele

There are two fundamental goals which guide development policies in modern democratic nations: the goal of establishing civic rights, responsibilities, and opportunities for everyone's participation in public affairs; and the goal of increasing production for the main purpose of eliminating poverty. These twin goals are not in conflict but reinforce each other. They serve as beacons for steering national policies.

The complexity of national life causes all sorts of deviations due to political storms, economic vicissitudes, inertia of traditional behavior, and the power of recalcitrant elites that tend to retard progress. Yet with all the ups and downs in the development path, these twin goals are becoming part of the thinking and the aspirations of more and more people in all walks of life.

Historical Perspective

In the newly developing world, these twin goals have become manifest in the formulation of national policy only during the last twenty years, since the last World War and the independence of many new nations from colonial rule. Twenty years, indeed, is a very short span of time in the history of nations. The changes have been profound and far-reaching in many vital spheres of people's lives: universal education and suffrage, political parties, trade unions and collective bargaining for wages and working conditions, emancipation of women, mobility of people horizontally over wide areas and vertically up the social and economic scale, and the introduction of modern technologies and organization in production, marketing, commerce, and all sorts of public and private services.

The order of magnitude of these changes in the newly developing world during the last twenty years is quite impressive and might be considered comparable to that experienced by the Western industrialized world during the hundred years between 1800 and 1900. This telescoping of the time dimension became possible because of two major factors: the

Rainer Schickele—United States. Ph.D., College of Agriculture, University of Berlin, in agricultural economics and policy; since 1967, visiting professor of Agricultural Economics at the University of Ceylon; associate of the Agricultural Development Council, Inc., New York; formerly director of the Land and Water Development Division of the FAO.

active guidance and promotion of social and economic development by progress-oriented government policies, and the transfer and adaptation of scientific technologies and democratic institutions from the West.

The Agricultural Lag

This spurt of development, however, is much more pronounced in urban than in rural areas, in industry and trade than in agriculture. Agricultural progress is lagging behind industry in the adoption of modern production techniques and of economic institutional arrangements required for a vigorous increase in productivity. This agricultural lag, in turn, retards industrial progress mainly because the large rural population is not generating a sufficient purchasing power to create the demand needed for absorbing the growing industrial output. Idle capacity in modern factories can be found in many developing countries. This experience discourages industrialization and diverts savings into nonproductive investments and capital flight abroad.

The interdependence of industrial and agricultural development is not readily seen. It is obscured by the glamour of industry. The political and economic leadership is typically urban oriented and tends to identify economic development with industrialization. Industrial expansion is more easily planned, financed, and implemented than agricultural expansion. Industry is spatially more concentrated, organizationally more centralized, technically more controllable in its input-output relationships, and financially more adequately served by present banking and credit institutions. In contrast, planning and implementing agricultural expansion is severely handicapped by its wide geographic dispersion, its decentralized management in millions of small family enterprises, and its high vulnerability to the vagaries of weather.

Another handicap is the almost universal inadequacy of infrastructural facilities in rural areas. All forms of transport and communication, market and credit facilities, schools and public health services, electricity and water supply are typically inferior to those in urban areas. Yet another rural handicap is the much stronger power of the local elite over cultivators and laborers with respect to social status and economic sanctions. Typically, small farmers are dependent upon the goodwill of their landlords or of their merchants and moneylenders, that is, upon a small local elite concerned with conserving the status quo and resisting innovations which tend to weaken their power position in the community.

In urban areas, the power of local elites is less direct and personal, more diffused. Workers have a wider choice of employment opportunities, of sources of credit; and they find it much easier to organize into unions, to bargain collectively with employers, and to participate in political parties and other group activities for promoting their welfare. Although we find, of course, wide variations in these group relationships, this contrast between rural and urban areas is quite typical for most newly developing countries.

We must be fully aware of the severity of these handicaps if we want to understand the rural development problems and devise policies for accelerating rural progress. In essence, national policies for reducing the agricultural lag must aim at placing farmers and agricultural laborers more nearly at par with urban workers with respect to such basic facilities as schools, public health, roads, transport, and communication, and such basic opportunities as education, vocational training, and participation in cooperatives, associations, and unions for group action. Without these facilities and opportunities, the interest and aspirations of farmers cannot be adequately reflected in the formulation of national development policies. Since we cannot bring the land to the city, we must bring the facilities to the farmers, to the rural villages and towns.

One of the most promising approaches for overcoming these rural handicaps lies in the concept of regional planning, in which Israel has pioneered with remarkable success.[1] Decentralization and diversification of industries and services and their dispersal into rural areas lies at the heart of the regional planning approach. The economic disadvantages involved in higher transport costs of raw materials and finished products and in smaller-scale operations are compensated by lower real cost of labor and housing and the avoidance of many diseconomies and social disadvantages of congested cities and overcrowded slums with their physical and mental health hazards.

This holds particularly for countries in their early stages of industrialization and with a high density of population in rural areas. Here, population pressure on farmland, on the one hand, and hopes for well-paid employment and exciting adventures in the city, on the other, often lead to a premature farm-city migration well beyond the labor

[1] For a constructive exposition of the concept of regional planning and its implementation, see Raanan Weitz and Avshalom Rokach, *Agricultural Development: Planning and Implementation* (Dordrecht-Holland, D. Reidel, 1968), Chapter 7.

demand of industry. This results in masses of underemployed casual workers, crowded into city slums of most appalling poverty, unsanitary conditions, and frustrated lives—indeed a poverty much more debilitating than what the migrants experienced in the "rural slums" from which they came. This phenomenon is typical of many urban centers throughout the newly developing world.

The urban-rural population ratio is considered as an indicator of economic development. But this indicator can be misleading if the farm-city migration goes too fast and the migrants are unemployed and worse off than before. The industrial stimulus of low wages is dulled by the unreliability, lack of training, and work discipline of a shifting, demoralized labor force. We could enumerate many other ramifications of such premature farm-city migration which render a too rapid population increase in urban areas distinctly undesirable and not conducive to economic development.

Another important aspect is often overlooked: the introduction of many modern farming methods increases rather than reduces labor requirements. Better and more timely tillage, application of fertilizer and pesticides, weeding, efficient water control for irrigation, harvesting, threshing, and transporting larger crops, diversification of crops, and introduction of livestock enterprises—these innovations require more labor, unless they are accompanied by an increase in labor-saving machinery. Such mechanization usually spreads more slowly because the investment required is heavier and of a longer-term nature. Hence, in the early stages of modernization, underemployment is often reduced rather than increased. In fact, in some areas, labor shortages have come in the wake of farm modernization.

Another part of the existing underemployment can be absorbed by the increasing demand for services required for handling and processing a larger volume of agricultural products as well as of production and consumer goods. These are all-powerful arguments for reducing the agricultural lag and for a national development policy which recognizes these interactions between the industrial and agricultural sectors. Their progress must be guided to remain in step.

Local Implementation of National Policies

Production Targets Ineffective The planning of production targets for individual agricultural commodities is becoming a much publicized feature of national development policy in more and more countries. In principle, this planning is rather easily done. We can start with the national output of the last few years, stipulate a certain rate of increase considered reasonable—say 4 or 6 percent for the next year—and announce this projected figure as the target for farmers to achieve. We can estimate the additional quantities of certain key inputs required, such as fertilizer, improved seeds, agrochemicals, etc., and provide foreign exchange allocations for them. That is essentially what is being done, with more or less refined techniques. Then, ministers, department heads, and party leaders stump the countryside exhorting farmers to achieve these targets. Sometimes they do, sometimes they do not, depending on the weather. If they do, the government claims the credit; if they do not, either the weather or the backwardness of farmers is blamed.

Just what do these targets mean to a farmer? All they mean to him is that he should produce more. Whether the target calls for 4 or 6 percent increase means nothing to him, simply because he knows that from one year to the next the weather and pests and diseases make for a much greater variation in output than the target calls for.[2] This is the nature of the agricultural production process, in contrast to industry, where the input-output relationship can be closely controlled.

We cannot even argue with confidence that if the farmer had not increased his input, his output would have been lower than it was. A severe drought or flood can ruin a crop regardless of the fertilizer applied. Some high-yielding crop varieties are more susceptible to damage from certain hazards than traditional varieties. This is the experience of the individual farmer. That this reasoning does not hold for the country as a whole (except for years of general crop failure, as in India in 1965 and 1966) does not concern him. What does concern him is the additional financial risk he takes in buying these modern inputs that may well make him richer if the weather is good but poorer if it is bad.[3]

[2] For instance, a national target of a 6% increase in rice production cannot possibly be implemented by telling every rice farmer to raise his output by 6%. To achieve such a global target, some farmers must increase production by 50%, others by 30%, and many by 10 to 20%, while many will not increase their output over the next year at all.

[3] His safest way to increase the output of a crop is putting more land under that crop. This is indeed what has been happening where farmers respond to the government's moral suasion and economic price and subsidy incentives. From the nation's viewpoint, such an increase is a net one only if previously idle farmland has been brought under that crop; if another crop has been displaced, that increase in one crop is offset by a decrease in another. To achieve a sustained higher

The point is that a national or even regional production target, expressed in absolute or percentage terms, has no operational meaning to an individual farmer. All it tells him is that the government wants him to produce more of that particular crop. Hence, the usefulness of specific crop targets under small family farm conditions is practically nil, except perhaps for their publicity value in focusing public attention upon the importance of agricultural development, and for a rough indication of the amount of modern inputs required to reach such targets. For these purposes, however, no sophisticated quantitative methods in arriving at these targets are justified; indeed, they may be misleading because they profess a degree of predictive accuracy they cannot achieve.

Still, it remains true that higher levels of production require larger quantities of modern inputs coupled with changes in the production process, in practices of new skills, in crop rotations and enterprise combinations, and in the accessibility of credit and marketing facilities. Furthermore, raising the output of particular products requires favorable intercommodity price relationships, cost-benefit ratios, and tenure conditions. These are the factors that control the individual farmer's production decisions and his future output. And these are the factors which national policies must direct in such a way that farmers can take advantage of them and increase output, especially of those products which are most urgently needed for economic development.

These factors, basically of an institutional and organizational nature, do not fit into the global quantitative planning models that deal primarily with the allocation of specific quantities of resources for the production of specific classes of commodities. The current trend of centralizing the national planning functions for all sectors of the economy into a national planning unit carries the danger of overemphasizing the global allocative planning of input and output targets and of neglecting the institutional framework planning for favorable price-cost relations, agricultural credit schemes, and tenure conditions; for the organization of research in adapting modern techniques to local farming conditions; and for the training of extension workers needed to make farmers willing and able to modernize their production processes.

A cursory examination of the agricultural growth rates achieved in

---

level of agricultural production, it is necessary, at least in the short run, to increase yields per acre; this holds even in the long run in countries where the potential margin of cultivation has in practice been reached.

various countries suggests strongly that high growth rates depend primarily on institutional framework planning (Japan, Taiwan, Mexico); where this type of planning has been weak, agricultural progress has been slow, regardless of the thoroughness of central allocative planning. **Planning from Below** In striking contrast to industry, the bulk of agricultural production, and especially of food, comes from millions of small farmers, from small-scale enterprises with a labor force consisting of one family. Some farmers hire a few workers during short periods, others release some family members for outside employment; but the prevailing farm unit in most countries is a family-operated enterprise, a situation that holds for the United States as well as for India. The production efficiency which a family farm can achieve is very high, much higher than people in developing countries can imagine. For instance, in the United States, an average farmer produces enough to feed his own family plus around 12 other families; in India, he produces food for himself and only one-third to one-half of another family. This goes to show that modernization and high efficiency of agriculture does not depend upon transforming family enterprises into large-scale plantation or factory-type units, as many people seem to believe. The examples of Japan and Taiwan show that in the newly developing countries also family farms can attain high efficiency, a fact which in these countries also is in striking contrast to industry.

Barring collectivization of agriculture, national policies for agricultural development must be geared to inducing millions of independent farmers to modernize their production processes. This fact alone calls for a widely dispersed and decentralized method of planning and implementing agricultural development policies.

Another characteristic of agriculture is equally important and points in the same direction: production is based on the biological growth of plants and animals. This growth process depends on microecological conditions which vary widely among localities and which can be controlled only within narrow limits. A particular fertilizer dose that proves profitable with one crop in one locality may bring a loss with the same crop in another locality, or with another crop in the same locality. This means that modern production techniques must be adapted in each area to its ecological conditions. Again, this characteristic contrasts with industrial production techniques, whose technical efficiencies are independent of climate, soils, temperature, and other aspects of physical environment.

All this may well be common knowledge to planners and government leaders. Yet this knowledge does not seem to be sufficiently reflected in the planning and implementation of development policies in most countries. Let us turn to the crucial problem we must solve to render national policies effective at the farm level. How can we plan from the bottom up, rather than from the top down? How can we find out what facilities, services, social conditions, and incentives the farmer needs for making him willing and able to work harder, invest more of his low income, and take what must look to him quite formidable risks? These are the things we ask the farmer to do if we tell him to modernize and increase production. What will make him do so?[4]

1. The farmer needs local facilities for moving more goods into and out of his locality, for getting modern inputs available in time, for grading, storing, processing, and selling farm produce. This means roads, transport, market halls, warehouses, processing plants. The kinds and amounts of these facilities and the financing of their construction must be determined locally; they cannot be planned in central offices.

2. The farmer needs research and extension services to demonstrate modern techniques and adapt them to local conditions. This means usually about one village-level extension worker per 200 or 300 farmers, who is guided by extension specialists working in close cooperation with researchers. The village-level extension worker is the crucial link between farming practice and scientific technology. This link is essential from the start, from the time modern techniques are introduced onward to the stage of highest technological development, because technology is constantly improving and so must farming practice.

3. The farmer needs credit and marketing services at favorable terms. This usually means well-managed cooperatives, because commerical banks are not organized to serve millions of farmers with small loans whose use is earmarked for specific purposes, nor are private merchants interested and capable to do so. Moreover, a loan on the farmer's crop is by far the best collateral security for loans of this nature. This means that credit handled through cooperatives must be secured by the crops sold to the cooperatives.

4. The farmer often needs economic incentives in the form of selective price supports and cost subsidies, at least in the early stages of modernization, when the risk factor involved in adopting new, unfamiliar techniques looms high in the farmer's mind.

[4] For an imaginative exposition of this problem, see A. T. Mosher, *Getting Agriculture Moving* (New York and London: Praeger, 1966).

5. Finally, he needs a rural social environment that encourages the development of his managerial capacities and civic responsibilities, his opportunities for self-improvement, and his participation in public affairs as a fully fledged citizen. This means land tenure conditions providing him with managerial freedom and security of possession of the farm, and protecting him against high rents and interest rates and other terms rendering him subservient to landlords, creditors, and merchants. It means schools and cooperatives and farmers' associations and political parties which he is free to use and in whose activities he can participate without retaliation and intimidation by a local elite bent upon preserving its traditional status of power and prestige.

These are the five basic needs of farmers for bringing about a rapid rate of progress: local transport and marketing facilities; research and extension services; credit and marketing services; price and cost incentives; and a favorable rural social environment. To meet these needs, national policies are required. To render these policies effective at the local level, they must be planned from below, and their specific implementation measures must vary according to the peculiarities of farming regions. Herein lies the most difficult and complex task of fashioning a set of national policies with built-in flexibility for their local adaptation.

For instance, fertilizer supplies are imported, but the provisions for distributing them to farmers and in time when they are needed have often been gravely neglected, largely because the central offices lack sufficient knowledge of where the bottlenecks are, and they have not planned for breaking them. As a result, large quantities of fertilizer have been wasted in bad storage. Improved crop varieties and doses of fertilizer have been promoted under local conditions where they fail to bring benefits, or where farmers cannot buy these inputs for want of credit, or where high crop-share rents make their use unprofitable to tenants. Price supports have failed to reach the farm level. Land reforms have failed to become effective due to lack of specific provisions necessary to overcome the power of the landlords and to strengthen the position of the tenants.

The lesson taught us by such experiences with national development policies is clearly that in order to make them function they must be planned much more from below, with a much greater concern for a combination of policy measures and provisions adjustable to fit local conditions. For this we must undertake fairly detailed studies of the salient features of each major farming region, not only of its ecological characteristics but also of its rural social structure, its facilities and public services, its tenure and the bargaining position, and the social status in which the typical farmer finds himself.[5] These are the most important local facts which must be ascertained, evaluated, and placed in the "feedback" from the rural community level to the national planners and administrators. This process is by all odds the weakest and administratively the least developed of all the planning and implementation activities. Yet the building up of this process of planning from below represents the most urgent and promising step for increasing the viability of national agricultural policies.

Some Difficulties Encountered

Let us examine briefly a recent approach to planning from below undertaken by Ceylon. Since 1965, the government has increased its emphasis on agricultural development. The national goal given the greatest publicity is self-sufficiency in rice and certain vegetable corps like chilies and onions. The "food drive" began with establishing national targets for rice production, which were based on the rate of increase in the last few years and announced in advance of the next crop season. The 1965 and 1966 crops were below the 1964 level mainly due to weather. Some districts, however, did better than others. The government instructed the administrative heads of each district (of which there are 22) to call meetings of all the agricultural officers and chairmen of the Cultivation Committees (consisting of 12 elected farmer-members for an area with about 250 to 300 farmers). In these meetings the harvest of the last season is appraised. Farmers and local officers are asked what they think might be possible to achieve in the next season. These district projections are aggregated into national totals and used, along with other data, to arrive at the national and district targets, expressed in total bushels and average yield per acre. All government district officers dealing with agriculture are instructed to do everything they can to help farmers reach these targets.

Up to this point, the program has no operational usefulness, except perhaps for the publicity surrounding this exercise, which gives officers and farmers a feeling of importance, a sense of urgency for raising output. The targets still have no meaning to individual farmers. If the target in a certain district calls for an increase from 42 to 45 bushels per

[5] For examples of how this might be done, see Rainer Schickele, *Agrarian Revolution and Economic Progress* (New York and London: Praeger, 1968), Chapters 12 and 13.

acre, this means nothing for the farmer who harvested 60 bushels last season, nor for one who obtained only 30.

What really matters are the specific programs carried out to help farmers in raising their yields. Cooperatives and Cultivation Committees are asked to canvass their members on the amount of fertilizers and improved seed they plan to use, how much credit they will need, how much tractor service they require to supplement their animal draught power, etc. These reports are sent to the national offices for use in arranging the distribution of these inputs to the various areas. The People's Bank is instructed to make credit funds available to the individual cooperatives according to their own forecasts of their members' requirements. The Extension Service staff is being strengthened at the village level and given short courses in the particular modern farm practices important in each district. Paddy-yield competitions are set up, and many of the winners get their awards presented personally by the Prime Minister or the Minister of Agriculture. Demonstrations of fertilizer use on cultivators' fields are arranged; the aim is at least one demonstration patch in each Cultivation Committee area. Schoolmasters are asked to organize groups of children to help farmers in transplanting and weeding of paddies.

This list is not exhaustive; there are several other programs for providing specific services and supplies to farmers according to their needs in the various localities. However, these are the specific and locally adjusted policy measures of direct operational usefulness. None of them is quantitatively tied to any specific production target for the district or the nation. These operational policy measures really got started only in 1966, after two poor crop years. No one knows how much of the yield increase in 1967 and 1968 can be attributed to these programs. It is obvious that the weather contributed a good deal, although its contribution is rather slighted in the publicity of the Food Drive. Still there can be no doubt that these measures did help, and that a sustained raise in output depends largely on the efficacy of these and other policy measures of an institutional framework nature.

The difficulties lie in the competent performance of such programs in developing countries. Many cooperatives function very poorly; so do many extension services. Their functions, however, are essential for progress, at least as long as no alternative institutions are in sight to fulfil them better. Hence, our task is to improve their functioning. There are many ways for accomplishing this goal, but they take time and confidence in the principles they serve. We need the courage of well-motivated leaders, both from the ranks of farmers and of government officials, to resist the power of self-seeking persons and temptations of corruption. Such leadership cannot be planned and installed by administrative regulations; it must be encouraged to emerge and can be fostered by moral suasion and social recognition of civic responsibility on the part of the community.

But there are practical ways for improving the performance of such institutions. Training of managers and technical and clerical staff for cooperatives, and paying them adequate salaries are necessary. It is unreasonable to expect the committee members, presumably all full-time farmers with no experience or time for running the cooperatives, to know what personnel with what training is needed. Nor are they prepared to pay salaries that will attract and keep good personnel. It is a legitimate function of government to train such personnel and carry a part of their salary, at least for a period of years.

These problems of cooperatives are common almost everywhere. But some countries are more successful in solving them than others, and thus are proving that something can be done about them.

Similarly, the extension staff is inadequate in numbers and training, especially at the field level, in most developing countries. They must know not only the present farming methods and the problems farmers face; they also must be trained in modern skills particularly important in the area. For the village level, vocational training of one or two years, periodically supplemented by short courses, might prove adequate; supervisory and technically specialized extension officers at the district and national level require advanced training. These extension workers must be the ones who organize and supervise, in cooperation with researchers on the one hand and leading farmers on the other, the use of credit, the field demonstrations of modern practices, yield competitions, and many other activities for accelerating the modernization of farming.

Large-Scale Farms and the Rural Community

So far we have explored the problems of implementing national policies for agricultural progress under family-farm conditions. But there are also rural areas where family farms are interspersed with large-scale farms where the owner or his agent manages the estate, and where the labor force consists of hired workers without managerial functions. These *centrally managed estates* include *plantations* of monocultural enterprises such as sugarcane, rubber, tea, and other usually perennial

crops, and *mixed farming estates* producing annual field crops, sometimes combined with livestock enterprises.[6] Some of the latifundia in
Latin America and most of the distinctly larger than family farms
throughout the world fall in this category of mixed farming estates,
including the collective and state farms in Communist countries.

For the theme of this chapter, the distinction between family farms
and large-scale farms is relevant in three respects. First, the implementation of production planning on large-scale farms is easier to administer,
because government contact with a few large farmers can influence a
comparatively large output, and because large farmers are better
equipped with capital and financial resources, are better educated, are
more commercially oriented, and are socially closer to government and
political leaders. For these reasons, many governments look to the large
farmers for spearheading agricultural progress, and offer them various
inducements in the form of concessions, credit, tax relief, import licenses, etc., which in some cases yield them very high profits on their
investments. This may readily lead to neglecting the needs of small
farmers for modernizing their production techniques.

Second, the large farmer is part of the local elite. By strengthening his
position in the rural community, the opportunities of the small farmer
for improving his managerial capacity, for participating in cooperatives
and group activities of his own choosing, are likely to suffer. The large
farmer finds it easy to increase his holding by acquiring land from small
farmers through purchase or foreclosure and offering them employment
at low wages. It is in the immediate interest of the large farmer to keep
a pool of underemployed laborers available for his expanding operations, to keep their wages low, and to prevent them from organizing
into unions. Hence, a national policy of aiming primarily at the large
farms for production increase is bound to weaken the bargaining power
and opportunities of family farmers.

Third, this weakening of the great majority of the farmers keeps them
poor and excludes them from sharing in the benefits of farm modernization. This results in keeping the demand for industrial goods well
below what it would be under a policy of modernizing family farms and
hence retards industrialization and general economic development.

Theoretically, it is possible to design a policy of promoting output
expansion on large-scale farms without incurring these undesirable side

[6]There are, of course, several intermediate types we cannot examine here. In
Israel, the kibbutz is typically a "mixed farming estate," while the farmers in the
moshav are typically operators of family farms.

effects, for instance by strengthening the bargaining position of farm laborers through unionization and laws prescribing minimum wage rates and adequate living and working conditions. This solution is rarely feasible from the start, since the large farmers are strongly opposed to it and will not accept government financial and other support offered with such conditions. Yet this solution is bound to emerge over time from the restlessness and frustration of small farmers and landless laborers, generating militant forces opposing the large landowners. This process was experienced, for example, in England and Germany and Mexico in the early part of this century, and is going on in some parts of Latin America and Southeast Asia at present.

Lest we lose a sense of proportion in weighing these conflicting arguments, we should realize that the normal course of events favors the large-scale farmers anyway because of their better access to capital, credit, and financial resources in general. The only encouragement to expand output they may require is to raise their awareness of investment and profit potentials in agriculture, making certain unproductive but highly attractive investment opportunities such as real estate and commodity speculation and capital flight much less attractive to them. This might redirect a good part of their savings into agricultural development investment.

At the same time, several policies aimed at family farms are of equal or even greater benefit to large-scale farmers. This, for instance, holds for price supports and foreign exchange priorities allocated to the import of critical farm inputs such as fertilizers and agricultural machinery, pumps, and other supplies. Hence there are effective policy measures available to encourage large farmers in raising their output measures which place little or no burden on the government budget and which do not compete for trained manpower and other resources required for a family-farm-oriented development policy.

Where these two policies do compete for scarce resources, the decision on how they should be divided between large and small farmers should aim at avoiding the undesirable side effects of neglecting the modernization of family farms. These small farms do represent the big majority of all farms, and they do produce the bulk of the food supplies in most non-Communist countries. Experience has proved that they can reach high levels of efficiency if institutional arrangements render farmers willing and able to do so.[7]

[7]In some areas, a considerable proportion of family farms are too small to support a family. They must be consolidated into viable units or provided with

Land Settlement and Rural Progress

There are two ways for expanding food production: raise yields per acre, and bring new land under the plow. Of these two the first is faster and cheaper; the second takes longer and is more expensive, but it is much more glamorous. Developing new land through jungle clearing, irrigation works, and settlement of farmers from overcrowded villages attracts popular attention. It appeals to politicians through the promise of employment opportunities, to engineers through the building of impressive dams, and to tenants, laborers, and farm youth through the hope of obtaining land of their own. It also appeals to financiers, who are much more interested in projects of massive investments than in many small loans for increasing crop yields on present farmlands.

In fact, over the last twenty years, acreage expansion accounted for over 50 percent of the total increase in crop production in many developing countries. Even densely populated India expanded crop acreage by 25 percent between 1948 and 1963, and this accounted for 59 percent of the total increase in crop output.

While some countries have practically reached their physical limits of new farmland development (e.g., Japan and Taiwan), there are many whose physical potential for increasing arable land is well over 50 percent, and in Latin America and Africa over 100 percent (e.g., Brazil, Venezuela, Colombia, Tanzania, Sudan).[8]

The case for land and irrigation development is pressing where masses of people are crowded on undersized farms while potentially productive land remains unused. Modern technology has made it possible to develop land by methods not known in the past. The real cost of land clearing and of construction of dams, canals, and tube wells for irrigation has been greatly reduced, and remote areas have become accessible by modern transportation methods.

Newly developed land without skilled farmers and community services is as useless as a car without a driver. Irrigation projects have fallen in disuse because farmers did not get the support of a well-functioning rural community required to make full use of the new land and water resources. Putting settlers on the land and letting them fend for themselves involves heavy cost in human frustration and economic waste

---

off-farm employment. In Japan, for instance, over 50% of the farm family's income is obtained from rural, industrial, and other off-farm sources.

[8]See United States Department of Agriculture, "Changes in Agriculture in 26 Developing Nations, 1948-63," Washington, D.C.: Foreign Agricultural Economic Report No. 27 (November 1965), p. 27.

because the land remains underutilized at a level much below its potential capacity. Farm settlement schemes offer a rare opportunity for pioneering with new farming practices, new tenure, and other institutional arrangements. The new land is free from an obstructive agrarian structure, from obstacles presented by undersized farms, absentee landlords, a poor and subservient tenantry. The project starts from a clean slate. Such settlement schemes must become pilot projects for rural development provided with a competent staff. Since ministers and directors are under popular pressure for giving the scheme high priority, the project manager can have ready access to top officials for securing current support, an opportunity that is all too rarely enjoyed by field officers in old farming areas.

Settlement schemes must function as catalysts and energize progressive forces far beyond the project area. Land development schemes without such a dynamic settlement policy are bound to yield disappointing results, often not more than a drop in the bucket, from the viewpoint of its effect upon total farm production and rural progress.

A Challenge to Statesmen

To achieve a good balance in developmental investment between the rural and the urban sectors is a difficult task. Leaders in government, business, and labor are city oriented; private investors are attracted to industry and trade but show very little interest in agriculture. Corporate finance, so eminently successful in industry, does not work in agriculture. Urban interests succeed much better in getting public investment in schools and roads than rural villagers. True, equivalent facilities in rural areas have a higher per capita cost. But these facilities are just as essential for raising agricultural productivity as they are for industrialization. Without them, agriculture will not be able to pull its weight along with industry and trade in the troika of progress.

This puts a heavy burden on enlightened leadership. Farmers and rural villagers are politically less articulate than are comparable interest groups in the cities. In modern times, the mark of a statesman lies in his championship for the inarticulate and economically handicapped. Such championship is not purely a labor of love; a statesman knows that by representing the interests of large masses of poor disadvantaged people in parliament and at the council table he can count on their support as they are in ascendency to political power.

Part One

**4. Regional Planning   S. Herweijer
as a Tool for Rural
Development
in Advanced
Countries**

Starting Points

In discussing regional planning as a tool for rural development it is necessary to indicate some starting points. In advanced countries the most important are the three following: more people, more prosperity, and more leisure.

More People   Every forecast of the future must start from a forecast of population, but this forecast has been proved most difficult to make. After World War II and especially in the sixties the problem of overpopulation has been called the most compelling of all for the coming generations. Quite recently all population forecasts were shown to have been too low, as a rule. However, in the United Kingdom the turning point was registered in 1965: the real growth of population was about 25,000 lower than the forecasts in question. A similar development can be seen in The Netherlands today, where official forecasts for the year 2000 evaluated in 1965, ranging some 20 million, are reduced now to the range of about 18 million.

Be that as it may, the growth of population is in any case a fact, and this growth may lead in densely populated countries, such as The Netherlands, to a so-called "structural overpopulation." The characteristics of such a structural overpopulation are a growing pollution of air, water, and soil as well as increasing noise.

More Prosperity   In connection with the physical consequences of this so-called structural overpopulation, there is also a frustration of cultural and psychical needs. The population optimum is not so much determined by the number of inhabitants to a square mile as by the cultural pattern and by the way the population of a region can work, live, and relax. This kind of frustration of nonphysical needs increases with the increase of prosperity.

There is thus a direct relation between the first starting point (more people) and the second (more prosperity). That prosperity increases is

S. Herweijer—The Netherlands. Agricultural engineer, Wageningen (1942); director of the Government Service for Land and Water Use; director of the Foundation for the Administration of Agricultural Land.
This paper has been composed in cooperation with E. Denig, engineer of the Government Service for Land and Water Use, Utrecht, The Netherlands.

inevitable, especially as a result of technical developments. The Dutch Central Economic Planning Office has calculated for The Netherlands that, with a growth percentage of 3.7 a year, the gross national product may be in the year 2000 3.5 times as high as it is in 1970. The private consumption level may be doubled in the same period. And all these predictions will be realized in relation to a continually decreasing work time, probably to 34 to 38 hours a week.

More Leisure Decreasing work time directly confronts us with the third starting point, more leisure, which poses a very important challenge. As various types of industry are eliminated by mechanization and automation, a mental changeover is becoming more and more necessary. Education, at present almost entirely vocational, must in future pay more attention to the instruction of how to live and how to use free time. At present we are not nearly prepared to meet the free time era from the pedagogic and the psychological points of view.

Free time is more and more regarded as being a kind of constitutional right of the individual, namely, free time in both meanings: as leisure time and as creative noncommercial activity. It is necessary to take into account these two types of free time when developing the rural areas.

Intensification of Land Use

The three stated starting points must lead inevitably to a more intensive use of the total living space. For this purpose we can draw a distinction among urban, recreational, and rural spheres.

Urbanization A quickly growing urbanization is characteristic of our time. World population increases per annum by 2 percent, but that of the towns by 4 percent. During the next 40 years we shall build more towns than were built during the whole of human history.

When we speak about urbanization, we most often mean the morphological way of urbanization, characterized by more or less continual building, and by a number of inhabitants of at least 10,000. But we also know social and economic ways of urbanization as well, as exemplified by the fact that the vocational structure is mainly nonrural. And finally we have a kind of cultural urbanization, that is to say, the pattern of behavior of the total population is becoming similar to that of a modern town inhabitant.

In all aspects we can expect a continually growing urbanization in the future. It is evident that the city of the future must provide good living conditions. In The Netherlands we have consciously chosen a so-called "concentrated deconcentration," a distributed setting of big towns and smaller towns. Three important motives in this policy are to provide a variety of residential environments and housing conditions; to maintain the possibility of public transport, this factor being a primary living condition for the centers of the cities; and to provide a rather high level of urban facilities, but evenly dispersed over the whole country.

Recreation With respect to recreation also we have to take into account a more intensive land use. Such intensive use can be realized best by creating special recreation facilities to meet the need of people to be in the midst of others in the open air. We can think in this connection of beaches and swimming pools (with 2,000 to 3,000 persons to a hectare), of specific recreation centers being highly visited (with 500 to 2,000 persons to a hectare) and town parks (with 50 to 500 persons to a hectare). The "Second Report on Physical Planning in The Netherlands," published in 1966, is careful to pay much attention to the recreational possibilities of all kinds of park areas, e.g., town parks, parks for city regions, and park and aquatic sports areas of regional or national importance.

The promotion of a high diversity of recreational possibilities and of an efficient use of the space assigned to recreational purposes also includes the fact that there must be possibilities of recreation and recuperation other than active athletic ones. Especially more intellectual people in our society show an increasing desire to enjoy rest and peace. Some seek this rest in contemplation; others are content to enjoy the scenery. Recreational facilities must provide for these preferences as well.

Rural Development Intensification of land use is also very clearly needed in relation to rural development. Particularly is this the case in areas under the direct influence of the urbanization process, where rural land use is greatly influenced by the presence of large consumer markets having an important spending capacity. The farms in those areas must be set up in a very commercial way, that is to say, with a business-like and professionally skilled management; with financially intensive equipment; and with long-standing buying and selling agreements.

The managers have to be flexible in psychological, technical, and financial respects and they must, so to say, "cultivate" their market even more than their land. In advanced countries the whole agricultural production process must and will develop slowly but surely—and even before the end of this century—in a way near to the industrial production pattern. Larger enterprises with more manpower, using the various forms of services by private firms and also consolidating under different conditions, will play an important part in this whole development. Farm enlargement develops quickly, and migration of farm labor will be considerable in the next few decades.

Importance of a Functional Structure
Up to now we have dealt with some aspects of land use resulting in a more intensive application of that use. It would not do, however, if we would try to concentrate all kinds of functions in one place or one area. Therefore a functional structure is obligatory. This means that we have in view the plural function of rural areas, the importance of conscious zoning, and the maximization of land use.

The Plural Function of Rural Areas Rural areas show a clearly plural character. Land is an essential production element in which factors like soil quality, ground water level, and size and shape of lots play a part. Roads serve the farmers as a necessary infrastructure with respect to the problems of farming, including transportation. But they are also a means of communication among the villages, and they have an increasing importance for the purpose of touring. Water management includes both a complex system of main canals for the supply and discharge of water, and individual drainage for farmers and market gardeners.

This plural character is intensified moreover by the fact that in advanced countries land is not only important for production, but also for consumption, that is to say, as a domain for working and living. As a result, ideas concerning the development of rural areas are rapidly changing. Care for agrarian production alone must make room for a pluriform policy with regard to rural areas. That implies that next to measures for the rural population, to ensure it an equal share in the general growth in prosperity, measures must be taken for the benefit of the urban population. For the farmers it includes measures for the improvement of the agricultural structure, industrialization of rural areas, social-cultural provisions, and improvement of traffic and transportation facilities. The measures for city people include provisions for recreation, nature preservation, and landscaping.

Although a rural area performs more than one function, it has a dominant function which varies, e.g., a function for agricultural production, for recreation, or as open space. The already mentioned "Second Report on Physical Planning" in The Netherlands makes distinctions among the mostly large-scale agricultural areas outside the immediate sphere of influence of town and recreation; the agricultural-recreational areas; and the rural areas within the urban sphere.

The Mostly Large-Scale Agricultural Areas The land use policy for these areas is first of all determined by the requirements of a sound agricultural structure. Regarding the constant process of structural change and adaptation in agriculture, the basic aim of government policy is to create such conditions that individual adaptations to new situations can be made readily. Within this program, land consolidation is very important.

In close connection with this comprehensive agricultural program operates a program of regional industrialization (economic development). The activities of these two sectors are complementary from the point of view of employment. Due to the special conditions of The Netherlands, with its rather extreme concentration of population and employment in the western part of the country, much attention must be given to a better distribution of economic activities over the country as a whole. It is a matter of common interest that the migration from agriculture in less developed parts of the country is counterbalanced by raising the level of nonagrarian employment in these regions. In this way, raising the standard of living outside metropolitan areas goes together with checking excessive congestion within these areas.

Agricultural-Recreational Areas Those parts of rural areas which offer attractive scenery have important recreational functions. Some of the most beautiful ones will be developed as national or regional park areas, necessitating a further development of recreational facilities. The character of these areas will be closely associated with their size. In extensive park areas there can still be large agricultural parts; not all areas with attractive scenery belong to park regions. Nevertheless, agricultural areas too will accomplish a mixed function of agriculture and recreation. In both types of regions—park areas and agricultural areas—the structure of agriculture will often have to be modernized. Therefore the possibilities of the comprehensive agricultural programs mentioned before are applicable here as well.

Rural Areas in the Urban Sphere In this era of urbanization, rural areas have an important part to play to divide elements between urban complexes and to provide a large variety of recreational facilities, especially for everyday and weekend recreation. These rural areas within and between the city regions (the so-called "buffer zones") should have the character of well-kept open spaces with such functions and such design that the cities themselves will have a direct interest in their preservation.

In a number of cases the proper organization of the areas around the cities actually demands reconstruction. This is particularly evident if recreation facilities have to be created in still largely agrarian buffer zones. Further, reconstruction is also often necessary if the agrarian land use is maintained, since the continuation of agriculture in these areas close to the city is possible only if the areas are not too small, and if they can boast of good external production conditions. For agrarian reconstruction of this type, land consolidation is the normal instrument.

Zoning In the future we shall need a conscious zoning either in direct or in indirect urbanization, that is to say, in the case of town building and in that of creating recreational facilities. In town building we must avoid individual nuclei growing together into an endless mass of settlements, where the rural areas will be eliminated almost totally. The point is to preserve open space. Open space has a positive function, serving at the same time more than one aim. It is not absolutely necessary that open space receive a recreational designation. Even a rural space can achieve a very good contrast with concentrations of population. We can thus say that agriculture is also one of the shaping elements of town building and should be appreciated as such.

But on the other hand it is doubtful whether open spaces near big cities may stand firm without special protective measures. In this respect the San Francisco Bay area story is interesting; urbanization developed so quickly and so irrationally that it has become no longer possible to maintain the necessary "green belts." Since 1964 the state budget of The Netherlands shows the need for creating buffer zones, as at present being developed in The Netherlands between Delft and Rotterdam, and between Amsterdam and Haarlem. In both cases it concerns recreation areas of some 2,000 hectares, while in the first case it is also the intention to preserve a small rural area. In both cases we think about a transfer of proprietorial rights to public authorities. It was decided to buy land with funds of the Ministries of Physical Planning and of Recreation and Social Affairs, by the Foundation for the Administration of Agricultural Land (of the Ministry of Agriculture), a foundation being put under the Service for Land and Water Use. Moreover, we are directing an interdepartmental Research Committee which has the task of advising the government in the future concerning the legislative, financial, and organizational aspects of land-property acquisition and the shaping of these regions.

Maximization of Land Use Functional planning is strongly promoted by aiming at maximum land use. A first goal is the differentiation of production. In advanced countries we cannot avoid the necessity for achieving rural production under the best conditions of soil quality, climatology, managment techniques, and economy.

A second aspect concerns the efforts to realize an optimal land use in the surroundings of the cities. We can compare this fact with the von Thunen rings. There exists a natural and comprehensible endeavor to realize maximum prices for the land. It is the task of the government to support these planned changes of development by means of a specific structural policy. But also in this way it is not possible to shield agriculture in such areas from being exposed to great tensions.

On the one hand we have pointed out already that a more intensive method of agriculture with an important commercial aspect may develop. A significant example in this line is the German *Grosskuhhof* project, founded by 60 farmers in the surroundings of the city of Essen, where 2,000 cows are producing milk of top quality. On the other hand we can establish the fact that agriculture falls off in the vicinity of an urbanized region. The expected rise in land prices is also often a reason to delay the sale of land, and consequently it becomes fallow land. This so-called *Sozialbrache* is a more frequent symptom if the region in question is more intensively urbanized. The consequent neglect of the parcels in question (a neglect also possible in the case of part-time and free-time enterprises) can be a danger for water management, for control of diseases and weeds, and for the appearance of the landscape.

Thus it is not surprising that measures are taken to preserve the rural areas in question. In international physical planning circles the question has been posed in the meantime, whether the survival of the private landed property system is possibly not the real weak point in actions to preserve agriculture in urbanized areas. However, the consequences of buying all the land concerned have to be studied very carefully.

Regional Planning
As a consequence of the plural character of rural areas, it is necessary to determine for many years in advance what should be achieved in one or more fields of activity. This means planning for the region as a whole, without overlooking the needs of national policy.

Regional Planning and National Planning Regional planning should be a part of national planning. In many countries, town planning and country planning are usually separately dealt with. Historically seen, this state of affairs is quite comprehensible. Yet, actually town planning and country planning are an integrated activity derived from economic, social, and political planning. As a matter of fact, points of view with regard to the distribution of income over various classes of the population; the system of taxation; the establishment of priorities in the development of agriculture, industry and services; the extent of autarchy; the increase in population—be these conditions dependent or not on factors in the spheres of public health, education, or religious attitude— are to a great extent directive of the development of the economy and social structure of a nation. Once these and other elements are interwoven with an integrated national economic and social plan, it becomes possible to draft derived divisional plans.

These divisional plans can be classified into national facet plans and regional plans. The national facet plans are the adoption of specific features, e.g., an agricultural plan, an industrialization plan, an energy plan, a recreation plan, an education plan, a traffic plan, a housebuilding plan. By preference these plans should be long-term plans. The value of these plans will increase if they do not depend too much on a few people (e.g., if they are not affected by a change of ministers) but are drawn up and promoted by the administration of the individual departments. The value of these plans is greater if they are developed in collaboration with other related ministries, and especially with the Ministry of Finance.

The annual divisional plans should be deduced from the long-term plans; if feasible, a further development of the long-term plan should be continuously studied while the annual plan is being implemented. The part of the plan that is short term should be realized, and the long-term part should be kept up to date. This as well as the adaptation of the divisional plan should be accomplished in order to adjust the divisional plan concerned continuously with the development of other divisional plans. The mutual dependence and mutual influence exerted among plans is of prominent importance and must be closely watched.

The regional plan has a character of its own and should preferably be an integrated one. The choice of the system of implementation depends on the prevailing conditions. A starting point could be an integrated survey of economic, social, and sociopsychological problems. According to such a study the priorities can be determined. Subsequently the facet plans for the region can be contrived. The study and implementation of the facet plans can be carried out either by a central service or by the separate departments. In a country with well-equipped and decentralized departmental services, a coordinated implementation of the regional facet plans by the departmental services will most likely be the preferable course of action. In that case the continuity is probably better secured, and a certain measure of continuation after completion will be possible.

Development of Agriculture In most advanced countries the problem of the development of agriculture is a complex one. In the framework of national production, agriculture should be developed in such a way that it contributes to the utmost to the national economy. Due to the fact that the production factor, land, is very difficult to appraise, many decisions will be of an arbitrary nature. Moreover, it is a long-term process. Not until 10 or 15 years after the moment that the most important decisions for the development of the region are taken will the influence on the economy of the region or the nation become visible.

In a world with a very rapid development of technical farming methods, of knowledge and capability of the farmers, and of possibilities of integration of activities, the short-run aspects are generally more overemphasized and overevaluated than the long-run aspects. As a result, many agriculture development plans executed after World War II are too small of scope, too conservative so far as farm size and farm structure are concerned, too much based on an economic trade system of autarchy and food shortage, and very often too little integrated with the other economic sectors, such as industry and services.

Agricultural development plans usually require a preparatory term of at least 5 to 10 years, and the same or even a longer period of implementation. After this period farming in the area concerned will have to be practiced for 15 to 25 years in accordance with a justified system. This implies that the plans must be flexible. We list three items on which agricultural development plans sometimes show shortcomings.

Development of Nonagricultural Employment Right from the beginning room must be left open in every agricultural development plan for the development of nonagricultural employment. The possibility of transfer of labor from farming in most areas is essential for a further development of agriculture. If such a transfer is not taking place, the result will be perceptible or hidden unemployment.

Farm Size For the same reason the size of arable and pasture-land farms in agricultural development areas should not be fixed too low. The size of the farms is dependent on the farming system applied, that is, on the size of the yields and the rate of labor productivity. In many countries, labor productivity shows an annual increase of 3 to 5 percent. It is anticipated that this growing percentage will go still higher. In arable farming there are many possibilities for mechanization and automatization; the same statement applies to livestock farming and horticulture as well.

Small holdings are justified in the future only if their existence is based on a high output of produce. From an economic point of view, however, it will be dangerous to put too much confidence in small farms. The quantity of national and international agricultural production may become higher than is justified by consumption. Large farms offer more scope for an increase of labor productivity without running the risk of an excessive increase of production.

Expectations of Soil Productivity Sometimes there are too high expectations about the productivity of some soils. In view of the fact that the surpluses of food in advanced countries might become a problem of a permanent nature, it cannot be considered wise to proceed with the reclamation or improvement of submarginal soils. It is scarcely possible to give a proper answer to the question of what exactly should be understood by submarginal. The criterion should be that spending of either labor or capital, at one time or annually, otherwise than to purchase the property under consideration, is expected to be remunerative. Also the plural function of rural areas has to be taken into account, and these submarginal areas can often be put to uses more productive than agriculture.

Rehabilitation of Backward Agricultural Areas Modern agriculture has to be ever more rationalized and mechanized. This method of farming requires larger holdings, better opening up of farming land, better water management, better equipment—in short, a radical improvement of the whole agricultural infrastructure which lies far beyond the possibilities of the individual farmer. Since the early twenties the Dutch government has been promoting such activities under the Land Consolidation Act. A decade ago, a long-term plan was drawn up for this purpose. It tends to the improvement of about 75 percent of our total agricultural area at a rate of 50,000 to 60,000 hectares per year.

The land consolidation projects started as mere technical improvements of moderate size. Gradually, however, they have developed into complete rural reconstruction plans covering areas of several thousands of hectares. Implementation goes hand in hand with slum clearance, the establishment of better social facilities, the introduction of new methods, the awakening of a new mentality, a greater social and cultural consciousness quite apart from the increase in the standard of living in the area. Great efforts are being made in order to reduce the number of small holdings. Besides, land consolidation is a means of allocating land for urban development and for the construction of motor roads and facilities for outdoor recreation and other public purposes without affecting agricultural interests. Naturally, the Dutch conception of land consolidation is not valid everywhere. But it is possible to draw attention to three general aspects in regional planning.

Survey of the Region   A survey is necessary of an area that should not be too small. Especially the question will arise for what reasons the total agricultural structure of one area will be better than that of another. To answer this question it is necessary to analyze the purely agricultural internal and external factors of production, internally the actual management of the farms themselves, and externally the conditions prevailing as regards the more collective items such as soil, water, means of transport, marketing facilities, etc.

Surveys must be combined and analyzed on a number of essential items, and considering all physical and cultural factors. From the point of view of a well-balanced national policy it is advisable to tackle in particular those areas where many factors are deficient. Before elaborating the detailed projects, a number of rough alternative development plans should be drafted. Of much importance here is the decision what to stress: the improvement of agriculture, or more particularly industrial activity.

Alternative Plans   Alternative plans ought to be drafted on the basis of cost-benefit calculations. In many countries these kinds of calculations show a very theoretical and speculative character. Therefore, in most countries, rougher methods of priority determination will very likely have to be based on a rough estimate of the cost, but the benefits will have to be based rather on feeling and guesswork than on real calculation. This implies that the decision of which areas will be designated will frequently be based for a large part on other considerations than those of a purely economic nature.

In addition the question may arise, whether in determining the priority of areas the highest cost-benefit ratio will have to be decisive, or whether social factors should also play a role. A combination of a more nuanced economic, social, and political determination of priority seems to be more justified than a determination of priority based on either element alone, or on not theoretically quantified economic calculations.

Farmer Participation   Human beings must be the starting point of any kind of planning, for they are the ones to participate in it. Especially and notably in the case of physical planning and rural development we have to start from a real and early consideration of the people concerned. But also after implementation, the farmers have to make good use of all investments.

It is clear that intensive systems of extension work are required for the achievement of all planning goals. It is essential that the farmers sympathize fully with the schemes which are implemented. Preparatory, executive, and follow-through committees will have to be established for this work, and local leaders will have to be nominated on these committees. Close cooperation between executive agencies and the local representatives will be a prerequisite for success. If such cooperation is realized, the remunerability of the invested money will prove to be much higher.

Conclusion

What do we conclude from the foregoing? Starting from the fact that we have to reckon in the future with more people, more prosperity, and more leisure, it is necessary to take into account a more intensive method of land use. This conclusion is valid not only in the case of urban, but also in that of rural development. In that connection we see the necessity of a functional shaping, a process to be directed by the authorities in concert with the participating population. Such long-term planning not only demands insight into the question of current and future needs and wants, but also asks for an efficient policy and the readiness of the population to sacrifice some things now in the expectation of having possible returns only in the future.

And with this the economic aspect appears. In advanced countries the object of a strong economic growth demands the use of all means of improving productivity. This is partly the task of the employers, but governmental authorities are able to support it in an important manner by efficient planning of land use and by adequate expansion of the infrastructure. In this connection a cost-benefit analysis can be important, although we have to express here values difficult to evaluate in money. This economic aspect must not be forgotten in the regional development policy, which should be based on regional studies. In this research at least four aspects have to be reviewed: the economic (agriculture, industry, trade, recreation); the urbanizational (in morphological and psychological ways); the sociological (cultural inheritance and cultural aims); and the ecological (the conditions of the nature and the setting).

Designing, executing, and administering regional development plans is becoming more and more a science. The time that it was a "one-man show" has gone; it is done no longer by a single technician but has been developed by a team of specialists. Agriculturalists, economists, physical planners, sociologists, and civil servants have to work together to get integrated plans. In an expanding economy agriculture is only a part, and often a small part, of a nation's overall economy; therefore separate agricultural planning is in the long run a dangerous enterprise. For the well-being of people in nearly every region there is a need for multipurpose planning. And finally we may never forget that planning cannot be restrained to the shaping of developments of the present. There does not exist a final situation, so we must leave ample possibilities for future changes.

Part One

Regional planning is increasingly becoming a tool for development, a fact that in turn has led to considerable advance in, and proliferation of, regional analysis and planning techniques. The bulk of research and practical application of these techniques is made in advanced countries, a fact which is clearly reflected in their nature. Emphasis is laid on analytical tools generally requiring large quantities of refined data and considerable mathematical sophistication. Attempts to apply such planning tools in the developing countries have often ended in failure. The more obvious reason is technical—the lack of sufficiently refined data. Recently, however, doubt has been expressed more and more frequently concerning the validity of planning methods relying primarily on analytical techniques as an approach to the development of underdeveloped regions. There is increasing suspicion, particularly on the part of those personally involved in development work, that even if the technical problems can be overcome, the results will be of little practical value. In this paper an attempt will be made to explore further this topic and to outline a conceptual framework for regional planning for underdeveloped countries and particularly for their rural areas.

Analytical Tools in Development Planning
The formulation of policy measures capable of inducing economic growth has in recent years become a highly sophisticated procedure, based on the use of mathematical models and various analytical techniques. The hope has been expressed that the more refined these tools become, the more effective will the planning process be.

The use of analytical tools for planning purposes is based on the assumption that it is possible to formulate the most effective measures for changing situation A in the present to situation B in the future, while still at situation A. The choice of both target and policy is made at the beginning, before the implementation takes place. In practice this approach means that once an area has been selected for development, the first step required, after setting the goals, is the preparation of a

Raanan Weitz—Israel. Ph.D., University of Florence, 1938; head of the Settlement Department, the Jewish Agency; head of the Settlement Study Centre, Rehovot; consultant to various international organizations.

survey in order to obtain the maximum relevant data. The second step is the formulation of the most effective policy measures by means of various analytical methods and mathematical models. This approach may be compared to the launching of a ballistic missile, whereby all the necessary data must be obtained and all the arrangements made in advance, so that once the missile is launched, it will hit the target without further intervention. Implicit in this approach is that situation B is both realistic and desirable and will continue to be so for the duration of the plan period. In other words, it is assumed that the best B can be chosen from the starting point A.

Recent attempts to apply this approach to regional planning have usually taken the form of comprehensive models of regional economies. These models are derived mostly from similar models of national economies, and are based on systems of mathematical equations expressing the quantitative relationships among factors operating in the economy. It is believed that if the model embraces a sufficiently large number of factors, it will describe the economy adequately. Such possibility seems to be practical due to development of modern computers which permit the inclusion of numerous equations in a single model. It is now possible to construct highly complex models that can include an ever growing number of variables, presumably approximating real-life conditions more and more closely. Such models may be regarded as mathematical guinea pigs, electronic simulations of reality, that enable the planner to experiment vicariously with the formulation of alternative plans of development. It is expected that further refinements of such models will eventually lead to the formulation of a universally applicable method of development planning.

Unfortunately, it is becoming increasingly apparent that the models as they appear at present are still unsuitable for practical application as tools for development planning. Two major reasons are usually cited by those who have had practical experience in the field [28, especially Part Two, "The Human Factor in Agricultural Development"]. First, there are many important factors, especially those which relate to the social and organizational spheres, that do not lend themselves to mathematical representation and that cannot be fitted to equations without losing their true meaning. Attributing quantitative values to these factors cannot but distort their meaning. Indeed, it is generally considered that the major difficulty in the practical application of analytical models is the assignment of relative values or weights to the different factors involved. This is true for all countries and for all levels of development, but it is doubly true in traditional societies living under conditions of a subsistence economy, where the basic information concerning the economic structure and the modes of behavior is still missing.

Second, a considerable number of factors cannot be foreseen and assessed in advance by the planners. These dynamic factors appear only during the transition from situation A to B. Therefore they cannot be included in a model which is prepared prior to actual implementation and which is, in fact, a static model. This criticism applies particularly in the case of a rapid development process involving structural changes, such as transformation of the production system. The achievement of structural change is, in fact, one of the major aims and purposes of development planning.

Recently several dynamic models have been evolved which are designed not only to take into account changes in the individual factors but also in the overall framework, i.e., in the values of the parameters or assumptions that underlie the entire system. It is quite possible that the development of such models will lead to the creation of a dynamic method of planning that will be applicable in this regard. This goal, however, has not yet been achieved.

Development Planning in Advanced versus Developing Countries
Apart from the technical limitations inherent in the mathematical mode of expression as such, there is a much more fundamental consideration which renders the approach to development planning in the advanced countries inapplicable in the developing countries. Development planning in the former group is designed for an efficiently operating economy. Its major concern therefore lies in the allocation of resources among the different regions and economic sectors of a given country, with a view to maximize the national product, employment, and income. To achieve this aim, governments apply various policies, mostly in the form of monetary and fiscal measures, such as taxes, subsidies, and price regulations. These are all aimed at the channeling of resources to their most productive uses.

Underlying this approach is the fact that the advanced countries have already reached the stage where supply is in excess over demand, and the constant gap threatens to throw the economy off balance. Consequently these countries seek to stimulate demand in order to meet the expanding supply. It is assumed that since the production system operates efficiently it can be expected to adjust automatically to the changes in demand.

Essentially this approach to planning maintains that once the demand is known or projected for a certain time range, it is possible to formulate the most effective policies and the required supply will be forthcoming. Implicit in this assumption is that the producers are both willing and capable of responding to the policy measures set by the government, and that there is a free mobility of the production factors among different uses.

This approach is not effective in the conditions of developing countries. Here the problem is not that of stimulating demand, but of creating an effective system of supply. This is particularly true for agricultural production, which is of prime importance in these countries. It is reasonably easy to calculate the quantity and composition of agricultural commodities which would be required to meet the demand. Estimates of nutritional norms and levels of income would give the planner a sufficiently accurate picture of what is needed. The difficulty lies in the fact that agricultural producers do not respond to this demand. This lack of response derives from a number of reasons, the most important being the existence of institutional barriers which prevent the producers from utilizing the existing resources in the desired manner. The present institutional arrangements in most of the developing countries seriously hamper the mobility of production factors. Outdated land tenure systems, lack of training facilities, poor communications, and inadequate supporting systems are but a few examples of this kind.

Moreover, policy measures evolved in the advanced countries are based on "modern" behavior patterns which do not hold in traditional societies characterized by completely different codes of behavior. Under such circumstances it is impossible to rely on the producers to adjust smoothly and efficiently to policy measures which are effective in "Western" societies. This limitation has been recognized by many scholars and development workers who have had to deal with situations of this kind:

It would appear that the splitting of *homo economicus* into a separate analytic entity, a common procedure since Adam Smith, in theorizing about growth in advanced economies, is much less suited to countries that have not yet made the transition to self-sustained growth [1].

... models, constructed around the Western concepts of employment, savings, investment, capital-output ratio and aggregate product, are superficial and not a relevant attempt to grasp causal relations in the under-developed countries. Many of the concepts used are not adequate to reality. For the rest, the almost lack of data means that the chosen parameters cannot be ascertained on the foundation of empirical knowledge; hence, they do not even pretend to be anything else than a demonstration of a general way of thinking. As this way of thinking is an inadequate characterisation of reality in the region, even their illustrative value is a figment of the imagination. As a guide to further research they will tend to direct it in an unrealistic, superficial and unreproductive direction and they contain a built-in policy bias [17].

One might compare the use of Western concepts and approaches to planning in developing countries to the situation where a captain tries to navigate a ship by operating the wheel on the deck while the rudder is disconnected.

What the developing countries need is, first and foremost, institutional reform, to lay the foundation for an effective supply system. Without prior institutional adjustments designed to bring about the necessary changes in a country's "way of doing things" and especially in its production processes, Western planning methods are to a large extent irrelevant. This has been noted, for instance, by Balogh:

In underdeveloped areas there are reasons, additional to those in fully mature industrial countries, to make uncertain the applicability of the simple Keynesian analysis. Institutional reforms eliminating these hindrances, or at least modifying and improving the defective agricultural framework, would seem as indispensable as direct controls which can discriminately deal with certain acute bottlenecks, without having to cut income. The great dormant potentialities of these improvements should be emphasized: They probably represent by far the most hopeful avenue of development, both in respect to the utilization of the vast idle manpower of all these countries, and at the same time also as one of the most fruitful and productive ways of employing scarce capital resources [3].

A Different Approach for Developing Countries

For the purpose of implementing rural development programs in developing countries an entirely different approach is required, one that is geared to their specific needs. Although the primary goal of such programs is often defined as raising agricultural output, this goal will not be attained unless many subgoals concerning institutional arrangements are fulfilled simultaneously. These subgoals relate, for example, to land use rights, organization of the rural communities, organization of the supporting system of services and facilities, or the spread of know-how among farmers. Such factors represent different elements of the institutional structure within which the economic forces operate. Unless this structure is properly adjusted, the effort to increase total production is bound to fail. This adjustment is the essence of the approach known as *institutional planning*.

The elements of institutional planning . . . affect the complex relationships of the peasant to the various spheres of his life. The important ones are: in relation to the State—administration; in relation to lands—land tenure and settlement; in relation to the financing of agricultural activities—agricultural credit; in relation to co-workers—cooperation; and finally, in relation to agricultural and economic development—education and extension [15].

In the developing countries it is not sufficient to determine the environmental conditions, to select the best possible way of utilizing material resources, and to expect the people to follow the chosen way of action. The emphasis should be placed on the people themselves, their aspirations and motives—sometimes known, sometimes only guessed at—and their capacity for utilizing the available resources. It is necessary to seek their participation, to provoke their interest, and at the same time to remove those barriers which prevent them from sharing in the development effort. The fundamental attribute of the approach required under such circumstances is its capacity to create such an institutional framework in which the people will not only be able to absorb innovations in the production process, but will be interested in doing so.

The rationale behind this approach is that development is not a goal unto itself but has as its object the people, their welfare, and their needs. Every development plan should therefore focus on man and his ability to utilize resources in a manner that will bring him the greatest benefit. Although this seems obvious, this attitude is relatively new, as Jacoby points out:

Before the second world war, the welfare of the people might also have been important and economic history included remarkable features marked by humanitarian and welfare spirit—but these features were side aspects of economic development . . . focussed on production and only production. . . . In colonial times the human factor was considered a tool, perhaps an essential tool, functioning in the big economic machine. . . . Modern development strategy considers the human factor not as a tool, but its economic and social rise as the final objective of development; institutional planning is determined to ensure the achievement of this objective [15].

Today this approach is gaining wide recognition. Nevertheless it has not yet been reflected in methods of development planning currently in use. A greater stress is needed on the fact that the human element should be an active participant in the development effort. Financial and technical measures are extremely important in any effort to increase production, but in the absence of active participation on the part of the people concerned, the effect of these measures will be relatively small. The individual producer should be regarded as a human being, not as another factor of production, and plans should be coordinated with the desires of the population for whom they are designed.

Apart from its emphasis on the human element and on institution building, the approach required for developing countries must also be capable of circumventing the limitations inherent in the analytical tools of planning. It will be recalled that these limitations refer mainly to the static character of analytical models and to the fact that many factors operating in the development process cannot be accounted for by such models. It is therefore essential to elaborate a method for planning that will meet the following requirements.

First, it must be integrative, that is, it must be capable of identifying all the factors affecting the development process and operating within it. Efficient planning depends to a large extent on the widest possible use of the largest number of factors that can be isolated, studied, and controlled. The planner is concerned, in particular, with the possible effects of change in one factor or group of factors on future situations. We have already pointed out that many of the most important—perhaps crucial—factors of development cannot be taken into account by current planning methods. They are often impossible to quantify, or else their quantification leads to biases in the evaluation of their role in development. It is therefore necessary to find another way of incorporating these factors within the planning process.

Moreover, each development phenomenon is usually analyzed and tested with the analytical tools of the various social science disciplines (economics, sociology, organization, etc.), each of which concentrates on a specific facet of the phenomenon and attributes to it a special significance. However, in order to understand the function of each facet and its role in the process of development it is necessary to assign "correct" weight to the various facets as they arise from the different disciplinal analyses. The desired planning method must have the capacity to carry out this complex weighting as an inseparable part of the planning process.

Second, it must be dynamic. This implies that the planning method must be sufficiently flexible and adaptable to absorb, *mutatis mutandis*, any changes, of either a quantitative or qualitative nature, on a factor or group of interrelated factors that are perceived during the time in which the planning is being carried out. The nature and number of the factors which affect a development plan and their interdependencies comprise an awesome complex. It is a complex which crosses the lines among disciplines, reaches beyond the quantifiable, and does not even remain entirely within the realm of objective reasoning. But it is only by attempting to grasp the meaning of the various operable factors and their dynamic relationships with one another that a sound base for development planning may be constructed.

So far we have established the theoretical background for institutional planning. We shall now see how this theory is applied in practice for the implementation of rural development programs.

Levels of Development Planning

Development planning can be carried out at three levels: the national level (macroplanning), the level of the individual farm (microplanning), or an intermediate level.

Planning at the national level generally deals mainly with the allocation of the basic factors of production among the different sectors of the national economy, with the aim of maximizing the economic benefits to the nation. At this level the plan is usually based on statistical data aggregated by groups and is designed to affect the entire economy. The goals of the national plan are usually of national significance and are of necessity based on the assignment of different weights to factors operating in different parts of the country. As a result, such an action by its very formulation cannot be effective in a particular location without suitable adjustments. It is therefore impossible to formulate a plan at the national level that will fit in with the specific institutional and human conditions of a particular area.

From the vantage point of the national level, the planner cannot examine adequately the elements of institution building needed for rural areas and formulate a feasible plan of action which will bring about the necessary institutional changes. It is impossible to understand the interrelationships among the various factors operating in rural areas by remote control, at least not with the tools of the social sciences available today. The only way to do so is via direct on-the-spot contact between the planner and the people. One example may serve to illustrate this point.

The creation of an effective supporting system requires the establishment of service centers in the rural areas. These centers can be established only on the basis of local information, including the social structures of village communities and their value systems as well as the economics of operating the different services and facilities. Such information can be obtained and evaluated only by planners in the field, who are familiar with local conditions and who are able to estimate the possible repercussions of their decisions. In addition, many development activities cannot be translated into terms of concrete projects at the national level. Most development projects, whether sectoral or multipurpose, usually are not designed to serve the entire economy and should be planned on the basis of the specific conditions in the given area.

The conclusion to be drawn from this state of affairs is that at the national level only the broad framework of the development policy should be formulated, while the details of institutional planning can only be worked out at a lower, intermediate level, i.e., the level of a region. Regional planning is therefore the tool for translating national development policies into operational terms reaching down to the smallest units of production.

Regional Planning as a Cross-Function
Regional planning is highly fashionable nowadays and is widely acclaimed in both advanced and developing countries. Unfortunately, this term is used in many different ways and in widely divergent contexts. On closer examination it appears that the term applies to two distinct operations. One is the integrated development of a single region, and the other is the breakdown of national plans into smaller units. This distinction is reflected in the recent classification of development regions proposed by the Resources for the Future study group on regional development:

1. *Single-purpose or limited-purpose region.* Normally involved here is the intensive development of a specific natural resource. A river basin developed mainly for irrigation falls in this category and is, as a matter of fact, the most common type of a single-purpose or limited-purpose development region.

2. *Frontier region.* This is usually a virgin or low-density territory, most frequently associated with large-scale natural resources development. In the more significant programs for such regions, projects are characterized not only by intensive resources development but also by industrialization and the building of a new town or series of new towns. Examples of this type of region are furnished by Guayana in Venezuela, Aswan in the United Arab Republic, and Lakhish in Israel.

3. *Depressed region.* A region in this category is usually chosen for national attention because levels of living are far below the average for the nation or because it is isolated from the rest of the nation due to cultural and economic backwardness. The region is normally designated as the problem area itself. Examples are Northeast Brazil, Southern Italy, and Comilla in East Pakistan.

4. *Metropolitan region and hinterland.* In countries around the world, metropolitan areas have become the subject for special planning and development efforts. Usually they are limited to relatively built-up areas and aim at achieving physical planning objectives. However, in some instances the regional effort has been concerned much more broadly with social and economic problems (e.g., problems of employment and in-migration), incorporating the surrounding hinterland in

addition to the metropolis itself. An example is the Calcutta regional program in India, involving four states surrounding the metropolis.

5. *Economic region or political jurisdiction established under a nationwide plan of regionalization.* In a few instances, all parts of a country have been divided into separate regions for planning and development purposes. Here a variety of standards for designating regions have been used. Normally a state, province or republic is employed because of the obvious advantages of using a well-established legal and organizational entity. In some cases, economic regions for development are designated on the basis of resources, trade patterns, and the like. Examples are the regionalization programs of Yugoslavia, Poland, Chile and Nigeria [5].

The first four categories belong to the first type of regional planning mentioned before—the development of a well-defined area. The fifth is identical with the second type, which concerns the regionalization of national plans.

The functions assigned to regional planning in the above mentioned categories may be designated as vertical and horizontal. The *vertical* function refers to the coordination of sectoral plans at the national level (macroplanning) with the planning of the individual unit of production (microplanning). Experience shows that there are always inconsistencies between the aims and projections of the two planning levels, which cannot be bridged over owing to the different methodologies used. As explained previously, national planning is based on statistical aggregates and averages, while microplanning is intimately linked with human behavior and social environment, factors which do not lend themselves to quantified expression. The task of integrating macroplanning and microplanning is assigned to the regional level.

The *horizontal* function consists of several operations, namely, (1) intersectoral coordination, (2) the translation of socioeconomic processes into physical terms, and (3) the translation of overall plans into concrete projects.

Most methods of regional planning being used today refer to either one of the two functions, and inadequately so. None refers to both functions simultaneously. Indeed, the term *regional planning* as used in most works published in the years after the Second World War has referred to those aspects of planning which here have been classified under the horizontal function exclusively. Included in this category are the works dealing with spatial organization analysis [4, 7, 18, 19, 22], location analysis [2, 12, 16], industry complex analysis [14], urban-rural analysis [3], all of which are elements of the so-called "Regional Science" [9, 13]. However, all these methods together are still short of fully elucidating many phenomena connected with the process of development at the regional level. Each of these methods deals with one aspect of horizontal planning mentioned previously, some of them with the first aspect, most with the second. None covers the full field of action designated as horizontal planning.

Attempts to deal with the vertical function of regional planning have been even less successful. Most of these took the form of endeavors to adapt methods of macroanalysis to the regional level. It could be said that they try to "descend" on the vertical ladder one step lower toward the microenvironment. A review of these methods is found in an article by Fox, published several years ago [8; for some specific applications, 6, 10, 11, 21]. Among them Fox lists area income and product accounts, macroeconomic models, input-output analysis, and linear programming. He cites several recent studies in which various attempts have been made to design models for an area economy such as the study of a metropolitan area by Leven, the econometric model of the United States designed by Klein, the input-output analysis of U.S. regions by Moses, and the combined models proposed by Clark and Chenery.

These methods are all based on the assumption that people react to incentives and regulations in a rational way which can be predicted. In other words, people can be categorized into analytical entities and treated as such. We have already seen that such methods are not adequate to deal with the human factor, especially in the conditions prevailing in underdeveloped rural areas.

Our conceptualization of regional planning centers on a full-scale merger of both vertical and horizontal functions within the framework of an institutional approach. It is our opinion that in planning the development of a region, both functions should be applied simultaneously because the development of a region cannot be separated from national development and it always involves the utilization of resources which must be coordinated to produce effective results. Regional planning operates accordingly on two fronts. First, it serves as a link between the macroplanning and the microplanning levels; second, it is designed to promote the utilization of resources within the area to the benefit of its residents. A *region* is the level where these two operations merge into a *cross-function*. [The concept of cross-function planning summarized in this paper was developed by the author in References 20, 23-29, 31, 32.]

The cross-function cannot be operated through the use of analytical tools alone, for the reasons outlined previously. It can be achieved only by means of an organization especially created for the purpose. A group of properly trained planners and implementors can solve most of the problems for which no answer has been given so far by analytical models. The capacity of such a group to carry out the tasks of regional planning is dependent on the fulfillment of four principles which must ultimately find expression in organizational terms [30].

1. **Coordination between Macroplanning and Microplanning** The coordination of macroplanning and microplanning constitutes the vertical function of regional planning. Macroplanning, as noted before, deals mainly with the allocation of resources among different uses, and takes into account in particular the economic considerations. Microplanning, on the other hand, is intimately linked with human behavior. The two methods cannot be accommodated within a single analytical framework. Their integration can be accomplished only by a regional planner who is at an intermediary level between the two planning systems. It is his job to blend them together and to bring about a synthesis in such a way that what is desirable at the national level will be also worthwhile and feasible for the individual producer. A regional planner must be aware of the constraints imposed by the overall national plan on the various regions (mainly with respect to the allocation of resources) and the demands made by the national system on them (e.g., the production of certain products in certain quantitites). He must also be well versed with the local conditions of the region.

Vertical coordination is usually the result of trial and error, pursuant to a "dialogue" between the regional and the national levels. Such vertical coordination must be carried out in all economic sectors of the region. With respect to the agricultural sector, for example, it implies the coordination of all types of farm enterprises with the sectoral plans for the region, as determined by the national development plan [23,31,33].

The dialogue between the national level and the regional level is not only important for regional development. The feedback effect of this dialogue for national planning is also of crucial importance; it changes national planning from mere wishful thinking into a practical tool for government policy.

2. **Horizontal Coordination** The integrated development in rural areas is the result of a system of relationships among the different economic sectors: agriculture, industry, and services. These relationships depend, of course, on the resources existing in each region and their exploitation, and on the region's stage of economic development. Plans for increasing agricultural production rely not only on the choice of the

most suitable crops to be grown on the farm, but also on the creation of service facilities and industrial installations as well as on the development of urban markets and transportation networks. Development plans formulated for each economic sector separately must be coordinated for effective implementation. In addition the plans must be translated into physical terms and then broken down into concrete projects suitable to the specific conditions of the region. These functions are the responsibility of regional planners.

In practice this implies the creation of an interdisciplinary team, with each member trained in a specific field (agronomy, economics, sociology, public administration, engineering, architecture, etc.). A team like this presents certain operational difficulties, since it is not an easy task to coordinate the activities of different experts when each is interested mainly in his own sphere of competence and employs his own professional methods. Opinions of experts from different disciplines rarely coincide, and experience has shown that even top-level specialists are sometimes unable to understand development issues that demand familiarity with concepts that are beyond their specific field of interest. Coordinating the activities of the team therefore becomes the task of the team's leader. The leader should be a "comprehensive planner" specially trained for this job.

3. Planning and Implementation   Planning should be conceived not as a one-time act, but as a dynamic process closely interwoven with implementation. Observations made during implementation provide the necessary data for evaluating the interaction among the various factors of development, particularly those which cannot be assessed beforehand, and for introducing necessary modifications. This feedback mechanism renders planning a continuous self-adjusting process, constantly adapting the original plan to new situations that arise, while retaining the final objective. At times this process may lead even to changes in the objectives.

According to this principle, regional planning may involve several successive stages: (1) the determination and formulation of the objectives and constraints of the development project, whether economic, sociopolitical, or a combination thereof; (2) the collection of basic data required to identify the factors which are likely to affect the development project; (3) the drafting of policies and formulation of detailed plans designed to attain predetermined objectives; (4) the preparation of the implementation stage, including the assignment of administrative bodies which will be responsible for carrying out the plan; and (5) the follow-up of the implementation stage, i.e., continuous observation and evaluation of the actual development process by means of which the appropriateness of the plan is tested. This may lead to a modification of the original plan or even to an alteration in the objectives.

Although the feedback mechanism is well known, and its significance appears obvious, it is rarely put into practical use by development authorities. In many instances experts from outside the development area are responsible for drawing up the plan, while the implementation is entrusted to organizations which have little or no contact with the planners. The lack of continuous coordination between the planners and the implementors at the practical level disrupts the continuity of the feedback mechanism and frequently makes the implementation of the plan impossible.

Recognition of the importance of this situation leads to far-reaching conclusions regarding the organization of the administrative bodies dealing with regional development, especially with respect to the working relations between policy makers, planners, and implementors. Only an adequate organizational framework that employs the feedback mechanism in its practical operations will be able to overcome the difficulties stemming from the emergence of unforeseen events during implementation. This is even more relevant at the time of the translation of the plan into concrete projects, which constitute the elements of development in practice. These projects should be a fulfillment in time and space of the processes set out in the overall plan, and this can only be done through the fullest use of the feedback mechanism.

4. Activating-Activated Relationship The knowledge and understanding of the factors of development which arise from the nature of the human element involved can be gained only via direct contact with the people concerned. Creating a direct relationship between those who are responsible for development planning (the activating) and those for whom the development effort is made (the activated) is the cardinal principle of institutional planning. It is this direct contact which provides the development team with the knowledge and the "feel" of those factors which elude the analytical tools.

A close relationship with the local population is extremely important, since the attitudes and reactions of the inhabitants of the region determine, to a large extent, the success of the development program. A clear understanding of the local attitudes and views frequently introduces new dimensions to projects and may often lead to revisions in the original plan, in order to adapt it to the needs and aspirations of the people. It is frequently impossible to predict people's reactions under certain conditions, and only through daily contact and mutual understanding is the development team able to adapt the plan to its human and material environment.

Expression of the above-described principles in concrete organizational terms makes the institutional approach an effective development tool. This approach enables those involved in regional development planning to overcome many difficulties and obstacles present in almost any comprehensive development project. It must be stressed, however, that the institutional approach does not exclude the application of analytical methods as tools for understanding many aspects of the development process. On the contrary, specific analytical techniques are indispensable to the planner. But they must be used within the context of an institutional framework capable of cross-function planning.

References

1. Adelman, Irma, and Cynthia Taft-Morris, *Society, Politics and Economic Development—A Quantitative Approach*. Baltimore: Johns Hopkins Press, 1967.

2. See, for example, Alonso, W., "Location Theory." In J. Friedmann and W. Alonso (eds.), *Regional Development and Planning: A Reader*. Cambridge, Mass: M.I.T. Press, 1964, pp. 78-106.

3. Balogh, T., "The Cause of Poverty." Paper presented to the Economic Experts' Conference of the Socialist International, Bergneustadt, mimeo, 1964.

4. Boudeville, J. R., "A Survey of Recent Techniques for Regional Economic Analysis." In W. Isard and J. H. Cumberland (eds.), *Regional Economic Planning Techniques of Analysis*. Paris: OECD, 1961, pp. 377-397.

5. *Design for a Worldwide Study of Regional Development*. A report to the UN on a proposed research-training program, Resources for the Future staff study. Baltimore: Johns Hopkins Press, 1966.

6. Edward, C., "Theory and Techniques for Integrated Area Planning," *Journal of Farm Economics 48* (1966), pp. 1279-1287.

7. Fox, K. A., *Econometric Analysis for Public Policy*. Ames: Iowa State College Press, 1958.

8. ____, "The Study of Interactions between Agriculture and Non-Farm Economy: Local, Regional and National," *Journal of Farm Economics 44* (1962), pp. 1-34.

9. The literature dealing with this subject is rather extensive, especially with regard to the influence of the city on its hinterland. See, for instance, the reader by J. Friedmann and W. Alonso (eds.), *Regional Development and Planning*. Cambridge, Mass: M.I.T. Press, 1964. Less attention has been paid to the analysis of rural-urban relationships.

10. Hirsch, W., "Design and Use of Regional Accounts," *Papers and Proceedings, American Economic Review 52* (1962), 365-373.

11. Hochwald, W., *The Design of Regional Accounts*. Baltimore: Johns Hopkins Press, 1961.

12. Isard, W., *Location and Space-Economy*. Cambridge, Mass: M.I.T. Press, 1956.

13. ——, *Methods of Regional Analysis: An Introduction to Regional Science*. New York: M.I.T. Press and Wiley, 1960.

14. ——, and T. Reiner, "Regional and National Economic Planning and Analytic Techniques for Implementation." In W. Isard and J. H. Cumberland (eds.), *Regional Economic Planning Techniques of Analysis*. Paris: OECD, 1961, pp. 19-38.

15. Jacoby, E. H., "Aspects of Institutional Planning as Part of Agricultural Planning." Paper presented to the Second Rehovot Conference, Israel, mimeo, 1963.

16. Losch, A., *The Economics of Location*. New Haven: Yale University Press, 1961.

17. Myrdal, G., "The Significance of the Population Development for Agricultural Planning in Underdeveloped Countries." Paper presented to the Second Rehovot Conference, Israel, mimeo, 1963.

18. Novacco, N., "Discussion Paper." In W. Isard and J. H. Cumberland (eds.), *Regional Economic Planning Techniques of Analysis*. Paris: OECD, 1961, pp. 399-405.

19. Prion, I., *Trends of Rural Cooperation in Israel*. Rehovot: Settlement Study Centre, Publications on Problems of Regional Development, 3, 1968.

20. *Regional Development in Israel*. Report submitted by the Israeli delegation to the OECD Seminar on Regional Development held in Herzlia, Israel, 1964. Paris: OECD, 1965.

21. Stone, R., "Social Accounts at the Regional Level: A Survey." In W. Isard and J. H. Cumberland (eds.), *Regional Economic Planning Techniques of Analysis*. Paris: OECD, 1961, pp. 263-293.

22. Ulmann, E. L., "Regional Development and the Geography of Concentration," *Papers and Proceedings of the Regional Science Association, 4* (1958).

23. Weitz, R., "Agriculture and Rural Planning: Its Organization and Implementation." Paper presented to the UN Conference on the Application of Science and Technology for the Benefit of the Less Developed Areas, Geneva, 1963.

24. ——, *Regional Planning—Report on a Visit to Turkey*. Jerusalem: Organization for Economic Cooperation and Development in Cooperation with the State of Israel Ministry for Foreign Affairs, Department for International Cooperation, 1964.

25. ——, Preface to *Crete Development Plan 1965-1975*. Tel-Aviv: AGRIDEV, 1965.

26. ——, "Rural Development through Regional Planning in Israel," *Journal of Farm Economics 46* (1965), 643-651.

27._____, *Regional Development Programming.* Washington, D.C.: Organization of American States Studies and Monographs, VII, 1966.

28._____ (ed.), *Rural Planning in Developing Countries.* Report on the Second Rehovoth Conference, Israel, 1963. London: Routledge and Kegan Paul, 1966.

29._____, "Sur le Principe du Développement Rural Intégral," *Economie Rurale,* pp. 1-4.

30._____, and Levia Applebaum. "Administrative and Organisational Problems of Regional Development Planning in Israel." Paper presented to the Annual Meeting of the Directors of Development Training and Research Institutes, Montpellier, France, 1967. Paris: OECD, 1967.

31._____, and J. H. Landau, "Comprehensive Agricultural Planning on the National, Regional and Individual Farm Level." Paper presented to the Second Rehovoth Conference on Rural Planning in Developing Countries, Rehovot, Israel, 1963.

32._____, with the assistance of A. Rokach. *Agriculture and Rural Development: Projection and Planning.* Rehovot: National and University Institute of Agriculture, Bull. 68, 1963.

33._____, and A. Rokach, *Agricultural Development—Planning and Implementation (Israeli Case-Study).* Dordrecht, The Netherlands: Reidel, 1968.

Part One

II. Agriculture and
Industry

6. The Role of
Industry in the
Development of
Rural Areas

Gabriele Pescatore

General Aspects of the Problem

The theme of this paper seems to call for preliminary discussion, in terms of its place in a wider concept. The concept of regional development admittedly refers to areas with a certain geographical, economic, and social homogeneity, or in which those homogeneous aspects combine to form a territorial pole of attraction. The evaluation of available resources, a first step in regional development planning, makes possible the identification of those areas which offer the best prospects for agricultural development and in which to initiate the development process, by giving priority to exploitation of the agricultural potential of those areas.

As regards regional development in the Mediterranean area, agricultural land suitable for use intensification occurs more frequently in flat country, in river valleys, or in coastal belts; these same areas are often also the most suitable for industrial development. Apart from geographical reasons, this circumstance is mainly attributable to the fact that in such areas the infrastructures required for integrated development are more easily created than elsewhere, and that access to major communication routes is easier, unless these infrastructures are already partially available through having been created concurrently with earlier agricultural development.

We therefore propose to deal with the problems involved in industrial development in areas where a radical change in farm policies has already been achieved, or is in progress, or is merely in the planning stage—areas having a potential for change that would provide higher levels of employment and income than the average for the region as a whole. In developing an area of high agricultural potential, the factors that condition the integration of industry and agriculture are quite different if agricultural development precedes industrial development as the sole and principal source of employment and income, as compared to cases when both sectors expand concurrently.

The pace and nature of the evolution of agriculture is also conditioned by the type of industrialization: the industries established may be

Gabriele Pescatore—Italy. Professor of Navigation Law at the University of Rome; President of Section of the State Council; President of the Southern Italy Development Board (Cassa per il Mezzogiorno); President of the Mediterranean Council of Regional Economies; Vice President of the International Council of Regional Economies.

linked directly or indirectly with agriculture, supplying equipment and other inputs, processing produce, etc., or they may be completely non-agricultural. Similarly, the impact of industrialization will vary according to its location, i.e., territorially concentrated (in industrial estates) or dispersed throughout the area, and to its labor requirements, leading to a varying degree of competition for local labor between industry and agriculture.

In the context of this wide variety of possible situations and in the light of experience of regional development in southern Italy, we shall try to analyze the more important aspects of the industrialization of rural areas and the principal relationships between agriculture and industry in regional development.

In southern Italy, industries are frequently located in areas of long-established, highly intensive cultivation (i.e., the traditional areas of intensive cultivation around large cities such as Naples, Salerno, Bari, Palermo). But there are also instances of industrialization areas where extensive land reclamation and irrigation projects have already been completed, and where radical agricultural transformation has influenced the entire economic and social structure of the relevant area. Industrialization can also go hand-in-hand with agricultural development (e.g., the Pescara Valley in Abruzzo and the Catania Plain in Sicily) or it may be superimposed so as to provide a qualitative contribution to the development process, sometimes on a quite unexpected scale (e.g., the Metaponto Plain and the Campidano district in the Ionian coastal strip).

In both these cases the main effects are (1) modification of cost relationships among production factors (especially labor); (2) competition for the use of limited local natural resources, such as water; (3) competition for the use of land, which inevitably pushes up land values; (4) development and localization of major infrastructures; and (5) change of agricultural pattern, farmers being forced to switch to cultivation methods and crops capable of competing with the alternative employment opportunities and higher wage levels created in the area through industrialization. If these circumstances lead to more rational choices and more profitable investments, they are a positive factor, helping to accelerate the process of evolution toward more efficient structures.

Furthermore, if industrialization occurs at an appropriate stage of the agricultural development process it can exert other important influences, outstanding among which is (6) a higher local demand for foodstuffs, deriving from the higher income of the local population engaged in industry and in the services. This refers especially to horticultural produce, meat, and milk—a vital factor for an irrigation district looking for new outlets for its produce. Moreover, (7) industrial concentration, if facilitated by special location incentives and by the provision of infrastructures, creates conditions that also favor the development of projects for processing agricultural produce, using infrastructures and economic integration possibilities that perhaps are nonexistent in an area devoted exclusively to agricultural development, and (8) the opportunity of supplementing rural family incomes with wages earned in industry or services leads to part-time employment, a vital form of adaptation by rural communities to the industrial life of the advanced countries.

These positive and negative effects, in their various combinations, influence the rate and intensity of agricultural development.

Relationships between Agriculture and Industry in Regional Development

The vast bibliography on this subject has provided a number of valid theoretical models, but at the practical level, in specific situations, none has resolved the long-standing dilemma of whether it is more advantageous to locate industry in areas with a high development potential, or already in course of development, or in areas which offer more limited development alternatives and which are in urgent need of economic and social advancement.

In support of the first proposition, we have the fact that the rate of development and the profitability of investment are favorably influenced by external economies as well as by economies of scale, through integration of industries that are technically complementary to one another. Those who favor the second proposition maintain that the effects of "polarization" and "irradiation" are too limited or too slow when they originate from a concentration-orientated development process ("development poles"), especially as regards the poorer areas of the region, which have less development potential. That is to say, both the centripetal force (which attracts mobile productive factors from the periphery, especially labor) and the raising of marginal labor productivity (which, due to the exodus, occurs in the peripheral areas), are very slow processes, conditioned by the intrinsic viscosity of the system; this situation often creates dualistic economies within the same region, with division into developed areas and backward areas.

But the two positions further diverge in the matter of choice of priority between the development of agricultural resources and industrial development. In this connection, the widest experience of regional development planning has been gained from instances in which absolute priority has been assigned to agriculture in the development process. There are two principal reasons for this: in agriculture the resources, being tied to the environment, are not subject to any substantial change, and are capable of more immediate utilization; and the infrastructures that are indispensable for agricultural development can, with appropriate modification, serve also for industrialization. This approach, however, while enabling the development problem to be tackled when global analyses of sectorial interdependences are not yet available, may lead to the creation of facts prejudicial to subsequent, better balanced development. In other words, by virtue of the inherent rigidity of crop combinations, optimum productive schemes in agriculture depend on available labor; furthermore, water and land resources cannot be rationally utilized unless development forecasts are available at least for the secondary and tertiary sectors in the area and in the entire region.

A different conceptual position is adopted by those who support the theory that industrial development should be allowed to precede the development of other economic activities; they affirm that this is the only way in which industry can assume the "load-bearing" role in the regional economy. This approach leads them to stress the need for prior solution of the problems of infrastructures, communications, and services which admittedly condition the establishment of industrial projects; they maintain that agriculture, whether advanced or still in the traditional stage, must adapt its structure to the new situation created by the arrival of industry. The fallacy of their reasoning is dual: it ignores both the direct dependence of the industrialization process on economic conditions and markets outside the area, and also the experience already gained from previous industrial development, either spontaneous or based on incentives, in most of the development poles of the Mediterranean area.

There is a third school of thought that sees the process of industrialization in developing agricultural areas primarily in terms of the creation of a closely integrated network of agrosupporting industries, as well as of efficient marketing facilities, both aimed at opening up new external markets for the produce of the area, and at keeping within the rural areas the added value derived from increased overall production. The development of agrosupporting enterprises, even if conditioned by seasonal processing cycles, by the productive potential of the relevant area, and by the area's location in relation to major communication routes, nevertheless gives a strong impetus to the industrialization process and affords the agricultural community an opportunity of earning more, without disturbing the cost levels of production factors.

From the many theories that have been developed on this problem, and taking into account the political factors and situations that must necessarily be considered in envisaging a plan of public intervention, one gets the feeling that generalization is impossible. Nevertheless, when industrial development comes as a further stage of a previously initiated process of agricultural development and socioeconomic advancement in a given area, there are certain factors that play a vital role in such industrial development: the qualitative orientation of investment; infrastructures; a more enterprising local population; the existence of laboriously accumulated "invisible capital" in the area.

It is true that cultivation policies will have to be reviewed in the light of the changed relationship among production costs, but it is also true that in the process of adaptation, agriculture benefits from the accumulation of extra-agricultural capital and from greater entrepreneurial capabilities, both essential conditions for deriving benefit from technological progress.

When, conversely, industry is introduced in an area where the agricultural development process has not even started, the two sectors remain separated for many years by a communication barrier that is very difficult to surmount. As a rule such industrial projects are highly capital intensive, launched by external interests with little regard for overall location requirements, and, because of the advanced technological level of the operation, recruiting locally only part of their labor requirements. Agriculture is first hit by the effects of the higher wages offered on the construction site, without important modifications of farm policies, except for some minor adjustments. On the other hand, in cases where agriculture has already reached an advanced stage by the time industry is introduced, one finds that farmers pass through a period of "reflection"; this is highly important, as it gives time for careful decisions on crop combinations, with the prime objective of achieving higher efficiency—especially in regard to production factors that have assumed primary importance in the new situation.

Industrial projects initially set up, especially if they belong to the primary sectors, are rarely followed by complementary projects. It should be remembered that in such cases there is a complete lack of all the essential prerequisites of integrated industrial development. The consequence is that considerable time is required both for the structural adaptation of agriculture and for industrial development itself. The situation is quite different in the case of an agricultural area, even undeveloped, where a group of integrated industrial projects has been set up on a preestablished rational pattern with large-scale capital investment. In this case the scale, intensity, and pace of the industrialization process are such that the entire economy of the area is vitalized: tertiary activity gains considerable momentum; the "spread" effect on small-scale industrial and artisan activity is vastly increased. In such a situation agriculture, even in the early stages of development, has much better conditions for advancement than when only two or three industrial projects are set up in the area.

Wages earned in industry supplement the incomes of farming families, and are often used for investment in farm equipment; land values increase and enterprising farmers are able to sell and reinvest the proceeds in land elsewhere, and engage in more profitable types of farming; demand for consumer goods increases, a process from which agriculture also benefits. Although farming may become more demanding, a more competitive type of agriculture emerges, capable of winning new markets, precisely because the process of change and adaptation has been accelerated; this process would have been much slower without such a powerful stimulus.

Relationships between Agriculture and the Processing Industry

A radical change in cultivation policies in fast-developing areas normally starts with a considerable increase in the volume of output, based on new crops for the relevant area and market. Thus the resulting need for market expansion through an efficient network of processing plants and marketing facilities becomes as vitally important as the usual methods of public policy aimed at improving natural resources (land reclamation, irrigation, etc.). Indeed, experience gained in the irrigation districts of southern Italy indicates that rationalization of marketing methods—including opening up new markets to absorb the increased production from reclaimed land—should accompany, if not precede, development of the production structure.

In areas where the cultivation of new crops is expanding, special marketing facilities are required to achieve a balance between demand and supply and to develop new markets, which otherwise would be difficult to find, or which would develop irrationally. The development of the processing industry and the adoption of new technologies has eliminated time and distance problems in the marketing of agricultural produce, opening up new prospects that enhance both the production potential and the income of the developed areas.

But the complementary nature and interdependence of the cultivation stage and the processing stage demand that the two activities be integrated as fully as possible through primary, secondary, and tertiary forms of cooperation; through bilateral forms of integration (production under contract), whereby growers and processers undertake to observe certain conditions, technical requirements, and agreed selling prices; and through associations giving farmers a share in the profits of processing and also the benefit of entrepreneurial skills and economies of scale which are necessary for competitiveness. It is only in this way that the industrialization of agriculture becomes an "instrumental variable" of development, to the mutual advantage of both sectors, and that harmonious growth may be achieved.

What has just been described constitutes the ideal model toward which agroindustrial integration can and should progress; but experience shows that this may require considerable time unless public intervention provides for all the exogenous factors that condition this type of growth: low-interest loans and various incentives, transportation advantages, market information, and the all-important technical assistance to farmers.

Those who, in the context of regional planning, support this type of industrial development for certain agricultural areas, carry their idea further: they are against promoting and encouraging other industries in those areas. But it should be remembered that the exclusive development of processing industries, with their seasonal character and providing only limited employment opportunities, does not solve the problem of finding work for that part of the rural labor force that is not needed for agricultural production.

The problem is very different when agricultural industrialization is being achieved in the traditional form. That is to say, instead of basing its operations on promoting the supply of agricultural products, it bases them, in its development and location, on the sources and areas of supply of raw materials, without any influence whatever on the technical orientation of farming, and severing the agricultural sector from industrial activity. Conceived in this manner, agricultural industrialization is very different from that first described, through being far from performing the primary role in area development.

Competition for Local Resources

This is a problem that has appeared in its multiple aspects in those development poles of southern Italy where there are concentrations of agricultural, industrial, and tourist industry development in parallel with rapid urban development. Apart from land, water is the resource in shortest supply, conditioning the intensity, rate, and type of intersectorial development.

The development of new water resources and the storage and adduction of water is limited in absolute terms by technical factors, and in relative terms by economic considerations. The fundamental problem, where local resources are limited or are capable of being increased only by costly long-distance transfer, is always that of choosing the utilization scheme capable of providing the highest net yield (updated cost-benefit ratio) to the community as a whole. This, however, presupposes knowledge of all the possible technical solutions for the storage and adduction of water, together with growth forecasts not only for agriculture but also for industry and tourism. It is only on the basis of this information that it is possible to make a rational choice among solutions aimed at maximum return on investment, or to establish—through assessment of water storage and adduction costs—the "maximum justified levels" of the cost of making water available.

While the methods described above are still in the experimental stage, in practice it is necessary to resort to comparisons based on empirical coefficients that indicate the degree of efficiency of utilization of water resources: this is an approximation method, permitting adjustments as the results of sectorial development are checked against the assumptions. It often happens, for example, that water initially intended for irrigation is transferred for industrial utilization as an additional source of supply, for as long as may be necessary.

Individual solutions can be found according to the logic of the facts, always provided that there is a clear reference to the planned pattern of a regional program, and that there is a supraregional authority capable of deciding on, and of finding, the most advantageous solutions.

Conclusions

1. In areas where the process of intensification of agriculture is already under way, the development of industrial activity conditions that process in appreciable measure. The consequent favorable effects on agricultural development depend on the extent to which agriculture is accorded priority of utilization of certain natural resources, and on

institutional arrangements for subsequent progress of agricultural development.

2. The development of industry provides a stimulus to agriculture to achieve more efficient crop combinations, through more rational utilization of production factors.

3. The type of industrialization most likely to impart a strong impulse to agricultural development is that applying to the processing and marketing of farm produce, on condition that such initiatives are planned and timed in a manner to orientate and expand agricultural development (and not follow one step behind it), and provided that there is close vertical integration of the two sectors, guaranteeing technical and economic efficiency.

4. The scarcity of resources such as water, in regions where a number of sectors are competing for them, requires expansion and productivity forecasts in the various sectors, in order to make possible prior selection of the more rational combinations of their use.

5. A final consideration with regard to an area where it is desired to develop the agricultural potential: the development of the area should be planned in the general context of development of an entire region, so as not to rule out other, more valid alternatives for the location of industry outside the area selected for agricultural development. As we have seen, this decision must take into account many variables that can radically influence profitability of investment, and therefore the effectiveness of a policy of direct and indirect incentives.

In this matter the methodology of territorial development planning is not yet sufficiently advanced. We can therefore proceed only on a basis of experience of the various types of development in agricultural areas where, in varying degrees, there is parallel industrial development.

Part One

II. Agriculture and
Industry

7. Agriculture
and Industry
in Developing
Countries

Joseph Klatzmann

It is the common belief of the political leader in the developing world that economic development is synonymous with industrialization. In this paper, I should like to submit that the best way to achieve development is, in fact, to assign the first priority to agriculture in developing planning.

The Problem: How to Achieve Economic Development of a Poor Agricultural Country

On a private basis, one can say that it is considerably more difficult for poor people to set aside savings than for rich ones. Inasmuch as savings are a prerequisite to investment, the objective of which is to earn more money, rich people can easily become richer and consequently widen the gap between themselves and the poor. In the case of countries the situation is analogous. The poorer nations need a faster rate of growth in order to reduce the gap between themselves and the richer countries. But a faster rate of growth requires a higher rate of investment, the means for which are lacking in the developing countries. External aid can contribute to the economic resources of a country, but it is not possible to rely only on foreign aid to achieve development. This is the "vicious cycle" which the developing countries face in their struggle to achieve economic viability and progress.

In order to achieve a faster rate of development, it would appear necessary to concentrate on those opportunities for investment which offer the highest output per unit of capital (taking into account the opportunity cost of capital). But this is a difficult task due to the lack of data available concerning efficiency of investments. It is easier by far to observe the more advanced nations, what they are doing and what they have done in the past.

Accordingly, the political leaders of the developing countries observe that the advanced countries are industrialized. Therefore, they conclude that reaching a given level of development in effect is equivalent to reaching a given level of industrialization. This point is not questionable. I am also of the view that developing countries must industrialize

Joseph Klatzmann—France. Ingénieur agronome; Docteur ès lettres; Professor of Agricultural Economics at the Institut National Agronomique, Paris; professor at the Ecole Pratique des Hautes Etudes (Sorbonne); member of the Académie d'Agriculture de France.

as quickly as possible. But the question remains: how to do it, and the most useful role that agriculture can play.

The common belief today in developing countries is that all stress and effort have to be put on industry at the expense of agricultural development. Further, inasmuch as the base of industrial development has usually been heavy industry, the creation of such an industry is frequently the main objective of leaders of developing countries. They dream of a big steel plant, to cite a common example.

In this regard, a well-known Polish economist explained the decision to triple the output of the chemical industry as part of his country's national plan. He pointed out that all advanced countries develop their chemical industry because they require even greater numbers of commodities from this industry. Accordingly, he explained, if Poland is to achieve rapid economic development, it will also need more chemicals, which necessitates, in turn, a high priority for the chemical industry in the national plan. But why triple the output? The answer provided was that three is a round figure. This manner of economic planning is far removed from the current sophisticated mathematical programming models, but at the same time it is nearer to economic practice.

To buttress his view in favor of immediate industrialization, the political leader of developing countries has found support among economists in the advanced countries. These economists claim that the developing countries have a comparative advantage vis-à-vis industry. Such advantage is said to stem from the fact that there are many obstacles to the accelerated progress of agriculture in developing countries. They hold that it is extremely difficult to modernize an agricultural system made up of millions of backward peasants. On the other hand, it is much easier to attain a high level of productivity in a modern plant, where the workers must follow the pace set by the machines. Therefore, it is to be expected that in the future developing countries will buy the surpluses of agricultural products from the richer countries and pay for them by increasing their exports of industrial commodities.

In actual fact, these theoretical—and questionable—arguments are usually not cited in the developing countries. The prestigious place of industry and the low regard accorded to agriculture (especially in those countries which are led by the urban bourgeoisie) are sufficiently cogent arguments in favor of industrialization. If, by chance, a planning expert insists on the necessity of doing more to develop the agricultural sector, he is met with the rejoinder, "You want to keep us in a state of underdevelopment."

Agricultural Development as a Precondition for Industrialization

In devising a development strategy for the less advanced countries, it is important that the process be started at the beginning, and not at the end. Otherwise bottlenecks can easily arise and seriously impede development efforts. The agricultural sector forms the base of the traditional economies of the developing nations. Assigning priority to this base offers a developing nation a number of potential advantages vis-à-vis industrialization.

Increase of agricultural production enables a country to reduce its imports and simultaneously to increase its exports of food and other agricultural commodities. The effect is to free other national resources for the purpose of importing industrial equipment, and in the long run to hasten the process of industrialization. In addition, the problem of international standards is a more tractable one in connection with agriculture as versus industrial products, as for example, setting international standards for bananas as opposed to steel.

While it is true that development of agriculture can foster economic development by helping to increase exports, this reasoning relies on the implicit assumption that more sales bring more foreign currency. Here we must consider the problem of the international market. Unfortunately, unstable prices of food and other agricultural raw materials on the world market can lead to highly undesirable results. The price elasticity of raw materials, measured at the producer's level, is usually low. Consider, for example, the difference between the FOB price elasticity of cocoa and retail price elasticity of chocolate. If increase of production exceeds increase of demand, prices drop so severely that a loss is suffered.

If a number of developing countries encourage production of the same agricultural export commodity, a situation might arise whereby they receive less foreign currency than previously from their sales, after having spent more foreign currency to buy the means of production such as fertilizers and machinery. To earn less after having worked more and spent more is surely not an effective incentive toward development.

The sine qua non lies in cooperation between developing countries in order to avoid overproduction. But these countries cannot act as a monopoly in order to maximize total income, because they would consequently come under strong pressure from their customers, the richer countries. What this implies is that, in practical terms, international agreements between sellers and buyers are necessary—however difficult they may be to achieve.

Another potential advantage of promoting agriculture centers on the problem of nutrition which is shared by all the developing countries to a greater or lesser degree. In these countries, peasants are poor for a variety of reasons, among which is that they do not work enough. But, frequently, the obvious reasons—namely, that they are lazy, dissatisfied with their conditions, or endure climatic severities—are not applicable. Frequently they are unable to work more because of their lack of proper nutrition, which in turn prevents them from producing more food and other agricultural products. This is the well-known vicious circle of poverty. Once this vicious circle is broken, the process of development can be initiated, not only in agriculture but also in industry. For the productivity of the industrial worker depends to a considerable extent on his physical ability, which is directly related to nutrition. If the problem of food production and the allied problem of adequate nutrition can be overcome, an important step forward will have been taken to promote industrial development.

At the same time, modernizing the agricultural sector would lead to a reduction of labor requirements in agriculture and allow for transfer of labor from agriculture to industrial plants. It is generally believed that at the beginning of the development process, the shift of labor from the villages to the big cities largely exceeds the needs of manpower in industry and services. As a result of this shift and other factors, agriculture is at times not able to fulfill its own labor requirements.

This may seem rather surprising, given the well-known state of underemployment in agriculture in developing countries. But it is not accurate to speak of either underemployment or a surplus labor force in agriculture in a general manner, without, for example, distinguishing the terms of the surplus, be it in hours or in numbers of people. Even if most of the agricultural labor force is unemployed a large part of the year, the total labor force available may be insufficient at certain peak periods—for example, at times of sowing or harvesting. Thus the flow of people from the villages to the cities can act to reduce agricultural production, because of the lack of sufficient manpower during peak periods.

From the other vantage point, the existence of such peak periods in agriculture can act to keep so many people engaged in agriculture that other sectors such as industry cannot fulfill their labor requirements. Modern agrotechnology, which requires a smaller labor force, can help to alleviate the strain wrought by peak periods to the mutual advantage of agriculture and industry.

Regarding the agricultural labor force, there is another factor which is frequently overlooked: the need for technically trained manpower in industry. In some areas, promotion of industrial development with a technically deficient labor force can result in disaster—particularly if minimal quality standards have to be observed. Once again, one must begin at the beginning. A modernized agricultural sector can provide industry with a labor force which would lend itself more readily to technical training than would the traditional peasant laborer. The intermediate stage of technical training within the agricultural area is not necessarily a loss of time and effort—on the contrary, it helps to lay the groundwork for subsequent technical training programs for industry.

An additional contribution of the agricultural labor force to economic development lies in its potential availability to engage in large-scale projects during nonpeak periods in agriculture. A decade ago, China succeeded in mobilizing millions of farmers, who were used mainly to build irrigation networks. This brought the peoples of the world to realize the gigantic potential of a large labor force in countries where climatic conditions prevent farmers from working more than 100 to 150 days per year in agriculture.

In some countries, such as Japan, a large part of the surplus labor is already used in the form of individual part-time factory work. But in developing countries, which do not offer the possibility of employing farmers part-time in industry, it seems that mobilization of the agricultural labor force would facilitate the development of huge projects at low cost, particularly projects related to the infrastructure of the country.

A considerable amount of thought—and ink—has been devoted to such projects. It seems that the opportunity cost of large-scale projects using underemployed manpower in agriculture is almost zero. At the same time, it is true that workers have to be paid, even when they work in projects for the benefit of their own villages. On the assumption that four kilograms of grain per day would constitute a suitable salary, some experts calculate what could be achieved upon the receipt of a gift of one million tons of grain from the rich countries (it might be added that the opportunity cost of the grain surpluses from the rich countries is very low).

But the real-life situation is not quite so simple. First, there are not many enterprises which can be carried out without industrial equipment, simply by using manpower and a few low-cost implements. Second, experience shows that mobilizing farmers and putting them to productive work requires an organizational ability of a high order, which is often lacking in developing countries. Third, the lack of incentive results in a low productivity of labor. These factors explain why so many similar efforts have failed in the past and why they must be kept in mind in connection with using the unemployed labor force in agriculture to carry out large-scale projects.

In sum, it appears that in many respects, agricultural development can provide a tenable basis for industrial development, a fact which means that development of the agricultural sector serves to hasten the process of industrialization. The same kind of situation arises when one confronts the choice between engaging in direct production or investing in an enterprise. From the standpoint of the developing countries the direct process is not the most efficient. Developing agricultural production is in fact investing in industry.

The previous discussion of the interrelatedness of agricultural development and industrialization assumes that progress in agriculture is a distinct possibility. Let us return momentarily to the statement that exports of agricultural commodities facilitate imports of equipment for industrialization. This argument fails completely if it can be demonstrated that it is impossible to increase agricultural production, due to the numerous obstacles encountered in a particular country.

Several years ago it would have been difficult to adopt a definitive position on this question. Those efforts that were being exerted to promote agricultural development were not producing the expected results. Today more and more countries are reaching the "take-off" stage of agricultural progress. The rate of increase of agricultural production in India, Pakistan, and Indonesia is rising and remaining at a higher level than their respective rates of population increase. The past efforts, marked by a long absence of visible results, were, in fact, long-term investments. Such examples help to illustrate the evolutionary process in which national efforts to promote agricultural development are followed by an increase in agricultural production. The net effect of increased agricultural production is faster industrialization, although it may be as long as 20 years' time before such an effect becomes apparent.

Targets in Agricultural Development
The proposal that first priority should be assigned to agricultural development does not imply that all efforts to initiate industrialization should cease. First, to assign greater priority to something, in any field,

simply means to change the ratios between factors making up a given pattern of operation. For example, if a consumer today attaches greater importance to the purchase of a motorcar, even if he assigns to this objective the highest priority, he does not consequently stop purchasing food. In the same vein, the man who offers first priority to food purchase does not begin to buy clothes only after all his needs for food are filled. In the same way, what we propose within the framework of a national plan is to devote a larger ratio of existing national resources to the development of agriculture. This does not imply that industry should be shelved even in the early stages of development.

However, a projected proposal for creating a new industry must be examined very carefully—is it economically sound to build a small-scale factory to produce fertilizers? Will there be a market, domestic and/or foreign, to utilize the output of a big factory? With regard to processing of agricultural commodities, the answer will be more often in favor of immediate industrialization. Today, the typical product which comes from the farm is no more than a raw material. Much has to be done, from grading to canning, to transform it into a consumer good, particularly for export purposes. Some of these processing activities must be carried out in the country of origin. There are many advantages to initiating industrialization via the processing of agricultural products insofar as the problem of quality is not forgotten.

Second, assigning priority to agriculture implies that all efforts should be made to increase agricultural production. But it is not by increasing the number of people working within the agricultural sector that such a goal can be attained. In order to increase output farmers need to employ industrial inputs, such as fertilizers and specific types of machinery. These inputs may have to be imported. But if it is possible to produce them in the country itself, important advantages are thereby gained, namely, opportunity for immediate industrialization and increase in general agricultural production.

There remains the problem of organizing the marketing of agricultural produce. Frequently, the lack of an efficient marketing organization is one of the main obstacles to the expansion of agricultural production. Development of agriculture therefore implies development of services and facilities to market the produce, and also to supply the means of production.

These various targets of agricultural development can be achieved only if the necessary infrastructure is ready to accommodate them—in particular a network of roads and adequate means of transportation. Creating an infrastructure in rural areas is a good way to initiate the process of industrialization, and also to build a technically trained labor force to work in industrial establishments. Thus assigning first priority to the development of agriculture does not imply that industrialization has to be delayed. The problem is rather to concentrate on establishing those industries linked to agriculture which will in the long term enable a faster industrialization of the entire economy. Such industries might be developed in the following areas: building a proper infrastructure in rural areas, producing modern inputs such as fertilizer, and processing agricultural commodities.

In connection with the last mentioned, rural industrialization which is based on the processing of agricultural products offers many advantages. In the long term, agriculture cannot constitute the sole base of economic development. A purely agricultural region would not be able to compete with other regions. The common pattern of concentration of industry in a few big centers constitutes a source of unbalanced regional development. Such planning also results in difficult economic and social conditions for those living in huge metropolitan centers.

Development of industry in urban areas implies that the unemployed agricultural labor population must perforce migrate to the cities. These workers suffer the psychological consequences of being uprooted. Further, there is the economic cost of building new housing for them in the large urban centers, while existing capital investment in the villages remains unused. Introducing industry into rural areas helps to reduce such transfers of population, helps to inculcate a new way of thinking based on economic rationality among the farming population, and provides resources for investment in agriculture (for example, when an industrial plant offers employment to a member of a farmer's family). In sum, locating industries in rural areas offers the following fourfold set of advantages: no uprooting of rural populations with its attendant psychological problems, and no need to build new housing facilities, in the short term; in the long term, a faster agricultural development and a balanced regional development. If it is true that developing countries need those industries which are linked to agriculture, there is reason to think that it is precisely these industries which are easily adaptable to rural areas.

But as in other areas of human endeavor, matters are really not so simple, and rural industrialization encounters serious obstacles (however, the cost of building a communications network in rural areas in order to promote faster industrialization should not be considered an obstacle, because it is a part of the required infrastructure). One problem that the national planning authorities face is that the projected advantages are not always advantages for the private entrepreneurs of industry. This problem would imply that rural industrialization requires state support.

Another problem facing the national planning authorities centers on manpower, that of attracting a sufficient number of qualified people to work in agriculture. We should remember that investments, whether directly or indirectly useful to agriculture, do not constitute only money, foreign currency, raw materials, and equipment. There must be a qualified corps of officers for the administration and supervision of the integrated operation. This statement may seem obvious, but such a problem does actually exist. The low status accorded to agriculture results in a reverse selection process: the most talented people turn away from agriculture. The same situation prevails in the developed countries, because of the fact that in these areas, agriculture is a declining activity. A brilliant student will be much more attracted by electronics than by agriculture. Those countries which decide to set a priority on agriculture have to find the means to attract brainpower to this area of endeavor.

It is not only a question of the highest level of civil service or research. Many developing countries with highly qualified people at the top echelons suffer from a severe lack of qualified manpower who are specially trained to do fieldwork. Experience shows beyond any doubt that a good extension service whose people work directly with the farmers is the key to agricultural progress. It is a very difficult task to be an extension service officer working in the villages. Such a man should have sound technical knowledge, for he can lose the farmers' confidence after a simple mistake; in addition he should be an amateur psychologist, and be honest and straightforward, to name but a few requirements.

It is difficult in a developing country to locate sufficient numbers of such people to work in agriculture. In order to recruit this type of person the planners must take into consideration the following objectives: replace the current negative attitude toward agriculture by a positive and imaginative regard; grant higher salaries to the people who work with the farmers in the villages; organize training programs for extension service officers; and last, provide sufficient incentive so that the latter will remain at their agricultural posts. All this is of primary importance, for fertilizers can be imported, but not extension service officers.

Outside the Developing Orbit

It is a well-known fact that industrial development in Europe became possible after what is known as the agricultural revolution. Progress in agriculture has enabled Europe to furnish its needed manpower for industry and to produce surpluses of food to feed its growing urban population.

In contrast to the European experience, we turn to the example of the Union of Soviet Socialist Republics. The purpose here is not to discuss the specific problems of agriculture in a socialist economy but rather to point out the consequences of neglecting agriculture in the early stages of economic development. The objective of the U.S.S.R. was to achieve fast economic growth. The need was to determine the surest way to maximize the rate of growth of the economy. A higher rate of growth requires more investment at the expense of consumption. Therefore priority had to be given to those industries producing investment goods. For example, steel had to be used to build new factories rather than to produce consumer goods. And the new factories themselves had to produce equipment to be rechanneled into investment in order to allow for an even higher rate of growth of production.

Less stress on consumer goods means, of course, less effort toward developing agriculture. The principle underlying such a policy—even if not always clearly expressed—is that a fast growth of the Gross National Product obtained at the expense of present consumption levels will enable the economy in the long term to produce more consumer goods than would otherwise have been possible. The results of such theoretical calculations are confirmed by the example of Japan, which exemplifies what it is possible to achieve with a high rate of investment.

However, it should be recalled that the volume of industrial production does not depend solely on the capital and manpower available for investment, as in the simplest production functions. The same implements can be made to produce more or less, according to the manner in which they are used by the workers. Labor productivity is not determined only by the nature and quantity of equipment in use, but also by the motivation and ability of the workers. In general, inadequate levels of nutrition and unavailability of specific consumer items reduce the incentive and even the physical ability of the worker to increase his productivity.

It is, therefore, possible to conjecture that, given a different development policy, one which laid greater emphasis on agriculture and the production of consumer goods, the U.S.S.R. would have obtained a higher productivity in the use of its resources, and consequently, a faster rate of growth of its economy. As paradoxical as it may appear, industrial development in the U.S.S.R. has been limited by too much investment in heavy industry.

Conclusions

The leaders of the developing countries are on the right track in their belief that industrialization is the key to economic development. They should strive to industrialize their countries as rapidly as possible. What we have tried to explain in this paper is that the best way to reach this goal is to assign the first priority to agriculture in their development plans. The direct way is not always the most efficient, as most elementary textbooks on economics, in their discussions of investments, will explain.

But assigning the foremost priority to increase agricultural production requires the development of industries which are directly linked to agriculture. Creation of such industrial enterprises and training of a labor force for industry are tasks which must play an integral role in the planning of developing countries. At the same time, the establishment of industries linked to agriculture in rural areas is not only beneficial for agriculture but also promotes a more balanced regional development.

Once the twin tasks of agriculture—namely, producing adequate food for the population and supplying a labor force to work in industry—are achieved, then general industrial development in its own right can be accelerated. But before the process of real industrialization can begin, the main roadblock has to be overcome: that of persuading the leaders of developing countries that assigning priority to agriculture does not mean that their country will remain forever a backward one.

8. Industrialization
of Rural Areas
in Developing
Countries

P. D. Malgavkar

The problem of locating and nurturing industries in rural areas in the socioeconomic and political context of developing nations is both difficult and challenging. India, which since 1951 has taken several measures to industrialize the rural areas, is an extremely good example in this field. Her progress along the path of development can be studied fruitfully, and conclusions with worldwide application can be drawn from her experience.

The first section of this paper briefly discusses programs of industrialization in India and attempts to analyze their impact on the rural areas, presenting data of some studies and reports. In the second section of this paper, a strategy for the development of industries in rural areas is suggested.

Some Attempts at Rural Industrialization in India

In the nineteenth century the Indian rural economy was self-supporting and self-sufficient. The village or chain of villages had a potter for making roof tiles and pots for household use; a blacksmith for making tools and plows; a carpenter for making carts, plows, and wooden articles; spinners and weavers for spinning and weaving cloth; etc. With the beginning of industrialization of the country from the start of the twentieth century, many of these village industries began to languish. During the first half of the twentieth century the urban population trebled while the rural population increased by only 70 percent.[1] Such an exodus can be explained only by the increasing opportunities for employment in the urban center and the withering away of occupations in the rural areas. "A 'dual economy' was emerging, dynamic in the cities but essentially stagnant in the farm-encircled villages" [2]. Naturally, the Government of India is aware of the insufficient develop-

P. D. Malgavkar—India. B.A. (Hons.); Final Diplomas of the British Institute of Management, England; Purchasing Officers' Association, England and Sales Management Association, England; Principal Director of the Small Industry Training Institute, Hyderabad, India.

[1]In 1961 the urban population of India was about 79 million and the rural population, 360 million. If we include towns below 20,000 population in rural areas, the rural population would be 378 million and the urban 61 million. The urban population includes population of all municipal/urban local government areas, and of towns with a population of 5,000 and over, having a density of no less than 1,000 per square mile, and having at least three-fourths of the working population in nonagricultural occupations.

ment of rural industrialization, and since 1951 attempts have been made to attract industries to the rural areas. A recent study of licensing of large-scale industries [5] shows that of 918 licenses granted during 1961-1965 to factories for which location could be ascertained, 145 related to factories which by their very nature have to be located near sources of raw material and have, therefore, no choice of location. Of the remaining number of 773 licenses, only 168 were granted for factories located in rural areas or towns with a population of less than 20,000.

Rural Industries Projects of the Planning Commission With this problem in mind, the Planning Commission of the Government of India formulated a rural industries projects program [3, pp. 1, 2, 12, 16, 19]. Rural industrialization comprises two separate processes, namely, (a) the location and development of the larger industries with a view to balancing regional growth and checking the tendency toward concentration of industry in large urban and metropolitan centers; and (b) the development of village and small industries, some of the latter being linked with large-scale industries as ancillaries. It is this second process that the Planning Commission activated through the Rural Industries Project Program.

Forty-five areas were initially selected to be covered by the Rural Industries Projects, and in 1965 four more areas were added. As each of the areas has a population between 300 and 500 thousand, the total population covered by these programs can be taken as about 20 million. During the Third Plan period a total sum of Rs. 48 million (equivalent to $6.4 million) was spent on various schemes and programs [4], such as training programs, common service facilities, departmentally run commercial schemes and production centers, loans to industries, etc. The program gathered momentum from the year 1964-1965 onward, as during 1963-1964 most of the time was spent in creating an organization and conducting initial surveys.

Up to March 1966 as a result of the program, financial assistance was provided to 3,084 existing units under private enterprise and to 472 existing cooperative societies. The total sum of financial assistance to these units up to March 1966 was Rs. 11.2 million (equivalent to approximately $1.5 million). These private units and cooperative societies had created additional employment opportunities for about 50,000 persons by March 1966. In the assisted (existing and new) industrial units and cooperatives, the value of production rose from Rs. 8.8 million (approximately $1.2 million) in 1964-1965, to Rs. 30.25

million (approximately $4.00 million) in 1965-1966. This excludes about 60 percent of the new units which had not gone into production until March 1966.

The Rural Industries Projects Program [4] was reviewed by the Planning Commission in 1966, i.e., four years after its inception, and in assessing the impact of the program it was realized that, first, the existing administrative and financial procedures and centralization of administrative powers adversely affected the implementation of the program. Second, project organizations were weak in respect of technical personnel and the frequent transfers of project officers and other staff considerably affected the smooth implementation of the program. Third, shortage of electric power delayed a number of units from going into production. It was further stated that suitable planning of the training program in relation to the requirements of the area and a vigorous following-up is necessary.

State Governments' Offer of Incentives In addition to the Government's Rural Industries Projects Program, a number of states offer incentives for the dispersal of industries [6]. The types of incentives offered include state government support for obtaining an industrial license, and relief from certain taxes, duties, and rates, including electricity tariff, sales tax, octroi duty, water royalties, and nonagricultural assessment. A guarantee is offered for obtaining loans, and contributions are made toward the cost of feasibility studies and industrial housing. An advance supply of building materials is also provided on loan. The states offer preferential treatment in the Government Purchase Program, assistance in technical training of personnel, and fiscal measures. The response to these incentives was not, at least in the initial stages, very encouraging. But the scheme is still too fresh to evaluate its impact on attracting industries to rural areas.

The Wardha Plan The development of an entire region with the active participation and cooperation of the people of the region was attempted by Professor D. R. Gadgil in what has now come to be known as the Wardha Plan [10].

Wardha is the smallest distict in Maharashtra State with an area of 2,434 square miles. The area has six towns. Its population is 634,000, of whom 454,000 are rural. The concept of "mandi centers," or market towns, emerged from the Wardha Plan. These centers are envisaged to be both the nuclei of rural services of all kinds and the growing points of resource-based and consumer goods industries. In all, there are 38 mandi centers in the district, and each mandi center is so located that no village is more than five miles from it. A road system, based on and connecting the mandi centers, was worked out in the Wardha Plan. Certain centers are naturally or historically indicated; in others, choice of location was possible. The creation of a close-knit economic system and adequate provision of required devices, aids, assistance, and amenities at appropriate centers is the ultimate aim of this plan. Closely connected with this predominantly communications-services plan is the plan for conservation and development of resources. Because of the long and continued neglect of soil, water, pasture, forest, etc., in this area, the problem of scientific conservation of resources is the core of developmental effort.

The size of the program is related to previous neglect of resources and of provision of facilities. The plan for increasing production and efficiency in particular activities follows next, and the two main parts of this plan are related to agriculture and industry. However, the initiator of the scheme himself commented that the plan "highlighted the difficulties of lack of coordinated effort and lack of adequate knowledge regarding local problems and their correct solution. Synchronization of effort was neglected under the existing system of implementation of individual schemes. Organization is seen to be of central importance everywhere. Without careful organization a large program of works involving considerable labor could not be carried through. And without such organization, employment benefits could not be canalized to appropriate sections" [2]. Incidentally, Wardha District is also covered under the Rural Industries Projects of the Planning Commission. The field study of the Wardha District carried out in June-August 1967 by the participants of the SIET Institute refers to overlapping of authorities and uncertainties in the different agencies in charge of industrial development. The district had not made much headway in rural industrialization.

Small-Scale Industries Program Machinery on hire purchase exclusively available to small industry [2] is supplied by the National Small Industries Corporation, which is a Government company. In the Corporation's statistics of 1964 [11] it was indicated that 54 percent of the total value of the machinery was supplied to enterprises in Bombay, Calcutta, Madras, and Delhi. An additional 20 percent were supplied to another seven towns. This indicates that hardly 26 percent of the total funds deployed by the Corporation have gone outside these eleven cities.

[2] Factories with up to Rs. 750,000 worth of machinery and equipment (Rs. 1 million if they are ancillaries).

The impact of these various measures on rural industrialization has thus been negligible. To quote Shri Jaya Prakash Narayan [8], "The total effect upon the countryside of fourteen years of industrial development since Swaraj and ten years of planning has been almost negligible both from the point of view of (a) creating employment, and (b) adding to the wealth of the rural communities and raising the standard of living of the rural population."

It will be seen from the foregoing paragraphs that the efforts to date have not yielded promising results. What, therefore, should be the strategy for development of industries in rural areas?

The Strategy for the Development of Industries in Rural Areas

Agroprocessing, Agrosupporting, and Household Industries To improve the state of the rural population, it is necessary not only to increase agricultural productivity but also to introduce first of all agroprocessing and agrosupporting industries as well as improving the techniques and technologies of the household and agroindustries now being practiced. This approach is feasible and practicable and can be introduced straight away in the rural areas, for it can be built up from the experience and strength of the rural people rather than planting therein industries completely unrelated to the rural background, atmosphere, and experience of the people. As these types of industries would contribute quickly to the improvement of rural production, rural income, and rural standard of living, these would be welcomed by the rural inhabitants, thus ensuring their speedy adoption and quick success in the development of the rural economy.

Such industries can be from the traditional sphere of rice mills, oil mills, sugar factories, establishments making sugar confectionaries, bakeries, fruit and vegetable canning and preservation units, dal (pulses) mills, or units engaged in making dairy products. They can, on the other hand, be more sophisticated, such as solvent extraction plants for oil extraction, or modern rice mills equipped with silos, pneumatic grain dischargers, elevators and conveyor belts, automatic parboiling equipment, rubber roller shellers, and automatic weighing and bagging machines. In the dairy industry, starting with the chilling of liquid milk, one can introduce bottling, spray drying, and making other milk products such as cheese and condensed milk.

In fact, a host of new sophisticated industries for the conversion, preservation, grading, storage, packaging, and ultimate utilization of agricultural products by the consumer can be thought of in lines such as packaging, freeze-drying, and dehydrating. Such industries would considerably enhance the value of the agricultural produce, reduce its wastage, spoilage, and destruction, and give better satisfaction and more nutrition to the consumer by giving him fresh and quality products. On the other hand, industries such as fertilizers and fertilizer mixes, pesticides, and fungicides, can provide nutrients and protection to the agricultural crops to ensure better yield and produce to the agriculturists.

Needless to say, the requirements for agroprocessing and agrosupporting industries, and also the needs of the farmers themselves, such as plows, harrows, weed killers, sprayers, seed drills, and water lifting pumps of various descriptions would encourage a number of engineering industries to come to the locality.

For persons engaged in the raising of livestock, fish, or vegetables or fruit, the industry of preparing animal feed, the preparation, preservation and packing of hay and paddy straw, the manufacture of balanced ready-mixed feed, as well as converting dairy output, poultry, pigs, and fish to be more suitable and attractive for the table would be very profitable. Efficient management and better returns for occupations would go a long way both to increase rural employment in industries and create more food for the population in general.

The next area is that of household industry. These are traditional occupations in which the rural families have been engaged since time immemorial. The main drawback in this industry today is that it provides subsistence occupation. No increase in this specific activity as practiced today produces a surplus for reinvestment and increased employment. In such household industries it is necessary to upgrade the technology. Fuller use of tools, intelligent attention to design, and standardization of parts may be very important: all this must be backed by a good marketing organization.

For instance, in the preparation of wooden household articles the introduction of a woodworking lathe will greatly improve the productivity of the worker, ensuring greater production and thus giving him an opportunity to save for further investment and improvement of his standard of living. For example, a worker producing wooden flour rollers for making a certain variety of bread was scarcely earning enough to meet his daily expenses when he was working with hand tools. When he introduced a woodworking lathe with a ¼ H.P. electric motor, his production jumped up so much that he could not only meet his expenses but save more than Rs. 100 (approximately $12.70) per month for reinvestment. Through his spare-time activity, he began to earn enough to establish himself gradually as an industrialist.

Most household activities are of this nature and allow enormous scope for improving their technology and techniques. The spectrum of household industry is vast, and includes handlooms, spinning and weaving, carpet manufacturing, production of indigenous sugar, manufacture of hooka tobacco, manufacture of materials from bamboo, canes, and leaves, handicrafts, etc. In each of these, with simple tools and a small investment in equipment, production can rise considerably, giving an opportunity to the individual worker to earn a better living and ensuring the possibility of reinvestment in further programs. There need be no set schemes to be introduced ready-made in such industries. One needs only to study of the present system of household industries to suggest the introduction of simple equipment, tools, and practices, and thus greatly improve productivity, ensure higher earnings, and create possibilities for further development.

Analysis of the 1961 census of Andhra Pradesh as well as review of the study on infrastructure for industry in India, as described in the following section, illustrates that a significant number of types of industries can advantageously be located in rural areas.

The Census of Andhra Pradesh From an analysis of the Census in 1961 of Andhra Pradesh, a representative State in Federal India, it can be seen that a significant number of industries are already located in rural areas [1]. Out of the total number of 18,663,400 workers, 2,323,600 or 12.76 percent were engaged in nonfarm, nonservice occupations such as mining, quarrying, or in manufacturing either in households or factories. The breakdown of these occupations in different groups of industries are given in Table 1.

We find that the textile industry dominates, followed by livestock and fishing, agro-based industries, forest-based industries, and minerals. The bulk of employment in the textile industry is accounted for by the handloom industry. Technological advancement, such as power looms and quality dyeing and printing, will improve the viability of this industry and yet ensure that it remains in rural areas. The livestock and fishing and forest-based industries are basically rural industries. The agro-based industries can all be developed and run economically in the rural areas. For instance, out of 228 sugar mills working in India in 1966, 124 were in rural areas, and another 41 were in towns below 20,000 population [7]. The mineral industry must obviously be situated near the mines. For instance, as of January 1, 1967, 32 out of 40

Table 1.
Industrial Breakdown of Nonfarm and Nonservice Occupations in Andhra Pradesh

	In Households	In Factories	Totals
Agro-Based	97,631	227,282	324,913
Forest-Based	238,395	38,124	276,519
Livestock and Fish	552,019	13,459	565,478
Textile	711,402	84,123	795,525
Mineral	109,324	53,374	162,698
Engineering	35,678	41,177	76,855
Chemical	6,252	9,213	15,465
Miscellaneous	64,453	41,672	106,125
Total	1,815,154	508,424	2,323,578

cement factories in India [13] (80 percent) were located in rural areas or towns below 25,000 population. In fact these five industry groups account for 2,125,100 employees out of the total of 2,323,600, or over 91 percent. All these five groups are mostly in rural areas and can very well thrive therein, provided that further encouragement is given to improve their technology and marketing skill.

The Relationship between Industrial Location, Size of City, and Infrastructure

A recent study [14] has attempted to find out if there is any consistency in the type of industries that in the normal process find it advantageous to be located in towns and cities of various sizes. Examining the high incidence of dairy, sugar, cotton ginning, wood, paper, glass, and pottery industries in the smaller (20,000 to 50,000 population) sized urban centers of Punjab, and of beverage, sugar, wood, structural clay products, glass, and pottery industries in small-sized urban centers of Uttar Pradesh, it was observed that the former group of industries is heavily drawn to specific nodes of resource availability, most of them being either weight-losing or perishable. Economically and rationally, their locations are determined by the main consideration of resource distribution.

The role of small towns as collection centers for raw materials of the region is a factor in the location of these industries. A number of industries showing widespread dispersion in different size groups were also identified. These are flour and rice milling, ice making and cold storage, structural clay products, repair of motor vehicles, casting and forging of different sizes, nonferrous metal products, electric appliances, and beverage industries. An analysis of the characteristics of these industries shows that ice making (cold storage) and repair of motor vehicles are highly localized types of activities, in the sense that the final consumption of their products and services are linked primarily with the area of production. In these cases, the mean of transferability is extremely low. Likewise, the structural clay products involve heavy transportation costs, and tend to meet the limited area demands.

Besides these two situations, another group of industries likely to be attached to rural areas is characterized as involving high labor content and high floor-space use. Examples are leather tanning, conduit pipes, paper and strawboard, crushers, and expellers. Because of the abundance of cheap labor, land, and floor space, efforts to channel this type of industry into rural areas may yield rich dividends. It was observed in the studies that flour and rice mills, cold storage, edible oils, textile processing and finishing, starch, inorganic chemicals, hume pipes, and steel rerolling are industries using heavy transport. This is a group which is also power and space intensive. Manufacturing operations in these industries are relatively simple and highly mechanized, and value added by manufacturing is low. Incidentally, these are direct raw-material-consuming industries as distinct from semimanufactured materials. As the transport costs are substantial, this group of industries tends to be located near the sources of raw material or centers of consumption. This group of industries is also suitable for rural areas, as it tends to meet a limited area of demand.

It was also observed that industries with high water use, though they may belong to different process groups in respect of the purpose for which the water is needed, have an intrinsic advantage in being located where water is available in abundance. The requirement of a large quantity of water necessitates that these industries be situated away from big urban development. Examples of such industries are textile finishing and processing, paperboard and strawboard, tanneries and leather finishing, starch, and canning, preserving, and dehydration of fruits and vegetables. These industries are therefore extremely suitable for rural development, as they can be sited by the side of a river or lake in rural areas. As the sources of electric power are also more likely to be in rural areas, industries demanding high electric power consumption are also very suitable for rural locations.

To sum up with the words of Shri Jaya Prakash Narayan, in his Note [3, Part 4, pp. 28, 29], on the "Problem of Rural Industrialization," "Rural industrialization would have to be based on two factors: (a) local resources, both human and material, and (b) local needs. 'Local' does not mean a single village; it might mean a village, a group of villages, a block, or a district—depending upon the nature of the industry and the technology used. There are to be no pre-conceived limitations or inhibitions of a doctrinaire or sentimental type in regard to such matters as the use of power and technology. The aim and total long-term effect of rural industrialization should be to convert the present lopsided purely agricultural communities into balanced agro-industrial communities."

We must, in short, have a multipronged program for industrialization if it is to penetrate and take root and develop the rural areas.

References

1. Census Commissioner for India, *India—Union Primary Census Abstracts*, Vol. I, Part II-A(ii). Census of India, New Delhi: Manager of Publications, 1961.

2. Gadgil, D. R., *Wardha Plan—A Commentary*. Kakawadi: Institute of Regional Development, 1965, pp. 11 and 12. Cyclostyled, 19 pp.

3. Government of India, Planning Commission. "Projects for Intensive Development of Small Industries in Rural Areas." New Delhi: Manager of Publications, July 1962.

4. ____ , Planning Commission, Rural Industries Planning Committee. *Review of Progress—Rural Industries Projects Program, 1965-66*. New Delhi: Manager of Publications, July 1967. Cyclostyled.

5. ____ , Development Commissioner, Small Scale Industries, Ministry of Industrial Development and Company Affairs, *Analysis of Licensing of Large Scale Industries—1961-65*. New Delhi: Manager of Publications, 1966.

6. Government of Maharashtra, Directorate of Industries, *The Package Scheme of Incentives for Dispersal of Industries*. Bombay: Sachivalaya, Annexe, 1964.

7. *Indian Industries*, Bombay: Indian Industries, 1967. 8th ed.

8. Jaya Prakash Narayan, "The Problem of Rural Industrialization," in *Projects for Intensive Development of Small Industries in Rural Areas*. New Delhi: Planning Commission, July 1962, 28 pp.

9. Johnson, E. A. J., *Market Towns and Spatial Development in India*. New Delhi: National Council of Applied Economic Research, October 1965, p. 3.

10. McRobie, George F., "The Wardha Plan: An Experiment in District Development." Hyderabad: SIET Studies, 1967. Duplicated.

11. National Small Industries Corporation, *Directory of Machines Supplied on Hire-Purchase*. New Delhi: National Small Industries Corporation, May 1964.

12. Participants of the Area Development Course, *In-District Study of Wardha District*, June-August 1967, conducted by SIET Institute.

13. Prakash Chandra, "Cement Industry in Perspective," *Commerce, 116*, no. 2979 (June 8, 1966), pp. 1566-1568.

14. Stanford Research Institute, School of Planning and Architecture, and the Small Industry Extension Training Institute, *Costs of Urban Infrastructure for Industry as Related to City Size in Developing Countries—India Case Study*, Chapter IV, "Relationship between Industrial Location, Size of City and Infrastructure Requirements." Menlo Park, Calif.: Stanford Research Institute, 1968, pp. 13 and 15.

9. Urbanization
Trends in
Northeastern
Megalopolis:
A Challenge
for Social Policies

Demetrius S. Iatridis

The process of urbanization in the United States during this century has been particularly rapid, erratic, and radical. Its effects upon the urban system are not yet adequately appreciated and understood, except in a piecemeal fashion which creates artificial conceptual dichotomies in physical, technological, economic, or social planning. As urbanization, that is, the proportion of the population concentrated in urban settlements or the rise in this proportion, nears a peak in most advanced industrial countries,[1] the complexity and interdependence of the various components of the country's urban system increase rapidly and generate synergically new systemic linkages and flows, new rural urban technological dependencies, and new conceptual challenges in understanding urban development. The very nature and scope of the urban scene have been radically affected, and urban policies planning is no longer perceived as a predominantly physical development problem at the local level but as a social and political problem of national significance.

Urban population dispersion and concentration, for example, is an issue which, though treated primarily as a concern of physical development planners, particularly those interested in regional planning, is now rapidly emerging at this advanced stage of urbanization as an issue which has predominantly social, political, economic, and cultural dimensions and which in many ways is at the core of the urban dilemma facing this nation. Urbanization trends of population concentration and dispersion not only contribute to new urban settlement patterns like Megalopolis but are directly linked to national social policies for urban growth.

In order to illustrate this, it will be necessary to examine the phenomenon of urban population dispersion more closely. Dispersion is perhaps one of the most challenging contemporary urban phenomena in this

Demetrius S. Iatridis—United States. Ph.D. Social Economy, Bryn Mawr College, 1954; Research Professor and Professor of Social Planning, Boston College; Director, Institute of Human Sciences, Boston College; faculty member of Urban Policy Conference Program, Brookings Institute; since 1967, Adjunct Professor of Ekistics and Social Planning, University of Rhode Island; Director, Graduate School of Ekistics, Athens, 1959 to 1966.

[1] In 1960 the United States ranked first in the world in total urban population, fourth in total population.

country and most significant for evolving effective urban policies. Within thirty years the United States will have moved in a single century from a largely agrarian nation to a highly urbanized society. Its urban population will have grown from 31 million to about 220 to 290 million, and the percentage of people living in SMSAs will be 85 percent as opposed to 35 percent (Table 1). Yet this process has proceeded in a somewhat erratic fashion.

The 1920s witnessed an urbanization peak, with great national prosperity, a declining birth rate, and extensive farm-to-city migration moving employment and people away from farming. The 1930s saw a period of economic depression and recession, the lowest birth rate in U.S. history, and some limited migration back to farms because of the lack of urban employment. The 1940s witnessed a sharp reversal of the economic trend, with a wartime economy producing an accelerated growth of metropolitan areas and housing shortages causing population to concentrate in the central cities and the developed suburban areas. The 1950s, in addition to sustained high birth rate, saw a decline in small towns and a continuation of metropolitan area growth, with considerable outward movement of central city populations as housing construction led to great suburban growth. In the 1960s metropolitan area population growth and economic activity have been at high levels, increasing national wealth, increasing leisure, increasing education, and increasing material affluence; service work has overtaken manufacturing employment in major urban centers, and employment in extensive land-

Table 1.
Number and Population of Major Urbanized Areas, Estimate 1920-1960 and Projection 1960-2000.

Census Year	No. of Urban Areas	Total Urban Pop. (millions)	Number of Urbanized Areas		
			Over 1 million	500,000 to 1 million	100-500 thousand
1920	70	34.6	6	9	55
1930	89	47.5	10	7	72
1940	97	52.2	10	9	78
1950	124	67.1	12	13	99
1960	159	90.7	16	21	122
1970	180	115.0	25	17	138
1980	192	147.2	28	27	137
2000	221	219.0	42	29	150

Source: J. Pickard, *Dimension of Metropolitanism*, Urban Land Institute Monograph No. 14, p. 19.

using industries has been curtailed significantly; the old central cities have become the central focus of social justice and conflict which result from an unacceptably slow diffusion of affluence; suburban growth has continued; and an exurbia is being created for certain population groups by a leapfrogging thinning-out of urban populations at the edge of built-up suburbs.

It now appears that if present trends continue, the urban population dispersion of the 60s and 70s is likely to become the leitmotif of the remainder of the century, and a key concept in urban social policies planning. These patterns of urban growth are resulting in the creation of new forms of urban settlements, such as the megalopolis, which, although not yet adequately studied, appears to be emerging much as the metropolis emerged a few decades ago. Of the world's emerging megalopoli, the oldest and most extensive is Northeastern Megalopolis (NEM).

Northeastern Megalopolis, as defined in the study of the Institute of Human Sciences, includes 63,000 square miles (some 700 miles long and 50 to 75 miles wide), 43 Standard Metropolitan Statistical Areas (SMSA),[2] a population of 44 million people, or 23 percent of the nation's total population, on 1.7 percent of the country's total land. The average density is 700 persons per square mile, but densities range from 3,900 in Connecticut to 100,000 persons per square mile in the Pennsylvania-New Jersey area (with internal fluctuations from 1,000 in 160,000 persons per square mile), with approximately 23 percent of the total area in urban use (residential-commercial-industrial buildings, streets, highways, airports, railroad, etc.). It includes four major clusters of urban regions: North (Boston-Providence), Central East (New York-Newark), Central (Philadelphia), and South (Baltimore-Washington-Virginia).

It is remarkable that in spite of the radical changes which have occurred in the last 120 years, NEM has maintained a steady share of the nation's population and a major role in the country's social, political, cultural, and economic leadership. In the last half-century, its popula-

[2]Portland, Lewiston, Manchester, Boston, Brockton, Fall River, Fitchburg, Lawrence-Haverhill, Lowell, New Bedford, Pittsfield, Springfield-Holyoke-Chicopee, Worcester, Providence-Pawtucket-Warwick, Bridgeport, Hartford, Meriden, New Britain, New Haven, New London-Norwich-Groton, Norwalk, Stamford, Waterbury, New York, Atlantic City, Jersey City, Newark, Patterson-Clifton-Passaic, Trenton, Wilmington, Baltimore, Allentown-Bethlehem-Easton, Harrisburg, Lancaster, Reading, Scranton, York, Wilkes-Barre-Hazleton, Philadelphia, Newport News-Hampton, Norfolk-Portsmouth, Richmond, Washington, D.C.

tion has fluctuated by only three to four percentage points, from 25 percent in 1920 to 23 percent in 1968, and estimates for the year 2000 are 22 percent.

This steady balance between NEM and the rest of the nation justifies the assumption that there is likely to be little change in the relationship in the next 30 years. This hypothesis is reinforced by NEM's strong, advanced, well-balanced, and diversified economic base, which includes growth industries as well as service and manufacturing, as compared with most other cities, which tend to be predominantly either service centers or manufacturing centers. NEM also boasts major national and international decision-making centers of government, science, and technology. Its indices of per capita income, education, and culture are higher than the national average. Its population grew from 25 million in 1920 to 44 million in 1968, and will reach an estimated 68 million by 2000 (Figure 1).

Two stages can be distinguished in the population dispersion which created NEM (and which is creating other megalopoli): a movement

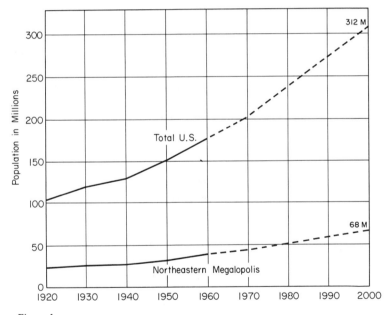

Figure 1.
Population growth: past, present, and future projection. Data compiled from County and City Data Book, 1967, of the Bureau of Commerce and the I.H.S. Megalopolis Research team.

from the cities to suburbia, and a further movement from suburbia to exurbia.

From the Cities to Suburbia

Technological and economic advances, which pushed labor off the farms and into the cities and contributed to the growth and densities of the city, encouraged the population dispersion to the suburbs. As early as the 1920s urban residents of major American cities were exploding back across city limits into the countryside. By 1960, 53 percent of the urban population in America lived outside the old central cities of metropolitan areas. Since 1950 this process has decreased the population of older cities, due to the out-migration of middle-income whites to the suburbs, even though nonwhite in-migration of previously rural or small-town people to the city has increased.

At this urbanization stage, suburbia, and not the central core of metropolitan areas, is the home of most Americans, and this trend will be more notable in the future. Between 1960 and 1965 the total U.S. SMSA population increased by 10.2 percent (a far greater percentage than the 7.7 percent growth of the total U.S. population). Of this increase, 17.7 percent was outside the central city (Table 2), whereas central city growth was only 3.2 percent. The outward movement of people has been matched by the outward movement of jobs, retail trade, manufacturing, and wholesale establishments. Between 1954 and 1969 more than 50 percent of all industrial and mercantile construction took place outside the core cities. Inner-city, multistory factories were becoming obsolete and noncompetitive. Traffic congestion in cities, and the ease of truck-highway transportation in the outer areas, led to the vast accelerating shift of industrial locations from old manufacturing rail centers into the suburbs, with their areas of inexpensive green land, access to principal markets, and residential exclusion (Figure 2).

From Suburbia to Exurbia

Parallel to the recent suburban population growth and in conjunction with it there is a moderate, but nevertheless significant, population growth beyond the suburban core into exurbia which will undoubtedly play a considerable role in urban population dispersion trends for the next thirty years. Although inadequately studied and statistically undocumented as yet, this outward population movement to lower densities in rural, nonfarm space surrounding suburbia already manifests itself in several ways (Figure 3).

Table 2.
SMSA Population Growth.

	1960 (,000)	1965 (,000)	% Increase 1960-1965
Total U.S. Population	178,458	192,185	7.7
Total SMSA Population	112,323	123,813	10.2
Nonmetropolitan Area Population	66,135	68,372	3.4
	Population Growth 1960 (,000)	Distribution within SMSA 1965 (,000)	% Increase 1960-1965
SMSA Population	112,323	123,813	10.2
Central City Population	57,790	59,612	3.2
Outside Central City Population	54,533	64,201	17.7

Source: Compiled from data of *U.S. Statistical Abstract* (Washington, D.C.: 1966), p. 19, and from data of the NEM project at the Institute of Human Sciences, Boston College.

The rural nonfarm population in NEM had increased 23.5 percent between 1950 and 1960 (compared to a 17 percent total population increase and a 15.1 percent urban population increase in NEM); the farm population of NEM decreased 48.1 percent (Table 3). The percentage of people living in rural areas and engaged in urban activities is on the rise. Thus, the ratio of nonfarmers in rural population in NEM has increased from 81 percent in 1950 to 91 percent in 1960. Even on a national basis the trend to nonurban areas is evident. The U.S. non-metropolitan area population growth during 1960-1965 was a significant 3.4 percent, almost half of the corresponding total U.S. population increase (Figure 4).

Several other indicators point clearly to a distinct preference of urban Americans for low, rural-like densities accompanied by urban facilities and services, and therefore for outward urban dispersion into rural space. This attitude is realistically supported by forecasts of increasing per capita income, economic development patterns, and technological (mass-media) communication advances. The population of the urbanized areas in the United States has increased 30 percent during the last decade, whereas the territorial growth of urbanized areas has increased 80 percent, almost threefold. Likewise in NEM urban population density dropped from 5,591 (1960) to 4,670 (1968) persons per square

TREND IN DISTRIBUTION OF SMSA POPULATION BETWEEN CENTRAL CITIES AND OUTSIDE, 1900-1975

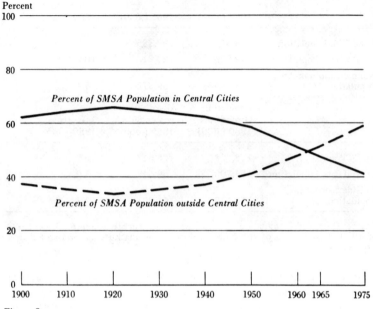

Figure 2.
Trend in distribution of SMSA population between central cities and outside, 1900-1975. Source: *Fiscal Balance in the American Federal System*, Vol. 2, *Metropolitan Fiscal Disparities*, Advisory Commission on Intergovernmental Relations, Washington, D.C., p. 30.

mile, although the population increased correspondingly from 39 to 44 million.

This trend away from the core suburbs to exurbia is likely to continue and accelerate further because of three major factors. One is the increasing suburban growth which, contrary to popular belief, is in its beginning rather than at its peak; another is the technological mass communication-transportation network, which enables urban dispersion into rural space accompanied by urban services; and a third factor is the housing and community preferences of urban Americans. The suburban growth rate was calculated at a significant 106 percent between 1960 and 1965 while the national population increase was only 41 percent. The high rate of population concentration in suburbia will probably be accompanied by a corresponding investment in facilities and services such as housing, including social overhead and infrastructure.

THE GROWTH OF U.S. POPULATION, 1900 - 1975

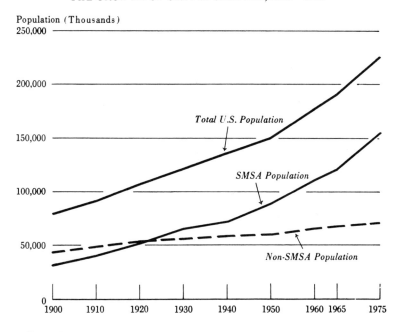

Figure 3.
The growth of U.S. population, 1900-1975. Source: *Fiscal Balance in the American Federal System,* Vol. 2, *Metropolitan Fiscal Disparities,* Advisory Commission on Intergovernmental Relations, Washington, D.C., p. 29.

In effect, suburban areas will probably absorb 79 percent of total national growth. The reason is not only that American cities have always grown at the fringes, but also that the post-World War II demographic forces have accentuated this trend. The earliest arrivals of the greatest baby boom ever experienced in the United States (from 1947 to 1960) are now old enough to marry and to occupy urban or suburban apartments. The present apartment squeeze in several cities of NEM and the inability of supply to keep pace with demand is partially due to this population growth. The apartment squeeze experienced in several cities of NEM and the accompanying rental increases in uncontrolled apartments has produced at least one major political issue, for example, in the 1969 New York mayoral election.

Prices, especially in relation to value received, have driven middle-class families from the city.[3] By the mid-seventies, when their first child is 2

[3]In New York City as of spring 1968, only 1.23 percent of rental apartments were vacant—the lowest figure since the years following World War II. The va-

Table 3.
Urban and Rural Population Changes in the United States and Northeastern
Megalopolis 1940-1960 (in thousands).

	Total			Urban		
	1940	1950	1960	1940	1950	1960
U.S.	131,669	151,325	179,323	74,423	96,467	125,284
NEM	29,302	33,415	39,098	24,175	28,248	33,282

	Rural					
	Nonfarm			Farm		
	1940	1950	1960	1940	1950	1960
U.S.	27,029	31,431	40,567	30,216	23,048	13,474
NEM	3,997	4,179	5,162	1,304	977	507

Source: Data compiled at the Institute from U.S. Census of Population: 1940,
1950, 1960.

to 3 years old and the second is about to arrive, many young baby-
boom parents will decide to buy suburban houses, strengthening another massive suburban building boom. Forecasts of employment distribution follow suit. If present trends continue, by 1985 one-half of
New York Metropolitan Region's jobs will be outside its core; by the
year 2000 probably two-thirds of the region's employment will be
outside the present core. The impact of this development and the concentration of such massive investment will have far-reaching implications for metropolitan and suburban local governments, for racial and
class polarization, for increased social conflict, and for regional urban-
rural interdependencies in NEM.

A second contributing factor is the rapidly improving mass communication media and transportation technology which accompany the outward population movement to rural space and later, after being institutionalized, act as a spur to further rural expansion. The communication
and transportation expansion forecast for the immediate future is likely
to shorten time distances radically and make possible greater access. A
complex communication-transportation network has already expanded

cancy rate of new apartments never under rent control had dropped from 4.37
percent in 1965 to 0.73 percent in 1968. With supply barely able to keep pace
with demand, rents have risen sharply in many of the 600,000 apartments not
under rent control in New York City (median increase approximately 26.5 percent with each new lease).

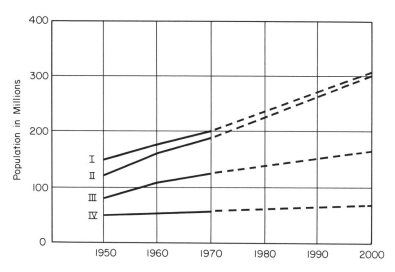

Figure 4.
Population growth and distribution in the conterminous United States. Compiled by I.H.S. from J. Pickard, Dimensions of Metropolitanism; Rand McNally Commercial Atlas; and U.S. Census of Population.

into rural areas of Megalopolitan complexes, providing new linkages and flows among urban centers in NEM and between metropolises and their hinterlands. Daily long-distance telephone calls increased from 3,366,000 in 1940 to 16,000,000 in 1965, and the percentage of American households having a telephone rose to 80.6 in 1965.

In nonmetropolitan areas telephone ownership rose from 61.1 percent in 1958 to 72.6 percent in 1965. Another important communication network index is the increase of households with TV outside SMSAs from 50 percent in 1955 to 89 percent in 1965. Transportation—especially the automobile—has always been an important linkage in the dispersion of urban population. Of the total 3,644,069 miles of highway in 1964, 3,152,577 were in rural areas. Passenger car registration rose from 9.2 million in 1920 to 90.4 in 1965, whereas registration of trucks and buses rose from 1.1 to only 15.1 in the same period. Air transportation provides a technologically more contemporary linkage which stimulates urban human settlement dispersion. Civil aircraft rose from 17,928 in 1940 to 162,083 in 1965; miles flown rose from 264 million to 2,562 million; and airports with lighted and paved runways increased from 1,422 in 1950 to 2,747 in 1965.

Technological and economic capabilities are obviously at the hard core of options available and determine the nature of the decisions made by population segments about housing and community life. But they are not sufficient by themselves. A third factor contributing to urban dispersion in rural areas is the psychological and social attitudes and preferences associated with social mobility, status, and prestige. Similarly, the style-setting symbols in the new generation are powerful elements in housing preferences and trends. Several studies seem to indicate that the majority of urban Americans, including those now living in the city, want a suburban single-family house when they have children. This urge for suburban life is not limited to America or the middle class. It has been reported in studies of European countries and of lower-income groups.

Other studies[4] indicate that the style-setters in the younger American generation also favor increased space and lower densities, particularly the new urban environment emerging now beyond the suburban core. Housing preferences indicate that graduates of professional schools clearly rejected the slum-ridden city, the old-style suburb they grew up in, and the glass-and-concrete high-rise apartments; and they were unsympathetic to proposals for raising families in cheek-by-jowl terraces or town houses. They preferred the dispersed urban way of life as opposed to life in small towns, central city, or suburb. They wanted space to move around in, room for privacy, and a living environment that brought them in contact with nature. There is mounting evidence that a substantial percentage of urban dwellers, including the style-setters of future preferences, are attracted to or pushed toward housing facilities farther and farther away from the central urban and suburban areas, i.e., to the relatively unexplored and easier-molded countryside. There is evidence suggesting that this trend will further accelerate in the next 30 years, leading to a more systematic megalopolitan development pattern. But it is clear that these urban dwellers do not leave the city for a rural existence. Along with land, space, and lower density, they want all their favorite urban facilities within a short driving distance from the house.

[4]George L. Peterson, "Subjective Value and Human Ecology," a paper presented at the Regional Science Association, Ann Arbor, December, 1964, at the University of Michigan. This study among graduate students of professional schools is a good example. Clearly, the notion that as the rich become invisible to the lower income groups, the professionals are looked upon increasingly by the middle class as the successes and provide the cues for imitation and social style-setting, has influenced the selection of young professionals-in-the-making in graduate school.

Actually, the density in cities and in metropolitan areas is dropping, not increasing, as the population grows; the reason being that the territory covered by the urban agglomeration is growing faster than the population. For example, the New York-Northeastern-New Jersey urbanized area grew by 51 percent from 1950 to 1960, whereas the population rose by 15 percent. In fact, urban population density in the United States has decreased from 5,408 persons per square mile in 1950, to 3,891 persons per square mile in 1960, despite the population increase. Consequently, the per capita land of urban dwellers has increased from 0.118 to 0.164 acre—an increase of 39 percent.

Policy Implications

This leapfrogging, unplanned urban population dispersion, which favors certain urban population groups, is at the root of many urban problems. Certainly it is a major cause of racial and social polarization in inner-city areas, and contributes greatly to the current urban crisis in finance, education, public welfare, housing, and city government. A brief examination of these problem areas indicates that adoption of a coherent social policy regarding population dispersion offers one of the most effective approaches to urban policies planning.

The problem of racial and social polarization and the urban ghetto is an excellent illustration of the need to view densities and urban population dispersion as instruments of social policy. Economically, socially, and culturally the core city has lost today much of its socializing function, because families trapped in the ghetto cannot enter the mainstream of urban life. Several students of the phenomenon argue, like Harvey Perloff, that social equalizers are now necessary to help these families make use of the traditional urban facilities and services to get on the urban escalator of social mobility. Low- and moderate-income families cannot afford and are excluded from suburbia or exurbia, and are trapped in the old central core of the metropolis.

Real estate practices, on the other hand, are responsible not only for the skyrocketing of land prices at the fringe of the metropolis (i.e., land acquisition and holding for speculation), which necessarily prevents lower- and moderate-income groups from moving into the suburbs, but are also responsible for racial polarization which is encouraged by their discriminatory practice. Zoning ordinances and density policies of most suburbs also contribute to this trend. The old central cities became the gathering grounds of the unskilled in-migrant, of the poor (black and white), and of the disadvantaged, while the predominantly white middle and upper class has concentrated in the suburbia and exurbia. The creation of two Americas—one black, located in the urban ghettos, and one white, predominantly middle class, located in suburbs—increases the economic and racial polarization of the rising urban population and intensifies the struggle for social and moral justice.

Urban dispersion has eliminated most of the employment opportunities for unskilled manpower (the typical in-migrant) in central cities and in conjunction with other factors contributed to urban poverty and ghettos. The old centers of metropolitan areas have lost much of their socializing function and their capacity to absorb the new in-migrants, economically, socially, culturally; to help them get on the escalator of social and cultural mobility; and to provide the families trapped in the ghetto with social inputs required to enter the mainstream of urban life. To provide job opportunities in the ghettos and to reestablish jobs near residences is a noble experiment which is not likely to have lasting effect, unless the broader industrial and urban population dispersion trend declines or is reversed. Even with massive government intervention and radical changes in housing policies—more encompassing than has so far been anticipated—the black-white polarization trend is not likely to be reversed.

"A Negro society largely concentrated within large central cities will be permanently relegated to its current status, possibly even as we expend great amounts of money and effort trying to gild the ghetto," noted the Advisory Commission on Civil Disorders. Indeed, cities' white population dropped from 31.1 percent in 1950 to 30.0 percent in 1960; for the same period the Negro population increased from 39.2 percent to 50.5 percent. The trend became more distinct in the 1960s.

According to the Bureau of the Census' sample surveys between 1960 and 1969, central cities gained nearly three-quarters of a million people. This net change was the result of an increase of 2.6 million in the Negro population, and a decline of 2.1 million in the white population. Nearly three-fourths of the total national growth in Negro population since 1960 has occurred in the central cities of the metropolitan areas. As a result, 55 percent of the total Negro populations now reside in central cities, compared with 26 percent of the white population. Insofar as future trends are concerned, it is interesting to note that only about one-third of the net gain in Negro inner-city populations—800,000 people—stemmed from migration from rural areas. The remaining 1.8 million is attributed to national increase of the population.

The white population in urban fringe areas increased in the period 1950-1960 from 14.7 to 22.8 percent; the corresponding Negro increase was from 6.1 to 8.4 percent (Table 4). The rate at which whites are leaving the city has accelerated sharply since 1964. Before 1964 they moved at an average rate of 140,000 a year. Since 1964 the net migration of whites from central cities is estimated at 800,000-900,000 a year. This trend is a distinct reversal of earlier trends in population distribution.

The financial crisis of cities is also related to the population dispersion. The old core cities are deprived of an effective tax base when middle- and upper-income groups reside outside the city limits. This financial crisis cannot be effectively solved without a reversal in the population dispersion trend or without radical changes in the political and tax structure of cities. Increased financial responsibility by state and federal government is long overdue. If present trends continue, the deficit of major American cities in ten years will rise to about 250 billion dollars. The greatest income source of American cities is the property tax. For as long as the old core city continues to be the gathering grounds of the poor and the disadvantaged, and as long as it breeds slums, it is impossible to solve the financial crisis. The poor and the underprivileged, the slum dweller, not only produce no income for the city but require more sophisticated and expensive services, such as education and public welfare, to enter the mainstream of urban life. The old core city which must finance these services from local resources is caught in the vicious circle of loss of income due to population dispersion accompanied by increasing costs to maintain urban facilities and services.

Education, therefore, is also related to the population dispersion trend. The quality of education is deteriorating in the old core cities

Table 4.
White and Nonwhite Population Distribution (percent).

White Population	1950 (100%)	1960 (100%)	Nonwhite 1950 (100%)	1960 (100%)
Rural	35.7	30.5	38.3	27.6
Urban	64.3	69.5	61.7	72.4
Central cities	31.1	30.0	39.2	50.5
Urban fringe	14.7	22.8	6.1	8.4
Other urban	18.5	16.8	16.4	13.5

Source: U.S. Statistical Abstract (Washington, D.C., 1966), p. 25.

because of inadequate financing and also because of the special nature of the educational task of educating the masses of ghetto and low-income children. The underprivileged require a special and high quality education, but our cities provide mediocre or poor educational facilities to this very population segment.

The deteriorating and outdated public welfare system in the old core cities provides another illustration of the social, economic, and political consequences of population dispersion and its potential as an instrument of social policies. The high concentration of the poor and the disadvantaged in the core city creates a particularly explosive and expensive situation for city governments. As the federal experts have found out, we cannot finance the antipoverty programs merely by taxing the rich. At any rate, there are not enough of them at the local level. The alternative to a redistribution of wealth from rich to poor is to put idle resources of the city economy to work and create new money. Available resources, however, are now scarce, so that the city—as is the case for the nation—must get resources for such social expenditure from general taxation, i.e., from the average taxpayer. The resistance, however, of the average taxpayer is well documented. It is extremely difficult to write legislation designed to solve minority-group problems and still be appealing to the majority. The most effective solution, of course, is the overhaul of the welfare system with the federal government acting as a kind of financial "guarantor," i.e., negative income tax, etc., against unacceptable low standards of living. The aim is to have the government provide money with which the individual citizens could purchase social welfare in the open market.

It is conceivable, then, that other urban needs of minority groups, such as housing, education, etc., might be met in the open market, the government acting again as financial guarantor. But we must, then, innovate socially and politically to ensure that such services are indeed available for all population groups in the free, urban market. Public responsibility is in such case essential to guarantee social and moral justice.

It should be evident that selection of urban growth and population distribution or concentration alternatives in NEM constitutes a tool for social planning and a social strategy well suited to provide a solid policies framework for the solution of urban problems. The crises in housing and open space requirements most clearly illustrate this conclusion. Of the 15 million additional housing units which will be required by

2000 in NEM,[5] at least 80 percent, or 12.0 million new housing units, will be located in suburbs and exurbs, as compared to 20 percent in central cities. These units will entail a residential investment of approximately 312.5 billion dollars, plus 156.2 billion dollars for social overhead and infrastructures, or a total of 468.7 billion dollars housing investment in suburbs and exurbs, compared with a total housing investment of 562.5 billion dollars in NEM.

The size of the investment, the number of new urban communities, and the anticipated suburban growth point to the need for more concerted and regionally conceived and implemented housing and urban community facilities and services, administered by inclusive and interlocking suburban local governments, and intramegalopolitan coalitions. The alternative is likely to be a spiraling of local tax rates in a problematic effort of suburbs and exurbs to underwrite low-density residential development.

Another illustration of future urban growth pressures upon resources is the spatial requirements for the accommodation of 29 million additional population in NEM by the year 2000. Although several analysts of megalopolitan growth have shown concern regarding space availability in the massive continuous, high-density, built-up corridor, current indicators do not justify this concern because NEM has ample space in toto for projected growth. The key question is the density projected or contemplated. It has been estimated at the Institute that an average of density 236,[6]

---

[5] The following assumptions were made at the Institute of Human Sciences in calculating housing cost and requirements: (1) 15 million housing units required by 2,000 to accommodate additional population and eliminate substandard housing; (2) one housing unit required for every 3 persons; (3) cost of one unit estimated at $25,000 (including finances, etc.) at 1960 price index; (4) cost of community facilities (including schools, parks, public buildings, service roads, management and maintenance, etc.) one-half of total housing unit cost; and (5) rate of deterioration of existing housing units in sound condition: 7 percent per 10 years.

[6] A density of 236 persons per square mile—extremely low as it is—has nevertheless been the actual average growth density in the 43 SMSAs of NEM between 1960 and 1968. The 43 SMSAs of NEM increased territorially 636 square miles from 1960 to 1968—or an annual average increase rate of 79.5 square miles. During the same period their population increased by 1,203,000 persons, or an annual average increase rate of 150,375 persons. This indicates an average density of about 236 persons per square mile—an incredibly low and wasteful urban density which reflects accurately actual experience only to the extent, of course,

1,000,[7] 2,000, and 8,000 persons per square mile creates an additional space demand of 118,000, 29,000, 14,500, and 3,500 square miles, respectively, to accommodate in NEM an additional 29 million people by the year 2000.

With the exception of the first density assumption—unlikely to materialize—the additional space required, ranging from 29,000 to 3,500 square miles, is available in toto in NEM (63,159 square miles). Even if the present built-up area is deducted, as well as public parks, high mountains, lakes, and areas not convenient for building, NEM still has ample space for projected growth. While space availability in toto is not likely to be a problem because NEM has an abundance of land far beyond that required to accommodate the next 29 or 45 million people, there would be distinct pressures upon several regions in NEM, i.e., those which grow at a faster pace and attract massive future population concentration because of social and economic benefits, such as suburbs and fringe rural areas.

There would also be pressures to act concertedly in the selection of the most appropriate areas for building and for open space, for the preservation of natural resources, and for the location of hospitals and transportation structures, such as centers for rail trains (tracked air cushion vehicles—TACV—or a gravity vacuum transit—GVT) or airports and highways, as well as to maintain a sound ecological and environmental balance. This building strategy suggests that river, ocean, and bay edges and seashores be preserved in a natural state under public ownership or control for public use. It also indicates that open space as well as land acquisition and costs can become a major block to development if preliminary steps are not taken. Several studies have established that the total cost of purchasing land now and paying interest on long-term loans would probably be lower than the total cost of the land at a later date.

Of course, present policies, programs, and plans depend for implementation upon governmental structures which now are painfully limited in scope, being spatially fragmented, independent, and uncoordinated. The multiplicity of types and jurisdictions of governmental units in

---

that the population growth was absorbed entirely in the territory added to the SMSAs.

[7]NEM as defined by Jean Gottman had actual density of 596 persons per square mile in 1950, and 700 persons per square mile in 1960. NEM as defined by the Institute of Human Sciences has a population density of 1,260-1,305 persons per square mile. Finally, the dispersed city population density ranges between 500 and 1,200 persons per square mile.

NEM makes concerted effort problematic and regional planning difficult. Regional, intramegalopolitan governmental coordination will require political and administrative innovations far beyond what current tradition envisions and encourages. A housing industry capable of mobilizing the required talent, money, and land is also a prerequisite. Open space, a critical resource presumed as a matrix within which urbanization occurs, land acquisition, and the development of land deployment programs are also vital to this strategy, which involves public policies of several states and intergovernment agencies.

Without public acquisition of land, sprawl in exurban growth will continue. But above all, a sound urban policy for NEM should avoid two extreme possibilities: further population concentration solely within presently urbanized areas of NEM, or accelerated population dispersion to its hinterland. On the national level, a sound urban growth policy must also avoid two similar extremes: further population concentration solely within NEM, or extensive population dispersion to the rest of the country. Population dispersion and low densities are currently a market necessity (at least for higher-income groups), but should not be confused with a desirable urban growth pattern in NEM.

Public policies must negotiate these two extremes so that ecological and open space considerations can be harmonized, and the organization of the urban residential areas and infrastructure to be added in NEM become economically realistic and socially complementary to urban policy strategy. Even a crude calculation of some of the facilities required for the additional 29 million people in NEM—such as offices, health or education centers, commercial services, entertainment, etc.—is sufficient to convince any analyst that grouping these facilities in appropriate large regional urban centers is socially more desirable and economically more efficient than dispersing them in exurbia, which will be the pattern if present population dispersion trends continue.

The effects of exurbia upon the younger generation have not yet been studied, but there are indications that isolation and inbreeding social transactions will influence the socialization process. Clustering of urban facilities and services in large urban centers appropriately located throughout NEM will enhance rather than reduce access by all population groups to educational, health, employment, and cultural opportunities close to residential facilities and public transportation.

What is needed above all is a broadly conceptual, interdisciplinary social policy framework to guide urban growth strategies. Such a framework can be effectively utilized only within a context of broader regional linkages and flows, "a *multi-nucleated* interlinked network" of regional urban centers within NEM integrated with urban-suburban-exurban governmental consolidations, if excessive population dispersion is to be checked. This naturally implies the creation of completely new urban communities which offer new urban ways of living[8] in conjunction with existing and proposed urban centers, with projected infrastructure facilities, and with the contemplated transportation networks.

The take-off point is the realization that NEM is exposed to most of the social, economic, and technological forces which generate change in the rest of the country. As the rest of the nation shifts from farm to metropolis, and as the metropolitan population shifts from city to suburbia and exurbia, the tendency for NEM and the nation to respond in parallel fashion grows even more marked.

Another aspect of this systemic pattern is the relationship between megalopolitan growth and metropolitan regions. As the megalopolitan urban regions emerge from colliding metropolitan expansions, and from new technological networks (particularly in telecommunications), the tendency of metropolises and megalopolis to respond in parallel and interdependent fashion grows. It is conceivable that megalopolis may serve increasingly as the intermediate link between national and metropolitan level forces which generate change in the country. The gap which now exists between national and metropolitan levels may well be filled by a megalopolitan unit which will bridge the two.

Selected Bibliography

Advisory Commission on Intergovernmental Relations, *Urban and Rural America, Policies for Future Growth.* Washington, D.C.: U.S. Government Printing Office, 1968.

Bureau of Census, *County and City Data Book, 1967,* and *Statistical Abstract Supplement.* Washington, D.C.: U.S. Government Printing Office, 1967.

Deutsch, Karl W., and Richard L. Meier, "The Confederation of Urban Governments: How Self-Controls for the American Megalopolis Can Evolve," Working Paper No. 77, Center of Planning and Development Research, Institute of Urban and Regional Development, University of California, Berkeley, June 1968.

[8] A long-range program of development of new urban communities or towns, as well as urban centers in outlying areas to accommodate urban population growth (with more balanced income, race, and ethnic groups) seems essential to provide subsidized housing units, replace urban substandard housing, and create socially and economically more balanced urban communities. Public expenditures for infrastructure can be invested into new urban areas and this can contribute to new development practices.

Gottmann, Jean, *Megalopolis: The Urbanized Northeastern Seaboard of the United States.* A Twentieth Century Fund Study. Cambridge, Mass.: The M.I.T. Press, May 1966.

Hauser, Philip M., and Leo F. Schnore (eds.), *The Study of Urbanization.* New York: Wiley, 1966.

Hoover, Edgar M., and Raymond Vernon, *Anatomy of Metropolis: The Changing Distribution of People and Jobs Within the New York Metropolitan Region.* Cambridge, Mass.: Harvard University Press, 1959.

Kulski, Julian Eugene, *Land of Urban Promise, A Search for Significant Urban Space in the Northeast.* Notre Dame, Ind.: University of Notre Dame Press, 1967.

National Commission on Urban Problems, *Hearings Before the National Commission on Urban Problems.* Washington, D.C.: Government Printing Office, January, 1968, vols. 1, 2, and 3.

Pell, Claiborne, *Megalopolis Unbound, The Supercity and the Transportation of Tomorrow.* New York: Praeger, 1966.

Perloff, Harvey S., "Modernizing Urban Development," *Daedalus, 96,* no. 3 (Summer 1967), 789-800.

Pickard, Jerome P., *Dimensions of Metropolitanism.* Research Monograph 14A and 14b. Washington, D.C.: Urban Land Institute, 1967.

Rand McNally & Co., *Commercial and Marketing Atlas.* New York, 1968.

Webber, Melvin M., in Webber, et al. (eds.), *The Urban Place and the Non Place Realm, Explorations into Urban Structure.* Philadelphia: University of Pennsylvania Press, 1964.

In 1933, Walter Christaller published his dissertation *Die Zentrale Orte in Suddeutschland*, which contained interesting studies about the existing settlement pattern in that part of Germany. This pattern resulted from human development during many centuries in which numerous changes in the economic level and technological possibilities took place.

This pattern, in which Christaller indicated the various functions performed by the different settlements during the present century, has been influenced by a great many factors among which possible means of transportation played an important role in addition to the requirements of government and administration. When Christaller wrote his book, the motor car had not yet become a common means of transportation, and its speed was limited because the highway and road system was insufficiently developed. Christaller refers to speeds of 40 km per hour, while we are used to much higher speeds nowadays.

Although there are local differences, the South German pattern with the hierarchy of cities systemized by Christaller can be observed in a great part of Western Europe. The distances between villages and between a village and a town ranged between 4 and 6 kilometers in highly developed areas. The population of the villages depended on the rural population of their service area.

Until the nineteenth century, land had been cultivated by animal and manual labor only. Consequently, agricultural plots had to be small, and a relatively large number of farmhands was required per surfacial area. Economic standards were low and there was no alternative employment except for minor opportunities in the upcoming industries. In general, people were satisfied if they could attain the subsistence level.

Conditions changed greatly during the twentieth century. Economic standards were raised; agricultural methods were modernized, rationalized, and mechanized. Small landowners could not compete with the owners of larger plots, and enlargement of scale through reallocation became a necessity. Consequently, employment in rural activities declined greatly and the population served by a village dropped seriously. In The Netherlands the proportion of people working in the primary sector, which was as high as 30 percent in 1900, declined to less than 9 percent in 1965.

Jac. P. Thijsse—The Netherlands. Civil Engineer, Technological University, Delft; Emeritus Professor at the Institute of Social Studies, The Hague; Planning Consultant; Professor at the University of Indonesia, Bandung.

In some villages the population decreased dramatically, causing some of the shopkeepers to leave, so that services in the villages also declined. All this naturally had a snowball effect. The farmers who formerly did their shopping in the nearest village preferred to go to town, where they had a larger choice. They could do this because their higher economic level provided them with other means of transportation by which they could cover larger distances in less time.

The pattern which stimulated Christaller to write his dissertation, and which had proved right and useful for a very long time, became obsolete under Western European conditions of the second part of the twentieth century. This example of obsolescence is no exception: the various curves related to the development of mankind have shown a very gradual course from the Neanderthaler to the period of our grandfathers. But around 1900 the development of many factors accelerated in such a way that living conditions changed intensively. This is the result of the tremendous increase of human knowledge. It is said that human knowledge doubled between 1950 and 1965, and it is understandable that new approaches are necessary.

Christaller's dissertation and his many successive publications have been and still are of basic importance for the development of new patterns. New patterns will also have to envisage the same fate of obsolescence which will occur more rapidly because of the accelerated changes.

A Rational Rural-Urban Pattern for The Netherlands (1957 Model)

Walter Christaller based his study on an existing situation which had resulted from human activities during many centuries. A different approach is to try to construct a model based on rationality which could serve an area in the most desirable way in the near future. This kind of pattern could be applied in newly reclaimed areas or in areas in which no human activities have yet taken place.

It should be clear that such a pattern is not a planning scheme; it should rather be used as a yardstick. The pattern which I presented in 1957 assumed a homogeneous area; in reality many factors such as topographical configuration, soil capability, existing settlements, and infrastructure will require diversions from the pattern as developed in the model.

The 1957 model was based on a series of assumptions. These were

1. The main principles to be followed are concentration and segregation of functions. This means regional concentration of industries in cities, but segregation of urban and rural activities.

2. The rural active population should be concentrated as much as possible in villages and towns. This might not be feasible for dairy and mixed farms, but there is a tendency that also the farm families of such farms will live in the villages or towns.

3. The village will serve an agricultural area. The character of the villages should be purely agricultural. This would include the possibility of agricultural industries in the villages, and also industries serving agricultural activities such as repair shops for tractors and other agricultural devices. The village should have a shopping center for everyday needs, primary schools, churches for all congregations, and community halls for associations whose members live in the service area of the village. It should not include secondary educational institutions or cultural institutions such as concert halls, cinemas, museums, etc.

4. Comparably the towns should serve an agricultural area which might be only a little larger than that of the villages. In the pattern we are discussing, each town is surrounded by six villages, and the town should cater for those services which are not available in the villages: secondary education, cultural institutions, etc. Moreover the town might have industries which are not directly based on agriculture. It might also perform tertiary functions, e.g., there might be a university, it might be the seat of administrative government, etc. Such functions depend on the suitable location of the town.

5. It is further assumed that the area is of a homogeneous agricultural character.

6. All agricultural activities are assumed to be performed in a modern way. Full use should be made of mechanization, motorization, rationalization, etc.

7. Transport is assumed to be completely mechanized with motor cars, buses, and mopeds (motorized bicycles) as means of transportation. These means may be private or partly or wholly public.

8. The pattern is based on a system of hexagons, in the middle of each of which a town is situated.

9. The six villages are at equal distances from each other, while the distances between village centers and the center of the town are also equal. Villages belonging to different hexagons are again at the same distance from each other.

10. The hexagon around each town is divided into seven parts. Each village will serve the part of the hexagon in which it is located. Its service area has the form of a pentagon. The town will serve the remaining central hexagon.

The pattern is shown in Figure 1.

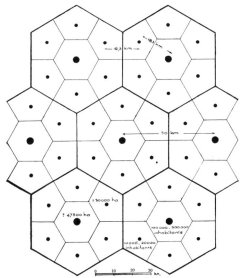

Figure 1.
Rural pattern, 1957.

The Scale of the Pattern

The motorization of all means of transportation is determinant for the scale of the pattern which will be based on the time necessary to be spent on travel (a) from home to work, and vice versa; (b) from home to the appropriate shopping centers, schools, etc.; and (c) from home to cultural and educational institutions of higher order, all of which should not exceed 30 minutes. Farmhands living in the villages will use mopeds with a maximum speed of 30 kilometers per hour. The greatest distance they have to cover to reach the farthest agricultural plot from their village would then be about 14 kilometers.

As the villages are at equal distances from each other and from the center of the town, this distance can be calculated and proves to be approximately 18 kilometers. The distance between two towns will then be approximately 50 kilometers.

Pupils will need not more than 30 minutes to reach institutions of secondary and higher education (which will be made available in the town). It is assumed that buses will run between villages and the town, and will cover the distance of 18 kilometers easily in 20 minutes. This time may be increased for those living on the remotest farms by about

10 minutes, necessary to bring them by car from the farm to the village. The same schedule applies for cultural performances and for nondaily shopping. As a rule, private cars will be used from the farm to the town for these activities. The maximum distance to be covered will then be 14 + 18 = 32 kilometers, and this will take less than half an hour.

Population

The area served by one village will be about 300 square kilometers, and that served by the town about 475 square kilometers. Experience in modernized areas taught us in 1957 that the total population in homogeneous agricultural areas, including those engaged in services, would vary between 30 to 50 persons per square kilometer. Consequently, the total population of the area served by one village will vary between 9,000 and 15,000. If we now assume that, according to the type of farming, 50 to 90 percent will live in the village, the result is that the village population will vary between 4,000 and 13,500. The smaller number was at that time sufficient to support the village economy under the then existing conditions in The Netherlands. It goes without saying that the population may be much higher in horticultural areas.

The population of the town, as far as it is based on its agricultural function, will vary between 7,000 and 21,000 if no intensified form of agriculture is used in the area. This is not probable, however, because the existence of the town itself will induce intensive vegetable and fruit farming in the close environment (provided that the soil and climatic conditions are suitable for the purpose). Consequently, the population working in the primary sector may also be higher. Furthermore, the majority of the town population may be employed in the industrial and service sectors. Depending on the regional, national, and international location, the topographic configuration and possible infrastructure, the population of the town may be quite high and even exceed a million.

If the location should be so favorable for industrial development that it would justify a larger population, this would contradict our assumption that we are dealing with an agricultural area.

Application of the Pattern

The pattern has been used to indicate that too many villages have been built in the Noord-Oost Polder in the enclosed Zuiderzee. According to the pattern, this area could easily have been served by two villages only, while eleven have been built. As a result, with the exception of the central main village, the development of the village population has seriously lagged. The population even declined in one village, and none of the village schemes were completely carried out, except in the central village, where people preferred to live. In the Oost Flevo Polder, which was reclaimed later, the number of villages was drastically reduced, although not yet completely in accordance with the pattern.

A third example of the usefulness of the pattern appeared when stimulation of industrial centers was being considered in the northeastern Netherlands, where economic development and employment are insufficient. In the province of Friesland, villages which applied to be designated as industrial centers numbered more than 30. According to the pattern, two centers would be sufficient. Drastic reduction proved to be impossible for political reasons; consequently 5 main centers and 6 subcenters were indicated. However, a large majority of the newly established industries chose the capital of the province. This shows that regarding industrial location the enlargement of scale is in accordance with the pattern.

Application of the Pattern in Developing Countries

Economic conditions in developing countries are of a totally different nature than those in present-day Western Europe. They are comparable with European conditions of many centuries ago, of the period when the pattern on which Walter Christaller based his studies and his theory started to develop. In our part of the world, economic conditions changed very gradually, and this change was not foreseen. We are stimulating this change in the developing countries, and we are expecting that, after a foreseeable period, the economic conditions there will be comparable to the present situation in Western Europe. Therefore when drawing up new schemes for developing countries in their present conditions, we should aim at designing a small-scale pattern which could fit our 1957 pattern to be used at a later stage of development, as soon as the improvement of the economic situation would allow enlargement of scale.

The small-scale pattern which is inherent in the present economic situation in many developing countries shows distances between the villages ranging from 4 to 6 km in densely populated areas. This may fit our 1957 pattern, into which it may be converted if one in six villages is maintained permanently. The other five may be considered temporary and may be destroyed at a later stage. The fact that many such villages are built with temporary materials makes such a policy possible without much loss of national capital.

Figure 2 shows how the small-scale pattern may fit into the 1957 pattern.

The Revised Pattern (1964)

The 1957 pattern was meant to be used as a yardstick and not as a planning scheme. It indicated the scale which would be rationally in accordance with conditions in The Netherlands at the time it was developed. The increasingly accelerated technological development required its revision after a period of six years because the assumptions on which it was based were no longer valid. There were several reasons:

1. Intensification of rural activities means that less land is essentially needed, even for increased production of vegetables, fruit, and flowers. The same applies to dairy farming, although not to the same degree. The Netherlands has long relied partly on other countries for staple food production, which used to require large areas. The activities of the European Economic Community may also stimulate this tendency. Units of large dimensions for ordinary agricultural production are expected to give satisfactory returns in the near future. Consequently marginal or unproductive farms will increase in number. As a result of these circumstances, agricultural land might be converted to other kinds of land use.

2. If the economy continues to rise, the proportion between work and leisure time will change. Several years ago the 6-day working week in The Netherlands was reduced to 5 days, and in less than twenty years from now, four days only might be necessary for work. This means that instead of 45 working hours and 35 leisure hours per week it may become 30 working hours and 50 leisure hours. Thus, apart from the formidable task faced by the Ministries of Education and of Culture,

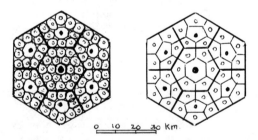

Figure 2.
Patterns of developing countries. ● towns; · permanent villages; ○ temporary villages.

Recreation, and Social Welfare in preparing the population to spend its higher income advantageously and to use its increased leisure time in a worthy and humanly valuable way, the provision of large recreation areas is essential.

3. The agricultural population, including farmhands, will be able to make use of motor cars (possibly sharing with others). Consequently, they can live at considerably larger distances from their work than when they used mopeds.

4. The increase of motor cars in many countries of the world results in an enormous volume of traffic, which for economic reasons should be limited as much as possible. Origin-destination surveys show clearly that the greatest volumes are caused by journeys between residential and recreation areas, and vice versa. The latter should therefore be located in close proximity to the urban centers.

5. It has long been realized that main highways should not cut through the cities but should pass them by. Roads radiating from the city should give access to the main highway system.

Taking these five factors into consideration, an effort was made to insert recreation areas close to the cities, in the 1957 urban rural pattern, and at the same time to develop a better system of communication.

Several alternatives are developed in Figure 3, which also show an increasing proportion of green space (recreation area). In Models A and B, the situation of the villages in accordance with the 1957 pattern is maintained. In the three other models, three villages are grouped together, moved out to the angle-points of the hexagons, and there combined with two villages from other hexagons. As a result each village is situated at equal distance of three cities and can benefit from all three. The maximum distances the farmhands have to cover to drive from their village to their work is about 20 kilometers. As they may use cars for transportation, they can cover this distance easily within 20 minutes. Time needed for transportation from the village to one of the three towns, a distance of about 35 kilometers, would not take more than half an hour by car. In this model, village population may range between 10,000 and 20,000. Consequently, institutions of secondary education would be required.

Models A and B, with the traditional location of the villages according to the 1957 pattern, are designed in such a way that a straight road between two adjacent villages in one and the same hexagon would not cut through the recreation area. These models give only a very limited

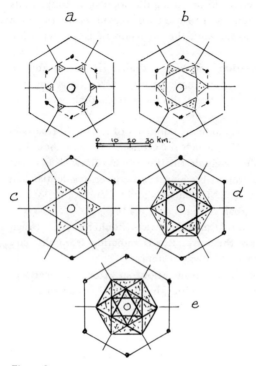

Figure 3.
Alternative models, 1964 pattern. Green space: (a) 6 X 1050 ha; (b) 6 X 3400 ha; (c) 6 X 5450 ha; (d) 66,000 ha; (e) 88,000 ha.

improvement regarding the fluency of traffic on the main highway system and the space for recreation has a limited capacity. If a larger space for recreation is needed, models C, D, and E could be used. These three also provide a much improved, shorter, and more fluid highway system. This highway system (Figure 4) would provide for outgoing connections from every town in 12 directions (Figure 5) without cutting through the agricultural units.

The secondary road system consists of connections between the towns and the highway system, and roads connecting the villages mutually, and villages with towns and the highway system (Figure 6).

The Capacity of Recreation Areas

The capacity of the recreation areas is a disputable subject. Data are available on daily visits to recreation areas. The Amsterdamse Bos, an

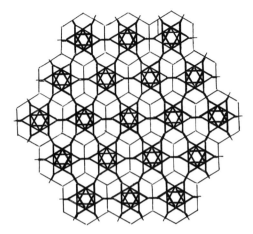

Figure 4.
Highway system, pattern 1964 and 1968. Scale 1:2,000,000.

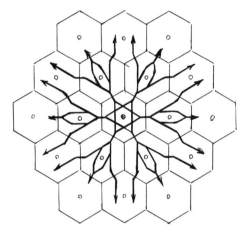

Figure 5.
Outgoing connections from highway system illustrated in Figure 4. Scale 1: 2,000,000.

artificial forest and park area near Amsterdam, with a surface area of 900 hectares, is simultaneously visited by 90,000 persons, or 100 persons per hectare. At such moments the area is too crowded and not pleasant. One might say that the fewer the visitors, the more pleasant is the area. But there are economic limits. Consequently, the more favor-

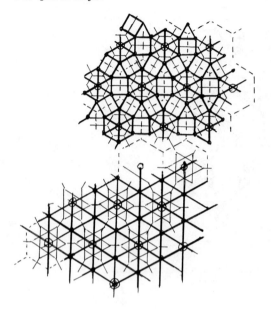

Figure 6.
Secondary road system. Top, pattern 1959; bottom, pattern 1964. Scale 1: 200,000. − primary highway system; O secondary road system; O hexagonal division; ○ town; · village.

able the economy, the larger the park area that may be allowed per person. Let us assume for the present that a density of 50 persons per hectare might be satisfactory. Let us also assume that all visitors come by car, and that every car will contain 3 persons, which is the expected average family size. Every car will need approximately 40 square meters of parking space. One hectare gross, including parking space, will thus be in accordance with 47 people. We may also assume that 80 percent of a city's population may use the area simultaneously; so for example, a recreation area of 6,500 hectares would be in accordance with 300,000 persons and consequently with a town of 375,000 inhabitants.

As we expect that the economic level will gradually rise, and the number of inhabitants of the towns will increase, we should be able gradually to increase the recreation area near each town. Therefore, it would be preferable to start directly with model C of Figure 3 and extend this in course of time to models D and E. Increase in recreational area will cause the area remaining for agricultural purposes to decline, but as mentioned before, the need for agricultural land will also diminish. In the case of model E, about 15 percent of the total area of a hexagon will be used for urban purposes, 5 percent for transport, 35 percent for recreation, while 50 percent will remain for (intensified) agriculture and dairy farming.

The main highway system which runs through the region in six directions has a mesh-width of 45 kilometers in three directions and a distance varying between 20 and 30 kilometers in three other directions (see Figure 4). This provides a more economical communication than, for example, the gridiron system.

A Third Phase of the Hexagonal Pattern (1968)

It is not likely that the 1964 pattern will be given pure application in Northwestern Europe within the foreseeable future, let alone that even more radical patterns based on the same system of hexagons will be considered, although this adoption might be rational against a background of more developed technological applications in the future. The existing pattern, which has grown historically, cannot be eliminated; and the scale of possible agricultural development in Northwestern Europe is too small for a really large-scale pattern to be rationally applied within a short time.

The 1957 and 1964 patterns, based on a homogeneous area, dealt with villages and towns. The villages were based on agriculture only in their service area, and as such they were all alike. There was no village hierarchy. The hierarchy of settlements came into the picture when towns were considered. The towns had different functions to perform, and their locational potentials varied. Consequently their population might vary between 50,000 and 2,000,000; but all towns had the function of being a cultural center. As a result of the increase of transportation speeds, it will be possible to omit the villages and to restrict the pattern to towns only.

It may well be that before the year 2000, speeds of 400 kilometers per hour will be reached by trains based on the Hover system. But even at speeds of 200 kilometers per hour, already achieved by traditional rail transport, the distance between towns acting as cultural, social, educational, administrative, or industrial centers could be extended up to 100 kilometers or more. In between, other towns will take over the functions performed by the villages in the 1957 and 1964 patterns. It may well be that most of the active population of the primary sector will then prefer to live in the towns. In that case, the longest distance from their homes to their plots will not exceed 42 kilometers, which on good roads can be covered by car easily within 30 minutes, the time span on which the former patterns were also based. This pattern is shown in Figure 7. Towns with main cultural and/or administrative functions are 100 kilometers' distance from each other. (These towns are indicated by the surrounding recreation areas.) Their cultural service area is four times as large as that of the towns of the 1957 and 1964 patterns.

As mentioned before, this pattern is not expected to be applied in Western Europe. However, it could be applied in large areas where agriculture has as far been impossible because of lack of water or eroded and lixiviated soils, where minerals and organic matter essential for agriculture have been leached out. There are very many large areas in the world in such condition. In many cases man himself has caused such deplorable conditions by misusing the soil. Scientific development will allow man the opportunity to restore such areas by providing water, biological regeneration, and fertilization. If such large areas are reclaimed or restored, the most efficient and rational pattern should be selected.

The author is well aware that many other patterns might also be considered. Instead of the hexagonal system, the rectangular system, mostly used in the United States of America and Canada, may well be developed. In this regard it is interesting to compare the rectangular system as described by Marion Clawson[1] with the hexagonal system. The latter undoubtedly has the advantage that the service areas maximally approach the circle, so that the average radius of the most remote plots is considerably smaller than in the square or rectangular system. Moreover, the main transportation system on motor roads and highways between towns, as developed in the hexagonal system, proves to result in smaller distances than in the square or rectangular systems, unless diagonal connections are added.

Figure 7 shows the possible connections from each town to all other towns based on the hexagonal system. The developed highways, projected in such a way that they do not cut unnecessarily through service areas, are only slightly longer than distances along a straight line. The percentage of difference ranges between 7.5 and 14.5, as illustrated in Table 1.

The various patterns outlined in this chapter have been based on settlements for specific areas, which might vary with regard to the functions

[1]Marion Clawson, "Factors and Forces Affecting the Optimum Future Rural Settlement Pattern in the U.S.A.," *Economic Geography 42,* no. 4 (October 1966).

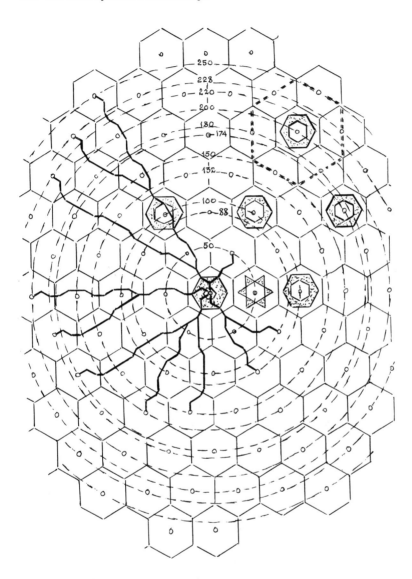

Figure 7.
Secondary road system pattern 1968. Scale 1:200,000.

Table 1.
Percentages of Differences in Distances.

Distances along a Straight Line	Distances along the Highway	Percentage
50 km	56.7 km	13
88	101.25	14.5
100	109.5	9.5
132	146.25	9
150	162.5	8
174	191.25	9.5
180	200	10
200	215	7.5
228	250.5	10
250	264.85	9.5
		Average 9

contemplated. For example, a town may serve a much smaller area for its agricultural center function than for the function as cultural, educational, or administrative center. Comparing the three patterns explained above, it is quite clear that service areas tend to grow larger because of technological developments. One of the intentions of this article has been to explain that dynamic changes can take place in one and the same hexagonal framework based on distances of 50 kilometers between towns. Development can start with the small-scale model of Figure 2. In the course of time this may be converted into the 1957, 1964, and 1968 models successively.

Amalgamation of Cities (Ecumenopolis)
The 1968 pattern may later also form the background for linear city development. Part of the agricultural areas should then be converted into residential, industrial, or recreational areas (Figure 8). In this way the density of population can be increased considerably.

A first step in this process is the amalgamation of two or three towns. Gradually this may be planned and developed into a string of cities such as have grown without much planning in the Conurbation Holland and Kita Kyushu in Japan. Ultimately this may lead to a network of cities covering almost the entire area, leaving little space for intensified agriculture. This may then result in Ecumenopolis, the concept of which was foreseen by Doxiadis. Land will then be available only for very intensified agriculture, limited to selected areas with the highest agricultural capability.

We must prepare ourselves for such conditions.

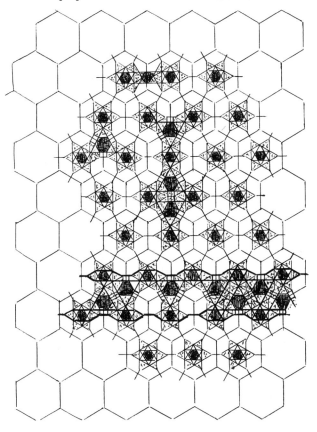

Figure 8.
Stages of amalgamation. Scale 1:2,000,000. ● urban areas; △ recreation areas;
〇 agricultural areas.

Part One

III. The Rural-Urban
Relationship

11. Rural-Urban
Relationships
and the
Development of
Rural Areas in
Developing Countries

Bert F. Hoselitz

The relationship between rural development and urban development is an important factor in the analysis of the developmental processes of different nations. As a whole, urban development has progressed further than rural development throughout the world, but several exceptions must be noted.

In Latin American countries, and sometimes in Middle Eastern countries, the majority of the population is in the cities. These cities have progressed internally, that is to say as far as law and order are concerned they are well organized, but they have not progressed in the same way as the cities in the advanced countries. Most of their populations are still new to city life, a large proportion having been born, brought up, and educated in the countryside and having only a few years at best, or a few months, of residence in the city. In these countries relatively little progress has been made in the standard of living in the cities or the countryside.

In the 1930s, economists thought underdeveloped countries would follow much the same paths to development as had the developed nations, and that by 1960 or 1970 they would have a rural population dependent on agriculture and an urban population dependent upon industry and services. We know now that this has not been the case, of course, particularly since the end of World War II. The urbanizing process has continued throughout the world, with utter disregard for the possible lack of capital and/or ability to establish new industries. The lack is most pronounced in the developing nations, and as a result almost all of them have an ever increasing number of unemployed persons. The situation is aggravated by continuing high rates of population growth and increasing immigration into the cities [3].

We must therefore determine first the relationship between the growth of cities and economic development, and second what can be done to reduce the ratio of growth of city populations and thus reduce the presently growing rate of urban unemployment which results largely from lack of integration of agricultural migrants in the large urban centers.

Bert F. Hoselitz—United States. Doctor Juris (Economics), Vienna, 1936; M.A., Economics, Chicago, 1945; Professor of Social Science, University of Chicago; Director, Research Center in Economic Development and Cultural Change, University of Chicago.

Contrasts in Urban Development

There have been three kinds of urban development: (1) that generally thought of as European, which includes, in addition to the countries of Europe, the United States, Canada, Australia, and New Zealand; (2) that of countries presently considered underdeveloped but in which urbanization is a continuation of prolonged high civilization in ancient times—India, China, countries of the Middle East, etc.; and (3) that in Africa, parts of East Asia, and Latin America, areas which had little or no contact with civilization and few cities worth mentioning before 1750 to 1900, when urban colonial centers of trade were established in these areas.

Urban development began when the population of the world was still small. Up to 1800, only some 2 or 2.5 percent of the world's population lived in urban centers, that is, in towns with more than 20,000 inhabitants. European urban development began in northern Europe in the seventh or eighth centuries A.D., and in southern Europe long before the birth of Christ. In what is now north and west Germany there existed some 200 "cities" in the Middle Ages, but only very few of them, that is five or six, had more than 5,000 inhabitants; the same was true in England, France, and Italy, and throughout the rest of Europe. How and why did these urban places develop? What special function could they serve that the countryside could not?

What distinguished these tiny cities was the presence of free citizens (as opposed to serfs or slaves) who participated in the economy, the defense, and the choosing of the administrating officials. The functioning of the European city as a community of defense, an independent economic entity, and a federation based on common participation in religious rituals is well described by Weber [9]. But these original *coniurati* on which city status was based in Europe, and which made eligible for membership in the city everyone who was not excluded by religious or serf status, form the bedrock of a tradition of urban consciousness which has remained alive all over Western Europe and which has been transplanted to those overseas territories inhabited by populations originating in Western Europe.

The existence of this long urban tradition in Europe meant that when the cities industrialized in the eighteenth and nineteenth centuries, individuals in the countryside experienced little hesitation about migrating to them. Once in a city, the laborer was free and self-reliant, and the city promised to protect him from molestation by others, as long as he obeyed its laws himself. Industrialization, which began about 1750 in Great Britain and spread to practically all of the cities of the advanced countries, was responsible for their growth, which has continued to the present day. Nowhere except in the developed countries did this industrialization occur.

Archeologists continue to discover ruins of ancient cities in the Far East and Middle East which indicate the existence of highly developed city life, but by today's standards the number of inhabitants was extremely small. Perhaps some of the present-day cities in these areas were originally ancient urban sites. Certainly cities in India, China, and the Middle East existed long before their counterparts were developing in Europe. But the percentage of the population in urban centers was probably much smaller than in Europe in the Middle Ages, and there were many less cities than in Europe. The Indian cities of Taxila and Sanchi, for example, existed in ancient times, but there were no cities within hundreds and hundreds of miles, although Indian villages were numerous. In Egypt, Thebes and Memphis, really large villages, existed for many hundreds of years, but there was really no city until the fourth century B.C., when Alexandria was built. The entire Nile Valley was dotted with villages, but urban places were extremely rare.

With the onset of capitalism, the cities of the Middle East, India, and China, for example, of course came to serve more and more as centers for capital. As capital was invested, the cities grew because peasants without land and property flocked to them. Some of these individuals found work and formed the base of the new working class in industry, but many of them—and as time went on, more and more of them—could not find jobs and therefore either returned to the countryside or remained in the cities as landless, propertyless, and jobless workers.

By the beginning of the nineteenth century, any urbanization which had existed prior to that time in Africa, parts of East Asia, and Latin America had virtually disappeared and since the time of its existence its impact upon the population of these areas had been negligible. For example, although Dekar and the Cape of Good Hope in Africa served as landing spots for European trading ships, and some exchanges of goods took place with the internal regions, the areas and population affected were extremely small. In Latin America, the relatively highly civilized states in Mexico and Peru were taken over and destroyed by the white conquerors, leaving the Indians with little more than a ruined economy. Latin America also had important landing spots for European ships, and even some inland cities which had developed around gold and silver mines, but these disappeared in the seventeenth and eighteenth centuries as their economic base of precious metals was exhausted. Only a few inland cities remained—Mexico City for example—and their role was purely an administrative and governmental one.

African cities are quite new and are growing very rapidly [1]. Although exact figures are not available, the urban population in Africa probably tripled between 1930 and 1960. There are several reasons for this, the major one being the transformation, almost overnight, of simple market towns dealing in native commodities into capitals of newly independent countries. The independent governments established many new ministries, resulting in increased numbers of goverment employees. Almost immediately there was a migration of many totally or nearly totally illiterate tribal and semitribal agriculturalists, often with only minimal or no skills, to the new capital cities, where because little industrialization had taken place they were unable to find the employment opportunities they sought. Many stayed on nonetheless, in the hope of acquiring a job sooner or later.

In a number of these capital cities, the population increased to more than half a million inhabitants. At the same time, the population of other African cities has also grown, again largely from the migration of agriculturalists for whom there are very few jobs. The industrialization which is taking place is totally inadequate to satisfy the demand for jobs, and the employment situation is much weaker than city size would indicate.

Some idea of the extent of the rapid urban growth occurring in Africa may be gained by examining Table 1.

The consequences in the last ten or twenty years are almost beyond imagination. There is a tremendous instability in these cities for a number of reasons.

1. New construction cannot possibly keep pace with the inflow, and it is common to find 6, 11, or even as many as 20 or more people living in a house built to accommodate two or three.

2. Since the availability of jobs is far behind the migration rate, the unemployed of course feel free to return home for seasonal agricultural work, and even someone with a job, especially if it is not too good a job, will leave to do important farm work he is expected to do at home. Because of the precarious living conditions in the town, and because of the mobility between town and country, the bond which links those who live in town to their village homes, however distant, remains very strong.

3. There is a strong contrast between European or Asian cities and

Table 1.
Prewar and Postwar Population of Selected Cities of Tropical Africa (thousands of persons).

City	Country or Territory	Prewar (a) (b)	Postwar (a) (c)	Percentage Increase
Abidjan	Ivory Coast	10 (1931)	251 (1963)	2410
Accra	Ghana	70 (1931)	522 (1966)	645
Addis Ababa	Ethiopia	150 (1959)	560 (1965)	274
Bamako	Mali	20 (1931)	165 (1965)	725
Bangui	Ubangi Shari	14 (1937)	111 (1964)	693
Brazzaville	Republic of the Congo	40 (1937)	136 (1962)	240
Conakry	Guinea	7 (1931)	175 (1964)	2400
Dakar	Senegal	93 (1936)	375 (1961)	303
Dar-es-Salaam	Tanganyiki	34 (1937)	190 (1965)	458
Douala	Cameroun	28 (1931)	200 (1965)	614
Freetown	Sierra Leone	55 (1931)	148 (1966)	169
Ibadan	Nigeria	387 (1931)	627 (1963)	62
Kano	Nigeria	89 (1931)	295 (1963)	231
Khartoum	Sudan	45 (1938)	173 (1964)	234
Lagos	Nigeria	126 (1931)	665 (1963)	420
Kinshasa	Republic of the Congo	36 (1938)	508 (1966)	1311
Luanda	Angola	40 (1934)	224 (1960)	460
Monrovia	Liberia	10 (1938)	81 (1962)	710
Nairobi	Kenya	65 (1939)	266 (1962)	309
Salisbury	Southern Rhodesia	33 (1936)	325 (1965)	884

(a) Figures in parentheses are the year of census or estimate.
(b) Prewar data from Walter Yust (ed.), *Encyclopedia Britannica World Atlas*, 1942, pp. 182-211, except for Abidjan, Bamako, Conakry, and Douala, which are from France, Minster d'Outre-Mer, 1957, p. 27, and Accra, which is from Gold Coast (Ghana), Office of the Government Statistician, 1950, *Census of Population*, 1948, Report and Tables.
(c) United Nations, *Demographic Yearbook 1966*, pp. 176-178.

African cities in the extent of disruption an African finds when he migrates to the city. In Europe or Asia, the new arrival meets many people who have been in the city for a long time or were even born there. The African migrant meets another African who is also new to the city. In addition, he finds a severe imbalance in the sex ratio, with many more men than women inhabitants; this problem is all the more important when we consider that most of the migrants are relatively young.

4. Although the skills required by city employers in Africa may be less advanced than those required by their European counterparts, they are still far beyond the experience of the African migrants, who usually have little or no education or knowledge of even the simplest modern tools. For this reason, their being hired as industrial workers is very rare. Therefore they choose either to follow various handicrafts or to be employed in a low-level job or in a service industry. For some of these jobs vocational education is important and usually missing in the background of the migrants. So a large number of them become traders who surround the urban markets, bringing and taking away their merchandise on their backs.

5. Racial diversity still plays a role. Although many Europeans have left Africa in recent years, some remain in a few business and engineering jobs. Moreover, we must remember that although these towns are inhabited primarily by Africans, they were built primarily by Europeans. And as jobs previously held by Europeans were taken over by Africans, the latter developed wider contacts, and the slackening of ethnic and family ties has resulted in the formation of wider groups bound together by vocational, political, and religious interests.

Contrasts in Employment

The differences among the three types of urban development carry over into differences in their employment situations. The already established towns in Europe and North America with a strong economic base developed into large industrial cities beginning around 1750 and continuing until about 1940. At the same time, many towns were established solely as industrial centers; many of these were ugly and remain as unappealing landmarks of the industrial age.

Although the ratio between the urban and rural population was disproportionate, the increase in urban population was not overwhelmingly great, agricultural migrants to the cities were able to find jobs, and no serious unemployment problem existed. This was true in all developed countries, including Japan. In the case of North America, many of the migrants came from Europe, often with excellent vocational training or experience. In addition, in the nineteenth century the need for unskilled labor was greater than it is today.

However, the cities continue to grow and the agricultural population is decreasing, as is the area of land cultivated. In 1945-1950 approximately 350 million acres of land were cultivated in the United States, but by 1964 this acreage had been reduced to 293 million [8, Table 4, p. 18]. Europe has seen a similar reduction of land in agriculture. This has been possible, despite growing total population, because of the growth in agricultural productivity per worker. In 1930, one farmer in the United States could produce enough food for 10 people; now he produces enough for 35 [8, Table 21, p. 35]. With growth in agricultural efficiency and mechanization, the bulk of the working population has been drawn into industry or the services, and thus finds its job opportunities primarily in the cities. This is true in Europe, North America, Australia, New Zealand, and Japan. Whether the *rate* of the shift of the working population out of agriculture and into the cities is appropriate is another question, but there can be no doubt that the trend continues in this direction.

The second group of cities, in the Middle East, India, and China, is overurbanized from the point of view of their employment situation, despite the fact that in Asia, excluding Korea, Taiwan, the Philippines, and Japan, only one in twelve persons is a city dweller—as against one in eight for the world as a whole, approximately one in three in North America, and one in five in Europe.

For Asia as a whole, approximately 13 percent of the urban population inhabits the smaller cities and more than 8 percent the metropolitan centers, but the proportion of the labor force available for industrial and service occupations is roughly 30 percent, some of which makes up the labor force for a sizable number of rural cottage industries and a few large-scale plants in the countryside. At a similar point of urbanization, the United States (1850s), France (1860s), Germany (1880s), and Canada (1890s) had roughly 55 percent of their labor force in nonagricultural—that is industry and service—occupations [7], without the serious unemployment situation which plagues Asian cities.

This fact indicates several things. First, it is a sign that in Asia urbanization has probably run ahead of industrialization and the development of administrative and other service occupations which are characteristically concentrated in cities. Second, it emphasizes the disproportion between the costs of urban growth and the maintenance of proper facilities for urban dwellers, as contrasted with the earning capacity of the people congregated in the cities. Third, it offers evidence that migration to the city is due less to the attraction of city jobs and city life than to the disenchantment with life in rural regions.

In general, the forces which tend to push people out of rural areas are associated with the increasing difficulty of making a living there. In Asia, many people also drifted to the cities because political insecurity made life in the country impossible or because bandits and insurgents destroyed their homes or their crops or took their land. In those countries spared the ravages of civil war and banditry, the push to the cities has resulted from the inability of limited agricultural areas to support the rapidly rising number of young people. Rural open or disguised unemployment became so impelling that the only means of escape was migration to the city.

In many Asian countries the migrants exchanged a precarious existence in the country for an equally precarious one in the city. The population grows not only in the countryside, but even faster in the city as a result of migration, while the development of urban industries and the creation of urban services proceeds at a slow pace, creating a number of jobs far less than the increasing number of available workers. Thus, the city has become a collection place for rural as well as urban unemployed. It is hard to determine where to begin attacking the problem.

India had approximately 500 million inhabitants in 1965 and a work force of 200 million, of which some 140 or 150 million, or 75 percent, were employed in agriculture. In contrast, the United States has some 200 million inhabitants and a work force of 75 million, of which 9 million or 12 percent are agriculturalists. India cannot expect to achieve this small a percentage of the work force in agriculture within several generations.

How do you compare the agricultural worker who produces enough for 3 or 4 persons with one who produces enough for 30 or 35? The United States accomplished the difference between these two figures in 130 years. India may do it faster, but at present nobody can even foresee when it will be able to produce even twice as much as it does now. The same is true in most underdeveloped countries; in fact the overall situation is often worse than the Indian one.

What do we see in these countries? Although their cities are old, they have relatively little industry. While the populations of their cities are smaller than those of the cities of advanced countries, considering the total industrial output they are still too large. Only a small percentage of the large population which flows into these cities can be absorbed by service occupations, and to an even lesser degree by cottage industries. It is predictable that a great percentage of the new population flowing into the cities will be unemployed. Just how many are already unemployed is disputed by various economists who have made surveys of these areas. The estimates for India, for example, are between 10 and 30 million unemployed, and those for other underdeveloped countries are comparable. The reason for the shortage of work is that capital is too scarce, so that even its full investment produces employment for relatively few persons.

African cities are urban centers for administrative and professional services as well as centers of trade and related services. And they are the focal points to which agricultural migrants have been flocking in large numbers for the past twenty years in the hope of finding jobs. However, capital-goods production has scarcely begun to develop—most of the increased production is of consumer goods to satisfy a constantly growing need. The cities grew but did not develop simultaneously into industrial centers. Africa has of course several mining towns, such as Elizabethville, which are quite large, but such examples are rare; production in Africa is still carried on, for the large part, in small enterprises such as shops. Although a great deal has been written about the growth of medium and large industry (employing more than 30 people), the existence of such large firms is relatively rare.[1]

What Can Be Done?

When we examine social development in general, we see that the process of rural exodus is of basic importance. Urbanization has progressed furthest in Western countries, less far in Eastern countries, and least far in Africa, but throughout the world the rate of growth of urban popula-

[1]W. G. Hoffman [4]. The tables on pp. 68-71 show the relationship between consumer-goods industries and capital-goods industries in developed countries in 1840, 1850, and 1860, with usually 60 to 80 percent of the manpower in consumer-goods industries and only 10 to 15 percent in capital-goods industries. As industrialization goes on, the capital-goods industries far outdistance the consumer-goods industries, as shown in the tables on pp. 79, 83, 89, and 92, which reflect the situation today after an interval of roughly 100 years. In the African cities, only the first stage of industrialization has been reached, i.e., the consumer-goods industries show a 70 to 90 percent industrial concentration and the capital-goods industries less than 10 percent.

tion is greater than that of rural. A major function of the process seems to be the shift from rural, traditionalistic forms of behavior to urban, rationalistic ones. Certainly the shift from the traditional to the rational is necessary to modernization. By now the advanced countries have succeeded in modernizing to the point where there has come to be little difference in the behavior patterns of the urban and rural populations, a fact which is beginning to attract more attention from research scholars [6].

The underdeveloped countries need to achieve the same kind of modernization; left to themselves, with no impediments to urban growth, they would probably continue to attempt this goal through urbanization, just as the advanced countries did. The question remains whether there is any way to achieve the shift without contributing more to the already severe problems of the cities in the underdeveloped countries.

Certainly we must avoid continuing on the present path if at all possible. Otherwise, in the next ten or twenty years the already desperate unemployment situation will be aggravated, because this will be the period in which recent increases in the rate of growth of population in these countries will begin to have an impact on the available labor force, as the children grow up and become of working age. For example, the labor force (age 15 and above) in South and Southeast Asia is estimated to have increased at the compounded rate of 1.0 percent before the 1950s, 1.5 percent during the 1950s, and 1.8 percent in the 1960s. These rates are expected to rise to 2.2 percent in the 1970s and 2.5 percent in the 1980s and probably the 1990s as well. If we exclude India and Pakistan, the absolute levels of these rates will have to be raised for each decade by about 10 or 15 percent [11]. When the expansion of employment opportunities already is unable to keep pace with present rates of growth in the labor force, what must be done to accommodate the even higher rates which lie ahead?

One new approach which has received some attention in Israel, India, Japan, and some Latin American countries, for example, is that of integrated or comprehensive regional development. The underlying principle here is to integrate the development of agriculture, industry, and the services within a defined region, taking into account the social, organizational, and political interaction of all these various activities [10].

Let us consider the case of an underdeveloped country, one which is divided into many regions, each with a large rural and a small urban population, and each with that small portion of its population actually engaged in producing services and industrial products living in cities. Assume that a method is found to increase the agricultural productivity of the region. This is certainly not an impossibility; for example, the experiments at Los Baños for increasing output from rice cultivation have been quite successful, and the knowledge gained through this and other experimental programs can easily be disseminated throughout the world by organizations such as the FAO.

With increased agricultural productivity would come an increase in the wealth of peasant farmers, but there would also be, if Western patterns are followed, a decrease in the number of peasants needed for farming as more modern methods were adopted, and these unemployed peasants would tend to migrate to large cities, further aggravating already existing urban problems. Thus, the first task is to prevent this situation. The unemployed farmer must be made to see the benefits, first of staying away from the city, and second of remaining in the area and utilizing or acquiring skills there which will ultimately assure him a job. In other words, a small urban center could become the center of development for the immediately surrounding area.

Under this plan, the urban center must first become a small industrial center, so that it can provide employment for workers no longer needed in agriculture, given increased agricultural productivity. It should also provide higher education and extensive health facilities, and perhaps technical services. In short, such a center must become a small center of both urban and rural life. The majority of the population of the area would be employed in agriculture, but there would also exist nonagricultural employment opportunities [5]. Such "rural towns" already exist—in Kerala, in India, for example. But their success depends very heavily on horizontal planning and coordination with different governmental departments so that each town has its own health facilities, schools, etc. Unless each town is completely equipped to serve its regional population, the purpose of creating such regional centers is defeated.

The population size and the number of these centers would depend to some extent on the population of the whole country, perhaps being greater in a densely populated country such as India, and smaller in a more sparsely settled country such as Iran. However, the existence of a regional authority is a necessity in any densely populated agricultural country. The regional centers could help to coordinate horizontally the vertical functioning of the different ministries, and they, rather than the principal large cities, would become the centers of industrialization and the expansion of service industries. All this may be difficult to achieve, but it may also be the only thing which can prevent the continuation and worsening of the present overurbanization patterns in underdeveloped countries.

It is true that in all probability capital-goods industry would continue to develop in the large cities which already exist, but much of the development of the consumer-goods industry would occur in the smaller regional centers, whose populations should not rise above 50,000 to 100,000 inhabitants.

As has been noted, several countries are considering or even attempting to carry out such a program although no marked success has been achieved as yet. Nevertheless, if such programs can be carried out successfully, avoiding an urbanization process which only leads to more unemployment, we would then have solved one of the most difficult problems facing virtually every underdeveloped country.

References

1. Balandier, Georges, *Urbanism in West and Central Africa: The Scope and Aims of Research, Social Implications of Industrialization and Urbanization in Africa South of the Sahara.* Paris: UNESCO, 1956, pp. 495-509.

2. Dewey, Richard, "The Rural-Urban Continuum: Real but Relatively Unimportant," *American Journal of Sociology 66* (July 1960), 60-66.

3. Frank, Charles R., Jr., "Urban Unemployment and Economic Growth in Africa," *Oxford Economic Papers 20,* no. 2 (July 1968), esp. 250-251.

4. Hoffmann, W. G., *The Growth of Industrial Economics.* New York: Oceana, 1958.

5. Namboodin, N. Krishnan, "A Contribution to the Study of Within-Urban and Within-Rural Differentials," *Rural Sociology 31,* no. 1 (March 1966), esp. 35-36.

6. Pahl, R. E., "The Rural-Urban Continuum," *Sociologia Ruralis, VI,* no. 3-4 (1966), 299 ff.

7. United Nations, Economic Commission for Asia and the Far East, *Economic Causes and Implications of Urbanization in the Recent Experience of Countries in Asia and the Far East.* Mimeographed document E/CN.11/URB/2, submitted to the Joint UN/UNESCO Seminar on Urbanization in the ECAFE Region Bangkok, August 8-18, 1956, pp. 9-10.

8. United States Department of Agriculture, *Changes in Farm Production and Efficiency,* Bulletin No. 233. Washington, D.C.: 1965, Table 4, p. 18.

9. Weber, Max, *The City*. Glencoe, Ill.: Free Press, 1958.

10. Weitz, Raanan, *A New Approach in Urban-Rural Relationships in Developing Countries*. Haifa: Mount Carmel International Training Centre for Community Services, 1964.

11. Ypsilantis, J. N., *World and Regional Estimates and Projections of Labor Force*. Geneva: ILO, 1966, mimeo.

IV. The Farm Unit	12. The Future of the Family Farm in Developed Countries	Hermann Priebe
	13. Social Factors in Rural Development Planning in Advanced Countries	A. K. Constandse
	14. Changing Social Patterns in Rural Communities in Advanced Countries	Henri Mendras
	15. The Family Farm: A Primary Unit of Rural Development in Developing Countries	Michel Cépède

Part One

IV. The Farm Unit

12. The Future of
the Family Farm
in Developed
Countries

Hermann Priebe

In the discussion of agricultural policies of developed countries, family farms are regarded nowadays with a critical eye. For a long time these farms had been the guideline for agricultural policy, their economic problems were often put into the background by social and political arguments in their favor, and traditional forms of life were idealized. Thus we realize that the response to this attitude has been a critical reflection. We can form an opinion on the future of the family farms only on the strength of a realistic reexamination of the views and experiences prevailing in the past.

Hitherto family farms have been able to hold their own, to a high degree, in the important transformation of economic and social life. While there have been created in the industrial sector large enterprises, based on division of labor and highly mechanized, agriculture has proved to be very adaptable likewise in its family farms structure. The farmer exchanged the draft animals for the tractor, and he became a full partner of the evolution of civilization, but the basic type of the family farm was maintained. In Western Europe as well as in North America, even nowadays family farms dominate agriculture, and, from an economic angle, they are reckoned among the most efficient farms of the world. Hence they are the starting-point of any investigation of the future, with reference to agricultural policy in highly developed countries.

The Concept of the Family Farm
The term *family farm* stands, in general, for a socioeconomic unit in which specific social conditions and farm size are correlated with one another. When defining and delimiting the term family farm, it must be taken into account that the organization and size of these farms are dependent on the stage of development of the country's economy as a whole, and thus likewise of agriculture. In the developing countries the bulk of the rural population lives on subsistence farms with little market production; such farms might be called something like a "prelimi-

Hermann Priebe—West Germany. Ph.D. and Professor of Agriculture; since 1959, Director of Seminar for Agrarwesen of University of Frankfurt, and Institute for the Study of Rural Structures of the University of Frankfurt; since 1956, member of the Gruener Beirat and of the Committee for the Improvement of Agrarian Structures, of the Federal Ministry of Food, Agriculture, and Forestry in Bonn; board member of the Society for the Development of Regional Structures; since 1958, Scientific Adviser to the EEC Committee in Brussels.

nary stage of the family farm." In all parts of the world there exist very different types of farming which are equal to one another inasmuch as families gain their livelihood in self-supporting small holdings; however, we would not make by this statement any comments on the organization of the farms, the methods of production, and the economic yield, which is often unimportant.

With the beginning of the land reforms which are nearly everywhere carried out at the start of a new economic and social development of the nations, a more precise definition of the term *family farm* is of importance. The prerequisite to this start in Europe was the release of the rural population from the obligations and charges of the traditional and feudal structures. The case of the independent peasant farm has been proved by economic as well as by sociopolitical arguments. In the controversy against the feudal system, there appear, in addition, emotional and ideological forces and motives. The discussion of the problem of the various types of farming begins to lose of its clearness, in the very moment of transition to a modern economy.

In the nineteenth century the contrasts between town and countryside, which were a feature of the beginning of industrialization, have brought about additional confusion in agricultural policy. The traditional rural forms of life were idealized and defended against working and living conditions in towns. This gave rise to unrealistic conceptions of the importance of a traditional agricultural system which was called "healthy" or "organic," and which was contrasted with modern mechanized units. Certain traces of these rural ideologies have not yet been completely overcome.

In the course of the last decades the term family farm gained in importance in discussions dealing with the conditions of land tenure in the countries of the Communist bloc. In these discussions the family farm was called to be the smallest independent unit of free economy and it was contrasted, programmatically, with the big collective and state farms and thus involved again in political and ideological argumentation. In this connection, family farms were often called to be the guidelines of agricultural policy, but precise definition was never given.

These one-sided sociopolitical and ideological arguments put forward for the family farm have given rise to fundamental misunderstandings. The idea that family farms are characteristic of a traditional structure is still perceptible, although since the beginning of industrialization such farms had developed into modern units with high productivity, in many European countries as well as in North America. It is possible to get a clear idea of the present condition and of the future prospects of family farms only on condition that we get free from former prejudices and face the actual economic facts.

In our new stage of agrarian policy it is more and more urgent to define the term *family farm* in an unbiased manner, all the more since structural policy has gained importance in addition to market and price policy. In order to assist agriculture in its structural adaptation to technical and economic development, many countries grant official funds for land consolidation and modernization of villages and farms as well as for improvement of infrastructure. For the purpose of selecting the farms deserving of encouragement and assistance, it will be necessary to apply specific criteria. For the Federal Republic of Germany a special commission, established in 1956 by order of the Federal Ministry of Food, Agriculture, and Forestry, has determined an exact definition.[1]

This definition is based on two main premises: (1) the farm is chief occupation and main source of income; and (2) the farm enables the owner to earn labor and capital returns comparable with those of other sectors of the national economy. Both these premises refer, as a rule, to the working capacity and the standard of life of a family with at least one or two full-time workers. We proceed, therefore, from a family consisting, in general, of two generations, so that working capacity is composed of different elements in the rhythm of the alternate generations. In this context the female members of the family are not regarded, on principle, as full-time workers.

The definition of the family farm is given a dynamic character if income expectations are taken into account. The objective is not to keep alive traditional farms, but, on the contrary, to encourage their further development. Thus the investigation into this problem cannot proceed from the statistical delimitation of specific factors—in particular, acreage—and cannot have in view the formation of specific systems of farming under a given formula, but must aim at adapting continuously the combination of the various factors to technical and economic development. Computation in each case must start from a volume of production (gross returns) that will make possible, with due regard to all necessary input, an adequate labor income for the family as well as a

---

[1] *Ausschuss zur Verbesserung der Agrarstruktur beim Bundesministerium für Ernahrung, Landwirtschaft und Forsten: Leitbilder für bauerliche Familienbetriebe,* in: *Förderung bauerlicher Selbsthilfe bei der Verbesserung der Agrarstruktur* (Frankfurt/M.: Institut für landliche Strukturforschung an der J. W. Goethe Universität, 1960), H. 4. 146-148.

satisfactory return on capital invested. Farm size thus represents an economic minimum volume which will be adapted to the growth of the national economy as a whole and to the general level of income. The required acreage and other input are to be derived from these elements; they are variable accordingly.

The upward limit of the family farm is, in general, not determined precisely. The definition given above, however, refers to the necessity of checking from time to time whether the volume of production necessary to meet the income claims does not exceed the working capacity of a family. Thus there is incorporated into the definition another dynamic element: the comparable number of working hours of other occupations. The family income ought to be earned solely by the able-bodied members of the family, without overburdening them, but giving them sufficient spare time, and without compelling children, retired farmers, and housewives to labor permanently on the farm.

Hence the definition proceeds from the social status of the farmer or, in general, of labor on family farms. On doing so, the family farm is understood to be an example of the self-dependent occupations, where the occupier works on his own responsibility and risk, and where management and practical work are combined with one another. Family farms, strictly speaking, are understood to refer to the working and living community of a family being mainly employed in agriculture with an average working capacity from 1.5 to 2.0 labor units. Whenever the economic size of such a farm makes possible a reasonable minimum income, we call it generally a full-time holding.

The transitions from the family farm to other farm types are fluid. Farm hands may be incorporated into the working community of the family, while the family continues to represent the core of the labor force and determines the rhythm of work. The upward limits of the family farm are overstepped only when hired laborers, with their families, form the majority and work is divided into managerial functions and practical activities.

Small family farms often represent transitions to other sectors of the economy. Some members of the family find work and income outside agriculture. There exist professional combinations with part-time farming. If the agricultural main occupation is maintained and only completed by other sources of income, we call it *farming with additional source of income* (*Zuerwerbsbetrieb*). If the family continues to run the farm, although there is no longer any member of the family working full time on that farm, we call it a *subsidiary earning holding* (*Nebener-*

werbsbetrieb), or rather a farm run as a sideline, where the motive of gain is not alone the determining factor.

In the general definitions the interpretation of the term *family farm* is largely concurring in the countries of Western Europe, and it virtually coincides with the interpretation prevailing in the United States. The definition chosen by the U.S. Department of Agriculture proceeds like-wise from a family who runs a farm independently and furnishes the main part of labor, on a holding which reaches a certain minimum volume of production.

When consistently adapting the dynamic elements of the family farm, such as production volume, income, and labor input, the result must be that all other factors have to become variable, too. The standard of living of the family will grow and the amount of work to be done in terms of time and toil must lessen. Thus the labor productivity must rise in order to make possible—in the same way as in the remaining sectors of the economy—that an increasing income combines with de-creasing working hours. Hence the appropriate factor combinations change continuously, and the stable statistical criteria of the past carry less weight.

The range of possible variations of optimum family farms is growing with the development of production techniques as well as of the econ-omy as a whole. These possibilities are most important and are deter-mined by such factors as soil and climate, line of production, share in the market, degree of mechanization, division of labor, and specializa-tion. Thus the term *family farm* applies in highly developed countries to a wide range of farming systems and acreage, varying from horticul-tural farms of a few hundred square meters to grain farming and pastur-ing covering several hundreds of hectares.

Economic and Social Position of the Family Farms
Opinion not only differs widely as far as the future prospects of family farms are concerned, but there are likewise taken quite contrasting views on their present social position and economic efficiency. Errors of judgment in this respect have their origin mainly in two causes: first, investigations based on overall averages for agriculture; second, the idea that, generally speaking, farm incomes are lagging behind. To begin with, it is necessary to define the statement of the problem.

When dealing with agriculture, overall averages of the national prod-uct, labor force, and income are not suited to estimate the value of specific types of farming. Although the majority of the holdings in the developed countries are family farms, we have to take, in the first instance, into account the great dualisms existing in all countries. Where the regions are highly developed from the point of view of trade and industry, farming too is highly developed; on the other hand, there are everywhere rural territories with only a small number of business enterprises, where many families live in traditional small holdings which are, in a high degree, self-supplying. This applies to North America as well as to Europe, and there especially to the Mediterranean countries, e.g., in southern Italy and in vast regions of France. In the Federal Republic of Germany, this applies to some regions in the hilly areas of central Germany, and in Great Britain, too, there are weakly developed hilly regions with traditional small holders. In the United States efforts are made to separate both groups in the statistics and to set the commercial farms apart from the bulk of smaller holdings, which have only a little share in the market.

For judging the present position of farming and the problems in the field of agricultural policy, we think it useful to distinguish between two different sectors of agriculture: (1) highly developed farms which are fully adapted to the system of the economy, based on division of labor, which, at a high level of productivity, produce entirely for the market and provide a full livelihood for at least one family; and (2) all other holdings which cannot provide such a full livelihood, and where, moreover, this goal is not striven for. In regions weakly developed from the point of view of the national economy as a whole, this applies to population groups who are not yet entirely incorporated into the division of labor, who cover therefore their basic requirements mainly as rural self-suppliers, and who have to be regarded more or less as the remainder of the former agrarian society. In the course of economic growth, many persons will be in a position to find employment outside agriculture; nevertheless many families will continue to run their farms as a part-time occupation. The whole group is very heterogeneous, but in terms of figures it highly surpasses in most countries the full-time holdings.

However, as far as the economic and sociopolitical problems are concerned, both these sectors of agriculture differ so much from one another that, strictly speaking, they ought to be distinguished by different terms. The usual statistical compilation of data leads to average values which are, in some cases, absurd. Nevertheless the associations representing the interests of farmers like to make use of such figures in order to support the dogma of the level of income lagging behind other sectors of the economy; in this way they intend to lay stress on their political demands for subsidies and higher prices. Recently many countries made efforts to elaborate exact methods for establishing income comparisons among agriculture and trade and industry. However, the so-called proof of a disparity in this field remains questionable. In view of the fact that in the majority of farms production and consumption overlap, statistics cannot provide sufficiently exact data. Besides, the income comparison between self-dependent farmers and employed persons in trade and industry refers to groups with quite different living conditions and personal resources.

The position of the family farms can be judged only if we make differentiated individual investigations in efficient farms. To this end, we have to get free, if ever possible, from the statistical average figures of agriculture as a whole, and we have to exclude the traditional farms producing only for their own consumption as well as subsidiary-earning holdings; *ex definitione*, such farms and holdings are not able to reach a complete income. Then the following problems have to be investigated with reference to the family farm: (1) Has this type of farm participated in the development of agricultural technology and in economic growth? or (2) are there other organizational patterns of farming which are, in general, superior to family farms?

It appears, from the "Green Reports" of German agriculture, that the income differences within agriculture are by far larger than the lag of incomes as against trade and industry, as indicated by Table 1.

These are group averages, which are classified in accordance with uniform location conditions. As far as fractional groups of the farms, with better or worse earnings are concerned, the farm income, in the Green Report 1968, per labor unit varies between DM 977 and DM 32,422. The earnings of individual farms vary even much more. It is well known that nowadays some farms of comparable size and location earn excellent incomes, others are nearly ruined. Modern agriculture offers growing possibilities and chances, and risks increase in the same proportion.

Table 1.
Lag between Agricultural Labor Income and Comparative Wage (= 100).

Green Report	1966	1967	1968
Overall Average	87	76	74
Group Averages	54-146	45-142	46-117

These important differences in productivity and income are found in farms of all sizes. They have their origin in the natural and economic location conditions such as soil, climate, terrain, and state of the market. They represent the large field for the business initiative of the individual farmer; they draw the line for him or offer him special advantages. As to the group averages which are arranged in the Green Reports in accordance with land value and regional location, these conditions have by far a stronger effect, as income-determining factors, than the size of the holdings.

All data available for German agriculture show that the highest incomes are not earned solely in the large-sized farms, but are spread among groups of all types of farming. However, these groups are subdivided only in accordance with acreage: in the Green Report 1968 there are 56 groups which are divided among farms of less than 20 hectares or more than 50 hectares, and medium-sized groups from 20 to 50 hectares. Only one-third of the nine groups with large-sized farms reach peaks, whereas large-sized farms are not at all found in groups with land of low value. One third of the 24 groups of smaller farms of less than 20 hectares likewise reach peaks and the remaining farms are divided among the groups with middle-sized acreage. In this context we would cite as an example the comparative study made by the Chamber of Agriculture, Bonn, and illustrated by Table 2.

These results can be verified by examples of individual scientific investigations. The series of publications *Neuzeitliche Familienbetriebe*

Table 2.
1,000 Family Farm Earnings during the Year 1966-1967.

Farm Size Arable Land (Hectares)	Full Labor Units	Gross Returns (DM/farm)	Net Return in % of Capital Invested			Incomes after Deduction of a Calculated Return on Capital (6.66%) (DM/labor unit)
			Upper 25% of farms	Lower 25% of farms	Average of all farms	
Under 10	1.51	42,400	15.8	−11.6	1.87	5,612
10-20	2.01	61,200	13.4	− 1.7	5.54	5,848
20-30	1.93	79,500	13.4	− 0.9	5.97	7,245
30-50	2.86	123,000	11.8	− 2.1	4.75	7,382
Over 50	4.58	216,500	11.2	− 0.5	4.83	9,950

(*Modern Family Farms*)[2] contains in its two first numbers the operating results of carefully selected farms, which furnish a representative
cross-section of various types of German family farms during the period
from 1958 to 1960 and 1962-1963. We compile hereunder the essential
results published in No. 2:
The great differences among farms of different land values, extent of
acreage, working capital, and regional location have been analyzed in
detail. This makes evident the successful adaptation, by means of the
choice of products and of productive equipment, and by cooperation
with other farms; despite quite different combination of factors, all
farms had secured labor incomes which exceeded considerably the average of the comparable wages at that time and an average interest on the
capital invested of 8.8 percent. Moreover, additional reserves of productive capacity are discernible in all farms.
  On the strength of the available data there is every indication that no
strict causality exists between farm size and profitability. This applies,
however, only to farms exceeding specific minimum sizes which are
nowadays the standard when dealing with the problem of farm sizes. It

Table 3.
Operating Results of Selected Family Farms 1958-1960.

Category	Average of 104 Farms	Range of Dispersion
Land Value (DM/hectare)	1,580	600 - 3,200
Gross Returns (1,000 DM/farm)	59	24 - 191
Full Labor Units	2.0	1.0 - 3.4
Hectares of Arable Land	17	4 - 47
Capital Invested (1,000 DM/farm)	149	67 - 322
Farm Income (1,000 DM/farm) (net production)	26	11 - 70
Net Return (in % on capital invested)	8.8	2.3 - 21.5
Labor Income per Labor Unit (after deduction of a calculated return on capital	20,500	8,500 - 61,000
Comparable Wages in Trade and Industry 1962/63 per Labor Unit	6,500	———

[2]*Neuzeitliche Familienbetriebe*, H. 1 and 2, issued by H. Priebe, Institut für
landliche Strukturforschung an der Johan Wolfgang Goethe-Universität Frankfurt/
Main, 1961 und 1966.

appears from the Green Report 1969 that the values for that level are within the sector of gross return varying from DM 30,000 to DM 40,000, and from 17 to 20 hectares of agricultural area. If, with growing farm size there is a small increase of income, this applies mostly to the income of the owner or farm manager, and much less to the interest earned on the capital actively engaged. It reflects, therefore, rather the existence of a bigger personal fortune than a higher capital yield, from the overall economic point of view.

In modern agriculture, the managerial efficiency of the farmer is the decisive factor for the formation of his income. The field of action of the individual farmer as well as the risk he runs is growing simultaneously with the development of agricultural technology. Analyses of income variations have shown that managerial abilities cannot be substituted either by capital or by acreage. The income differences increase considerably with growing farm sizes, and they often differ many times over with adjacent farms. The old idea that incomes proceed more or less fatefully from existing bases of production or farm sizes corresponds rather to the system of farming applied prior to the industrial age. In modern agriculture, conditions are rather reversed. The farmer himself organizes his farm, he determines not only the type of farming but to a large degree even the farm size. Under such circumstances, farm size cannot any longer be defined in physicostatistical terms; it is rather an economic unity.

Family farms have undergone, up to the present, considerable changes, as we have seen from the examples cited above. The statement of the problem of their position makes it possible for us to summarize the following facts:

1. The prevailing trend of modern agriculture to increase farm sizes has not given up so far the system of family farms; on the contrary, it is a trend aiming at extending more and more the family farm.

2. The changes in the structure of farm size—first of all in statistics dealing with the acreage—have taken place up to now chiefly within the sphere of the family farms.

3. The enlargement is only in a smaller degree a matter of acreage and of available technical equipment. Primarily it concerns the production volume, which can be achieved nowadays by means of very different factor combinations.

4. It is not possible to furnish proof that, under comparable conditions of location, the family farms show, as a rule, an income lag. In particular, it is not possible to discern, in the light of the return on capital

invested, the threshold of transition from the family farm to larger holdings working with farm laborers. The old problem of farm size— family farm or large estate—has lost something of its importance; as far as full-time family farms are concerned, only a specific minimum size is essential.

5. Family farms have had their full share of development in the technical and economic field; however, they achieve their economic success mainly by means of other factor combinations than larger holdings working with hired laborers and by means of increasing cooperation with other farms in respect to production and marketing.

6. We see in the prevailing structural development of agriculture in highly developed countries a tendency of concentration upon the type of family farm. Owing to the fact that they have enlarged their areas and increased their working capital, many holdings have become, from the bottom, modern family farms, and many large farms, by means of dismissing their farm hands and by fully mechanizing their holdings, have developed into family farms.

It appears from the available data that we have no reason to doubt the adaptability and competitive capacity of the family farms. These farms have not been kept alive by state assistance; on the contrary, the German high-price policy for cereals has rather favored the larger farms. Nevertheless many family farms have had their full share of the general economic development so that the completely motorized modern family farm, without special state assistance, has become the predominant type of farming. This applies to the majority of the countries of Western Europe.

Discussion of the Family Farm in Agricultural Policy

The adaptability and efficiency shown hitherto by the family farms are really not sufficient to reassure us as to their future. Often in the course of discussion of agricultural problems there has been expressed a critical opinion of their prospects. We think it instructive to look into the cause of this attitude.

The agricultural policy of the highly developed countries is now on the point of freeing itself from the conservative principles concerning the preservation of the structure and the individual farming families. In this connection, many persons are laboring under the misapprehension that a traditional structure with prevailing family farms is the cause of the disequilibrium of the market and of the general income lag and that increasing subsidies and high prices chiefly serve the purpose of maintaining out-of-date structures and submarginal farms. If they proceed from such considerations, the call for a fundamental change of structure would be logical, since it raises the hope to solve in this way simultaneously a great many problems in the field of agricultural policy.

The first wrong premise of these considerations is the general lag of income in agriculture. No doubt, it is easily possible to prove the opposite. In German agriculture the average income in 1968 has quadrupled since 1956. Farming offers the picture of quick modernization and adaptation to the latest developments in agricultural technology and in the field of economic progress; as for increase in productivity, according to the index of the gross domestic product per capita since 1950, farming is at the top of all sectors of the economy, with the figure of 247 (overall average: 219).

Nevertheless the Farmers' Association has succeeded so far in maintaining the dogma of the general income disparity and in rendering it the basis for programs of agricultural policy. The program established for agricultural reform by the European Economic Community even proceeds from the—easily refutable—premise of the constant increase of the income lag in farming. Hence, the family farm runs into all sorts of embarrassments and becomes the scapegoat of an agricultural policy which, based on wrong ideas, arrives at wrong data for price and market policy. The blame for all the difficulties is put on the conservative structural policy and on the predominance of family farms. Revolutionary ideas are conceived for a novel type of production system. As far as the countries of the European Economic Community are concerned, some proposals have been submitted which outline a radical departure from all types of farming existing hitherto.

Farmers' associations are indignant about these proposals and reject them, but their arguments show them still prisoners of their own propaganda. It is impossible for them to admit that the economic position of many family farms is favorable, and they try therefore to defend these farms more on ideological and emotional grounds. This line of action intensifies the impression that the family farm cannot be defended from the economic point of view. Thus the idea gains more and more acceptance with the public that the sole way out of this muddled state of agricultural policy is a fundamental change of structure, and that this change alone can free the general public from the need to subsidize agriculture.

In this connection, enlargement of farm size becomes something like a magic formula, and there is talk of a necessary "industrialization" of farming. This idea may be successful, if the concept is interpreted to be a mental process of more intensive rationalization, and if we want to find out suitable types of farming, not in the field of ideology but from the point of view of the country's economic efficiency. But too much attention is given to technical capacities and not enough to the favorable experience of existing family farms. Here again the idea of the general disparity prevails.

The uncritical use and inadmissible generalization of scientific models contribute to this state of affairs. There is failure to notice that the authors of such models proceed from the assumptions that all farms are established anew, that technical capacities are utilized in the optimum way, and that the managerial work, as an operating factor of importance, can be taken into account only in average estimates. In this way the special features of the family farm, as well as the advantages of higher flexibility and adaptability connected with independent management, pass unnoticed. Nevertheless it is possible, thanks to the clause *ceteris paribus,* to render the models unassailable; it is even possible to banish from them as disturbing elements all other factors and motives of human action and to do without their verification by empiric control.

In this way agricultural policy will run the risk of getting lost in model thinking, in new abstract ideologies. Other concepts and practical experiences are dismissed as reactionary. Instead of verifying the models by empiric control and of adapting them again and again to actual working conditions, efforts are now made to adapt the structural reality of European farming to the supposed optimum models.

Factors of Further Development
Neither romantic ideas of the past nor speculations about the future can be of any help to us in planning future development. To begin with, we have to face the fact that the great performance achieved by European agriculture is mainly due to the work done by the family farms. It is certain that there will be many changes in this sector; however, should we no longer put confidence in the inventive faculty and managerial initiative of the farmers? We think, in any case, that the experience we have gained in the past does not entitle us to cast far-reaching predictions for an entirely new development. Let us try, first of all, to find out the changing forces and to ask pertinent questions.

1. It is probable that change in attitudes will have more far-reaching effects than technical development. As a matter of fact these two factors are correlated in certain respects. At any rate, we have to base our assumptions on the fact that traditional values and behavior patterns of the rural population have lost their weight. Social guidelines are no longer sought in the sphere of rural life but in the living conditions of other occupational groups. In this respect we see that urbanization as a mental process gains ground everywhere, and that owing to this process the rural population takes it for granted that they are entitled to participate in the general development of civilization.

In this connection we have likewise to point out that, in contrast to conditions in the past, the choice of a trade is no longer a matter of course, as it was in former times. Nobody is born any longer to follow an agricultural occupation; on the contrary, one must have a propensity for this trade and decide to learn it. This may result in a far-reaching change of the structure of rural families and the outcome might be that we cannot reckon everywhere with a labor potential of 1.5 to 2 of full-time workers of two generations. The small family, then, would probably not be equal to meet the growing requirements of a modern family farm and would thus more and more depend on cooperative associations.

On the other hand, the dissolution of the traditional social structures must be judged in a positive sense, with reference to the selection of the most capable persons. However, there is no guarantee for the future that people will be interested to follow the trade of a farmer. Only on condition that they can reckon with attractive working and living conditions will they do so. This aspect will influence the coming generation more than any other when deciding on the future of the family farm. What has agricultural technology to offer them in this respect?

2. It is expected that owing to technical progress there will be forthcoming in the field of agriculture vast possibilities as well as great changes. In the majority of farms the highest stages of technical development have not yet been reached. On the other hand it is impossible to survey completely the further development of agricultural technology. For this reason all future models are of a temporary character only and at best they indicate in outlines the trend of development.

As far as the problem of the effects of the progress of agricultural techniques on the family farm is concerned, we have to differentiate in various respects. Progress in the biological field does not significantly affect farm size. Improvements in the sector of plant and animal breeding, of feeding, manuring, plant, and animal hygiene, gain ground nowadays within a relatively short period so that we call it, in some cases, autonomous progress. They take effect without changing, to an essential degree, the structure of production; and as regards their propagation and proper application, knowledge and ability of the farmers are more important than capital investment.

On the other hand, mechanotechnical progress requires considerable investments and adequate volumes of production. As it is generally known, the reduction in costs to the full extent is attained only at specified minimum units. This state of things gives rise to a series of problems for the family farm: (a) Is its working capacity sufficient for choosing optimum production units? In this connection, it must be examined if, in certain periods, more workers are required than are normally available. (b) How is it possible to reduce the risks which result from the forced specialization of farms in specified production units? (c) How is it possible to even out the demands on labor? For soil cultivation this means leveling out peaks of overwork and depths of underemployment. As regard livestock production, the present problem is how to provide for leisure and vacations within the course of routine work.

By means of the method formerly applied of combining several production branches in the same farm, it is certainly possible to reduce risks and to create better preconditions for evening out the demands on labor. However, in view of the size of optimum units, the limits of the family farm are generally exceeded in this way. As far as it is possible to discern up to now, efforts are made to solve, in different directions, the problems arising in this matter by means of cooperation of various farms or by professional combinations, i.e., in the field of organizational-technical progress.

3. Apart from all changes, we must not lose sight of basic strengths. The social type of the family, which has proved its undiminished force, can be considered to be an element of constancy. Specific basic conditions of the agricultural production likewise appear to be stable: there exist no preconditions for establishing a production which is fully controllable and which functions as continuously as a purely mechanical process; agriculture is always tied to the soil; it depends on the rhythms of life and climate and cannot achieve the continuity and concentration as these qualities are found in trade and industry. The economic success, personal managerial ability, initiative, and interest of the individ-

ual must take the place of the managerial methods of the large enterprise in industry. Agriculture will continue to offer favorable openings for self-dependent callings.

The importance of self-dependent work in family farms could be justified at all times, from the point of view of the economic efficiency of the farm. Adam Smith realized this fact in the eighteenth century, and it applies equally well to modern agriculture. So far, the character of self-dependence, the power of maintenance of self-dependent farmers as compared to farm laborers, has been one of the factors of the attraction exerted by the agricultural calling. As far as prospects are concerned, the points at issue are from the technical angle, whether the individual farming family will be in a position to achieve optimum conditions of output; and from the social angle, whether independent farming will not lose many of its advantages in consequence of its personal bonds and burden of work.

In former times, professional independence found expression in a greater degree of individual freedom of movement and decision-making, as compared with persons in a dependent position. Nowadays increased incomes and reduced working hours give persons in every walk of life a feeling of great freedom of movement. Self-employed persons, on the other hand, have lost to a large extent the employees who could easily be recruited in former times, and they find themselves now tied in a higher degree to their work. At the same time the professional requirements are now more varied and the risks have increased. It is true that the static system of economy of the past had drawn more narrow limits of income, but that system offered a higher degree of safety. Thus the feeling of strong personal ties and at the same time intellectual and physical overstrain becomes a danger for many self-dependent callings. This danger threatens the family farm, too, more than many other factors.

As far as solutions of these problems are concerned, they can be found out only in the organizational field. In the family farm, too, the farmer has to picture himself primarily as a "manager." This holds good for the use of his personal working power and of the productive equipment as well as for the marketing of the products. It is necessary to expand organizational connections across several farms and sometimes across several trades. For the time being it is an open question how far it will be possible to preserve spheres of independence, and how far the concept of the family farm is still justifiable.

Cooperation among Enterprises

In the course of the development from the predominantly autonomous self-sufficient farms of the agrarian state to the production unit of modern agriculture, which requires a considerable amount of working capital, the cooperation of farms has increased more and more in importance. The agricultural cooperative societies were the first institutional organizations. Meanwhile there have been created various new forms of cooperation among farms, in particular in the field of utilization of technical equipment and of marketing. It is quite logical to attach likewise great importance to the future development of such cooperation.

There is, on the other hand, nowadays the danger to overassess the value of cooperation as a panacea and to raise it to the dignity of a new ideology in the field of agricultural policy. Cooperation is a natural concomitant symptom of an economy based on division of labor; this statement does not only apply to family farms. The decisive point in this connection is to know the forms in which it is justifiable on material grounds and where the appropriate limits between individual and joint responsibility are located.

In discussions about questions of agricultural policy, cooperation among farms is viewed from an angle which is too narrow and one-sided in the light of an objective of business management for enlarging production units, whereas cooperation has hardly been thought out carefully from the point of view of its entrepreneurial and social problems. Some people hold that full cooperation, i.e., the merger of farms into a joint production unit combined with full renunciation of their independence, would offer the greatest advantages. In this way, the individual ownership may be maintained formally, but practically land utilization must be tied up for a long period.

In the case of full cooperation, the system of family farming is virtually given up. Reliable experimental data in this matter are not yet available. The kibbutzim in Israel represent a special mental and political attitude, and hence it would hardly be possible to transfer this system to other countries. Rarely do we come across examples where farmers voluntarily give up their independence to form a cooperative society for the purpose of maximizing their incomes, and almost regularly such associations are bound to specific preconditions. On the other hand, in nearly all highly developed countries there are manifold forms of cooperation, showing a variable degree of integration, but combined with preservation of a certain proportion of independence as regards management of the agricultural unit. The advantages of such cooperation can be assessed only theoretically. It should give us food for thought that collective farming is propagated mainly by persons who are not directly concerned with the subject, and who are not bound to pass the resolution on their own behalf.

We think that the problems to be dealt with in fully cooperative (collective) large-scale farms should not be seen alone in the initial decision of the persons concerned, the more so as it is possible to encourage this decision by means of subsidies. The real problems are contained in the actual cooperation, in the day-to-day decisions taken in the field of allotment of the work to be done, and in the organization of the production process. In the case of decisions on matters of principle it is quite conceivable that such decisions are taken in accordance with democratic rules, but such a system would be too cumbersome when applied to the daily allocation of work. To assure the production unit its effectiveness and full economic success, we think that it would come to resemble a production unit operating with paid workmen and placed under vigorous management. Owing to participation in profits and share in ownership, the members will doubtless be able to hold a different status from that of mere wage worker. However, just this circumstance would not facilitate. in our opinion, their readiness to fall every day into line and to submit themselves to the authority of the management. The more such a full joint enterprise is created for the benefit of all members, the less the individual person has the possibility to participate in the management, or to retire from such an enterprise without suffering any loss.

Thus there is many an indication that the economic advantages of large-scale production units which have been calculated theoretically are offset and even outweighed by practical and psychological difficulties. The disadvantages will certainly diminish in about the same proportion as members turn to work in other occupations and continue to participate solely as partners and shareholders. Under such conditions, however, another point would come into question: how to obtain the necessary labor. To say the least, it is an open question whether working for wages in agriculture will remain attractive in an industrial society, even if farm laborers receive the same amount of wages as in industry.

In this context the various problems relating to trade and industry as a whole should also be put forward. The fully cooperative large-scale farms do not only require of the farmer members the renunciation of their independence; but they likewise cause a weakening of the position of other trades in their environment. The creation of full cooperatives means that interconnections among independent units will be weakened while inward integration within the farm will be intensified. This will lead to prejudices against service-rendering trades and often likewise against the subsidiary-earning small holdings which otherwise might participate in the cooperation among farms. The consequence is that all economic relations in the immediate environment will be weakened. This will counteract the development of trade and industry as a whole in rural regions and will hit back at agriculture if a sound basis for efficient infrastructure as well as public and private services are impaired by small population density and slackness in economic activity. The remaining farmers will then run the risk of being isolated from the economic and social point of view, and we are doubtful whether maximum income will still be worth the effort, when social relations have reached a minimum level.

There are many reasons to believe that the prospects are less in large-scale fully cooperative production units rather than in the ingenious combination of independent units with cooperative work. The different branches of production offer variable chances in this respect. New forms will be developed for this purpose likewise in the legal and organizational field. Thus the family farm type will continue to change and may obtain a new strengthening owing to cooperation.

Combined Occupations
In addition to cooperation within agriculture, the persons concerned take into account to an increasing degree, while keeping the family farm as a base, chances of earning money by working in other jobs, inasmuch as the development of trade and industry in rural regions will offer such opportunities. In practice the result will be that the target of the full-time holding will be replaced by that of securing full paid employment to the persons concerned.

For the individual farmer it is often more advantageous to have a combined occupation for earning his livelihood, instead of enlarging his acreage and having recourse to cooperation. He is at liberty to continue cultivating his land in the same way as before, and to improve his income with little capital investment and little risk by taking on an additional job, perhaps for certain periods to begin with. It is first of all possible in specialized arable farming to utilize periods with little farm work for taking up other occupations. If steady jobs are available in trade and industry, the activity in these sectors will then often become the chief occupation, and the farm will be run as a sideline. A great deal of forms of transition exist nowadays in the field of combining occupations.

The concept "family farm" may be applied in this context in a larger sense, as long as a small independent unit of production and a basic amount of landed property are conserved as additional security and support of the way of life of the family. Various motives may be advanced in favor of the conservation of the family-type farm. The feeling of traditional bond is receding more and more, and we see that the former methods of operating farms as a sideline with the help of women and retired farmers are abandoned more and more in the same proportion. Instead, modern specialized operating methods are coming forward in this sector; such methods are fully developed in the course of cooperation with other enterprises, and they require only a small amount of labor. The young generation keeps up part-time farming for various reasons: many persons are looking for an occupation in their spare time which may at the same time be a compensation in case of one-sided, specialized, main functions; with other persons, the conservation of property as a secure investment or for the improvement of their incomes are perhaps also matters of importance.

In the Federal Republic of Germany the majority of all farmers have decided on combined occupations inside and outside agriculture for earning their livelihood; of the 1.4 million farms stated in the agricultural statistics, 25 percent at best are run as full-time holdings. Owing to the great variety of combination forms, it is impossible to draw a precise delimitation, all the more since constant change is a characteristic feature of this sector. However, this very factor contributes to safeguard for the future the necessary mobility and adaptability of land tenure. We have to expect, in the course of technical progress, that many family farms which still provide a full livelihood for one family, will continue to be run in future as a sideline, unless they are totally merged into other farms. New forms of cooperation between full-time and part-time holdings will be conducive to the continued development of both sectors. Thus the tasks to be undertaken in the future are found here, too, first of all in the field of organization, in the development of management in the broadest sense of the term.

Part-time farms are of importance in all highly developed countries, and their future depends primarily on the regional development of trade and industry. Nowadays the promotion of these farm types can doubtless be considered as an efficient means for slowing down the increase in production. It appears from the latest investigations undertaken in the Federal Republic of Germany[3] that part-time farms are run with less intensity: the input of productive and capital equipment is about 33 percent inferior to the amount provided for this purpose in comparable full-time holdings, and the output per unit of acreage is smaller in the same proportion. This statement, however, does not reveal anything as regards profitability. It may be quite satisfactory, because there is no necessity to insert in the calculation the high minimum cost of full labor units and equipment, but fractional labor units, e.g., a small number of working hours a day or a week, and machines utilized in the framework of a cooperative society. As far as the family is concerned, they wish to increase first of all their total income to the highest possible extent and not to derive the maximum amount of marginal profit from farm work. Hence full-time farms and part-time farms aim at quite different targets and have quite different production forms as well as different labor and capital intensity.

It often occurs that part-time family farming is subject to a negative assessment, since experience and knowledge gained by scientists and extension workers in the course of studies made in full-time farms have been absorbed without verifying the accuracy of the figures and data with regard to part-time farming. The study of the vast subject of rural families employed in combined occupations is still in its initial stage, and there is still a wide field remaining for research for economists and social scientists. In this connnection it is safe to assume that this domain will certainly offer unforeseeable possibilities as a result of the development of technology, the further reduction of working hours, and the increasing trend to acquire a second residence as well as a spare-time occupation.

Conclusions

1. The family farm is threatened to a less degree by technical and economic changes than by the prejudices held against this type of farming. They are a response to the conservative agricultural policy with ideological defense of traditional forms and a consequence of mistaken ideas regarding a general lag of income in agriculture.

2. In reality, the family farm has proved to be as constant as it has been adaptable. Family farms have participated to full extent in the technical and economic development and have evolved, without outside

[3]Green Report 1969.

help, into modern productive units which are able in all respects to enter into competitior. with other farming types and which, on principle, are not inferior to them in productivity.

3. The socioeconomic basic type of the family farm has held its own in the course of development, from the subsistence farm of the agrarian society to a productive enterprise of modern agriculture, but as regards its economic importance, there has been a continuous expansion. Starting from the basis of independent occupation, the field of activity of the family has spread more widely and the input of the factors of soil and capital, as well as the output of performance and income, have increased. The definition of the term *family farm* is often misunderstood as a static entity; on the contrary, this definition must proceed from dynamic elements and aim at the continuous adaptation of the combination of factors to technical and economic development.

4. So far there are not discernible any factors which call for a sudden transition to novel types of farming. When reflecting upon further development in agriculture, it often happens that the importance of technological units is overrated and that that of the entrepreneurial qualities is underrated. The central task incumbent on agricultural policy is not the creation of technological maximum units, but the encouragement of qualified and skilled farmers. Supposing that the structural development continues in an evolutionary manner, we shall see that the amplitudes of oscillation in optimum family farms and their organizational possibilities for cooperation inside and outside agriculture will increase.

5. Further development of family farms has its limitations in the capacities of human beings. Growing demands upon special knowledge in all fields of production, marketing, and management, increasing risks and personal ties, as they result from taking advantage of the increasing extent of economic opportunities, may lead to overcharge the individual person and the farm family as in other independent occupations. Solutions in this respect must be looked for in the organizational field by means of specialization and cooperation for the purpose of freeing human beings from overwork as well as of creating economic units for production and marketing.

6. There are two distinct trends which may be suitable for new organizational solutions: cooperation of various agricultural units, and the occupational combination between agriculture and other sectors of the economy. The individual farmer, in his capacity as entrepreneur or manager, has to look for the best solution under specific circumstances

for turning his qualities and his personal work as well as his acreage and productive equipment to account.

7. Cooperation among family farms is possible in various forms and by making use of a variable degree of integration. In all probability the best solutions will likewise be found in the combination of individual and cooperative work, whereby it will be necessary to look for novel organizational and legal forms.

8. Small-scale family farms are taken, to an increasing degree, as a basis for combined working and earning opportunities which are offered in other occupations, inasmuch as such chances exist in the course of development of the economy as a whole in rural regions. The tapping of new sources of income by working temporarily in a second occupation often involves for the individual farmer less capital investment and risk than the enlargement of the farm acreage or the cooperation with other units. Combined occupations, in particular part-time family farms, have to be considered for various reasons as future forms of agricultural enterprise in highly developed countries.

9. Full-time family farms in the narrow sense will hold their own in the near future in the nucleus of agricultural structure among large-scale production units on the one hand and small part-time family holdings on the other. However, it is not possible to show the importance of these units in terms of figures since the development of the next 10 to 20 years will be influenced by factors which are not yet perceptible. We would leave the domain of well-founded forecasting if we should try to predict, even if only for a decade, definite figures as regards specific types of farming.

10. As far as further development is concerned, we must not view it from the angle of determinism and perhaps in strict causality to specific technical facts. The future is determined by acts of decision of human beings, by their ways of thinking and behavior. This applies likewise to the family farm. Its future depends on how it is valued by the farmers themselves, by the politicians, and by the public at large, and what measures will be taken in the field of agricultural policy. It is just possible that pseudoprogressive dogmas of agricultural industrialization will lead agricultural policy to new ideological adventures, and will deprive the family farms of all types of their material and psychological basis. Even such an event, however, would offer no proof that family farms are not viable.

13. Social Factors
in Rural
Development
Planning in
Advanced
Countries

A. K. Constandse

This article is a distillation of findings of studies carried out by the author and some of his colleagues, and of viewpoints developed in lectures held about these problems or subjects narrowly related to them. The experience is for the main part drawn from the situation as found in The Netherlands. Some findings from a cross-national research project, carried out in nine European countries and one state of the United States, together with information from other sources, are convincing enough to permit us to assume that the views in this article apply to a situation in quite a number of advanced countries. Of course this article cannot pretend to be more than a rough sketch, necessarily exaggerated in places, and not taking into account the pluriformity of situations, differences in farm policy from country to country, etc. The two most important studies on which the article is based are A. K. Constanse, *Boer en Toekomstbeeld* (*Farmers and the Image of the Future*), Bull. no. 24, Department of Social Sciences at the Agricultural University, Wageningen, The Netherlands, 1964; and A. J. Jansen, *De Sociale Gevolgen van de Mechanisatie in de Landbouw* (*Social Implications of Farm Mechanization*), Bull. no. 30, in the same series, 1968.

This text was written in October 1968. Although the author's main line of thought is still valid in his own view, there has been a rather fast evolution in the ideas of the policy-makers with regard to agricultural development, with the result that policies are less dualistic now than is suggested in the article.

There is a general awareness among the policy makers in our world that rural areas in both developing and advanced countries tend to lag behind the urban regions in economic and social development. There is general agreement that measures have to be taken to eliminate this lag. Although the task to which modern society sets itself is certainly not an easy one, in the main lines the measures which are necessary are not difficult to define: agriculture should be modernized, production and productivity should be enlarged, rural people should be educated, and because an increase in productivity of labor implies a reduction of the labor force within agriculture, job opportunities outside agriculture should be created, either by industrializing the countryside or by facilitating migration to urban areas, while in both cases rural people should be helped to adjust themselves to conditions of life off the farm.

A. K. Constandse—The Netherlands. Ph.D., Rural Sociology, University of Utrecht, 1960; head, Socio-Economic Research Department of the Zuyderzee Development Agency; lecturer in the Sociology of Physical Planning at the University of Tilburg; 1962 to 1968 Managing Editor of the journal *Sociologia Ruralis*.

Furthermore, in order to assure a satisfactory way of life for those who remain in agriculture, that is, a way of life which can compete with the stereotype of urban life, which sets rightly or wrongly the standard for what is considered as desirable, it is necessary to give rural people easy access to all the amenities which are characteristic for an urban-industrial society, or at least to give them indemnities or substitutes which prevent the growth of feelings of inferiority and of frustrations. The more underdeveloped a rural society is, the more backward, the more clear it is for the policy maker to see what his task is (which, it should be stated again, does not mean that the accomplishment of his task is any easier). If people cannot read they should be taught to read; if people do not use fertilizer they should be induced to do so; if there is no industry it should be established. There cannot be any misunderstanding about *what* should be done, the problem is *how*. Since the latter problem, for the developing countries as well as for the developed countries, will be amply dealt with in other chapters of this book, it might be useful to concentrate in this contribution on an aspect which gets less attention because it is for most of the rural areas not yet relevant but may become soon, as soon as a high level of technological and economic development has been reached. It concerns the question of what should be done in case the farmers have done about everything that is possible within the limits of an existing farm structure to achieve a good income and to lead a good life, but in which they nevertheless do not succeed to arrive at that level of life satisfaction which they not only desire as such, but to which they claim a right of assessment, in the awareness of being citizens of a welfare state. An attempt will be made to describe in which way such a situation can come about.

The Family Farm in Advanced Economy

Not taking into account the countries in which farming is socialized, in all advanced countries the most typical farm unit is the family farm, and even if hired labor is employed the enterprise is seldom of the industrial type; it is the family forming the core, and comparatively speaking, the farm is more close to the artisanal form of enterprise than to the industrial. Before the era of industrialization this type of farm fitted well into the total societal pattern, but in our days the persistance of it, amidst the enormous structural changes in the organization of production, is remarkable and even anomalous. Supposing that the peculiar conditions under which foods and fibers have to be produced (caused by dependence on soil, climate, and the necessity to work with living organisms) would make it impossible to introduce industrial patterns of production into agriculture, this would explain once and for all the existing farm structure. In fact, many people and in particular the farmers themselves use this explanation as a justification for the situation. But the undeniable fact is there, that if we take together the total of activities which form the process of production of foods and fibers, agriculture *is* for the main part industrialized. In the system of agribusiness the farmers form a minority and in the most advanced agricultural systems the task of the farmer is reduced to such an extent that only the field operations and the care of the animals fall under his responsibility; but even those operations he often does not carry out himself. So if there is truth in the forementioned supposition it applies only to a very restricted part of the production process.

Independent of the validity of the belief in the necessity to maintain family farms, it is certain that the initial wish of the farmers to continue their operations, in basically the same forms as had been existing for ages, has always received support by the society at large; either as a vague notion or as a well-defined theory, there has been always some basis for an ideology on which the policy makers built the guidelines for themselves. It is not the intention of this contribution to attack this ideology or to criticize the farm policies. But without mentioning the ideology as a datum it would be impossible to find an explanation for the present situation in farming. Under the influence of the beliefs concerning the significance of the family farm, and of course also because of the power of agricultural pressure groups (which has been existing for different reasons not to be discussed here), the policy makers have done much to keep the family farm in existence, sometimes directly by price supports or tariff barriers, sometimes and with more lasting effect indirectly, by intensive extension programs, promotion of general and vocational education, scientific research for finding better products and improved methods of production and marketing, and finally, by setting up land consolidation and land reconstruction projects. As such, these policies could be unbiased and could be used for the benefit of any farm system. But one should look at the contents of the programs and the aims of the projects: farm boys were trained for entrepreneurial roles, for a future life as all-round farmers, not as specialists; farm workers were, until recently, not trained at all; extension programs were looking for ways of rationalizing, mechanizing, intensifying, specializing, or diversifying existing farms in such a way that they could escape the cost-price squeeze and stay in existence; consolidation and reconstruction projects, although sometimes aiming at an increase of the size of the farms and trying to eliminate the submarginal ones, first of all tried to achieve a strengthened position of the family farm; scientific research, although by its very nature more neutral, nevertheless helped also the family farm, the most striking example perhaps being the successful attempts to construct ever smaller agricultural machines designed for the needs of the small enterprise, while there are ample possibilities to build low-cost machines with high capacities.

In the main, if we exclude effects of general economic depressions, war, or sudden changes in marketing possibilities for certain products for whatever reason, one can say that the assistance given to agriculture by the governments has been successful. Agriculture and therefore conditions of rural life could be improved, it appeared, considerably without changing too much of the existing farm structure, and even now in many areas there is still a great deal of space for changes for the better. Social research has revealed very clearly that not lack of intelligence and ability of the farming population, not the quality of the soil or bad climatic conditions, should be held responsible for low yields, low income, or even poverty, but lack of education and of skill, traditionalistic culture rebuking innovation. In those areas where the mentality of the population was changed, where the modern, dynamic culture pattern of industrial society was adopted, new farm practices were introduced with remarkable results. Higher yields, higher quality of the products, and a better market orientation improved farm life, not only because of a higher income, but also through a relief of the burden of hard physical labor and too long working days.

Although the modernization of the countryside disrupted the local community and destroyed the folk culture, the integration into the larger society made farm life in general much more bearable. Particularly because there were areas and individual cases in which, without any change in the farm size, by specialization and by better farm methods spectacular improvements were shown; and also because it appeared in many cases possible to build up modern processing industries, either through cooperative action of the farmers themselves or by integration with private enterprise, again without changing the original farm structure, nothing seemed to contradict the idea that the family farm could remain a viable economic unit in the modern industrial society. Moreover there was hardly any experience with any other way of organizing the production of food and fiber, there were no incentives to start experiments with change, and, perhaps with the exception of the case of Israel, all countries in which new types of farm enterprise were created were in the capitalistic countries for political reasons unpopular a priori. This latter circumstance made serious research impossible because in case of failure of these systems no distinction was made between the causes, which could be of a political as well as of an organizational-economic nature.

The Problems of Farm Size and Structure

Notwithstanding the success described, the sky remained not cloudless. After the first big jumps ahead the effects of the law of diminishing returns began to be felt; each increase of production demanded ever higher investments, and although the limit at which new investments or innovations have no effect is certainly not yet reached, the rising cost of production is not accompanied by an equal rise of the level of returns. Since the prices of the agricultural products hardly rise, the only way to increase or maintain the farm income is to be found in attempts to keep the cost of production low. Because labor becomes expensive, the productivity of labor should be increased; labor should be replaced by capital. This process of replacement has been going on for many years now, and up to a certain limit it caused no difficulties for the family farm. The labor force in agriculture could be reduced in the first place by transferring a part of the work which was originally done by hand, on the farm, to industrial plants, outside the farm. The remaining work on the farm itself could, with the help of machines and the use of chemicals, be done with fewer people. Of course it cannot be maintained that the enormous changes, which are mentioned here in just a few lines, did not at all affect the farm size structure. The high capital investment needed for the acquisition of the machines made a certain minimum size of the farms, below which the machines could not be efficiently used, inevitable. Many smallholders left agriculture or went into part-time farming. In areas where the pressure on the land was not too high, many farms were enlarged by buying or renting more land. But in general it can be said that the farm size did not change to such an extent that the demands of fully mechanized enterprise were met, at least not in the most efficient way; many farms are overmechanized, the machines underemployed. In a number of areas in the advanced countries the point is reached at which there is no more space within the existing operation to further mechanize and rationalize, and at which the labor force has been reduced to the absolute minimum of one person.

The reaching of this point leads to the curious situation that not the smallholder, not the uneducated, not the peasant, forms the most important social problem, but the average and sometimes above average farmer with a middle-sized farm. If he is well educated, has acquired all necessary skills, and is integrated into the larger society, his level of ambition will be relatively high. He will demand a reasonable income; he will try to give his children a good education; he will want to enjoy the good life, will need time for leisure activities, for vacationing. Instead, by firing his hired help he has less leisure time than before. He has to work harder than ever, he has to carry the burden of high investments, and still his efforts are not rewarded with a higher income. Because of all the financial and intellectual investment in the future he has fewer alternatives which are acceptable for him, than the poor man who has nothing to lose and who may find a better living off the farm. This situation may lead to frustration. He has been taught to be an entrepreneur, he has followed the advice given by the extension service, but nevertheless his position is, relatively speaking, not improved. He does not want to leave the farm, but on the other hand he sees no future in it; he wants his son to become a farmer, but he does not know whether he should encourage him to do so. He is likely to put the blame on the society at large, and more specifically on the government.

The "Dualistic Policy" of Rural Development

Although this picture does not apply to the majority of the better farmers yet, research in several places has demonstrated that we are faced here with a problem now which may become a major problem in the near future. The policy makers are aware of it, but they know also that it will be difficult to find a solution; they show a certain evasiveness in this respect, which leads to what may be called a "dualistic" policy.

Because of the existence of the ideology which we mentioned earlier, the policy maker who wants to develop the countryside is interested in the first place in the well-being of the farmers; he takes the existence of the farmer as a datum and tries then to see what should be done. A quite different approach could be to find an answer to the question: What is the most rational way to produce foods and fibers? and then to decide what role the farmer could play in this process of production. The study of alternatives for the organization of agriculture would then

not be left in the hands of outsiders, daydreamers, or political ideolo-
gists; the discussion could be carried out at a higher level; and the
chances would be better for the planners to find clearer guidelines for
the action in the future. In the present situation one could say that
everyone who criticizes the family farm is immediately classified as
someone who is in favor of large-scale farming, either by collectivization or by handing over the land to big firms; in other words: he is
against the farmers.

Whereas any suggestion for a change in development policies, when
launched from outside the agricultural world, is suspect as soon as it
contains an element which threatens the independence of the farmers,
from the inside no plans which might involve a basic change in the farm
structure are to be expected. The leaders of a group have too many
vested interests, they will not undermine their own positions, not dig
their own graves. Even if we do exclude the important effect on policy
making of those agricultural pressure groups who do not want any
change at all and who just insist on higher prices for agricultural products, even then there are enough arguments left for finding some justification in a continuation of the policies of the past. In the first place
there is the fact that there are people who make a good living on
relatively small farms. The officers of the extension services know them
well and use them as examples of what can be achieved if a farmer is a
good farmer. In the second place there will be always people who put
such a value on independent living, that they do not mind that they
have to work harder than others while perhaps they earn less. These
two types of people provide the inspiration for the agricultural leaders,
the extension services, and also the policy makers, to continue to defend the family farm. It is, however, doubtful that there is any educational system that can make all the people the best, and one can even
ask whether it might not be true that the best are so extremely successful because there are so many others who do things not so well. It is
also doubtful whether in the industrialized society a sufficient number
of people will be willing to lead a hard life without other rewards than
to be independent.

Without dwelling further on these last two arguments and without
developing any specific viewpoint against or in favor of the family farm,
it will become clear now what is meant by "dualistic policy." It is a
policy which enables and induces the farmers to modernize their enterprises with the aim to make agriculture profitable and to arrive at a
situation in which it can maintain itself, on the basis of its own re-

sources, in the total economy. But it is also a policy which tries to keep the relatively small farm in business and does not undertake any action to create organizational structures which would facilitate a more industrialized way of farming, which would prevent overmechanization and lessen the burden of too high capital investment, and which would free the farmer of many problems that he cannot possibly solve all on his own.

Again, this description may sound exaggerated and it probably is: the dualistic policy is not so simple that it can be described in a few lines, and there are many variations and changes in it. Therefore, one illustration may be given in order to make the picture more fair.

In several areas where farms used to be considered as large and prosperous, mechanization of the operation has increased to such an extent that as independent enterprises the same farms are now too small. In making attempts to escape from the trap they have fallen in, more and more farmers decide to work together with others, to buy machinery together, to exchange services, in a few cases to combine the operations completely. They realize in fact that only an enlargement of scale of the unit of operation can help them out. But on the other hand they try to stay independent, they fear to be absorbed in a large enterprise in which they would have less freedom on the decision-making level. Therefore they go only halfway, invent forms of cooperation from which they can always withdraw again, refuse to sign written contracts. One could say that the "horizontal integration," as this may be called, is looked upon not as a first step to larger operations, but as the last opportunity to keep the independent operation of the family in business. The number of partners in the combinations is in most cases restricted from two to four, and the majority of the agreements are made between farmers who have kinship ties. The partnerships have for these reasons often a very unstable character, remain limited in their effects, and can cause quarrels which are for others a new proof for their belief that the family farm is the only satisfactory way of enterprise in agriculture.

For a long time these developments have been ignored by the extension services; they became interested only recently, but they are still hesitant to give advice in this field. In some countries the creation of machine pools is encouraged; in France the government started to take measures to facilitate the conditions for group farming. These last phenomena indicate a change of attitude, but still one cannot speak of a firm policy free of dualism, choosing for the one way or for the other.

Still land-reclamation projects and land-consolidation or land-reform schemes, although trying to follow the technical developments by enlarging the average size of farms, create new family farms. The question may be put whether a policy free of this dualism, liberating the farmers of their uncertainty concerning the future should not aim at either the creation of family farms but guarantee at the same time a reasonable income, or promote the creation of large-scale units of production, not necessarily large farms, in which the former farmers would be employees; different kinds of organizational structures can be thought of. It would be of importance with regard to the future of farmers and farming if development planners would try to create conditions in which the development of industrialized farming would be facilitated.

It may seem that the reasoning so far is, notwithstanding the pretention only to plead for a choice between two alternatives, biased in favor of industrialized farming. There is, however, another problem with which the development planning has to cope.

Diversified Land Use of Rural Space
Rural areas in advanced countries, and in particular those around and in between metropolitan regions, are no longer the domain of agriculture only. For a long time the physical planning has been urban planning, even if it was called "town-and-country planning." In regional plans the parts in agricultural use and reserved for that use in the future were indicated on the maps as "open space." While for the built-up areas as well for the natural landscapes a number of regulations for the land use was set up, farmers enjoyed a relative freedom in that respect. Measures taken in the agricultural areas were for the main part in the interest of agriculture only (soil conservation, water management, etc.). This is not surprising, because in the first place agricultural land use was for a long time the best way to preserve and maintain the landscape and did not lead to such chaotic and destructive results as the activities of urban people did. In the second place the rural areas were isolated and served no other purpose than agricultural production.

At the present time the rural-urban dichotomy is disappearing quickly; the statistics show an enormous growth of the category of people called "rural nonfarm," and furthermore the city dwellers indulging in outdoor recreation are spreading in continuously growing numbers over the countryside. The town planner has come to realize that town and country are inseparable, have become a functional unit; consequently, he gets interested in the contents of the open space. At the same time the technological developments in agriculture are such that agriculture is no longer the guardian of pastoral beauty. Large ugly buildings, silos, and factories replace the pretty farmhouses and barns; forest belts are cut; wild vegetation is destroyed; airplanes spray poison over the fields. This leads to a clash between agricultural development planners and town and country planners. Since in the advanced countries the farm population forms in many cases less than 10 percent of the total population and may decrease in the future to a proportion of 5 or even 3 percent, it is very improbable that this small group will be able to dispose freely of the greater part of the total area of a nation. For preservation of the landscape and for recreational purposes, already several countries have made up regulations which prevent agriculture from making optimal use of the technological opportunities available for further rationalization of the production. Again, a dualistic policy threatens to be born: on the one hand the requirement that agriculture increase the productivity to such an extent that it can compete successfully with other sectors of the economy; on the other hand the demand to make sacrifices in the interest of the public. The development planner should be aware of this dichotomy; the policy maker should draw the full consequences of decisions made once the interests which have to prevail are set.

Agriculture viewed upon not as a means to produce foods and fibers only, but also as a public service, has no reason to be ashamed of permanent government support. When agriculture because of the conditions it has to work in cannot be economically profitable, then it is in the good company of many other public services, like health care, art, education, and traffic provisions, which cannot exist from direct retributions only, and which need the substantive help of the taxpayer.

A New Approach to Physical Planning of Rural Areas

From that viewpoint there is perhaps a necessity for zoning of the countryside: there should be regions, the best agricultural regions—which are, happy coincidence, often the least attractive for tourism—where every effort should be made to bring agriculture at the highest level of productivity and for which the best organizational forms should be chosen; there should be regions which should be kept in such scenic conditions that they are attractive for recreation, while the farmer, doing the best he can on his family enterprise, should receive support from public sources; finally, there should be regions which serve recreational purposes first of all, and if such regions cannot be exclusively parks or forests, but require some agricultural land use too, the agricultural work should be carried out by personnel employed by the government or operator of the "park."

Of course it will be extremely difficult to realize plans along these lines, but on the other hand the dualistic policies which have been discussed in this contribution will cause increasing problems in the future. One danger is the frustration of the farmers which may lead—and has led already—to political radicalism and open revolt; another is the taxpayer who will get tired some day of subsidizing a business which appears to be unable to stand on its own.

In the regions of the first type, the real agricultural regions, the planner would meet the problem of the viability of the countryside in even sharper forms than in the present situation. The regions would be very sparsely populated and few other sources of income outside of agriculture would exist. But, because of the possibility to concentrate fully on the profitability of agriculture, the per capita income in such regions could be increased perhaps to a point where it compensates for the lack of "urbanity." In the regions of the second type the farmers, once having a clear view of their function in society and thus liberated of their feelings of inferiority and of being discriminated against, might work with more pleasure and feel more safety. The farmers in the third type would not be farmers in the traditional meaning of the word, but there is no reason to expect that they would do worse than employees of the state forests and national parks.

These remarks in connection with social factors in rural development planning deal, as has been said in the beginning, only with one aspect. The intention of writing these pages has been no other than to try to add some new elements to the discussion on the problem of farm structure.

Part One   14. Changing   Henri Mendras
                        Social Patterns
IV. The Farm Unit   in Rural
                        Communities
                        in Advanced
                        Countries

Industrial societies are seeking a civilization for which they have not as yet found a firm framework of moral and social values, or definite forms of social life. That is why traditional peasant values and ways of life, and social institutions in rural communities, still appeal so strongly to emotion and remain so strikingly evocative in our urbanized, industrialized world. Village society is still seen as an ideal—and often idealized—social model; industrial societies would like to have something comparable in their vast cities.

As a country becomes urbanized and industrialized, village communities undergo profound changes. With rare exceptions, one no longer finds in Western Europe coherent instances of closely knit village communities, in which face-to-face relationships are predominant and each individual knows everyone else. We propose, after describing a model of the traditional village community and the changes it is undergoing today, to try and envisage a local community of the future, with reference mainly to French instances we have studied.

The Traditional Rural Community

A traditional village society is characterized by three fundamental traits: self-sufficiency, cultural homogeneity, and social diversity. To take self-sufficiency first, it was threefold—demographic, economic, and social. The villagers kept to themselves and had little to do with the outside world, and everyone in the village knew everyone else. They did not seek to marry "outside the fold." Endogamy was not absolute in single villages, but a group of villages appeared as an endogamous group. Demographic self-sufficiency went hand in hand with economic autarchy. The traditional family farm was adequate to fill essential needs. A certain amount of exchange was necessary, but it was limited to the confines of the village or, at most, neighboring villages. The blacksmith, the carter, the weaver, the tinker, and all other traditional handicrafts

Henri Mendras—France. Docteur ès lettres, Sorbonne and Institut d'Etudes Politiques, Paris, and University of Chicago; professor of Sociology and Political Science at the Fondation Nationale des Sciences Politiques; professor at the Institute of Political Studies, Paris; director of research at the National Center of Scientific Research; director of the Rural Sociology Group (CNRS); has served as a UNESCO expert in several countries.

were available to cater to the needs of the farms, and of farming families.

Once these requirements had been met, contacts with the outside world were minimal. In order to pay taxes and buy salt and other products that had to be procured from outside, it was enough to sell part of the crop, but still on a self-sufficiency basis: the villagers did not produce for purposes of sale, but sold "surplus" produce. Sometimes, when no surplus produce was available, "commercial" crops were added to the subsistence crops or a part of the work force went to work outside, to bring in a salary. Living among themselves, more or less cut off from the outside world, the villagers had their own way of life. Each little territorial unit had its own "culture"; this fragmentation of rural societies is apparent in the many dialects which are the product and instrument of each "culture." Language, words, pronunciation often differed from district to district and from village to village. This diversity extended to customs, ideas, and general outlook.

This social and cultural self-sufficiency presumed general agreement within the social group—a consensus of beliefs, outlook, moral values, and behavior. All social groups and individuals shared this way of life and were in agreement on good and evil. When the vicar delivered his sermon at Sunday mass, the whole population of the parish would be present; he spoke a language understood by all, from the lord of the manor to the beggar. No doubt a big landlord would also have ways of thought and standards that differed from those of the main peasant group, but in essentials he shared the peasants' ethos, just as he spoke the local dialect with them.

Demographic and economic self-sufficiency and homogeneity of "culture" were counterbalanced by a profound social diversity. To begin with, there were men and women, young and old. In traditional village society, some social functions devolved on the young, others on the adult, and others still on old people. There was sharp cleavage between the tasks of the sexes. Young people looked after the social side, organized the festivals. The adults were in charge of economic life, while the old people passed on the cultural heritage and saw to it that the traditions and the rules of behavior were observed [13].

The village also comprised various social groups and categories. The peasants formed a majority, but they were very diversified. The holdings of the poorest smallholders were barely adequate to keep them alive. They had to have other work as well, as artisans, or to emigrate in winter. Then there were medium, big, and very big peasants. There is a striking contrast between a one-hectare holding, without even a horse and cart, and a forty-hectare estate with several brace of oxen or horses and a large domestic staff. In most regions there was genuine social stratification among the peasantry.

Besides the peasants, the village comprised other social categories. First came the notables, who lived off the land without themselves cultivating it. They included the landowners, whether noble or bourgeois, and many notaries, lawyers, and bailiffs, as well as priests, teachers, and doctors. The countryside industries were run by forgemasters, by master glaziers, by textile manufacturers and merchants, and by small manufacturers who produced a variety of goods. These notables formed a relatively numerous group, with far-reaching power and prestige. In second place came another fairly numerous and diversified group: the handicraftsmen, merchants, or purveyors of services who produced or repaired everything required. The artisan-manufacturers such as weavers, joiners, and wheelwrights marked the beginnings of rural industry. The latter's expansion in the late eighteenth and early nineteenth centuries led to an increase in this "peasant-worker" class. Third came the administrative personnel such as tax collectors, gendarmes, council clerks, and those employed on the big estates, in the manufactories, and in trade. Finally, there were often a good many people without means of production. Those who could do only manual labor were servants and hired farmhands, artisans' helps, or, if unfit for such work, beggars. Begging was an appreciable source of income in the old villages.

This social diversity lay at the root of a lively and satisfying social life. Within the local community, people could fill most of their needs. It was Marcel Maget [7] who described the village as an "inter-cognitive" society, where everyone knew everyone else; these personal relations gave village society a peculiar "transparency." Thanks to intercognition, this combination of diversity and homogeneity imparted that extraordinary vitality described in literature dealing with eighteenth- and nineteenth-century village life, that contrasts so strikingly with the boredom and social lethargy that seems to have taken possession of the countryside today.

Seasonal Migrations

Although at all times the farming population accounted for only a fraction of people living in rural areas, the growth of the population in the nineteenth century led to an upsurge in all nonagricultural occupations, such as rural industry and seasonal migration. The subprefect of Riom wrote in 1848: "In the country of Saint Gervais (Auvergne) there are only two industries, apart from professions indispensable for the daily needs: linen-making and periodical emigration, which help to make up for the inadequacy of agriculture. Some 850 bricklayers and 50 sappers leave in March and return in November with hard-earned savings from the Lyon, Orleans, and Champagne areas."

In the southern Alps, seasonal migration was essentially of an agricultural nature [2]. The mountain folk with their herds descended southward, where they found a different climate. In the plains, the women and children minded the herds while the men took farming jobs. Thus the mountain dweller saved on food while keeping his herd alive. A nineteenth-century author maliciously remarked that "the mountain dweller, very frugal at home, becomes a big eater and a big drinker when food is part of his salary, in winter . . . ."

Whether migration was industrial and restricted to men, or agricultural and on a family scale, village agriculture was reduced to a subsistence level, being left to old people, women, and children, while the men went to earn their living elsewhere. It was in the men's interest to go alone. They could then make the most of their small village capital: the dwelling provided the family with housing, and the little farm provided them with food. If the men had tried to sell their modest assets, they could not have made enough to install their families in town by buying something comparable there.

Seasonal migration was economically justified, as sociological analysis confirmed, but it had serious drawbacks. In their villages, these peasants owned something and held clearly defined positions, whereas in the towns, owning nothing and being unskilled, they became "proletarians" employed on work sites or in transportation, and they hardly led pleasant lives. Moreover, the women were left in sole charge of the farm and children. The seasonal migrant was therefore faced with a hard but rational choice. Many mountain communities have kept in close touch with the outside world through seasonal migration [8]. Traditional migration broke down geographical barriers and mountain isolation. P. Rambaud [10] stressed the fact that life in these mountain communities was so "deeply moulded" that all mountain folk felt the need to "go out into the world."

The foregoing is of course no more than a schematic reconstruction; the picture differs widely from region to region. But it helps comprehension of the factors that broke up the old order of things. By means of urban industrialization, society introduced social disorganization factors into the countryside, progressively destroying the foundations of traditional civilization. It would exploit to its own advantage a disorganization that would cause the local communities to lose their autonomy [5].

Exodus and Changes in the Nineteenth and Twentieth Centuries

Demographic self-sufficiency could endure as long as migration affected only the overflow population—the excess of births over deaths. A genuine exodus, however, involves more than the overflow, and this breaches demographic autarchy. In parallel, economic self-sufficiency is broken, since city markets keep growing, and in order to satisfy them, agriculture is increasingly oriented toward commercial production. In many regions, however, there was a massive exodus without loss of traditional economic self-sufficiency; those who remained continued to cultivate their land for food. But in most cases the exodus did not affect all social categories equally, causing an imbalance and thus changing the model we have just outlined.

Partial exodus of the population is not always a factor of imbalance, provided that it affects all social categories without distinction. The social model may still function on a smaller scale if its economic bases remain relatively sound and the fundamental social roles are filled. In most cases, however, the bulk of those who left belonged to social categories without which local communities could not function on traditional lines. All available statistical data and local research prove that it is the young people who leave in great number and at all periods. Recent research bearing on the French farming population shows that half the young agricultural workers aged 15 to 30 left the land between 1954 and 1962. The natural result is an aging process entailing well-known demographic results, particularly a decrease in the birth rate. In a society with an excessive percentage of old people, it is obviously difficult to have a balanced, satisfying social life.

A second resulting phenomenon is sex imbalance. The men initiate a rural exodus; they migrate on a seasonal basis, or for good. The women have no reason to go because they cannot find outside work; they remain more closely integrated in the traditional social and family life of the villages. But when the rural exodus has gathered momentum, women are more inclined to go; at this stage men prefer their village occupations and their farms, whereas women are more attracted by tertiary forms of urban employment. Research by the INED [3] has shown that 56 percent of recent provincial migrants to Paris were women.

These trends result in disproportionate age pyramids, with more men than women, more old people than young. In extreme cases, one finds hamlets without young women, and farms run by old or unmarried people. Particularly the mountain regions show a marked masculine predominance in France; the ratio may reach 124 men to 100 women between the ages of 25 and 34 [4]. From the angle of social relations in the village, aging and the absence of women lead to major difficulties, for social life depends on young people and women; if young men have difficulty in finding wives, no social life is possible.

All the social categories do not leave the village in equal numbers, or at the same time. A differential pattern of exodus by social categories can be given, but this is purely theoretical, varying in each region according to social history. The many local research programs we have reviewed are usually vague on this point. Often the big notables are the first to leave. They lived both in the village and in town, often only on income from their land, but began to devote more time to their nonagricultural pursuits. The manufacturer concentrates on his industry, leaving his estate to be managed by a farmer or a butler. The notary and the lawyer devote more time to business, to which they add real estate and banking, advising their clients on investments. The children go into the administration, politics, or business. All tend to spend more and more time in town, returning to the village only when on holiday, in summer.

They therefore lose political control of the village, which passes to a new category of notables. Peasants who have made money give up direct farming to lead a bourgeois life, and gradually turn their farms into small manors. Small-town bourgeois acquire land on a bigger or smaller scale, to imitate the departed notables. Yet these new notables in turn head for the cities, for the same reasons as their predecessors.

Unskilled men, unattached to the village by capital possessions, particularly the seasonal farmhands, go at the same time as the big notables. As a result of population growth and agricultural modernization, it is more difficult to find work on the farms, while industrial development provides urban employment. The artisans, too, are ousted by cheaper industrial production; the village weavers, for instance, tend to move to town manufactories, where they can do better than in the villages. The farmworkers and artisans constituted the "proletarian army" that enabled industry to expand in the second half of the nineteenth century.

The peasant smallholders whose farms were too small for modernization were likewise unable to adjust to the changed agricultural economy, and somewhat later they followed the farmhands.

Influence of Industry

Ph. Pinchemel [9] studied three cantons in Picardy. Disregarding the seven small market towns located in that area, one finds that the purely rural population dropped by half in a century, from 1836 to 1936. Yet this drop went hand in hand with a comparatively stable number of farmers in the three districts: 1,836 farmers in 1836, 1,832 in 1872, 1,493 in 1911, and 1,221 in 1936.

An important nineteenth-century professional category has, however, disappeared completely today: the *menagers* (homesteaders) who in 1836, with 878 families, accounted for two-thirds of the total number of agriculturalists. In some villages, they outnumbered the genuine farmers. The homesteaders were small farmers who owned a house, a garden, poultry, perhaps a cow and a small plot—not more. Their holdings were not true subsistence farms; in order to live, the *menager* had to work for a big farmer who gave him some help, in particular lending him a plow and horses for tilling his field. There were close and complex bonds between the big farmers and the homesteaders. The latter often engaged in a handicraft such as weaving, chairmaking, etc., living off his little holding, his work as a hired laborer, and his handicraft.

The hired farmworkers numbered 4,274 in 1836, 4,884 in 1872, 4,417 in 1911, and 1,131 in 1936. Thus until 1911 the agricultural population, comprising independent farmers and wage-earners, remained almost stable, even increasing slightly. Then came a sharp fall, exceeding 50 percent, in the number of farmworkers, whereas the decrease in the number of farmers was slight.

The artisans, totaling 6,427 in 1836, fell to 3,460 in 1872, 2,569 in 1911, and 1,143 in 1936, a 6:1 ratio. Thus the rural exodus was essentially nonagricultural. There were spinners, weavers, stocking-makers, loom menders, rope makers, dyers, fullers, etc. Interpenetration between agricultural and industrial activities was complete. In 1873, the number of home-based artisans began to decrease, and small manufactories appeared. These began to merge until in 1911 they were less numerous. There was a short woodworking and chairmaking period between 1872 and 1911; in the latter year sugar mills, breweries, and a fertilizer plant were set up. In 1936 the manufactories had completely disappeared. The passing of a century had witnessed a profound social change. Integration between agricultural and textile production had given way to agriculture backed by agrosupporting and processing industries.

Artisans providing services, merchants, and the liberal professions remained about as numerous as before, moving from the villages to the cantonal centers. The artisans became slightly fewer and began to do different work: the blacksmith and upholsterer were replaced by the farm-machine mechanic. The merchants showed a relative increase, from one in 60-70 inhabitants to one in 50, but in absolute numbers they were fewer. The liberal professions and state employees (notaries, doctors, tax collectors, gendarmes, teachers, etc.) increased from 1 in 100 in 1836 to 1 in 34-39 in 1936.

Summing up, Pinchemel distinguishes between "strong villages" and "weak villages." The former were villages of eighteenth-century laborers, a rugged peasantry which either stood up to crises or took the initiative, increasing their holdings by buying land and preventing the homesteaders or hired workers from becoming farmers. In the "weak" villages, there were only homesteaders and hired men, unable to expand, who left their land to the big farmers of "strong" villages. Sometimes a single farmer from outside would quickly achieve a concentration of land to his profit.

In other words, in some villages the agrarian structure stood up to the changes because the larger holdings were able to modernize, while other social categories, such as the homesteaders, had to go. In villages where the poorer peasants and artisans were in the majority, the social structure lingered on until it finally broke down and big farmers from neighboring villages bought up the smallholdings.

Local society, composed mainly of agriculturalists, was exposed to the direct influence of industry.

The Present Situation
Comparing a village in 1830 to one in 1960, one finds that, with the departure of all those social categories, only big or medium farmers are left. There is no longer any social diversity; this diversity was a prerequisite of the traditional social life, and the rural exodus caused the latter to disappear.

More and more, the countryside is populated by agriculturalists, since the other social categories have moved to urban areas. Village institutions such as schools, churches, and cooperatives also tend to move to the market towns. Both trends become more pronounced and induce a change of scale in rural society: formerly, the village was a valid framework for analysis of the traditional form of society, whereas nowadays the framework for such research is the village group. A scale of about one kilometer now approximates to ten kilometers.

The departure of different social categories at different times not only shook up the social scene, but also the balance of power. The notables held political and social sway over the community as a whole; it was they who ensured contact with the outside world. When they left, these functions became vacant. In France, the small-town bourgeois or rich peasants who took over or split up the estates naturally tended to inherit the positions and become notables; when they, too, went away, they left them to the teachers and doctors. These three generations of notables each wielded their influence in their own way, slowing down or speeding up the exodus as their interests dictated [12].

The departure of the notables, whether noble or bourgeois, brought down the keystone of the village hierarchy. Now the weight of influence passed from an influential minority to the most numerous group: the peasants. Thus the community principle of diversity and hierarchy disappeared. All became socially equal; there was no chance of social betterment, and any young man who wished to change his status or "get on in life" had to leave the village.

With a decreasing population, it is difficult to maintain communal institutions such as the village hall, the school, and the church, particularly when the population is wholly agricultural [1]. In the latter case, the village council has to deal with farming problems only. Professional organizations such as farmers' and producers' associations and cooperatives have disappeared; the village council is staffed by the same people as those organizations, the two categories tend to coincide, and there is duplication. The village council is emptied; there are no candidates at council elections; the budget is too small to permit any action; the same is true of the church and farmers' union. A community of a couple of hundred people cannot carry traditional institutions, not to speak of new ones such as community or welfare centers.

Paradoxically, a waning population and social life coincide with a proliferation of institutions, which cease to play a part in communal life. The exodus feeds itself by destroying the structures and mechanisms that made village life worthwhile for villagers. In different countries, much local research has been done covering the existence of churches and schools, the clientele of the various trades and professions, though these have not yet led to conclusions, or even to reference norms [11].

The rural exodus was paralleled by a phenomenon that would link agriculture with urban industrial production. One may reasonably wonder whether technical progress in agriculture has not more or less substituted itself for the fundamentals of traditional community life. The old social interplay, based on diversity, would, after many social categories had disappeared, be rebuilt with those who remained: the farmers. New values would emerge: the central figure would be the big farmer, who by introducing up-to-date agricultural techniques would gain growing influence and assume the status of the former notables [6]. This reshaping of village life is well known to agricultural propagandists who, when seeking to introduce a technical innovation, know they must first convince a "big" peasant. When this is done, the others will follow suit sooner or later.

With technical progress, agriculture turned resolutely toward market production. Traditional self-sufficiency was replaced by increasing dependence on outside markets—the cities. Agriculture became closely bound up with industry—the supplier of fertilizers, machinery, agricultural engineers, etc. Thus the social systems of these local communities, no longer self-sufficient, would gradually become integrated into global society.

One may object that the foregoing is to some extent exaggerated. In many parts of Europe one can find survivals of the old ways of life and social systems, including the landlord-tenant and other traditional relationships, but one soon finds that these survivals are not based on social realities, but rather on rejection of change. Such rejection occurs mainly in backward areas, where agriculture has not changed sufficiently to induce the emergence of new social structures. When the big village landlord is the descendent of the old nobleman (and not a rich peasant who introduces mechanization) and continues to farm his land by means of a large group of tenants or farmers, instead of consolidating it; when thereby agricultural production still keeps a good many people alive (albeit precariously), traditional social relationships may be preserved and, in fact, fight a rearguard battle against the new, global social design. This produces the "vicious circle" well known to experts of underdevelopment: its main elements are traditional social structures, rejection of technical progress, and hostility to the outside world, relative impoverishment of the community, ill-will toward anything that threatens a scheme of things that has become a "refuge."

The rural world in the developed countries is today characterized by the coexistence of two types of rural communities: on the one hand those which, following the emergence of a social system based on technical progress, adjust themselves to the economic requirements of global society; and on the other, those who have stayed on the fringe of social evolution and observe, at least to some extent, the ways of life and ways of thought inherited from traditional life. Each type no doubt prevails in some entire regions, yet the observer is often confronted with a more complex reality: the two types exist side by side within a group of villages, or even in the same village; two social groups are in opposition. For instance, one group of agriculturalists has adapted its production system to the exterior market, whereas the members of another group, who have found employment in a neighboring town, continue to cultivate their own smallholdings, or work on a day basis, in their spare time.

Unexpectedly, it is usually the second group that is more inclined to perpetuate the old way of life; they seem willing to let the full-time farmers take charge of village life and, indeed, replace the former notables. The full-time farmers may in that case either try to use the village institutions to their own advantage, or effectively, if they feel that agriculture is threatened, step in to preserve the traditional ways. It is a transitional stage; small communities are unsuitable for the coexistence of "identical" people. The result is a sense of frustration and aspirations to return to the traditional way of life.

The transitional social models which have superseded the traditional models have served mainly as vehicles for agriculture's economic mutation. Possible patterns for the future should now be envisaged.

A Model of a Local Community of the Future

The picture of the countryside as a workshop of agricultural production still endures. If the notion of "countryside" is broadened to include the small country towns, we find that the last fifteen years have witnessed a dwindling, both relative and absolute, of the agricultural section of the total active population of the rural areas, and we revert—in a different way—to the situation at the outset of the nineteenth century: there are fewer and fewer farmworkers in the countryside, and the latter is becoming less and less a workshop of agricultural production.

Our analysis now bears on a different unit. The nineteenth-century peasant society could be termed either a "village" society or a "peasant" society; conversely, the rural communities of today and tomorrow cannot be termed villages, but rather "rural areas" centered around a small, essentially tertiary, yet also rural town. The diversity of the nineteenth-century village now reappears on a different plane: there are ever fewer agriculturalists, but a very considerable tertiary population working in trade and in the services, a secondary population engaging in minor local industries, and a residential, nonproductive population.

The ideal model of the rural community of tomorrow could be a small town with a population of about 5,000—not exceeding 10,000— surrounded by essentially agricultural hamlets and farms, with an additional residential population scattered round the area. This structure, though on a quite different scale, might be comparable to a nineteenth-century village with a population of about 1,000, centered around its church and village hall. The center of our modern rural town would be far larger, due to the growing diversification of industrial civilization.

There would be one fundamental difference: in the new model, global society would be within easy reach of any member of the community through the mass communication media: television, press, cinema. It would seek them out in their homes, in contrast to the old villages, where the only "media" were the notables. The new structure would thus be urban rather than rural. Except for a lower density, it would be rather like a city suburb.

Thus the dominant organizational factor of the rural community of tomorrow would not be tradition or natural resources, but its proximity to and relationships with the ruling urban society. Rural concentration is paralleled by the tendency of the urbanized areas to expand outward. Towns are becoming less and less "walled centers, where people live" but rather, despite density of urbanization, loosely knit habitats. The description of a rural community might also fit an urban community. Seen in this perspective, there is no difference between a genuine rural-type community, far from any town, and a suburban community with a very small percentage of agriculturalists.

Let us take a closer look at this rural or suburban community. The agricultural population would vary from 50 percent of the active population, in areas that might remain "agricultural workshops," to 2 percent of the active population in some suburban communities. The residual population would be residential, working in the cities or suburbs, drawing a pension, or possessing independent means.

In a rural community proper, the active, nonagricultural population may be residential, commuting greater or lesser distances. In highly industrialized areas such as northern or eastern France, Holland, Belgium, and parts of Germany, there is not much difference between urban and rural residence for industrial and administrative workers. In less densely populated areas, however, the active agricultural population is numerous: these areas are "genuine countryside." The residual population may be increased by seasonal tourist and vacational migration—the reverse counterpart of the seasonal migrations of farm workers in earlier periods.

The secondary residence phenomenon is developing in the coastal areas and seaside resorts as well as in the rural areas proper. Migration on retirement seems to be assuming growing importance in our society, since increasing expectation of life and duration of retirement causes more and more people, belonging to the "third-age" category, to live on their earnings, as consumers only. Many would rather live in the country than in towns. The number of these temporary or permanent nonproducer, consumer residents is increasing steadily in the countryside; they have needs that must be filled, and money to spend. This calls for a build-up of services, including trade, and catering to recreational and cultural requirements in the small towns, involving a fairly numerous service population.

Finally, telecommunications should enable some activities to be moved from town to country. A large bank, for instance, could store its securities in any outside location, provided communications were quick and easy.

In a mountain region, the residential population would consist essentially of summer vacationers or winter sports enthusiasts. This would be a borderline case: a picturesque area, with facilities operated by a few guides and hotel keepers for tourists who come skiing, or to give their children a "taste of fresh air."

Agriculture always has been a subsistence occupation, providing agriculturalists with enough to eat. A typical instance was the eighteenth-century countryside; the French revolution of 1789 broke out partly because the village folk had not enough to eat. In those times, governments were worried about food shortages in the countryside; nowadays, it is the other way round—goverments have to cope with problems of agricultural overproduction.

In the new communities, the old problem may return—modern villages, besides procuring industrial products, may have to procure food, like any urban district. A possible future development may be a revival of individual food production: all local residents without professional commitments, and having external sources of income, would devote some of their spare time to gardening or poultry keeping. Tinkering and minor handicrafts are on the increase, in both town and country. Standardized mass production does not meet every personal and special requirement; a whole new subsistence production, both agricultural and of the handicraft type, will also gain ground.

Conclusion

Having reviewed the present-day organizational trends of rural communities in the industrialized countries, one finds that the rural society of tomorrow may be moving toward renewal—on a larger or regional scale—of the essential traits of the old villages. We refer to traits that were disappearing in the upheavals caused by industrialization and the rural exodus: (1) cultural homogeneity, born of participation in global, not purely local, civilization; (2) social diversity, due to the many rural services and residential population; (3) coherent social relationships built up on cultural, sporting, political, religious, and other pursuits; (4) agriculture, whether of the commercial or subsistence type, which would again be the pursuit of a minority; (5) overlapping and coexistence of agricultural and nonagricultural occupations within the same family, with some persons engaging in both; and (6) seasonal migration, which would play a capital role as an element of contact with the outside world, and of population growth.

On passing from the old pattern to the new, however—from a population of 500 to a population group of some 10,000—the old intercognitional relationships among everyone would not be possible. Distant, functional (or secondary) relationships would be set up, and elementary, urban-type groups, with new personal relationships, would appear.

Some readers may find this likening of late twentieth-century rural society with that of the eighteenth century somewhat far-fetched, and attribute it to a nostalgic hankering for the old order; let them consider the validity of the available elements of observation, and the coherence of the model we present.

To explore further along these lines, the Rural Sociology Group of the CNRS, Paris, has undertaken comparative research in social change in a test group of French rural communities, and has set up conceptual analytic machinery which makes possible systematic comparison of the social systems and constitutive subsystems of any community, study of the autonomy and coherence of each system, and the arrangement of these systems according to a special suprasystem whose autonomy and coherence permits appraisal of the viability and independence of the community studied.

The pattern of the rural society of tomorrow is obviously, like that of the traditional community, conceived on very general lines, permitting extreme diversity of the social forms and structures that will emerge in different countries, in function of geographical data, external economic and social pressures, the traditions and spirit of the population, and social structures inherited from the past. It would be a serious error to suppose that our industrial society will create a uniform pattern to which all local communities must conform. Indeed present research in the Rural Sociology Group of the CNRS shows that each social system tends to interpret and adapt the elements forced on it by global society.

Let us take television: it is the same for all French people, but different village communities use it in different ways. In a Vendée village, where the notables still hold influential positions and assure contact with the outside world, television plays the part of a notable who discloses to the peasants the outside world that acts like a magnet on their children. The reaction to television is like that toward the lord of the manor or the curate: gratitude at providing a link with global society and culture, the lack of which is felt. In a village of the Beauce region, however, social life is nonexistent; people shut themselves in their houses, whose windows open onto an inner courtyard, while only the door opens onto the street. In this society, television brings the outside world into the home without a neighbor intruding, thus perpetuating the isolation of each family and the lack of social communication.

Conversely, in an Armagnac village, where people like to talk and conversation is a popular social activity, an art in which everyone participates, television offers new subjects of conversation and opportunities to exercise one's judgment. Thus, according to whether a society is hierarchic, fragmented, or sociable, television is utilized by each group to perpetuate its own traditions and preserve its own special character.

There is no more urgent task in this late twentieth century in the industrial countries than to study the mechanisms of transmission and preservation of these provincial or ethnic originalities. Adequate intellectual instruments should be created to describe traditional diversity, and to provide the means of expressing and predicting the diversity of tomorrow. If the rural sociologist fails to apply himself to this task, a time may come when peasant populations disappear and he is unable to answer one of the major questions posed by our civilization; he will have to seek refuge in folklore or in the psychosociology of agricultural work—that is, renounce being a sociologist.

References

1. d'Aragon, C., "Le village et les pouvoirs." In J. Fauvet and H. Mendras, *Les paysans et la politique*. Paris: Colin, 1958, 532 pp.

2. Blanchard, R., *Les Alpes et leur destin*. Paris: Bayard, 1958, 283 pp.

3. Chevalier, L., *La formation de la population parisienne au XIXème siècle*. Paris: PUF, 1950, 312 pp., Cahier de l'INED No. 10.

4. Duplex, J. (ed.), *Atlas sociologique de la France rurale*. Paris: Colin, 1968.

5. Giraud, A., H. Bastide, and G. Pourcher, "Mobilité géographique et concentration urbaine," *Population*, 1964, pp. 227-287.

6. Cf. Juillard, E., *La vie rurale dans la plaine de Basse-Alsace*. Paris: Le Roux, 1953, 581 pp.

7. Maget, M., "Remarques sur le village comme cadre de recherches anthropologiques," *Bulletin de psychologie* 8 (7-8) (April 1955), 373-382.

8. Mendras, H., *Six villages d'Epire*. Paris: UNESCO, 1961, 92 pp.

9. Pinchemel, Ph., *Structures sociales et dépopulation rurale dans les campagnes picardes de 1836 à 1936*. Paris: Colin, 1957, 236 pp.

10. Rambaud, P., *Economie et sociologie de la montagne: Albiez-le-Vieux en Maurienne*. Paris: Colin, 1962, 292 pp.

11. Sauvy, A., G. Ghez, P. Georges, and L. Chevalier, *Dépeuplement rural et peuplement rationnel*. Paris: PUF, 1949, 108 pp., Cahier de l'INED No. 8.

12. Cf. Thabault, R., *Mon village*. Paris: Delagrave, 1954, 252 pp.

13. Varagnac, A., *Civilisation traditionelle et genres de vie*. Paris: Michel, 1942, 403 pp.

15. The Family
Farm: A Primary
Unit of Rural
Development
in Developing
Countries

Michel Cépède

The family farm is generally recognized as a primary unit of the rural society in the so-called "western" world. It has played an important role in the past development of the countries in this group. Nevertheless many modern economists consider a rural structure based on family farms as a brake upon economic progress. Our problem is whether the family farm may be used as a primary unit of rural development in developing countries. Analyzing, by way of introduction, the role of the family farm in the development of the rural "western" world, one should recognize that the main values of a family farm system are contrary to those which Adam Smith considered as causes of the wealth of nations.

The family farm system should be discussed from four different angles: (1) the family farm and economies of scale; (2) the family farm and employment; (3) the family farm and agricultural production; and (4) the family farm and conservation of natural resources (fertility, soil conservation). Only after having considered these problems will it be possible to discuss if and how the family farm can be a primary unit of rural development in developing countries.

The Family Farm and Development

Western European politicians, like those of North America, not only recognize the primary importance of family farming within the rural economy of their advanced countries; they unhesitatingly assert that their policy must be based on this established fact. The Treaty of Rome, and even more the declaration of the Conference of Ministers of Agriculture of the European Economic Community (Stresa 1959), support this statement. The U.S. delegation to the Organization of Economic Cooperation and Development declared (Paris 1963) that "maintaining and strengthening the family character of U.S. farming is a primary objective of American rural development policy."

Yet in the view of "modern" economists, family farming appears as a relic of an outdated past. In proposing its adoption as a basic unit of

Michel Cépède—France. Ph.D., Economics and Political Sciences, Paris, 1944; Hon. Ph.D., Agricultural Sciences, Gembloux, 1967; currently Professor at the Institute of National Agronomy; Membre Correspondant of the Agricultural Academy, France; Foreign Academic Member of Academy des Georgofili, Florence.

rural development in the developing countries, are we not merely attempting elsewhere what has proved unsuccessful in our own countries? There are "experts" who still recommend, round the world, policies which have invariably ended in failure.

The Family Farm and Development in the United States Nevertheless, the role played by the family farm in one striking instance of development—the three-century buildup of the North American economic system—should give us food for thought. The fact is that, despite the sarcasms of early nineteenth-century economists, aimed at the philosophy of the American colonists [16] and at "Jeffersonism," the proportion of family farms in this society, which can hardly be termed underdeveloped, today amounts (rating as family farms those that employ less than 1.5 years of salaried work per annum) to 96 percent, while family farms account for 80 percent of U.S. agricultural production. Moreover, the family farm thus defined, selling on the market $10,000 worth of produce, or more, per year, is the fastest-growing group of agricultural units [1].

What, then, according to E. G. Wakefield, should have retarded the economic development of a country like the United States, whose agriculture was based on family farms? "The passion for owning land which prevents the existence of a class of laborers for hire" and creates "a barbarizing tendency of dispersion of producers and national wealth." Wakefield further pointed out that those people were opposed to the division of labor—the specialization which, as Adam Smith taught us, was the big factor in the growth of productivity: "Free Americans who cultivate the soil follow many other occupations. Some portion of the furniture and tools which they use is commonly made by themselves. They frequently build their own houses, and carry to market, at whatever distance, the produce of their own industry. They are spinners and weavers, they make soap and candles, as well as, in many cases, shoes and clothes for their own use. In America the cultivation of land is often the secondary pursuit of a blacksmith, a miller or a shopkeeper." Reading these remarks, one wonders how the United States was able to develop.

The Social Cost of the Division of Labor

The division of labor, despite its accepted function as the motive power of the post-Adamite economy, involves a social cost which should give pause to those who wish to promote development "of the whole man and of all men" (Francois Perroux). John Ruskin, who, as one perhaps too readily forgets, taught political economy in Manchester, wrote in "The Stones of Venice" (1851-1857) that through division of labor "the small part of intelligence that is left to man is inadequate to make a pin; it is used up in the production of a pin-point or a nail-head. It is certainly a good and desirable thing to make many pins in one day," but he reflected that if we could only see with what sand the pin-points were polished—sand of the human soul which must be considerably magnified before its nature can be discerned—we might well conclude that here, too, there was a certain amount of waste.

We should therefore ask ourselves if the social cost involved in the division of labor is assessed by the societies, groups, and individuals whose development we wish to encourage, at a price comparable to the progress in productivity which it is supposed to bring about.

In establishing this comparison, we cannot trust unreservedly the criteria used by economists in calculating growth. The growth of the gross national product is systematically overestimated during the transition period from a subsistence economy to a market economy, from a family economy where self-supply and self-consumption are naturally important, to an economy which procures its means of production, including manpower, on the market, and which markets its products in the form of merchandise. Not only are men justified in preferring a less market-governed economy; one finds that the classic criteria of economic growth show progress, while the structural change that has intervened may have brought about a general regression. Pigou drew the attention of his students to the misleading character of these criteria: he reminded them that if, being single, he married his housemaid, he would be reducing the gross national product, whereas if he divorced and asked his ex-wife to render him the same services against payment of even a minimal salary, he would be increasing it. This is a very precise illustration of the transition from a subsistence economy to a market economy or, in the first instance, vice versa.

Though Pigou's illustration may seem oversimplification, it is too important for our problem to be passed over lightly. Measuring growth by this or that criterion may be acceptable provided there is no structural change—in other words, no development. But our problem is precisely one of development, and the process cannot be measured by indicators of growth, indicators laid down in a different economic structure: that of the developed world. We often lack criteria for measuring the most important human aspects of our problem, and we construct models with the available statistical data. These models are useful in bolstering our arguments, but we must be wary of believing that our model is the only true and rational one, and of rejecting what appears not to conform to it.

We certainly concur with Lord Kelvin in admitting that without a yardstick we do not know much, but to believe that we know everything because we have been able to measure some of the aspects of the problem is worse. A "technician" tends to reason on a basis of available data, which are thereby given preferential consideration. Perusal of the absurd reports contained in field studies show how unsuited our instruments are to the realities they are expected to measure. When some economists go so far as to state that there is no reason for preoccupation with "social prices," "political prices," self-consumption, part-time work, female labor, etc. because, in the absence of statistics which should reflect the complex aspects of these facts, we can no longer apply the simple arguments of "pure economics," they come very near to denying those realities. They are deluded by a "scientific alienation" [6] similar to that denounced by Feuerbach as a "religious alienation" [15]. They rely on their models, which they brandish aloft as "rational idols," to describe a reality whose complexity they refuse to recognize because they are incapable of analyzing it. This approach is unscientific and fallacious, just as that of the faithful and priests, denounced by Feuerbach, is "anti-religious" when it leads to the estrangement and not to the true liberation of man.

To deny what is not readily measurable and does not fit a theoretical model inevitably makes one think of the man who, having lost one of his keys in a dark street, goes to look for it under the street lamp, because there, at least, he can see clearly. To assess the prosperity or nonviability of a family economy in the sole light of criteria set for a market economy is a good example of muddled thinking.

That is why we should not allow ourselves to be too impressed by the classical economists' criticisms of the family farm and its accompanying rural structures and values. We have only to note that, despite Wakefield's predictions, Jeffersonism has not retarded U.S. economic development and that, despite the predictions of Karl Marx [14, Part 8, Chapter 33], the American colonist, like the European peasant, has resisted being forced to become a wage earner effectively enough to ensure that in American, as in French, agriculture there is less than one wage earner to every four "actively engaged" persons; this suffices to cast doubt on the validity of certain contemporary views that do not stand up to the test of reality.

Figures for the 1959 census for the United States are given in Table 1. If we take only the full-time farmers into consideration, we shall have for the commercial farms 1 wage earner to 1.9 owner-farmers, and for all farms 1 wage earner to 2.35 owner-farmers.

The Family Farm and Economies of Scale

Turning to South America, we find that in the pampas of Buenos Aires Province the family *chacras* are making headway at the expense of the big *estancias* that employ wage earners. We may therefore question the validity of criticism of the family farm on grounds of economies of scale. We might here point out that the family farm should not be confused with the smallholding, as too often occurs. A farm employing hired labor is of course likely to be bigger than one which employs only family members, but the "family" character of a farm is of a sociological nature and is unrelated to size.

A family farm is one that is cultivated by the farmer's family members without usually employing hired labor. In order to allow for exchange of services, seasonal work, replacements, etc., I think the most suitable practical statistical criterion would be the following: a family farm is one which, run by the farmer and his family members, does not employ more than one and one-half years of hired labor per annum. Such a family farm may considerably vary in size, according to the number of work units provided by the family members and invested capital— whether own capital or procured through loans from neighbors, co-operative organizations, or otherwise.

Nor is a family farm necessarily owned by the farmer. Whether the holder be owner or tenant does not matter so long as the management decisions are taken by an independent operator whose family provides the work units. The question may arise in regard to "sharecroppers" who, if subject to the decisions of their landlord or his representatives,

Table 1.
U.S. Agricultural Statistics 1959.

Actively Engaged Persons	Total (*thousands*)	On Commercial Farms	Others
Full-Time Farmers	2,450	1,930	520
Part-Time Farmers	980	610	370
Wage Earners	1,050	1,010	40
Total Active Agricultural Population	4,480	3,550	930

cannot be considered "family farmers." Again, in cases of vertical integration of production under contract, one may question whether the integrated agriculturalists remain "farmers." To say that family farms are predominant in a European country where 50,000 hectares of tomatoes are grown under contract with a single firm is entirely misleading. On the other hand, the farmer who, with his seven sons, runs a big farm in the east Parisian region on intensive and highly mechanized lines, without hired labor, and the American farmer whom I visited near Champaign, Illinois in 1955 and who, assisted only by his son in working his 160 acres, was earning $17,000 a year from them, are family farmers. J. P. Madden [12] found that one-man cultivation of 640 hectares (corn on fallow land) is as efficient as any larger unit; a family farm run on such a system could obviously not be smaller.

D. R. Bergmann [2], who quoted Madden in a recent report, also gave instances which seem to show that the size beyond which reduction of average total costs is minimal (i.e., beyond which there are no economies on the internal scale) is larger than that which can be operated by a family of normal size. It is true that Bergmann warns us from the outset that "this work is a doctrinal note and not a study of statistical data"; that it applies to France and can be extended, as the title indicates, only to northwestern Europe. When he shows how, by setting up Agricultural Groups for Common Working (GAEC) some farmers have tried to exceed family farm level, to find ways of cutting costs through economies of scale without creating a class of wage earners, he recognizes the ideological importance of the movement. He then voices an opinion which is highly important for our problem: "It seems essential to us not to extrapolate the results of this experiment to the underdeveloped countries where economies of scale hardly exist and where the necessary economic and cultural equality to avoid exploitation phenomena seems unlikely to be found. In the poor countries, the group agriculture one finds is of a quite different nature—based not on democratic consensus, but on rigid discipline."

For the present we shall concern ourselves only with the following: (a) that the rejection of salaried work poses an ideological problem, and (b) that the arguments based on "economies of scale" are not determinant, particularly in developing countries.

The Family Farm and Employment

A point to make is that existing data for assessing employment in agriculture are dangerously inadequate and may lead to serious errors. It may occur, for instance, that in the absence of reliable data on female employment, statistics on the number of male agricultural workers are prepared in the developing countries along the same lines as in the so-called developed countries, where the method is likewise questionable [5]. Let us emphatically say that in some countries, such data would only have significance insofar as the number of women who actually work the land is accidentally equal to that of the men who watch them doing so, or merely direct the work without doing any physical labor themselves. In a rice-producing country men certainly drive the animals that tread the rice fields, and hold the plows that sometimes till them. But in replanting, a man directs and supervises a team of women who perform this most tiring work.

The method consisting of working out, not the number of workers employed on the farm, but the number of hours of work or their equivalent in "man-work-years" (PAT) also has a serious fault: that of the distribution of work throughout the year. To assess a farm's productivity on a basis of work-hours would mean overrating farms that employ seasonal workers without having to assure them of year-round employment. As a borderline case, there was the astonishing productivity per work-hour on one farm the owner of which, in 1947, on 24,000 hectares, employed only 40 permanent workers, with 120 seasonal hands for the harvest. But if all the farms in the United States were to employ such methods, one wonders what would happen to the seasonal workers during the remainder of the year, and whether a social cost on such a scale should not be taken into account in assessing productivity per worker.

In a developed economy the community can shoulder such costs, but should the economists not take them into account before making pronouncements on the superiority of large-scale farming with mass-scale seasonal employment? Modern capitalism has a marked tendency to collectivize social costs in order to make possible the private appropriation of higher profits. One may wonder whether such pronouncements do more than provide a "scientific" disguise for a piece of trickery. But in the developing countries, the collectivization of social costs is not and, moreover, often cannot be assured, while uncovered costs exist nonetheless. In the pampas of Buenos Aires Province, the workers of the thresher-harvester companies are employed about one month a year at very high salaries, more than tenfold those of the full-time workers (peones) of the big grain estancias. These seasonal workers, however, cannot be content to earn a great deal less during the remainder of the year and thus lose status, so they stay unemployed nearly eleven months a year in the suburbs of the federal capital.

To economists who indignantly exclaim that these men's attitude is irrational and blameworthy, one could reply that when your skill entitles you to a high rate of pay, it does not follow that you are bound to accept the values of the "economic society" any more than it is necessary to rise to leisured class status in order to belong to a civilization in which values other than the economic are taken into account. When men's destiny is at stake, the economy cannot be content to minimize costs and maximize monetary profits, in disregard of the social cost.

Here we have a recurrence of one of the traditional features of agriculture, leading one to evoke F. Toennies' dichotomy between *Gemeinschaft* (community) and *Gesellschaft* (society); the first is characteristic of rural life, the second of urban life. The purpose of agriculture would be to provide a living for the members of the community, while industry and commerce create goods which are exchanged among the members of society. Agriculture provides employment for women, children, old people, the physically handicapped, etc.; it does not pick and choose its workers, but employs its family members. Its productivity is the lower and it fills its community role the better because it provides employment for its members without requiring a definite amount of work from them.

Employment and work are two notions that should not be confused. In the labor market, those termed "seekers of work" are in reality looking for employment, and those who, paradoxically, are called "givers of work" are those who require work from the workers to whom they offer employment. But—and this point is essential for our present argument—it is not true that the antithesis is between agriculture and other sectors. These problems do not arise in agriculture only, nor even in the whole of agriculture.

As regards seasonal labor, building and several other outdoor trades have features in common with agriculture. Artisans in industry and trade, and also in agriculture, likewise have community aspects. A family farm is a household enterprise in agriculture. The problems of employment and underemployment are posed in terms of social structure: capitalist enterprises versus household enterprises, i.e., in agriculture, capitalist farms versus family farms, and not as an antithesis between agriculture and industry within the economy [7].

If, as Karl Marx put it, the unemployed constitute the "reserve army of the proletariat," then the recognized and registered unemployed are the "readily available contingent" or "first reserve" of that "army"; there remains the enormous "hidden reserve" of "agricultural under-employment"—the "disguised unemployment" that would weight intolerably on the whole economy if it had to be subsidized. In terms of economic mechanisms, this is disparity among standards of life, to the disadvantage of agriculture. But here again, it is not agriculture as a sector that is involved, but family farming as a handicraft-type, "community" social structure responsible for those whom the sectors that operate more on the lines of a "society" cannot maintain in a capitalistic exchange economy. "Disguised unemployment" is a phenomenon of the family economy, and also of estate or plantation economy; it is nonexistent in enterprises that employ mainly wage earners, i.e., that procure in the labor market the labor force they use. But if so, how can one fail to take into account the social costs that are absorbed by the family structures, despite the apparently better results of the capitalist enterprises? This applies particularly to economies whose development has not yet reached a level at which the social costs can be shouldered by the community, as they are in up-to-date capitalism.

The Family Farm and Agricultural Production

It is well known, on the other hand, that the smaller the area worked per worker becomes, the higher the gross product per acre. On lands of equal fertility, capitalist farming employs less labor per hectare than family farming. It often also invests more capital, because it has found that investment in mechanization is more profitable than engaging even seasonal labor; faced with the workers' unwillingness to accept the terms offered them, the operators have been led to increase their capital investments. This is, more or less, what Mario Bandini expresses in an African story: some twenty years ago, he met a rich chief who had a hundred wives; when congratulated, but also questioned on the reasons of this abundance, the chief replied that he was generous and when he found a young girl without a job, he married her and sent her to work on his lands. Some ten years later the chief had only four wives; again questioned by Mr. Bandini, who asked him whether there were no more poor girls and land to cultivate, the chief answered: "Of course there are, but I have since bought a tractor."

As Sismondi remarked, a capitalist enterprise seeking profit, which he, in a different sense from that of the Physiocrats, termed the "net product," is often led to sacrifice the "gross product." It furnishes both less "employment" and less "production."

The big Cuban pre-Castro cane sugar plantations, and many others too, kept their old cultivated areas at a low gross yield in order to reduce labor costs, employ workers at harvest time only, and keep the cost of sugar production as low as possible. But, as René Dumont pointed out, younger, better tended plantations could have provided steadier year-round employment, and yields could easily have been doubled.

L. Malassis [13] writes: "It thus seems that the amount of labor determines the cultivation system on the small farms and the cultivation system determines the amount of labor on the big farms." The fact is that the overpopulation on small farms leads to a greater number of per-annum working hours to each hectare. These are family farms, otherwise they would not be overpopulated—despite, but also because of, obvious underemployment. That is what J. B. Chombart de Lauwe and F. Morvan [8] had also found in the Chateaulin area of Brittany: when one moved from holdings of less than 5 hectares to those of more than 25, the number of workers per 100 hectares fell from 105 to 18.7, the number of per annum working hours per hectare from 1,500 to 480. Working capital also fell, but less markedly, from 210,000 to 119,000 francs, and gross yield from index 163 to 88 (average for the area: 100).

Are these observations transposable to the Third World? Although examples, such as that of the sugar plantations, may lead one to think so, this is perhaps not generally true. The contrary seems even less probable, so that the conclusions of L. Malassis deserve careful consideration. He points out that "if the family farm stands up better to slumps than commercial agriculture"—an argument often put forward in Europe in favor of family farms—"this is not due to its economic superiority, but to its social structure and to the peasant family's capacity for tightening their belts." It is also true that "the small farm contributes more (per hectare) to the aggregate farm income and thus to the national income." He adds that "under present conditions of production, the small farm is of more interest to society than to the producers themselves."

The Family Farm and the Conservation of Natural Resources
If the family farm, by virtue of its handicraft-type structure, were induced to intensify its cultivation system, another consequence of

major importance for developing economies would supervene, since one of agriculture's main problems is that of conserving fertility.

It may seem evident that, with the growing demographic pressure and man's demand for ever-increasing production from the same areas, the latter will eventually be exhausted. This pattern, which is consistent with the law of diminishing returns and its corollary, Ricardo's theory of land rent, may be illustrated by examples of areas, formerly populated, which man has had to abandon to the desert, whereas conversely, the demands on English agriculture, for example, have decreased, and its fertility seems to have increased markedly. A. Woelkoff [17] had already stressed in 1905 that more than half of mankind then lived between the twentieth and fortieth latitudes north, i.e., in an area that excludes the whole of Europe and the big industrial concentrations of the period, and which contains the principal deserts of the northern hemisphere. To conclude from the foregoing that this zone is, in the biological sense, the most favorable to human life and that the deserts there are the consequence of human multiplication, is only a step away. It does not seem, however, that these zones were ever densely populated; if they were, it was either on the basis of a food-gathering economy, or—more frequently—of a pastoral economy and sometimes of an extensive agricultural economy, but not on a peasant economy, the only genuine agricultural one.

Peasant agriculture was born by investing labor in the soil to increase natural yield and is naturally of a land-improving nature. "It requires of its farmers," remarked Lecouteux, "to leave in the soil, after the completion of each crop rotation, an excess amount of fertilizer which, not being immediately assimilable, creates a reserve of humus or mould which has a beneficial effect on the physical properties of the soil and builds up, long beforehand, the assimilable elements for future harvests." This agriculture, having an improving effect, is naturally intensive, as P. Gourou [11] points out: "Whereas a barbarian people, in response to an increase in its population, sees no other solution than to seize the lands of its neighbors, the Far Eastern peasant, who is civilized, responds to the growth of the population by improving his agricultural techniques and increasing yields."

The sedentary peasant, who belongs to a "people of time" [19], asks himself, "What will things be like *here*, tomorrow?" Conversely, there are "peoples of space" who are ready to wander, i.e., to seek elsewhere tomorrow what they have used up here today. The nomad, in a food-gathering economy or a pastoral economy, is naturally tempted to introduce an agriculture that will exhaust more resources than nature can restore. This destructive agriculture exploits nature as if it were a mine, which, as Turgot has put it, is not a productive unit but a fruit to be picked once and for all. Great destructions due to this "mining agriculture" have occurred in regions occupied by more or less stabilized nomads, or by those who conquered peasant peoples. They forced on the latter a type of agriculture which they would not have chosen freely, for, although they became agriculturalists, these "herdsmen" did not become "peasants" but transposed to agriculture the ways of thought and the "culture" of "peoples of space."

Another aspect of the Toennies dichotomy appears in the antithesis between the "sedentary" and the "nomad," the "peasant" and the "herdsman." We are aware of the drawbacks of oversimplification implicit in this dichotomy; the three "Homeric," "Hesiodic," and "Aristophanic" poles of Carle C. Zimmerman [18] are an indispensable minimum to classify the different types of societies. Toward the Hesiodic peasant, the Aristophanic bourgeois behaves no better than the Homeric herdsman or warrior. The essential character of a society of "economic-minded" men, orientated toward the market and capitalist profit, is disdain of the "freely available," and this society therefore tends to expend wastefully the "apparently freely available" natural resources that are indispensable for economic life and for life itself. The market economy favors extensive agriculture because, being of the mining type, it lowers the apparent cost prices. It was this capitalist agriculture that Karl Marx had in mind when concluding as follows Section IV of Book I of *Das Kapital*: "Moreover, all progress in capitalistic agriculture is a progress in the art, not only of robbing the labourer, but of robbing the soil. . . . The more a country starts its development on the foundation of modern industry, like the United States, for example, the more rapid is this process of destruction. Capitalist production therefore develops technology and the combining together of various processes into a social whole, only by sapping the original sources of all wealth: the soil and the labourer." Capitalist agriculture, he further opined, "annihilates the peasant, that bulwark of the old society, and replaces him by the wage labourer" [14, Chapter 15, Section 10].

Conclusions
The weaknesses of family farming, in the light of criteria of the capitalist economy, should not weigh heavily against its advantages for an

economy "of the whole man and of all men." Developing economies cannot afford the luxury of social costs involved in seeking economic growth exclusively on a basis of classical criteria.

A subsistence economy and the handicraft enterprise cannot be replaced by a market economy governing human labor without causing hardship that only costly social institutions can attenuate or relieve. Full employment, and full use of the natural factors of production, conservation, and development of human resources and of soil fertility, intensive production—these are considerations which for developing economies should have priority over growth of profits, which is often illusory.

Even if the family farm appears as a rejection of salaried status, it does not follow that it eliminates all forms of exploitation of man by man. Friedrich Engels [9] held that the family, as an economic unit, was a social structure based on "the avowed or disguised slavery of women." We know today that, in cases of the enslavement of one sex by the other, the victim has not always—though no doubt more frequently —been the woman, and a democratic family in which sex equality is respected does not seem impossible to us [3]. But whereas the elementary family consists of two adults only, a family farm may involve a more or less enlarged family, within which there is division of labor among individuals by sex, age, and perhaps status.

The traditional hierarchic structure of an enlarged family is not often favorable to technical progress, though it is not alone in having to bear this consequence of gerontocracy. Such a structure discourages individual initiative; egalitarian distribution tends to inhibit effort, which therefore must depend only on the cohesion of the family group and on its will to attain its objectives. Thus in many cases such a group produces only under the stress of necessity. The incentives of the market economy have little effect on the productive effort, the more so since income from sales is traditionally spent on outward show, or hoarded. If in the Mediterranean area and Western Europe the family farm has been able to provide the necessary basic supplies for industrial growth and urban development, this is because towns were places "where income from the land was spent" [10]; it was in order to raise money for payment of tribute and lease that the peasants sold in the market and produced more than they needed for their own consumption. In Asia, the situation before the colonial period showed certain analogies. In the two Americas, as in Africa, the urbanization phenomenon has not been linked with supplies to bourgeois landowners from the production of "their peasants." When peasants produced crops for export, this was due to other pressures, if not to the existence of capitalist plantations. Development thus poses special problems when based on family farming.

What will be the role of family farms in the economies of developing countries? This role would not be an exclusive one but that of primary units; that is, they would be integrated in a certain number of institutions, starting with the family as a basic unit and extending to national and international organizations. There is no doubt that if we wish to eliminate feudal or capitalist solutions, we must develop cooperative forms of integration. Only cooperative organizations can provide family farms with supply services for production, and with facilities for processing and marketing. Such cooperative organizations would also provide responsible representation of the primary units in relations with regional development boards and the state administration, which in the absence of such representation, and in dealing with small primary units, might feel tempted to misuse their power.

Research for promoting technical advancement, education, vocational training, and extension services would remain a matter for public preoccupation, but cooperation can play a useful part in these fields as a reception and transmission structure. Agreements among the planning authority, the cooperatives, and the family farms could, moreover, provide the latter with the means of production and guarantee adequate income from peasant labor by promoting the expansion of lines of production, orientated according to the community's priorities [4].

Going beyond the rejection of salaried status in general and transposing to the economy as a whole the need to avoid the unfavorable consequences of division of labor, one might envisage a society structure in which all family cells belong to consumer cooperatives, and also to cooperatives that assure them of the means of production and of exchanging their products with those obtained by other workers, so that all are assured of full satisfaction of their basic needs. It is because agriculture provides steady employment for members of the family community, in conditions that prevent work being turned into a merchandise, while filling mainly a basic need—that of food, which a market economy cannot do because it values only penury—that agricultural development can and should, as many believe, be founded on family farming as a basic unit.

Family farming provides the developing countries with the means of building an economy in which work (as we have said) is not a merchandise and where foodstuffs are not treated as mere goods either, because eating and working are matters too serious to be left a prey to market fluctuations. Thus the developing countries can avoid repeating the tragic mistakes of the capitalist economy.

References

1. Beal, George M., "The Character of Changes in Agriculture in North America." Working paper, First World Congress of Rural Sociology, Dijon, France, 1964. Mimeo.

2. Bergmann, D. R., "The Evolution of Farming in the Developed Countries of North-western Europe." Colloquy of Bressanone, Italy, August 31, 1968.

3. Cépède, M., "De la propriété foncière a l'exploitation familiale," *Revue Socialiste*, no. 132, Paris, April 1960.

4.____, "L'Exploitation familiale paysanne," *Revue Socialiste*, no. 133, Paris, May 1960.

5.____, "Analyse statistique de l'emploi agricole. Développement économique et Agriculture," *Economies et sociétés, Cahiers de l'ISEA, II*, 1 (January 1968), pp. 41-57.

6.____, and A. Madec, "Contribution de la sociologie à l'économie rurale," *Sociologia Ruralis, VI*, no. 2 (1966), Van Gorcum—Assen, pp. 156-178.

7.____, and G. Weill, *L'Agriculture—l'administration française*. Paris: PUF, 1965.

8. Chombart de Lauwe, J. B., and F. Morvan, *Les possibilités de la petite entreprise dans l'agriculture française*. Paris: SADEPP, 1954.

9. Engels, Friedrich, *Origin of the Family, of Private Property and of the State*. Paris: Costes, 1936. Tr. into French by M. Bracke (H. M. Desrousseaux).

10. Friedmann, G., *Villes et campagne, CNRS*. Paris: Colin, 1954.

11. Gourou, P., *La terre et l'homme en Extrême-Orient*. Paris: Colin, 1940.

12. Madden, J. P., *Economies of Size in Farming*, Agricultural Economics Report 107-USDA. Washington, D.C.: U.S. Department of Agriculture.

13. Malassis, L., *Economie des exploitations agricoles de grande et de petite superficie*. Brussels: CEE, 1958.

14. Marx, Karl, *Das Kapital, The Modern Theory of Colonization. Oeuvres de Karl Marx, Economie I*. Paris: La Pléiade, 1963, Part VIII, Chapter XXXIII.

15. Olman, Bertell, "Alienation and the Law of Value," *Le Capital, cent ans après—Cahiers de l'ISEA*, Paris, June 6, 1967, pp. 89-124.

16. Wakefield, E. G., *England and America*. London: R. Bentley, 1833, 2 vol.

17. Woelkoff, A., *Verteilung der Bevolkerung auf der Erde unter dem Einfluss der Naturverhaltnisse and der menschlichen Tatigkeit.* Gotha: Petermann's Mitteilungen, 1905.

18. Zimmerman, Carle C., *Outlines of Cultural Rural Sociology.* Cambridge, Mass.: Harvard University Press, 1948.

19. Zimmerman, E. W., *World Resources and Industries.* New York and London: Harper, 1933.

Part One

V. Agrarian Reform
and Cooperative
Institutions

16. Man-Land
Relationship and
Rural Development
in Overpopulated
Countries

V. M. Dandekar

It will be useful to begin by identifying the overpopulated countries of
the world and getting a quantitative notion of the burden of the world
population they bear. The overpopulated countries are of course the
countries of South and East Asia. Even if we exclude Japan, which in
spite of its high density is now a highly developed country, the countries of South and East Asia account for over half the world's population. But they possess less than one-seventh of the world's agricultural
land. The man-land ratio in these countries averages 107 persons per
100 acres. In contrast stand the countries of Oceania, Southern Africa,
and the River Plata countries of South America. These countries have
over 20 percent of the world's agricultural land; but they support less
than 2 percent of the world's population, the man-land ratio being 2.5
persons per 100 acres. Somewhat better populated are the United
States, Canada, Mexico, and the Soviet Union. They have over 30 percent of the world's agricultural land; but they support less than 15
percent of the world's population, the man-land ratio being 15 persons
per 100 acres. The two groups of countries together have more than
half the world's agricultural land but they support barely one-sixth of
the world's population. This is exactly the opposite of the situation in
South and East Asia.

Overpopulation and the Asian Drama

Myrdal (*Asian Drama*, New York: Pantheon, 1969) surely knows these
facts. But he chooses to look at them differently and dispute the fact of
overpopulation in South Asia. He says:

... in South Asia as a whole the density of population in relation to
cultivated land is about the same as in Europe, if the Soviet Union is
excluded. The agrarian density, i.e., the number of persons engaged in
agriculture per unit of cultivated land ... is, of course, considerably
higher than in Europe. Typically, there are not much more than two
hectares per agricultural family in South Asia as against some five
hectares in Europe. To bring this comparison into the right perspective,
allowance must, however, be made for the huge difference in agricultural technique. In South Asia, human labour and bullocks are still, in
the main, the sole source of power. In comparison with Europe, the

V. M. Dandekar—India. Director, Indian School of Political Economy, Poona;
1966 to 1968, Director of the Gokhale Institute of Politics and Economics,
Poona; since 1954 active with FAO in study teams and as consultant in many
underdeveloped countries.

crop pattern in South Asia also implies a more labour-intensive agricultural production. . . . When taking into account both the more labour-intensive techniques applied and the choice of crops requiring more labour input, the agrarian density in South Asia is perhaps not surprisingly high, even if we should be aware of the opposite causal relation, and that labour-intensive patterns are partly a function of the high man/land ratio" (p. 432).

This is a strange argument and is equivalent to denying that a man is poor by pointing out that he eats so little, clothes less, and has no roof over his head, and implying that probably his needs are small. It is surprising that it should come from one who understands so well the phenomena of circular and cumulative causation [ibid., pp. 1843 ff.].

Having dismissed the fact of overpopulation in South Asia, Myrdal naturally denies that overpopulation is the main cause of poverty in this region. He says:

. . . certain facts . . . dictate caution in accepting without important qualifications this common view that South Asia is severely "overpopulated" and that the density of population, resulting in "unemployment" and "under-employment" is the main cause of poverty in the region . . . the very low average agricultural yield per hectare in the larger parts of South Asia contradicts the impression that, throughout the region, rural pauperization is mainly the result of too much labour being devoted to too little land. If the overall view is taken, the agriculture in the region, in spite of the labour intensity in regard to production methods and crop patterns, has rather to be characterised as an "extensive" one. The implications of this conclusion is that, *even without radical changes in technology, it should be possible to extract very much larger yields from the available land by raising the input and efficiency of the labour force* [ibid., pp. 431-433, italics original].

This again is a strange argument. In South Asia, agricultural yields are very low and labor is underutilized. The two facts are put together and conclusion is drawn that greater labor input would lead to much larger yields. Why then does labor remain underutilized? Because "the behaviour patterns of labour are deeply rooted in attitudes that, deriving strength from the institutional framework of society, have hardened into mores" (ibid., p. 1242). In plain English, agricultural yields in South Asia are low because the people are lazy and would not work even for a better life. One wishes that the situation were as simple, for then, as Myrdal expects, "educational reform and the exhortative elements in government-sponsored propaganda and agricultural extension work" would do the trick and "have the effect of making people work longer and harder" (ibid., p. 1295). Unfortunately, the situation is a little more complicated.

Let us for a moment look again at the comparison between South and East Asia and Europe. Europe is the only world region where the density of population in relation to agricultural land comes anywhere near the same in South and East Asia, though even in comparison with Europe, the density of population in South and East Asia is at least a quarter higher. But there are more important differences between the two regions. First, over the years, Europe has accumulated a vast amount of nonagricultural capital which gives employment to over 70 percent of its population. In contrast, the nonagricultural capital accumulated in South and East Asia is meager and provides employment to less than 30 percent of its population and at a much lower level of labor productivity than in Europe. Second, over the years, a great deal of capital has also been accumulated in European agriculture embodied in developed soil and water resources, agricultural machinery and equipment, milk and meat-producing animals, infrastructure in roads, buildings, and power, and, finally, an advanced agricultural technology.

It is this accumulated agricultural capital which is responsible for the higher yields in European agriculture. In contrast, the accumulated capital in South and East Asian agriculture is meager and basically explains the low agricultural yields in these countries. Further, because this low capital-stocked, low-yielding agriculture is burdened with at least two-and-half times population per unit of land as in Europe, the labor productivity in Asian agriculture is vastly below the same in European agriculture and is often below the minimum subsistence of the population. This is the simple fact of overpopulation in South and East Asia. It creates fundamental difficulties in the economic development of these countries which the Western countries have never experienced.

The contrast between Europe and South and East Asia is not of ancient origin. Indeed, four centuries ago, conditions in the two regions could not have been very different. How did it then happen that, during the past four centuries, while Europe was able to accumulate vast amounts of agricultural and nonagricultural capital per head of its population, in South and East Asian countries, the ratio of capital to population probably declined? In other words, how did it happen that, in the past four centuries, while the rate of capital accumulation in Europe kept ahead of the rate of population growth, in South and East Asian countries, at some point of their recent history, the rate of capital accumulation fell behind the rate of population growth? These are important questions. They are relevant to an understanding of how and why the South and East Asian countries fell into the situation of overpopulation which is another name for poverty. If Myrdal had addressed himself to these questions, he could have justified better the subtitle to his *Asian Drama,* namely, *An Inquiry into the Poverty of Nations.*

Process of Capital Decumulation

What concerns us immediately here is that the process of accumulation of capital is a cumulative process. Once a country achieves a rate of capital accumulation higher than the rate of population growth, it is easier for it not only to sustain but even to improve the rate of capital accumulation. Unfortunately, the reverse process is also cumulative. Once the rate of capital accumulation falls behind the rate of population growth, it becomes increasingly difficult to sustain that rate. The reason is simple. With capital accumulation lagging behind the growth in population, the output per capita falls and surplus over subsistence of the population is reduced. This causes the rate of capital accumulation to fall. The process becomes cumulative, and surplus over subsistence is reduced to zero resulting in zero net savings and investment in the economy.

The process does not stop there because population continues to grow almost independently of the rate of capital accumulation. When output proves inadequate for the subsistence of the growing population, the population begins to live by capital consumption. A state of cumulative deterioration soon sets in with negative net savings and investment and a steady reduction in the stock of capital. To see that this in fact happens, one merely has to notice the state of repairs in which land, equipment, living houses, livestock, and finally the health of men lies in these countries. Of all the disinvestment that occurs, the most serious is that one which occurs in man himself because, through a long process of malnutrition and hunger, it ultimately reduces the productive efficiency of labor below its own subsistence. Existence of such low-efficiency labor is the characteristic feature of overpopulation.

The fact of overpopulation and consequent malnutrition is indeed more serious than appears from the average man-land ratio for a country or a region because the pressure of population is not uniformly spread over the whole land surface. The land resources are generally very unevenly distributed among the population. At one extreme, there are a few large farms owned by a few persons, and there, therefore, the pressure of population is very light. Naturally these farms produce a surplus over the subsistence of the population they support. At the other extreme, there are numerous small farms owned by a large majority of the population. Here the pressure of population is excessive. The farms fail to produce enough for the subsistence of the population, and capital consumption becomes inevitable. In between, there is a whole continuum of farms with the pressure of population on land increasing from one end to the other and consequently the surplus over subsistence going from a positive high to a negative low. Somewhere in the middle, there is a point where the surplus over subsistence is zero.

This point provides an analytically convenient division of the over-populated agriculture into two sectors: (1) a sector which is not over-populated and which therefore produces a surplus of varying degree over subsistence of its population; and (2) another sector which is overpopulated, which fails to produce a surplus over the subsistence of its population, and in which therefore dissaving and disinvestment of varying degree prevail. For analytical convenience, we may also include in this sector the section of the population which has no land of its own. The point of division between the two sectors is of course not fixed and static. With growing pressure of population, the margin between the two sectors recedes and the surplus-producing sector continually shrinks.

The two sectors are not physically segregated, and a great deal of traffic, both in land and labor, takes place between the two. Traditionally, the surplus-producing and land-surplus sector rents out parts of its land-resources to tenants in the other sector. This is a peculiarly feudal arrangement evolved to meet the situation of overpopulation. It maximizes employment by creating conditions of pseudoself-employment for all. It should be noted that the family labor of a tenant works on the same principle as the family labor of an owner-cultivator and therefore may work beyond the point where its marginal productivity equals its subsistence and indeed up to the point of zero marginal productivity. It follows that tenancy also achieves, for a given technology, maximization of the output. This is obvious under sharecropping. Here, both the landlord and the sharecropper are interested in maximizing the output because their respective returns depend upon the size of the output. Under tenancy, with a fixed rent, the landlord is usually able to pitch the rent so high that the tenant would not derive even bare subsistence unless he maximized the output.

But the arrangement is not conducive to development and growth in agriculture. The reasons are simple. The landlord class aims at maximum exploitation of the labor of tenants. Because of the pressure of population on land this is possible and easy. In their turn, the tenants subsist by exploiting the land and extracting maximum out of the soil without returning anything to it. It is thus that tenancy, under conditions of overpopulation, leads to a continuous process of capital consumption both in land and man.

The process is strengthened and accelerated when the feudal institution of tenancy is combined with concepts of freehold property and unrestricted rights of alienation in land. For then, the landlords find it possible and profitable to invest their surplus in acquiring more land for renting out and in the allied activities of moneylending, trading, and shop keeping. Growing poverty and hunger in the other sector provide ideal conditions to pursue these activities, and, for a competent operator, the returns to investment in these lines far exceed any conceivable returns to capital accumulation and improved inputs in agriculture. But basically their function is exploitation, and they inevitably result in accelerating the depravation of both land and man. This is the historical process by means of which agriculture in overpopulated countries has reached the present level of low productivity of both land and man.

Reversing the Historical Process

The problem is how to halt and reverse this process. Communism presents a logically well-conceived solution. Over the years, through a process of trial and error, it has also developed a well-tried operational procedure to achieve the desired solution. Briefly, it consists of three stages, the first of which is expropriation. Its purpose is to abolish the feudal institution of tenancy and to destroy politically the landlord class. The second stage is redistribution of the expropriated land in equal holdings. Its purpose is to win allegiance, support, and participation of the agrarian masses and also to demonstrate the absurdity, under conditions of overpopulation, of distributing land in equal holdings on the principle of land for everyone. The third stage is consolidation or collectivization of the land so distributed into sizable areas under cooperatives or communes. It is in this final form that the reorganized agrarian structure is able to meet the challenge of the situation. There is no doubt that the communist strategy can break through the vicious circle of poverty and rescue an overpopulated agricultural country out of the conditions of overpopulation. North Vietnam offers a shining example of what even a small Asian country can achieve by employing this strategy.

But it takes a determined government, supported by a country-wide political cadre and endowed with leadership with rare political acumen, for a country to be able to take this path. Governments wanting in these qualities or what Myrdal refers to as "soft" governments must work within the institutional framework of private property in land. Having accepted this, it is necessary to pursue a logically consistent solution. It seems that the solution to the problem should meet three requirements: First, it must create conditions which will promote agricultural growth by capital accumulation and adoption of advanced technology in agriculture. Second, it must employ all available labor either in current cultivation or in direct capital accumulation in agriculture until it finds employment in the growing industry. Third, it must improve the mobility of labor so that its transfer from agriculture to industry is facilitated.

The case against tenancy is obvious. As we have seen, though tenancy maximizes utilization of labor, it is not conducive to growth in agriculture; instead, it results in the exploitation of both land and man. Governments of overpopulated countries, therefore, rightly desire to curb tenancy. Sharecropping, in particular, is often sought to be abolished and replaced by tenancy with fixed rent. In a sense, this is strange because the landlord takes much more active interest in cultivation under the system of sharecropping than under tenancy with fixed rent. Nevertheless, sharecropping is sought to be abolished on grounds that, under the system, the points of contact between the landlord and the sharecropper are too numerous; that, indeed, the sharecropper is often hardly distinguishable from a serf; and that, hence, regulation of conditions of sharecropping and prevention of exploitation become difficult. These are undoubtedly legitimate grounds and fully justify the attempts to abolish sharecropping.

However, it is often not realized that effective regulation of tenancy with fixed rent is also not easy. It is sought to be regulated by regulating rent and protecting the tenant from arbitrary eviction. The two measures must, of course, go together because one without the other is meaningless. But the two measures together amount to a measure of price control in a situation of acute shortages, and it is not easy to enforce effectively in so unorganized and far-flung a market as exists in land. Hence, the conclusion seems inescapable that tenancy must be abolished first because it is not conducive to agricultural growth, and second because its effective regulation is difficult under conditions of overpopulation.

The abolition of tenancy is usually a double-edged measure. On the one hand, tenants of a certain standing are declared the owners of the land they have been cultivating; the landlords are dispossessed, usually with adequate compensation. On the other hand, under certain conditions, landlords are allowed to resume land for personal cultivation; the tenants, usually of short standing, are evicted from the lands they cultivated. The first process leads to a considerable redistribution of the ownership of land, and the surplus-producing sector is substantially reduced. The second process throws out a number of tenants from the land they cultivated, and their burden falls on the overpopulated sector. But, on balance, the result is a more equal distribution of land than before, though inequality persists. Both the processes lead to an expansion of owner-cultivation, which indeed is the principal aim of the abolition of tenancy.

It should be recognized that legal prohibition of tenancy constitutes an important limitation of the concept of private property in land. An allied and needed measure is the prohibition of mortgaging of land. Continued enforcement of these measures, under conditions of overpopulation, is not easy. As soon as tenancy and land-mortgaging are legally prohibited, they begin to appear in several concealed forms. One familiar form is one in which tenants are declared as farm servants and a mortgage is shown as a conditional purchase, a situation not easy to prevent. Nevertheless, legal prohibition of tenancy and mortgaging helps to direct attention of landowners to possibilities of owner-cultivation. But real positive impetus to owner-cultivation can be given only if, simultaneously, opportunities are created for capital accumulation and introduction of advanced technology in agriculture. In the absence of such opportunities either the old institutions of tenancy and land-mortgaging reappear in new forms, or large farms, which cannot be cultivated by the family labor of the owners, are broken by sell-out and capital is withdrawn from agriculture. Land is more evenly distributed; exploitation of man by man is reduced; but exploitation of land by man continues.

Emergence of Capitalist Agriculture

If, simultaneously with the abolition of tenancy and land-mortgaging, opportunities are created for capital accumulation and introduction of advanced technology in agriculture, owner-cultivation receives a positive impetus and expands rapidly. Owner-cultivation in larger farms can of course be undertaken only by using hired labor. This becomes possible and indeed profitable because capital accumulation and advanced technology maintain the marginal productivity of labor above the wage it must be paid. A surplus accrues which the owner finds it profitable to plow back in agriculture either in the form of greater capital accumulation in the exisiting farm or expansion of the farm by acquisition of more land. The process gathers momentum and capitalist agriculture emerges.

This creates a new situation. Inequalities in the distribution of land, sought to be reduced by the abolition of tenancy, reappear in a more aggressive form, strengthened by more potent economic forces. But the capitalist development initiates the process of modernizing agriculture leading to an increased productivity of land. To the extent it absorbs labor from the other sector, it also relieves the pressure of population in that sector. Of course, it can never equalize the pressure of population in the two sectors. The reason is that the capitalist sector cannot employ hired labor beyond the point where its marginal productivity equals the wage it must be paid. Hence, the marginal productivity of labor in this sector necessarily remains much above the same in the other sector. In other words, the other sector continues to be overpopulated with marginal productivity of labor much below subsistence.

Certain forms of capital accumulation in agriculture, such as those embodied in the development of soil and water resources, result in an effective expansion of the land-capital resources and hence in an increased demand for labor. Certain cultural practices coming along with advanced agricultural technology, such as increased use of fertilizers, as also the mere fact of increased output, may also result in increased demand for labor. To that extent the development of capitalist agriculture in the surplus sector may further relieve the pressure of population in the other sector. But this is not true of several other forms of capital accumulation in agriculture. Mechanization of cultivation generally is labor-saving. Certain cultural practices coming along with advanced agricultural technology, such as use of weedicides, are also labor-saving. The immediate effect of such forms of capital accumulation and technological advances is to reduce the demand for labor in agriculture. Judging by the experience of capitalist agriculture in developed countries, one must suppose that development of capitalist agriculture will, on balance, have the effect of reducing demand for labor in agriculture. Myrdal is overstating the case when he asserts that *"Technological reforms do not decrease the opportunity to improve labour utilization but, on the contrary, increase it"* (ibid., p. 1295, italics original). This is possibly true of the economy as a whole, and in the long run, but not of a single sector such as agriculture.

The process of displacing labor by capital can assume a serious proportion if capitalist agriculture develops in a situation of a free market in land, for then capitalist agriculture may expand by acquisition of more land from the other sector and displace part of the labor subsisting thereon. Hence, in the long run, development of capitalist agriculture, though it will modernize agriculture by promoting capital accumulation and adoption of advanced technology, may displace labor and make the problem of overpopulation in the residual sector even more acute.

To prevent such a development, it is often suggested that ceilings, that is, maximum size limits, should be imposed on even owner-cultivated holdings. An explicitly stated purpose of such ceilings on holdings is to obtain the surplus land for redistribution. In fact, the surplus that can accrue from any feasible ceiling is small and negligible for purposes of redistribution. Hence the main effect of ceilings on owner-cultivated farms is to prevent the growth of capitalist agriculture. Realizing this, it is often suggested that, if it is not feasible to reduce the existing holdings by imposition of ceilings on existing farms, the ceilings should at least be made effective on future acquisitions. This would prevent the expansion of present holdings beyond a certain limit and thus put a curb on the development of capitalist agriculture.

An important consequence of ceilings on holdings follows from the fact that, whatever its justification, a ceiling on landholdings is a ceiling on how far a peasant may go so long as he remains a peasant. Therefore, effective ceilings on landholdings will, sooner or later, drive out of agriculture ability and enterprise which cannot be contained within the ceiling. Such ability and enterprise move out of agriculture into the nonagricultural sector where there are no corresponding ceilings. This may make the agricultural sector politically weak and may have serious consequences on agricultural growth. This is generally recognized. But unrestrained growth of inequality in the agrarian economy may also have serious consequences. Hence ceilings on landholdings continue to be advocated though a concession is made that they should not be too low and that, in fact, they should be sufficiently high to attract ability and enterprise. In general, the ceilings will have to be much above what are called "family" holdings, that is, holdings which can be cultivated chiefly by the family labor of the owners. In order to attract ability and enterprise, the holdings will have to be large enough to be cultivated on capitalist lines with the employment of hired labor. Subject to this important qualification, there will be an advantage in imposing ceilings on holdings because it will prevent excessive labor-saving mechanization in agriculture.

Organization of Agriculture in the Overpopulated Sector

Equal attention needs to be paid to the size of landholdings in the other, namely, the overpopulated, sector. Here, by definition, the landholdings are uneconomic in the sense that, in spite of the adoption of improved cultivation practices, they fail to produce a surplus over the subsistence of the population they support. Hence, the population subsisting on these farms inevitably lives by capital consumption, causing continuous depravation of the land resources. This is generally recognized, and, therefore, along with the ceiling on landholdings, a floor to the landholdings is also advocated. However, there have appeared no practical proposals as to how a floor to the landholding may be enforced.

A common prescription for the ills of uneconomic holdings is to organize them into cooperatives, but this is easier said than done. A primary difficulty is that the uneconomic holdings are not all located in large compact blocks to be organized in effective farming cooperatives. Further, even if this primary difficulty is resolved by consolidating the uneconomic holdings in large enough blocks by exchanging them with other holdings, the real difficulty remains because it is rooted in the situation of overpopulation. The main advantage of the individual peasant holdings, in conditions of overpopulation, is that they afford conditions under which labor may be employed without reference to its marginal productivity. This advantage is lost in the process of cooperativization because conditions of employment in a cooperative farm are usually governed by considerations of marginal productivity. Consequently, even the family workers of the members of a cooperative cannot be employed beyond the point where the marginal productivity equals the minimum subsistence wage.

Of all the problems of a cooperative farm, under conditions of overpopulation, the most serious is how to employ usefully all its labor resources. Obviously, all the labor cannot be utilized in current production. Therefore, a part of it has to be utilized on works which directly create capital in agriculture. It is by this means alone that a cooperative farm may be able to create additional employment and utilize the unemployed labor resources disguised as self-employed in overpopulated family farms. However, to be able to discover, plan, and execute meaningful capital works in agriculture, the cooperative farm has to extend to sizable agricultural regions. In other words, cooperativization cannot be confined to only the uneconomic holdings but must include all the farms in a given region. This goes too close to the communist solution to be attempted by a "soft" government.

Hence, if uneconomic holdings are not desirable but they cannot be organized into cooperatives, there is no alternative to eliminating them by squeezing them out of agriculture. This is not easy, if for no other reason than that it would be inhuman to expropriate the small farmer without giving him any alternative means of livelihood. Nevertheless, it must be recognized that uneconomic holdings are harmful both for the land and the population which subsists on the land. It is also not easy to help the small farmers out of the uneconomic size of their operation. Hence, even if it may not be possible to eliminate the uneconomic holdings forthwith, facilities must be given to the small farmers to move out of agriculture whenever they see alternative opportunities. One of the difficulties in their being able to move out is the lack of mobility resulting from their attachment to land. They are unwilling to sell their land until they are satisfied that the alternative opportunities are adequate and reliable.

The normal process has been for the uneconomic farmer to lease out his land to a tenant, himself to move out into an alternative employment, and finally to sell out his land when he is satisfied that the alternative employment is adequate and secure. A blanket ban on leasing out of land, as we have recommended above, may hinder this process. This must be avoided. Hence, though renting out to tenants should in general be prohibited, the uneconomic holders should be exempted from such prohibition. They may be permitted to lease out their holdings. Being small and themselves likely to move out of the village after leasing out, they are unlikely to exploit the tenant. The tenant may be given the normal security of tenure subject to the right of the small owner to resume his land if he desired to return to agriculture. This will improve the mobility of the uneconomic farmers and will enable them to gradually move out of agriculture.

For the same reason, creating new uneconomic holdings has to be avoided. If land becomes available for distribution or redistribution, it should be utilized, as far as possible, to enlarge some of the existing uneconomic holdings to an economic size rather than creating new uneconomic holdings. This is not done. Instead, the landless persons usually receive a high priority, and the land gets distributed in new uneconomic holdings. Such holdings are not adequate. They are harmful to the land and they reduce the mobility of the persons concerned by tying them down to small pieces of land. The problem of the landless is important and serious; but, under conditions of overpopulation, it cannot be resolved by providing land to everybody.

Conditions for Agricultural Development in Overpopulated Countries

An essential condition for agricultural development in overpopulated countries is to organize agriculture in economic holdings, that is, holdings which create a surplus over the subsistence of the population subsisting on them. Taken together with ceilings on holdings, this means that agriculture will be organized in not-too-small and not-too-large individual farms. Evidently, this is the most desirable form of agricultural organization in overpopulated countries. But this will have to be supplemented by appropriate organizations which will enable farmers to make decisions in larger units wherever they are needed. For instance, in irrigated areas, management of water and enforcement of an agreed cropping program will obviously require joint decision and action on the part of a number of cultivators.

Even in unirrigated areas, an agreed cropping program may greatly facilitate cultivation, protection, and watching of crops. Spraying and dusting of crops with pesticides and weedicides may also have to be enforced jointly. Construction of certain soil and water conservation works and their maintenance may again have to be a joint responsibility. In submarginal lands, suitable for pasture and woodland development, joint management may have to be extended to certain production aspects as well. For instance, for pasture cultivation, it may be convenient to plow and sow with improved grasses an entire block of land without recognizing the individual proprietary boundaries. For woodland development, suitable blocks of land may be planted, protected, and exploited jointly.

There are certain ancillary aspects of farm management as well where joint decision and action will prove beneficial as, for instance, provision of essential supplies, services, and credit and processing and marketing of farm produce. The particular activities where joint decision and action may be necessary and beneficial will, of course, depend upon the nature of land use. Nowhere will it be necessary to abolish individual proprietary rights in land; but appropriate organizations among the owner-cultivators will have to be set up to look after those aspects of land and water management, and farm business in general, which will require their joint attention.

This is not difficult but will require much detailed work on the ground and among the people. If this is not attended to, ceilings on holdings will act only as a negative check to agricultural growth. It may then be advisable to give them up and let agricultural development proceed on capitalist lines without restraints. This is what Myrdal recommends when he says: "it may be preferable to make a deliberate policy choice in favour of capitalist farming by allowing and encouraging the progressive cultivator to reap the full rewards of his enterprise and labour while approaching the fundamental issues of equality and institutional reform from a different angle and by different policy means" (ibid., p. 1380). As he points out: "It would create a climate in which efficiency could be more readily recognized and rewarded. Scarce supplies of technical skill could be rationally allocated by relying more on the initiative among the progressive farmers themselves. Productivity-raising technological reforms would be more readily assimilated. Price policies would be more effective" (ibid., p. 1381).

However, by no stretch of imagination can this "be recognized as a quite radical 'land reform,' " as Myrdal wants us to believe (ibid., p. 1381). Like the "soft" governments of the South and East Asian countries, he too cannot give up the radical appearances and wants to give his recommendation the same kind of "deceptive facade" of which he accuses the "policies and practices now prevailing" in these countries. He suggests: "High priority in this scheme should be accorded to a program to *give a small plot of land—and with it a dignity and a fresh outlook on life as well as a minor independent source of income—to members of the landless lower strata*" (ibid., p. 1382, italics original). This is a peculiarly Asian solution to an Asian problem, namely, try and forget the problem.

Let us therefore remind ourselves that if in a situation of overpopulation capitalist agriculture is to be promoted and encouraged, there is not land enough, at the same time, to give a small plot of land to members of the landless. The landless will inevitably remain landless. In fact, their numbers may grow. It is good that they remain landless rather than be tied down to small pieces of land. There are many who own small plots of land but little dignity or fresh outlook on life. Small plots do not do any good either to the men or the land; they merely reduce the mobility of labor. The fundamental issue of equality cannot be resolved by such means.

But people are willing to be patient if a more elementary issue is attended to, namely, the right to a living through gainful employment.

This requires a twin policy. First, the capitalist sector in agriculture, as in industry, must be regulated to protect the interests of the labor hired in that sector. Second, the capitalist sector in agriculture, as in industry, must be taxed sufficiently to enable all the residual landless labor to be gainfully employed on works which will create capital in agriculture and infrastructure from which ultimately the capitalist sector will profit. Myrdal does not think that this is feasible. He says, "Such a scheme would be resisted politically the more effectively since at both the village and the state levels the power belongs to those who would have to make the most sacrifices, at least initially" (ibid., p. 1362). In the event, their power shall break and the "soft" governments resting on that power shall be crushed under the weight of masses of hungry and unemployed people.

Myrdal is probably right in his assessment that in South Asia, "the opportune moment for a radical reshaping of the agrarian structure has passed" (ibid., p. 1367). But, if the "soft" governments of South Asia and their Western advisers do not see the plain logic of overpopulation, that opportunity might yet present itself again.

17. Agrarian Reform: Erich H. Jacoby
Planning,
Implementation,
and Evaluation

No Real Progress Without Land Reform

Agricultural development in most underdeveloped countries is the only safe way to general economic development. In the majority of the countries in the underdeveloped regions of the world, 75 to 85 percent of the whole population is engaged in agriculture and rural pursuits. Agricultural planning, therefore, is the hard core of economic planning, and it is a very favorable indication for future development efforts that the President of the World Bank, in submitting the World Bank Report for 1968, has promised a shift of the resources of the Bank more to education and agriculture with less concentration on roads, railways, power, and steam mills. This, however, is not sufficient. Development planning should not only be planning for expansion of agricultural production but also for increasing productivity, which cannot be achieved by exclusive investments in the mere mechanics of agriculture.

With the need for emphasis on productivity, elements enter into our consideration which are partly distinct from the world of pure physical factors. An increase of production per man-hour in the long run will be obtained only if the human element has sufficient motivation to produce more. This means that the producer has to be convinced and satisfied that additional efforts will bring him greater returns. The expansion of agricultural production should not be confined to those upper strata of rural society which at present are reached by the extension, credit, and marketing services and which will have the financial resources to apply fertilizers, modern equipment, and better seed. There is little doubt that, as for instance in India, some dynamic developments in limited areas have occurred by institutional changes due to the decline of absentee and noncultivating landlordism, which was the dominant characteristic of agriculture before independence, and consequently in some areas a marked increase in owner-cultivation has been observed during the last decade. Unfortunately, however, this change for the better was concentrated in areas where former absentee landlords have resumed the land for self-cultivation, and where a large-scale eviction of tenants has been carried out. A development of this kind is conducive neither to equity and mass welfare nor to agricultural devel-

Erich H. Jacoby—Sweden. Studied law and economics in Germany and Denmark; Research Professor at the University of Stockholm, the Institute of International Economic Studies; formerly Chief, Land Reform and Settlement Branch, FAO.

opment on a country wide scale. Therefore, more than a routine approach to agricultural education is required to break the stagnation in the villages.

As long as education and agriculture are focused on the present agrarian structure, it will in the best case generate the two-tier system where the privileged on the upper tier produce an ever-increasing surplus while those on the lower tier, comprising the bulk of the rural people, remain bound in agricultural stagnation with a declining standard of living. It is here that the need enters for structural reform and, more specifically, for land reform. Its link with economic development is obvious since only the correction of the agrarian structure can make possible a depth-effect of agricultural education and extension and open up the remote villages for the application of advanced agricultural methods. It has been said over and over again that the limiting factor for many promising fertilization programs and irrigation schemes has been the lack of understanding and cooperation on the lower strata of the agricultural community which are not benefited by the effects of technological progress.

If the new policy of the Bank would include an attack on the strong structural barriers to the application of the results of science and technology in the rural communities and support the planning and implementation of land reform in its broadest meaning, the breakthrough of socioeconomic progress in the underdeveloped countries would be a possibility in the foreseeable future.

Planning of Land Reform
In the pattern of agrarian reconstruction of underdeveloped areas, land reform therefore is the focal point. It is the total effort directed toward the reorganization of the institutional framework of agriculture and having as its end the achievement of economic and technical progress in consistency with the prevalent social philosophy, values, and creed of the community concerned. Just because land reform is a key issue in development, it cannot function in isolation, and therefore it cannot be disassociated from the whole economic process. Land reform, as all rural development schemes, has to be integrated into the pattern of economic planning. Agrarian reconstruction, therefore, has to be seen within the broad framework of a totally reorganized institutional and economic system and should not be narrowed to the focus of land redistribution proper and tenure reform. Neither should these problems be considered in isolation from general development trends nor from

the struggle against hunger, since land reform in itself is an essential part of the armor at our disposal in multiplying and broadening the effects of land development and land-use programs.

The planning of a land reform program determines its final result. It is of great importance even at its planning stage to be aware of the fact that the increase of productivity includes planning for the human factor. The man on the land has to be the center of all institutional planning if we wish to have more than a sporadic expansion of agricultural production. Before the Second World War, the welfare of the people might also have been important for some private enterprises operating in underdeveloped regions, and we know remarkable features of welfare planning on rubber plantations in Malaya and Indonesia; but these features were side aspects of economic development and little more than tolerated additions to hard efficiency and capitalistic calculations. The results of planning of this kind are evident: all over Asia, Africa, and Latin America we find booming commercial agricultural enterprises surrounded by large low-production areas significant for their economic stagnation and poverty.

Planning for the improvment of the agrarian structure will create the foundation for a broadly based agricultural development. To this end, the economic planner has to see the cultivator in the whole context of his economic and social relationships. It will not be sufficient to provide him with the incentive of tenure security based on equitable tenure relations. The blueprint for land reform will also have to include adequate credit, marketing, and educational facilities and a satisfactory infrastructure; in other words, the planner will have to apply an integrated approach which also has to include the concept of land development. If the land reform planner recognizes that the background of the existing agrarian situation is the poverty and misery of the bulk of the agricultural population, he will apply the broadest possible concept of rural development.

Land reform as it is understood here embraces programs of various kinds, as for instance redistribution of land, improvements in existing tenure legislation and systems of land tenure, resettlement schemes for defective settlement patterns, land taxation and land consolidation operations for the reorganization of farm units. In Africa the adjustment of tribal communities to the conditions of socioeconomic programs is of fundamental importance.

In view of the complex character of land reform programs and the great variety of measures which are available, the planner will have to face the question as to whether a developing country should give its attention to all aspects of land reform simultaneously—which in the majority of cases cannot be done because of the limited staff and financial resources available—or whether it should establish priorities for some kind of programs or districts and to determine where the emphasis should be centered.

A considerable knowledge of the agrarian situation and the economic climate and potentialities of the country is required in order to make the right choice among alternative approaches and solutions. The determination of the policy program will be the final conclusion of—as it is hoped—a correct analysis of the agrarian situation.

There are fewer chapters of economic history which provide us with so many examples of badly planned and unimplemented or faulty policy programs than the field of structural reform, which has always been the focal point of controversial interest. Many mistakes and failures could have been avoided if the planning agency had determined in time the first priorities in an integrated approach, such as land redistribution, settlement, tenancy regulations, land consolidation, ceiling operations, and/or land administration. This is also valid for the complementary programs such as agricultural credit, extension, the provision of marketing facilities, or any other important institutional features relevant to land reform.

How to decide about the priorities? One of the most significant discussions at the World Land Reform Conference in Rome in 1966 took place between the Japanese delegate and experts from underdeveloped countries on the problem of tenancy regulations. While the Japanese delegate recommended tenancy regulations as the most suitable first step in a land reform program, since these are more easily accepted than land redistribution, participants from underdeveloped countries contradicted the Japanese point of view; they were perfectly right, since their weak administrative machinery could not secure equitable tenure relations by the implementation of rent control, and therefore land redistribution for them was the preferable approach. This position has been confirmed by the experience of India, where tenancy regulations with rent control were frustrated by the superior economic power of the landlords, while the expropriation of the land of the Zamandaris has been on the whole a success.

The obvious interdependence of land reform with agricultural and industrial development, technical progress, and employment possibilities will prevent the conscientious planner of land reform programs from confining himself to the narrow concept of tenure relations, farm sizes, and farm structure. There actually does not exist a single relationship in the context of the agrarian complex which will not be affected by a land reform program. Land reform interacts with such development of the infrastructure as communications and rural electrification, and will exert a considerable impact on the base of rural migration and the status of farm women.

Such a comprehensive effort, of course, requires high-level policy decisions, and the land reform planner therefore will have to clarify the fringe effects of his proposed program, taking into consideration the main elements and objectives of the country's economic policy. In individual cases it will not be sufficient to formulate the program in accordance with the concepts of mere social justice and equality, since consideration has to be given to technical aspects such as those providing motivation for additional efforts to increase productivity.

It is of crucial significance that land reform planning concentrate on the problems of administration and implementation of the program, since its final result will depend to a considerable extent on the administrative capacity of the country concerned; a land reform program which in its objectives is going beyond this capacity is dangerous, and its final effects will be frustration and defeat. The planner, therefore, will have to make a realistic assessment of the capacity and potentiality for growth of the administrative body, taking into consideration the possibilities for proper training activities.

How can the land reform planner gain the factual knowledge of the details of the agrarian situation and the administrative capacity? A clear analysis of the "economic and administrative realities" is a precondition for successful land reform planning—no less than a survey of the physical resources is necessary for the planning of land development. An appraisal of the economic and social conditions which surround the human factor in a defined area is required to ensure the success of the whole operation. In this way the planner will get unbiased information on the socioeconomic aspects of the area in relation to the people concerned; specific attention must be given to the demographic situation, to the income distribution pattern and its effect on the peasants, to the actual availability of and the access to the resources for the individual peasant and to the kind of resource utilization; institutions and creeds which govern availability of and access to resources are equally subject to the survey.

We have in some underdeveloped countries quite satisfactory statistics about the actual income distribution, but only the institutional survey will explain to us the reasons why the income distribution is in this and not in another way: it will identify the obstacles to socioeconomic progress and on the strength of such information the planner can proceed to the design of land reform and institutional planning—with both feet on the ground.

Of equal importance is the survey of the administrative realities and potentialities with respect to the implementation of a land reform program. The planner will have to make a sober appraisal of the numbers and qualifications of the staff available in the light of the political and administrative needs of the land reform program. The hard core in the work of land reform has to be done by national officials working at the field level where the primary changes will be carried out and contact with landowners and peasants is essential: the decisive battle for or against land reform is fought almost everywhere there, and, unfortunately, at this level, the risk of friction and bribing is the greatest. The planner has to take this into consideration and will have to supplement his socioeconomic program with an effective administrative plan.

In planning for the administration of land reform programs, the designer of the program will have to give specific attention to the concept of institutional planning in order to provide the most favorable conditions for the human factor in agricultural production. Institutional planning concerns the reconciliation of the peasant's position with the economic realities of the country. This task is interlinked with the building of the administrative machinery which has to be geared to the provision of services to the peasant with a view to strengthening his capacity to resist the superior economic forces which have suppressed him in the past; the administration of credit and extension programs, therefore, has to be integrated in the program of the execution of land reform as a whole. But even this is not sufficient since the most active participation of the peasant in development activities and in the execution of land reform has a strategic place in the program: this means the planning of cooperative organizations and peasants' associations.

Finally, the planner who has the ultimate responsibility for the successful completion of the program will have to think of suitable measures to establish an effective system of accountability and evaluation both of the implementation and the subsequent effects of the program. Since no land reform program is better than the administrative machinery which is designed to carry it out, the blueprint of the reform has to decide on the type of administration for land reform and on the question whether country wide or phased implementation is more suitable in the light of the administrative potentialities of the country.

Implementation of Land Reform

The implementation of land reform programs will encounter many difficulties. The principal reason is that the forces opposed to land reform, which have been unable to defeat it on the levels of political decision and planning, will attempt to frustrate it at the stage of implementation. The first, and probably the greatest, obstacle to the implementation of land reform is the prevailing mentality of the status quo, the compulsion which tradition and custom impose on human action, and the scale of values which is recognized by the leading groups of the community. These three components can be considered as a barrier to progress against which the administrative offensive has to be directed.

In many underdeveloped countries the odds are not favorable for the success of controversial reform programs, which are designed to defeat vested interests often strongly represented in the government itself; the fact that the available administrative machinery is weak and also probably divided on the merits of the reform is an additional complicating factor.

After the experiences of the two postwar decades it can be said with some certainty that in the course of the administration of a land reform program, the establishment of peasant organizations and the formation of local government bodies to assist its execution is of crucial importance. In many underdeveloped countries, particularly in Latin America, it is necessary to separate the local political authority from the economic and social power of the landlord. The importance of such a step is obvious since almost everywhere in the developing world the big landowner is the center both of political and administrative influence and control. In Latin America, the big hacienda is generally more than a system for producing farm products; it is actually a unit of government, an agency for developing and maintaining the infrastructure, for providing communication, and for what little there is of education. Furthermore, the hacienda acts as a center for supply, financing, and marketing, and its master has policy and judiciary functions as well.

In the light of the political and administrative obstacles to the implementation of land reform, the organization of an effective executive machinery appears to be an absolute precondition for the success of the whole program; this machinery has to cope with the possible evasion of the law (for instance by concealing facts, ficticiously dividing properties, and finding loopholes in the law), with the frightening of the peasants, or with simply ignoring the provisions of the law. Of greatest importance, therefore, is the establishment of an information department to reach the most remote villages in order to inform the peasants about the content of the reform legislation and encourage them to insist on their rights. This action, of course, has to be supported by organizational measures, as for instance the setting up of mobile tenure litigation courts which visit the villages and make decisions uninfluenced by local pressures and by the organization of effective appeal procedures. The peasants have also to be protected from fear of reprisals, which can be ensured only by the creation of local supervisory committees of carefully balanced composition, the reshuffling of executive officials to reduce local pressures, and the establishment of state agencies to act as intermediaries in the buying and selling of land.

At this stage a crucial decision has to be made: is it preferable to have in areas of agrarian conflict an administration which acts with rough and ready methods leading to a speedy execution of the reform legislation, but causing some limited injustice (in the sense of unequal treatment for people in similar circumstances depending on the local situation), or to have a more homogeneous administration with greater justice which, however, will lead to delays of such magnitude that the whole reform is jeopardized?

In my view the choice between both methods is not difficult: the perpetuation of the present agrarian situation would be the greater injustice, and therefore the rough and ready execution is preferable. But even if this decision has been made, the shortage of skilled administrators remains the greatest difficulty in countries where middle-class education does not exist. An additional difficulty is that the small number of administrators available to the government are largely members of the landowning class with an ideology opposed to the spirit of the reform.

These facts justify the setting up of a separate administrative machinery to implement agrarian reconstruction programs in order to avoid overloading the normal administrative machinery. It will also be difficult to convince the "hard" core of a traditional Ministry of Agriculture in the underdeveloped countries of the need to invite the active participation of the peasants in development activities in general, and specifically in the administration of land reform, which can be achieved only by the strengthening of cooperative organizations and peasant associations.

Without the realization of such a progressive concept, land reform programs will frequently remain on paper or at best uncompleted. Land reform programs have to be executed in a spirit favorable to the peasant—actually with a bias in favor of the peasant in conflicting situations. Any changes in the administrative concept will need more than an expansion of staff; it will require a new start in the administrative sphere by people who are not motivated by the experiences of the past. Examples of the integration of peasant organizations in administrative procedures are the village land commissions of Japan, the farm tenancy committees in Taiwan, the village tenure committees of Burma, and the cultivator committees in Ceylon.

The majority of developing countries have decided to establish separate administrations for land reform and resettlement schemes, since they believed that existing administrations were not suitable for the implementation of progressive land reform legislation and would not ensure the continuity which a land reform program requires. Decisions of this kind have been made by Burma, the Philippines, Ethiopia, the United Arab Republic, India, Chile, Bolivia, Venezuela, and Colombia. The main justification for this administrative approach is the necessary concentration on specific policy issues involved in agrarian reconstruction programs. At a later stage, of course, the new specialized administrations might make a badly required contribution to the renewal and regeneration of the existing administrative systems in the agriculture of the underdeveloped world.

But even if there has been established a specialized agency or department for land reform, there still remains the shortage of skilled administrators; a decision has to be made whether it is nevertheless better to make an attempt to carry out the land reform program on a country-wide scale or to be content with its execution in phases. Many countries have phased the implementation of their programs because of the shortage of administrative resources in terms of trained personnel and finance, as for example, the Philippines and some of the Latin American countries.

Phasing can be qualitative in relation to the land reform program, such as taking tenancy reform first, or quantitative in terms of areas, which means that land reform is proclaimed or implemented district by district. There is much to be said for the phasing of land reform, a method which makes it possible to concentrate scarce resources, increase the security of tenurial reform, train an effective staff, and build up adequate complementary services by districts. But from the psychological, political, and social points of view the phased implementation of agrarian reconstruction programs can be quite risky, particularly in areas where accumulated discontent has led to unrest and where the urgency for reform can easily give rise to a revolutionary situation. From an economic point of view the phasing approach might discourage investments and production since the landowners are reluctant to invest in view of the expected reform measures. Finally, the implementation of land reform in one district might encourage frightened landowners in other districts to resort to evasion practices, as for example, the eviction of peasants and the dispersal of land above the expected ceiling limits.

The difference between success and failure of land reform can depend on the man at the lowest stratum of the local administration—the field level. This official needs detailed knowledge both of the objectives of the legislation and of the practical problems which he has to face, and last but not least, the integrity required to carry out his work successfully. Most important for him to have is the bias in favor of the peasants because of their weak bargaining capacity and the unfavorable balance of economic power in the village. It is therefore of crucial importance to strengthen the field service of the land reform administration by increasing the status and income of these officials and training them in the objectives of the legislation with the view to strengthening their resistence to the local pressure of landlords and traders.

To summarize, it can be said that the functions of administrative services are different at the stages before, during, and after land reform; the advancement of land reform causes changes in administrative objectives, and the psychology of the staff, therefore, must be sufficiently flexible to adjust themselves to the needs required.

The type of land administration as organized in territories once under British control has proved to be an excellent pre-land reform administration, oriented on revenue collection and land development; but land administration during the implementation of a land reform program, and particularly of a land redistribution program, has to identify itself with the objectives of government policy. Usually, this demands a new agency or a reorganization of the entire administration from the highest to the lowest level, and the active participation of those who will benefit from the implementation of the land reform program. Land administration after land reform will mainly be concerned with the defense of its achievements, training, and education of the beneficiaries, and with the reorganization of the farm structure, essentially consolidation operations.

Evaluation of Land Reform Programs

In another context, we have already emphasized the importance of an effective system of accountability and evaluation, which can provide the administration with a true account of progress, achievements, and failures and enable it to make the necessary adjustments in legislation and government services, in time to ensure the achievement of the objectives of the reform. Evaluation of government action is always useful, but it is particularly necessary in a sphere as controversial as land reform. In the institutional field, it has to be organized to the specific needs of a distinct program as for instance land reform programs, community development schemes, and educational programs. This makes evaluation more expensive from a budgetary point of view, but its contribution to the success of the whole program will exceed by far the relatively modest costs of an evaluation procedure.

In the case of land reform the evaluation will have to state whether the administrative machinery executes the legislation in the light of its clearly defined objectives and provides appropriate services to the rural producer, or whether shortcomings in the administrative machinery—as for example incorrect interpretation of the legislation, lack of staff resources, or bias contrary to the objectives of land reform—are responsible for failure. Such an appraisal of the administrative aspects of agrarian reconstruction programs—the so-called transitional evaluation—will have to be carried out concurrently with the execution of the program. It will deal mainly with the following aspects:

To what extent does the implementation by the administrative machinery serve the immediate objectives of the legislation? What are the difficulties encountered in realizing them? Does the program during the period of implementation remain in step with the trend of general economic development, or has it to be adjusted?

Did the administrative action produce the desired effect on the population? How do various groups affected by land reform legislation—the losers, the beneficiaries, and the administrative staff at the field level—react, and to what extent are favorable or unfavorable conditions for implementation established or promoted?

The evaluation should also examine whether unexpected side effects of the implementation—desirable or not—are observed, and to determine the reasons and, if requested so, to recommend remedial action.

Implementation of land redistribution schemes might, for instance, lead to eviction of tenants and increase insecurity, as happened in India in the beginning of the 1950s; there is little doubt that the existence of an independent evaluation service at that time would have prevented a great deal of injustice and human misery.

The evaluation of the ultimate effects of land reform, the so-called subsequent evaluation, has a much broader scope than the transitional one; it will actually comprise the full part which land reform has to play within the framework of the desired agricultural and economic development. This type of evaluation, therefore, has to be geared to the directive of the intended and resulting changes, taking into consideration the ultimate goals of land reform. The questions to be raised might be the following: What have been the effects of land reform on the underprivileged sections of the rural community? Has land reform resulted in the progress of the village economy and has it—directly or indirectly—also improved conditions in the nonrural sectors of the economy?

There has been some argumentation in favor of restricting the evaluation to the effectiveness of the implementation of the program, and it can hardly be doubted that the restricted approach has the advantage of greater practicability; it concentrates limited administrative resources on the most important issue, but it misses, in my view, the examination in terms of the general direction to which the agrarian program is oriented. The authorities responsible for the operation of the program are entitled to learn from the evaluation agency about the effects, including the long-term effects, which may arise as a result—expected or otherwise—from the change in the agrarian situation. Important as it may be to know whether the law has made the desired changes in the tenurial status, it is not sufficient; the evaluating agency, therefore, has to examine both the changes in the entire system of agrarian structure and their effects on the production function and the social balance of society. If the ultimate effects of land reform are not evaluated, the government cannot ascertain whether the legislation was correct and whether its implementation has produced the intended results. This is the most important consideration in a crucial socioeconomic situation which possibly calls for new decisions on the policy-making level.

In practical terms, it is not enough to learn that the intermediary landholders have been abolished, since the planning authority has to know the effects of this measure on production factors and income distribution. In the case of a land consolidation program, it is not sufficient to be informed whether, or to what extent, the excessive fragmentation of holdings has been eliminated, since it is also essential to know the effects of land consolidation operations on the application of advanced farming methods, increase of productivity, employment, working hours, income, etc.: future policy decisions might depend on such information.

The comprehensive approach to evaluation requires a complex analysis which, as its opponents insist, involves of necessity complicated arrangements and delays. The difficulties, indeed, are serious, but they should not be a deterring factor; they can be solved by an adequate organization of evaluation based on the requirements of the individual case. There can be no doubt that first priority lies with transitional evaluation, which is concerned with the immediate objectives of legislation and the effectiveness of its implementation, and that staff resources have to be allocated accordingly. But at the same time it must be recognized that transitional evaluation is but a half-measure and that only the comprehensive concept of evaluation can give appropriate guidance to governments.

While we ask for an independent evaluation agency, we are aware of the fact that every evaluation contains a subjective element and therefore a certain bias, but the process of evaluation itself has to be a scientific one involving the collection of facts and their systematic interpretation; it has to be concerned both with the means and ends of the program. To a certain extent ends cannot be evaluated since they are established a priori and have a strong subjective element; but the means to achieve particular ends can be objectively evaluated.

The special position of the evaluation organization is a very important aspect of the whole evaluation program. The personality of the individual evaluator should not be concealed behind the organization carrying out the appraisal since both the government and the reader of the report have to know whether the evaluator has the knowledge to appraise the situation correctly and his approach in the formulation of the questions.

Within the framework of the assumptions on which the evaluator bases his appraisal, the most advanced scientific methods have to be applied to identify the facts, to bring the latter into proper relationship to one another, and to facilitate the interpretation of the existing agrarian situation on the basis of the established objectives of the legislation. The ideal evaluation is based on the reconciliation of the subjective approach of the evaluation and the scientific analysis of facts. There does not exist any possibility for the elimination of the subjective element from the evaluation process since there is no fully objective economic science; social economics and social engineering have a purposefulness based on political ideologies; to deny this is in itself a subjective approach and reveals a negative attitude to the dynamics of social and economic development. The colorless evaluation report which merely states facts and does not draw conclusions is practically useless and certainly inferior to one which arrives at some conclusions from a stated and well defined point of view.

The methods applied in an evaluation of land reform programs should ensure (1) that the approach is elastic and closely related to the subject under evaluation and that the methods applied match the interaction of the various factors involved in the situation; and (2) that the agrarian situation concerned is covered over a period of time and not only at one point of time.

The organization of properly equipped evaluating agencies is still in the stage of experiment in most countries. While the main purpose of evaluation is to provide the government with impartial and current information on all aspects of the program, it must be kept in mind that the evaluation of agrarian reform measures is focused on highly controversial issues and affect very sensitive antagonistic groups in society. The organization of an evaluation agency, therefore, should be guided by (1) a maximum degree of independence from the agency responsible for the implementation of the program, so as to be beyond suspicion of partiality; (2) professional capability and reputation for objective research; and (3) a limited but highly qualified staff.

A relatively high degree of centralization might prove particularly useful for the organization of the evaluation activities in the field of agrarian reform programs. A central evaluating agency would be able to work out a series of specific economic, social, and technical concepts for the appraisal of land tenure conditions and for the use of data available in the area under evaluation. It should likewise be able to establish a set of suitable criteria in accordance with the various environments which will be subject to investigation. Once this has been achieved, studies and surveys by universities or other research institutions (preferably in the field of long-term research) should be requested.

The central agency should give first priority to and have exclusive responsibility for the transitional evaluation of land reform programs, which calls for the highest authority and might confront local institutions close to the implementation of the program with a number of difficulties. In most cases of transitional evaluation, representative results can be achieved by investigations of a relatively small number of carefully selected typical villages.

By executing its responsibility for transitional evaluation of land reform programs and the coordination of evaluation activities concerning the ultimate effects of land reform, the agency could gradually assume additional functions which are of greatest importance in the sphere of land reform: it could train a qualified and efficient staff of observers and evaluators and serve as the high level advisory agency for the formulation and implementation of agrarian policies.

Bibliography

Annual Report, World Bank International Development Association. Washington, D.C., 1968.

Progress in Land Reform. Third Report, New York: United Nations, 1962.

Progress in Land Reform. Fourth Report, New York: United Nations, 1966.

Report on the 1966 World Land Reform Conference, Document of the United Nations Economic and Social Council, E/4298. New York: United Nations, March 1967.

Report of the Working Group of the Government of India and the Food and Agriculture Organization of the United Nations on Methods for Evaluation and Effects of Agrarian Reform, New Delhi: Ministry of Food and Agriculture (Department of Agriculture), Government of India, August 1958.

Report on the Second Rehovoth Conference, "Rural Planning in Development Countries," Routledge-Kegan Paul, August 1963. London: 1965.

Jacoby, Erich H., "Evaluation of Agrarian Structure and Agrarian Reform Programmes." Rome: FAO Agricultural Studies, No. 69, 1966.

———, "Agrarian Reconstruction." Rome: FFHC Basic Studies No. 18, FAO, 1968.

Part One

V. Agrarian Reform
and Cooperative
Institutions

18. Organization of
Rural Cooperation
in Developing
Countries

Otto M. Schiller

It is one of the most important tasks in developing countries to overcome the stagnation in the traditional sector of agriculture and to achieve by modern methods and techniques an increase of agricultural production and an improved standard of living of the rural population. The organization of rural cooperation is of outstanding importance for the realization of this aim. But the possibilities to induce the progress of agriculture by the adoption of cooperative methods may sometimes be overestimated. The question should be examined first of how far rural development can be promoted without systematic organization of cooperation in the one or the other form.

Individual Approach without Organization of Cooperation

In the developing countries the traditional sector of agriculture is generally characterized by relatively small farming units. As far as Latin America is concerned, large-sclae farms existing there since long ago, many of them not managed by modern methods, could be taken as a part of the traditional sector of agriculture as well. But in the countries of Latin America, too, a large part of the rural population is using the land in small-scale farming units. Whether in developing countries the smallholdings in traditional agriculture are managed by owner operators or by tenants depends upon the existing land tenure system and upon the progress of land reform.

It would be wrong to assume that all small-scale units in traditional agriculture in developing countries are submarginal farms. In accordance with the land tenure systems of these countries there is as a rule a category of family farms with a sufficient size as well. In this part of traditional agriculture some progress can be achieved by an individual approach, too, be it by an intensified extension service or by other methods. The so-called package program in India, for instance, is based on individual extension service, although some functions are carried out by the existing or newly founded cooperative societies. Investigations in the hinterland of the big steelwork of Rourkela in India have shown

Otto M. Schiller—West Germany. Studied agriculture and economics at the Universities of Berlin, Breslau, and Königsberg; since 1960, Professor of Comparative Agrarian Policy and Rural Sociology at the South Asia Institute of Heidelberg University. This article was written shortly before his death in 1970.

that small farmers even without intensified extension service may respond to incentives from outside in a quite reasonable way. It was found that rural families, with a family member employed in the steel-work and sending surplus money home, are using their additional income in a much higher degree than expected for production purposes and even for the education of children.

It is evident that under certain circumstances individual incentives and individual advisory work, even without organizing the cooperation among the farmers, may have some remarkable results. Nevertheless, it is a fact that generally without an effective cooperation among the farmers it will not be possible to materialize agricultural progress in such dimensions as required by the rapid growth of population and by the social needs of rural population in these countries. In considering the organization of cooperation between the farmers one should distinguish between (1) the traditional forms of cooperation (precooperatives) existing in the developing countries from historical times, (2) the classical forms of cooperation according to the rules of the cooperative system developed first in Western countries (e.g., Raiffeisen societies), and (3) new forms of cooperation and integration which only in recent times have evolved here and there partly on the cooperative and partly on another institutional basis.

Traditional Forms of Cooperation (Precooperatives)

For the traditional forms of cooperation among small farmers or the precooperative stage of development there are interesting examples in the old communal organizations of the Indios in Latin America. Apart from their social and administrative tasks they have also some functions in the use of land. A number of families may join to lease the land and use it jointly. In other communities only the pasture land and the wells are used on a common basis. In some parts of Africa the tribe or extended family are the basic elements of the rural social order, and the cooperation among their members is a typical feature of their use of land. There may be fields belonging to several families and used by them jointly. In other regions there may be working groups doing some of the fieldwork on the land which otherwise is used individually.

In some parts of the developing countries irrigation is one of the preconditions for an efficient use of land. Many forms of cooperation exist in the irrigated areas, because there are various processes which cannot be carried out in isolation. Thus, in South Asian countries small groups of 2 to 5 farmers join in farming operations in which the whole group tills the field of one farmer first and then turns to the field of the next one. This way a certain piece of land may be tilled in a very short time, which means a better utilization of the managerial advantages connected with a more efficient use of water. In this respect the psychological effect of working in company may also play a role.

Common property and common use of wells have an old tradition, for instance, in Indian villages. The common use of draft animals may be mentioned as another example of such cooperation. This is necessarily the case when farmers own only one draft animal each and therefore have to cooperate in order to make up a yoke. In many cases it leads to joint work or joint planning of individual work. But the processing of agricultural products as well may lead to some forms of cooperation, as for instance in the processing of sugarcane on a common basis. In many cases the traditional cooperation in India is based on the joint family system.

Precooperatives on the basis of extended families and traditional communities, however, will not lead in all cases to a transition to modern cooperative societies. Modern cooperative societies, in theory, are supposed to be an organization of the weak to give them the power of uniting against the strong. Often, the precooperatives in traditional societies are controlled by the dominating village families. Traditional cooperation, in practice subordination, is one of the several means of the more powerful families to exercise influence and authority over smallholders, tenants, and laborers. In such cases it seems unlikely that the precooperatives will provide a basis for modern cooperation. Nevertheless, it seems to be necessary to mention the traditional forms of cooperation as well, because in organizing modern forms of cooperation these traditions may be of great use.

Classical Forms of Cooperation (Cooperative Societies)
In nearly all the developing countries nowadays the cooperative system of the modern pattern exists, although in some countries only in the initial phase. It is true that in most developing countries the introduction of a modern cooperative system was not based on further development of old traditional forms of cooperation, but induced by impulses coming from outside. This is the case, for instance, in all those countries which formerly were ruled by a colonial regime like most of the countries in Asia and Africa. In these countries the cooperative system and the corresponding legislation in most cases have been intro-

duced by the foreign administration and influenced by the foreign model of cooperative societies.

A typical example is Indonesia, where in 1915 the Dutch regime had enforced the first Cooperative Act, which was quite similar to the cooperative legislation in The Netherlands. Later on the necessity was felt to modify the law to have it adapted in a better way to the local conditions of the Far East. After independence in Indonesia a new cooperative law was enacted in 1958 based on local legal conceptions. Another example is India, where the British colonial system already in the beginning of this century had initiated the introduction of a rural cooperative system in general based on the pattern of the German Raiffeisen cooperative system of credit societies.

In most cases the credit requirements of small agricultural producers were the main reason for the introduction of a cooperative system in developing countries. The transition from subsistence to money or market economy—one of the preconditions for agricultural progress—requires some capital investment which the small agricultural producer in general cannot materialize out of his own resources. In many cases, therefore, the transition to a money economy is accompanied by an increasing indebtedness of the smallholders for whom the only source of credit supply usually is the private moneylenders, be it the representatives of the rural upper class as the former landlords or the rural tradesmen or professional moneylenders.

In connection with this situation quite difficult organizational problems may evolve when starting the organization of rural cooperative credit societies. If the indebtedness of the farmers cannot be lifted up before they are becoming members of the new societies, they will hardly be in a position to fulfil their obligations toward the cooperative society. If the dependence on the private moneylenders continues, they may have to sell their products to them at low prices and may have to get some credits for consumption purposes as well from them.

It would be desirable that the credits supplied by credit societies to their members would be used mainly or exclusively for production purposes. If, however, credits for consumptive purposes can be made available only from private moneylenders, the dependence on them will continue with all its disastrous consequences. It is typical for the situation in India, for instance, that one of the main items of the credit requirements of the farmers up to the present days are the extremely high expenses for family ceremonies.

It cannot be expected that with the organization of the credit societies the necessary capital needed for the credit activities will already in the initial stage be made available by the thrift and savings of the members. It has to be considered that the lack of capital and the low standard of living are typical features of rural population in developing countries. The capital needed by the credit societies for their activities must therefore to a great part be provided by government agencies or banks. In many countries only in recent years special banks have been established for rural credits supplied to the farmers through the cooperative or other channels. At a later stage, when the formation of cooperative capital by the savings of members is advanced, the organization of secondary cooperatives and of central or apex banks may help to reduce the dependence of primary credit societies on state help.

In the initial stage of rural cooperative societies the role of state help is not restricted, however, to the credit supply. Under the conditions as they exist in most of the developing countries, the so-called cooperative movement is actually not a development from below, but must be initiated by some action from above. In many countries there are ministries for cooperatives or government agencies whose task it is to organize and supervise the cooperative societies. It depends upon the political and social order of the respective country whether the influence and the participation of government officials in the activities of the cooperative societies in the course of time will be reduced or will become an essential element of the cooperative system. In India, for instance, nowadays there are tendencies to replace state help more substantially by self-help and to come to the so-called deofficialization of the cooperative system.

The supply of credits for productive purposes in many cases results in the transformation of primary credit societies to multipurpose societies which are taking over the supply of means of production as well as the marketing and sometimes the processing of agricultural products. One of the typical forms of credit are the so-called crop loans by which seeds, fertilizers, means of plant protection, etc. for the current crop season are supplied by the society. The loans are paid back when the product is sold on the market with the help of the society. In many cases such loans are not given in cash but in kind to secure their proper utilization for the planned purposes. The risk that the supplied means of production may be sold on the black market is usually not high.

In a number of developing countries in recent years a new form of credit similar to crop loans has been developed, namely, the so-called supervised credit for production purposes. It means that the supply of credits is combined with a special advisory and supervisory service for which trained personnel are employed to supervise the proper use of the credits. If this service is efficient enough, it is not necessary to observe the approved rules for credit limits on the basis of tangible security but to calculate the additional income which can be expected from the proper use of the credits.

There are regions in the developing countries where not the credit needs but the requirements of the market have been the main reason for the organization of rural cooperative societies. For instance, in regions where the main agricultural product is a typical cash or export crop such as textile plants (cotton, jute, and others), oil plants, or such commodities as tea, coffee, and spices, the marketing and processing of the product must be organized in a reasonable way. To a great part these commodities are produced in plantations or other forms of large-scale farms. In recent times, however, more and more small producers as well are participating in the cultivation of cash crops. In some developing countries, special cooperative societies have been established for the marketing and processing of such products. These are usually called producers' cooperatives, and may also include ownership and management of a processing plant, in a similar way as is the case in plantation enterprises. The cooperatives may also work on a contract basis with a processing plant as an independent enterprise. A typical example for the first case are the cooperatives of sugarcane producers in India which are combined with sugar factories, and which are working in general with good success.

The transformation of primary credit societies to multipurpose societies with activities in various fields may result in some changes of principles. The original principles of credit societies of the Raiffeisen model were, for instance, a relatively small size, an unlimited liability, and a management on honorary basis. But activities in the sphere of marketing and processing require larger units of operation, and with the increasing number of members in most cases it is unavoidable to turn to limited liability and to the employment of a paid manager.

In cases where government agencies only are supplying the cooperative societies with capital, there is no need for unlimited liability, which may scare away wealthier farmers. The government departments, being responsible for the promotion and expansion of the cooperative movement, scarcely will hold members liable for debts of the society, so as not to discourage other farmers from joining cooperative societies. Unlimited liability is not suitable in such cases where several specialized single-purpose societies (credit, marketing, etc.) are existing and farmers want to be members of more than one cooperative society.

The main problem of rural multipurpose societies is to find qualified managers to work in rural areas. Accounting especially requires more skill in multipurpose societies than in single-purpose societies. The process of a certain commercialization of cooperative societies is also going on in Western countries. As experience has shown, the enterprise will lose its cooperative character if the commercialization goes too far and no efforts are made to preserve the cooperative spirit. The experiences made in India with the establishment of large-scale cooperative societies with a membership of more than 1,000 persons were not encouraging. It is also possible to preserve relatively small units of primary societies and to have some of the functions in marketing and processing carried out by large-scale secondary societies. There are examples of this type in Turkey and Malaysia. In other cases the processing activities are left to private commercial enterprises which are working on a contract basis with the farmers themselves or with their primary societies.

New Forms of Cooperation on a Cooperative or Other Institutional Basis
It is a typical feature of modern development that new forms of rural cooperation are coming up which are organized other than on a cooperative basis. This is necessary, for instance, in all such cases where the cooperation is organized by small groups which do not have the minimum number of members required by the respective cooperative law. These may be small groups of mutual aid without any special legal form or groups registered as societies or associations under the civil code of the respective country. Such small groups may engage in the common use of machinery, but they may also organize some joint action in the fieldwork of small farmers. Interesting examples of group farming are given in Japan and Taiwan and may come up also in other countries.

It is remarkable that in Taiwan, for instance, some of the functions which otherwise are the task of cooperative societies in recent times are partly carried out by farmers' associations or farmers' clubs. Similar steps are taken in Thailand as well. Another interesting example for the cooperation on other than a cooperative basis is the so-called Gezira Scheme in the Sudan.[1] This is a partnership between the government,

[1] See Chapter 31, "The Development of the Gezira in the Sudan," by Arthur Gaitskell.

the so-called Gezira Board, and the small tenants using the allotted land individually on contract basis.

It may be mentioned in this connection that quite recently in Iran by a new legislation the start is made to establish, besides the existing cooperative societies, stock companies for the progress of agriculture. Small farmers getting the land allotted on the basis of the land reform legislation are induced to contribute their land to the joint enterprise for the purpose of ensuring the application of modern methods and modern machinery in large-scale units. There are not yet experiences available about the work of these new organizations. But as in the case of similar institutions established quite recently in Japan, it seems to be doubtful whether these are actually forms of cooperation of small farmers, because they are contributing their land but not necessarily their labor to the common enterprise. In Japan the new term *corporate farming* is used for the activities of such institutions.

In the developing countries there is a tendency to transfer to cooperative societies in addition to the traditional activities some functions in the sphere of agricultural production. In the countries of the Near East, for instance, as in Iran, Iraq, Syria, and Egypt, the necessity was felt to establish cooperative societies in connection with the measures of land reform. The landlords who formerly were leasing their land out to small tenants working for them under quite unfavorable conditions have lost their leading role in agricultural production. With the transfer of ownership rights to former tenants or rural laborers some functions, such as the supply of seeds or credits, the maintenance of the irrigation system, etc., which formerly were partly the duty of the landlords, were to be organized in a new way. Those who are getting the land allotted are obliged therefore to become members of a cooperative society which is taking over these functions. It is the unusual case of obligatory membership to a cooperative society, but it seems to be necessary under the given circumstances.

It can be observed, not only in land reform areas, that here and there cooperative societies are taking over some functions in agricultural production, i.e., in farming operations and animal husbandry. It may be called cooperative promotion of agricultural production, or individual farming on cooperative lines. An interesting example of this new type of cooperative activity is given in Egypt, where in recent years, in a great part of the villages, so-called unified crop rotation has been introduced. The small farmers have to adopt on their small plots of land a certain crop rotation prescribed in a uniform way for a whole group.

The result is that in the respective villages the main crop of the country, namely, cotton, is cultivated in blocks of at least 8.4 hectares where all the plots belonging to the block and used individually are cultivated with cotton in the same season and in a uniform way. This may result in substantial advantages not only with regard to plant protection, but also in irrigation and in the possible use of machinery. Certainly, in the beginning there are great difficulties with the introduction of a unified crop rotation in a number of individual holdings. Furthermore, the restriction of individual decision-making may have some substantial disadvantages as well. Nevertheless, the Egyptian method is an interesting model for the application of cooperative methods in farming operations preserving individual ownership and individual use of land.

For the introduction of cooperative or collective farming in new settlements the experience of Israel is of most instructive value for other countries. But the well-known kibbutzim with their collective farming and their common way of life are to a high degree the result of the unique conditions and the specific human factors in that country. It means that this successful model can hardly be applied in any other country, regardless of the fact that some sporadic examples of similar rural communities with collective use of land and a common way of life exist in a few communal farms of Protestant sectarians in the northern part of the United States and in Canada.

But in Israel besides the kibbutzim there are the ordinary cooperative societies called moshavim, and a small part of them are using the land jointly (moshav shitufi). With the help of Israeli experts a few new settlements in Burma have been organized in a similar way. The ejidos in Mexico are characterized by communal ownership of land, but as a rule they are using the land individually. Only in a small part of them joint managerial methods are applied in the use of land or in animal husbandry.

In India efforts have been made in recent years to introduce a new form of cooperative farming with joint use of land. These experiments are not restricted to new settlements, as is the case in other developing countries, but are also extended to old settled villages. It is of special interest that the attempt has been made in India to perform the transition from individual to cooperative or collective farming in the existing villages of the traditional type, and to organize this way the cooperation of small farmers on a new basis. The results of these experiments are not encouraging up to the present time. But cooperative farming with joint use of land is still an essential part of the Indian program of rural development. The great efforts made by the Indian government to promote cooperative farming may bring some fruitful results in the course of time. For the time being some progress of this type of rural development can only be achieved by essential privileges offered by the government to the members of newly founded cooperative farming societies. These are usually small groups of not more than 10 to 20 farmers, and there are many cases of fictitious cooperatives.

Tunisia is another country where in recent years agricultural production cooperatives with joint use of land have been established on a large scale. A new model of rural cooperation has been developed there by combining already existing large-scale farms formerly belonging to foreign owners with the plots of land of the surrounding small-scale farms establishing in this way large-scale cooperative units. But it is not a voluntary decision of the members to join the new units of agricultural production. If they are included in the program they have only the choice to join the new societies or to contribute their land on a lease basis.

There are also some sporadic examples of agricultural production cooperatives in some countries of East Africa and Asia. But in general it can be stated that up to the present time joint use of land on a cooperative basis in the traditional section of agriculture, i.e., in old settled villages, has not yet proved to be a suitable way for rural development in developing countries. It is the principle of production cooperatives that the members should contribute not only their capital, mainly in the form of land or land use rights, to the common enterprise but their and their families labor force as well. There is a certain tendency to deviate from this principle by the employment of hired labor. In such cases it may be advisable to organize production cooperatives only for the transitional period of land reclamation and resettlement, and to turn afterwards to other forms of cooperatives with individual use of land.

At the present stage of development the organization of cooperation in other forms than production cooperatives, such as cooperative promotion of agricultural production, interfarm cooperation, group farming, and the intensified extension service seems to be more adequate to the requirements and the mentality of rural populations. The application of the classical and some of these new methods of rural cooperation can be regarded as one of the most important means to promote the progress of agriculture in developing countries.

Bibliography

Digby, M., *Cooperative Land Use. The Challenge to Traditional Cooperation*. Oxford: Blackwell, 1963.

Food and Agriculture Organization, *Agricultural Credit through Cooperatives and other Institutions*. Rome: FAO Agricultural Studies, 1965.

Ghaussy, A. G., *Das Genossenschaftswesen in den Entwicklungsländern*. Freiburg: Rombach, 1964.

International Cooperative Alliance, *The Role of Cooperation in Social and Economic Development*. London: Asia Publishing House, 1966.

International Research Centre on Rural Cooperative Communities (CIRCOM), *The Role of Cooperation in Rural Development. Papers Presented to the International Symposium, Israel, Tel-Aviv, March 1965*. Tel-Aviv: CIRCOM, 1966.

Schiller, O., "Die Kooperation in der Landwirtschaft." In P. von Blanckenburg and H. D. Cremer (eds.), *Handbuch der Landwirtschaft und Ernährung in den Entwicklungsländern*, Vol. I. Stuttgart: Eugen Ulmer, 1967.

———, *Cooperation and Integration in Agricultural Production*. London: Asia Publishing House, 1969.

Smith, L. P. F., *The Evolution of Agricultural Cooperation*. Oxford: Blackwell, 1961.

Srivastava, G. P., *Traditional Forms of Cooperation in India*. New Delhi: Publishers Private Limited, 1962.

Texier, J. M., "Traditional Forms of Collective Activities." In *Modern Cooperatives and Traditional Rural Societies: Notes and Opinions by a Group of Experts, International Research Centre on Rural Cooperative Communities (CIRCOM)*. Tel-Aviv: CIRCOM, 1968.

19. Land Reform and   Shlomo Eckstein
Cooperative Farming:
An Evaluation
of the Mexican
Experience

There is general agreement about the importance of both land reform
and cooperation as means of promoting rural development and welfare.
The experience of Mexico is especially illuminating in this respect, for
two reasons. First, large-scale programs have been launched there in
both spheres: Mexico's land reform is perhaps one of the most far
reaching—and most debated—ever undertaken in the Western Hemisphere, and its collective ejidos, though much less publicized, are
matched in scale and scope in few countries.

Second, and more important, cooperative farming in Mexico emerged
as an integral part of the land reform movement there, during one of its
most intensive phases of development. It is this interrelationship which
ties the two topics together in the present paper.

The Agrarian Reform in Mexico has been described and analyzed at
great length, and an abundant literature has been published on the
subject. However, after five decades of execution, many issues raised by
the Reform itself have as yet remained unsettled. They are being debated both in Mexico, which is eager to consolidate the Reform, and in
other countries, equally eager to derive from the Mexican experience as
much insight as might prove applicable to their own specific agrarian
problems.

Among these unsettled questions, the internal organization and functioning of the *ejido,* as related to the general goals of the land reform, is
no doubt one of the most interesting and of immediate concern to all
countries embarking on reform programs. It is the purpose of the
present paper to evaluate one possible route—cooperative farming of
the new settlements—in the light of the experience gained in this field
by the *collective ejidos.*[1]

Shlomo Eckstein—Israel. Ph.D., Harvard University, 1964; Associate Professor
and Chairman of the Department of Economics, Bar Ilan University, Israel; CIDA,
Land Tenure and Agrarian Reform Study Program, on Mexican Project, 1966
to 1968.

[1] The term *collective ejido* was probably ill chosen from the very outset, mainly
because of its association with alien political systems. What is actually meant is an
"ejido producers' cooperative," which may but need not, and generally does not,
encompass an entire ejido. However, the term "collective ejido" is so popular
nowadays that we preferred to use it rather than introduce confusing though
more precise terminology.

Like so many aspects of land reform, the issue of collective farming has given rise to a most ardent controversy, with positions taken at both extremes: from those who see in it the only solution to the rural problems of less developed countries, all the way through to those who consider it a catastrophe for the campesino sector.

Before embarking on the subject, however, let us review briefly the Mexican background.

Historical Background

The Mexican Revolution of 1910 was essentially agrarian. One of its major achievements was the Agrarian Reform, incorporated into the Constitution promulgated in 1917. In synthesis, the Reform consisted of two basic provisions: (1) All villages in need of land will receive the necessary land, which will be taken from public lands wherever available, or by expropriation from adjacent properties. The land thus granted constitutes the *ejido*, and is considered the holding of the village; it cannot be mortgaged, leased, or sold, and rights thereto are transmitted to the ejidatario (member of an ejido) perpetually on an usufruct basis. (2) The *latifundia* is declared contrary to public interest, and should disappear. At the same time, constitutional guarantees are given to all smallholdings in operation, which shall not be subject to expropriation under any circumstances. The maximum size of these holdings is fixed in the same Constitution, at 100 to 150 hectares of irrigated land, or their equivalent. As a result, the agrarian structure would eventually consist of two major tenure groups: ejidos and private small farms.

In fact, by 1968 about 55 million hectares had been granted in 25,000 ejidos to close on two and a half million ejidatarios. The situation at present is far from equitable or otherwise optimal, but roughly speaking about one half of all agricultural land is being held by the ejido sector, and the other half by the private sector.[2]

Although the general concept of the ejido—untransferrable land held jointly by the village—emerged very early from the constitutional law itself, there was no clear idea for a long time of how exactly it would function in practice. Moreover, no unique trend can be observed in this respect. Different methods of organizing the ejido were advocated at different periods over the last five decades, reflecting shifts in both the

[2]This is a gross oversimplification. For a more detailed analysis see S. Eckstein, *El Marco Macroeconomico de la Reforma Agraria Mexicana*, published jointly by CIDA (Washington) and CDIA (Mexico), 1968.

agrarian and agricultural policies pursued, and the role assigned to the ejido as means of implementing these policies.

Until 1934, about 10 million hectares had been distributed to one million ejidatarios. However, the ejido was considered to be only a temporary solution, providing supplementary income for farm laborers working on nearby estates, or providing bare subsistence to the lowest rural strata. It was believed incapable of any superior performance, and thus it was excluded from the more prosperous agricultural regions and also from the irrigation districts constructed by the government. These were confined to the peasant, middle, and upper classes tilling land of their own private property.

Accordingly, the actual functioning of the ejido was at that time more of a social and welfare concern than one of overcoming an impediment to agricultural development. In 1922 an attempt was made to impose "communal exploitation" on all ejidos by administrative regulation, but already in 1925 this was counteracted by a radically opposed law which established the system of ejido tenure as it has remained, with minor changes, to the present. Formally, ejidatarios are free to decide in general assembly whether they wish to farm their land individually, collectively, or in any other form. But in the reality of rural Mexico—and, in fact, of all developing countries—public support and encouragement of any specific farming system greatly determine its chances of success. Much of the history of collective farming in Mexico has thus turned out to be a function of the prevailing political attitude toward the collective ejido.

The Cardenas administration (1934-1940) introduced a radical shift in the entire approach to the agrarian problem, which gave rise to substantial policy changes. The ejido was henceforth considered the basic agrarian unit, called upon to emancipate the peasant not only socially but also economically, providing him with his entire income on levels higher than those known hitherto. Furthermore, the ejido was to turn from a subsistence farm to a commercially productive unit, supplying local and foreign markets. The nation's agricultural economy was to be based in the future mainly on the output of the ejido sector.

The new outlook was reflected in the redistribution of large and important tracts of land: twenty million hectares granted to 770,000 ejidatarios in the 6-year term. The relative share of ejidos grew, between 1930 and 1940, from 13 to 47 percent of all cropland, from 13 to 57 percent of all irrigated land, and from 4 to 53 percent of agricultural capital. In return, their share in agricultural output rose from 11 to 44 percent.[3]

The new policy found expression not only in the quantity of land distributed but mainly in its quality and significance to the national economy. The Agrarian Reform had encompassed, until then, only backward haciendas, mostly self-sufficient and of low efficiency. The areas that were expropriated in 1936-1938 had until then been tilled by well-established and efficiently organized large-scale farming units, producing basic crops for local and foreign markets. If these estates were to be broken up into small ejido parcels and tilled individually, as was being done elsewhere, they would have been turned immediately into primitively farmed corn fields, causing serious damage to the whole economy. No one was ready to take responsibility for such results.

The alternatives were either to squeeze the Reform into the straight-jacket of the existing primitive ejido organization, or else to try to organize the ejido so as to make it capable of applying superior methods of production—and thus to carry the Reform to its logical conclusion.

Implementing collective farming within the ejido was believed to provide the necessary organizational framework. It is important to remember that the idea was accepted not without fierce debate, which has lasted to the present day. At that time, it was incorporated as an integral component into the new agrarian program. It was during this period that about 700 to 800 collective ejido societies were established in some of Mexico's most fertile regions, then expropriated by the Reform Authorities. In fact, only one new group has been created since, comprising seven collective cattle-growing ejidos (1959).

After 1940, agrarian and agricultural policies changed in several respects. The rate of land redistribution declined, as more emphasis was being given to measures aimed directly at increasing the potential for agricultural output: appreciable public investments in large-scale communication and irrigation projects, agricultural credit, fertilizer industries, and improved seeds. On the whole it seems that the private sector received the greater part of these improved inputs, reflecting a departure from the previous outright and almost unconditional support of the ejido sector. Between 1940 and 1960 ejidos' share in irrigated land

[3]Salomon Eckstein, *El Ejido Colectivo en Mexico* (Mexico: Fondo de Cultura Economica, 1966), p. 46.

dropped from 56 to 41 percent, in agricultural capital from 31 to 21 percent, and hence in agricultural output from 44 to 33 percent.[4]

This change in basic agrarian policy left its mark also on the collective ejido, which was henceforth gradually abandoned and eventually opposed. Far from being the "favorite child" as under the Cardenas administration, it was now looked upon as the *enfant terrible* of the Agrarian Reform. On political grounds it was opposed because it was considered a dangerous Communist cell in a highly explosive rural environment. The economic merits of the individual system were now enhanced, based on principles of economic liberalism and private initiative. Others approached the issue on pragmatic grounds: the Mexican peasant, they argued, was socially unprepared for, or psychologically indisposed toward, cooperative farming—good though that may be in itself. Consequently, it was further argued, collectivization only fostered corruption, mishandling of funds, bribery, social domination, and political terror.

The official policy therefore aimed at guaranteeing each ejidatario the possession and use of his personal parcel, while at the same time he was free to pool it with his neighbors if he so wished. More important still than the local measures against the collective was the political atmosphere which turned strongly unfavorable. The sudden turn of the official tide from extreme protectionism to complete apathy and abandonment at the very initial stages proved disastrous to many collective societies. Those that did not succumb altogether suffered a considerable setback in their development. To all, it was a severe test of performance and viability.

Comparative Economic Results

Notwithstanding the difficulties with which the collective ejidos had to cope, as a whole they have proved their effectiveness, as was shown in a recently published study.[5] It will prove worthwhile to review the major findings.

The empirical part of the analysis was based on the statistical data contained in a sample of 2,133 census questionnaires, corresponding to 667 ejidos in 1940, 815 ejidos in 1950, and 651 private farms in 1950. The sample consisted of collective, semicollective,[6] and individual

[4]Eckstein, *El Marco Macroeconomico*, p. 128.

[5]Eckstein, *El Ejido Colectivo*.

[6]In the collective ejido society all farming is done jointly; in the semicollective or "mixed" society, part of the work is done (or part of the land is tilled) in

ejidos, small and large private farms, chosen in 88 (out of Mexico's 2,340) counties. The counties were those where collective and/or semi-collective societies had been registered in a special survey conducted in 1953.

The 88 counties, scattered in 11 (out of a total of 32) states, were regrouped into 16 regions—10 high-income regions and 6 low-income regions. The gap between these two groups of regions is very significant, with respect to both resources and income per ejidatario. The comparative analysis was carried out by the regional units. Hypotheses about the overall pattern of performance were tested by counting the number of regions with "successes" and "failures" in each case, without weighting. In spite of the great differences found among all 16 regions, a clearly distinguishable pattern emerged between the two income groups, regarding the comparative performance of collective ejidos. This was borne out significantly with respect to all aspects analyzed: income, aggregate and resource productivity, and employment.

Income   In seven to eight of the 10 high-income regions, collective ejidos reported in 1950 greater income per ejidatario than did individual ejidos—in most cases 20 to 25 percent more, in a few up to twice. By contrast, they were surpassed by the latter in almost all of the six low-income regions. Income differentials between the two income classes had grown between 1940 and 1950. Moreover, whereas in the high-income areas the income gap between collective and individual ejidos did not change materially during this period, in the low-income group individual ejidos improved while collectives deteriorated.

The following pattern thus emerged: in those regions where ejidos were endowed with adequate natural resources, especially irrigation, capital, credit, and a minimum of technical assistance, collective ejidos were generally more efficient than individual ejidos operating under similar conditions. Furthermore, they compared favorably with neighboring private farms, large and small alike. In contrast, in poor regions, without irrigation and sufficient credit, individual ejidos seemed to make better use of their limited resources.

In the better endowed regions, collective ejidatarios derived higher income levels than individual ejidatarios, because due to their larger

---

common, whereas the remainder is done (or tilled) by each member on his own. In the following review the two subgroups are treated as one, loosely referred to as "collective."

scale of operation they managed to be more efficient, as measured with respect to both their aggregate and their resource productivity. By major resources, economies of scale manifest themselves in different ways. In this respect it is important to remember that the national average of the ejido parcel was 5.3 hectares of dry farming and 1.1 hectares of irrigated land.

Land The collective use of land permits more equitable land distribution, more rational crop planning and rotation, smaller irrigation costs, a more efficient control of pests and diseases, and the greater availability of complementary inputs. It furthermore facilitates the introduction of new lines of production, such as vineyard and livestock, which cannot be grown on tiny units.

Productivity per unit of land was measured in terms of physical yields of major crops; value of agricultural output per hectare of cropland and of irrigated land; average and residual value of farm produce per unit value of land, as compared with availability of complementary inputs.

Labor Labor can be more efficiently utilized in the collective society, due to better possibilities of dealing with seasonal unemployment, of division of labor, and of specialization, management, extension service, and adult education. On the other hand, it was precisely in the management of members' labor that some of the major difficulties arose: mismanagement, mutual distrust, and social discord appeared in some societies. These obviously reduced the potential technical and economic advantages.

Evidence was found in both directions. Many societies succeeded because they produced genuine capable leadership; many failed because they fell prey to dishonest executives. In the high-income regions, but not in the low-income regions, collectives obtained higher average and residual value products per unit of labor than individual ejidos. In some cases, this was due to a greater amount of complementary inputs per unit of labor, denoting greater intensity of work.

Furthermore, labor on the ejido, including that of the low-income groups, obtained more output from each unit-worth of accompanying inputs than did labor on both small and large private farms, in most of the regions analyzed.

Capital It is in the use of capital that the collective offers the greatest economies. Most installations, irrigation equipment, machinery, and agricultural credit in general can be profitably operated only on a scale that exceeds by far the ejido parcel. Private business providing these services have often turned into rural monopolies, doing the peasant more harm than good. In some countries, rural cooperatives formed by individual farmers have filled this gap, but in Mexico these have had little success, unless they covered also the farming process itself. Alternatively, state-controlled institutions have been created for this purpose, like the Irrigation Districts, the National Storage System, and the Agricultural Banks. The Ejido Bank operates formally through local ejido credit societies, which were expected to function as genuine credit cooperatives. In reality, however, except for the collective societies, credit is provided on an individual basis. This, again, is in marked contrast with the pattern observed in other countries, where cooperation in credit is not dependent upon joint farming.

The collective society has stimulated saving and capital formation to a much greater extent than has the individual ejido. Consequently, it has accumulated considerably more capital, mainly agricultural machinery. In addition, in the high-income regions the collective also utilized this capital more efficiently, deriving from it a higher net rate of return, mainly by putting in larger amounts of complementary inputs.

Agricultural Machinery One of the collective's major contributions was the fact that it made possible and promoted the mechanization of the ejido: by encouraging saving and investment, and by providing an adequate scale of operation. This can also be achieved by the establishment of state or private machine centers, but available empirical evidence seemed to prove that the direct cooperative ownership and operation of machinery was by far the most important source of mechanical traction used in the ejido.

Data for 1950 indicated a positive correlation between income and mechanical equipment, but only for higher values of the latter. The use of agricultural machinery is apparently subject to substantial economies of scale, and it will affect income positively only when applied in greater quantities. At the same time, machinery was also positively correlated with the amount of complementary inputs, reflecting the fact that mechanized ejidos also farmed more intensively, particularly in the staple crop areas of the Laguna and the Yaqui. This, rather than the mere availability of mechanical equipment, accounted for the observed higher incomes.

Unemployment and Diversification
However, these very advantages of large-scale production have aggravated in many instances the problem of unemployment, open or disguised, and this for two reasons. First, by the saving in labor require-

ments due to a better organization of the work, and secondly, by the introduction of agricultural machinery, made possible by cooperation. In both cases the "saving" proved rather useless where alternative employment was not made available at the same time.

The new system was expected to be very flexible in its adjustment to unfavorable resource combinations. Much hope was pinned on the possibility of absorbing surplus labor in widely diversified activities—agricultural, industrial, and of public services. That the system did not prove to be so flexible was because the local society was left prematurely to its own devices in tackling problems of such complexity. The potential for diversified employment was undoubtedly there, but it was not realized. It seems to be a fact that the matter never received the close attention and careful treatment it deserved from the authorities—probably because the magnitude of the problem and its consequences were not fully appreciated.

The above considerations apply, with minor variations, to most developing countries embarking upon large-scale land reform projects. The collective system certainly offers economic advantages, but they are not always explicit; whether they will actually present themselves depends on the fulfillment of a series of conditions, quite similar to those that proved critical in the particular case of Mexico.

Social and Political Obstacles
Collective ejidos did not realize their full potential capacity, and developed much less than they were capable of developing and expected to develop. Moreover, many of them divided and disintegrated altogether, presenting today a rather deplorable situation. It is most common nowadays to find one ejido divided into several subgroups of ejidatarios, some collective, others semicollective or mixed, and again others operating as individually farmed credit associations, whereas several ejidatarios work their parcels on their own, untied to any one group. Why did this happen, in spite of the economic advantages which the collective system seemed to offer? The answer lies in the numerous political and social problems that emerged in the collective societies, and which can be grouped under three main headings: political climate, internal conflicts, and mismanagement.

The decisive factor, in our opinion, was the withdrawal of public support during the critical stages of the societies' development. In many cases the collective group was openly attacked and compelled to parcel out its collective land. The indirect effects of political disfavor were as unfortunate, even in those cases where the authorities merely assumed a "nonintervention" attitude. Internal discord and improprieties would not have spread to such a degree were it not for the general feeling of indifference and apathy which the peasant felt in the government. The history of the collective societies is replete with conflicts among the members themselves, which subsequently resulted in their division and segregation. If this phenomenon is directly attributable to lack of internal harmony and cohesion, its ultimate causes were in many cases of an external origin. Antagonistic peasant organizations that disputed the control of an ejido initiated discord there, in order to incite some groups to split off from the others. It was not difficult to find in the ejido a dissatisfied member, feeling discriminated against or rejected by the assembly, always ready to join the "opposition," if this would help him occupy a place on the political scene, local or regional, or personally to benefit from the disintegration of the society.

This segregationist tendency was reinforced by eminently internal factors: lack of mutual confidence; disagreements and clashes on diverse issues; rivalry among opposing kinship groups (*compadrazgo*); the unwillingness to accept orders from a foreman, even though he was elected by the assembly, especially when he seemed to be inefficient as leader or administrator, or of dubious behavior. That is why at present we find ejidos separated into five, some of them up to ten, credit groups, some collective and others individual, where before there could exist only one cooperative credit society per ejido.

Matters were made worse by the many acts of dishonesty, the misappropriation of funds and illegal diversion of products, that interacted as both cause and effect with external meddlings and internal strife. Fertilizers and insecticides received but not delivered, machinery disappearing mysteriously, accounts not reasonably justified—all these necessarily led to a weakening of social identification, a strengthening of mutual mistrust, and a demoralization of the entire group. It is not surprising that under these conditions the peasant refuses to cooperate and prefers to work for himself, even if this proves to be economically less productive—at least he alone will enjoy the fruits of his efforts.

In these circumstances the collective organization of the ejido could well become self-defeating, at least as long as the danger existed of dishonest employees and leaders abusing the economic and political power thus concentrated in their hands. The questions arise: Is this degenerating process inherent in the collective system? Is it inevitable and irreversible? The facts observed in the field seem to prove that it is not. Most cases of corruption appear to have been initiated and spread from outside the ejido. They would not have multiplied or become so general had the atmosphere not been suitable for it; they could have been reduced considerably had effective sanctions been applied at all levels.

In the above review, social and political obstacles to the proper functioning of the societies have been described at great length, because of the important lessons to be drawn from this experience for similar programs in the future, both in Mexico and elsewhere.

Nevertheless, it would be wrong to conclude that in the social sphere all results were negative. Many positive achievements have been registered, and they are very encouraging: well-integrated collective societies, of great entrepreneurial initiative and ability; members with a highly developed social conscience and responsibility; honest leaders, capable and respected; and a long list of social capital investments undertaken by the societies such as schools including free breakfasts, medical services, housing, and many others. One indicator that depends wholly on the ejido's own initiative is the following: 55 percent of all collective ejidos covered in the mentioned study provided their members in 1950 with medical services, as against 24 percent of individual ejidos in the same regions, and 9 percent of all ejidos in the country.[7]

Generalized Evaluation

Land reform programs everywhere have three major goals in common: attaining sociopolitical stability through a tenure framework sanctioned by public opinion and national institutions as just and "progressive"; raising the income and living standards of the great peasant masses; and accelerating the rate of agricultural growth. The weights attached to these goals vary among nations and over time as the power of political forces, the pressure of social problems, and the urgency of economic needs shift with respect to both their relative gravity and the nature of their interrelationships.

The basic question is: Are these three goals compatible? Regarding the Mexican Agrarian Reform, the question can be posed in the following terms. The ejido is an irreversible result of political and social pressures, which came to a dramatic expression in the Revolution. In this respect it has fulfilled its function. But has the ejidatario, on the whole, achieved an acceptable standard of living? Does he participate fully in agricultural development? Recent studies seem to indicate a negative

[7]Eckstein, *El Ejido Colectivo*, p. 482.

answer, although the problem is not exclusively of the ejido sector, but of a large portion of both the ejido and private sectors confined to small plots of land and very limited resources.[8]

The necessary conditions for rural development can be grouped under three headings: resources, know-how, and interfirm organization. The first two are insufficient, if the scale of the operating unit is too small for their adequate application. Unlike industry, where scale is determined mainly by the technological and economic variables, in land reform it is determined by its sociopolitical goals and may thus turn into a highly limiting factor when entered as a constraint into the growth function. It is here where the incompatibility among the three major goals may arise, that "organization" must be added as a necessary condition, and where collective farming is offered as a possible solution.

It is by no means the only one. State farms are one alternative. Public or private enterprises for essential services—machinery, credit, marketing—are another. Cooperation is a third, highly attractive and widely publicized. The production cooperative would appear as an ideal starting point, to bridge the gap between the competing ends of tenure, income, and productivity.

The function of collective farming being so obvious, and the role it has to fulfill so important, why is it meeting with such strong opposition? Criticism is launched at three levels: at the political level, for fear of leftish doctrines; at the socioeconomic-philosophical level, for belief in private initiative as the only effective driving power for development; and at a pragmatic level, for fear that it simply does not work in the world of hard rural reality.

Regarding the political level, one point comes out clearly from the preceding review: the success of the collective system depends to a large extent on its depolitization. By this we do not mean that "politics must be kept out of the societies"—it cannot be and should not be so kept out. Peasants as citizens must manifest themselves politically, and this is an undeniable part of the process of development. Furthermore, peasant organizations unfold in a political environment, and it is the backing of these organizations that has upheld and supported the societies, both in developed and in developing countries. Finally, a favorable political climate is required if the system is to prosper, as well as a clearly defined agrarian policy. What is intended, then, is to depoliticize the issue of the system of organization, not the members of

[8] For the problem of the "minifundio," see Eckstein, *El Marco Macroeconomico*, pp. 109 ff.

the societies, neither the society itself nor the forces that generate the agrarian and agricultural program. Not the politician must decide where and when it would be convenient to introduce any particular type of cooperation—this decision concerns the economist, sociologist, and microplanner. But it is up to the policy maker to determine the broad aims to be obtained and the resources to be allocated to this end.

Regarding the need for a personal motivating power of development, it is clear that not only a theory of cooperation is required, but a "mystique of cooperation" as well that would inspire the peasant with enthusiasm and hope and thus turn the collective system into an instrument of economic and social progress. That this is at all possible was amply proven in Mexico during the Cardenas regime. This brings the discussion to the pragmatic level. There exist in agriculture considerable economies of scale, of both a technological and an economic nature. On the other hand, the larger the scale of operation, the more numerous and complex become the social problems, which invariably appear in all cooperative enterprises and more so in those of agricultural production: social friction, resistance to teamwork, real or imputed incompetence and dishonesty of the local leaders, and the like.

These obstacles, which could be called social disadvantages to scale, counteract the technological and economic advantages. In the final analysis, the effectiveness of the collective system will depend on the balance between these two groups of elements, which can be either positive or negative. Naturally, not all economic variables enter the scale function positively, neither is antisocial behavior always unavoidable in group work; but for analytical purposes, it is convenient to maintain this dichotomy.

Since we are dealing with a social organism and not a line of automatic equipment, acceptance and hence viability of the system will depend, not on the objective balance of the technician, but on the subjective evaluation of each group of peasants. They will carefully weigh the tangible and effective benefits that may result from any form of cooperation against the social problems which they feel they will have to face. These are related facets; the exercise of power by local leaders might be readily accepted when the benefits directly attributable to the functioning of the society are substantial, but it can turn into an insurmountable obstacle when the material advantages of cooperation are not that obvious.

This is why the merits of the collective system are not universally valid in all places and at all times. In mechanized farming, large-scale plantations, or cattle raising, cooperation among peasants is a determining factor; on the other hand, primitive subsistence farming will not benefit greatly from joint work, even if the cooperativist spirit is deeply rooted.

In the social sphere one cannot generalize either. Certain groups have a highly developed sense of social motivation, while others respond only to purely individual inducements. This depends on the social and psychological characteristics of the peasant population in different parts of the world, as well as on their habits, customs, and experiences. Those who have been repeatedly deceived by immoral leaders will not easily be lured into a cooperative venture, even if it might appear to be very profitable. The most important fact is that neither the positive nor the negative elements are constant; on the contrary, they change constantly and what was true yesterday need no longer be true today. It is precisely in these changes that man can and must intervene, inducing those possible transformations that will bring us closer to the final social and economic goals of development.

Consequently, both the technological economies as well as the social diseconomies in any program of rural development must be considered integral variables rather than predetermined constants. When it is desired to raise agricultural productivity, by intensifying and diversifying it, and by providing it with appropriate natural (land and water), capital (credit and equipment), and human resources (improved techniques and know-how)—then the cooperative organization of production not only is justified but can become a major instrument of promotion. However, if one intends to launch the collective gospel as a panacea for all rural problems, without basically modifying the structure and methods of production, nothing much will be achieved and the mystique of cooperation will evaporate very soon in an economic vacuum, not without leaving a bitter aftertaste of failure and frustration.

Similarly, the planner can and must treat directly the social variables; they will be affected by his economic measures anyhow. Positive steps, such as careful and detailed microplanning at the local level, training courses, and an adequate extension service, can avoid many difficulties which appear when solutions are improvised to problems after they have arisen, mostly by incompetent personnel. Preventative measures, such as simple accounting statements to be periodically posted, rigorous auditing, and the severe punishment of mismanagement should certainly reduce immoral acts and the mistrust they cause.

The experience witnessed in Mexico as well as in several other countries also seems to indicate the possibility of collective farming as an initial preparatory stage, aimed at promoting agricultural development in reform areas, although it might eventually transform into family units supported by a cooperative service system. Since this is a highly probable growth pattern, it should be provided for in the microplanning of the reform settlements, so that such a transition be made technically possible in the future.

Toward the Future

In the light of all that has been said, both on the limited success of collective ejidos in Mexico, as well as on the objective difficulties of implementing collective enterprises on a large scale, should the conclusion be reached that the system is not suited to the real world of developing countries? Could it be—as some affirm—that in these countries the peasant is not yet sufficiently developed culturally and socially for adapting himself to a cooperative framework? We think that the experience gained in Mexico proves the contrary. During the first years in which they operated, almost all the cooperatives were successful and prospered, proving the viability of the systems as such. Certainly the peasant of 30 years ago was not more educated and better adapted to the requirements and temptations of a modern economy than his counterpart is today.

The collective society is a complex and delicate organism that requires special attention and definite support from the authorities and organizations with which it operates. This must not necessarily be interpreted as implying preferential treatment in the allocation of resources, but a favorable political atmosphere in which to grow and develop. It can hardly flourish among indifference and neglect; it is inevitably predestined to failure in a hostile domestic environment; it has reasonably good chances of success when adequately oriented and supported.

The greatest advantage of the collective organization lies in providing an institutional and operational framework which facilitates the joint application of all the elements that produce agricultural development, including the intensification and diversification of farming activities, the creation of complementary occupations, and the formation of social capital. In addition to internal economies of scale, it generates external economies which bring the aims of rural progress more into reach.

But this framework must be filled, and therefore to launch a "collective program" implies a serious obligation that cannot be lightly taken.

If the natural and social environment makes it at all feasible; if the decision is taken at the highest political level to encourage and support it; if the necessary resources can be made available to provide it with an appropriate infrastructure, convenient credits, technical assistance, and training facilities; and first and foremost, if able and devoted personnel can be found, technicians, planners, and extension workers who see in this a social challenge—if all these conditions prevail, the great efforts that are required to put the collective system successfully into operation will not only be justified per se, but will play an important role in the solution of agrarian and agricultural problems in many a developing country.

Part One

VI. Extension
Service

20. **Rural Extension**   J. M. A. Penders
in the Advanced
Countries

In order to gain a clearer view of the development of rural extension in the advanced countries, a more detailed comparison between the development of rural extension in the United States and that in The Netherlands may provide more guidance than a mere comprehensive description. Since 1950 an ever-increasing cooperation in the field of rural extension took place in the North Atlantic area (OECD, EEC), which has laid a foundation for appraisal of the respective rural extension services through mutual comparison. Besides, great more or less parallel developments arose with regard to agriculture and rural life. Finally, a study of the development of rural extension in the advanced countries could certainly provide guidance for developing countries, mainly agrarian in their structure, where rural extension has to fulfill a predominant role.

Extension, Vocational Teaching, and Research
In both countries, vocational teaching was introduced first as a public service, followed by research and last by rural extension. These different institutions, however, show differences as to their origin, character, and consequently their mutual relationship.

In the United States, vocational teaching on the academic level straight away received a firm basis in the more or less autonomous institute of the agricultural university, the so-called land grant college. Around this school were successively grouped applied research, apart from a few national or regional research institutions, and extension; the university was extended in order to accommodate these partly independent institutions which, however, were linked to one another. Nonacademic vocational teaching institutions as part of the general high school, which does not come under the Department of Agriculture, are not included here. The extension staff scarcely participates at all in research.

The first agricultural university in the United States was founded in 1862; at present there is one in each state. In 1887 an association of these universities was formed to ensure their coordination. The desire to obtain concrete results of research, disseminated by lecturers in short

J. M. A. Penders—The Netherlands. M.Sc., Agricultural University, Wageningen, 1937; formerly Director of Agricultural Extension, Ministry of Agriculture, The Netherlands; presently Project Manager, United Nations Development Program of the FAO in Turkey.

courses, gave rise to the foundation, beginning from 1887, of agricultural experimental stations. Rural extension proper took its origins from the catastrophic cotton-plant disease ravaging the southern states, which forced the federal Department of Agriculture to recruit a special staff of competent personnel in order to help control this disease on the spot. This pioneering feat, embodying the demonstration method as a new extension feature, aroused public attention and gave the incentive for the employment of the first county agent in 1906.

In 1914, a cooperative rural extension service was established by law for the entire country in cooperation with the federal (national) Department of Agriculture and the agricultural universities of the individual states (provinces) and the counties (subdivisions of provinces). The aim of this service was to extend information and primary research results obtained at the universities and the related research stations. It was intended to make the entire rural population benefit from these results by means of information adapted to practical requirements. Close relationships among extension, teaching, and research are ensured at and centered around the state university level. Within the state, that is to say, the district or local level, and at the nonacademic level, the mutual cooperation among extension, teaching, and research is far less pronounced. The central and departmental authorities play only a minor part in the coordination between extension, teaching, and research.

In The Netherlands, the agricultural university was founded at a later date, and we see first of all the development of nonacademic, specifically church-sponsored, agricultural teaching. The first state secondary agricultural school was opened in 1876; in 1891, the first agricultural teachers took up their functions; and in 1893, agricultural winter-schools were instituted, followed by elementary agricultural schools from 1921 onward. The agricultural university was established in 1918. The teacher of agricultural subjects at elementary and secondary schools can in fact be considered as the pioneer of rural extension.

Rural extension is based on a grounding of vocational teaching in some form or other. The first agricultural experimental station came into being in 1877. After some itinerant agricultural teachers had been working in the service of provincial agricultural societies in the 1870s, the great European crisis in the 1880s gave the government the incentive of appointing, in 1890, the first state agricultural teacher, later called state agricultural advisor acting as agricultural extension officer. Research and extension are chiefly directed by the authorities, in close organizational cooperation, under the supervision of more or less specialized departments of one ministry.

In this context extension too participates actively in research on the regional level, and furthermore contributes to no small extent to the research carried out by central research institutes. Coordination with the specialized division of agricultural teaching is ensured by the person of the Director-General of Agriculture. Particularly in horticulture the relationship between extension, vocational teaching, and research is very close, as the regional horticultural extension officer may at the same time be the principal of the state horticultural high school and director of the experimental station.

There is no formal link between the agricultural university on the one hand and applied agricultural research and rural extension on the other. This fact is explained by the European concept of university teaching which must be "free," that is, not socially committed. With the exception of Scotland, there is no tie between rural extension and the agricultural university in any other European country. Meanwhile a certain change has become noticeable in this respect: the agricultural university in The Netherlands strives to obtain more freedom in agricultural research and is developing certain initiatives in order to be more directly concerned in the preservice and postgraduate training of extension personnel.

Agricultural Extension, Rural Home Economics Extension, and Rural Youth Extension

In the United States, an integral rural extension service was established from the outset. As early as 1900, the work of a rural home economist, Martha van Rensselaer, aroused interest in that branch for extension which obtained a further impetus during World War I. At the same time, rural youth associations were founded around the turn of the century, and later initiated the vigorous development of the 4-H Club. Simultaneously with agricultural extension in the southern states, the pioneers in this field appealed also to the cooperation of rural youth. The pioneer of the agricultural extension service in the United States, S. A. Knapp, discouraged by the distrust he encountered when working with adults, turned to the youth, and in doing so also succeeded by using the demonstration method in pushing his ideas among the older generation.

On the occasion of the institutionalization of the extension services in 1914, all three categories of extension were taken into account. Due to the influence of laws promulgated later, including those of 1946 and

1955, which promoted extension with regard to the marketing and consumer education, respectively, for underdeveloped areas and in which home economics was given an important place, we find a situation in the United States where the professional home economists are nearly as many in number as the agricultural extension agents. Evidently, the coordination between rural extension, home economics, and rural youth extension is promoted due to the fact that all three branches are part of one service.

In The Netherlands, rural home economics education as well as rural home economics extension services were started later, that is, after 1930. Home economics extension services received their first impulse as a result of the crises of the thirties. After that date, rural women's organizations and home economics education—the major part of which is on a church-sponsored basis—developed vigorously; extension services for women are mainly supported and carried out by these two organizations. In addition, a Foundation for Rural Home Economics Extension was brought into being, which provided extension classes in areas inadequately covered by the schools. Rural home economics education, which developed vigorously and in intensity approaches agricultural education, comes, just as the above-named Foundation for Rural Home Economics Extension, under the jurisdiction of the Ministry of Education. The chair for Home Economics at the Agricultural University in Wageningen established in 1954, and that for the Foundation of Home Economics Research established in 1955, do, however, come under the authority of the Ministry of Agriculture. Home economics extension received a second impulse in 1956, when regional development schemes were set in motion. The number of home economists rose, in a period of 5 years, to approximately 60, and the funds used for home economics extension rose from 7 to 30 percent of the total regional development funds. The total number of professional personnel in home economics extension is, by the way, only 5 percent of that of agricultural extension, as are funds allotted to the two branches of activity. In regional development areas, a more integral agricultural extension scheme is being applied.

Rural youth work in The Netherlands undertaken by the responsible organizations is of more recent date, from 1930 onward. In the postwar years, a foundation has been brought into being, with the help of Marshall Aid funds, for the coordination of certain projects for rural youth. There is no formal link with agricultural extension despite numerous informal contacts. As compared to the United States, rural youth extension is much less intensive here, a circumstance which is due among other causes to the fact that agricultural teaching in this country lays a heavy claim on rural youth. According to estimations, 90 percent of the future farmers now enjoy an agricultural education with a gradual rise in the level of the teaching. Manual aptitudes and practical skill occupy an ever more important place in the curriculum, and meanwhile the level of general education is also raised.

It should be noted that vocational teaching in agriculture in the United States at the nonacademic level is a part of the general high school education, although in a section for vocational teaching, whereas in The Netherlands, vocational teaching takes place at specific vocational schools.

The Functional Structure of the Extension Service
Rural extension in The Netherlands is more specialized than it is in the United States, which partly coincides with the more specialized character of the intensive system of agriculture; at the same time it can be explained by the more instructive character of extension. The ratio of all-round agricultural advisers to specialized extension officers in The Netherlands is 1:2. In the United States this ratio was at one time 5:1. In recent years, however, a strong trend can be noticed toward increasing the number of specialized extension workers in the United States as a consequence of greater specialization in agricultural production. This is not only the case on state (provincial) level but also regionally, within a province, per agricultural area that may comprise several counties (provincial subdivisions). At the same time farm management (organization) extension has been expanded, in view of the rapid changes in the traditional relation of production factors (land, labor, capital) to elaborate management plans based on budgetary techniques worked out by research. The local extension staff in the individual county is growing. The coordination of extension keeps pace, among other causes, due to the nomination of a number of general regional supervisors who stimulate the entire extension program. In addition, there is an almost automatic coordination on the state level, since there is only one extension service.

In The Netherlands, too, we have noted a shift in emphasis toward farm management (organizational) extension alongside a high degree of specialization in extension in the past few years, as agriculture in The Netherlands is also faced with a rapid change in the relation among production factors. The coordination of individual extension services for agriculture, horticulture, and animal husbandry is growing gradually on the national as well as on the provincial level, as a result of the activity of the agricultural extension councils. These were started in 1953 with a secretary, a coordinating agricultural extension inspector on the national level, and a coordinating agricultural extension officer on the provincial level.

The extension services in the United States are more decentralized than in The Netherlands, a fact to be ascribed to the difference in organization and financing of the service. In the United States, this activity is the result of the cooperation of (1) the federal authorities; (2) the agricultural university at the state level; and (3) the county at the local level.

The former contributes 40 percent, the other two contribute 30 percent each toward the cost of the extension services. Relatively speaking, the contribution at the regional level increases and that of the central authority decreases. During the last ten years, the federal contribution rose by approximately 100 percent while at regional levels (state and county) it rose by 250 percent. The staff at the federal or national level is relatively small, i.e., less than 100, of a total of approximately 15,000 total staff, 11,000 of whom are working at local levels. Although general directives are issued from a central point, as is also programming, the policy is determined, for the major part, at state and county levels. The federal authority ensures that less prosperous areas also get their share financially.

In The Netherlands, there is a Government Extension Service whose expenses are for the main part borne by the central authority. Since 1935, a trend toward a decentralized policy has made itself felt, as well as a trend toward intensification of the formal cooperation with the professional agricultural organizations. This trend has been promoted by the agricultural extension councils in which farmers', market gardeners', and agricultural workers' organizations participate. Formal cooperation with private industry in the United States is more intensive than in The Netherlands, and this is not limited to agricultural societies. However, it must be stated that financial contributions are not made by the agricultural organizations or institutions at the regional level, but that they are made by the county or state authorities. This implies that the nonagricultural rural population, as well as amateur gardeners in towns and particularly rural women and rural youth, all benefit by the extension services. With the agricultural organizations as such cooperation is casual. At the local level, in the counties, extension committees have been established with representatives of different branches of farming and industrial activity. These representatives do not come only from the formal agricultural organizations and societies, and their activities extend beyond the agricultural sphere.

Extension Staff

The number of staff of the rural extension services in the United States keeps rising steadily, particularly due to the shift of emphasis toward individual and group methods of extension in view of radical structural changes in rural areas. Their number rose from 1,500 in 1913, shortly after the inception of the extension services, to 5,500 in 1920; 6,000 in 1930; 9,000 in 1940; 12,000 in 1950; 14,000 in 1957; and 16,500 in 1960.

Their number at the federal level is approximately 100, at the state level 5,000, and at county level a good 11,000. The number of specialists who are working chiefly at the state level amounts to 2,500. Of the total number, approximately one-tenth is engaged in rural youth extension, a third in home economics extension, and half in agricultural extension. On an average, the local agent covers 1,000 farms, about 500 of which are run on a commercial basis; in this work he is assisted by the above-mentioned specialists on the state level.

In The Netherlands, the number of permanent staff in the extension service rose from 50 in 1910 to 100 in 1930; approximately 400 in 1940; 1,200 in 1950; reached a maximum of 1,500 in 1958, and decreasing thereafter until a constant number of 1,400 employees was reached. Approximately 400 farms of over 3 hectares (7.5 acres) are covered by each extension officer. Extension services are therefore more intensive in The Netherlands. Home economics extension is relatively much less intensive in The Netherlands. In the regional development plans which comprise one-seventh of the area under cultivation where home economics extension is in full development, there are some 60 home economists working temporarily in addition to 150 temporary rural extension workers. In addition, there is limited number of staff of the Foundation of Home Economics Extension, as already mentioned, and of the Information Office of the Council for Nutrition. Socio-agricultural extension has been introduced in The Netherlands, in the service of the agricultural organizations concerned, during the past few years; in the United States it finds its counterpart in the extension services proper.

In contrast to The Netherlands, the entire extension staff of the

United States is academically trained, with the educational requirements increasing. If, ten years ago, a bachelor's degree was sufficient, a master's degree involving an additional two years of study is now considered even more desirable (in half of the states at county level), or even required (in half of the states for an extension function at state level). Postgraduate studies are regarded as very important. The so-called sabbatical leave is a helpful means in this respect. Agricultural colleges and training centers for extension devote considerable attention to extension as a scientific subject. In the United States, candidates can obtain a master's degree in extension as such in thirty states, and a doctor's degree in extension in four states. In addition to this "standard" program of the agricultural faculties, training and study centers for extension have been founded on a national level with financial support from institutions such as the Kellogg, Ford, and Rockefeller Foundations, and the centers for "Agricultural Communications" in Michigan, for "Extension Administration" in Wisconsin, and for "Comparative Extension" in New York.

In The Netherlands, only one-seventh of the total manpower of the rural extension services has had an academic training. However, the need for academically trained extension workers is growing. Postgraduate induction training for the young academically trained extension workers was started in 1957. In the meantime, in-service training takes place through regular meetings and study tours abroad. At present the establishment of a Chair for Extension at the Agricultural University of Wageningen is being considered.

There is a large number of extension officers, so-called "assistants" with a certificate from agricultural secondary schools, who form the main source of recruitment for local extension officers. Requirements keep growing with regard to this category too. Moreover, induction and in-service training in and by the extension service is given serious consideration to this category of extension personnel, who are supervised by academically trained extension workers at the regional and national levels.

The Scope of the Extension Services

The field of activity covered by the American extension services is very far flung, and it keeps spreading. It is not only attuned to the agricultural population but in principle is available to the entire population, and is in fact directed at the rural population in which the purely agricultural element is numerically decreasing. In The Netherlands, the agricultural extension services are completely attuned to that part of the population which is actively engaged in agriculture, and hitherto has been almost exclusively directed to the owners of agricultural and horticultural enterprises. Extension services for agricultural workers have begun to develop in recent years only. Rural home economics extension and rural youth extension too are chiefly directed to the agricultural population.

With regard to actual agricultural extension, we find that in the United States more attention has been devoted to the production per man rather than to the production per acre because of the production conditions prevailing there. The production per acre has, however, assumed greater significance in recent times. In The Netherlands, we find that an opposite trend has developed in recent years. In both countries the average profit margin is dropping and the variation of the profit margin between the individual farms is increasing due to greater demands made of farm management.

Farm organization as a production factor, in addition to farm management, will determine results to an increasing extent. In view of the rapid changes in the interrelation of the production factors, farm organization in extension will grow as compared to farm operation in extension. With regard to the budgeting techniques developed for this purpose, the United States has progressed further with their program planning, a form of budgeting technique to be considered as a transition between a simpler form of budgeting and linear programming. In The Netherlands, however, the simple form of budgeting based on certain branches of the farming activity, namely per surface unit and per livestock unit, is finding a wider application; at present it is already applied in a third of all farms. In the United States, individual and group extension has been increasing since 1953 with the help of additional personnel in its integrated farm and home development program. This program devotes greater attention to farm and home management than hitherto. The latter branch is still in its infancy in The Netherlands.

A particular aspect of the American extension service—and this is equally true of agricultural and home economics extension—lies in the significance imparted to systematic extension, work with regard to the marketing of agricultural produce, in addition to relevant research including so-called utilization research. This is all the more significant in the light of the ever smaller percentage of the consumer price paid for foodstuffs received by the farmer. This type of extension work covers not only the farmers but also the processing industries and commerce, as well as consumer education. This latter is of particular significance in the large cities. In 1946, the extension services were entrusted with this task by virtue of special legislation. For this purpose the extension services were supplied with the results obtained by researchers and specialists.

In The Netherlands, where the agricultural cooperatives are relatively more developed, and where cooperative producers' organizations have been established, agricultural extension has no direct task in this field, although a closer contact of the extension with these organizations would appear desirable. For in The Netherlands, too, the proportion of the consumer price obtained for foodstuffs received by the farmer is on the decline although to a lesser extent than in the United States; marketing plays an ever growing role in order to find the most advantageous possibility of marketing an ever growing production.

Last, extension work in backward agricultural areas is given special attention both in the United States and The Netherlands. We can observe even a striking analogy, in chronology and structure. In both countries the gap between more advanced farms and agricultural regions and the more backward ones is continuously widening. An analysis, carried out in the United States in 1954, demonstrated that one-third of the farms, particularly the smaller farms of the southeastern part of the continent, obtained a relatively low income. In these regions, the number of farmers producing for the market to the extent of $3,000 gross reaches scarcely one-fifth of the total; in the other regions of the country, at least three-fifths of the farmers attain a production figure exceeding $3,000. By virtue of a special law of 1955, a special task was set aside for the extension services in these areas. From 1956 on, schemes of regional development were launched by means of particularly intensive systematic and integrated extension schemes. At the present moment, there are 200 pilot counties in thirty states.

In The Netherlands, the cost-price reports of the Institute of Agricultural Economics demonstrated that there were great differences in cost price between agricultural areas with regard to milk, which forms a stable and relatively important source of income for the smaller mixed farms and, moreover, which represents 30 percent of the total agricultural production, one-third of which again must be marketed abroad. A study of the Department for Regional Socio-Economic Research of the IAE has demonstrated that a third of the entire land under cultivation was backward. It is estimated that two-thirds of the land under cultivation are in need of land consolidation measures. In The Netherlands too, pilot areas have been started since 1956, two-thirds of which coincide with land consolidation schemes; intensive, systematic, more or less integrated extension work has resulted which takes into account aspects of agriculture as such, home economics, and socio-agrarian aspects. At the moment there are about 100 such pilot areas distributed over all provinces comprising one-seventh of the entire land under cultivation.

A few years ago The Netherlands introduced systematic agrosocial extension work by intermediary of the professional agricultural organizations which recruit their own personnel. In the United States, extension in regard to social aspects in agriculture and rural life is carried out by the normal extension services.

The Working Procedure of Extension
In the United States, the population under the influence of the structure of the extension services exerts great power, both individually and collectively, upon the objectives of rural extension, more so than the Dutch population does in The Netherlands. The collective influence makes itself felt through the local and regional extension committees which establish the advisory program. In agricultural as well as in home economics extension, the farmer or the farmer's wife will in the first instance determine what he or she wants to achieve, not the extension worker. The extension worker, however, puts before the person advised wider possibilities of choice by pointing to various alternatives by means of analyses of farm and household and alternative budgets with a view to a judicious organization. Here we see an analogy with the working methods of agrosocial extension in The Netherlands. Dutch agricultural extension is more instructive in its method, although we see a growing emphasis in farm management extension on the elaboration of alternatives from which the farmer must make a choice himself.

An example of the difference—and this is a difference in degree only—of attitude between the two countries is that the American farmer will state that he wants to earn a certain additional amount of money in order, for example, to enable his son to study, upon which the extension officer will indicate how this additional amount might be earned through a different organization or operation of the farm. In The Netherlands the agricultural extension worker will point out to the farmer the possibility of earning a larger income to begin with, without going into any further details, whereupon the farmer will decide whether to carry out the necessary conversion measure and take the necessary steps in his farming activity. Agricultural extension in The Netherlands, therefore, is based on the viewpoint that the economic motive as such is of interest to the farmers concerned; besides, it is more instructive in character. On the other hand, there is a gradual development, as a consequence of in-service training in group "dynamics." Extension workers evolve a more conscious attitude of allowing the farmers themselves to decide on the objectives of extension, an attitude that has been imparted added impetus by the structure of the pilot-area schemes with their regional committees established for that purpose in which the farming population is represented.

Conversely, American extension services adopt in this matter a more dynamic attitude which does not await the passive group or individual choice (decision) of objectives. In this matter, too, a convergence of the extension methodologies in the two countries can be observed.

Extension services in America have chiefly relied on mass methods promoted by the so-called information service. That extension in the United States has greatly developed by means of television, radio, and the written word must partly be explained by the large distance among the various farms. There is one wireless broadcasting station for about 70,000 inhabitants. Nearly half the advisory staff regularly attends a radio program of its own. In spite of the expansion of television, the radio continues to keep a place of its own, for example, in the stable, in the motor car, on the tractor, and in various rooms, this means of communication having thus found a peculiar, more specific function. Three-quarters of the country dwellers have now at their disposal a television set. The advisory service is highly familiar with this means of communication, which lends itself very well to the propagation of work simplification, consumer education, and public relations programs for agriculture.

In The Netherlands, where there are already a great many television sets (one set per ten inhabitants), this extension aid is hardly ever used for this purpose, contrary to England, France, and Germany. That television specially lends itself for instruction has become clear from studies in the United States and England. In both countries television in schools is purposely applied and subsidized as an aid to learning. During the past ten years the conviction gained ground that, as problems become gradually more plentiful, these methods are not effective. The extension staff was therefore expanded through the farm-and-home development plan embodying group and individual methods in extension as well as visits to the farms. In The Netherlands we can, to a certain extent, observe a certain reversal of the development. After the introduction of individual and group methods rendered possible by the relatively intensive extension services, mass methods developed in the postwar period. This was partly to be related to the growing demand for these services which could no longer be satisfied by routine and service and advisory work. One keeps seeking the optimum balance in applied methodology which differs from region to region and according to the educational level of the agricultural population and the subject requiring priority.

The American extension services are quite clearly addressing themselves to the farm family as a whole. This is the prerequisite of the development of a combined, and to a certain extent integrated, extension service for the benefit of farm and household management. In The Netherlands, this method is beginning to find an entry into some regional development plans, although extension is still chiefly directed to the agricultural aspect.

In the United States, work with small groups, numbering between ten and twenty participants in clubs under the guidance of male and female leaders, plays an important part, particularly in home economics and rural youth extension. Adult male and female leaders who volunteer for this work, which they carry out free of charge, are selected and trained for this activity. This aid enhances the effect of professional extension work to no small extent. If the work of these local leaders, who number almost one hundred times the professional advisory workers, were to be expressed in money according to current rates, the resulting total would be of the same order of magnitude as the amount spent on the entire extension services. An analogous institution in The Netherlands is found in the discussion evenings under the guidance of the local extension agent. Generally speaking, however, rural women's and youth clubs are of larger size, so that group work is far less intensive.

Extension Programming

In the United States, extension has been based for some time past on a program established, in the first instance, by the local extension commission, taking into account the priorities in extension. The annual plan of work of the extension services is largely established by the extension services themselves. The extension program on the state level chiefly comprises a compilation of the county programs into which must be integrated activities considered to be urgent by the state extension personnel. This is the case also with regard to recommendations made by the federal extension staff in this matter. Program experts are active both on the regional and on the state levels. Programming as a whole has not been efficient enough in the past, since the organizers tried to please everybody. This defect was recognized and endeavors have been made in recent years to introduce changes in this field also as a result of the rapid structural changes of agriculture and rural society.

On the national level, a commission, in which regional representatives also participated, established a scope report some years ago. In this report some major points were enumerated to which the extension services will have to devote their attention in the near future. On the basis of this report, the individual states have established regionally adapted, more specific programs, which finally give rise to more detailed local programs. As a consequence, we can observe a systematic interrelation from the local to the provincial and the federal levels, and vice versa. Programming moreover acquires a sounder basis, since it is based on preliminary investigation resulting in an up-to-date analysis of agricultural and rural areas, which in turn supplies the basis for a program of work. This time-consuming fundamental programming, the preparatory work of which is done with the aid of selected professional experts on behalf of the extension committee, is carried out only periodically in so-called "program projection."

In The Netherlands, extension programs have been established for agriculture by the extension services for some years past. This program takes account of the wishes of the professional extension staff. In the pilot areas, programming has developed in a manner so as to comprise an ever more integral extension. In these latter schemes, committees comprised of representatives of the profession elaborate programs of points of action, as regards both a long term plan and an annual extension program. The programs gradually proceed from an analysis of the factual situation and trends to be expected in the near future, to an evaluation of the results achieved. From 1961, a new general programming procedure for the entire field of agricultural extension was introduced on the basis of general directives laid down by the national agricultural extension council. Its implementation constitutes a concerted effort of the agricultural extension councils at the national and provincial levels, in which the national extension service as well as the farmers' and agricultural workers' organizations are represented.

There will be national, provincial, and regional programs, which will be the more specific and detailed the lower they are in the hierarchy. It is desired that this programming should result in a proposal for the com-

position of the budget. The extension will, possibly with the cooperation of research organizations, carry out preliminary research, on the
basis of which the organized agricultural profession can indicate the
extension subjects to be attributed priority. The extension service as
such will have to elaborate the detailed plan of its activity, the so-called
annual plan of work, and will have to evaluate the results. Within the
framework of this new initiative, 1961 has served as a trial year.

Evaluation of extension has been carried out in the United States for
quite some time, both from the public relations aspect as well as from
that of improving the extension activity. This latter frequently comprises only statistical reports on extension activities such as number of
visits, meetings, participation in meetings, and so on. Evaluation of the
actual effect of extension is still at the stage of preliminary research. In
The Netherlands, too, this evaluation is still in its infancy.

21. **Agricultural
Extension and
Education in
Developing
Countries**

Francis C. Byrnes
and Kerry J. Byrnes

Wherever one goes in the developing world, one is likely to find growing restlessness about and mounting criticism of the ability of local agricultural educational systems to cope effectively with development problems. While agreeing that development depends upon education, most development specialists find themselves attacking existing educational systems as being dysfunctional. Typically, rather than attempting to correct the problems, they launch ambitious programs to train already educated people, either at home or abroad, in what they need to know or be able to do if they are to help achieve particular development goals.

Several factors confound the issue [17]. First, there is the development specialist's concepts of development and what is necessary to bring it about, as well as his tendency to reflect his experience-bound and culture-bound criteria when he evaluates the operations and products of a given educational system. Second, representatives of different socioeconomic sectors of the developing country frequently identify with diverse expectations of and commitments to development. Their concepts of development vary as widely as do those of foreign development advisers. Third, national leaders may differ radically in educational background, ranging from that which is strictly indigenous to holding one or more advanced degrees from abroad. This range significantly influences the heterogeneity of their concepts of development and what they see as priorities.

National leaders in the developing countries frequently request and support training efforts in specific areas as development stimulants. Less frequently do they recognize the felt need for such activities as a symptom of inherent short-comings in their national educational systems. As a result, the existing educational systems continue, changing

Francis C. Byrnes—United States. Ph.D., Communication Arts, Michigan State University, 1963; Head, Office of Training and Communication, Centro Internacional de Agricultura Tropical, Colombia; member of the field staff of the Rockefeller Foundation.

Kerry J. Byrnes—United States. M.A., Communication Arts, Michigan State University, 1968; currently graduate research assistant in the Department of Sociology, Iowa State University, pursuing Ph.D. in Sociology of Communication in relation to development.

slowly if at all, producing "educated" persons who subsequently must be trained if their "education" is to become viable.

At the same time, while some may benefit from their training, many encounter great difficulty in finding opportunities to use their new knowledge and skills fully, or in gaining the administrative and technical support necessary for their training to become functional. Moreover, their training becomes dysfunctional to the extent that their acquired knowledge, skills, and even orientations (values, beliefs, attitudes, opinions, etc.) are foreign to those of their educated, elder superiors, who tend to perceive new concepts as threats rather than as valuable resources.

Correction of this situation is vital to the efficiency of development progress in the developing countries. The dissipation of energy and time in criticism and defense of national educational systems and their products cannot be constructive. It is time to think positively, to focus attention on some emerging concepts of development and their implications for agricultural extension and education. Included among these concepts are the following propositions:

1. The essential variable and target of development is people.

2. The development of and by people requires new approaches to the organization and management of people and resources—in short, social innovation, the creation of new ways to facilitate and direct change.

3. Social innovation depends upon a willingness to approach problems with an open mind, and upon a recognition of the need to acquire the data necessary for planning and decision-making.

4. This recognition and willingness is conceptualized as the total systems approach and includes continuing appraisal of what education must contribute to changing people, institutions, and processes.

5. The objectives of education must stress changes in the behavior of the student and define clearly the level of performance expectations. These objectives and performance expectations must be derived from the basic manpower requirements of the developing country and specify how the learner's changed behavior will help fulfill these needs.

6. Indigenous models of education and extension are required to produce the kinds of persons the developing countries need, now and in the future. For too long we have wrestled with the conceptual, methodological, administrative, and even diplomatic problems that result from trying to transplant and adapt models from the developed countries [10]. Whatever the model, the relevant functions to be performed

include "(a) the development of new materials and knowledge, (b) the transfer of innovations into use on the land, and (c) the building of human resources to perpetuate the evaluation, transmission, and use of new technology" [26].

Implicit in much of the above is the need for objective application of research to the development of viable educational systems. Unfortunately, relevant research is limited, and much of this reflects the assumptions associated with the study of educational processes and establishments indigenous to the developed world. Nevertheless, we shall present some empirical data related to agricultural educational efforts in the developing countries. We focus on the preparation and performance of the change agent, the extension worker whose response to the farmer's requirements puts to a test the relevance of the knowledge, skills, and orientations which agricultural educators assume are necessary and are acquired in the educational process.

The relevance of the extension worker's response depends upon his competence: the quality of being adequate or sufficient for the purpose. We hypothesize that the more underdeveloped a country's agriculture, the more competent must the extension worker be—and in more areas of competency. The illiterate farmer in the developing country depends almost solely on the extension worker. He does not have the diversity of communications media (telephone, radio, television, newspapers, farm magazines, etc.) or ready access to other information sources (experiment stations, local commercial input distributors, supervised credit advisers, etc.) that are available, for example, to the farmer in Iowa. If the extension worker cannot competently respond to the farmer's questions or if he gives wrong advice, the farmer and many others suffer.

Agricultural education and extension also involve the organizational dimension of the agricultural college and the extension service. This dimension is treated briefly under communication competency later in this chapter. Though we are primarily concerned with appropriate behavioral objectives and performance expectations for extension workers in developing countries, the discussion carries implications for the development of effective "indigenous" models of agricultural education-extension organization.

Innovation, Validation, and Change Agent Competency
Those who study the diffusion of agricultural innovations (i.e., purportedly "improved" varieties, practices, and/or packages of these)

usually focus on the farmer and his social and physical environment in seeking explanatory variables for the acceptance or rejection of recommended innovations. They rarely, if ever, consider the role of change agent competency as a possible explanation of why farmers accept or reject new technology. They do not ask: How does the change agent (e.g., extension worker, village level worker, agronomo, etc.) objectively ascertain that a particular innovation has a significant advantage for farmers in microenvironments other than the area or areas where the innovation was developed? or, Where the farmer fails to adopt or tries and later abandons an innovation, had the change agent failed because of his inability to teach the farmer how to use it?

These questions emphasize the problems of validating both the innovation's minimax advantage and the worker's change agent competency. By minimax advantage we mean an innovation's significant advantage for the particular environment of a given farmer. This depends on, but is not limited to, whether adoption of the innovation is a sufficient condition for (1) minimization of costs in the production of crop and/ or livestock yields that are significantly greater than those obtained by the farmer using his present technology; and (2) maximization of profits sufficiently large that net returns (balance to the farmer after repayment of input costs) are significantly greater than those obtained by the farmer using his present technology and its associated input costs.

Additionally, as the farmer's "test of relevance is whether a practice proves superior on his farm or on his neighbor's farm, and not on the experiment station farm" [6], the extension worker must be able to demonstrate in the farmer's environment that adoption of the recommended agricultural innovation achieves the minimax advantage. One way to determine that adoption of the innovation is a sufficient condition for the minimax advantage and to minimize risk of failure in the demonstration of the innovation to the farmer is to test the innovation in an environment similar, if not identical, to that of the farmer. This requires of the extension worker competency in at least four areas:

1. Technical competency, or the level of knowledge (the ability to recall specific bits of information and facts and a familiarity with terminologies) and understanding (the ability to apply principles and generalizations in a given specific problem-situation) which the extension worker possesses relevant to the crops or livestock the farmer produces, the production practices involved, and the physical environment in which the production takes place. This includes, but is not

limited to, the ability to diagnose typical problems and abnormalities correctly, plus knowledge and understanding in the application of proper treatments.

2. Economics competency, or the ability to weigh (e.g., calculate cost-benefit ratios, interests, etc.) alternative production input and product commercialization strategies to determine whether adoption of the innovation is sufficient for the minimax advantage. An effective strategy must be based on, and can go no further than, the availability of the necessary production input and product commercialization factors. Included among possible production input factors are guaranteed product demand and market price, certified seeds, fertilizers, insecticides, and herbicides, credit, irrigation, crop and/or livestock insurance, technical competency, etc. Included among possible product commercialization factors are accurate and timely information on product demand and market prices, farm-to-market roads, transportation, storage, packaging, wholesale and retail outlets and functionaries, etc.

3. Science competency, or a basic understanding of the philosophy of science and the ability to conduct a simple replicable field experiment which objectively tests whether adoption of the innovation is a sufficient condition for the minimax advantage.

4. Farming competency, or the willingness and skills to perform the range of physical tasks involved in producing a specific crop or animal. This includes, but is not limited to, the extension worker's ability to perform at least the range of physical tasks within the existing competency of the farmer. Also, as mechanization advances, the extension worker must acquire the relevant knowledge, understanding, and skill in the operation and maintenance of various energy-driven machines and processes.

After the extension worker has employed these four competencies to validate an innovation's minimax advantage, then he is ready to demonstrate it to farmers and to seek its adoption. At this time, a fifth change agent competency becomes vital:

5. Communication competency, or the ability to specify and coordinate specific behavioral objectives for relevant audiences whose changed behavior is necessary for the minimax advantage. This includes, but is not limited to, the ability to plan, prepare, and present appropriate messages for and to obtain feed-back from the relevant audiences, which may include in the farmer's environment: the landlord, the credit agency, the input distributor, the wholesaler, retailer, or even the consumer. The most appropriate message for the farmer audience, of

course, is an innovation whose minimax advantage has been validated in an environment similar, if not identical, to the farmer's.

Support for the hypothesis that agricultural development requires competence on the part of the extension worker usually emerges as fortuitous or qualitative data in case studies of development projects [1, 13, 31, 32]. However, case studies usually lack control over numerous intervening factors. In each of the sections that follow, we discuss one change agent competency, reporting available data and related problems.

Technical Competency
The notion that effective extension work involves more than one dimension of change agent competency is not new. Lacking in most attempts to demonstrate the tenability of the hypothesis, however, have been independent measures of the change agent's competency and the "success" of the extension effort studied. These studies have assumed, instead, that the perceptions of extension supervisors, administrators, and even extension workers alone validly measure (1) which of a group of extension workers are more "knowledgeable" and "successful" and which are not; and (2) the area(s) in which a given number of extension workers need training if they are to become "knowledgeable" and "successful."

Warren [39] used the subjective judgments of the supervisors and administrators of a population of Oklahoma extension workers to measure whether a particular extension worker had been successful or unsuccessful. He reports that "the more successful employees of the Cooperative Extension Service . . . had taken a significantly greater amount of course work in the areas of education, sociology, mathematics, science, communication, and economics."

Contado's recent study of communication fidelity between farm management technicians (FMTs) and rice farmers in Leyte, the Philippines [9], included approximate measures of both adoption and technical competency. In order to include (1) the communication purpose or objective of the extension worker's communication behavior, and (2) other farmer responses in addition to adoption, he developed a measure of communication fidelity: the extension worker's effectiveness based on farmer response (awareness, conviction, trial, and adoption) to practices recommended by FMTs. This measure, the quotient of the farmer's response index and the FMT's communication input index, represent the degree of accuracy with which messages encoded by FMTs are decoded by farmers.

As his measure of technical competency, Contado used a test developed by Cuyno [8] at the International Rice Research Institute (IRRI) in the Philippines. Contado's analyses revealed a nonstatistically significant tendency for highly competent FMTs to obtain high communication fidelity. However, Contado also found statistically significant inverse relationships (i.e., negative correlations) between technical competency and the number of years the FMT had been on his present station, the number of years he had been a FMT, and authoritarian personality. Contado concludes "that the longer the change agent is in the service and in his present station, and the more autocratic he is, the less likely he will be to make a high score in a test on knowledge in rice production."

Contado infers that a "rusting" effect possibly operates from being in a station and on the same job for a long time or "that those who had remained for a long time in a particular station and in the same position were those who had failed to demonstrate superior ability that would merit consideration for transfer or promotion." It is also possible that the FMTs had never been competent in rice production. In addition to the kind of knowledge and understanding which can be measured by written tests, a vitally important aspect of technical competency is the extension worker's ability to identify and to diagnose correctly the typical problems and abnormalities which the farmer may have. If the extension worker does not recognize the problem, he can be of little help to the farmer. Further, if he does not know but is unwilling to say, "I don't know," he will guess at either the diagnosis or the treatment, or both. At this stage, the farmer becomes the victim of the extension worker's imagination.

Data [3, 23] from the International Rice Research Institute's rice production training programs illustrate the point at issue. The Institute tests an incoming trainee's ability to identify such symptoms as grassy stunt virus, tungo virus, bacterial leaf streak, bacterial leaf blight, dead heart, rice blast disease, white head, and such specimens as brown planthopper, striped stem borer, pink stem borer, greenleaf-hopper, lindane granules, and rice bug. A similar exercise is repeated at the end of training.

During seven programs, each of a week's duration, 95 North Americans averaged 12.5 percent correct answers on the first day and 81.1 percent on the sixth, while 73 Filipinos averaged 34.9 percent correct answers on the first day and 85.2 percent on the sixth. These data illustrate three significant points: (1) Many rice workers lack the technical competency necessary to teach farmers how to increase their rice yields; (2) where outside agencies try to help national workers, the specialists provided may be less competent than the personnel they are to assist; and (3) when instructional objectives are crystal clear and appropriate methods used, significant behavioral changes can be achieved in a relatively short period.

Economics Competency
Economics competency involves the ability to calculate whether adoption of an innovation is a suffcient condition for the minimax advantage. The literature provides numerous examples of the necessity to recommend innovations having the minimax advantage, otherwise they were not adopted beyond a possible trial stage.

Contado asked each of the local FMTs whether the practices he recommended to farmers in his areas were perceived by farmers to be as costly as commercial fertilizer. On the other hand, farmers were asked if they perceived the practices recommended by their local FMT to be as costly as commercial fertilizer. The FMTs reported that most of the practices they recommended to the farmers were not as costly as the use of fertilizers. The mean of the FMTs' responses fell in the range of "no, not really" and "maybe yes, maybe no." On the other hand, farmers reported that the practices recommended by their local FMT were generally somewhat more costly than the use of fertilizer, the mean of their responses falling in the range of "maybe yes, maybe no" and "most of the time." The differences in perceptions of cost of recommended practices were statistically significant.

Studies of the Farm and Home Development Program at the University of the Philippines College of Agriculture further illustrate the influence of economic factors in extension projects. Of 25 farm practices introduced to 380 farmers, Feliciano [14] reports that 8 were adopted by about 40 to 50 percent. The principal reasons farmers gave for adoption were (1) the compatibility of the practice with the farmer's needs and goals, (2) the seen and proved effectiveness of the practice, (3) use of effective extension techniques, such as the result of demonstration, (4) ease of doing the practice, and (5) availability of necessary resources. The reasons suggest that the farmer's management decision-making is economic-oriented.

Some authors suggest that the extension worker as an information source, just as the farmer's information-seeking behavior, is a critical intervening variable. Myren [28] reports that Latin American farmers search for information: "Even those on small peasant holdings appear to have a considerable desire to produce more efficiently and are interested in information on how this can be done." On the other hand, Myren [29] considers, in another article, the credibility of the information source. "What, then, would adequate information for a farmer about a new practice consist of? First of all, the idea must appear to be credible—it must make sense when considered in the light of his past experience. That is, it must not sound illogical or impossible. But much more than this, the source of the new information must be considered trustworthy by the farmer, and this judgement will be based again largely on his past experience and the observations of people whom he trusts—these may be neighbors, extension agents or even farm magazines which have developed a reputation for honesty and trustworthiness."

Evidence from persuasion research [20] indicates that responses to a message are significantly affected by cues to the communicator's credibility (i.e., his expertness and trustworthiness). Preliminary analysis of more than 900 documents in the Diffusion Documents Center, Michigan State University, however, indicates that few of these documents report use of expertness or trustworthiness as variables in agricultural diffusion studies. Similarly, few studies have considered the relative advantage of the innovation to the farmer as a factor influencing adoption.

In contrast to the inductive approach, implicit in Myren's orientation, to the communication of information, Campbell [4] proposes that extension services take a deductive approach which would include (1) the interpretation of market outlook and changing price relationships, (2) the provision of more specific information about the relation between inputs of various resources and likely output, and (3) the interpretation of major changes in agricultural policy. Campbell's rationale is this:

Many extension programmes have been based on the assumption that farmers use inductive thought processes almost exclusively. Demonstration plots and experiment farms have been used to provide factual information about production practices. If the conditions prevailing on a specific farm are similar to those obtaining on the experiment farm, the operator of that farm might appropriately apply the practice demonstrated on his own farm. The weaknesses of this approach stem from the fact that no two farms have identical physical, economic, and managerial resources and on no privately owned farm can conditions on the experiment farm be duplicated.

If one accepts the fact that farmers can and do reason deductively, the problem of the extension service becomes infinitely easier. The task then is to provide the farmer not with isolated approved farm practices or bundles of practices which he can adopt by emulation, however ill-suited they may be to his immediate situation, but rather to provide him with the information he needs to work out the best plan for his own farm taking into account his personal goals and the resources at his disposal.

In a similar vein, Dandekar [11] proposes that the extension services take a more deductive approach in communicating information to the farmer:

As it is generally understood, the function of extension seems to be to communicate to the farmer techniques and technology which either are supposed to be known, or are imported fresh from abroad or at best are produced in highly exclusive laboratories and experimental stations. The farmer hardly, if ever, participates in the evolution of these techniques and technology, and therefore seldom understands their experimental character.... What is required ... is some arrangement by means of which at least a small number of progressive and intelligent farmers in each district or smaller area may participate actively in the research experimentation and a forum where they may regularly report the findings of their experimentation in a scientific manner.

These proposals for a deductive approach to communicating information to the farmer indicate a possibly needed emphasis in extension services. But the effectiveness of a deductive approach to communicating information on economic conditions would depend on two factors: (1) the economics competency of the extension worker, and (2) those factors affecting the farmer's response to "economic incentives." Let us consider the latter point.

A growing body of evidence supports the proposition that farmers respond to "economic incentives" [40], but it is not clear (1) whether the farmer has the same meaning as the extension worker for such economics terms or concepts (e.g., "economic incentive") as the latter may use to communicate to the farmer, or (2) how much "incentive" constitutes an "economic incentive" for the farmer. Some data from the developed world indicate that farmers vary in the degree to which they comprehend economics terminology.

Felstenhausen [15] measured the degree to which farmers and high school students in a Netherlands farming community comprehend economics terms and concepts. The comprehension was higher for economics concepts which represent events or relationships that are a part of personal experience than for theoretical concepts. Farmers tended to score higher than students on those concepts observable within a limited space in time from market-place activities or in the course of making individual farm management decisions. Felstenhausen concludes:

Agricultural information people should not expect to reach all farmers in a community like Bennekom with the same degree of effectiveness by presenting all material at one level of difficulty or via one medium.... Information generally understood may still not reach some farmers if transmitted only through mass media and groups. This implies, for example, that programs such as agricultural extension which are committed to helping all farmers, should use several levels of approach and not just one. In some cases, separate programs may be needed for farmers who are non-readers and non-joiners.

What do we know about farmers' comprehension of economics concepts in developing countries where the differences between subsistence and commercial farmers are even greater than among the commercial farmers of Bennekom? Though lacking such information, extension workers have tried to "convince" or "persuade" the peasant farmer and villager to adopt innovations assumed to be "improved." In the face of perceived resistance by farmers to adoption of the recommended innovations, not only extension workers but also those charged with allocation of resources for agricultural development, the administrators of extension services, "have eagerly adopted the idea that peasant farmers are not rational economic men" [40].

Some agricultural economists are now seeking answers to the question: How much "incentive" constitutes an "economic incentive" for the peasant farmer? Hill [19] proposes that farmer response to extension efforts in developing countries "is going to be slow at the outset unless relatively simple combinations of improved practices are available, capable of increasing yields by at least 25 to 50 percent on good soils with good water supplies. Increases of 50 to 100 percent would be still better." Hill suggests "that in most circumstances, research workers set as their initial target the development of combinations of improved practices that will at least double yields on the better land."

Hill's hypothesis deserves empirical test. Wharton [41] outlines a conceptual framework for handling the problem and reports data to support Hill's hypothesis. Wharton observes that while agricultural innovations are a potential force for change in subsistence agriculture, peasant farmers resist adopting varieties, practices, and/or combinations of these which they perceive as not maximizing survival. The risks and uncertainties associated with yield, cost, and market price variabilities combined with low levels of income (output) and subsistence levels of living produce a strong "survival" element in decision-making. What is important for the farmer under these conditions is his expectation of output variance if the innovation is adopted compared with the current output variance obtained under conditions of the farmer's present technology. "The subsistence farmer has learned that any recommended technological introduction has associated with it a different expected variance on his fields—a variance which may be wider than that on the fields of the research station. Under these circumstances the determining factor is the comparison between the expected variance of the new technology and the known variance of the traditional technology."

If the farmer sees or expects the negative variance in yield per acre (i.e., the worst that the innovation would yield) to be below what he perceives as a necessary yield to provide for the minimum subsistence needs of his family, the farmer will resist adoption. Thus, "even though the average expected yield may be considerably higher than his average yields with current varieties and practices, the variance in expected yields with the alternative technologies as viewed subjectively by the individual farmer are far more important in determining the adoption of the new seed, practice or factor input."

These considerations lead Wharton to hypothesize that adoption is more likely to occur when the negative standard deviation of yield distributions is above the traditional average output, i.e., that the worst the innovation could do is still better than what the farmer now gets on the average.

Science Competency

Adequately preparing an agricultural graduate in the developing countries is in many ways the task of equipping him with the necessary concepts, skills, and motivations to engage effectively with the physical reality of the immediate environment in which he works. He must not only be taught to look, but where, when, how, why, what to look for, and how to recognize it when he sees it. While he learns much of this in training aimed at increasing his technological knowledge, economics sophistication, and farming skills, he also needs some grounding in the methods and philosophy of science to make these competencies more fully operational.

The frequent lack of preparation of agricultural graduates [8, 24, 35] coming to the United States for graduate work prompted the Agricultural Development Council [37] to remind prospective grantees that they will be expected to increase their mastery of the three rudimentary skills—perception, analysis, and synthesis.

Whatever the methods employed to enable an agricultural student to acquire some science competency, the minimum goal should be to help him develop an intelligent skepticism about situations, observations, statements, and data. He needs to know what kinds of questions to ask of the data he will be expected to communicate as a teacher or an extension worker. This skepticism is based on acquaintance with assumptions about and an understanding of variability, probability, and process (as opposed to viewing all relationships in terms of cause and effect). With these basic concepts of science, he is more likely to seek empirically supportable explanations for relationships among phenomena, to communicate these explanations to others, and to develop confidence in his ability to make predictions and check data.

If the extension worker desires to maximize his effectiveness in the field and to protect his credibility as an information source, he needs more than these basic concepts of science. He needs to be able to conduct simple, replicable field trials. While it is possible for the extension worker to employ economics competency to work out, prior to recommending an innovation to the farmer, the strategy which combines production input and product commercialization factors to minimax advantage, only after testing the innovation locally can the extension worker ascertain whether a promised minimax advantage empirically obtains. "Experienced agricultural scientists know that small, subtle differences in environment can have very great effects on crop yields. These differences must be recognized and cultural practices adjusted accordingly. Because unreliable advice is worse than none, the scientist needs to be reasonably sure he is right before he gives advice, and the best way for him to acquire this confidence and trustworthiness is to test his ideas in well designed experiments carried out in the particular area" [36].

Extension services generally recognize the extension worker as a liaison between research worker and farmer, although less frequently have these services realized that innovations developed by research must be tested for their relevance in the farmer's environment. To the extent that the extension worker is to fulfill this function, not only must his science competency be adequate for the level at which he is expected to perform, but he must also see his job as that of communicating back to the research worker information on the innovation's performance in the farmer's environment.

We do not know whether extension workers in the developing countries see their job in these terms—communicating to the research worker information about the farmer's problems and data on the performance of innovations in the farmer's environment. The problem, however, is not only that of role perception but of administration, coordination, and support. "A serious missing link in most research and development schemes in the hot-humid tropics of Latin America is the production or subject-matter specialist. . . . Even though field-extension organizations exist, the depth of training of most extension agents is insufficient for the problems they face. Research personnel are often severely limited in their understanding of extension needs and practices. The feedback of farm-production problems to the researcher is usually inadequate" [34].

The extension worker may aspire to higher levels of science competency although this may not be necessary in his work. But higher levels are required of those who carry on research, and they frequently do not have the motivations, skills, and/or concepts which situations demand. The research worker too often lacks the ability to generate hypotheses grounded in theory, to plan statistically sound experiments, or to analyze effectively the resulting data. Unfortunately, data may be of little value because the experimental plots were poorly supervised and farmed. The resultant data are confounded by the uncontrolled influence of such variables as weeds, insects, diseases, lack of water, or other random misfortunes (some of which the scientist may be totally unaware because of the infrequency with which he visits his field plots).

Somewhere, somehow, the agricultural research worker must become committed to engaging with the physical reality of his research in the field rather than at his desk. Simultaneously, he must approach agricultural problems from a scientific viewpoint. In these two respects, at least, his needs and those of the extension worker are nearly identical. The implications for agricultural education are obvious.

Farming Competency

One of the development problems which national agencies face is recruiting, training, and managing a field staff of extension workers. Not only are there frequently not enough well-trained persons to fill all of the jobs [21, 22, 38, 42], even those available usually lack the rural background which would make them most immediately useful.

Richardson [34] points out the Colombia's agricultural colleges graduate each year about 90 students with the degree of "ingeniero agronomo" to help serve a rural-farm sector population about equal in size to that of the United States' farm population of 7,500,000. "The number of Latin American students graduated each year in the agricultural sciences is approximately 1,000. . . . These individuals are to assist in serving a population of approximately 115 million whose livelihood is derived from, or is immediately related to, agricultural production." For purposes of comparison, in 1963-1964 alone, the United States graduated 7,050 students with B.S. degrees in agriculture and closely related disciplines, 1,759 with M.A. or M.S. degrees, and 569 with the doctorate. The tally includes agriculture, agricultural economics, agricultural education, agricultural engineering, forestry and veterinary medicine.

Chaparro and Allen [7] point out that even in countries with large rural populations and a public policy encouraging their education, fewer than 25 percent of the agricultural graduates come from rural areas. The new extension worker must not only acquire farming competency but also learn about rural customs, values, and ways of thinking [27]. Where the graduate lacks preparation in these areas, he feels insecure and inadequate in his role of extension worker. This problem is brought out in Cotterill's study[1] of persons who had completed their courses in two Colombian agricultural colleges and were involved in information-dissemination activities (mainly extension and technical assistance) within 12 to 18 months after leaving the classrooms.

Cotterill asked each person to rank, in order of importance, a set of personal characteristics related to performance of his current work role of "agronomo," and this same set of characteristics in order of the suitability of his university preparation. Appropriate statistical analyses revealed that the personal characteristics for which the respondent perceived an unsuitability of university preparation were those he now saw as important to performing the "agronomo" role. In other words, the more important he perceived a characteristic for performance of the "agronomo" role, the less he perceived his university to have prepared him in that characteristic. This inverse relationship is found for such characteristics related to farming competency as ability to analyze problems in the real world; ability to communicate with uneducated persons; understanding the relation between the "agronomo" career

[1] Data gathered by Ralph Cotterill in Colombia during 1967-1968, performing dissertation research. At the time this chapter was written, Mr. Cotterill was completing his doctoral program in the Department of Agricultural Economics, Michigan State University, East Lansing.

and reality; ability to work without much supervision; practical farming skill in the field; and knowledge of rural sociology.

While the respondents generally felt that their university had suitably prepared them in such areas as mathematics, soils, control of insects and diseases, statistics, biology, chemistry, zoology, agricultural economics, and irrigation and drainage, their technical competency in any of these areas falls short of that required by the development needs of Colombian agriculture. As in other Latin American universities, in Colombian agricultural colleges, "The undergraduate is often equally trained in nearly every phase of agriculture from agricultural engineering through agronomy and animal science to food technology and rural economics. This system combined with insufficient training in critical analysis, tends to produce a generalist inadequately prepared to direct critical thought to the solving of the problems which will confront him" [33].

The importance of such qualities in an extension worker is reflected in other studies by Castillo [31]. When extension workers demonstrated a readiness to carry on above and beyond the call of duty, the farmers' skepticism was substantially reduced. Actions that were perceived favorably included getting into the paddy to plant rice, remaining in the barrio to work on Sundays and holidays, and arriving for evening classes despite heavy rains and bad roads. Not surprisingly, Contado found that FMTs in the high communication fidelity category were significantly more likely to consider the value "enjoy working with farmers" as of high importance in their job than did FMTs in the low communication fidelity category.

But to "enjoy working with farmers" is not enough. The extension worker must have the farming competency necessary to cultivate an innovation the way it should be cultivated, even if the practices required appear strange to the farmers. Contrary to the frequently expressed criticism that agricultural graduates perceive themselves as being too important to engage in such undignified work as farming, we believe that much of this avoidance behavior results from feelings of inadequacy and insecurity—they simply never had opportunity to learn farming skills.

Communication Competency

For the past 15 years, we have been involved in planning and conducting communication workshops, seminars, and training programs for diverse groups of persons interested in the problem of how to use communication to direct change in the developing countries. Among these persons were thousands of U.S. Agency for International Development-sponsored participants from some 70 countries; dozens of U.S. technical assistants about to go abroad for the government, foundations, or industry; and, more recently, several hundred foreign nationals, principally Southeast Asians, in training at the International Rice Research Institute (IRRI). Whatever the audience, we structure a communication training program so that the trainee learns

1. To state his communication objectives in terms of specific behavioral changes in the audiences relevant to the problem at hand.

2. To observe, listen, and question for insight on the decision-making criteria of relevant audiences and the rationales supporting these criteria and consequent behavior.

3. To be a communication strategist, i.e., to recognize individuals and situations available for, ready for, and receptive of communication as potential facilitators of achievement of the behavioral objectives and to specify how psychological, sociological, and cultural dynamics which affect attention, interest, understanding, acceptance, behavioral change, and selected social action may be employed to activate and coordinate the behavior of facilitators.

4. To be a communication technician, i.e., to develop, evaluate, and adapt as necessary decision-making criteria for selecting appropriate means (content, treatment, code, channel) for communication of messages to activate the facilitators.

5. To assess and coordinate the behavior of communication efficiency through monitoring the social and physical environment for response and reaction (feedback) to communicated messages.

6. To understand and control one's own behavior and mental orientations as significant communication variables.

7. To have a sense of urgency for development and to assume personal responsibility within the realm of one's sphere of daily influence.

These communication training objectives constitute a detailed statement of the dimensions of communication competency, the appropriate role of which has not always been recognized by those in extension. Prior to 1952, United States extension workers generally assumed, and the methodology specialists under whom they trained advocated, that the more methods or channels employed in extension work, the greater the likelihood of success. In short: the more message production the better.

In 1952, administrators and editors of the United States extension services, supported by a grant from the E. K. Kellogg Foundation, established a national project [30] with the objective of increasing the effectiveness of extension programs in the United States through identification, integration, and translation of the findings of human behavior research into approaches and materials which the extension worker might use to improve the quality of his skills in communication decision-making.

As a major dimension of this new project, a series of intensive two-week and three-week training programs was undertaken for carefully selected members of state extension staffs. Their behavior during training documented repeatedly the great extent to which the United States extension worker advocates adoption of innovations rather than teaches the farmer "how." Many extension workers evidenced considerable distress about and resistance to the notion that communication competency or effectiveness depends in part in defining clearly behavioral change objectives for specific audiences relevant to the problem at hand. Illustrative of not uncommon violent reactions to this idea was one home demonstration specialist who declared loudly: "But I don't want to change anybody; I just want to help people help themselves."

Unfortunately, this philosophy is part of the package of assumptions, organizational structures, and operational procedures which the United States has exported as an extension model. In a study of the impact of foreign programs on the organization of Chile's extension effort, Brown [2] states that there has been

a wholesale transfer of extension philosophy and methodology from the United States, especially regarding administrative and institutional arrangements for carrying out extension functions. From its inception as a ministerial bureau the Departamento de Extension Agricola has borne many similarities to its counterpart in the United States. In the early years this similarity was more in philosophy and method (i.e., demonstrations, farm visits, meetings) than in structure and was largely a result of the fact that some of the department's people had been to school in the United States. Over the years the similarity has increased. The division of the country into pseudo regions and zones approximating U.S. counties, the introduction of subject matter specialists, supervisors, and home agents, the initiation of 4-H clubs for rural youth and the organization of work along project and campaign lines were all instigated by U.S. advisers.

Rather than stressing acquisition of communication competency among workers, the specialist advocated extension methodology as the royal route to maximizing the likelihood of the farmer accepting a recommended innovation. Brown states that underlying this emphasis on methodology is a notion

that the basic communications task (i.e., extension) is one of persuasion and attitude change. This may be appropriate to a modern agriculture in an industrial nation, but it ignores the economic, institutional, and other situational constraints that greatly limit the utility of a strictly informational or educational program for the vast majority of Chilean farmers. Besides advocating a wholesale transfer of modern U.S. institutional forms, this kind of advice denies the history of these institutions in our own country by implicitly ignoring the fact that early extension workers in the United States were very much involved in controversial and political activities. It is, for example, quite impractical for Chile to maintain a purely informational extension program that stays away from "political" issues. . . . The surest way to make extension irrelevant and ineffectual in Chile is to isolate it from land reform, credit, and other development programs that are and will be underway in the countryside.

Other writings [16, 18] suggest that Chile is not alone among the developing countries as recipients of ineffectual, and irrelevant, transplants. However, organizing extension efforts around "political" issues neither makes them relevant or effectual. Instead we believe that extension efforts organized around competency are relevant and potentially effective. But if competency is not to be misdirected, a mechanism is required to assure that it is well utilized. This role we conceive for a subdimension of communication competency, communication strategy, or consideration of behavioral changes required in other audiences if the farmer is to be facilitated in the adoption of innovations.

In fact, thinking in terms of communication strategy, the extension worker is more likely to see that in some cases the appropriate audiences for message are not the farmers but rather landlords, input distributors, bankers, friends and neighbors, etc. who may play a significant role in response to the farmer's information-seeking behavior or who can facilitate or frustrate the action he wishes to take.

Conclusions into Practice

In the absence of the change agent competencies necessary to validate a hypothesized minimax advantage following adoption of a recommended innovation, we most probably find (1) extension educators who stress, in pre-service and in-service training programs, extension methods rather than acquisition of the competencies described; (2) extension administrators who consequently send inadequately trained extension workers to "teach" farmers rather than to obtain behavioral changes among other relevant audiences; (3) extension workers who (a) tell farmers and villagers what to do rather than asking them what they do and why they do what they do; (b) talk about and advocate practices assumed to be "improved" rather than (i) demonstrate innovations for which the minimax advantage has previously been validated; and (ii) teach the farmer the "how" and "why" of the recommended variety or practice; and (4) farmers who increasingly learn to resist extension workers.

In short, extension efforts tend to be promotional rather than educational, persuasive rather than informative or instructional; the farmer is told he ought to increase production but the extension worker lacks the competencies necessary to instruct the farmer in the "how" and "why" of the innovations he recommends. As a result, "resistance to change" can be "resistance to extension workers."

Except in a few instances, structures (e.g., ministries, agencies, institutes, organizations, bureaus, etc.) in the developing countries concerned with agricultural problems lack the communication and administrative links to coordinate effectively research, education, and extension.

Considering the problems of the education-research link, Peterson and Frazier [33] observe that "Educational institutions and experiment stations are usually separate organizations with little cooperation between the two. The extension programs introduced in several countries are also too frequently carried as separate programs, not embodied in a unified effort of research and education. Consequently, the extension personnel lose the stimulus of contact with a large body of scientific fellows and must expend much energy in locating sources of new information. Also, research and teaching programs suffer from lack of contact with professional colleagues working daily with real agricultural problems."

Similarly, with reference to research and extension activities, Hill [19] points out that "One of the important missing links in the extension service of many developing countries is the person we call the subject-matter specialist. He is the man with an advanced degree who makes it his business to know both the scientific and the applied side of his particular field. He shuttles back and forth between research workers and extension workers. In too many developing countries there is not a sufficiently close working relation between research and extension. When the research worker holds an advanced degree, not to mention a white-collar job, and the extension worker has a high school education or less plus a thin veneer of special training, the gap between the two services is often hopelessly wide. The subject matter specialist as we know him can help bridge this gap."

Lionberger and Chang [25], analyzing the modern-day agricultural success story of Taiwan, point out that the high levels of productivity have been achieved "by the use of systems (agencies) for developing and disseminating scientific farm information very different from those used in the United States. . . . This success of a different system is a fact that U.S. technicians, generally dedicated to the land grant college system, sometimes find difficult to recognize." They describe the system most developed and most extensively used in Taiwan as "composed of a series of more or less crop-specialized, publicly-supported research organizations for developing scientific farm information. These systems, in turn, are connected in a variety of ways to a more or less dual extension system designed to carry new scientific knowledge about all crops and livestock of concern to farmers." One extension operation is publicly supported; the other is financed by local farmers' associations. Where one's assumptions no longer hold and the "stateside" model of extension does not fit, as is usually the case in the developing countries, it is time to develop indigenous models of agricultural research, extension, and education.

In Retrospect

What, then, can we conclude about the role which agricultural education can play in facilitating acquisition and maintenance of the competencies required in agricultural development, particularly for those who work with farmers? Development requires knowledge and persons competent to produce needed knowledge if it does not exist. This requires research; if competent research workers are not available, they must be produced. This may require establishing new institutions or orienting old ones to prepare people who can study the farmer's production input and product commercialization problems.

If this research is to be relevant to the problems of agricultural development, we need mechanisms that increase the likelihood that the resulting innovations are capable of solving the farmer's problems regardless of his environment. This is one of the roles we see for the extension worker. Performance here assumes, however, that the extension worker has the necessary competencies, such as already described. Without these, he cannot objectively test an innovation for its local advantages.

Where such tests produce positive results, the extension worker, given adequate communication competency, can develop appropriate communication strategies and messages for the farmer and various supporting audiences. Where negative, the relevance of future research may depend upon how well he can report this to the research institution. Thus, the relevance of research, the justification of education, and the effectiveness of extension depend upon the extension worker having, at least to some degree, the technical, economics, science, farming, and communication competencies described.

Unfortunately, the majority of agricultural educational institutions in the developing countries probably are not so oriented to these goals, or do not have the human resources to pursue them. They may feel they also lack the physical resources, but this, too, is part of the problem. Chances are that the most readily available, low-cost efficient classroom—the farmer's field—is rarely used.

Universal agreement with the point of view about agricultural education or extension described here is not expected. Our experiences at home and abroad have documented time and again that the heterogeneity among institutional settings is much too diverse and complex for any particular model of extension. We have presented, instead, a set of characteristics which we believe to be minimal for the success of any agricultural education or extension model. While we do not expect anyone to disagree about the importance of competency, some may disagree about which competencies and how much of each are important. Others may argue that we have neglected the most important virtues or characteristics of agricultural workers—a dedication to service, an interest in agriculture, and a desire to help one's fellow men. Such characteristics are desirable, but we cannot accept them as substitutes for competency.

Finally, we recognize that it may be difficult to find all of the five competencies—technical, economics, science, farming, and communication—combined in a single agricultural graduate, or to marshal the resources necessary to provide the learning opportunities so that he may acquire those missing or inadequate. To the extent that it is not possible, and this certainly may be the case in many developing countries where workers in agriculture have minimal education, then the agricultural development organization must provide the missing competencies through domestic or imported specialists, teams of specialists, and/ or cooperative arrangements with other entities.

Although we all probably know better, there is a pervasive tendency, at home and abroad, to try to solve all developmental problems through a single disciplinary approach. What is needed is an approach that mobilizes, energizes, and qualifies the range of persons and institutions in the total system, or all of the relevant, interacting systems. This means attention to research, education, and extension, yes, but also to multitudinous production input and product commercialization factors. We need a broader viewpoint, and we need better information about the competencies required to make the total system effective.

References

1. Aler-Montalvo, Manuel, "Cultural Change in a Costa Rican Village," *Human Organization, XV*, 4 (Winter 1957), 3-5.

2. Brown, Marion R., "Agricultural 'Extension' in Chile: A Study of Institutional Transplantation," No. 54, The Land Tenure Center, University of Wisconsin, Madison, September 1968, mimeo.

3. Byrnes, Francis C., and William G. Golden, "Changing the 'Change Agent'—A Step Toward Increased Rice Yields," The International Rice Research Institute, Manila Hotel, Manila, the Philippines, September 30, 1967.

4. Campbell, Keith O., "Farm Decision-Making and Its Implications for Agricultural Extension." Paper prepared for the Australian Agricultural Extension Conference held at Hawkesbury Agricultural College, Richmond, N.S.W., August 13-17, 1962.

5. Castillo, Gelia T., "Some Insights on the Human Factor in Overcoming Barriers to Adequate Food Supply." Paper read at Symposium on Overcoming Barriers to Adequate Food Supply, Philippine Association of Nutritionists, March 5, 1964.

6. _____ et al., "A Development Program in Action: A Progress Report on a Philippine Case." Revised version of paper presented at the Seminar on Life and Culture in Asia, University of the Philippines, December 5, 1963.

7. Chaparro, Lavaro, and Ralph H. Allen, "Higher Agricultural Education and Social Change in Latin America," *Rural Sociology, XXV*, 1 (1960).

8. Constantino, Josefina D., "The Filipino Mental Make-up and Science," *Philippine Sociological Review, 14*, 1 (January 1966), pp. 18-28.

9. Contado, Tito Egargo, "Communication Fidelity between Farm Management Technicians and Rice Farmers in Leyte, Philippines." Unpublished Ph.D. thesis, Cornell University, Ithaca, N.Y., 1968.

10. Cuyno, Rogelio V., "Assessing the Rice Production Competency of Agricultural Change Agents: Developing of a Measuring Instrument." Unpublished M.S. thesis, University of the Philippines, College of Agriculture, Los Banos, 1967.

11. Dandekar, V. M., "Motivating Farmers to Increase Agricultural Production." Comments on Items C. 7 of the Provisional Agenda, Seventh FAO Regional Conference for Asia and the Far East, Manila, 1964.

12. Dommen, Arthur J., "India Crop Yield Barely Increased by U.S. Skill-Farming Experts Can Show Only Modest Results after Six Years of Innovations," *Los Angeles Times*, November 8, 1967.

13. Einsiedel, Luz A., *Success and Failure in Selected Community Development Projects in Batangas* Study Series, No. 3, Quezon City: Community Development Research Council, University of the Philippines, 1960.

14. Feliciano, Gloria D., "The Human Variable in Farm Practice Adoption: Philippine Setting." Paper read before the Philippine Sociological Society, February 22, 1964.

15. Felstenhausen, H. H., "Economic Knowledge and Comprehension in a Netherlands Farming Community." Bulletin No. 26, Social Science Division, Agricultural University of the Netherlands, Wageningen, 1965.

16. ____ , "Fitting Agricultural Extension to the Development Needs of Colombia." No. 21, Land Tenure Center, Bogota, Colombia, October 1968, mimeo.

17. Gusfield, Joseph R., "Tradition and Modernity: Misplaced Polarities in the Study of Social Change," *American Journal of Sociology*, 72, 4 (January 1967), 351-362.

18. Grunig, James E., "Information, Entrepreneurship, and Economic Development: A Study of the Decision Making Processes of Colombian Latifundistas." Unpublished Ph.D. thesis, University of Wisconsin, Madison, 1968.

19. Hill, F. F., "Developing Agricultural Institutions in Underdeveloped Countries." In *Agricultural Sciences for the Developing Nations*, publication No. 76 of the American Association for the Advancement of Science, Washington, D.C., 1964, pp. 141-161.

20. Hovland, Carl, I. Janis, L. Irving, and Harold H. Kelley, *Communication and Persuasion.* New Haven: Yale University Press, 1953, p. 35.

21. Interamerican Development Committee for Agricultural Development, *Inventory of Information Basic to the Planning of Agricultural Development in Latin America.* Regional Report. Washington, D.C.: Pan American Union, October 1963, pp. 61-66, 79-86.

22. International Bank for Reconstruction and Development, *A Review of INCORA and Its Program in Colombia,* Colombia, October 26, 1967, Appendix B, pp. 104.

23. International Rice Research Institute, *Annual Report,* Manila: Manila Hotel, 1967.

24. Lewis, A. B., "Thoughts on the American Training of Graduate Students of Agricultural Economics from Less-Developed Countries." Paper issued by the Council on Economic and Cultural Affairs, Inc. Expanded from comments made at the Conference on International Exchange of Persons, Institute of International Education, Washington, D.C., 1959.

25. Lionberger, Herbert F., and H. C. Chang, "Communication and Use of Scientific Farming Information by Farmers in Two Taiwan Agricultural Villages." Research Bulletin 940, University of Missouri, Agricultural Experiment Station, May 1968.

26. Moseman, A. H., "National Systems of Science and Technology for Agricultural Development." Paper presented at University of Minnesota, June 9, 1966.

27. Mosher, Arthur T., "Learning to Think About Farming." Paper issued by the Council on Economic and Cultural Affairs, Inc. Address given before the Allahabad Rotary Club and later printed in *The Allahabad Farmer*, 1952.

28. Myren, Delbert T., "Training for Extension Work in Latin America," *America Latina*, VII, 2 (April-June 1964).

29. _____, "The Role of Information in Farm Decisions Under Conditions of High Risk and Uncertainty." Symposium on the Role of Communications in Agricultural Development. Mexico City, October 1964, p. 99.

30. National Project in Agricultural Communications, "The First Seven Years, 1953-60." East Lansing: Michigan State University, March 1960.

31. Niehoff, Arthur H. (ed.), *A Casebook of Social Change*. Chicago: Aldine, 1966.

32. _____, and J. Charnel Anderson, *The Primary Variables in Directed Cross-Cultural Change*. Alexandria, Va.: Humrro Division No. 7, January 1965.

33. Peterson, J. B., and R. D. Frazier. "Plant Agriculture in the Emerging Nations." In *Agricultural Sciences for the Developing Nations*, publication No. 76 of The American Association for the Advancement of Science, Washington, D.C., 1964, pp. 33-50.

34. Richardson, Ralph W., Jr., "Training of Scientific Personnel." In *Rural Development in Tropical Latin America*. Ithaca, N.Y.: State College of Agriculture, 1967, pp. 403-412.

35. Schulman, Sam, "Intellectual and Technological Underdevelopment: A Case Study—Colombia," *Social Forces*, 46, 3 (March 1968), 319-327.

36. Stackman, E. C., Richard Bradfield, and Paul C. Mangelsdorf, *Campaigns Against Hunger*. Cambridge, Mass.: The Belknap Press of Harvard University Press, 1967.

37. Stevenson, A. Russel, "Graduate Study in the United States: An Introduction for the Prospective A/D/C Fellow." New York: The Agricultural Development Council, 1968.

38. Villanueva, B. M., "Community Development Techniques and Administration at the Project Level." In Buenaventura M. Villanueva (ed.), *Elements of Rural Development*, Laguna College of Agriculture, University of the Philippines, 1963.

39. Warren, Alexander G., "A Study of Some Training Factors Associated with the Success or Failure of Cooperative Extension Workers." Unpublished D.E. thesis, Oklahoma State University, Stillwater, 1960.

40. Welsch, Delane E., "Response to Economic Incentives by Abakaliki Rice Farmers in Nigeria," *Journal of Farm Economics*, 47, 4 (November 1965), 900-914.

41. Wharton, Clifton R., Jr., "Risk, Uncertainty, and the Subsistence Farmer: Technological Innovation and Resistance to Change in the

Context of Survival." Paper prepared for the Joint Session American Economic Association and Association for Comparative Economics, Chicago, December 28, 1968.

42. Yudelman, Montague, *Agricultural Development in Latin America: Current Status and Prospects*. Inter-American Development Bank, October 1966, pp. 47-52.

Part One

VII. Implementation
of Rural
Development

22. Modernization
Processes and Rural
Development in
Developing
Countries:
An Anthropological
View

Jack M. Potter

The study of modernization and rural development in traditional societies has become in the last two decades one of the most important foci
of research for social and cultural anthropologists [4, 5, 7]. The central
problems for anthropologists engaged in this research have been to
understand the structure of traditional peasant societies, their similarities and differences, and to study how they are being modified in the
contemporary world by modern cultural, social, and economic influences, and by planned rural developmental programs [1]. A few applied
anthropologists have served as advisers in formulating and evaluating
rural development programs [3], but the majority have been less
immediately concerned with practical problems and have devoted their
efforts to descriptions of the processes of change occurring in particular
societies and to general theoretical discussions of processes of modernization. The results of both kinds of anthropology should be of interest
to those engaged in rural development. The following is a summary
statement of major elements in the modernization processes as seen by
anthropologists, plus a few general conclusions that might possibly be
of use to those engaged in planning and carrying out rural development
programs.

Processes of Modernization

The major sources of change in peasant societies are the cultural, technological, scientific, and ideological influences which have come in part
from the Western industrialized nations, and in part from the elites of
the new countries themselves. This process of change began several
centuries ago with the first expansion of the West, but it has accelerated
to a breakneck pace in this century. Everywhere modern economic,
cultural, and ideological influences are eroding traditional societies at
national and village levels. Already peasant societies can no longer be

Jack M. Potter—United States. Ph.D., Anthropology, University of California,
Berkeley, 1964; Associate Professor of Anthropology, University of California,
Berkeley. Part of this article (pp. 000-000) is adapted from my introductory
article "Peasants in the Modern World," which appeared in *Peasant Society: A
Reader,* edited by Jack M. Potter, May N. Diaz, and George M. Foster (Boston:
Little, Brown, 1967), pp. 378-383.

found in what may be called their "classical" forms: change has carried them beyond this point. This transformation is one of the great social revolutions in history, comparable to the rise of civilizations, and it will have enormous effects on the human condition. Until recently, life in a peasant village was the most prevalent form of human existence, and probably more people have lived and died there than in any other social context.

In the modern world, traditional peasant societies are anachronisms, and it is inevitable that they disappear. Peasants themselves have demonstrated time and time again that they prefer a different, and what they believe to be a better, life. Poverty, illiteracy, oppression, disease, an early death, and a backbreaking life of sweating over a piece of land have little nostalgic value to peasants, a great many of whom will take every reasonable opportunity to escape to the new life of the city. Modern technology as well as human desires have conspired to hasten the end of the traditional peasant.

Ever since its appearance in eighteenth-century England, industrialization has been the main force changing the traditional peasant order, and for most overcrowded and impoverished peasant societies in the world it is seen as the only alternative to a miserable and increasingly unsatisfactory existence. The phenomenal increase in population over the last century has created a problem that is, simply stated, one of too many people trying to live off too little land. With an ever-increasing population pressing against limited resources, many peasants are forced to seek a livelihood outside their traditional communities. Only with the expansion of industry, a sharp drop in the birth rate, and the improvement of rural life can remaining peasant societies escape their serious dilemma and achieve some measure of human dignity.

Urbanization accompanies industrialization. Classical peasant societies have always contained cities, but these preindustrial cities are changing from centers of commerce and handicrafts, and residences of traditional elites, to new centers of industry. It has been from the new urban centers that most modern influences have entered the countryside.

With the beginnings of industrialization, cities not only change in type; they also dramatically increase in size as peasants are attracted by jobs in the new industrial plants and by the novelties of modern urban life. The migration of peasants into urban centers that is occurring on a dramatic scale all over the world is often a traumatic experience for the peasant. The move from the small, personal world of the peasant community, where one is in the bosom of family, friends, and kinsmen, into the impersonal and confusing life of the city, is an adaptation often difficult for the peasant to make. Made cautious by centuries on the land, the peasant often makes the move from village to city over several generations. At first young peasants leave the village to find temporary work in the city. Since this is at first a risky business, because of depressions and other imponderables to which modern economic systems are subject, the peasant may initially retain his village kinship ties and his right to property as something he can fall back upon if he loses his job or in some other way fails to make it in the city.

Often "making it" in the city is difficult because the peasant usually has to enter the urban job market at the lowest level as an unskilled laborer. Peasants rarely become members of the bourgeois middle class upon moving to the urban areas. In the mushrooming industrial cities the peasant finds that economic development does not proceed fast enough to absorb all migrants, and frequently he ends up unemployed, living in an urban slum where life is sometimes even worse than in the countryside. Only gradually, after he achieves some success and job security in the city, does the peasant finally break his ties with the countryside—which by that time have outlived their usefulness and become burdensome. It is largely through the influence of city migrants that modern political and social attitudes of the city, usually heavily influenced by Western culture, are introduced into the peasant village, where they begin gradually to change traditional attitudes and customs.

The commercial network is another important avenue by which economic and technological innovations reach the countryside. New manufactured goods such as electric appliances, canned foods, and new clothing styles are made available to peasants in the market. The desire to acquire these new manufactured goods and all the other gadgets of modern industry gives rise to new expectations and furnishes the incentive for peasants to take advantage of new economic opportunities. As commerce and industry develop, the market nexus increasingly penetrates the subsistence sector of the peasant economy, and soon the peasant is caught up in market networks that extend to market towns, cities, and the outside world.

As the extension of the market network opens up wider trade channels to the world outside the village, agriculture frequently becomes commercialized. Participation in the market gradually changes traditional peasants, to whom agriculture was a way of life, into farmers, or agricultural businessmen, whose activities become a business for profit.

The impersonal forces of the city and the market, though inexorable, are not the only ways in which peasant life is being changed in the contemporary world. The elite groups which control the new nation-states, imbued with the idea of progress, deliberately attempt to transform their peasantries through programs of planned change. Rural extension and community-development programs, in which efforts are made to introduce new farm technology, new crops, better sanitary and health facilities, birth-control methods, and so on, are common in most of the emerging nations. These attempts at social engineering meet with uneven success, sometimes because they are poorly planned and executed, and sometimes because the peasant's basic caution and conservatism do not permit him to change as rapidly as the more advanced sectors of his nation wish.

Peasants are crucial in the industrialization of new nations. In the initial stages of industrialization new nations have to raise capital to finance the building of factories, the importation of machinery, and the acquisition of necessary industrial skills. Since agriculture lies at the base of traditional economies, some capital accumulation must come from this source. The peasants, therefore, must not only furnish the food requirements of an expanding urban labor force; they must also produce a surplus which can be sold abroad to obtain foreign exchange that will finance part of the industrialization program. At the same time, peasants must supply the manpower to create the urban labor force for the new factories and new service establishments.

Ultimately, modernization and industrialization so transform traditional peasant societies that almost all features which characterized the traditional peasant social, economic, and cultural order are significantly altered. The structural semi-isolation of the village community becomes less pronounced, and class groupings, occupational associations, and other horizontal ties become more important in the peasant's life than his traditional village. Traditional kinship groups, like the extended family and the lineage, where they exist, give way to the nuclear family, which is better suited to the social and geographical mobility acquired in modern industrial society. The old cultural separation between the Great and Little Traditions is blurred by modern communication facilities, which tend to create a common mass culture. The fatalistic attitude of traditional peasants gives way—although slowly—to an achievement orientation as it becomes more and more possible to acquire newly created wealth and status in the wider society. Communal custom as a means of social control is replaced by the bureaucratic legal and political systems of the new states. The political and social independence of the local community is lessened as the modern state apparatus extends its power down to the local level. In all these ways the "part-society" characteristics of traditional peasants are significantly altered as the peasant becomes an organic part of a new social order.

At present there seem to be two main routes by which peasants enter the modern world, with many variations. The first peasant societies to be transformed into modern societies were those of Western Europe during the eighteenth and nineteenth centuries. In these, the transformation took place in laissez-faire fashion, because of industry and commerce. A similar, though by no means identical, process is taking place in those new nations which are trying to modernize within a democratic framework. India is perhaps the best example.

A second and contrasting alternative is the Communist route, pioneered by the Soviet Union and followed by the Communist countries of Eastern Europe, China, North Korea, and North Vietnam. These countries illustrate one of the great themes in contemporary history— the violent transformation of traditional peasant societies into modern nation-states by Communist-inspired and Communist-led revolutionary movements in which peasants take active part. This should dispel the widespread notion that peasants are inherently passive, meek, and non-violent, a notion already proved false by the violent eruptions that have occurred throughout history in many peasant societies, including traditional Europe. The increased political awareness of peasants has not, of course, been manifested solely in Communist-led movements; the Mexican Revolution is a case in point.

The Stages of Rural Development

The crucial tasks of social change preparatory to rural development are similar in most traditional societies. First, a new elite group motivated to modernize their society must gain effective political power to pacify and unify the society. A common social prerequisite for rural development, given the increasing politicization of peasant populations, is land reform.

Land reform has social as well as narrow economic effects. Land reform usually eliminates or weakens the power of the traditional landed elites, who control most peasant societies and who usually block efforts at rural development because such plans threaten the prestige, power, and wealth of their class. The distribution of land temporarily assuages the land hunger of peasants and also ties the peasantry to the new political and social order. The new middle peasant class now becomes dominant in the rural areas and land redistribution is able to maintain, at least temporarily, a viable standard of living for most of the rural population. At least it eliminates the worst cases of poverty among tenants and landless laborers.

Having reached this point, plans can be made for the development of the rural sector of the population on the basis of some ideological guideline. The elite group must make a judgment as to the future shape of their society and begin to implement this decision. Ideology is important in rural development, not only because ideologically influenced decisions determine to some extent whether the end product of planning will more closely resemble family farms or factories-in-the-fields, but also because the social force needed to overcome social resistance and to mobilize a conservative peasantry to participate in development programs can apparently come in no other way. Nationalism plus some form of socialism is the usual creed adopted in most developing countries.

Another decision must then be made as to the overall strategy that is to be adopted in modernizing the society and the role the rural sector is to play in this. Three choices are possible: (1) to emphasize the development of heavy industry and leave agriculture to fend for itself; (2) to give equal weight to the industrial and agricultural sectors; or (3) to stress rural development at the expense of industrial growth.

The first strategy is that followed by the Soviet Union and by China until the failure of the Great Leap Forward in 1958-1959. The second is probably the more usual choice made by most developing countries. And the third choice, while probably best for many developing countries, is rarely if ever made because of the prestige and importance given to industrialization.

The second strategy, to develop industry and at the same time to devote considerable resources to agriculture is the more usual course of action. The aim is to foster industrial and commercial development rapidly enough to create the jobs necessary to absorb the excess rural population. At the same time, agriculture is improved by increasing capital expenditures for fertilizer, insecticides, seed selection, and the building of irrigation works. To facilitate the process of agricultural development, communication and transportation facilities to the rural areas are built and efforts made to improve marketing and rural credit facilities. The aim is to improve the livelihood of rural dwellers so that they will be able to buy the industrial products and the services furnished by the urban sector of the economy. This assumes that industrial development is divided between heavy industry and light consumer-goods industries. If capital is insufficient to finance the production of consumer goods, dependence must remain on the production of these goods by the traditional handicraft sector of the economy in the urban and rural areas.

Ultimately the urban industrial sector is supposed to gradually absorb a large percentage of the population engaged in agriculture. The mechanization and modernization of agriculture is supposed to allow increased production from a smaller group of farmers.

Difficulties with the Standard Model of Development

This classical model of development, based upon the experience of the developed countries of the West and Japan, is the one usually followed by most developing countries. It is, however, becoming increasingly clear that this classic model of rural development is unrealistic for many developing countries. Usually development has not proceeded along the guidelines supplied by this model. Industrial development, even though it is frequently overemphasized at the expense of agriculture, does not proceed at a rate sufficient to employ the urban dwellers, let alone draw off the excess population from the rural areas. Migrants who leave the countryside to escape an intolerable life are left unemployed and live in urban slums, creating serious social and political problems in the cities.

In the countryside, problems also arise because traditional handicraft industries and the usually neglected consumer-goods industries are not able to fill the increased demand for new consumer goods by the rural population. At the same time, unchecked population growth wipes out all economic gains made through the program of development. It is becoming apparent, for example, that very few of the emerging nations will be able to industrialize rapidly enough and create the jobs necessary to absorb the excess rural populations that can never be employed in agriculture, and few nations will be able to modernize agriculture to an extent that less than 10 percent of the population will be engaged in agriculture. There is no assurance whatsoever that the developing countries will pass through the same stages followed by Western nations and emerge from this process of change with social and economic institutions similar to those of modern European countries and Japan.

The world does not need, nor can it support a large advanced industrial plant in every nation. The industrial plants of the United States, Europe, the Soviet Union, and Japan alone are fully capable of producing most needed industrial goods for the entire world. And in the future, new developments in automated industrial plants will increase this capacity and utilize only a small, skilled labor force. The world no longer requires that every nation become industrialized on the scale of the United States, Europe, the Soviet Union, and Japan.

The significance of all this is that in the future it will no longer be possible to rely on the pull of industry and commerce to reduce rural populations significantly. For the foreseeable future most of the world's large rural populations will remain exactly where they are. And this makes rural developmental planning even more important than at present, when it is sometimes regarded as a stop-gap measure to care for the rural populations while they are gradually eliminated by the growth of industry and urban life. The traditional solution to the rural problem by some economists of simply finding ways to encourage and speed the process of getting the peasant out of the country and into the city is no longer a rational policy. The rural populations will be with us and will increasingly have to receive priorities in capital investments and planning which are now given to the urban areas. Ways will have to be found to bring the benefits of modern urban life to rural dwellers. Industry will have to be built on a decentralized basis to supply employment for rural people not engaged fully in agricultural activities. Although the forms of rural societies of the future are at present difficult to predict, they are probably foreshadowed by the new kinds of rural social and economic organizations, such as the kolkhoz, the kibbutz, the ejidos, and the Chinese communes, which have appeared in some of the developing countries.

Rural planning must proceed on the basis of some estimate of the future course of social evolution. The difficulty with most rural planning in underdeveloped countries at present is that changes in technical, social, and ideological patterns are occurring at such astounding rates that it is difficult to keep pace with events. It is, however, becoming clear that the shape of future rural societies in many of the developing countries will be quite different from that found in contemporary industrialized nations. And it is doubtful that the same programs and policies that have been followed in these countries will be relevant for the future when conditions will be very different. The notion that all societies must develop through the same stages toward a condition which approximates Western nations is a misleading survival of nineteenth-century unilineal evolution that still exerts unsuspected tyranny on our thinking. Just as classical agrarian societies developed a multiplicity of social and cultural patterns on generically similar agricultural bases, the future shape of the modernizing agrarian countries will exhibit considerable diversity. And in formulating rural development plans diversity should be accepted as a basic axiom.

Rural Development: The Contribution of Anthropology

The primary way in which anthropologists can be of assistance to rural development planners is to help them understand the cultures undergoing change as interrelated wholes and to help predict what consequences particular changes might have for other parts of people's lives. Anthropology's primary message is that it is necessary to understand a rural culture before one begins to change it. Unless rural development planners have an intimate knowledge of all aspects of a culture, unnecessary difficulties will occur for both the planning agency and the people involved. For example, even an apparently simple matter like the introduction of a new food crop often has far-reaching implications that can be predicted only after careful analysis. A change in a major crop might affect the religious life of a people, the division of labor within the family, the yearly work-cycle, and so on. Cultures are very delicate and intricate mechanisms that are not to be loosely tampered with by agents of change, however well-meaning, if they do not know the social and cultural framework of the people whose life they are trying to improve.

Often planning goals can be achieved more easily if they build upon elements of the existing social order rather than attempt to work against it. A case in point is the initial failure of the Chinese commune experiment partly because they tried to ignore or destroy the traditional Chinese marketing structure without offering any viable alternative [6]. Even with totalitarian political power and the help of effective propaganda programs, many development plans are impossible to implement because those directing them do not understand or choose to ignore the existing institutional framework. Institutional adaptations which have been developed by peasants over the centuries are ignored by planners at their peril. It is simply not possible to begin with a clean slate. This does not mean that rural planners should adopt an overly conservative policy. It is obviously impossible to maintain many elements of the status quo. It simply means that programs of rural development should be adjusted to local conditions whenever possible if this adaptation is consistent with or contributes to the achievement of developmental goals.

It is also essential for those engaged in rural development to have some understanding of the characteristics of peasants, the kind of people with whom most of them deal. Recent anthropologicial research on world-view and interpersonal relations among peasant populations is almost unanimous in agreeing that because of their exploited social position and long historical experience, most peasants tend to be cautious, noncooperative, and highly suspicious of the motives of persons within their community as well as of people from the outside. Such characteristics make it difficult for them to supply the leadership and develop the kind of community spirit and cooperative efforts that seem to be required in most of the new social and economic organizations advocated by rural development planners [2]. It is not impossible to develop leadership and foster cooperative organizations among peasants, but planners must recognize that such programs go against the grain of most peasant societies and great effort is required to overcome this built-in social resistance.

Another important result of recent anthropological research of significance for rural development is the analysis and description of the complicated ways in which inhabitants of peasant villages are connected to their larger society. Villages are not isolated or self-sufficient social, cultural, or economic units and cannot be understood in such terms. Villagers have important ties with persons of status outside the village on which they depend for aid and support and for help in dealing with persons and institutions in the wider society. They are also involved in complex regional marketing arrangments and religious activities, and have ties of friendship and kinship that reach out across the countryside to other villages and to towns and cities. In many peasant societies the market town-tributary village areas form natural communities in the context of which most of their life activities take place. The implications of these findings is that in many, if not most, peasant societies the village is not necessarily the most important unit for planning and that larger units, market town areas and regions, should be the basic units for developing a rural society.

Rural development must also proceed against the background of structural changes in the overall society and must be coordinated with urban planning and industrial development. It is naive in the extreme to believe that well-meaning activists can enter a single village community, organize the village, drum up community spirit, and have the villagers pull themselves up by their own efforts. Rural development is part of an overall program of structural change which involves planning at the total societal level, and to be effective rural development requires the exercise of economic and political power and cannot be implemented through enthusiastic persuasion alone.

The task of planned rural development can and should be a cooperative effort between those engaged directly in planning, and anthropologists. The anthropologists can help planners by supplying information about the social, cultural, and economic characteristics of rural societies and their inner dynamics. He also can do follow-up studies to evaluate the effectiveness of planning efforts and help overcome difficulties in the program. Many of the younger generation of anthropologists now see this practical application of their studies as the central concern of their discipline.

References

1. Foster, George M., *Traditional Cultures and the Impact of Technological Change.* Boston: Little, Brown, 1962.

2.____ , "Peasant Society and the Image of Limited Good," *American Anthropologist, 67,* 2 (April 1965).

3.____ , *Applied Anthropology.* Boston: Little, Brown, 1969.

4. Potter, Jack M., May N. Diaz, and George M. Foster (eds.), *Peasant Society: A Reader,* Boston: Little, Brown, 1967.

5. Redfield, Robert, *Peasant Society and Culture: An Anthropological Approach to Civilization.* Chicago: University of Chicago Press, 1956.

6. Skinner, G. William, "Marketing and Social Structure in Rural China," Parts I, II, and III, *Journal of Asian Studies, 24* (November 1964), 3-43, *24* (February 1965), 195-228, *24* (May 1965) 363-399.

7. Wolf, Eric R., *Peasants.* Englewood Cliffs, N.J.: Prentice-Hall, 1966.

Part One

VII. Implementation
of Rural
Development

23. Farmers'
Organizations in
Planning and
Implementing Rural
Development

Solon Barraclough

Discussions of the role of farmers' organizations in development are more frequently distinguished by ideological fervor than by rational analysis. Perhaps the most important reason for this in the poorer countries is that the organization of the traditionally powerless peasant majorities would threaten deeply held values and the existing social structure itself. It is also because the lack of conceptual clarity concerning both farmers' organizations and the development process allows anyone to interpret the relationships between them pretty much as he wishes.

To some people, farmers' organizations suggest poorly armed peasants in heroic guerrilla actions. Others envision demagogues inciting rural mobs to mindless destruction and reigns of terror. Still others have in mind small producers patiently trying to improve their lot through cooperatives and community efforts while the larger progressive commercial farmers working through their agricultural societies diffuse technical knowledge and educate governments to follow enlightened policies. And there are many who, after counting the potential number of rural voters, hope that organizing the farmers would provide political support to maintain stability and to keep themselves in power while development proceeds.

There is little I can do here except to indicate a few of the issues in organizing farmers for rural development and relate them to experience, especially in Latin America, where I have been working. I wish to make three major points. First, evaluation of the role of farmers' organizations in rural development depends fundamentally upon one's value premises of what development is all about. Second, the functions of farmers' organizations in the development process may range from pressing forward their members' interests both within the traditional social systems and by forcing revolutionary changes in it, to the social mobilization of the rural population and the creation of new economic institutions. Third, while the role of farmers' organizations in specific

Solon Barraclough—United States. Ph.D. Economics, Harvard University, 1950; Professor of Agricultural Economics at Cornell University; formerly Director, Inter-American Agricultural Development Committee's studies of land tenure and agricultural development in Latin America; presently Project Manager of the Agrarian Reform Research and Training Institute, joint project of the United Nations and the Government of Chile, in Santiago.

instances may in part be attributed to chance and leadership, the key to making useful generalizations must be sought in analysis of social and historical circumstances.

The Ideological Problem

What role have farmers' organizations had in planning and implementing rural development, and what role should they play? The answers to these questions largely depend upon one's concepts of development, of social change, and of history itself. Development implies a historical process by which a country becomes less like Ethiopia, Burma, or Guatemala and more like the United States, Sweden, the Soviet Union, or Japan. But like which one of these, and in what respects? No simple index of change such as gross national product per capita can begin to measure the complex transformation of productive processes, institutions, values, and attitudes implied by economic growth and social change. Any attempt to become concrete introduces numerous value judgments. All development concepts are in a sense ideological [23].

Development ideologies without exception stress the goal of increasing per capita production of goods and services. They also usually emphasize greater national unity and independence along with improvement of the welfare of the population. Moreover, most developers profess to believe in the integration of hitherto marginal groups such as the peasantry into the national community, greater individual opportunities for social and economic advancement, a more egalitarian society and active popular participation in political decision-making. One has only to read the constitutions and development plans of many poor countries, the United Nations Charter and its "Declaration of Human Rights," or the Charter of Punta del Este to realize what a high priority is assigned to these other dimensions of social change. Even the United States Congress affirmed its adherence to an ideology of popular participation and democratic institutions in development when it inserted "Title IX" into the Foreign Assistance Act of 1966 [33].[1] My own experience in several less-developed countries indicates that many influential politicians, intellectuals, and student leaders place as high or higher priorities on some of these other social and political goals of development as on that of simply increasing production.

[1] Title IX says: "In carrying out programs authorized in this Chapter, emphasis will be placed on assuming amximum participation in the task of economic development on the part of the people in the developing countries, through the encouragement of democratic private and local governmental institutions."

If widespread popular participation in a more independent, egalitarian, and integrated society are part and parcel of one's concept of development, as it is of mine, then the role of farmers' organizations in the process must be judged in this context. The relatively rapid expansion of agricultural production and productivity recently attained in several countries such as Guatemala, Peru, or Pakistan, where the welfare and participation of the mass of the peasantry have not significantly changed, would not be sufficient in itself to qualify as being rural development. A broad concept of development such as that envisioned in the charters, declarations, and resolutions of the United Nations and its specialized agencies, and which I adopt as an explicit value premise for this analysis, implies by definition strong independent farmers' organizations representing their members' interests with real participation by the small peasant-producers and landless laborers who make up the overwhelming majority of the rural population in most poor countries. Elitist development values, on the contrary, not only do not require democratic peasant and workers' organizations but are invariably threatened by them.

A farmer is considered here to be anyone who makes his living primarily from farming. While the English term "farmer" implies a farm operator or entrepreneur, I find it unreasonable to exclude farm laborers, small tenants, and sharecroppers who in poor agrarian countries often make up the majority of the rural population. A farmer than may be a large landlord at the apex of the social, political, and economic pyramid, a middle-class farm operator, or a low-status small-holder, tenant, or laborer. In most Latin American countries, 60 to 90 percent of all "farmers" are low-status small producers and laborers, while a very few large owners control practically all the land. All are farmers by our definition.

As this paper deals with the role of farmers' organizations in planning and implementing rural development, a word must be said about planning. By a rural development plan I mean a conscious political program to achieve developmental goals. In this sense, a development plan is not a precise blueprint or a self-consistent model of the behavior of a few "economic" variables, other things being equal, but a practical program of action. Perhaps the most important lesson to be learned from the hundreds of development plans prepared during the last two decades is that those having real impact not only had political support based upon involvement in planning by those wielding political power but also counted on participation in the preparation of the plans by those responsible for carrying them out [40].

If rural development requires the cooperation and support of a wide range of farmers for its success, it goes almost without saying that participation in the planning process by organizations representing these groups is highly important. The relative failure of many well-intentioned rural development programs, even within the limited objectives imposed by political constraints, can in large measure be attributed to disregard of this simple rule. Examples would include such projects as resettlement in Brazil, agricultural credit for low-income producers in Peru, and land reform in the majority of countries that have adopted agrarian legislation as an act of grace without an organized peasantry to provide political support and to participate in planning and carrying out the reform program.

Kinds of Farmers' Organizations

Sociologists sometimes distinguish between movements and organizations. The Salvadorian peasant insurrection in 1932, suppressed with some twenty thousand killed, the Colombian rural violence after 1945 with its widespread property destruction and hundreds of thousands of peasant dead, and the bitter revolt by the Brazilian backland followers of the messianic Antonio Consejero at the end of the last century are regarded as movements [36]. They are seen as being collective reactions in defense of threatened norms and values. They are assumed to occur without clear goals or organizational structure but as consisting of leaders and the led. On the other hand, organizations are characterized by explicit external goals, a bureaucratic structure, and role differentiation such as exhibited by most landowners' associations, unions, and cooperatives [15].

In practice this distinction between movements and organizations is rather artificial. It is a matter of degree and not of kind. What appear to be spontaneous peasant movements are found upon closer examination to show many organizational features, while most farmers' organizations have at one time or another attracted a measure of spontaneous support of the kind attributed to a movement. For our purposes, a farmers' organization merely implies a group of people directly depending upon agriculture who act together in pursuit of collective goals, implicit or explicit, and the existence of a bureaucratic hierarchy of some kind to facilitate their achievement.

Such organizations may take forms ranging from corporate enterprises and large landowners associations to farm-workers' unions, credit societies, cooperatives, peasant leagues, or political movements and parties. Numerous typologies have been proposed based on such criteria as ideology (Catholic, socialist, etc.), clientele (peasant, landlord, sugar producers, etc.), goals and functions (credit, marketing, political action, production, etc.), and legal form (cooperatives, corporations, unions, etc.). Instead of commencing with an elaborate classification, however, I will stick to common usage and hope that a pattern will emerge.

It should be obvious that the legal codes of individual countries are often the determining factor of what form a given organization takes. For example, Juliao's decision to organize peasant leagues instead of agricultural workers' unions in northeast Brazil after 1955 was largely because these could be legally recognized immediately under the civil code while the law impeded creation of effective peasant unions [19]. This was changed by the Rural Labour Statute of 1963, and over 2,000 peasant unions were organized in Brazil in the year preceding the military government which practically prohibited them again in 1964.

Before attempting to summarize the functions of farmers' organizations in rural development I will sketch very briefly the experiences in three countries—Chile, Mexico, and the United States. Neither development nor farmer organizations happen in isolation but only within a particular historical and social context. Moreover, while farmers' organizations have analytically separable functions in development, the same organization may simultaneously play several roles. For these reasons it is important to see how they evolved in a few particular cases before making broader generalizations.

Chile Just a century ago the Chilean National Agricultural Society (SNA) was organized in Santiago (for the third time since 1838) by a group of large landowners. The Society's legal charter stated its objective to be the promotion of agricultural technical education and progress. A glance at the organization's first bulletins for 1869 and 1870, however, shows an at least equal concern about such mundane matters as the emigration of unskilled farm laborers to higher paying jobs in Peru, foreign markets and prices for wheat, the availability of credit, costs of farm inputs, and national land policies [5]. During its long history the SNA has played an important role not only in fomenting technical agricultural education but also in influencing legislation affecting all aspects of the national economy. Among other things the Society has been successful until very recently in proscribing effective agricultural labor unions, in blocking agrarian reform, and in preventing the effective organization of competing political pressure groups representing other strata of the farm population.

While the National Agricultural Society in Chile has played an important role in planning and implementing agricultural policy, its membership has never included more than a very small percentage of the country's farmers. In 1955 the large and medium-sized farmers, the only ones who might conceivably have been represented by the SNA, amounted to only 9 percent of the total number of farm families in the country, although they controlled over 90 percent of the land in farms [9]. The SNA's most recent data indicate that its membership controls about two-thirds of the country's agricultural production.

Small-holders and farm laborers have not participated in Chilean farm organizations until relatively recently. The communists organized some of the first farm workers' unions in the narrow North Central Choapa valley in 1925. Workers on the large sheep estancias in sparsely settled Patagonia, mostly migratory seasonal labor, had formed an effective union with the aid of the socialist party before World War II, taking advantage of more liberal legislation regulating industrial unions. The socialists and communists had also aided in organizing the Mapuche Indians, the majority being small semisubsistence producers living on reservations in south central Chile, and the subsistence farmers living on communal-held lands in the arid north, where many worked part-time in neighboring mines and had already participated in union activities there. In the early 1950's the vineyard workers in Chile's most important wine-producing area organized with the support of progressive Catholic intellectuals and carried out a partially successful strike for higher wages [28]. A few groups of small farmers had been included in farmers' cooperatives, but these were generally dominated by large landowners and tradesmen with the primary objective of taking advantage of favorable credit and tax provisions [18].

While farm workers' unions had gained considerable momentum and membership during the opening months of the "Popular Front" government elected in 1938, they were practically prohibited by a presidential decree in 1939 as a result of a political transaction with the large landowners. In 1947 legislation was adopted reaffirming the main points of the 1939 decree virtually proscribing farm union activities. This law was not repealed until 1967, although it was in effect ignored, beginning in 1965 [1].

Rural organization took place on a wide scale after the Christian

Democratic government was elected in 1964 with a populist program and an ideology that placed considerable emphasis on the integration into the national society of "marginal" groups such as the small-holders and farm workers. The government introduced new agricultural union legislation and actively promoted farm labor unions and organizations of small-holders. Within four years well over half of the country's farmers had been organized into unions, credit societies, precooperatives, cooperatives, and land reform asentamientos. The government, the major political parties, and various groups aided by the Catholic Church and foreign agencies such as the United States-based International Development Foundation all competed for the peasants' affiliation. Real wages of farm workers increased substantially on the average. Some credit was diverted to small producers and a strong land reform law was adopted; it was implemented rather cautiously with slightly more than 5 percent of the country's farm families having received land by early 1969.

Proponents of these new low-status farmer organizations see them as indispensable for future rural development. Large landowners and other conservative groups, on the other hand, view with alarm the exponentially growing number of strikes, the rural unrest, their higher production costs, and the competition among peasant groups for membership and patronage accompanying this proliferation of farmers' organizations; they declare that agricultural development may have been set back for decades as a result.

Mexico In Mexico the only nationally recognized important farmer organization at the time of the 1910 revolution were those of the few large hacendados who owned nearly all of the land. Discontented intellectuals instigated the revolt against the Diaz regime with considerable middle-class help. The revolution soon spread to other social groups and was pushed considerably further than many of its founders intended to go by bands of armed peasants long resentful of the loss of their traditional village lands and their increasingly inferior status. The most charismatic of the peasant leaders, Emiliano Zapata, organized peasant armies in the state of Morelos that not only waged a successful guerrilla war but at times occupied the nation's capital. Zapata's 1912 "Plan de Ayala" for returning the hacienda lands to the peasant communities was followed by a de facto land reform in his own state of Morelos. This provoked the adoption of a national land reform law in 1915 and Article 27 of the 1917 constitution. During the subsequent five decades, peasant ejidos acquired nearly half the agricultural land in the country. Although the individual peasant had been virtually powerless in Mexican society, peasant movements had been instrumental in bringing about a profound social revolution [24].

Zapata was murdered by his political enemies only two years after adoption of the 1917 constitution promising land to those who worked it. Peasant organizations, however, played an increasingly important role in Mexican politics and rural development during subsequent years. Sometimes opposed by the government and sometimes encouraged by it, sometimes allied with urban labor unions and sometimes in conflict with them, often competing bitterly among themselves for influence and patronage, these low-status farmers' associations were a political force that had to be taken into account. Peasant organization was further stimulated by the fact that, under the terms of the agrarian code, committees composed of peasants had to be formed at the community level in order to petition for land.

During the Cardenas regime, from 1934 to 1940, about 800,000 peasant families were established on ejidos, more land being distributed in these six years (some 18 million hectares) than during the previous two decades. Cardenas depended heavily upon peasant organizations for political support and distributed some 60,000 rifles to peasant militias to enable them to defend the reform against armed bands mobilized by landlords, conservative clergy, and other political opponents. In the rich irrigated cotton-producing Laguna area the Cardenas government worked closely with peasant associations in expropriating the large estates and in establishing collectively operated ejidos complemented by a peasant-owned and managed insurance company and peasant-controlled marketing organizations. The government established the Banco Ejidal to provide credit for these and other ejidos throughout the country. Peasant organizations not only influenced government policy but were a principal instrument for carrying it out.

After 1940 the influence of middle-class commercial, industrial, and professional groups increased rapidly as they consolidated their position in the new social structure. Organizations of the larger commercial farmers became relatively more powerful and government policy gradually shifted from encouraging strong peasant organizations to one of manipulating credit, patronage, and political influence in order to assure compliant peasant support for official programs. The Ejidal Bank began to give preferential treatment to splinter groups within the collective ejidos, and peasant leaders were provided with government salaries

and opportunities for individual upward mobility in return for supporting the official line instead of pressing peasant demands.

With the cooptation of its leaders the powerful national peasant confederation (CNC, or Confederacion Nacional de Campesinos) that had
been organized under Cardenas became more and more integrated into
the structure of the governing party while the lion's share of new agricultural investments went to benefit the larger commercial farmers and
not the peasant ejidatarios. In the northeastern development area,
where the Mexican government invested large sums in new irrigation,
much of the land was distributed to politicians and entrepreneurs with
government connections instead of to peasant committees as stipulated by law. The peasants then organized an independent union to
pressure for land and in 1958 symbolically occupied some of the properties. They eventually gained enough public sympathy to force expropriation of many of the new latifundios (large land-holdings) [14, 24,
26, 29].

United States Farmers' organizations in the highly industrialized
United States, where only about one person out of every twenty is now
farming, can hardly be expected to have the same role in rural development programs as in Mexico or Chile. Most United States commercial
farmers belong not to one farmer organization but to several, many of
them highly specialized. A typical United States commercial farmer
may be a member of the Farm Bureau, the Grange, a commodity-
oriented association such as the Dairyman's League or the Apple Growers Association, various federally and state-sponsored organizations
such as soil conservation districts, farm credit associations, grazing districts or irrigation districts, plus a farmers' cooperative for purchasing
farm inputs. He might also participate in privately owned corporations
of the "agribusiness" complex. The modern industrial state is an organizational state.

Only low-status farm laborers, tenants, and subsistence farmers are
likely to lack effective organization in the United States structure.
These are relatively unimportant numerically in many farming regions,
although they still constitute a majority of the rural population in some
parts of the south and southwest. Even this situation seems to be changing with Chavez's recent success in organizing Spanish American and
other low-status farm labor in California, the progress of the various
civil rights organizations in the south, and rapid out-migration to the
cities.

Historically, however, there are many parallels with today's less-developed countries in the early struggles of United States farmers to organize in their own interests, as well as in the efforts of the government to mobilize farmers. The "committees of correspondence" and local militias that initiated the American Revolution in New England were in large measure organizations of farmers and tradesmen. Shays's Rebellion in western Massachusetts and the "Whiskey Rebellion" in central Pennsylvania were organized by farmers disgruntled with the impact of credit, monetary, and tax policies. The farmers of central New York organized and rioted in the early nineteenth century to abolish quitrents and similar quasifeudal obligations left over from the Dutch land system in that area. Farmer political pressure was partly instrumental in obtaining passage of the Homestead Act and the creation of the Land Grant College System [37].

Following the Civil War farmer resentment in the Midwest against exploitation by the railroad companies, high interest rates and tight credit led to the organization of the Patrons of Husbandry (The Grange), the Farmers' Alliance, the Greenback and Free-Silver movements, the Populist Party, the Farmers Educational and Cooperative Union, and the American Society of Equity. These essentially farmer organizations succeeded in bringing about many fundamental changes in agrarian policy such as the regulation of freight rates in interstate commerce. While most of the numerous farmers' cooperatives established in this period, including an experiment with cooperative banking in California, did not survive for very long, they were the forerunners of a more effective cooperative movement and had considerable success in breaking monopolies in some local situations. The Farmers' Union, the Non-Partisan League, the American Society of Equity, and later the Farmer-Labor Party not only succeeded in starting a powerful farmers cooperative movement in the Midwest but also put many western state governments directly into the business of marketing and storing farm products and inputs [6, 35].

The post-World War I slump in export demand for farm products followed by the Depression of the 1930s further stimulated farmer organization. The Farmer Labor Party, the Farmers' Union, and other relatively radical organizations did much to create the political climate for the Bank Holiday and subsequent New Deal legislation designed to improve agricultural prices and raise farm incomes. The more conservative Farm Bureau, however, working closely with the state and federal governments, with the Federal Extension Service, which it had helped to create, with the business community in general, and especially with local Chambers of Commerce, became highly influential both in planning and implementing the New Deal and subsequent farm legislation. The Farm Bureau had been organized in part to forestall a threatened political union between hard-pressed farmers and urban labor. In 1950 the Farm Bureau included only about one-fourth of the nation's farm operators, but its membership consisted mostly of the better-off commercial farmers [37]. Small farmers' and farm laborers' organizations, on the other hand, became relatively less important as the United States became increasingly prosperous, urban, and industrialized.

These three brief case histories provide a basis for generalizations about the functions of farmers' organizations in rural development. I will refer back to them in the following section.

Functions of Farmers' Organizations

As rural development planning is a political process, farmers' organizations contribute to planning to the extent they influence political processes and decisions. They contribute to the implementation of development plans by mobilizing farm people to work for collective goals and by creating new institutions required for development. This provides the broad framework for analysis of their functions.

Interest Articulation Farmers' organizations often function as pressure groups. The examples cited of the Chilean National Agricultural Society, Zapata's peasant army, and the American Farm Bureau Federation illustrated this clearly. Interest articulation, to use Almond and Coleman's terminology, was a primary function of these and of many other farm organizations mentioned earlier [3].

When farmers' organizations include wealthy landlords and large commercial producers their influence in planning may be very great in countries with traditional agrarian structures in which large landowners generally have a virtual monopoly of local political power along with high social status and prestige. These landlords would be influential individually even without formal organization. In agrarian societies where most wealth is in the form of land and where the control of land and labor is the main source of political power, it should surprise no one if through organization the landowners often constitute a powerful pressure group such as the Chilean National Agricultural Society. The rules under which traditional societies operate are made, applied, and abjudicated taking the large farmers' interests into account. In fact, legislatures in agrarian countries may be partly composed of large landowners' representatives—for example, Hirashima estimates that 96 percent of the members of the West Pakistan Provincial Assembly and of the Pakistan National Assembly in 1962 were occupationally and socially wealthy agriculturists or landlords, although many also had other businesses or professions, and most lived in the cities [7, 21].

The administrative bureaucracies are often recruited from the families of these large landowners; in Ecuador about 80 percent of the professional and technical personnel of the Agrarian Reform Agency (IERAC) came from relatively wealthy landowning families [10]. Many of the judges and lawyers in the judicial systems of such countries have similar social origins. The principal newspapers, radio stations, and other means of mass communications are likely to be controlled by large landowners or by their organizations. The educational systems and other socializing institutions, such as the established Church, tend to be attuned to the preservation of traditional social relationships. In short, large farmers' organizations may be the dominant influence in rural development planning.

It would be naive in the extreme, however, to assume that all farmers' organizations could so easily influence the political systems in which they operate. Most farmers in the developing countries are low-status, small producers and workers—i.e., peasants. Almost by definition they are subordinate to the large landowners and urban groups. They are often both illiterate and voteless. In Latin America, for example, the majority of the present-day governments came to power not through elections but by means of some kind of military coup. Rural illiteracy is two or three times higher than urban, and in countries such as Haiti and Guatemala, because of literacy requirements, over three-fourths of the farm population could not vote even if elections were held. Even if they can vote, the peasants' choices are often so limited that their participation in elections has little significance for national planning.

Peasant organizations, therefore, frequently resort to tactics such as strikes, demonstrations, and violence in order to articulate their interests and influence policy. In 1960-1963 demonstrations and strikes organized by peasant unions in La Convencion, Peru, under Hugo Blanco's leadership, occurred when permanent laborers on the large plantations in the area simply refused to continue providing practically wageless labor services to the landlords. The plantations were worked by two classes of laborers, the arrendires, who had been given rights to use relatively large plots of unimproved land (10 to 15 hectares) in return for rendering labor obligations on the plantation, often from 300 to 600 days per year; and the allegados, who were given use of much smaller areas within the arrendires' plots and who paid their labor obligations to the arrendires. As money wages on the plantations often amounted to only about four cents daily and markets for their produce were improving, it became economically advantageous for the arrendires to use their own and their allegado labor in their own plots. Some actually increased their incomes while on strike. Although the movement was ruthlessly suppressed with armed force and the leaders jailed, it was effective in influencing development planning. A special decree was promulgated dividing the large holdings in the immediate area and selling them to the peasants. Soon afterwards a first attempt at national agrarian reform legislation was speeded through the legislature [32].

The show of strength by the Ligas Camponesas and other peasant unions in northeast Brazil, where a strike of over 200,000 farm workers took place in 1962, resulted in many concessions by the landlords and in the stimulation of several national and regional proposals for agrarian reforms [11, 19]. It also probably was one factor causing the military take-over two years later that reinforced the power of the more traditional large farmers' organizations at the expense of the peasants.

The fourteenth-century English peasant risings, the peasant movements in sixteenth-century Germany, and numerous more recent peasant movements throughout the world were in some ways comparable to those in present-day Latin America [27]. Sometimes they achieved limited success in articulating peasant interests within the existing political systems, sometimes they were followed by repression and a worsening of the peasants' situation, and sometimes they contributed to social and political revolutions, as happened in twentieth-century Mexico, Bolivia, Cuba, Russia, and China. While the differences among these revolutionary changes were at least as notable as the similarities, in all of them organized peasants played an important role.

In revolutionary situations where various elite groups are fighting for power, the weaker ones such as the new middle classes and emerging industrial entrepreneurs may turn to the peasants for support, encouraging their organization and even arming them, as happened in 1953 in Bolivia, and as Cardenas did in Mexico. The peasants then have relatively strong bargaining power for a brief period during which they may be granted major concessions such as land. Once the revolution is consolidated, however, only rarely have peasant organizations maintained their newly won influence for long. As Landsberger and Hewitt point out, the sources of weakness and cleavage within peasant groups are always present [30]. They are easily taken advantage of by better educated groups—the opposition to peasant interests by other more powerful social groups is usually strong enough to keep peasant organizations from maintaining much political influence [16]. In Venezuela, peasant organizations enjoyed a brief period of relatively strong power when the Perez Jimenez dictatorship was overthrown, but they soon became more instruments for carrying out government agrarian policy rather than for shaping it much in the same way as had happened earlier with the CNC in Mexico [25]. Even where the official ideology is strongly oriented in favor of the peasants as in mainland China or Cuba, the scanty information presently available does not indicate that it is easy for peasant organizations to maintain an independent political role.

Social Mobilization As explained earlier, rural development implies the mobilization of farm people including the peasantry for the achievement of collective goals. Karl Deutsch has defined social mobilization as "the process in which major clusters of old social, economic and psychological commitments are eroded or broken and people become available for new patterns of socialization and behavior" [26]. Deutsch's concept agrees with my premises here concerning the nature of the development process.

After old settings, habits, and commitments have been broken, however, the rural population must be inducted into new patterns of group relationships, socialization, and behavior. In other words, farmers' organizations are not only necessary to influence rural development planning, but also to carry out the plans. This explains much of the emphasis placed upon organizing the peasantry by many developmentally minded governments. Moreover, governments not particularly committed to participatory development often feel compelled to mobilize political support from the peasants and encourage their organization for this reason alone.

Experience shows that government promoted mass-based farmers' organizations do not always act in the way their instigators hoped. It is true that relatively independent peasant organizations frequently become coopted and subverted in order to make them increasingly serve as instruments of official policies, such as happened with the major peasant unions in Venezuela and Mexico. Offsetting this tendency, however, is the fact that the leaders of government and landlord-inspired peasant organizations often discover that the only way they can maintain grass-roots support is to press forward more and more strongly the aspirations of their membership. In Chile, for example, the government, political parties, and church groups have all been attempting to mobilize the peasantry, partly for their own purposes and constituencies. The rival organizations, however, sometimes disconcert their sponsors by showing considerable independence and uniting on bread and butter issues such as higher wages and more sweeping agrarian reform while largely ignoring the ideological disputations that did so much to create them in the first place [1]. Such shows of independence by supposedly grateful and loyal organizations may be highly frustrating for planners and politicians. They can be regarded only as positive by those who see development as being too important to leave to the technicians.

Paradoxically, the very conflicts engendered by peasant organizations pressing forward their demands and the countermeasures taken by groups representing vested interests may speed up social mobilization and community solidarity. For example, in practically all traditional societies the structure of privileges, wealth, and power associated with land ownership is of immediate concern to almost everyone. When population growth, new production methods, changing markets, and values threaten the old order, as is happening now in most of the world's agrarian countries, both peasants and landlords can be more readily rallied to defend what they consider their natural rights inherited from the traditional society than to support any other single issue. The ensuing conflicts may be so great as to slow down growth in agricultural production for several years, as happened in revolutionary Mexico, Bolivia, and Cuba. On the other hand, it must be recognized that when traditional peasants organize to achieve common goals such as land and the abolition of labor services made intolerable by an increasingly commercial society, they rapidly acquire many of the new patterns of commitments and behavior Deutsch sees as an essential part of social change. Peasant solidarity in La Convencion, Peru, for example, was found to be relatively high following their partially successful struggle with the landlords and police [12].

One does not have to be a Chinese Communist to recognize the large measure of truth in Liu Shao-Chi's statement: "Only through the people's own struggles and efforts can their emancipation be achieved, maintained and consolidated . . . ." [20]. His observation is consistent with sociological theory as well as with experience in many countries professing highly diverse ideologies.

Production and Exchange Complementary to their functions of applying political pressure and of social mobilization, farmers' organizations frequently engage directly in production, investment, buying, and selling. The American Farm Bureau, for instance, has interests and influence in numerous businesses serving its membership such as insurance companies, processing plants, and supply houses. Throughout Latin America one finds business corporations of all kinds in which large farmers' associations have made important investments including radio stations, newspapers, and banks as well as agricultural businesses.

Of more interest to the present analysis, however, are farmers' cooperatives and similar economic organizations which at least in theory have objectives of wider income distribution and democratic participation as well as economic performance. For this reason farmer-owned or -controlled economic institutions based upon cooperative principles are often viewed as being more consistent with dominant development ideologies in poor countries than are capitalist-owned businesses such as corporations, partnerships, and limited liability companies.

The farmers' cooperatives of the United States and Western Europe, especially those in Scandinavia, are frequently seen as models for the developing countries. Others hope to emulate the successful cooperative agricultural structure in Israel with farmers' organizations like the moshavim and kibbutzim, although many Israelis do not believe the latter institution to be exportable. The Yugoslavian experience with labor-management has attracted wide interest in the developing countries and is seen by some as a form of economic organization that could be adapted to conditions in Latin America and similar developing regions. Agricultural organizations based on Soviet-style collectives or Chinese type communes all have their advocates.

In spite of widespread agreement about the desirability of farmers' cooperatives, actual experience has frequently been rather discouraging in Latin America. The collective ejidos in the Laguna region of Mexico mentioned earlier lost much of their initial dynamism after 1940 when government policies became more favorable to private investors and the official ejido bank no longer aggressively favored the collectives but preferentially granted loans to splinter groups within them. The Bolivian land reform never resulted in a strong farmer cooperative movement, although a great many agricultural cooperatives were legally constituted and given slight government assistance. In Cuba the cooperative sugar plantations created to operate the expropriated companies were soon replaced by state farms. One of the principal reasons given by the government for this change was that as some of the cooperatives were much richer in capital and land than others large inequalities of income distribution were being perpetuated. The Puerto Rican proportional profit farms did not evolve into cooperatives but became more and more like corporate plantations with some profit-sharing aspects. The 90,000 beneficiaries of the Venezuelan land reform have never been integrated into a dynamic cooperative structure, although there exist several individually successful cooperatives associated with the reform.

The farmers' cooperatives that have developed outside of a context of national agrarian reform show similar characteristics—one can point to numerous limited successes but one can show no cases where a powerful cooperative movement embraces a major part of the farm population permitting low-status farmers to exert significant market power. Japanese small farmers in Brazil have organized an efficient and powerful marketing cooperative (COTIA), but it is an exception within the country's latifundia-dominated agrarian structure [34]. Milk marketing in much of Costa Rica and grain marketing in parts of Argentina are cooperatively organized. Successful cooperatives are gaining influence in the La Convencion area of Peru following the partial agrarian reform there. Numerous small farmers and handicraft producers' cooperatives have been formed in Ecuador with Peace Corps aid, as in many other countries.

The typical Latin American farmers' cooperative, however, exists primarily in order to take advantage of preferential tax and credit laws. In fact it operates in almost every respect as a privately owned business. Even if its members are of more or less equal social and economic status the cooperative tends to function somewhat as an extended partnership or limited stock company for the benefit of its owners but without much member participation in management. More frequently there are both small and large producers in the same organization. In this situation the cooperative tends to be operated for the benefit of its richer members who take advantage of their superior social position and education to obtain produce and labor from the weaker ones [18]. For example, owners of pisco-processing plants in the Chilean Elqui Valley organized a cooperative among their small suppliers of pisco grapes in order to exercise more effectively their monopsony powers as sole buyer [17].

Critics of cooperative farming can cite examples of where such efforts have failed, often after a few years of initial success. A typical case is Los Silos in Chile, a former property of the Catholic Church, where after four years of apparently successful operation the members decided they would prefer to have their individual family holdings, an outcome not unrelated to national political disputes at the time. Such failures are usually attributed to internal jealousies and dissensions, the absence of sufficient individual incentives, corruption, administrative incompetence, and the peasants' individualism and desire for their own land.

Naturally, peasants who have never known any other land system than one of private property and who have been born and raised in a culture that recognizes land ownership as a primary source of power, security, and prestige do not readily change their values and aspirations. Vicos, a communally owned and cooperatively operated hacienda in Peru, seems to have a better chance for survival because it is partly based on the pre-hacienda Indian community and has strong outside support from Cornell University. In northeastern Brazil, a cooperatively operated sugar plantation, Tiriri, was supported by SUDENE (the North-eastern Development Authority) and is in a region where planta-tion workers are much more accustomed to work collectively than are peasants in areas of diversified farming and small-holdings.

Nonetheless, it is very difficult for isolated cooperatives of these kinds to survive for long or to spread spontaneously in societies that are primarily oriented toward individually owned holdings and where the economic and social structures are designed primarily to serve the needs of traditionally organized enterprises. As was illustrated by the Laguna (Mexico) experience with collective ejidos, their dynamism depends partly upon a deliberate government policy to support them and the creation of new institutions to service them. In a hostile institutional environment they will always be subject to erosion and attack, espe-cially if they show signs of economic success that would enable them to compete with and possibly threaten existing institutions.

Recent experience with agrarian reform in Chile further illustrates some of the difficulties that have prevented cooperatives from achieving more prominence in rural Latin America. The agricultural development agency responsible for aiding small farmers (INDAP) stimulated the organization of numerous cooperatives. One of the INDAP-promoted regional cooperatives, Marchigue, in a poor overpopulated coastal area 100 miles south of Santiago, used government credit and technical assistance to develop several dozen cooperative units producing broilers, pork, and handicrafts for the Santiago market. The operation was so successful that the cooperative was supplying close to 10 percent of the city's broiler production after only three years of operation. At this point, established private producers became alarmed and engaged in a series of maneuvers to stifle the cooperatives' competition, cutting off its supply of baby chicks and creating numerous other obstacles to its marketing and purchasing. Only government intervention has kept the operation on its feet. If a fully integrated cooperative structure is not soon established with control of its own incubators, feed mill, slaughter house, and market outlets the cooperative will probably decline if there is any let-up in government support.

Also in Chile the government adopted the asentamiento as a transitional tenure system for managing expropriated estates. While the asentamiento is not legally a cooperative, it operates very much as one, and one of the aims of creating it is to prepare the peasants for cooperative management of their lands. During a three to five-year period the agrarian reform corporation (CORA) and a committee elected by the reform beneficiaries on each asentamiento manage the unit jointly while necessary investments are being made and the beneficiaries are being trained to take over full management responsibilities. In mid-1969 there were nearly 500 of these asentamientos in operation with an average of over 30 families each. These land reform units generally include individually operated small garden plots as well as cooperatively operated crop and livestock enterprises. By law after the asentamiento period the unit should be converted into an agrarian reform cooperative. The beneficiaries decide whether the land will be divided into individually owned small-holdings, held cooperatively, or a mixture of the two (except where technical reasons make subdivisions impossible). The reform agency, however, has attempted to encourage not only cooperative organization but also cooperative land ownership.

The asentamientos have generally functioned fairly well. Production and incomes have increased markedly. While peasant participation in management decisions varies greatly from one to another, on the whole it has been impressive. Nevertheless, several problems have emerged similar to those encountered in the other cooperative experiences mentioned above. In addition to the internal weaknesses of peasant cooperatives that so many sociologists have documented and critics have gleefully pointed to, the four problems mentioned below are particularly noteworthy because they could be remedied by appropriate public policies, and they explain in part the internal difficulties of these kinds of peasant organizations.

There is a tendency for a new social stratification. The land reform beneficiaries on the asentamientos frequently restrict their membership as much as possible even when more intensive production creates additional employment opportunities. As a result, nearly one-third of the asentamiento labor in some zones is hired without participating in the profits or the management decisions of these cooperatives, although in other zones vigorous CORA leadership has convinced the members with rights to land to grant participation in the asentamientos to laborers without land.

It seems obvious that if producers' cooperatives are to achieve their aims, all of their workers should participate in their economic benefits and decision-making on more or less equal terms. While the permanent workers on the large estates are most frequently the beneficiaries of land reform, they are usually fewer in number in Latin America than the holders of small subsistence-sized units and unattached farm laborers. As a consequence, reform beneficiaries often find it economically advantageous to employ laborers who have no rights to land in the asentamiento and in a sense "exploit" this low-cost labor much as the large landlord did before them. Theoretically the problem could be avoided by rigorously separating the rights of ownership from those of control, management, and participation and requiring that participation rights be the same for all labor employed by each cooperative enterprise. This is very difficult in practice in traditionally organized societies.

Another problem, observed almost everywhere peasant cooperatives have been formed, has been a tendency for government officials to manage things too much themselves without allowing as full participation of the asentamiento members in decision-making as would be possible or desirable. As the number of land reform beneficiaries has increased more rapidly than the number of government officials, the asentamientos have necessarily been left more on their own in recent years, but government paternalism continues to be notable. Excessive paternalism, of course, runs counter to the objectives of establishing cooperatives but is highly likely where government officials and other professionals aiding cooperatives come from a higher and much better educated social class than do the peasants. It appears to most officials easier and more efficient to build cooperatives from the top down instead of from the bottom up as the latter course requires patient and skillful educational and promotional efforts.

The result of simply imposing a cooperative structure without the necessary educational work being carried on simultaneously is usually an organization that is cooperative in name only. The same is true of cooperatives that combine in the same organization higher social classes and low-status peasants. In the case of the Chilean asentamientos the promotional problem has been made even more difficult by lack of a clear-cut policy of whether in the long run they would be based upon individual or group ownership of land and other capital.

Closely related to the problem of paternalism is the relatively high government cost of the land reform cooperatives per family benefited. It is axiomatic that long-run survival of cooperatives requires that they be economically competitive with other forms of organization, and that the costs of creating new job and employment opportunities should not be higher through the cooperative than they would be in other lines of investment. Moreover, if the cooperative is not merely to be a link in a centrally planned "command" economy, markets and prices have to be relied upon in large measure to influence investment decisions and re-source allocation (how to influence market prices so that they reinforce development goals as much as possible is still another problem). The practice of subsidizing cooperatives through low or negative interest rates and underevaluation of investments and inputs often work against the objective of attaining competitive economic performance. If sub-sidies are provided for cooperatives, and there are many justifications for these considering the peasants' previously underprivileged position and the prevalence of special privileges, subsidies, and monopolies in the rest of the economy, it is generally preferable from an economic stand-point that they be explicit and direct.

There would be several advantages in the creation of a substantial national fund or bank from which cooperatives or labor-management enterprises such as the asentamientos could rent capital on the basis of reasonable plans and requirements. Assuming competitive interest charges, this would help to achieve a rational resource allocation. It would also help to force the cooperatives to be fully aware of their costs and to keep accurate financial accounts. Moreover, it would pro-vide a built-in motor for growth and expansion as the national coopera-tive fund could be expected to grow constantly through returns on its capital approaching its marginal productivity in the economy which in many developing countries might exceed 10 percent. If, on the con-trary, each cooperative is given an initial endowment of its own capital practically without cost, the temptation to consume the returns on capital instead of investing them are understandably great given the low initial income levels of their members [39].

Another problem of the asentamientos and other peasant producers' cooperatives throughout Latin America is the absence of a strong cooperative marketing and processing structure integrated with the peasant producers' cooperatives. As it is they are largely dependent on the agrarian reform agencies and the traditional private sector for inputs, credit, sales, and services. Political changes could leave them at the mercy of the private sector and a more hostile government bureaucracy as happened in the case of the Laguna collective ejidos. Existing monopolies and monopsonies can be counted upon to hamper peasant cooperatives' effectiveness in every manner imaginable. There is probably some critical size below which a cooperative sector can not possibly hope to operate dynamically within a capitalist economy. In any event, the "rules of the game" must be such that the cooperatives really have a chance to compete on equal terms with private business. This means they must have real political power at the national level where laws and regulations are made and economic policy is formulated and enforced.

In theory, there is no reason why farmers' cooperatives could not compete successfully with privately owned enterprises and eventually control a major part of agricultural marketing and production, bringing many advantages in participation, welfare, and efficiency. In practice, it is doubtful whether cooperatives will play an important role in most developing countries until there have been drastic agrarian reforms and other political changes creating an environment that is more propitious for cooperative endeavor.

Farmers' Organizations and Social Structure

Implicit in the foregoing discussion has been the predominant role of social structure in determining the kinds of farmers' organizations that arise, the functions they have, and the values by which their contemporaries judge their roles in development. Analysis of the changing social structure and other historical circumstances constitutes one of the few useful tools available to the social scientist for predicting what kinds of organizations are probable or possible in particular situations. This is no place to enter into metaphysical debates as to whether society creates values or values shape society, whether history calls forth leaders or leaders make history. It is a fact that development involves changing both society and personalities. An understanding of social structure—of institutions and the changing relationships among them—provides a key for making generalizations about the process.

The principal structural influences on farmers' organizations are, of course, closely associated with agrarian institutions, especially land tenure [8, 38]. For example, population growth, urbanization, the closer incorporation of hitherto isolated rural areas into national and world markets, and changing values and technologies are dynamic factors producing pressures for change in Latin America's agrarian structure. They have caused profound social dislocations, leaving many peasants dissatisfied with their lot and often even worse off than before. Meanwhile, traditional land tenure systems have persisted, and the resistence to changing them is strong [2, 8, 22, 31].[2] In these circumstances peasant movements and organizations frequently have revolutionary implications. Where the agrarian structure is dominated by large landlords and quasifeudal institutions, as is the case in most of Latin America, even if the immediate goals of the peasants are seemingly very modest ones, such as a greater security of tenure or the abolition of compulsory labor-services, they are in effect revolutionary because their attainment implies profound changes in values and institutions.

The form farmers' organizations take, however, will likely be different in an agrarian structure dominated by large commercial plantations, as was Cuba's, than in one dominated by the traditional latifundia-minifundia structure such as the Andean highlands. In the former the demands of the workers tend to be for better wages, improved working conditions, fuller employment, and more participation in profits. In the latter the peasants may place a higher priority on obtaining their own lands.

In Chile there has not been much direct peasant pressure for land except by the Mapuche Indians, who lost much of their territory only a century ago. In areas of commercial agriculture the workers have shown more interest in pressing for better wages, working conditions, and job security than land, although most sharecroppers are apparently anxious to press for ownership of their farms. Those laborers who have usufruct rights to land on the more traditionally organized estates have been highly receptive to promises of owning their own land through agrarian reform. Nevertheless, although they have joined with the poorer tem-

---

[2]Contemporary social scientists, at least in the United States and Western Europe, do not seem to put very high priority on the analysis of social structure in relation to developmental change, although there are some notable exceptions. Concerning the relationships of social structure to peasant movements and revolts, however, a few excellent studies have been published recently, notably, Barrington Moore's and Eric Hobsbawm's historical analyses and a stimulating essay by Hamza Alavi. I know of almost no comparable analyses relating to structural factors to the functioning of other types of farmers' organizations such as cooperatives, although a group of us made an attempt to touch on this problem in the CIDA studies of land tenure and development in Latin America.

porary estate laborers in organizing unions, there has only been relatively mild direct union pressure for land reform. This may in part be explained by the fact that the poorer laborers often realize their chances of getting property rights would be slight even with reform and hence prefer to press for better wages and privileges. Small subsistence farmers, with some exceptions such as the Mapuches, have been more readily organized around demands for credit and markets than for land which their experience indicates may never be available [1].

Once the traditional quasifeudal agrarian structure in Latin America is substantially modified, the functions of even revolutionary peasant organizations may shift from supporting structural changes to fighting for their own interests within the political system and to the mobilization of the peasantry for developmental and other political goals. In Mexico, Bolivia, and Venezuela the peasant unions became less aggressive as political pressure groups for peasant aspirations once considerable land had been distributed to their leaders and membership.

The existence of numerous underemployed landless workers, very small holders, and tenants, however coupled with mass urban unemployment and limited urban job opportunities, will inevitably result in new conflicts and tensions in most of the now less-developed countries. In present-day Mexico there are more poor landless laborers now than at the time of the revolution, for example. Unless these poorer farmers can press forward their interests strongly enough to be provided with job opportunities, they will be left far behind by urban and other better-off rural groups. Substantial amelioration of the employment problem in developing countries, however, would require profound structural changes [4].

Farmers' organizations have played an important role in planning and implementing rural development. What their roles have been or should be depends primarily on one's value premises, historical circumstances, the social structure, and whether the organizations represent small farmers and laborers or more privileged farm groups.

My own conclusion is simple. If the major portion of the low-status peasant producers and farm laborers who constitute the majority of the underdeveloped world's population are to benefit directly and soon from economic growth, they must organize. Once organized, they must press forward their interests effectively. Their organization is also necessary to mobilize farm people for achieving development goals. Presumably, the lessons of experience if properly understood could contribute to the success of their efforts.

388 Solon Barraclough

References

1. Affonso, Almino, Emilio Klein, Pablo Ramirez, y Sergio Gomez, *Movimiento Campesino Chileno*. Santiago: ICIRA, 1969.

2. Alavi, Hamza, "Peasants and Revolution," *Socialist Register*, 1965.

3. Almond, Gabriel, and James Coleman, *The Politics of the Developing Areas*. Princeton: Princeton University Press, 1960.

4. Barraclough, Solon, *Employment Problems Affecting Latin American Agricultural Development*. Department of Agricultural Economics, New York State College of Agriculture, Ithaca, N.Y.: Cornell University, 1968, mimeo.

5. *Boletin de la Sociedad Nacional de Agricultura, 1*, no. 1 (October 1967) Santiago: Libreria Del Mercurio, 1973.

6. Buck, Solon Justus, *The Granger Movement* Lincoln: University of Nebraska Press, 1913, paperback reprint, 1963.

7. CIDA, *Tenencia de la Tierra y Desarrollo Socioeconomico del Sector Agricola: Ecuador*, Washington, D.C.: Pan American Union, 1965.

8. _____, *Tenencia de la Tierra y Desarrollo Socioeconomico del Sector Agricola: Argentina, Brazil, Chile, Colombia, Ecuador, Guatemala y Peru*, Washington, D.C.: Pan American Union, 1966.

9. _____, *Tenencia de la Tierra y Desarrollo del Sector Agricola: Chile*. Santiago: ICIRA, 1966.

10. _____, *Tenencia de la Tierra y Desarrollo Socioeconomico del Sector Agricola: Peru*. Washington, D.C.: Pan American Union, 1966.

11. _____, *Land Tenure Conditions and Socio-Economic Development of the Agricultural Sector: Brazil*. Washington, D.C.: Pan American Union, 1966.

12. Craig, Wesley W., *From Hacienda to Community, An Analysis of Solidarity and Social Change in Peru*, Latin American Studies Program Dissertation Series No. 6. Ithaca: Cornell University, 1967.

13. Deutsch, Karl, "Social Mobilization and Political Development," *The American Political Science Review, LV*, 3 (September 1961).

14. Eckstein, Solomon, *El Ejido Colectivo en Mexico*. Mexico: 1966; Fondo de Cultura.

15. Etzioni, Amitai, *Modern Organizations*. Englewood Cliffs, N.J.: Prentice-Hall, 1968.

16. Feder, Ernest, "Societal Opposition to Peasant Movements." Seminar on Latin American Peasant Movements, New York State College of Labor and Industrial Relations, Cornell University, Ithaca, N.Y. 1968, mimeo.

17. Garcia, Antonio, "Las Cooperativas Pisqueras del Valle del Elqui." Santiago, Chile: ICIRA; 1968, mimeo.

18. _____, *Las Cooperativas Agricolas y Campesinas en Chile*. Santiago: ICIRA, 1969.

19. Hewitt, Cynthia N., *An Analysis of the Peasant Movements of Pernambuco, Brazil: 1961-1964*, Seminar on Latin American Peasant

Movements, New York School of Labor and Industrial Relations, Ithaca, N.Y., 1969, mimeo.

20. Cited by Hinton, William, *Fanshen* New York: Monthly Review Press, 1966.

21. Hirashima, Shigemochi, "Political Factors in Land Reform." Unpublished paper, Cornell University, January, 1967.

22. Hobsbawm, Eric, J., *Primitive Rebels*. Manchester: Manchester University Press, 1959.

23. See Horowitz, Irving Louis, *Three Worlds of Development*. Oxford University Press, 1966. Also Gunnar Myrdal, *Asian Drama*. New York: Panthenon, 1968.

24. Huizer, Guerrit, *On Peasant Unrest in Latin America*. Washington, D.C.: CIDA, UP-65/071, June 1967.

25. See _____ "Popular Participation in Land Reform" (with special emphasis on the role of Peasant Organizations in Latin America), International Labor Office preliminary draft, Geneva, 1968, mimeo.

26. _____ , *The Role of Peasant Organizations in Mexico*. Washington, D.C.: CIDA/ILO, 1968, mimeo.

27. Landsberger, Henry, *A Framework for the Study of Peasant Movements*, Latin American Studies Program Reprint Series, Reprint No. 20. Ithaca: Cornell University, 1968.

28. _____ , and Fernando Canitrot M., *Iglesia, Intelectuales y Campesinos: La Huelga Campesina de Molina*. Santiago: Editorial del Pacifico, 1967.

29. _____ , and Cynthia N. Hewitt, *Preliminary Report on a Case Study of Mexican Peasant Organizations*, I. L. and R., Cornell University, Ithaca, N.Y., 1967, mimeo.

30. _____ , *Ten Sources of Weakness and Cleavage in Latin American Peasant Movements* (mimeo), to be published in Rodolfo Stavenhagen (ed.), Latin American Peasantry (forthcoming).

31. Moore, Barrington, *The Social Origins of Dictatorship and Democracy*. Boston: Beacon, 1965.

32. Quijano Obregon, Anibal, *Los Movimientos Campesinos Contemporaneos en Latino-America*. Santiago, Chile: 1965, ILPES, mimeo.

33. *Report to the Congress on the Implementation of Title IX*, Washington, D.C.: AID, May 10, 1967, mimeo.

34. Saito, Hiroshi, "Cooperative Agricola de COTIA, Brasil," *Las Cooperativas como Metodo de Desarrollo de Regiones y Comunidades*. Washington, D.C.: Pan American Union, 1964.

35. Saloutos, Theodore, and John D. Hicks, *Twentieth Century Populism*. Lincoln: University of Nebraska Press, 1951.

36. For a summary of these movements see Santos de Morais, C. *Grupos de Presion del Agro-Movimientos y Organizaciones de Trabajadores Rurales*, Memoria del Seminario Nacional de Reforma Agraria para Sacerdotes, Instituto Nacional Agrario de Honduras, Tegicugalpa, March 10-14, 1969.

37. Shannon, Fred A., *American Farmers Movements*. Princeton: Van Nostrand, 1957. An Anvil Original.

38. For an interesting discussion of some of these structural influences, see Arthur L. Stinchombe, "Agricultural Enterprise and Class Relationships," *American Journal of Sociology*, September, 1962.

39. Vanek, Jaroslav, *The General Theory and Perspective of Labor Managed Economies*. Ithaca: Cornell University Press, 1969.

40. See, for example, Waterston, Albert, *Development Planning*. Baltimore: Johns Hopkins Press, 1965.

Part One
24. Types of
Yitzchak Abt
Agricultural Projects
VII. Implementation
Used in Developing
of Rural
Countries
Development

After years of effort to lay a foundation for sustained growth of agricultural production in developing countries, an effort which is beginning to bear fruit,[1] planners should pause and take stock of their experiences. In many developing countries the situation has at best remained static. Despite consistent growth of food production in Latin America, Asia, and Africa in recent years, there is as yet no clear evidence of sustained growth per capita. In fact, total and per capita agricultural indices show that in the face of the steady population growth the index of per capita production has, actually, somewhat declined.[2]

Taking cognizance of the major causes limiting agricultural growth in developing countries and the impracticability—especially in Asia, Central America, and the Caribbean areas—of bringing extended new areas under traditional cultivation, the inevitable answer to the problem of at least maintaining the per capita production levels lies in modernization.

Until recently, efforts to modernize traditional agriculture have been channeled into three major types of projects: (1) production campaigns; (2) establishment of large commercial or administered farms; and (3) socioeconomic planning of family farms and rural communities. Recently, an additional dimension to rural development, namely, the concept of integrated rural area planning, has been successfully applied. Many planners consider that this concept is destined to play a highly important role within the general context of development dynamics. It should be pointed out that the implementation of any of the three types can be, and has been, linked with the implementation of national or regional development schemes such as irrigation and/or settlement carried out as part of agrarian reform.

Production Campaigns

Generally, production campaigns pursue two sets of objectives: (1) introduction of improved technology in the cultivation of traditional subsistence crops (maize, rice, wheat, sorghum, cassava, etc.) or tradi-

Yitzchak Abt—Israel. Agronomist, Stellenbosch University, South Africa (1954); Deputy Director, Center for International Cooperation in Agriculture; member of the Research Team, the Settlement Study Center.

[1] Lester R. Brown, "The New Era in World Agriculture," *Foreign Agriculture,* January 1969.
[2] W. W. McPherson (ed.), *Economic Development of Tropical Agriculture* (Gainesville: University of Florida Press, 1968).

tional industrial crops (cotton, sugarcane, oil crops, etc.); and (2) promotion of newly introduced cropping and husbandry practices as part of an effort to diversify agriculture and develop multicropping systems where conditions permit. The principal aim of all production campaigns is to increase regional or national production through greater productivity resulting in higher yields. Generally, production campaigns have been backed by price-support programs, subsidization of commercial inputs, and organization, or upgrading, of the credit and marketing arrangements. A vital prerequisite is, of course, concerted agricultural extension and action programs linked to timely supply of inputs.

One of the merits of production campaigns is that they permit concentration of human and financial resources for the fulfilment of a defined objective. To some extent, the present "green revolution" in some developing countries is an outgrowth of specialized production campaigns. Undoubtedly, the development of hybrid and synthetic varieties and the availability of new effective pesticides, herbicides, and fertilizers have stimulated the development of operational systems which incorporate novel practices.

The usual time lag between the introduction of modern inputs and their acceptance by traditional farmers can be, at least in part, traced to the inadequacies of the extension services in many developing countries. In a region, for example, such as northeast Thailand, the extension service is confronted with a situation whereby 25 percent of the farmers had never heard of fertilizers and over 50 percent had never used them. An effort to introduce an improved rice variety has met with resistance because of the farmers' preference for the native glutinous rice. The much greater input requirements of the improved variety have to be substantiated. On "costing-out" the introduction of new inputs for rice culture in that region, especially of fertilizers and pesticides, it is clear that such technology can be applied only where high yields are assured through irrigation throughout the growing season.

In some countries attempts to introduce second crops grown under irrigation in the dry season—oil crops, for example—have failed because of the inability to convince the farmers of the long-range reliability of the proposed innovation. This has been observed where technological achievements of the research stations have not been sufficiently promoted among the traditional farmers.

Shortcomings of extension services are known to have adversely affected the outcome of a number of production campaigns. In some countries extension services are not sufficiently attuned to the needs of the cross-section of the farming population, placing rather exaggerated hopes on the demonstration effect of large farms or plantations.

The traditional farmer is generally reluctant to accept innovations if he is not convinced of their absolute profitability. It is the more advanced and progressive farmers who are more receptive to new techniques leaving the traditional farmer to trail far behind. Often this has enabled the former to capture the market previously served by the traditional farmer. This has been the case in many countries where large operators, benefiting from livestock-production campaigns, established large-scale production units and eased the small farmers out of the market.

At the root of the problem is a dearth of extension personnel to help implement production campaigns. Often, the result is that local extension personnel channel their promotional efforts into commercial progressive farms by allocating investments in such a way that these farms, in effect, turn out to be the only beneficiaries of the campaigns.

Montague Judelman in his study of agricultural development in Latin America quantifies the shortage of extension personnel on the continent, pointing out that in 1965 there was roughly one trained agronomist per 2,000 active persons in agriculture, whereas a ratio of one per 500 should be regarded as a practicable minimum.[3]

Even under ideal physical and economic conditions the ability of some of the dairy production campaigns to achieve the set objectives within a reasonable time has been limited by the lack of know-how by traditional farmers to manage dairy farms. Therefore, when planning a national production campaign, the time factor necessary to train farmers and the subsequent requirements of intensive on-the-farm extension work must be carefully taken into consideration.

A major problem facing the traditional farmer is the high cost of inputs. Fertilizer is generally more expensive in Latin America than in the industrialized countries of the world.[4] In Brazil for example, 100 kilograms of corn will buy 6 kilograms of nitrogen; in the United States the same amount will buy 16 kilograms, and in Mexico, which is an exception for Latin America, 22 kilograms. Much of Mexico's more rapid progress in agriculture results from its heavier use of fertilizer. The price of mechanized equipment in developing countries is generally

[3]Inter-American Development Bank, *Agricultural Development in Latin America: The Next Decade* (Washington, D.C., 1967).
[4]M. Judelman, *Agricultural Development in Latin America: Current Status and Prospects* (Washington, D.C.: Inter-American Development Bank, October 1966).

very high. In 1963, a 50-horsepower tractor cost an English farmer 315 metric quintals of wheat; a Colombian, 575; a Chilean, 800; and an Argentinian, 1,300.

The timely and economic supply of inputs for a national production campaign in the larger developing countries is a mammoth task involving many problems. In one East African country, for example, the maize campaign called for the introduction of farm machinery to ensure timely cultivation and a potential yield growth of over 150 percent. It was found, however, that the break-even point was at a yield improvement of 100 percent. Obviously under such conditions full mechanization could be applied only on the few—if any—very efficient commercial farms. The need is therefore to determine, before the production campaign is undertaken, the optimum package of farm inputs in relation to costs, and other limiting factors. Moreover, in regions with unreliable rainfall, irrigation facilities must be secured. Failure to do so is exemplified in the case of Laos, where efforts to expand the production of the IR 8 rice in the Vientienne plain have thus far resulted in the planting of a mere 6 percent of the suitable land with this variety, because of the inadequate rain distribution and lack of irrigation facilities.

In some developing countries production campaigns have been accompanied by unforeseen resource dislocations. In Latin America and Africa, for example, production campaigns for maize, cotton, and sesame led to the dislocation in the distribution of professional manpower, with detrimental results for some of the other agricultural branches. In Venezuela, the 1961 successful maize production campaign had stimulated maize production, but with a negative side effect of uneconomic growing of maize in ecologically unsuitable regions. In many countries, success of production campaigns could be attributed solely to a system of heavy price supports. Introduced to overcome shortages, these were difficult to cancel or to reduce even after production of the commodity fully met market demand. This was due to the inbuilt pressures that the support system had created.

Production campaigns have been more successful in smaller developing countries, particularly those having a better-developed infrastructure. Israel, for example, has achieved outstanding success in promoting the production of cotton, sugarbeet, horticultural products for export, and grain. A successful wheat production campaign is at present due to a breakthrough in auxilliary irrigation practices and the introduction of improved varieties.

Better overall success can be expected in countries where the economics of the various ecological regions and their comparative production advantages have been carefully weighed. Other essential factors are an efficient extension service, catering to the needs of the cross-section of the farming population, and marketing and credit organizations capable of matching the upgraded agrotechnology.

In many countries production campaigns produced results other than those which can be assessed statistically. For example, government encouragement of commodity promotion has, in some cases, restored farmers' confidence in government policies. They paved the way to the establishment of primary producers' associations, making the achievement of the "immediate income targets" (better food basket) possible. This, in turn, has enabled planners to proceed with the programming of further investments for diversification of agriculture, such as investment in irrigation and drainage works, designed to lead to the eventual introduction of the multicropping system.

There are outstanding prospectives for the "green revolution" and its contribution to welfare, especially in tropical areas. At the International Institute for Rice Research, Los Baños, the Philippines, Dr. R. Bradfield produced in one year 17 tons of grain (3 crops) and 5 tons of rice per hectare. Given the climatic advantages of tropical countries, there is no reason why similar results cannot be achieved in many other equally suitable ecological regions.

Whatever the success of production campaigns in terms of material returns, their socioeconomic residual effect has been significant. They have enabled farmers to become acquainted with modern inputs and their use. Frequently, the campaigns led to the bolstering of the effectiveness of the rural credit and marketing systems. They have, in some cases, stimulated the initiation of ecological and economic regional research, useful in pinpointing the relative advantages of individual regions. Finally, they have impelled the extension services to formulate specific actions programs and have subsequently streamlined financing operations for such purposes.

Commercial and Administered Farms
Prereform agriculture is generally characterized by large holdings; absentee ownership; extensive land use; and stagnant technology entailing a minimum of cash outlays. The management—semifeudal or hired— is often mediocre. Theoretically, holdings of this nature could be modernized, but in practice the restraints have been virtually unsur-

mountable. One of the main reasons for the stagnant technology and inefficient management is the fact that, for their owners, the holdings are a symbol of social prestige as well as a bulwark against inflation. In this context there can be little room for incentives to produce more. Even if there are improvements in technology and overall farm income, the rural labor force benefits very little, if at all, from such improvements. There have been attempts to break this vicious circle by promoting redistribution of property through land taxation, to enable the more enterprising elements to take over such farms and engage in commercial farming.

Establishment of large, heavily mechanized, commercial farms has not always brought results commensurate with the investment. Conceived as a shortcut for agricultural development, large farms were hoped to serve as models of high productivity, producing enough food for the big cities as well as for export and employing large numbers of laborers to boot.

Some governments awarded potentially lucrative concessions to foreign firms, often from industrial countries, to undertake farm production on large-scale units. They relied on their initiative, resources, and knowhow to create the hoped-for breakthrough which would lead to rapid modernization of farm production and marketing. Unfortunately, in many cases the inapplicability of farm equipment and methods, the lack of adequate understanding of the institutional framework, bad labor relations, and the unfounded optimism that modern technology would be a magic wand for better yields had led to disappointments.

Postcolonial state-run farms have proved to be the least efficient, mainly because of lack of competent management, bureaucracy, and inflexibility in adaptation to local conditions. Many of them have, in effect, become a burden on the economy. In most cases, these farms have not fulfilled the expectations of providing permanent large-scale employment, rather employing labor only for the planting and harvesting seasons.

One of the main problems of large commercial farms has to do with the tendency to overmechanize. For traditional crops, the break-even point is reached at a relatively high yield. This is especially apparent in those developing countries where the management is inefficient and unit costs of traction work are often double what they are in developed countries. It follows, then, that large-scale commercial farming should be undertaken only for the relatively high-value industrial and horticultural crops, e.g. cotton, tobacco, fruit plantations, etc.

Nevertheless, operation of large farms has brought substantial benefits to some countries. They have pioneered in commodity target production, and they have been the mainstay of specialized export crops, as is the case in the plantation system today in many postcolonial countries. Many countries have adopted policies to preserve the plantations despite political pressures to divide these farms among the plantation workers or peasants. New systems of profit-sharing have been evolved for farms which are recognized as commercially important to the national economy. Even countries undertaking agrarian reforms have found it wise to seek private initiative and capital to open up new areas by allowing enterprising investors to develop large commercial farming. This has particularly been the case in countries which could not afford to invest public funds in extensive land development. The special lease system used in the Mahiyangana Project in Ceylon aimed at developing new lands by granting lessee rights to farmers of the private sector. In this way private capital was mobilized for the development of spearhead crop production zones.

One of the companies adopted a novel program of farm development which incorporated a rural housing project based on the provision of land adjacent to each house. By undertaking real estate development, the company has enabled farm workers to become fully fledged settlers while assuring for itself a stable and reliable labor force. Moreover, the farm will be operated on a profit-sharing basis. The project will assure for the company a regular supply of tobacco and rice for processing. Hopefully this interesting socioeconomic undertaking will be an important precedent in linking welfare targets to commercial interests.

However, there is evidence that the original optimism of some governments that the plantation management could be induced to and could succeed in diversifying agricultural production proved in most cases unfounded. This was due to the fact that specialization of management skills was so narrow as to preclude expansion into other production spheres. The incorporation of administered production units as a built-in element of development schemes is a contemporary strategy of considerable value. In some countries large units are being developed as demonstration-cum-training farms aimed to help bridge the gap between the achievements of agricultural research and the farmers.

One variant of this system are the Youth Training Farm projects, which are, in fact, forerunners of new settlements on hitherto undeveloped lands. The projects have been used in settling trained youth in some Asian and West African countries. Working on pioneer farms, the youth manually clear and prepare the land for farming. This has proved to be a rather expensive and wasteful method, especially because it involves the payment of per diem subsistence allowances to trainees. Hence, it is desirable that such farms have at their disposal some developed land prior to the commencement of training programs. This would permit the farms to reach the take-off point earlier. Moreover, estimates show that the cost of land development by efficient use of heavy machinery is cheaper than the payment of subsistence allowances.

Large-scale administered farms have played a significant role in the priming of new settlement projects in Israel. Farms established as administered units were parceled out to settlers after their viability had been proved and the newcomers trained in the techniques of modern farming. Establishment of such farms in undeveloped and unsettled areas has offered to potential settlers the combined advantages of training and concurrent wage-employment. In the absence of experimental stations, the farm staff carry out local crop trials, establishing at least tentatively the best crops suited for their areas. In some cases this has offered the possibility of drawing up a commercial crop plan, which although containing an element of risk, frequently proved its feasibility.

In Latin America, for example, the Fincas Escuelas, demonstration and training farms, have been the forerunners in the practical application of modern agriculture in new settlement areas. They have trained numerous prospective farmers and have been active in the dissemination of new techniques among farmers of the surrounding communities. Rapid turnover of trainees, who spend only one or two seasons at the farms, permits training at a relatively low cost, which is to some extent recovered through the sale of farm produce.

Large, well-managed farms, utilizing modern production techniques and research data, have been important instruments for the promotion of improved seed production and stock breeding. In Israel, for example, seed-production farms, located in different ecological development regions, have been the forerunners in the introduction of new plant varieties and of improved technology. A seed production farm in Petrolandia, northeast Brazil, has evolved improved varieties of sorghum, maize, and vegetables and introduced formerly unknown crops such as alfalfa.

Planned Modernization of Family Farms and Rural Communities
Modernization of farming communities in developing countries is viewed here as an externally stimulated process of transition from the

tradition-bound agrarian society to one which is becoming increasingly aware of the benefits of advanced technology and services and increasingly skilled and effective in their use.

At the core of the process is planning at the farm and community level. According to the type of community dealt with, planning might be confined to the introduction of a few relatively simple innovations, or extended to cover much broader socioeconomic aspects of the community's life. Whatever the scope, the basic objective always aims at raising the income of the community to a higher-than-subsistence level.

The projected benefits deriving from the introduction of traction animals and other basic inputs into an African village are illustrated in Table 1, which shows that a modest investment of about $500 is potentially capable of producing a considerable quantitative and qualitative improvement in the villagers' diet and of a rise in annual family income from the present $100 to $325.

For a more inclusive scope of modernization, directed toward the development of market-oriented production, a three-pronged strategy has been evolved, aiming to bring about agricultural growth of a community consistent with predetermined income targets. The strategy is based on (1) seasonal crop planning; (2) development of services (extension, marketing, credit); and (3) organization of timely supply of all the required inputs. The three-pronged approach has been successfully applied in the establishment of immigrant villages in Israel. Known as moshav olim, these villages of about 80 families each are initially organized as precooperatives. The Settlement Authority plans and implements a carefully directed credit program for each season. In Venezuela[5] and Chile a similar approach was used for consolidating villages within the framework of the national agrarian reform. In Argentina,[6] the same strategy was adapted in planning the La Vanguardia project, involving the consolidation of 70 middle-class farms around the town and experimental station of Pergamino.

Seasonal crop planning of farms is based on the assumption that the best way to ensure effective utilization of modern inputs is by providing each individual farm with a seasonal crop plan. Obviously, effective implementation of the crop plan will require intelligent participation of

[5] For detailed description of the approach, see Inter-American Committee for Agricultural Development (CIDA) Research Paper No. 7, by Leonardo Luiz Pineda, a case study of Venezuelan Agrarian Reform Settlement. W. C. Thiesenhusen, December 1968, pp. 34-38.

[6] Proyecto La Vanguardia 1965, Inta, Pergamino Argentina.

Table 1.
Comparative Data for a Traditional and Transitional Model Family Farm in Africa.

	Traditional Manually Worked Farms (existing)	Transitional Farm Employing Traction Animals (projection)
Cultivated Area, in Hectares	2.00	4.80
Investment, Total, $U.S.	217.00	552.00
1. Agricultural	127.00	444.00
2. Nonagricultural	90.00	108.00
Value of Output, $U.S.		
1. Value of output, including that of home-consumed produce	127.00	530.00
2. Cost of inputs	—	190.00
Gross Margin, $U.S.	127.00	340.00
Value of Output Components, $U.S.		
1. Cash	60.00	403.00
2. Value of home-consumed produce	67.00	127.00
Food Basket for Adult per Day		
1. Calories	2,235	2,385
2. Proteins, plant, in grams	61.6	66.0
3. Proteins, animals, in grams	5.8	14.6
4. Cost of purchased food, $U.S.	38.00	30.00
Manpower Input, Workdays per Annum	210	366
Indices		
1. Value of (output) per workday, $U.S.	0.60	1.45
2. Gross income per workday, $U.S.	0.60	0.92
3. Gross income per hectare, $U.S.	63.00	71.00
4. Gross income as % of value of output	100.00	64.00
5. Disposable income	100.00	325.00

Source: *Traditional Family Farm. A Plan for Transitionary Agriculture in Malawi* (Centre for Agricultural Cooperation with Developing Countries, Israeli Ministry of Agriculture, March 1969).

the local extension personnel and of the farmers themselves. Each farm unit benefits from the services provided by the directed credit system. This system is a nonselective one, differing in this respect from its American prototype. Its principal function is disbursement of approved inputs and services on credit repayable to a public settlement authority or a bank. While the system is taking root, its scope can be conveniently expanded to include provision of credit for diversified community expansion programs. The marketing and transport arrangements are designed to impart to the developing community an early bargaining capability. Initially these arrangements need not take on the form of full-fledged cooperatives; in fact, good results have been obtained with precooperative types of organization.

In practical terms, the community will strive to market its produce in bulk, at guaranteed prices agreed upon with the processors. The community will also strive to acquire its own transport in order to prevent the middlemen from reaping the benefits of guaranteed prices by virtue of their monopoly on transport. A characteristic feature of this kind of modernization program is that it calls for a technician-to-farmers ratio which might be as high as 10 technicians per 1,000 farmers. A rather narrow specialization in such fields as field crops, bookkeeping, village store management, marketing, and transport, and intensive instruction in each of these subjects, make quick training of technical personnel practicable.

A more comprehensive planning phase, which, among other things, utilizes the advantages of scale, is used for communities comprising at least 300 families. Such communities had been planned and established within the framework of agrarian reform in the Dominican Republic, Chile, Venezuela, and Equador, as well as in Zambia and Nepal as part of their land settlement programs. The standards of social amenities and rural community services are planned to equal those enjoyed by urban communities, especially in matters of health, education, recreation, and municipal services. Their cost to the farmer should be compatible with his income, and their operation should be gradually taken over by the farming community.

Primary services are established in each village. On the other hand, schools, health clinics, recreation amenities, and economic organization—marketing, credit, transport—are set up in rural service centers, each serving a community of from 300 to 600 families. The size of the community being served enables the centers to reduce the unit cost of services.

Basically, the planning concept rests on the fulfillment of certain quantitatively expressed socioeconomic objectives formulated as a result of juxtaposition of macroeconomic, political, national, and social considerations. The two principal arms of this planning process are the agroeconomic and the social plans; it is the interaction of these plans at various levels that makes the evolvement of a practical implementation program possible.

Briefly, the agroeconomic plan projects optimal farm types and sizes, which, as market analyses will show, will be most practicable for the attainment of the predetermined income goals. Determination of farm types and sizes will permit the phased planning of investments and the drawing up of a seasonal credit plan.

The social plan is based on the findings of the social survey—demography, occupational structure, mores, social organization, and stratification—to determine the optimal settlement and housing patterns, and lays the groundwork for the development of the village institutions, educational, cultural, and economic. Some of the institutions will be expected to serve specific project implementation aims, while others will be a permanent fixture of the community.

Figure 1 shows the juxtaposition of the agroeconomic, social, and physical planning elements entering into the actual physical planning of communities and project installations. A subsequent assessment of the physical requirements, including the estimated cost of establishing or up-grading services, will make calculation of investment requirements possible. This system has satisfactorily been applied in the design of

Figure 1.
Agroeconomic, social, and physical planning elements required simultaneously in community planning.

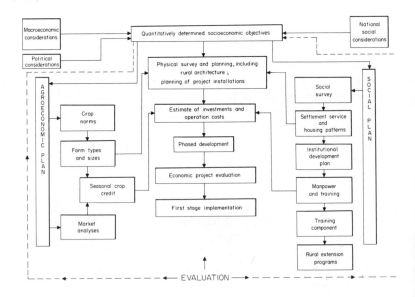

irrigation projects carried out in conjunction with land settlement or agrarian reform projects.

Development will be phased commensurate with availability of capital and trained manpower. Implementation through all stages will be accompanied by an evaluation and feedback for possible modification of the set objectives.

This approach to rural development requires outstanding professional leadership and interdisciplinary coordination. It is sufficiently challenging to professional workers, but requires carefully planned in-service training for all personnel. Inherent in this type of project is the need for substantial institutional innovations at both the local and the national levels.

The concept of integrated rural area planning adds an additional dimension to this approach. It pursues the aim of synchronous development of the agricultural (farm) and urban (rural towns) sectors of a functionally defined rural area. It is based on the bringing together of two development components: rural and urban. The first is symbolized by agroeconomic development, agrarian reform, and agricultural settlement, while the second is exemplified by the development of industrial processing of agricultural produce and of diverse services for the farming community.

The diversified character of planned development envisaged by this concept—of agriculture, rural and urban infrastructures, agricultural processing industries, other industries and of various kinds of services— cannot fail to exert a powerful modernizing influence on the agricultural sector. In the process, stagnant rural towns can be linked to agricultural development and benefit from the introduction of processing industries, which will provide an impetus for the development of other industries and of services. The concept can be best implemented by an area development authority acting in close cooperation with a national development or planning agency.

An example of integrated rural-urban planning involving the establishment of a new town is the Lachish region of Israel. There, the initial investment in agriculture and in the development of the infrastructure of the regional center came primarily from public sources. Another example is the development plan prepared for the revitalization of the city of Catamarca, in northwest Argentina. This rural-urban development plan envisages the provision of greater employment opportunities to some of the 3,000 technical-school graduates who hitherto had to seek work in distant metropolitan areas. The plan also aimed to arrest the growth of the poor rural periphery around Catamarca by resettling these families on viable farm units in the adjacent Piriquitas Valley. An agricultural plan provided a link-up of vegetable farming with a dehydration plant established in the city; in addition, livestock farming was to be linked to a meat processing plant in the town.

Conclusion

The scope and scale of rural development projects should reflect national agricultural policies. It should be borne in mind, however, that particularly in the less developed countries development projects in turn have the potential of exerting an impact on national development, even if the development policies have not been fully formulated. Thus, project implementation provides experience and data valuable for the formulation of national rural development policies. Market-oriented agrarian reform projects, based on simple technology and innovations, have influenced the workings of national institutions and financial agencies.

Project implementation invariably leads to the introduction of some institutional innovations, sooner or later mirrored in national organizational strategies. This has been the case, for instance, where interagency cooperation for the development of irrigation facilities has led to the establishment of national irrigation policy-making agencies. Project implementation often encounters unanticipated difficulties. The efforts which go into the solution of problems that have come to the surface can be extremely valuable in fields other than those covered by the project itself. In all cases, a project should be defined in terms of its wider implications on the economy of the surrounding areas. The aim should be to avoid dissipation of manpower, capital resources, and energy on very limited goals. Only by defining the functions of a project in its wider implications can wasteful duplication be avoided.

It would seem that all three types of projects have an important role to play in modernization of agriculture. Each has its advantages and flaws. In cognizance of this, the choice and place of alternatives must be carefully considered in relation to national and local conditions. National production campaigns seem to be an important means of providing an impetus to stagnant agriculture and of stimulating changes and innovations on the institutional level. The development of large commercial or administered farms, either as export enterprises, as training-demonstration farms, or as improved seed-production centers, is undoubtedly important for rural development. These farms often play the part of initial pacemakers for modernization. The development of family farms in relation to predetermined income targets is a forerunner in the development of market-oriented rural communities.

In the light of the contemporary "green revolution" in many parts of the world, integrated rural area planning seems to be the ultimate aim for which rural development should strive. This strategy aims at developing marketing and processing centers in rural areas where farm products can be efficiently processed, commercialized, and marketed. Not less important is that these growth centers are also planned to afford employment opportunities for people displaced from agriculture, thus providing an alternative to migration from rural areas. Rather, these people can participate in a concerted development effort based on an ever-growing output of a more efficient farming community and the development of other resources in the same region. Thus, integrated rural area planning becomes a forerunner of rural-urban development.

Selected Bibliography

Clark, C., and H. Haswell, *Economics of Subsistence Agriculture*. New York: Macmillan, 1966.

Efferson, J. Norman, "The Planning and Operation of Land Distribution Programs in Developing Countries." Unpublished paper, 1968.

Hunter, G., "Assistance to Agricultural Development in Northeast Thailand with Special Reference to the Use of Present and Potential Irrigation." Mimeo. 1969.

Institute for Planning and Development, Israel Ministry of Agriculture, *Rural-Urban Integration. An Approach for Developing Countries Based on Israeli Experience*. Tel-Aviv, 1968.

Pineda, Leonardo Ruiz, "A Case Study of a Venezuelan Agrarian Reform Settlement." Report paper, Pan-American Union, 1968.

Planificacion para el desarrollo integral de areas restringidas, Pergamino, Argentina: Piriquitas Catamarca INTA, 1966.

Schultz, Th., *Transforming Traditional Agriculture*. New Haven: Yale University Press, 1964.

Survey of the Alliance for Progress, "Problems of Agriculture," Washington, D.C., 1967.

Weitz, R., and A. Rokach, *Agricultural Development—Planning and Implementation*. Dordrecht: Reidel, 1962.

25. Problems and Policies of Agricultural Development: The United States Experience

Peter Dorner

Agricultural development in the United States occurred under a number of special circumstances, many of which cannot be duplicated elsewhere. To this extent, the U.S. experience serves only in a limited way as a guide for agricultural development efforts currently being undertaken by many countries. The United States was endowed with rich resources—an abundance of fertile land, minerals, rivers and forests, and great open spaces. The relatively small indigenous Indian population was eventually brushed aside by the European settlers. Land was the measure of opportunity, and the terms of access to it was the battleline of freedom. Land under cultivation increased about as rapidly as the total population. The hard realities of the frontier stimulated a reassessment of old values and attitudes, and the replacement of those irrelevant to the circumstances with new styles of life and new institutions for organizing human efforts [44].[1]

A relatively scarce labor supply—but abundant land—provided a near optimum testing ground for the liberal philosophies of the eighteenth century concerning private property, competition, freedom, and democracy. Immigrants came in large numbers, especially after 1820. Over 2,000,000 streamed across the Atlantic from 1820 to 1850, and in the next 10 years 2,600,000 more arrived. From 1850 to 1920, immigration increased the U.S. population by over 31,000,000. These immigrants were an uprooted but energetic people, well aware of the advantages of markets and trade. In addition to the skills they brought from their homelands, the early settlers also adopted some of the crops and cultivation practices of the American Indians. As one historian has observed: ". . . it is not going too far to say that it was the union of

Peter Dorner—United States. Ph.D., Harvard University, Economics, Agricultural Economics, and Economic History, 1959; Professor of Agricultural Economics and Director, Land Tenure Center, University of Wisconsin. The author wishes to acknowledge the helpful comments received from a number of friends and colleagues on earlier drafts of this manuscript. Especially helpful were suggestions made by William Thiesenhusen, Raymond Penn, Kenneth Parsons, Don Kanel, Hugh Cook, Arthur Mosher, Raymond Christensen, Benjamin Villanueva, Lester Schmid, John Bielefeldt, Francis Kutish, Solon Barraclough, and Noble Clark. Responsibility for the final product is, of course, my own.

[1] Numbers in brackets refer to references at the end of this manuscript.

American Indian and European farming that produced the beginnings of American agriculture and provided the essential basis for its ultimate development [11] ."

In retrospect, one can also see the contribution that U.S. agriculture made to national economic development. It provided the necessary food for a growing population and an increasing per capita demand. With the growth of industry, it released labor for nonfarm employment. It provided large sums of foreign exchange and domestic capital [20]. In the early years and through the 1790s, tobacco ranked first on the list of American exports. Later cotton became the predominant export, representing 61 percent of all exports in 1860. After 1860, grain exports became dominant, especially wheat and corn, while meat and meat products came to rank third in importance [11]. U.S. agriculture likewise provided a growing market for the manufacturing and service industries.

Despite the many favorable circumstances for U.S. agricultural development, some broad lessons can be gleaned from it that are relevant for today's developing countries. During the past 150 years, our agriculture has been transformed from a largely self-sufficient system to one deeply interdependent with the rest of the economy. In this respect, the U.S. has certainly traveled the road over which all nations must pass on the way to economic development [44].

In the sections to follow, I can only illustrate a few of the highlights of this transformation process.[2] The next section presents some measures of growth and changing sources of farm output over time. For several reasons, statistical measures to be employed here emphasize the past 50 years. First, data are more readily available for this period. Second, the major changes in sources of growth and productivity increases have occurred during this modern era. The third section examines some of the major landmarks in development—the underlying public policies and the group action of farm people in bringing about the growth shown in Section II. Finally, problems growing out of this transformation are outlined in the fourth section.

[2]In a country with an agricultural sector as large and diverse as that of the United States, it is difficult to deal briefly and meaningfully with agricultural development over an extended historical period. There are wide variations among regions; there are also large differences for farms of varying type, size, and tenure class within regions [27]. In light of this diversity, overall averages and development trends need to be interpreted cautiously.

Changes in Farm Production and Its Sources

Three Sources of Increased Output   As in all agricultural systems, the expansion of farm output in the United States was, for many years, the result of increases in the traditional production factors—labor and land. In fact, growth in the farm population and expansion of the cropland base remained the major factors in the growth of farm output until near the beginning of World War I [34]. Farm capital was of course being created and accumulated during this long period—livestock herds were built up; buildings, fences, and drainage systems were constructed; farm-produced animal power in the form of horses and mules grew apace.

Also in the decades from 1830 to 1860 a number of inventions and improvements were introduced that revolutionized agricultural development. After this period food scarcity and famines were no longer accepted as inevitable. The mechanical reaper, the mechanical raker and binder attachments, the steel plow, the grain drill, the corn drill, and the threshing machine were some of the key developments in farm mechanization in that period [11].

Gross investments in agriculture (for improvements to land and buildings, implements and machinery, harness and saddlery, and livestock inventory changes) increased from $51 million (all measured in 1910-1914 dollars), in 1800 to $190 million in 1850 and to $631 million by 1900[3] [33].

The U.S. farm population reached its peak of 32.5 million people about the time of World War I. Actually the farm population was fairly stable from 1900 to 1940, varying between 30.5 and 32.5 million. Cropland harvested reached its highest acreage in the early 1920s [31]. A major source of increased output during the period from about 1920 to 1940 was the shift in the type of power used by farmers. Tractors and trucks replaced horses and mules at an accelerating rate throughout the 1920s, 1930s, and 1940s. Large amounts of labor and other resources were released from raising feed for horses and mules to the production of products for human use. The direct effect of mechaniza-

[3]It is of great significance for development to recognize that much of this capital was produced through the direct efforts of farmers themselves—converting their own labor into capital structures. It is also of interest to note that the fluctuation of farm product prices and the attendant changing prospects for profits from farming did not greatly influence this capital growth process. "Between 1870 and 1900 prices paid to farmers were declining much of the time, yet during those years real capital formation proceeded at a faster pace than at any subsequent time" [26].

tion accounted for half the rise in farm output from 1919-1921 to 1938-1940 [34].

This shift in the type of power continued to be an important source of increase in farm output in the 1940s. However, in the early years of World War II increases in crop production per acre became the dominant source, followed by increased production per livestock unit. After 1950, these two accounted for practically all of the increase in farm output.

Three distinct but overlapping periods of U.S. agricultural growth, each characterized by a different major source of output expansion, can therefore be identified: (1) expansion of cropland, farm labor, and animal power up to about 1920; (2) displacement of animal power with tractors from 1920 into the 1940s; and (3) increased production per crop acre and per animal unit after 1940. The first stage was based on land and human and animal power; the second stage was based on the tractor and mechanical power; the third stage was based on developments in the sciences of chemistry, nutrition, and genetics.

The major source of increased output during each stage was of course operative in other stages as well (Table 1). The shift to mechanical power declined in importance after 1940 and ceased to be a measurable source of farm output after 1960. Increased production per livestock unit (as well as increased number of breeding units, which together reflect the change in net livestock production) became increasingly

Table 1.
Sources of Increased Farm Output in the United States.

	Percentage Distribution of Increases			
	1919-21 to 1938-40	1939-41 to 1949-51	1949-51 to 1959-61	1959-61 to 1980
Reduction in Farm-Produced Power	51%	22%	10%	0%
Change in Crop Production per Acre	34	37	87	73
Change in Cropland Used	−4	15	−28	−13
Change in Net Livestock Production	19	26	31	40
Change in Total Farm Output	100	100	100	100

Source: Raymond P. Christensen, William E. Hendrix, and Robert D. Stevens, *How the United States Improved Its Agriculture* (Washington, D.C.: ERS Foreign-76, U.S. Department of Agriculture, March 1964).

important over the decades. Except during World War II, change in
cropland used had a negative influence since acreage was being withdrawn and diverted, largely the result of government farm programs.
According to the estimates shown in Table 1, changes in crop production per acre will remain the most important source of increased farm
output throughout the 1970s as it has been since the 1940s. Fertilizers,
new varieties, insecticides, herbicides, improved tillage, and increasingly
efficient farm management are the underlying factors increasing production per acre.

Consequences of a Changing Input Mix The changing input mix and
the accelerated output expansion since 1910-14 are evident in the data
shown in Table 2. These trends, especially since about 1940, have resulted in basic changes in the organization of farming. In the mid
1930s, the farm population was only slightly under the peak it had
reached shortly before 1920. But in the next 25 years it declined by
more than one-half, and in 1968 it stood at about 11 million people—
less than 6 percent of the U.S. population. Since 1940, there has been
an average net outmigration from the farm population of about one
million people per year [30]. Farm numbers have shown a similar
pattern of decline. After a peak of 6.8 million farms in 1935, numbers
decreased steadily; the 1964 census recorded only 3.2 million farms in
the U.S.[4] Average farm size remained relatively unchanged from 1900
to 1935 (averaging 155 acres in the latter year), but it more than
doubled in the next 30 years (averaging 352 acres in 1964) [42].

Dramatic increases in labor productivity occurred (Table 2) but not
uniformly for all farm products. Between 1940 and 1968, production
per man-hour increased as follows: feed grains, 892 percent; cotton,
722 percent; oil crops, 542 percent; food grains, 459 percent; and
tobacco, 174 percent. Livestock enterprises also show a wide range in
labor productivity, with production per man-hour in poultry increasing
by 641 percent; in dairying by 400 percent; and in meat animals by 203
percent [31]. Differences among enterprises in per-acre yield increases,
the level of mechanization, and the consequent reduction of labor inputs account for most of these variations.

Commercialization of Farming These developments signified an increasing commercialization of farming. In 1820 each farm worker

[4]Some were eliminated from the statistics over the years by changes in the census
definition of a farm. But the great bulk were combined into larger units. For
example, in 1966, about 58 percent of all farmland purchases in the United States
was for farm combination and enlargement [30].

supplied farm products for 4.12 persons (including himself). It took 100 years to double this to 8.27 persons in 1920. The next doubling came in slightly over 30 years (16.40 by 1952), and the figure doubled again in the following 12 years (33.25 in 1964). By 1968 each farm worker supplied farm products for 43.4 persons[5] [31].

The increasing commercialization of farming is also evident in the fact that nonmoney farm income constitutes a declining proportion of total gross income.[6] In 1910, 29 percent of realized gross farm income consisted of the value of products consumed on the farm and the imputed rental value of the farm dwelling. In 1940 these items still accounted for 26 percent of gross income. The figure then dropped to 16 percent in 1950 and to 12 percent by 1968 [27, 37].

All farmers, however, did not benefit equally from increased labor productivity and commercialization. As shown in Table 3, less than one-third of all farms receive more than 85 percent of all cash receipts and government payments. Many operators of the smaller farms are increasingly dependent on earnings from off-farm employment to supplement their modest farming incomes. The number of these small farms, however, is diminishing rapidly.

Farm Policies in Historical Perspective

The preceding section emphasized several measures of growth and productivity in U.S. agriculture; in this section we will discuss the public policies and collective action underlying these changes. Any greatly condensed historical sketch of this kind can do no more than indicate a few landmarks in this development. Likewise, this brief account will undoubtedly make the process appear more rational and orderly than was actually the case.

Since the scope and nature of agricultural policies changed as the national economy developed, it will be useful to view this history as

[5]These statistics should be interpreted with some caution. Included in the calculations is labor time used on the farm in the production of farm products. Since many of the input-producing as well as the product-processing and marketing functions have been transferred to off-farm industries, farming becomes increasingly specialized in the transformation of purchased inputs into raw farm products in need of further processing, packaging, etc. If all labor time directly engaged in these agricultural support activities were included, the increases in labor productivity would be less dramatic. However, the above figures do reflect accurately the increasing commercialization of farming.

[6]Nonmoney income includes value of farm products consumed directly in farm households and gross rental value of farm dwellings. Changes in farm inventories are not included.

Table 2.
Agricultural Input and Output Trends in the United States, 1910-14—1969 [31].

	1910-14	1920-24	1930-34	1940-44	1950	1960	1968-69[a]
Crops and Livestock (1957-59 = 100)							
Cropland used for crops	94	103	107	104	106	99	94
Principal plant nutrients used	12	13	15	28	55	111	232
Crop production per acre	69	68	64	80	84	109	127
Livestock production per breeding unit	na	58	68	77	86	105	118[b]
Man-Hours (1957-59 = 100)							
Man-hours labor used for farmwork	217	217	210	191	142	92	66
Farm production per man-hour	24	26	29	41	61	115	182

Total Outputs and Inputs (1957-59 = 100)							
Farm output	52	57	60	78	86	106	120
Production inputs	85	92	93	99	101	101	111
Productivity^c	61	62	65	79	85	105	108
Number of Machines (in thousands)							
Tractors (excluding steam and garden)	9	377	995	1,861	3,394	4,685	4,810
Motor trucks	6	258	894	1,193	2,207	2,825	3,160
Grain combines	0	0	0	271	714	1,042	850
Corn pickers and picker-shellers	0	0	0	129	456	792	625
Pickup balers	0	0	0	0	196	680	790
Field forage harvesters	0	0	0	0	81	291	327

aData for 1968-69 are preliminary.
bLatest year available is 1966.
cOutput per unit of input.

Source: *Changes in Farm Production and Efficiency: A Summary Report, 1969.* U.S. Department of Agriculture Statistical Bulletin No. 233, revised June 1969. Washington, D.C.

Table 3.
Number of Farms and Farm Income by Value-of-Sales Classes, 1960, 1964, and 1968 [37].

Value-of-Sales Class and Year	Number of Farms		Cash Receipts Plus Government Payments; Percentage Distribution	Farm Operator Family Income		Off-Farm Income
	Thousands of Farms	Percentage Distribution		Total Income	Realized Net Farm Income	
All Farms						
1960	3,962	100.0	100.0	$ 5,102	$ 2,962	$ 2,140
1964	3,442	100.0	100.0	7,151	3,802	3,349
1968	3,054	100.0	100.0	9,627	4,841	4,786
Sales under $5,000						
1960	2,465	62.2	12.7	3,638	1,128	2,510
1964	2,013	58.5	9.4	5,086	1,197	3,889
1968	1,613	52.8	6.2	7,145	1,267	5,878
Sales of $5,000 to $9,999						
1960	660	16.7	14.7	4,878	3,305	1,573
1964	533	15.5	10.9	6,304	3,477	2,827
1968	420	13.7	7.4	7,795	3,695	4,100
Sales of $10,000 to $19,999						
1960	497	12.5	21.2	6,626	5,368	1,258
1964	482	14.0	19.0	8,072	6,010	2,062
1968	495	16.2	16.9	9,331	6,454	2,877
Sales of $20,000 and over						
1960	340	8.6	51.4	13,920	12,076	1,844
1964	414	12.0	60.7	14,745	12,014	2,731
1968	526	17.3	69.5	16,656	12,956	3,700

Source: U.S. Department of Agriculture, Economic Research Service. *Farm Income Situation*, July, 1969.

representing three somewhat distinct yet overlapping periods. Policies of the first period, after independence and through the 1860s, emphasized the establishment of a system of land tenure and settlement. From the 1860s through the 1930s, agricultural policies focused on the provision of services which would convert the farmers' raw stake in the land into valuable market opportunities. Finally, beginning in the 1920s and continuing to the present, policy emphasis has been on production adjustment and control, farm price policy, and maintenance of farmers' purchasing power relative to other groups in society.[7]

Land Policies Although the economic organization of U.S. agriculture is characterized today as a family farm system, large landed estates were established in some of the original colonies. However, in the course of the Revolutionary War, many of these large estates were confiscated and divided. "Under the leadership of frontier 'radicals' like Jefferson," quitrents, entail, and primogeniture were abolished, leading to more democratic modes of land tenure [11].

In the southern colonies, however, there developed a system based on large plantation holdings producing cotton with slave labor. Although small farmers greatly outnumbered the planters, the plantation system determined the economy of the region, and the planters dominated the colonial governments [11]. After the Civil War, a sharecropping system developed on the remains of the old plantations. Except for these deviations in parts of the South, the family farm emerged as the predominant form of land tenure in the United States.

The federal land policies which developed were conditioned by struggles among different economic groups. "On one side were those who urged that the Government should dispose of its land with prudence; in the opposite camp were those who demanded a generous land policy. Starting with the first viewpoint in dominance and gradually swinging to the other extreme, the clash of these divergent views constitutes the central theme of the history of American land policies during the eight decades preceding the enactment of the Homestead Act of 1862.... As early as 1800 the political pressure of the frontier farmers, a group traditionally disposed to demand 'liberal' land legislation, had begun to show its influence, and within 20 years their cause had definitely won" [11].

There were also marked regional conflicts over questions of land policy [6, 17]. The Homestead Act of 1862, which provided full title to 160 acres of public land after five years of residence on the land, was

[7] For detailed accounts, see References 2, 7, 11, 13, 14, 23, 43, and 44.

passed only after many years of debate and after the secession of the South "had removed from Congress the bloc of States' rights advocates who opposed Federal farm aid" [44]. This act was actually "an acknowledgement of practices already established" [44]. Long before its passage, settlers were establishing farms on the frontier—"squatting" without legal title to the land they farmed. The Pre-emption Act of 1841 provided a procedure for securing their rights and obtaining legal title.

Service Policies   Life on the frontier was difficult. There was a pressing need for more efficient transportation systems to move farm products to the eastern cities and ports, and to transport people and manufactured goods to the west. Water and road transport became increasingly inadequate. Railroad construction began in the late 1820s, but was confined largely to the eastern seaborad until about 1840. By 1850, however, the first railroad reached Chicago; a great spurt in railroad construction followed, and the first transcontinental line was completed in 1869. Railroad construction was financed through massive land grants and direct money subsidies from the federal government, European investments, and the sale of railroad bonds. At first, the railroads followed the western migration. But later, and especially with movement west of the Mississippi River, the railroads preceded and in fact often determined the migration and settlement routes [11].

A great variety of transport systems was used in the course of westward expansion—roads, canals, rivers, and railroads. A high density of roads (typically located every mile and dividing the landscape into square-mile blocks) was needed to serve the dispersed, small-scale, family farm system of settlement. This variety and density of roads and other means of transport made possible a mushrooming growth of rural towns—centers of agricultural service and marketing activities within a reasonable travel distance of the majority of farm people.[8]

The development of viable economic opportunities (as against the mere subsistence opportunities on the land) proceeded slowly. Many additional services were required. Several legislative enactments in 1862 were of great significance for the development of U.S. agriculture. In addition to the Homestead Act already mentioned, the Morrill Act established land-grant colleges, providing federal grants of land for the endowment, support, and maintenance of at least one college in each state teaching agriculture and engineering. The U.S. Department of

[8]I am indebted to Arthur Mosher for calling my attention to the key significance of these developments for U.S. agricultural growth.

Agriculture was also established in 1862. This department evolved into a great agricultural research, education, and service institution and has served as an important catalyst in all the major agricultural developments over the past century.

Subsequent developments in the area of agricultural research and education included the Hatch Act of 1887, which provided funds to all states for the support of agricultural experiment stations[9]; the Smith-Lever Act of 1914, establishing the Cooperative Agricultural Extension Service[10]; and the Smith-Hughes Act of 1917, which provided federal money to support the teaching of vocational agriculture and home economics in the high schools. These laws led to the specialized system of agricultural research and education in the United States.

The enactment of legislation in each case marked the culmination of long, often bitter, struggles going back in one form or another, to the early days of the Republic[11] [5]. In all cases, as a result of the federal system, which gave individual states the residual power and autonomy in these areas, some experience had already been developed. For example, several states had established colleges of agriculture in the 1850s, before the Morrill Act. In the 1870s, a few states created experiment stations where scientists were employed to conduct research on farm production problems. Before the formal establishment of an extension service, extension work was being carried out through special short

[9] In later years, additional funds were provided by the federal government to aid the state experiment stations in carrying forward all types of agriculture-related research, including studies in economics, sociology, and home economics.

[10] Although initially affiliated in some states with one of the major farm organizations, today the Cooperative Agricultural Extension Service in each state is closely integrated with the land grant college (now university), and is financed by federal, state, and local funds.

[11] Even after the legislative fights had been won, the early history of these efforts was replete with difficulties. At least one of these difficulties is illustrated by the following experience as told by Murray D. Lincoln, the first extension agent in the state of Connecticut:

Nobody knew what an extension agent was supposed to do. So I asked Dr. Jarvis, who was in the Department of Agriculture, what I should do. He said, "Good Lord, I don't know. Just go down there and find out what the source of income of the farmer is and try to improve it."

One of the first farmers I was told to meet was in Stonington, Connecticut.

As I met this big, raw-boned Yankee farmer, almost without introducing myself, I said to him, "Good Lord, man, what is your source of income in this area?"

And I have heard this story quoted later, but it actually happened. He looked at me and said, "Source of income, young man? We don't have any around here. We live on lack of expense" [44].

courses at colleges, "through lectures, correspondence, publication of bulletins, field experiments, demonstrations, and exhibits at fairs." And by 1916, "421 public high schools throughout the country had agricultural departments" [11].

It is significant, however, that the various groups pressuring for agricultural research and education eventually sought the help of the federal government. "Agricultural schools and colleges, organized experimentation, extension work, and elementary and secondary school training in agriculture all began locally, and though State and local governments have supported them to the present day, in each case Congress was called upon to furnish national leadership and financial aid" [11].

Another policy focus in the area of services to agriculture was the provision of credit. The transformation of the vast land area into productive commercial farms required large amounts of capital. Farmers depended on borrowed funds for many of the required investments. But commercial credit terms available to farmers were a major source of dissatisfaction throughout the latter half of the nineteenth century. Corporate finance methods were not applicable to the individual proprietor of a family farm. Credit available from commercial banks, insurance companies, and merchants carried a high rate of interest and was available only on a short-term basis. Expensive renewal fees pushed costs even higher. And in many areas, credit for any purpose was hard to come by [4].

The financial panic of 1907 and the report by the President's Country Life Commission appointed in 1908 helped highlight farmers' credit needs and problems. After more years of agitation, the Federal Farm Loan Act of 1916 established 12 regional federal land banks to provide long-term credit in larger amounts and on more favorable terms (e.g., providing for long-term amortization of mortgages) than that available from other sources. Local cooperative farm loan associations with farmer-borrower shareholders were, and remain to this day, the vehicle for implementing lending activities under this act.[12]

[12] Additional regional banks were established in the 1930s to provide production credit for farmers and loans to farmer cooperatives. This specialized cooperative farm-credit system is administered through the Farm Credit Administration established in the 1930s. In this cooperative system, farmer borrowers own shares in the local associations, which in turn own the stock of the regional banks. The regional banks obtain funds through bond issues sold in the regular money markets. This specialized farm credit system is supplementary to other sources. The bulk of farm credit continues to be supplied by commercial banks, individuals, insurance companies, and merchants, but this system does provide an important

With the severe depression of the 1930s, an additional innovation was made in the field of farm credit. Direct government loans were made to farmers who could not get credit from other sources—often considered the least credit worthy by commercial bank standards. In the early years, the emphasis was on rural rehabilitation, resettlement, and loans to permit tenants to become owners. Supervision and management counseling has been a key feature of these programs. In 1946, these emergency, high risk, supervised credit operations were coordinated under the Farmers' Home Administration. This agency was given federal funds and was later authorized to insure loans made by private lenders. In the 1960s, its role was expanded to provide loans for rural housing, for water and sewage facility construction by the smaller cities and towns in rural areas, and for other rural development needs.

This brief sketch of the major developments in federal farm policies and programs points up the diverse nature of the services provided.[13] All these policies grew out of the experienced needs of the time and were actively sought by farmers. In fact, one point that must be emphasized is the significant role played by farmers' organizations throughout this history [22]. The early battles were over free access to and security on the land. With increasing commercialization of farming following the Civil War, competition intensified and farmers addressed themselves to issues of speculators in commodity markets, high railroad freight rates, shortage of credit and high interest rates, and monopoly power of the railroads and other industrial firms with which they dealt. The initial push toward action in these areas grew out of activities sponsored by the Grange, a farm organization founded in 1867. A series of laws, still referred to as the Granger laws, resulted from this pressure by farmers. Later, rural leaders helped lead the fight to enact additional antimonopoly legislation and establish railroad regulatory bodies. Another major consequence of this antimonopoly movement was the rapid growth in farmer cooperative buying and selling. Many of these early

alternative source of funds. Also, this specialized system introduced new guidelines and criteria for all credit agencies in serving more adequately the particular credit needs of farmers.

[13] Many of the programs have not been discussed at all—e.g., rural free delivery of mail, soil conservation services, rural electrification, crop insurance, statistical reporting of crop and livestock production, and prices, etc. Also, since we focus on federal policies, we omit the important actions taken by state governments in the development of services and regulations governing agriculture in the several states. The references cited at the end of this manuscript should be consulted for more elaborate treatments of all these topics.

efforts at performing the function of the middleman failed, but they paved the way for the cooperative movement of later years [11].

Production Adjustment and Price Support Policies In the 1920s, a new emphasis was introduced in farm policy debates. During the World War I, farm commodity prices and land values soared. Following the war, prices of farm products fell sharply relative to farm production costs. Land values also declined after 1920, but farmers who assumed large mortgages while land prices were high found their repayment capacity greatly reduced. Exports declined, prices dropped even further, farm failures and foreclosures increased, and farm surpluses appeared. Given these circumstances, several new ideas became popular: production adjustment and farm income equity. Adjustment later was translated into production regulation and control, while the concept of income equity found expression in the term "parity"—reestablishing the relationship between farm product prices and farm production and living costs that existed in the period 1910-1914.

The catastrophic depression of the 1930s intensified the search for solutions which finally culminated, at least in broad outline, in the present programs of farm production control and price supports. Farm groups became more militant during the 1930s, organizing strikes, violent resistance to farm foreclosure sales, marches on state capitols, and similar actions. Whereas earlier policies were intended "to induce growth, to foster development," the policies in the 1930s emphasized remedies "to be used in treating internal ills" [16].

Basic agricultural adjustment legislation enacted in the 1930s has been modified in subsequent years. The strong demand for farm products in the 1940s shifted emphasis from controlling to encouraging production. Demand remained relatively strong throughout the postwar years until near the end of the Korean War.

By late 1952 there were again clear signs of mounting surpluses. Yet the task of agricultural adjustment in the 1950s had become different and in a sense more difficult than in the 1930s. In the 1930s, a low level of effective demand accompanied high levels of unemployment in the economy. But in the 1950s, even at relatively full employment and with high levels of demand, farm surpluses mounted. The new technologies widely adopted on farms had increased greatly the productive capacity of the agricultural sector. Land was dwindling in importance as a factor in the farm production process; so was farm labor. With this increased productive capacity and with a greater flexibility and substitutability in the input mix, production control became more difficult.

To complicate matters, United States agriculture is characterized by a wide range in farm size and in levels of technology employed (Table 3). Consequently, there are great differences in the per unit cost of producing a given farm commodity, in the volume of output per farm, and in the income per farm family. When prices are set high enough to provide the farmer producing a small volume with a reasonable income, they give the farmer producing a large volume and using modern techniques a tremendous windfall [1, 18]. Furthermore, the higher the price supports, the greater the production restrictions required if large government stocks are to be avoided.

In the 1950s, in an effort to aid developing nations as well as to reduce accumulated stocks by expanding foreign shipments, Public Law 480 was introduced. Under this legislation, farm commodities are sold abroad for local currencies and donated for emergency and relief purposes. Important additional policy changes were made in the 1960s. Price support levels on basic crops were lowered and a system of direct payments introduced. Lower domestic prices have increased commercial exports and decreased the need for export subsidies. The direct price support payments provide a greater incentive for farmer participation in acreage diversion programs and consequently a better supply control mechanism. However, federal payments for voluntary withdrawal of land from production remain the primary vehicle for supply control.

Summary This history of selected highlights indicates the relationship between these broad policies and the general circumstances prevailing at the time. In the first phase of development, policies emphasized the creation of opportunities on the land. Given the large land mass and open spaces, procedures were required whereby people could gain access to and secure rights on the land. But the opportunities thus created were of a subsistence nature; the next phase of policy concentrated on services to transform these raw opportunities into commercially viable occupations—transport systems, markets, research and education, and credit occupied the center of the stage. Finally, as productivity increased and as the economy changed from agricultural self-sufficiency to a complex industrial-market economy with concentrations of economic power, policy emphasis shifted again and focused on the level of return to agricultural producers and the governmental regulation and control of market forces needed to achieve these ends. In each phase, direct action by farm people through their organizations provided an important thrust for the enactment of new policy.

Problems Resulting from the Agricultural Transformation

The production performance record of agriculture in the U.S. economy is a highly successful one. That performance was significantly influenced by private developments in the industrial sector. From the early mechanical inventions to the technological revolution of recent decades, the industrial sector, with the strategic support of public investments in research and education, played a significant role in agricultural growth.[14] In the course of its development, agriculture became increasingly dependent on off-the-farm factors such as modern capital inputs, research, extension, communication and transportation facilities, markets, credit, and legal and social services.

One outstanding feature of U.S. agricultural development has been the general lack of public planning. There have been no five-year plans or production targets. Yet agriculture has contributed impressively to capital formation and to the economic development of the nonagricultural sector [20]. In recent years, the U.S. Department of Agriculture has performed a basic production planning function for the agricultural sector through the administration of the price support programs. But primary reliance is placed on income inducements to elicit the willing participation of millions of farmers.

The underlying philosophy was well expressed by Parsons: "In the Anglo-American tradition, we tend to place major reliance upon general working rules in economic affairs, which define the limits within which voluntary discretion is permitted. This is what we mean by liberty and opportunity. In our tradition, as we move toward specifying the terms of particular acts, we specify what is to be avoided. In totalitarian systems, by contrast, principal reliance is placed upon working rules which define specific performances. The society that places major reliance upon rules which define the terms of specific performance embraces a duty state. A society which relies principally upon working

[14] It is also well to remember that the United States was able to and did indeed borrow heavily from Europe. For many years the United States gained from its reliance on the research undertaken in European universities. Students from the United States went to European universities for their Ph.D. work; just as many students from the less developed countries today come to Europe and the United States.

rules which define only avoidances leaves room specifically for freedom and opportunity" [21].

Despite the good production performance achieved under this opportunity-oriented system, many problems have emerged from the transformation of U.S. agriculture and the concomitant development of a predominantly urban-industrial society. These problems can be divided into those facing the commercial farming sector, and those residual poverty problems associated with the continuing agricultural transformation. The problems in these two areas are, of course, interrelated.

Commercial Farm Problems In 1966, farms with annual sales valued at $10,000 or more, which I will call the commercial farming sector, comprised about 32 percent of all U.S. farms and produced over 85 percent of all farm products (Table 3). Four major problems can be identified.

1. Increasing Capital Requirements. With the continued shift of farm tasks to nonfarm firms, and with the increased mechanization of planting, harvesting, and the handling of crops and livestock in and around the farmstead, labor productivity in farming continues to increase at a rapid rate. This means that one man can work increasingly larger acreages and handle more livestock; consequently, the trend of farm enlargement continues. With increasing land values and increased investments in machinery and livestock, capital requirements for an efficient farm operation mount. It is not uncommon to find investments of from $100,000 to $200,000 and more on well-operated family-sized farms, and most farms do continue to be family owned and operated.

A two-phased problem arises—acquiring sufficient finances for growth and expansion within the lifetime of the farm family, and the even more difficult problem facing young people trying to get control over sufficient capital to establish themselves on an adequate-sized farm. New methods of financing may be needed which permit a sharing in the equity financing of the farm business by people outside the immediate farm family. Vertical integration, farm incorporation, increased reliance on contracts, and resource rentals may be the forerunners of a new system. Whether the family farm system as we know it today survives or evolves into some new system will very likely be decided by the competition from alternative forms of economic organization. Many are concerned about the entrance into farming of the large industrial corporation [28]. The family farm is today the dominant form of economic organization in agriculture because of its good performance, but its continued relative advantage will depend on how the financing of farm enlargement and farm transfer are worked out in the future [8, 9].

2. *The Continuing Production of Surpluses.* Although government-held stocks of major farm commodities (wheat, feed grains, cotton, and dairy products) have been substantially reduced in recent years, the excess productive capacity in agriculture remains. Full utilization of that capacity would result in ruinous farm product prices, or exorbitant government costs in trying to maintain prices at reasonable levels. A substantial unutilized capacity in U.S. agriculture still exists (e.g., between 30 and 40 million acres of land continue to be withheld under government programs), and the continued rapid increase in productivity per acre and per animal unit, as well as per man, practically assures that this excess capacity will remain for the foreseeable future.

This situation reveals several basic inconsistencies in policy. The overwhelming emphasis on productivity and economic efficiency of earlier years is somewhat misplaced under these circumstances. This has led some to question the continued emphasis on production technology research. Likewise, new irrigation developments in some of the western states seem illogical at present. The federal government, pursuing a policy begun in 1902, appropriates large sums of money each year to reclaim and develop land for growing farm products. The President's National Advisory Commission on Rural Poverty found it "impossible to reconcile federal expenditures for reclaiming and developing land with federal expenditures for taking land out of production while surpluses of certain farm products mount" [19].

Benefits for some farmers and some communities undoubtedly accompany both the increased adoption of advanced production technology and new irrigation developments. But other farmers and other communities suffer a loss of incomes and opportunity as a result of these public investments. Consequently such developments may generate greater national costs than national benefits. One study estimated that the accumulated public investment in federal reclamation projects in the western states up to about 1955 has been responsible for displacing 5 percent of the farm workers in the southeast, the area with the largest concentration of rural poverty [25].

3. *A Continuing Cost-Price Squeeze.* In the United States, the income elasticity for food is very low. "Evidently, the income elasticity for that part of food produced on American farms is less than 0.15 percent, meaning that on the average, a 1 percent increase in per capita income causes less than a 0.15 percent increase in expenditure on food. . . .

Food consumption measured in pounds per person in the United States, a nation where only 16 percent of the consumer's expenditures are for food (with less than half of these for food per se—the majority being for services incorporated with food) has hardly increased in the last 40 years" [15]. People do not consume greater physical quantities after a certain income level is reached. They do change the composition of their diet and demand more services associated with the food they buy. Consequently, total demand for food in the United States grows at a rate exceeding only slightly the rate of population growth. Given the rapid growth in productivity and the tendencies to surplus production, these demand characteristics have led to downward pressures on farm prices since the end of World War II.

At the same time, costs of things farmers buy have been increasing. The farm cost-price relationships over the years are expressed in the "parity ratio." This measures the percentage ratio of prices received for farm products to the percentage ratio of prices paid by farmers for goods used in production and family living, all on a 1910-1914 base. The adjusted parity ratio reflects, in addition to prices received in the market, the government payments made directly to farmers. From 1940 to 1949, the simple average of the annual adjusted parity ratio was 107; it fell to 92 for the decade 1950-1959; and it averaged only 82 for the years 1960-1967 [10]. This deterioration in farm cost-price relationships did not lead to lowered net incomes on all farms. Those farmers who were able to enlarge their operations and take full advantage of the productivity increasing technology were able to increase their earnings (Table 3). But the operators of smaller farms could not keep pace and had to rely more heavily on off-farm earnings. As a result, many left farming entirely. Although the large and growing farms could maintain good incomes, the cost-price squeeze inherent in the present U.S. demand and supply relationships does present a continuing threat and is the fundamental rationale underlying the farm price support-supply control programs.

4. *The Struggle for Bargaining Power.* Despite strong farmer organizations and the substantial political power wielded by farmers, especially until very recent times, farmers have lacked bargaining power in the marketplace relative to that exercised by industry and labor [12]. This seems to be an inherent quality of the development process, and was clearly recognized by the early economists[15] [20].

15 It was also noted by Marx when he said "While the country exploits the town politically . . . wherever feudalism has not been broken down by an exceptional

The economic power that farmers have achieved in the market has come primarily through governmental assistance—commodity loans, withholding surpluses from the market, marketing orders for milk and fresh fruits and vegetables, and other actions. Farmer cooperative organizations have exerted the greatest bargaining influence in commodity lines—especially milk—in which marketing is regulated under federal or state marketing orders. But farmers, through their organizations and with the help of sympathetic members of Congress, continue to press for a greater voice in the determination of farm prices in the marketplace. Major breakthroughs in this area appear unlikely for the near future. Given the tremendous productive capacity, the wide geographic dispersion of production of all major farm commodities, the difficulties of withholding perishable commodities, especially meat, from the market, and the conflicting regional interests, farmers will continue to be more dependent on federal farm policies than on their own collective bargaining in the market.

Rural Poverty and Related Issues In 1966, 20.8 percent of farm households in the United States were living in poverty.[16] For nonfarm households, the percentage was 17.6 [10]. The incidence of poverty (in both the farm and nonfarm population) is much higher among nonwhites. However, poverty is by no means confined to the nonwhite population. Of the 14 million rural poor reported by the National Advisory Commission on Rural Poverty, 11 million are white [19; see also 40].

The underlying causes of rural poverty and the interrelations between the agricultural transformation and the problems in many of our large cities are most complex. Although the latter issue will not be discussed here, the rapid adoption of labor-saving technology and the massive displacement of people from farm employment obviously intensified the problems of poverty in the cities.

In addressing the issues of rural poverty, we are dealing with a much larger population than that actually on farms. While the farm population is under 6 percent of the U.S. total, the population classified by the census as rural constitutes about 30 percent of that total. Only

---

development of the towns, the town on the other hand, everywhere and without exception, exploits the land" [quoted by Owen, 20].

16 Poverty is defined by the Social Security Administration poverty-income standard; it takes into account family size, composition, and place of residence. For example, households are defined as poor if their income falls below the cost of a certain minimum consumption standard—$2,185 in current prices for a nonfarm couple under 65 years of age, $3,335 for a nonfarm family of four, and so on [10].

slightly more than one in four rural poor families lives on a farm. Others live in small towns and villages or in the open country but are not employed on a farm [19]. Yet poverty for many of these people resulted from the rapid transformation of agriculture.

People who are most likely to be adversely affected by this transformation are those who remain on farms but who are unable to adjust to the new technological requirements, and those who leave the farm but who are ill prepared to move into good paying jobs in the industrial sector. In part, these adjustment problems are associated with the lower levels of formal education among farm people. Despite the attention given to rural education throughout our history, educational levels are lower in rural than in urban areas throughout the country. In 1960, 57 percent of rural farm white males 20 to 24 years old had completed high school, compared to 68 percent of urban white males in this age group. The corresponding percentages for nonwhite males were 16 and 45. This educational disadvantage is most pronounced for nonwhites and for people, white and nonwhite, living in the South [10].

The situation in the South is also related to the land tenure system. Had a system of family owned and operated farms emerged after the Civil War, rather than the sharecropping arrangements which retained the political and economic power concentrations of the old plantation system, the operating farmers, both black and white, would have had control over taxation and local investments in schools and other required infrastructure. Farmers and laborers released from such a family farm system might well have been more adequately prepared for urban life [24].

Relative to the 1920s and 1930s, higher skill levels are now required in most employment. Today there are far fewer rungs on the ladder of economic opportunity within reach of those lacking education and specialized training than in the earlier decades of this century. Many of the people who have been pushed and/or pulled out of farming face a labor market demanding skills they do not possess. Thus the poverty problem, both rural and urban, would be less acute if (1) rural migrants had been better trained—if the agricultural sector had not released so many unskilled workers who could not meet the skill requirements at the particular technological stage of development that industry was passing through; and (2) if racial discrimination were absent from the scene [24].

Within the farm population, poverty is concentrated among two groups. First, a substantial number of operators on small farms are poor. Over 50 percent of all farms in the United States have gross sales of less than $5,000 per year with realized net farm income of only slightly over $1,000 (Table 3). In 1964, 55 percent of all farms with less than $5,000 in annual sales—but only 44 percent of all U.S. farms—were located in the South. Not all of the families living on these farms are poor; some operators are in semiretirement, and some have well-paying nonfarm jobs. However, most of the remaining farm poverty is concentrated among operators of these small farms [10, 40].

Second, hired farmworkers are also more likely to be poor. In 1966, the 757,000 hired farmworkers averaged 212 days of farmwork and 13 days of nonfarm work with total wages from both sources averaging $2,102 for the year.[17] The hired farm work force contains a disproportionate number of nonwhites—27 percent in 1966; this contrasts with 13 percent of nonwhites in both the total farm and the U.S. population. Almost 50 percent of the hired farmworkers live in the South [38].

Regionally, the South has a high concentration of both farm and rural nonfarm poverty. Outside the South, Indian reservations, especially in the Southwest and the northern Plains, contain enclaves of rural poor, along with parts of New England and the Upper Great Lakes. Pockets of rural poor Mexican-Americans exist along the southern border [3, 19].

Several large geographic areas with substantial numbers of rural poor have always been marginal farming areas; among them are the hill and semi-mountainous areas of Appalachia and the Ozarks, and large areas in the northern Lake states. In addition to small farm agriculture, people in these areas depended heavily on employment in mining and forestry. Major adoptions of labor-saving technology in mining were made in the 1950s, and during this same period competitive forces in farming led to farm combination on a massive scale. Thus in the decade 1950 to 1960, the Appalachian region had a 52 percent (334,900) drop in employment in agriculture, forestry, and fisheries, and a 59 percent (265,400) drop in employment in mining.[18] Despite employment growth in manufacturing, construction, and trades and services, the area had 32,600 fewer employed in this five-industry grouping in 1960 than

[17] The hired farm working force is much larger than 757,000. But this number had hired farmwork as their primary employment and source of income.
[18] The Appalachian region includes a large part of western and northern Pennsylvania, all of West Virginia, and parts of Ohio, Kentucky, Tennessee, Maryland, Virginia, the Carolinas, Georgia, and Alabama.

in 1950. The Ozark area ended the decade with 53,440 fewer jobs and the northern Lake states with a decline of 30,779 [32, 35, 36, 41].

As a consequence of rapid labor displacement from agriculture, as well as from mining, large areas of the United States have had an absolute decline in population. Small rural towns have experienced the same squeeze as farmers on small farms. As population declines, it becomes more difficult and more expensive to maintain high-quality public services and to support a desired variety of private retail trade and other local establishments. Between 1940 and 1960 more than 1,200 U.S. counties lost population. Approximately 80 percent (960 counties or almost one-third of the U.S. total) had no population center of over 5,000 persons in 1960. And between 1959 and 1964, in 1,315 non-metropolitan counties private nonfarm employment either declined or increased by less than 100 jobs [10].

The problems discussed here are extremely complex. They do not lend themselves to quick solutions. Most of these problems are not new, but all of them were intensified by revolutionary changes in agriculture over the past three decades. Policy makers are beginning to recognize these problems as major issues in economic development. In recent years, we have adopted as one measure of economic progress the number of people lifted from the misfortune of being poor.

Historically, there was a strong faith in the ultimate justice and maximum welfare to be derived from a free-enterprise exchange economy. A man earns what he gets and gets what he deserves. This faith has been badly shaken—especially by the severe depression of the 1930s. In recent decades, we have placed our faith in the efficacy of fiscal and monetary policies to maintain high levels of effective demand and employment. But after three decades of prosperity interrupted on only a few occasions with minor recessions, and especially after seven years of very rapid economic growth, we find over 30 million people (14 million of them rural) still in poverty—unattached to the growing points within the system. They remain on the outside looking in.

Although high levels of employment and aggregate demand are a key to any solution, the problems of the poor and the unskilled cannot be resolved by sole reliance on general fiscal and monetary policies. Particular and sharply focused programs that deal with their special needs are also required. Thus greater attention is now being given to those tough questions of human development, income distribution, and the structure of economic and political power and opportunity.

References

1. Ackley, Gardner, "U.S. Economic Developments and Policies and Their Impact on Agriculture," *Journal of Farm Economics, 49,* 5 (December 1967), 1019-1031.

2. Benedict, Murray R., *Farm Policies of the United States, 1790-1950: A Study of Their Origins and Development.* New York: The Twentieth Century Fund, 1953.

3. Brophy, William A., and Sophie D. Aberle (eds.). *The Indian: America's Unfinished Business. Report of the Commission on the Rights, Liberties, and Responsibilities of the American Indian.* Norman: University of Oklahoma Press, 1966.

4. Brown, Philip S., "Money." In *After a Hundred Years: The Yearbook of Agriculture 1962.* Washington, D.C.: U.S. Government Printing Office, 1962.

5. Carstenson, Vernon, "Profiles of the USDA—First Fifty Years." USDA Graduate School, Growth through Agricultural Progress, lecture series in honor of the United States Department of Agriculture Centennial Year, Washington, D.C., 1961, pp. 3-17.

6. Clawson, Marion, and Burnell Held, *The Federal Lands: Their Use and Management.* Baltimore: Johns Hopkins Press, 1957.

7. Cochrane, Willard W., *Farm Prices: Myth and Reality.* Minneapolis: University of Minnesota Press, 1958.

8. Dorner, Peter, "Discussion: Problems in Domestic Policy." A discussion of papers presented under the general title of "The Family Farm in Domestic and Foreign Land Tenure Policy." *Journal of Farm Economics, 44,* 2 (May 1962), 545-549.

9. _____, "The Farm Problem: A Challenge to Social Invention." *Journal of Farm Economics, XLII,* 4 (November 1960), 911-926.

10. *Economic Report of the President Transmitted to the Congress February 1968 together with the Annual Report of the Council of Economic Advisers.* Washington, D.C.: U.S. Government Printing Office, 1968.

11. Edwards, Everett E., "The First 300 Years." In *Farmers in a Changing World: The Yearbook of Agriculture 1940.* Washington, D.C.: U.S. Government Printing Office, 1940.

12. Galbraith, John Kenneth, *American Capitalism: The Concept of Countervailing Power.* Boston: Houghton Mifflin, 1952.

13. Griswold, A. Whitney, *Farming and Democracy.* New Haven: Yale University Press, 1948.

14. Hathaway, Dale E., *Government and Agriculture: Public Policy in a Democratic Society.* New York, London, Toronto: Macmillan, 1963.

15. Heady, Earl O., *Agricultural Problems and Policies of Developed Countries.* Oslo: Johansen and Nielsen, 1966.

16. Hibbard, Benjamin Horace, "Objectives in Our National Agricultural Policies," *Journal of Farm Economics, XX,* 1 (February 1938), 37-48.

17. _____, *A History of the Public Land Policies.* Madison and Milwaukee: University of Wisconsin Press, 1965.

18. National Advisory Commission on Food and Fiber, *Food and Fiber for the Future.* Washington, D.C.: U.S. Government Printing Office, July 1967.

19. National Advisory Commission on Rural Poverty, *The People Left Behind.* Washington, D.C.: U.S. Government Printing Office, September 1967.

20. Owen, W. F., "The Double Developmental Squeeze on Agriculture," *The American Economic Review, LVI,* 1 (March 1966), 43-70.

21. Parsons, Kenneth H., "Institutional Aspects of Agricultural Development Policy," *Journal of Farm Economics, XLVIII,* 5 (December 1966), 1185-1194, also, Land Tenure Center Reprint No. 28, Madison, Land Tenure Center, University of Wisconsin, 1966.

22. Penn, Raymond J., "The Rural Community and Its Relation to Farm Policies." Land Tenure Center Paper No. 32, April 1967.

23. Schickele, Rainer, *Agricultural Policy: Farm Programs and National Welfare.* New York: McGraw-Hill, 1954.

24. Thiesenhusen, William C., "Population Growth and Agricultural Employment in Latin America." Paper presented at a conference on Population Problems and the Development of Latin America, University of Wisconsin, Madison, May 3-4, 1968.

25. Tolley, George S., "Reclamation's Influence on the Rest of Agriculture," *Journal of Land Economics, XXXV,* 2 (May 1959), 176-180.

26. Tostlebe, Alvin S., *Capital in Agriculture: Its Formation and Financing Since 1870.* A study by the National Bureau of Economic Research. Princeton: Princeton University Press, 1957.

27. U.S. Congress, Joint Economic Committee, *Policy for Commercial Agriculture: Its Relation to Economic Growth and Stability.* Papers submitted by panelists appearing before the Subcommittee on Agricultural Policy, 85th Congress, 1st Session, November 1957. Washington, D.C.: U.S. Government Printing Office, 1957.

28. _____, Senate Small Business Committee, Monopoly Subcommittee Hearings at Eau Claire, Wisconsin, July 22, 1968. See testimony by Sydney D. Staniforth, "Economic Considerations on the Probable Future Form of Business Organization in Farm Production," and Philip M. Raup, "Some Issues Raised by the Expansion of Corporation Farming."

29. U.S. Department of Agriculture, *Parity Returns Position of Farmers: Report to the Congress of the United States Pursuant to Section 705 of the Food and Agriculture Act of 1965,* 90th Congress, 1st Session, 1967. U.S. Senate Document No. 44. Washington, D.C.: U.S. Government Printing Office, 1967.

30. _____, *Handbook of Agricultural Charts: 1967.* Agriculture Handbook No. 348. Washington, D.C.: Government Printing Office.

31. _____, *Changes in Farm Production and Efficiency: A Summary Report, 1969.* USDA Statistical Bulletin No. 233, revised June 1969. Washington, D.C.: Government Printing Office.

32. _____, Economic Research Service, cooperating with West Virginia Agricultural Experiment Station, West Virginia University. *An Economic Survey of the Appalachian Region with Special Reference to Agriculture.* Agricultural Economic Report No. 69. Washington, D.C.: U.S. Government Printing Office, April 1965.

33. _____, *Agriculture and Economic Growth.* Agricultural Economic Report No. 28. Washington, D.C.: U.S. Government Printing Office, March 1963.

34. _____, Agricultural Research Service, *Changing Sources of Farm Output.* Production Research Report No. 36. Washington, D.C.: U.S. Government Printing Office, February 1960.

35. _____, Economic Research Service, in cooperation with Michigan Agricultural Experiment Station, Michigan State University. *An Economic Survey of the Northern Lake States Region.* Agricultural Economic Report No. 108. Washington, D.C.: U.S. Government Printing Office, February 1967.

36. _____, Economic Research Service, in cooperation with the Pennsylvania State University, College of Agriculture, Agricultural Experiment Station. *Employment, Unemployment and Low Incomes in Appalachia.* Agricultural Economic Report No. 73. Washington, D.C.: U.S. Government Printing Office, May 1965.

37. _____, Economic Research Service. *Farm Income Situation.* July 1969.

38. _____, Economic Research Service. *The Hired Farm Working Force of 1966. A Statistical Report.* Agricultural Economic Report No. 120. Washington, D.C.: U.S. Government Printing Office, September 1967.

39. _____, Economic Research Service, Development and Trade Analysis Division. *How the United States Improved Its Agriculture.* ERS Foreign-76. Washington, D.C.: U.S. Government Printing Office, 1964.

40. _____, Economic Research Service. *Rural People in the American Economy.* Agricultural Economic Report No. 101. Washington, D.C.: U.S. Government Printing Office, October 1966.

41. _____, Economic Research Service, cooperating with the Agricultural Experiment Station, University of Arkansas. *An Economic Survey of the Ozark Region.* Agricultural Economic Report No. 97. Washington, D.C.: U.S. Government Printing Office, July 1966.

42. U.S. Department of Commerce, Bureau of the Census. *U.S. Census of Agriculture.* Various years.

43. Wilcox, Walter W., and Willard W. Cochrane. *Economics of American Agriculture,* Second Edition. Englewood Cliffs, N.J.: Prentice-Hall, 1960.

44. *World Food Forum Proceedings.* The Inaugural Event commemorating the 100th Anniversary of the USDA, 1862-1962. May 15-16-17, 1962, Washington, D.C. See especially statements by Kenneth H. Parsons, Walter W. Wilcox, Erven J. Long, Oris V. Wells, and Murray D. Lincoln.

26. New Settlement and Land Consolidation in The Netherlands

Charles A. P. Takes

Settlement in newly reclaimed lands and land consolidation in existing cultivated areas are two important, though quite different, activities in the field of rural development in The Netherlands. Settlement in new lands has occurred for many centuries, as land reclamation was already practiced in the Middle Ages, but there was hardly any planning in the way in which newly reclaimed areas were settled. Even the settlement of the Haarlemmermeer, a large lake of 18,000 hectares (45,000 acres) near Amsterdam, which was pumped dry in 1852, still took place in a voluntary and uncontrolled way. People from various parts of the country who settled in this new polder had a very hard time trying to build up a new life for themselves and their families.[1]

The need for careful planning of settlement projects and for assistance to settlers in building up a new territory was recognized only in the twentieth century when the reclamation of the Zuiderzee was undertaken. It is this type of planned new settlement, represented in The Netherlands by the Zuiderzee Reclamation Project, which will be dealt with in this paper.

Land consolidation, as a government-guided and government-sponsored activity in The Netherlands, dates back to 1924, when the first Land Consolidation Act became operative. The original aim was to reallocate holdings, which by gradual opening up of the land and by repeated subdivision of farms had been fragmented, and to counteract the tendency toward a further splitting up of the land. Gradually, however, land consolidation developed toward a complete reconstruction of rural areas, including the improvement of water management, road systems, public utilities, location of farm buildings, landscaping, recreational facilities, and enlargement of uneconomic small holdings.

For many years the settlement on new land in the Zuiderzee project and the consolidation of holdings in the old land were planned, organized, and carried out completely independently from each other. In recent years, however, the two activities are linked in the sense that priority in obtaining a farm in the new land is given to a number of farmers from land consolidation areas who are prepared to place the

Charles A. P. Takes—The Netherlands. Ph.D., Municipal University, Amsterdam; Deputy Director and Rural Sociologist of the International Institute for Land Reclamation and Improvement, Wageningen.

[1] H. N. ter Veen, *De Haarlemmermeer als kolonisatiegebied* (Groningen: P. Nordhoff, 1925).

land they leave behind at the disposal of the land consolidation authorities, for the enlargement of other farms in the block.

For the rest, however, land settlement and land consolidation in The
Netherlands are still so different with respect to organization, planning,
and execution that it will be necessary to describe them separately in
the relevant sections of this paper.

Main Characteristics of the Physical,
Social, and Economic Structure of The Netherlands

For a clear understanding of the importance of settlement and land
consolidation activities in The Netherlands, it is necessary to have some
background knowledge of the prevalent physical, social, and economic
conditions of the country, particularly those of the agricultural sector.

The Netherlands forms part of the delta of three West European rivers,
the Rhine, the Meuse, and the Scheldt. Accordingly, the country is very
low and flat. The total land area is 33,000 square kilometers (13,000
square miles) and has for about one-third of its extent an altitude below
the mean sea level. A second third part is lying between the mean sea
level and 10 meters (30 feet) plus, and—apart from a few undulated
areas and hills (less than 1 percent of the total area)—the remaining part
does not reach higher than 50 meters (150 feet). The lower two-thirds
are almost completely flat and would be inundated regularly by the sea
and the rivers if they were not protected by a range of natural sand
dunes and artificial sea walls along the North Sea coast, and by river
dikes alongside the main rivers. At present, more than 2,000 pumping
units are used to keep the land dry.

Since about the year 1200, 375,000 hectares (940,000 acres) of land
have been gained from the sea, and 140,000 hectares (345,000 acres)
by pumping of lakes.[2] These figures do not include the areas in the
Zuiderzee Reclamation Project. Up to the present time, in this project,
four out of five big polders with a total area of 165,000 hectares
(410,000 acres) have been pumped dry. The fifth one, which will
probably be reclaimed by 1980, will have an area of 60,000 hectares
(150,000 acres).

Most of the land area of The Netherlands has been brought under
cultivation. In the higher diluvial parts forests and heath land were
reclaimed, particularly in the eighteenth and nineteenth centuries. The
remaining areas of forest and wastelands cover less than 9 and 5 per-

[2]Johan van Veen, *Dredge, Drain, Reclaim, the Art of a Nation* (The Hague:
Martinus Nijhoff, 1955), 4th ed., p. 58.

cent, respectively, of the total land area of The Netherlands,[3] and are carefully preserved for recreational purposes for the still growing population of this, at present, the most densely populated country of the world[4] (12.7 million inhabitants on a land area of 33,400 square kilometers, which means an average density of more than 380 per square kilometer or 985 per square mile).

The flat low-lying country, with its predominantly fertile deltaic soils, moderate sea climate, and rather regular distribution of precipitation throughout the year, has received from nature suitable conditions for agriculture. In former centuries, therefore, agriculture has been a very important means of living in The Netherlands. On the other hand, the location of the country on the North Sea coast, opposite Britain, and on the mouths of three West European rivers with important hinterlands, was a favorable factor for the development of shipping and trade. The seventeenth century was the "golden age" for Dutch navigation and commerce.

In the nineteenth century, particularly after 1870, industry too developed as an important means of living for the rapidly growing population of the country. Although The Netherlands is poor in minerals, industry could develop because of its shipping and trade facilities and its labor surplus from the rural areas.

Basic and auxiliary materials were imported and high-grade finished products were exported. The industrial development was, in turn, conducive to a further development of shipping and trade. The process of transition from a predominantly agricultural to an industrial country is still going on. In 1889 the percentage of the Dutch population living from agriculture was still about equal to that living from industry (31.8 and 31.5 percent, respectively); in 1920 these figures were 22.9 percent for agriculture and 36.9 percent for industry; and in 1960, 10.5 and 42.2.[5] It is expected that the percentage for agriculture will continue to decrease, possibly to 5 percent or even less.

It should be noted that after World War II the number of people having agriculture as their main occupation is not only decreasing proportionally, but absolutely as well. Whereas the total working population of The Netherlands increased 7 percent from 3.9 million in 1947

[3]*Maandstatistiek van de landbouw* (Centraal Bureau voor de Statistiek, 's Gravenhage) Vol. 16, No. 2 (February 1968), p. 50.

[4]Apart from a few miniature states, such as, for instance, Monaco, which have a greater population density.

[5]*Landbouwcijfers 1968.* Landbouw-Economisch Instituut, 's Gravenhage, 1968.

to 4.2 million in 1960, the number of people engaged in agriculture decreased 38.6 percent from 728,000 to 447,000 during the same period.[6]

The most rapid decrease took place in the category of paid farm laborers. Before the war, wages for agricultural laborers were considerably lower than those of industrial workers. Although after the war these wages were gradually put on the same and even later on a higher level, there were still other conditions, such as more regular and shorter work time, paid holidays, better housing and public facilities, recreational facilities, etc., which attracted many young people from the countryside to work in industry, trade, transport, and other occupations in town. In the same way many farmers' sons preferred a paid job outside agriculture rather than a future of hard work, low income, and difficult living conditions on their fathers' small farms.

The rapid decrease of farm labor could partly be compensated by mechanization and rationalization. On many small holdings, however, mechanical equipment could not be used in an economical way. Table 1 shows that the group of farms with an area of less than 10 hectares, in particular, is decreasing rapidly. The only group that showed a continuous and considerable increase is that of the farms between 10 and 20 hectares, which indicates that much of the land that became available by the abandoning of small farms was used for the enlargement of others. Since 1959 the group of farms between 20 and 30 hectares also shows a perceptible increase.

In animal husbandry and horticulture Dutch agriculture has specialized in the production of high-grade export products like butter, cheese, condensed and powdered milk, bacon, eggs, poultry, vegetables, seed potatoes, fruits, flower bulbs, flowers, and woody nursery stock. Much of the horticulture is practiced in heated glasshouses, a very capital-intensive form of production.

The transition from agriculture to other occupations has been greatly stimulated by the postwar industrial boom, resulting in a state of full employment and even shortage of labor in many branches of industry and trade. Agriculture could keep pace only by more specialization, rationalization, intensification, and mechanization. At the same time a process of physical and mental urbanization set in. An area of 6,000-8,000 hectares is needed every year for the construction of new industrial sites, residential districts, roads, recreational areas, etc., the great-

[6] 13e Algemene volkstelling 31 mei 1960. Deel 10, Beroepsbevolking, B, Voornamste cidfers per gemeente-Centraal Bureau voor de Statistiek. Mitgeversmaatschappig nl. de Kaan N. V., Leist, 1964, pp. 14-15.

est part of which can be obtained only by withdrawing it from the cultivated land.[7] The isolation of rural areas is disappearing rapidly, both owing to the improved traffic provisions and the development of other means of communication, viz. telephone, radio, television, newspapers, professional journals, etc. Small farmhouses, left by farmers who abandoned their farming occupation, are often bought nowadays by townspeople as a "second house" in the countryside, where they spend their weekends and holidays. The contacts between urban and rural people are intensified, and the urban way of life is adopted more and more by the rural population.

It is against the background of the postwar development trends described above that we shall have to consider the land settlement and land consolidation activities in The Netherlands.

New Settlement in the Zuiderzee Reclamation Project

Objectives of the Reclamation Project Since the middle of the nineteenth century several proposals for the reclamation of the Zuiderzee, or part of it, have been made by different persons. They all recommend the scheme as an advantageous venture for the promotion of agriculture, commerce, shipping, etc., and thus for the strengthening of the economy of the country. On private initiative the Zuiderzee Society was founded in 1886 with the aim of examining the possibilities of the scheme in a more scientific way. By order of this society Dr. C. Lely, a young civil engineer, made a new technically feasible design which he completed in 1892.

However, it was not until 1918, when Dr. Lely was Minister of Waterstaat (Waterways and Public Works) for the fourth time, that Parliament approved the execution of the project under the responsibility and with the financial means of the state (Figure 1). By that year the circumstances were favorable for getting the approval to the scheme. In the last year of World War I it had become very clear that The Netherlands were not able to produce sufficient food for its population. A project, therefore, which would increase the country's cultivated area by 225,000 hectares of very suitable land for agriculture was considered favorably. Second, a serious flood disaster on the coast of the Zuiderzee had struck the province of North Holland in 1916. It was considered that by the construction of the strong enclosing dam included in Lely's

[7]*Statistisch Zakboek 1968,* Centraal Bureau voor de Statistiek. Stoatsmitgeverij, 's Gravenhage, 1968, p. 2.

Table 1.
Change in Size of Farms, 1950-1965.

Size of Farms (hectares)	1950 Number	Index	1955 Number	Index	1959 Number	Index	1965 Number	Index
1- 5	101,737	100	94,241	93	87,726	86	74,200	73
5- 10	64,275	100	65,820	102	62,206	98	52,465	82
10- 20	48,693	100	50,050	103	53,884	111	55,221	113
20- 30	15,746	100	15,667	99	15,789	100	16,571	105
30- 50	8,775	100	8,612	98	8,675	99	8,740	100
50-100	1,968	100	1,873	95	1,872	95	1,948	99
100 and more	165	100	155	94	160	97	171	104
Total	241,359	100	236,418	98	230,312	95	209,316	87
Total Area (X 1,000 hectares)	2,297	100	2,280	99	2,283	99	2,236	97

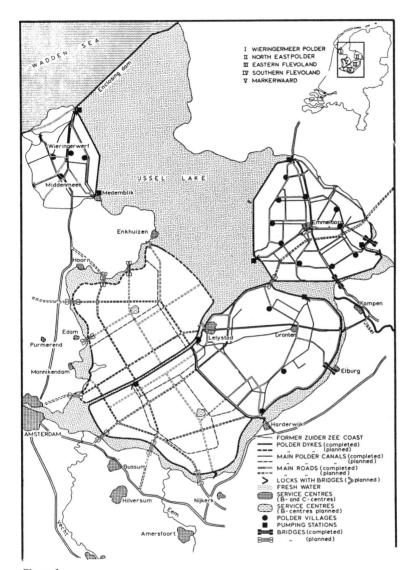

Figure 1.
General map of the Zuiderzee Reclamation Project.

plan the coastline would be shortened by 320 kilometers, and that it would then no longer be necessary to strengthen and maintain the existing dikes over such a large distance for protection against future flood disasters. The construction of the dike would also make it possible to shorten the overland connection between the provinces of North Holland and Friesland considerably. A further argument in favor of the scheme was that the water management of the agricultural areas in the said provinces would be improved and that navigation would benefit from the control of the water level.

It is interesting to notice that during the execution of a long-term project like the Zuiderzee Reclamation Scheme, the importance of certain objectives was decreasing or increasing, and that new objectives were added to the list.

For instance, in the period between the two world wars the creation of new employment possibilities by the works was considered of great importance; after World War II, however, when there was a state of full employment all over the country and in many sectors of the conomy even a shortage of labor, this argument lost its value. In the postwar years the importance of the creation of a big fresh-water reservoir, the Yssellake, was also recognized more and more for several reasons, such as pushing back the infiltration of salt water in the North Sea Canal, the supply of drinking water and fresh water for agricultural use in the surrounding provinces during periods of drought in summer. Another example: After the Northeastpolder had been pumped dry an inadmissible lowering of the groundwater table in the adjacent old land was experienced. In order to prevent similar difficulties in the fringe areas of the southern polders it was decided to space wide oblong lakes between the old and the new land (see map). Now, these lakes appeared to get an important function, not only for navigation, drainage, and water supply, but in particular also for the recreation of both the Dutch people and foreign tourists. On nice summer days hundreds of thousands of people enjoy themselves by swimming, sailing, fishing, and waterskiing on the lakes and by camping along their shores.

There has also been a considerable change of opinion in The Netherlands concerning the allocation and use of the newly reclaimed land. The original objective was to create a kind of "model agricultural area" where well-selected farmers, under optimal conditions of soil fertility, water control, parcelling, transport, and storage could practice modern mechanized farming methods which would lead toward maximum production results. Gradually, however, the idea was winning through that the new land could be better used for helping to solve the problem of shortage of space in the old land. Accordingly, in the settlement of the Northeastpolder, preference was given to a number of farmers from some islands in the southwest of the Netherlands, which had suffered severely from the flood disaster of 1953. After the repair of the dikes of these islands, an agrarian reconstruction was carried out. For the enlargement of farm holdings which were too small, land could be made available only by the resettlement of a number of farmers to the Northeastpolder. In the same way a preference for settlement in the new polders was given to farmers from different parts of the country who by town development, construction of roads, air fields, etc. were forced to abandon their farms, and to tenant farmers who were unable to find new land elsewhere when their landlease contracts ended.

Presently, in Eastern Flevoland 50 percent of the new farms are allocated to farmers from land consolidation areas, 25 percent to the victims of town expansion, etc., and only 25 percent to free applicants. Nevertheless, all the settlers still have to meet minimum requirements concerning professional knowledge, personal suitability, and financial capacity.

A next and very important step toward the new objective of using the reclaimed land for the relief of spatial problems in the old land was included in the "Structure Plan for the Southern IJsselmeerpolders," published in 1961.[8] This plan recommended the allocation of the southwestern parts of Southern Flevoland and the Markerwaard for an expansion of the overpopulated urban and residential districts of Amsterdam and 't Gooi and for recreational purposes. It is for this same reason that the planned central town of Lelystad in the polders will be stimulated to grow into a much bigger industrial and urban center than it would have been had it remained a mere service center for the surrounding rural polder area.

The Institutional Structure of the Zuiderzee Development Authorities After the Dutch Parliament had accepted the Act on the enclosure and partial reclamation of the Zuiderzee, a special governmental agency was founded in 1919: the Dienst der Zuiderzeewerken (Zuiderzee Project Authority). This agency was under the responsibility of the Ministry of Waterways and Public Works, and was entrusted with the tasks of planning and budgeting the technical construction works and

[8] An English version of this publication was issued in 1964: A Structure Plan for the Southern Ysselmeerpolders. Rijkswaterstaat, The Hague, 1964. Rijkswaterstaat Communication No. 6.

supervising their execution. As a rule the construction of the different parts of the project, such as dikes, pumping stations, sluices, bridges, canals, roads, etc. was given to private contractors.

With the bad experiences in the development of the Haarlemmermeer in the nineteenth century in mind, it was recognized that for a successful agricultural and socioeconomic development of the Wieringermeer much work would have to be done of quite a different type than the civil engineering works performed by the Board of the Zuiderzee Works. This was the reason why a second governmental agency was founded in 1930: the "Directie van de Wieringermeer." This agency took care of, in particular, the detail drainage and further preparations for cultivation of the new land, its temporary exploitation (until the permanent settlers arrived), the selection of settlers, allocation of holdings, the planning of farm buildings and all the facilities needed to make the area livable, such as service centers, electricity, water supply, etc. This agency, which was established in Alkmaar, a town near to the Wieringermeerpolder, moved to Zwolle on the other side of the former Zuiderzee as soon as the development of the Northeastpolder had to be undertaken. At present its work is mainly connected with the two parts of the big Flevoland-polder, and its name has been changed to Rijkdienst voor de IJsselmeerpolders (IJssellakepolders Development Authority).

The question may be posed as to whether it is logical and efficient to have two different governmental agencies in charge of the Zuiderzee Reclamation Project. From the foregoing it will be clear that the existence of the two agencies can be explained historically. The first works to be carried out were of a typical civil-engineering nature. In a later stage, activities in the agricultural, socioeconomic, and architectural fields were also required. It is true that, in principle, one big agency covering all aspects of the reclamation work would be preferable, but in practice the existing situation has never led to serious disadvantages or problems, because both governmental agencies have clear-cut tasks, which mostly have to be carried out in continuation of each other. It is mainly in the field of planning that close cooperation and mutual agreement is required. For this purpose there are, and always have been, close contacts between the two agencies by means of committees and by individual contacts between their directors and staff members. Both agencies work under the responsibility of the same minister (Public Works).

A civic body, the Openbaar Lichaam Zuidelijke Ysselmeerpolders,

Southern Ysselmeerpolders Public Authority) has further been established, which is the precursor of the normal municipal authority, and is mainly entrusted with local administrative functions and duties (public health, schools, police, civil registration) during the first stages of development of a new polder. The Wieringermeer and the Northeastpolder have already obtained the normal Dutch municipality status.

Principles of the Physical Planning of the Polder Areas

The General Plan of the Zuiderzee Project The general plan for the Zuiderzee Project as based on the scheme developed by Dr. C. Lely is comprised of (a) the construction of a barrier dam across the Zuiderzee between the coasts of the provinces of North Holland and Friesland, and (b) the endikement and drainage of five polders having a total area of 225,000 hectares (560,000 acres).

After the completion of the barrier dam the whole inlet sea south of it became a big fresh-water lake because the IJssel (a branch of the Rhine) and some smaller rivers continued to bring fresh water to the lake. Direct precipitation as well as water discharged from the surrounding agricultural areas are other sources of fresh water entering the lake. At low tide in the North Sea the sluices in the Enclosing Dam are opened and the superfluous water of the lake is discharged by gravity. At high tide the sluices are closed so that salt water cannot penetrate into the lake.

The necessity for the rivers to discharge their water into the sea is one of the reasons why the whole basin south of the barrier dam could not be reclaimed, but there were also other reasons. The northern part of the former Zuiderzee has rather infertile sandy soils and is considerably deeper than the southern part. It was, therefore, neither attractive nor technically easy to construct new polders in this northern part, with the exception of the Wieringermeer. Moreover, as has already been mentioned, it is of great economic importance to The Netherlands to dispose of a large fresh-water reservoir, the IJssel-lake.

The Physical Planning of the Individual Polders In planning the layout of each polder, various factors have to be taken into account, such as the shape of the polder as it is determined by the general plan of the project, the system of canals needed for drainage and shipping, the parceling system, the settlement pattern, the road system, and the requirements of landscaping and recreation. From this list of factors it will be evident that the design of a polder plan requires a great deal of teamwork among specialists in different fields. Where so many different interests must be coordinated into a harmoniously designed plan for the area, the final layout will necessarily bear the characteristics of a compromise.

Within the context of this paper it would go too far to give a detailed description of the polder planning.[9] It may be useful, however, to say something about one element of the planning which has been subject to considerable change from one polder to the next, viz., the settlement pattern.

The Settlement Pattern   In accordance with the prevalent situation in The Netherlands, farmers' dwellings and barns in the new Zuiderzee polders are built on the plots themselves and not in the villages. By the time the settlement of the Wieringermeer and the Northeastpolder took place (before and immediately after World War II, respectively) it was still a common practice for most farmers who had a farm of about 20 hectares or more on clay soils to employ one or more permanent farm laborers, and some semipermanent and seasonal laborers in addition. It was considered necessary for at least the chief permanent laborer to live at a distance of no more than a few hundred meters from the farm of his employer. As a result, in the above-mentioned two Zuiderzeepolders small blocks of laborers' dwellings have been built and dispersed over all the polder area. The remaining permanent laborers, as well as the semipermanent and seasonal farmhands, were settled in the villages, where their families had the advantages of living near to the school, church, shops, and social amenities.

As far as the villages were concerned there was not yet much of a planning in the Wieringermeer. It was considered that in similar rural areas of the old land, villages were located on distances of 3 to 4 kilometers, but in this new polder the distances could be somewhat greater, namely, 4 to 5 kilometers because of better roads and better means of transport. Accordingly, 14 places were reserved on crossroads for the eventual development of villages or hamlets. It was intended that on one of these places the main center of the Wieringermeer would be built. In fact, however, only three villages were founded.

Important private enterprises, shops, and other economic facilities were established in the first village that was built, and so this village

[9]For more detailed information on these subjects see my publication: *Physical Planning in Connection with Land Reclamation and Improvement,* Publication No. 1 (Wageningen: International Institute for Land Reclamation and Improvement, 1958), Chapter 4.

became the economic center of the polder. The village that was planned to become the main center was built later on and thus received only the function of administrative center. The situation which grew in this way—the presence of only three villages located very near to each other in the central part of the polder, and a division of the central function between two of them—has in practice proved to be not ideal. Therefore, for the second Zuiderzeepolder, the Northeastpolder, a more careful plan was designed, consisting of a small town, Emmeloord, which was to serve as the only clear central town, surrounded by ten villages, regularly dispersed over the polder area and located at distances of 7 to 8 kilometers from each other and from Emmeloord.

By the time this plan was designed and executed the new development of "enlargement of scope" had not yet set in, but in the first few years following the establishment of the 10 villages in the Northeastpolder it was found that the village population grew much slower than was expected, and it was soon realized that several of the villages would never get a population of more than 400 or 500.

In order to prevent a similar situation from arising as was the case in the Wieringermeer, where none of the villages became the clear central town, the development of Emmeloord was stimulated purposely. All kinds of facilities with a central function for the whole polder area, such as secondary schools, hospitals, banks, wholesale trades, rural industries, etc., were allowed to be established only in Emmeloord. In this way it grew to be a lively rural center having at present a population of almost 11,000, which is about one-third of the total population of the whole polder (32,000).

Both the Wieringermeer and the Northeastpolder have a more or less isolated location in the whole of the Zuiderzee Reclamation Project. Accordingly, their settlement plans were able to be designed separately. This was no longer the case for Eastern Flevoland, which will form part of one big polder area, the Zuidelijke IJsselmeerpolders, the three parts of which will be separated from each other only by a dike and a canal, respectively. Consequently, the planning of the larger towns in these three polders had to be done at one go for the whole of the Zuidelijke IJsselmeerpolders.

As this vast new area of 157,000 hectares would be surrounded on three sides by the old land it had to be investigated, first of all, for what distance the existing towns could be expected to serve a central function for parts of the new polder area. This was done by analyzing the service facilities of a dozen towns surrounding the southern basin of the former Zuiderzee.[10] It was found that regarding their central function, two categories of towns could be distinguished: seven of the smaller towns had a more or less sharply defined area of intensive influence, usually an approximately circular area with a radius of 5 to 10 kilometers, where the services provided by the centers are intensively used. These centers were called B-centers to distinguish them from the smallest centers (A-centers), the villages, which provide only services of the lowest order for daily use. The five larger towns had an area of intensive influence similar to that of the B-centers, but in addition they had a much larger area of influence with those facilities of a higher order which were not available in the latter. These larger services centers were called C-centers. As, in general, this influence did not extend further than 20-25 kilometers, it could be concluded that only relatively small parts on the outskirts of the southern Polders could be serviced by these five existing C-centers, and that in the middle of the whole area a new C-center would need to be established. In the same way it was found that in addition to this main town (which is called Lelystad after the founder of the Zuiderzee Reclamation Scheme) a smaller center (B-center) would be needed in each of the three southern polders. These three centers will be comparable with Emmeloord in the Northeastpolder. At present, one of these, called Dronten, already exists in the Eastern Flevoland Polder.

As far as the planning of ordinary villages in Eastern Flevoland is concerned, lessons were drawn from the experiences in the Northeastpolder. It was considered that the number of farm laborers would be much smaller in the new polder. For the remaining laborers the advantages of living in good-sized villages with enough facilities for the primary needs are of greater importance than having to drive a few kilometers further to their work under the present good conditions of modern transport. Therefore, the number of ordinary villages in the southern polders will be drastically reduced as compared with the Northeastpolder. Besides Lelystad and Dronten, only two villages have been built in Eastern Flevoland.

The described planning of the settlement pattern in the Zuiderzeepolders has been based almost exclusively on the assumption of the creation of a rural area inhabited by farmers, agricultural laborers, and

[10] Ch. A. P. Takes, "Bevolkingscentra in het oude en het nieuwe land," thesis, Municipal University of Amsterdam, N. Sampson N. V., Alphen a/d Rijn, 1948, 161 pages. Publicaties van de Stichting voor het Bevolkingsondersvek in de Drooggelegde Linderseepolders No. 12.

people with a service function toward these agricultural producers. In the southern polders this will be different, as has been mentioned before. Lelystad is expected to attract different industries and, accordingly, to grow into a town of 100,000 inhabitants or more, and in the southern parts of Southern Flevoland and the Markerwaard many people will settle who will work in the urban agglomeration of Amsterdam and the surrounding area and in new industries to be established in these new polders. No detailed or definite plans for the settlement pattern of these urbanized areas have been published as yet, but they certainly will add a new and interesting element to the layout of the new land.

The Social Structure of the Settler Community

Selection of Settlers As the new land in the former Zuiderzee is created by The Netherlands government and therefore is financed by the whole of the Dutch people, it has been a principle, right from the beginning, that settlers should be carefully selected, in order to prevent failures and consequently a waste of money. Therefore, high demands concerning theoretical knowledge and practical skill and experience for managing the type of farm they applied for were made upon the applicants. They also had to be in good health and in the age group between 26 and 50. A further requirement was that the farmers should be married or engaged. Information was collected not only about the farmer's moral and social reputation, but also about that of his wife. To be sure that the settlers would be able to bear up against any eventual misfortunes in the first years after settlement they were required to have a certain amount of capital available per hectare, which should partly be possessed by themselves and partly could be borrowed. Special attention was also paid to the applicant's experience in performing management functions in professional and/or social societies and clubs or as a member of governing bodies or committees. Such experience was required because it was thought to be very useful for quick community building in the new living area.

It was possible to make such high demands upon the applicants because, after the hesitation in the first period of settlement of the Wieringermeer had been overcome, the interest in becoming a tenant in the new polders appeared to be very great. In the Northeastpolder there were often more than twenty applicants for each farm to be rented. In this polder a priority was given to those farmers' sons who had worked

at least two years in the reclamation of the polder, the so-called "pioneers." It is not surprising that as a result of the sound selection of
settlers, failures practically never occurred after settlement.

With respect to the selection of nonfarming settlers, the following may
be observed. Agricultural laborers are tested only on their skill. For
shopkeepers and craftsmen, the general Dutch standards of professional
skill, commercial knowledge, and solvency are required, and in addition
the colonization authority carefully considers the need for and possibilities of such people.

Community Building   As a result of the careful selection, the group of
farmers in the new land is, more than anywhere else, composed of
people who have a modern outlook on life. Being modern became a
norm here. The people in the polders keep an eye open for all kinds of
innovations and experiments; they are, in general, more dynamic than
the average farmer in the old land. As the people come from different
parts of the country, with their own habits, traditions, and dialects,
there is a tendency, particularly in the beginning, to keep social contacts preferably with other settlers originating from the same place or at
least from the same province. After some time, however, the factor of
same origin becomes less important. The common modern attitude and
common interest stimulate people to join cooperative societies and to
establish various forms of social relationships with each other. Children
of settlers are in school together with children from different areas of
origin. They gradually lose their dialect and traditions, so that a new
generation of polder inhabitants grows up with their own attitudes and
tongue, which is closer to the official Dutch language than any of the
provincial dialects spoken in the areas of origin.

Certain specific problems have arisen as a result of the methods used
to select the settlers. As most of the settlers were young married
couples, the age structure, at least in the beginning, was unbalanced.
There were many young children below the age of 12, very few teen-
agers, many young adults, and hardly any old people. Consequently,
there was a great need for primary schools in the first few years; but
children who were somewhat older had to go great distances, often even
to their parents' original homes, to find secondary or technical schools
because the number of these youngsters was insufficient as yet to make
the establishment of such schools worthwhile. It was also very difficult
for such youngsters to find companions for social intercourse. The
absence of people over the age of 50 meant that the stabilizing element
which these people form in every normal community was lacking. In

this respect the arrival in the Northeastpolder of farmers from the reconstruction areas in Zeeland was highly valued, because these settlers were, on the average, older than the already present settlers.

It is not possible within the context of this article to go into detail about all the other aspects of community building. Where necessary and possible the Zuiderzeepolders Development and Colonization Authority assists, stimulates, and subsidizes the establishment of churches, medical and veterinarian services, schools, community halls, etc. Certain activities for which well-organized national agencies exist, such as, for instance, agricultural extension, are executed in the polders by these agencies in close cooperation with the reclamation authorities.

Land Consolidation in the Netherlands

Objectives of Land Consolidation   There are various possibilities for individual farmers to increase their productivity, e.g., by using better farm equipment, fertilizers, better seeds and seedlings, etc. Apart from these internal production factors there are, however, a number of other factors which, in general, cannot be improved by the individual farmers themselves. These external production factors include the parceling system (number, shape, size, and location of the different plots belonging to the same farm), water management, the road pattern for transport to and from the different plots, the location and suitability of the farm buildings, and the supply of public utilities such as electricity, piped water, and telephones.

In the beginning of the twentieth century, on the initiative of the Royal Dutch Heath Society, small groups of farmers started to change plots and unite them into larger and better shaped holdings. It was soon recognized, however, that much better results could be obtained if this reallocation of land was accompanied by measures for the improvement of the soil, of water management, and of the road pattern. For this the actual cooperation of the government was indispensable. The passage of the first Land Consolidation Act in 1924 made this governmental activity possible (Figure 2). Later on, as the population of the country grew, the aims of land consolidation were broadened. Within the framework of town and country planning, land consolidation became very important for the reconstruction of the countryside, and then attention had to be paid also to landscaping and recreational facilities.

At present land consolidation is an important instrument in the government stimulated process of the abolition of small uneconomic farm

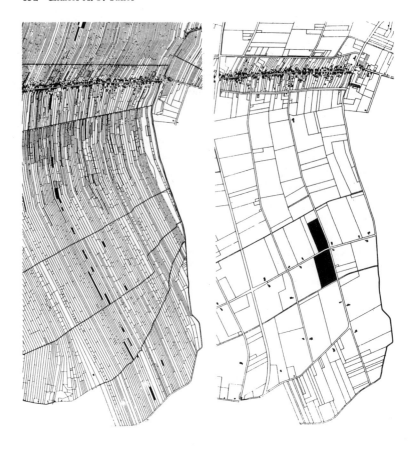

Figure 2.
Detail of the land consolidation project Vriezenveen. The dispersed black parcels on the left map (old situation) were owned by one farmer. The right map illustrates how these parcels have been replaced by two adjacent plots in the new situation. The small black dots on the right map represent farms which were resettled from the village center. Source: Annual Report 1967 of the Government Service for Land and Water Use.

units and the enlargement of the remaining farms. The Land Consolidation Act had to be modified twice: in 1938 and 1954.

The Organization and Procedure of Land Consolidation   By the Land Consolidation Act of 1924 a committee was established which would be in control of the land consolidation activities and would advise the government concerning all matters of this kind. This committee, the Centrale Cultuur-technische Commissie (Central Committee for Land

and Water Use) consists partly of representatives from different ministries and partly of representatives from private farmers' organizations. It was not until 1935, when the Cultuur-technische Dienst (Government Service for Land and Water Use) was established under the Ministry of Agriculture and Fisheries, and working under the supervision of the above-mentioned committee, that land consolidation was able to develop substantially.

The central direction and office of the Government Service for Land and Water Use is at Utrecht; it has a bureau in each of the eleven provinces of The Netherlands. The service stimulates and supervises the execution of the projects, the technical works of which are actually carried out by private land development bureaus. The Government Service for Land and Water Use cooperates closely with other governmental bodies, such as the Cadastral Land Consolidation Service and the State Forestry Service (Staatsbosbeheer). Scientific agricultural, hydrological, and economic research in aid of land consolidation is done by the Institute for Land and Water Management Research at Wageningen.

Land consolidation projects can be brought about either by voluntary agreement between all landowners in the area, or by the force of law after a vote, taken under the landowners. If the landowners who are voting affirmatively either constitute more than 50 percent of the total number of landowners, or together own more than 50 percent of the land, the project will be carried out. It is only the latter type of land consolidation "by force of the law" which is realized on a large scale. This is illustrated by Table 2, which indicates the total number of hectares up to the end of 1967 in the different stages of progress for the two types of land consolidation.[11]

Table 2.
Land Consolidation.

Land Consolidation	Applied for	In Preparation	In Execution	Completed
By Mutual Agreement		11,530	21,540	22,500
By Force of the Law	1,289,600	443,600	502,560	268,910

[11] Annual Report 1967 of the Government Service for Land and Water Use. (Jaarverslag 1967 Centrale Cultuursechnische Commissie Cultuursechnische Dienst, Herverkavelingscommissie Zeeland, Stichting Beheer Landbouwgronden. Cultuursechnische Dienst, Utrecht, 1968. 100 pp.

For a clearer understanding of the terms "applied for," "in prepara-tion," "in execution," and "completed," it will be necessary to give a brief description of the procedure by which a land consolidation proj-ect is realized. An application for land consolidation "by force of the law" can be made with the provincial government by either public authorities, such as the national government, a provincial government, a municipality, a polder board, or by private organizations such as an agricultural organization. An application can also be made by a group of landowners comprising at least one-fifth of the total number of cadastral landowners of the area in question. After receiving an applica-tion the provincial government asks the advice of the Central Land and Water Use Committee concerning the urgency of the project. The Gov-ernment Service for Land and Water Use carries out a survey of the land use, tenancy relations, and other social and agricultural problems of the area in question. A provisional plan for the necessary improvements and an estimate of costs is made on the basis of this survey. The expected "rate of return" and the "social leeway" of the area, measured on a certain point evaluation of five different social factors, are decisive for the urgency of the project and its place in the priority scheme.[12]

The provisional plan may be modified by eventual wishes or by objec-tions from interested parties. Before it is put to the vote of the land-owners, informative meetings are organized in the area during which experts from the Government Service for Land and Water Use give detailed explanations about the different aspects of the plan. Up to the present the votings have been favorable in a great majority of the cases.

If the voting has ended with a positive result, the provincial govern-ment sets up a so-called Local Committee which consists of local author-ities and informal leaders, and which is assisted by some experts. This local committee, in fact, is in charge of the execution of the project. A list of rightful claimants is drawn up, and the value of each claimant's land is determined by expert valuators who are appointed by the local committee. Objections may be raised against the results of their work, and it is possible to appeal against decisions. The same can be done in a much later stage, when—after the technical works have been carried out—the plan for the new allocation of land in the block has been

12 Farmers' incomes, location in an economic development area, location in an area with an unfavorable geographic location, number of slum dwellings, and connections with public utilities. *A Priority Scheme for Dutch Land Consolida-tion Projects*, Publ. No. 6. (Wageningen: International Institute for Land Reclama-tion and Improvement, 1960).

designed. In order to prevent objections, special desires of individual landowners concerning, for instance, the location of their new property, are taken into account if possible. If an agreement cannot be reached, the investigating judge or the court will decide. Finally the notary will draw up the new title deeds, which are then entered in the land register.

Farm Enlargement Although some of the cultivable land in a land consolidation project may get a different destination, e.g., for new roads, watercourses, town and village development, landscaping and recreational facilities, farmers usually are not allotted a total area of land which is smaller than they had before. On the contrary, the execution of the project is considered an excellent opportunity for trying to increase the size of farms which are too small. The land necessary for this farm enlargement can be obtained in three ways, one of which has been mentioned before: the resettlement of farmers from land consolidation schemes to the new Zuiderzeepolders. This resettlement may be done either directly or indirectly. The latter means that a farmer gets a farm elsewhere in the former territory when land becomes available by the migration of landowners to the Zuiderzeepolders. This indirect method may be useful, for instance, if the type of farming in the land consolidation area is so different from that in the Zuiderzeepolders that the change would be too great. The second way of obtaining land for farm enlargement is by reclaiming eventual wastelands located in the land consolidation block. As there is hardly any wasteland left in The Netherlands, this way is not very important.

Of much more importance is the third way: the buying out of landowners who voluntarily decide to abandon their farming occupation, a process that is stimulated by the government. The Land Consolidation Act of 1954 provides for the possibility of paying a farmer, over and above the purchase price, a lump sum as capitalized loss of income. Farmers of 50 years and over who have a low income receive in addition a monthly pension, up to the age of 65, which guarantees a reasonable living standard. From that age onward he receives the state old-age pension, like every Dutchman. A special government Foundation for the Administration of Agricultural Land purchases and administers the land for farm enlargement and makes it available for the reorganization in land consolidation blocks as soon as it is required.

Land Consolidation: Preparation and Follow-up It will be evident that the realization of a land consolidation scheme which, in fact, means a complete reconstruction of the rural area in question, requires quite a bit of adaptation to the new situation on the part of the people living in the project area. Therefore, it is of the utmost importance that since 1956 the different governmental extension services carry out a program of regional development which covers largely the areas where land consolidation has been or will be carried out. Extension courses and other activities are organized, both in the sphere of farm management and in the sphere of agricultural economic, social, and household problems. In some cases the regional development measures taken have helped to remove any initial resistance by the inhabitants toward a proposed land consolidation scheme.

It is also important, particularly with reference to the farm enlargement measures, that the government organize occupational retraining for those people who wish to abandon their farming occupation.

Financing Land consolidation is an expensive activity. On the average the total cost per hectare amounts to about $1,000. It is evident that this cannot be fully financed by the landowners themselves. They pay, in principle, only for the increase in the value of the land resulting from the improvement, which in general represents about 30 percent of the total costs. For this they get a credit redeemable over a period of 30 years. The government subsidies are usually 60 to 70 percent of the total costs. Since 1964 the Development and Reorganization Fund of the European Economic Community has contributed toward the financing of technical improvements of individual farms on the one hand, and toward the liquidation of smallholdings on the other.

In 1967 the total gross investment in land consolidation and other land improvement works amounted to nearly 300 million Dutch guilders ($83 million); and 55,000 hectares (137,000 acres) were consolidated. A further acceleration of the activities will be hampered by limitations of funds, staff, and technical capacity. Of the total area of nearly 1.3 million hectares for which land consolidation has been applied, nearly 270,000 hectares has been completed. From these figures it is evident that for many years to come land consolidation may go on in The Netherlands.

Bibliography

An Assessment of Investments in Land Reclamation from the Point of View of the National Economy, Publication No. 7. Wageningen: International Institute for Land Reclamation and Improvement, 1960. 65 pp.

From Fisherman's Paradise to Farmer's Pride. The Hague: Netherlands Government Information Service, 1959, 116 pp.

Land Consolidation Act 1954. Utrecht: Government Service for Land and Water Use. Reprint from *Food and Agricultural Legislation 3*, 4 (1954) (F.A.O.), 40 pp.

A Priority Scheme for Dutch Land Consolidation Projects, Publication No. 6. Wageningen: International Institute for Land Reclamation and Improvement, 1960. 84 pp.

A Structure Plan for the Southern Ysselmeerpolders. Rijkswaterstaat, Communications No. 6. The Hague, 1964. 32 pp.

Constandse, A. K., "Reclamation and Colonization of the New Area," *Netherlands Journal of Economic and Social Geography, 54*, 2 (February 1963), pp. 41-45.

Jacoby, E. H., *Land Consolidation in Europe*. Publication No. 3E. Wageningen: International Institute for Land Reclamation and Improvement, 1959, 142 pp.

de Soet, F., "Rural Development in the Netherlands," Ministry of Agriculture and Fisheries, The Hague, 1959. Reprinted from *The Way Ahead, 6-7* (1956-1959). 24 pp.

Takes, Ch. A. P. *Physical Planning in Connection with Land Reclamation and Improvement*. Publication No. 1. Wageningen: International Institute for Land Reclamation and Improvement, 1958. 79 pp.

_____, "The Settlement Pattern in the Dutch Zuiderzee Reclamation Scheme," *Tijdschrift van het Koninklijk Nederlandsch Aardrijkskundig Genootschap, 77*, 3 (1960), pp. 347-353.

_____, "Recent Rural Development and Problems in Holland," *Netherlands Journal of Economic and Social Geography, 54*, 2 (February 1963), pp. 34-41.

_____, and A. J. Venstra, "Zuyder Zee Reclamation Scheme. Post-War Developments in Planning and Execution Especially as Regards Layout and Colonization," *Journal of Economic and Social Geography, 51*, 7 (July 1960), pp. 162-167.

van der Bom, F. L., "The Water Management in The Netherlands," *Annual Bulletin, International Commission on Irrigation and Drainage*, New Delhi, 1967, pp. 47-68.

van Veen, Johan, *Dredge, Drain, Reclaim: the Art of a Nation*. The Hague: Martinus Nijhoff, 1955. 200 pp. 4th ed.

27. Agriculture's Contribution to Economic Development: The Italian Experience

Giuseppe Barbero

The study of Italy's economic development is probably of some relevance for a number of developing countries, which have recently come to the foreground in the international scene, gaining political independence and attempting to assert themselves as nations, not only with regard to the outside world but also internally and finding themselves up against the difficult task of integrating regions, groups, and sectors often quite dissimilar as to history, values, interests, and culture. For the history of Italy as a nation dates back only to 1861, when as a result of a number of favorable circumstances, the various states, formerly extending over small or large parts of the peninsula, disappeared to make place for the Kingdom of Italy.

Political unification meant the appearance on the European scene of a nation of about 30 million people and the initiation of a process of economic integration of a number of states, each marked by its own set of institutions, degree of economic progress or backwardness, and socioeconomic structure. The task before the ruling class of the time was indeed a formidable one. The new state immediately set out to adopt a single set of institutions and in so doing it chose the easiest way, if perhaps not the most rational one, by extending over the entire territory the laws and administrative regulations of the Kingdom of Sardinia, which had assumed the political and military leadership of the unification movement. Among other measures, trade barriers were eliminated and the tariff system of the State of Sardinia became that of unified Italy. Thus the premises for a national market and for intensified internal and external trade were established. But it also meant that some regions came to enjoy advantages over those which had a weaker economic basis. The economic unification proved to be a much more difficult and longer task than political unification, to the point that it is still today a national policy issue [1]. One aspect of the "economic dualism" of Italy, exemplified by the well-known North-South antithesis, is at least partially rooted in the economic and social

Giuseppe Barbero—Italy. Professor of Agricultural Economics and Dean of the Faculty of Economics and Banking, the University of Siena; promoter and Director of the Socioeconomic Research Center for Agriculture in Venice, 1964 to 1968; served with FAO in various instances, both in Rome and in field assignments.

differences existing prior to 1861, and was worsened by successive economic events and economic policy. The big attack on the regional split between North and South was initiated only after World War II, but in spite of the public effort produced since that time and the remarkable rate of progress shown by the southern regions, the gap still exists.

At the time of Unification, the Italian economy was definitely dominated by agriculture: approximately 70 percent of the working population was engaged in agriculture. Italy had practically none of the mineral resources so valuable in those times, and the few industries were mainly rural-based industries, both in the sense that they dealt with agricultural products such as silk, wool, hemp, cotton—the latter mainly imported, except at the time of the American Civil War when internal production was expanded—and later sugar beet, as well as in the sense that it employed to a large extent members of rural families and seasonal agricultural laborers. Techniques of production both in agriculture and in industry were generally primitive; railroads had been built only in the northwest; the merchant marine was old fashioned, due to the very small proportion of steamships. By and large the situation was slightly better in the North than in the South, with the Center holding an intermediate position in practically all aspects of economic and social life. Several factors have been singled out to explain why the North was better off: the advantageous geographic position with regard to the other more advanced European states; a richer natural endowment in the broad sense of water resources and more flat and fertile land; relative ease of communications; a social structure freer of feudal ties as evidenced by the existence of more enterprising landowners and merchants as against a prevalence of absentee landlords in the South.

Looked at as a whole, Italy's higher degree of backwardness was also apparent with regard to the rest of Europe: the industrial revolution in England was one century old; France and Germany, although themselves "late joiners," could boast great progress in agriculture, industry, fixed social capital (railroads in particular), and social organization. It was particularly to England and France that the State of Sardinia had looked during the Risorgimento, in the ten years preceding the unification, not only for political purposes but also for the formulation of her economic policy, marked by a free trade approach. This policy, later extended to the whole of Italy, favored the more advanced or the less backward regions. When, about twenty-five years later the new state, following the changed mood in the European scene, turned to a protectionist policy and the capitalists (industrialists) of the North found a natural alliance with the capitalists (large landowners) of the South, the economic split could not but deteriorate further.

Methodological Remarks

The main theme of this chapter is an attempt to measure the contribution of agriculture to Italian economic development in the century following its political unification. The relatively long period under consideration allows only a summary presentation of the changing relationships between agriculture and the rest of the economy. As such, it lacks many details and omits treatment of problems, pertaining particularly to the social structure and to socioeconomic policy.

This chapter is nothing more than an application of the method proposed by Simon Kuznets for the measurement of agriculture's contribution to economic development [13]; it claims therefore no theoretical or methodological originality of its own. The emphasis is entirely on the assembling and analysis of statistical and other information referring to the main components of the relationships between agriculture and the rest of the economy. Agriculture's contribution to economic development is treated under four major headings: growth of total output; growth of output per worker; purchases and sales; transfer of resources (capital and labor). Some preliminary observations seem necessary regarding the ambiguity of the concept of the contribution of one sector to the rest of the economy—as Dr. Kuznets himself takes care to do—as well as the limitations of the sector definition as used in the context, and of the time series on which most of the analysis is based.

First, the term *contribution* must be understood here not in its broad sense of allocating to the various economic sectors the great structural variations within the economic system and in international relations which accompany any process of economic development. The objective is a narrower one, to isolate and measure the amount of resources originating in the agricultural sector and used by other sectors, through the introduction of new activities or the enlargement of previous ones. But even this narrower concept does not do away completely with the problem of allocation, because a higher volume of resources can be attained in one sector and released for the growth of the entire system only inasmuch as the other sectors are ready to use them. A sector is not an independent entity but part of a whole, and whatever changes take place within it condition, and are conditioned by, what happens in the rest of the economy and internationally. A certain amount of arbitrariness in allocating the growth of the system is thus unavoidable.

As to the question of sector definition, it is well known that operational definitions to suit specific national and regional income accounts are generally based on the aggregation of economic activities and as such cannot avoid arbitrary decisions as to where the activities belong. The difficulties are perhaps even greater in the sectoral distribution of labor forces, because of a number of persons working in activities classified under different sectors. When the analysis extends over a long period of time, one must add the shortcomings deriving from changes in definition in censuses as well as in other statistics.

As to statistics, it must be recalled that most of the time series referring to the earlier periods, up to the beginning of this century, have been worked out in recent times and often rest on indirect indicators and estimates [5, 6].

The above limitations are being underlined not because they are such as to deprive the analysis of any significance, but rather to make clear that the figures given in the following pages are to be taken only as gross indicators of order of magnitude.

Contribution to Growth of Total Product

Agriculture accounted for almost 70 percent of the active population and about 55 percent of the gross domestic product in the first five years after Unification. In 1961-65, one century later, the corresponding figures were 27.3 and 14.2 percent, as shown on Table 1.[1]

During the same period the gross agricultural product in real terms more than doubled, in spite of the drawbacks of two wars and of the slow rates of growth for long periods, as Table 2a shows. The average contribution of agriculture to the growth of gross national product over the century can be estimated in the region of 20-25 percent. But considering the length of the period under review and the great changes which have marked the formation of the Italian industrial state, it is worth examining the contribution of the agricultural sector during shorter historical periods. The contribution of a sector to the growth of the national product in each specified period depends on the initial ratio of the products of the sectors and on the ratio between growth

---

[1] Figures have continued to decline rather rapidly in the last few years; for example in 1968 employment in agriculture was down to 22 percent of the total; and gross agricultural product, in current terms, fell to 11 percent of gross domestic product.

Table 1.
Agriculture's Share in Gross Product and Working Population, 1861-65 to 1961-65.

| Period | Working Population[1] | | Agriculture's Share in | |
	Agriculture, forestry and fisheries	Total	Working population (%)	Gross product[2]
1861-65	10,826	15,638	69.2	54.6
1901-05	10,248	16,873	60.7	45.8
1921-25	9,665	17,597	54.9	38.2
1936-40	9,098	18,759	48.5	26.0
1946-50	8,281	19,168	43.2	32.8
1951-55	8,212	20,043	41.0	22.0
1961-65	5,447	19,971	27.3	14.2

[1] Thousands; active population up to 1946-50; persons employed, for the following periods.
[2] Percentages derived from current prices estimates.
Sources: [20] up to 1946-50; [8, 9] for the following periods.

rates of the products during the period. In the early stage of development, when agriculture predominates, the contribution can be a substantial one even if the rate of growth is a relatively slow one, while at later stages the contribution may be very low, even if the sector progresses rapidly, on account of its small percentage of total national product. This is confirmed for Italy by the figures in Table 2a (last column). In the first 40 years, from Unification to the turn of the century, contribution of agriculture was between one-third and one-half; this average range, however, conceals a much larger contribution in the first two decades against a rather small one after 1880, when agriculture underwent a severe crisis. In the first decade of the new state there was a great upsurge of exports of primary and manufactured agricultural products, while in the last two decades of the century gross product of agriculture remained almost constant, in real terms, and the modest growth of the national product was due almost exclusively to the expansion of industrial production.

At the beginning of the present century, agriculture's contribution drops to about 15 percent, mainly because of the remarkable performance of the nonagriculture sectors. The decline continues in the following periods, with the exceptions of the war and immediate postwar years, for the same reason.

In the interwar period agriculture progresses but little, due to the sharp reduction in foreign trade, flows of capital and know-how. After World War II, the rate of expansion of agriculture is unprecedented, as the period is marked by trade liberalization, great investment in fixed social capital, rapid development of mechanization, and the introduction of new technology, mainly of the production-increasing type, available and easily adaptable from other countries. An abundant labor supply completes the picture and provides the motivation for this big production drive. But if one keeps in mind that, after the postwar recovery, the nonagricultural sectors already generate a gross product almost four times as large as agriculture and that their rate of expansion is again almost four times as large, it is no wonder that agriculture's contribution is down to 7 percent.

In view of the previously mentioned "economic dualism," one would expect a different behavior of the agricultural sector in the main geographic subdivisions and a corresponding diversified contribution to the formation of regional products. Available regional income statistics, however, do not permit such an analysis, except for the most recent period, as shown in Table 2b.

The breakdown by the three main regional subdivisions indicates that agriculture has played a strikingly different role in each one. Thus it can be seen that while in the Northwest agriculture's contribution was practically nil, in the South and Islands it was in the region of one-fifth. Roughly one could say that in the latter region agriculture has had in the period after 1950 a role equivalent to that performed by the whole sector, at the national level, at the turn of the century. This result is of particular significance if one recalls that at the time of Unification the weight of agriculture, both in terms of products and of labor forces, was approximately equal in the three great regions.

Table 2b tells us that at the beginning of the 1950s the ratio of net products of the nonagricultural and of the agricultural sectors was 1.7 in the South and 5.8 in the Northwest. If the starting point, at least in pure quantitative terms, was roughly equal, then the nonagricultural sector of the North must have enjoyed a faster rate of growth during the first 90 years after Unification. Consequently the South has had to rely on agriculture to a much higher degree throughout the history of the unified state, in spite of a less favorable endowment of natural resources. This explains why during periods of stagnation or of depression, owing to the weakening of export markets and the fall of agricultural prices, mass emigration from the South, mainly directed to the Americas, became the only feasible alternative.

Table 2a.
Agriculture's Contribution to Growth of Total National Product 1861-65 to 1961-65.

Periods	Initial Ratio[1] P_b/P_a	Percentage Change (%)[2]			Agriculture's Contribution (%)[3]
		r_b	r_a	r_b/r_a	
1861-65 to 1901-05	0.97	61.0	34.5	1.77	36.8
1901-05 to 1911-15	1.16	54.6	11.5	4.75	15.3
1911-15 to 1921-25	1.61	20.4	5.7	3.58	14.7
1921-25 to 1936-40	1.84	49.1	6.4	7.67	6.6
1951-55 to 1961-65	3.79	83.6	24.9	3.36	7.3

Sources: [2, 8, 13, 20].

Table 2b.
Agriculture's Contribution to Regional Net Product, 1951-55 to 1961-65.

Regions	Initial Share[1] P_b/P_a	Rates of Change (%)[2]			Agriculture's Contribution (%)[3]
		r_b	r_a	r_b/r_a	
Northwest	5.75	104.3	-0.5	-208.60	-0.1
Northeast and Center	2.78	104.6	26.9	3.89	8.5
South and Islands	1.71	85.1	36.6	2.33	20.1
Total for Italy	3.05	100.4	24.3	4.13	7.3

Sources: [2, 10, 13].
[1] Ratio of gross product of nonagricultural sectors (P_b) to gross product of agriculture (P_a), at the beginning of each period; constant terms; housing and government services excluded from gross product of nonagricultural sectors.
[2] Percentage change during each period: r_b = nonagricultural sectors; r_a = agriculture.
[3] Obtained from equation: $$\frac{1}{1 + (P_b/P_a \cdot P_b/r_a)} = \frac{1}{1 + (P_b/P_a \cdot r_b/r_a)}$$

For Table 2b, estimates are based on net product at 1963 prices; consequently, for the national territory, initial ratio and percentage changes do not coincide with those given in Table 2a.

Contribution to Growth of Product per Worker

Table 1 shows how the agricultural labor force (expressed in terms of population active in agriculture) have declined throughout the period, not only in relative terms but also absolutely; it is easily seen that the most pronounced drop belongs to the last postwar period. Agricultural labor forces in 1951-55 were still about 75 percent of those of 1861-65; ten years later the proportion was down to 50 percent. This trend is also shown in Table 3a, in terms of yearly rates of change: the decrement of the agricultural labor force is evident, although at modest rates, in all periods up to the last world war; it greatly accelerates afterward. As the product of agriculture increased somewhat in all periods, it follows that countrywide product per agricultural worker has been constantly moving upward. Yearly rates of change, however, are far from homogeneous among periods and between the two sectors. Only in the first 40 years and in the more recent period has the yearly increase of product per worker been higher in agriculture than in the rest of the economy. In the early 1950s the ratio of product per worker in agriculture and in the nonagricultural sectors was less than 0.4, even worse than that estimated for the very first years of the new state.

In spite of the above events, the contribution of agriculture to the increment of product per worker is a substantial one: it ranges from 61 percent in the second half of the last century, to 25 percent approximately in the last period. However, the figures presented in the last column of Table 3a need some illustration. The contribution of agriculture in the early period is a remarkable one only because countrywide productivity increases are exceptionally low, particularly in the nonagricultural sectors. The period is marked by a very small overall increase in nonagricultural employment: the free trade policy put great stress on the few manufacturing industries, forcing the stronger ones to adopt more efficient techniques and the weaker ones to disappear. Railroad building and housing development in some urban centers were not enough to pull some of the excess labor force out of agriculture. The decline in the agricultural labor force observable in the last decade of the century is therefore due not to people leaving stagnant rural areas to move to developing centers, but rather to the flight abroad of desperate farmers and agricultural laborers.

When, at the beginning of the century, industrial production starts moving upward at a sustained rate, the contribution of agriculture to the increment of product per worker drops to about one-quarter and this level is maintained afterwards if we disregard the reversed trend of the war years; but, while up to 1940 this can be explained by the slowing down of the rate of growth of the nonagricultural sectors, in the postwar period one must note the great increment in agricultural

Table 3a.
Agriculture's Contribution to Growth of National Product
per Worker, 1861-65 to 1961-65.

| Periods | Product per Worker[1] | | | |
| | Absolute values (lire)[2] | | Rate of change per year (%) | |
	A	B	A	B
1861-65 to 1901-05	2,158	4,714	0.89	0.39
1901-05 to 1911-15	3,066	5,512	1.24	3.14
1911-15 to 1921-25	3,467	7,510	1.11	1.35
1921-25 to 1935-40	3,873	8,567	0.75	1.35
1951-55 to 1961-65	370	1,080	6.50	4.15

Sources: [2, 8, 9, 13, 20].
[1] Data based on gross product of the private sector (at 1938 prices) up to 1936-40 and on net product (at 1963 prices) for the last period.
A = agriculture, forestry, and fisheries; B = nonagricultural sectors (excluding housing).
[2] Thousand lire for last period.
[3] Active population up to 1936-40 and persons employed for the last period.
As government employees are excluded, percentages are higher than those given in Table 1.

Table 3b.
Agriculture's Contribution to Growth of Regional Product per Worker,
1951-55 to 1961-65.

| Regions | Product per Worker[1] | | | |
| | Absolute values (000 lire) | | Rate of change per year (%) | |
	A	B	A	B
Northwest	491	927	4.19	5.35
Northeast and Center	330	771	7.37	5.15
South and Islands	298	666	6.86	4.34
Total for Italy	340	802	6.48	5.07

Sources: [2, 10, 13].
[1] Data based on net product of the private sector at 1963 prices.
For further explanations see Table 3a.
[2] Persons employed. As government employees are excluded, percentages are higher than those given in Table 1.

Agricultural Labor Forces (%)[3]			
Initial period	Final period	Rate of change per year	Agriculture's Contribution (%)
0.61	0.61	−0.14	60.9
0.61	0.57	−0.14	23.3
0.57	0.55	−0.45	34.2
0.55	0.48	−0.40	24.7
0.44	0.30	−4.19	25.2

Agricultural Labor Forces (%)[2]			
Initial period	Final period	Rate of change per year	Agriculture's Contribution (%)
0.25	0.15	−4.24	9.5
0.46	0.30	−4.84	26.0
0.57	0.43	−3.57	39.4
0.44	0.30	−4.19	23.0

product per worker and the substantial shift of agricultural workers to nonagricultural and more productive occupations.

In conclusion, even in more recent years, in spite of the fact that agricultural product is only about 14 percent of the total product, the contribution of the sector to the increment of total product per worker is still a substantial one. The regional breakdown of such contribution, presented in Table 3b, provides a further proof of the internal structural differences.

In the Northwest, for example, the contribution to the increment of product per worker was after 1950 one-tenth only, while it rose to about four-tenths in the South. The explanation is at hand. In the Northwest, at the beginning of the period, most of the labor displacement from the agricultural to other sectors had already taken place because it is here that the industrial basis of the state concentrated since its inception: agricultural employment was as low as 25 percent as against about 57 percent in the South and the Islands. Labor reduction in agriculture continues at a high rate, but in the face of a stagnant agricultural aggregate product and high increase of product per worker in the nonagricultural sectors, the contribution of agriculture cannot be but modest. In these years the state initiated a big effort in the depressed South to overcome its traditional disadvantages: the emphasis was at first on agriculture and general infrastructure (roads, reclamation, irrigation, public services), and only at the beginning of the 1960s was attention directed to incentives for the location of new industrial plants in these areas, a development soon checked by the recession that hit the economy around 1964.

The larger weight of agriculture in the economy and the high increase of product per agricultural worker, coupled with a smaller increase of productivity in the nonagricultural sectors, explain the high contribution of agriculture mentioned above. Once again the northeastern and central regions hold an intermediate position marked by a contribution of agriculture to the increment of total product per worker of about one-fourth. Taking an interregional view, one could probably add to the active side of the South a further contribution: the manpower that moved to the northern regions (and to other countries) to take on more productive employment there.

A further conclusion which can be drawn from the above analysis is that agriculture during this period of general economic expansion has played a great role only in those regions where the agricultural basis was still large and where the expansion of the other sectors was not great enough to match the productivity increases obtained in the industrial Northwest. And this in turn can be taken as a confirmation of a critical observation concerning the Italian economic growth in this period: the country has experienced productivity advances in all sectors, but unevenly distributed among regions so as to widen rather than to lessen regional disparities.

Purchases and Sales

Agriculture, through purchasing goods and services from other sectors and through selling its own products, "makes it feasible for other sectors of the economy to emerge and grow and for international flows to develop . . ." In turn the strengthening of the above market relationships helps agriculture to operate more efficiently [13].

We will consider first the position of agriculture as a buyer, and start by examining the historical trend of the purchases made by the sector, countrywide and by regions. Time series of gross and net product are given as percentages of gross saleable output in Table 4; therefore, the complement to 100 of the percentages relating to gross product gives a relative measure of the sector purchases of goods and services, while the complement of the last column gives a relative measure of the purchases plus capital consumption.

The relative weight of purchases—and of purchases plus depreciation— seems to have been fairly constant up to around 1930. Purchases, however, have increased at an accelerated rate since then and have come to represent around 20 percent of saleable output in 1963-66. In the first part of the 1930s the higher percentage is also a consequence of the depression, i.e., of the unfavorable terms of trade resulting from the low prices received by agriculture; but, especially after 1950, the quantity of goods and services purchased by agriculture has moved up rapidly. In 1963-66 purchases were about four times as high as those in 1921-25.

The regional breakdown, for the most recent period, shows that the volume of purchases in the North and in the Central regions, both absolutely and relatively, is far greater than in the South. This is in part related to differences in natural conditions, irrigation facilities, in product mix (livestock and fodder production being concentrated in the North); but it is also an indication of differences in socioeconomic conditions and levels of technology, as evidenced by the fact that the trend toward a higher volume of purchases from other sectors is observable in the South as well [23].

Table 4.
Gross and Net Product of Agriculture as Percentages of Gross Saleable Output.

Periods	Gross product (%)	Net product (%)
Italy (1861-65 to 1961-65)		
1861-65	92.2	88.2
1881-85	93.2	89.2
1901-05	92.7	88.2
1921-25	94.2	88.7
1931-35	89.7	83.6
1936-40	89.0	83.6
1951-55	86.3	79.4
1961-65	81.7	74.7
Regions (1963-66)		
Northwest	73.7	64.4
Northeast and Center	76.9	70.4
South and Islands	86.3	78.4
Total for Italy	79.7	72.3

Sources: [5, 8, 10].

As to the implications of the above trends in terms of contribution to economic growth, it is clear that the expenses of the agricultural sector represent revenues for the home and foreign firms producing goods and services needed by the agricultural sector. Thus, in the second half of the last century, on the average, expenses incurred by agriculture to purchase goods and services from other sectors (and abroad), including depreciation on capital items, amounted to about 18 percent of the gross product of all other sectors. The figure can be reduced to 15-16 percent, approximately, to take into account imports.

Turning now to the most recent period of observation, one finds that in spite of the large increases of all purchases (a growth of about 6 times in real terms) and of the wider range of products and services offered to the agricultural sector, the net value of such purchases represents only 4 to 5 percent of the gross product of nonagricultural sectors. Obviously, for individual firms or branches of industry the demand forthcoming from agriculture absorbs a sizable part of their total sales. For example, from the 1959 input-output table, three sectors and subsectors stand out as depending to a greater or lesser degree on agriculture's demand for current materials and services: feed industries, which service animal production, chemical industries, trade, and auxiliary services. If capital goods are also included, then one must add the mechanical industries, whose sales of tractors and other forms of machinery and implements (net of imports) in 1959 represented about 10 percent of their total sales for domestic gross investment purposes; and the "building" activities, which had a relationship with gross investment in agriculture of about the same magnitude [7, 17].

As the volume of agricultural produce reaching the market increases, greater opportunities arise for activities dealing with the transformation of such products in form, space, and time. A greater volume of commercialized produce, however, is not only or not always dependent on a larger farm product, but it is also related to changes in farm population, food habits, and ways of life at large, as well as in innovations or improvements in transportation and marketing channels.

In the earlier phases of economic development the processing and marketing of agricultural products cannot but play an important role in internal and foreign trade. One should expect also that the contribution to economic growth stemming from the farm products coming onto the market is more important than the contribution due to purchases by the agricultural sector, because the latter correspond to a relatively small, although expanding, fraction of the agricultural saleable output.

The scanty information available for the most distant periods do not permit working out direct estimates of the extent of trade of domestic agricultural products and consequently of the market contribution to economic growth derived therefrom. The indirect estimates which seem warranted for the Italian situation as of the first decade after Unification do confirm Dr. Kuznets' speculation that the proportion of net income from agriculture released "as a basis for demand for consumers goods (or, to a more limited extent, of producers goods) from other sectors in the economy and from foreign countries" must have been close to four-tenths. The decade from 1865 to 1875 was in fact characterized by a growing agricultural production and by an expanding volume of exports, fed by agricultural products or by manufactured goods from agriculture. The specific conditions of Italian agriculture do not, however, lend support to a high degree of autoconsumption, as assumed by Dr. Kuznets. Population and income shares of those times suggest that at least 50 percent of net agricultural product came to the market, so that the proportion of net total product released by agriculture was about 28 percent (0.50 X 0.55). Assuming that the net product of the other sectors was entirely marketed, the share of agriculture in total marketed net product must have been 28 percent out of 72 percent, or four-tenths approximately.

For the period 1961-65, due to a higher and more specialized production, to lower agricultural population, as well as to partially modified buying habits, the extent of autoconsumption by agricultural producers and landowners was reduced to about half, or approximately 27 percent of agricultural net product; but the resulting higher proportion of sales corresponded to only 10 percent of total net product and to little more of the total marketed product, given the small weight of the agricultural sector in the economy [12].

The reduced importance of the demand for consumption of nonagricultural goods stemming from people receiving agricultural income is thus evident; however, one must not overlook two important facts. In the first place, available statistics show that at the end of the 1930s the share of agriculture in total marketed product was still as high as 20 percent, and higher than that in postwar recovery years. The decline then is a consequence of the fast rate of growth and of the structural changes occurring in the more recent period; in the second place, from observations made earlier, it is obvious that the contribution of agriculture even at present must be widely different on a regional basis, i.e., while negligible in the Northwest, the share of agriculture in total marketed product is probably still around 20 percent in the South.

As a further qualification to the changing weight of agriculture through time, with special regard to exports, it can be added that in the first decade after Unification the agricultural industries (textiles, tobacco, food, and beverages) accounted for about 60 percent of the gross product of the industrial sector and that around 1880, prior to the economic crisis, total exports were made up by agricultural products for about one-quarter and by manufactured goods (derived from agricultural products) for about 60 percent [22]. In the first part of the 1960s agricultural industries accounted for only 15 percent of the gross product of the industrial sector and 20 percent of the manufacturing industries.[2]

Agricultural exports (primary products and manufactured goods), from a high of 84 percent of total exports in 1880, declined to about 56 percent in 1910-14, to 40 percent around 1938, to 30 percent around

[2]But at present, only a small part of the raw materials needed by the textile industries comes from domestic agriculture.

1950, and to only 13 percent in 1964/65 [12, 15]. For long periods then agricultural exports have had a strategic role in the country's economic development, because it is mainly through them that the country has established economic relations with the industrialized countries and has imported the resources, the tools of modern technology, and the know-how necessary to build up an industrial base.

After a century, and particularly after the big spurt in industrialization of the 1950s, the structure of international flows is obviously quite different. Exports concern primarily nonagricultural consumption and investment goods, and the country has come to have *vis-à-vis* the developing countries the same position that France, England, and Germany once, or the United States more recently, had with regard to Italy. About half of Italy's imports of agricultural products come from developing countries (including the socialist ones) and about 95 percent of the exports to these countries are made up of nonagricultural products [12, 15].

Terms of Trade Terms of trade can be looked at from two different, but complementary, points of view: (a) the trend of relative prices resulting from the ratio of implicit prices of gross (or net) agricultural product and total domestic product; and (b) the trend of the ratio of prices received by farmers for their produce and those paid by them to purchase production goods. The first aspect, embracing the entire economy, reflects the relative purchasing power of the income gained by the sector. The second aspect, being restricted to trade relations connected to agricultural activities only, bears upon a narrower concept of purchasing power.

The trend of relative prices is far from uniform, due to the disturbances introduced by two world wars and sectoral and general economic depressions; but nonetheless a trend against agriculture is noticeable. Taking 1861-65 as 100, the terms of trade in that respect dropped to a low of 83 in the quinquennium 1906-1910; since then the trend has been very irregular with a sharp rise during World War I, a very sharp decline in the period 1931-35, followed by a peak of 164 during war years; after 1950 from a level of 83, through ups and downs, they have moved somewhat against agriculture. Although adequate data are lacking, it is probably in the first 40 to 50 years of the period that agriculture has witnessed the highest deterioration, because during the crisis of the 1880s agricultural prices fell sharply [8, 20].

The second aspect of the terms of trade can be analyzed only on the basis of time series referring to the period after 1950 [8, 12]. During this period terms of trade have been generally in favor of agriculture due to the relatively stable level of prices of current inputs and machinery, at least up to 1962. If terms of trade for agriculture have deteriorated in more recent times, it is not because farmers have to pay higher prices for farm inputs, but mainly because of the decreased purchasing power of farm income, in terms of prices of goods and services produced by all the other sectors.

Factor Contribution

Factor contributions are the result of transfer of capital or labor resources from agricultural to other sectors. Transfers of capital, "or rather of funds financing the acquisition of material capital," will be considered first. They can be of two different types: the compulsory type, "through taxation of a kind in which the burden on agriculture is far greater than the services rendered by the government to agriculture"; or the lending type, the "utilization of savings originating in agriculture in financing the growth of the nonagricultural sectors" [13].

Transfers by Taxation   The flow of direct taxes paid by receivers of agricultural income in Italy at present is only a very minor fraction of the total flow of direct taxes accruing to the central government or to the local governments (provinces, municipalities, etc.), not only because of the small weight of the sector in the economy but also because of the deliberate government policy aiming at reducing the tax burden on the sector as a whole or on some depressed areas and low-income groups. But soon after Unification the land tax was over 50 percent of all direct taxation and about 21 percent of all fiscal revenues of the state and the local governments [18, 19]. The burden was, however, unevenly distributed among regions and very likely among taxpayers because the new state had inherited a variety of taxation procedures and of Land Books (Cadastres) from the former states, each of them compiled with different criteria and degrees of precision.

If one keeps in mind that the ruling class of those times was mainly composed of large landowners, it is no wonder that discussions about the absolute level and the regional disparities of the land tax were the subject of hot political debates for almost three decades and became secondary to other national issues only after the enactment of a law providing for the gradual establishment of a uniform cadastral system and, perhaps even more important, when industrialists gained some weight in national economic and political affairs.[3]

The other components of direct taxation were the taxes on buildings, on inheritance, and on non-real estate revenue; the last mentioned, negligible at the beginning, became as large as the land tax as soon as in the second decade after Unification. But more than half of total fiscal revenue was made up of indirect taxes, falling to a small extent on business (registration fees and sales tax) and to a large extent on the meager incomes of the masses of consumers, i.e., the agricultural population (excise duties, monopolies on salt, tobacco, and lotto, tax on "grain milling," etc.). Regressiveness was obviously an outstanding feature of the fiscal system of the new state.

To ascertain whether or not tax revenues derived from agricultural income have contributed to finance public works of general interest and investments in the nonagricultural sector, we may turn to the pattern of public expenditure prevailing in the early periods after Unification. Available information, however incomplete, supports the view that only a marginal quota of public funds extracted from agricultural income through taxation was returned to the sector in the form of services and of infrastructure. Almost 60 percent of public expenditure, up to the end of the century, took the form of interest payments on public debt and of salaries and other expenses of the public administration; about 25 percent went to military expenses; little was left then for investment outlays such as public works, which in some periods did absorb as little as 10 percent of total public expenditures. As for agriculture, it is easily shown that even considering only general services (education, hospitals, roads, transport) its share was far smaller than its contribution to the fiscal revenue. A similar observation can be made with regard to the share of the Ministry of Agriculture in the state budget, which as late as 1900 was only 0.3 percent.[4]

Defense and warfare swallowed a substantial part of the meager state

[3]The cadastral system, which took almost 80 years to be completed for the entire national territory, has been in recent times subjected to criticism for its lack of flexibility in ensuring an equitable distribution of the tax burden, in periods of rapid variations in land use and income-producing capacity. To be sure, complaints about present disparities stem also from the discretionary powers of local governments in levying local taxes on land property and agricultural assessed income, over and above those collected by the central government.

[4]After 1870, however, the state and more often local institutions took steps to establish a few experiment stations, to promote vocational training schools and the early examples of what is today classified under advisory work.

budget of the early periods; of course, orders and purchases made possible by this type of appropriations had probably a role in supporting the introduction and the growth of modern industries (steel and mechanical plants). But the agricultural sector did not enjoy any direct advantage from military expenses. The high weight of public debt in the annual budget was mainly due to foreign loans, secured to finance military operations preceding and following Unification.

The share of agriculture in direct taxation begins to decline in the 1880s because of measures taken to lessen the burden on landed property and of the greater tax revenue derived from other sectors. The tax burden on agriculture becomes less in terms of total fiscal revenue and of national product, but not in terms of gross agricultural product (Table 5). In other words, up to the middle of the 1950s direct taxes paid by agriculture rose faster than the gross product, but they have come to yield but a very small fraction of total fiscal revenue. In the last decade, due to the rapid growth of the other sectors and to the exemptions granted to some social groups and areas, fiscal pressure in agriculture resulting from direct taxation, has rapidly declined. Furthermore, most of the taxes are collected and retained by local governments, so that it can be stated not only that direct taxation of agriculture is nowadays much less than the amount of public funds allotted to the sector, but also that local taxes are to a much greater extent than formerly returned to contributors, as services performed by local agencies.

As to indirect taxes, it is well known that they continue to be the main source of fiscal revenue up to present times; but if nowadays taxes on business transactions are one of the mainstreams, excise duties on basic consumption goods were for a long time, even after 1880, the backbone of fiscal policy, so that the agricultural population, in spite of the depressed incomes, continued to contribute to the public budget in a much greater proportion than that of the public services received.

Transfer of Savings Originating in Agriculture
The quantitative assessment of savings realized in the agricultural sector and used in financing the growth of nonagricultural activities is difficult, because of the lack of specific data as well as conceptual problems. First, estimates of aggregate national savings, and gross and net investments, are available, but the place of agriculture in the various periods can be arrived at only through speculations. Second, one must recall that savings are realized not only by the state and by firms but also by

Table 5.
Direct Taxes Paid by Agriculture (Selected Years).[1]

Years	Taxes as a Percentage of		
	Fiscal revenues	Gross agricultural product at factor cost	Gross national income at market prices
1866	21	4.0	2.3
1880	20	4.5	2.4
1890	13	4.3	2.0
1938	7	5.1	1.3
1954	5.5	5.4	1.0
1959	3.8	5.2	0.8
1966	1.6	3.0	0.3

[1] State and local taxes, including collection costs. Figures up to 1890 are slightly underestimated because they do not include taxes paid by tenants on their nonreal estate income, the amount of which is difficult to separate from the total yield of this tax.
Sources: Data derived and adapted from various publications: [5, 12, 18, 19].

families; agricultural income accrues also to families, the heads of which are not engaged in agriculture (for instance, nonresident or absentee landlords); in more recent times, a number of "agricultural" families do get some nonagricultural income, as a reward for services performed outside the sector, by one or more of their members. Third, attempts to measure the amount of savings originating in agriculture must be related to the rather complex social stratification observable in Italian agriculture and to the saving propensity of the various groups, in each period and through time. Finally, one must remember that gross and net investments in agriculture are underestimated, because of the so-called "labor capitalization," whereby labor services with zero or very low opportunity cost are converted voluntarily or through institutional pressure into capital formation. To a large extent, such investments as terracing, tree planting, and stone-clearing, to which the landscape of several Italian regions owes so much, have been made by peasants whose only wealth was a large family work force.[5]

The average propensity to save was very low throughout the second

[5] Many such investments, although still an essential component of the landscape values, have ceased to be assets from an agricultural point of view because of radical changes in resource availabilities and costs, which make increasingly unprofitable the utilization of such lands for farming purposes.

half of the last century and particularly so in the first quinquennium after Unification, savings being negative in several years and less than 1 percent on the average [6]. In the second half of the 1860s the average rose to approximately 3 percent; the yearly rate of growth of the national product being about 1 percent, the incremental capital output ratio was approximately 3 to 1. One can assume, however, a lower capital output ratio in agriculture because of two reasons: the importance of labor capitalization and the possibility of increasing output through the adoption of new techniques requiring modest capital investments. In the other sectors and particularly in manufacturing and heavy industries, in the context of an open economy and foreign competition, resulting from the adoption of a free trade policy, capital needs were higher. To this one must add capital requirements for the expansion of the railroad network. Assuming then an incremental capital output ratio twice as high in nonagricultural sectors, the rate of growth being approximately equal in the period 1866-70 and the agricultural sector providing about 55 percent of the net national product, it follows that capital needs in agriculture were about 36-37 percent of total capital needs.

As to savings, we must rule out the possibility to save on the part of dependent workers, in agriculture and elsewhere, for the reasons mentioned earlier. Savings out of agricultural income could be obtained almost only by the larger landowners, either direct managers or landlords with small tenants and sharecroppers, and by the capitalist tenants. For the distribution of total savings between agriculture and the other sectors we can proceed on the basis of two extreme assumptions: (a) equal rate of savings; and (b) rate of savings in the other sectors twice as high as in agriculture. With the first assumption, savings originating in agriculture would have been about 55 percent of the total and therefore in excess of internal capital needs; agriculture's contribution to the capital needs of other sectors would have been slightly less than 30 percent. With the second assumption, agriculture's savings would have barely covered internal needs. Although quantitative indications are hardly available it would seem more reasonable, taking into account the structure of the economic system of the times and the socio-economic position of the landowners, to attribute to agriculture as a whole a rate of savings not much lower than in the rest of the economy and consequently to place agriculture's contribution to the capital needs of the other sectors in the region of 20-25 percent.

Several indirect elements concur to justify the above statement. First, in 1866 contributors to direct taxation (land tax, housing tax, and non-real estate tax) were forced to subscribe to a public loan of an amount equal to half the gross investments of those years. Second, the state put on sale the lands expropriated from the Church and lands of the public domain in order to raise public revenue: although it was hoped that small proprietors, tenants, and other agricultural workers would take advantage of the sale to enlarge their holdings and climb the social ladder, for a number of reasons, including the inadequacy of the administrative machinery and the socioeconomic weakness of the small cultivators, the lands on sale were acquired almost exclusively by large and medium landowners.

National income time series show a gradual increase in the rate of savings for the rest of the century, but it is only after 1900 that the total rate of savings becomes 10 percent or higher. In the first decade, as already pointed out, the other sectors enjoy a period of rapid growth of the order of 4-5 percent per year, while the agricultural product, with its rate of 1 percent, lags behind.

The incremental capital-output ratio is still around 3 to 1. Even assuming the same ratio for agriculture as in the rest of the economy, capital needs of the agricultural sector drop to only about 15 percent of total capital needs. As to the origins of savings, it is reasonable for this period to assume a rate of savings in agriculture considerably lower than elsewhere, say about one-half. Consequently agriculture's contribution to total savings can be estimated at 30 percent or a little less, and its contribution to the capital needs of the other sectors falls to about one-sixth. In this period, due to mass emigration fed mainly by rural people, probably part of the savings left the country together with the emigrant.

In general, along with a gradual diversification of the economy, a variety of means were used to channel agriculture's savings to feed other sectors' needs, the same means that to a smaller or larger extent are still employed nowadays. First, savings are mobilized through land sales among small owners, when the seller intends to move out of agriculture and uses the sale revenue to get established elsewhere, whether he opens a shop or uses the money for other purposes (housing, consumption, education). Second, a similar transfer takes place when the seller is a landlord who sells part of his land to finance other endeavors or again for consumption, probably of the conspicuous type. Third, small postal deposits or local bank deposits (savings accounts) which directly or indirectly flow to central accounts or larger banking institutions are finally used to finance business activities. This was certainly true, and still is, even in the case of cooperative local banks, which originally developed to cater to agricultural needs, with members drawn from farm families, but slowly moved to finance artisan shops and small business enterprises.

No doubt one must also take account of capital transfer in the opposite direction, prompted by purchases of land by professionals or businessmen, who sometimes get interested in agriculture and invest in it part of their earnings as a security or for prestige or other purposes. Such examples are often publicized, particularly when they give rise to unconventional types of farming or forms of organization; however, in spite of their individual weight and attention gained, they are of much smaller impact than the movements in the opposite direction, which are more silent but much greater in number. Thus the net movement of savings out of agriculture was indeed a positive one for a long period, and it is only in more recent times, in the 1950s and the 1960s, although for reasons other than the ones mentioned above, that the movements of savings in and out of agriculture tend to balance out.

Coming now to the more recent period (1951-65), we find a high rate of growth of the overall economy (5.5 percent), together with an unprecedented rate of growth of the agricultural product (2 percent) and an average rate of savings of about 15 percent [2, 3]. The resulting incremental capital-output ratio, estimated at about 2.7 to 1, is lower than in the periods previously examined, but one must allow a higher ratio (around 4) for the agricultural sector because of the large investments in such undertakings as reclamation, irrigation, land clearing, settlement, mechanization, new buildings, etc. Capital needs in agriculture for the period under consideration were on the average about 11 percent of the total.[6]

As to savings, assuming a rate equal to one-half that of the other sectors, or approximately 8 percent, agriculture's contribution to total savings comes to about 11 percent. A rate of savings of 8 percent is considerably lower than the estimated average propensity to save of all families whose head is a dependent worker in nonagricultural sectors, according to a recent report of the Central Institute of Statistics, based

[6]The ratio of investments in agriculture to total gross investments rose to 12 percent or more in the first quinquennium due to the heavy public involvement in the land reform program and in the program of extraordinary works for the development of the southern regions, but declined afterwards and has been about 8 percent in the 1960s.

on the 1963 survey of family budgets [11]. The indirect evidence which the above source provides, lends support to the view that an average rate of savings of 8 percent on agricultural income is probably to be taken as a minimum. The agricultural labor force is made up for more than 70 percent by farmers and family members whose average yearly expenses approximate the situation of dependent workers in the other sectors. Furthermore, the rate of savings in the southern regions, where families dependent on agriculture for their livelihood are in greater number than elsewhere, is higher, *ceteris paribus,* than the rate estimated for the regions having a more diversified economic base.

If the above is true, and certainly more specific information would be needed before it can be taken as a factual conclusion rather than as a working hypothesis, then investments made and savings originated in agriculture in the more recent period have at least balanced out. This statement will probably seem odd to those that know how big is the state role in supplying agriculture with capital investments. Some additional observations, however, will make it more plausible. First, the statement applies to Italy as a whole, and it is indeed possible that a regional breakdown would show that investments and savings do not balance everywhere. Second, one must keep in mind the various types of channels through which savings, originated in agriculture, are mobilized for investments elsewhere. In addition to the lists presented earlier, one should stress the fact that since 1950, and particularly so after 1955, labor has moved out of agriculture at a very high rate.[7]

Part of those who migrate (geographically and/or professionally) carry with them some funds derived from sales of land and of other forms of capital as well as inheritances or shares in capital accumulation. The use of banking facilities and post offices for current accounts, savings accounts, and time deposits is nowadays much more common than it used to be. Starting a small business on the side which ultimately may substitute farming is also much easier, particularly in areas of tourist attraction or of intense traffic. It is even reported that the alert farmers at times convert agricultural credit, obtained on easy terms, into state or other kinds of bonds yielding the current rate of interest. The state, therefore, in supplying capital for investments in agriculture, performs a useful redistribution function, even if it is doubtful whether the funds supplied are any larger than the amount of savings originated in agri-

[7]From a high of 8.2 million people in 1951, agricultural labor forces have dropped to 4.2 million in 1968.

culture and if the steps followed in doing so are more intricate than would be the case with more efficient banking and credit institutions operating in the agricultural sector.

Transfer of Labor

In the previous sections reference has already been made to the fact that since Unification the percentage of labor working in agriculture has dropped from about 69 percent in the first part of the 1860s to 25 percent only in the middle of the 1960s; in absolute terms, between those two dates, the reduction has been from 10.8 million to approximately 5 million workers. As can be easily seen from Table 1, the more noticeable changes have taken place only after 1950; they are related to the rapid rate of economic growth which is typical of the more recent period.

It would be erroneous, of course, to conclude from the above figure that agriculture's contribution to the growth of other sectors, as far as provision of labor is concerned, is simply the difference between the number of persons working in agriculture at the initial and the final dates. In examining the Italian case, in addition to the rate of natural increase of population and the possible rate differentials between agriculture and the other sectors, attention must be directed to two other variables, emigration and changes in the ratio of active to total population, because they had a very significant effect on the amount and structure of employment of the various periods. The role of emigration is easily assessed: total resident population since Unification has risen from 26 million to 52 million; during the same period, total net emigration can be placed in the region of 10 million.[8]

The ratio of active people to total population has constantly declined during the century; it was as high as 58 percent in 1861-65, while it dropped to 38 percent in the first part of the 1960s [20]. Such a decline is the result of number of causes—legislation on child labor, changes in the school-leaving and pensionable ages and in the number of women seeking employment—with which we cannot deal here. The decline was probably more pronounced in the nonagricultural sectors, although statistics are not available to prove it.

However, what matters here is that workers migrating from agricultural families and agricultural employment have provided the greatest

[8]The number of expatriates rose sharply at the beginning of the century and reached a peak of 870,000 in 1913; however, there was also a high number of people repatriating each year.

part of the net addition to the labor forces of the other sectors since Unification: approximately 75-80 percent up to 1940, and as much as 95 percent after 1950. Over and above its share in emigration, agricultural families have probably provided the other sectors with about 9 million workers from 1861 to 1965. The transfer of workers can be considered as a capital contribution to the nonagricultural sectors, because each worker leaving agriculture embodies some investments in past rearing and training financed mainly out of income accruing to agricultural families.[9]

Estimating in money terms the amount of this contribution is a very difficult task; the very dissimilar unit values which have been obtained by various authors for the same country and dates are there to prove it. The unit figures suggested by Dr. Kuznets, equal to 10 times the current product per worker and obtained by assuming a certain age of transfer and a certain proportion of the product per worker spent yearly for such a purpose, seem too high for Italian conditions, and it is also doubtful if the method is not too crude to take into proper account the many changes in diet, family participation in schooling costs, age of migrations, etc., which have occurred over such a long time span.

For our purposes it is probably enough to stress the fact that the contribution of Italian agriculture stemming from the transfer of workers increased over time, while the other forms of contribution show an opposite trend. This is apparently explained by two concurrent events: (a) the gradual increase of the average rate of migration to other sectors, which rose from about 0.3 percent per annum in the 1860s to 1 percent in the interwar years and to about 3.5 percent in the 1960s; and (b) the trend toward a higher product per agricultural worker in real terms. Whatever value is attributed to the investments in human capital transferred by migrants, the total amount of "capital" thus made available to other sectors has been an increasing proportion of the agricultural product, and of total national income, throughout the period under consideration.

References

1. Caracciolo, A. (ed.), *La formazione dell'Italia industriale.* Bari: Laterza, 1969.

2. De Meo, G., *Produttivita e distribuzione del reddito in Italia nel periodo 1951-1963.* Rome: ISTAT, 1965.

[9] The term *agricultural* is used here to qualify families whose head is an agricultural worker.

484   Giuseppe Barbero

3. ____, *Redditi e produttivita in Italia 1951-1966*. Rome: ISTAT, 1967.

4. Gerschenkron, A., *Economic Backwardness in Historical Perspective*. Cambridge, Mass.: The Belknap Press of Harvard University Press, 1962.

5. Istituto Centrale di Statistica (ISTAT), *Indagine statistica sullo sviluppo del reddito nazionale dell'Italia dal 1951 al 1956*. Rome, 1957.

6. ____, *Sommario di statistiche storiche italiane 1861-1955*. Rome, 1958.

7. ____, *Primi studi sulle interdipendenze settoriali dell'economia italiana (tavola economica 1959)*. Rome, 1965.

8. ____, *I conti nazionali dell'Italia*. Nuova Serie-Anni 1951-1965 Supplemento al *Bollettino Mensile di Statistica*, No. 3 (March 1966).

9. ____, *Occupazione in Italia negli anni 1951-1965*. Supplemento al *Bollettino Mensile di Statistica*, No. 12 (December 1966).

10. ____, *I conti economici territoriali dell'Italia per gli anni 1963-1966*. Supplemento al *Bollettino Mensile di Statistica*, No. 7 (July 1967).

11. ____, *Indagine statistica sui bilanci delle famiglie italiane anni 1963-64*. Rome, 1968.

12. Istituto Nazionale di Economia Agraria (INEA), *Annuario dell'agricoltura italiana*, V (1951) and following issues.

13. Kuznets, S., "Economic Growth and the Contribution of Agriculture: Notes on Measurement." *Proceedings of the Eleventh International Conference of Agricultural Economists*. London: Oxford University Press, 1963.

14. Lutz, Vera, *Italy—A Study in Economic Development*. London: Oxford University Press, 1962.

15. Ministeri del Bilancio e del Tesoro, *Relazione generale sulla situazione economica del Paese*. Rome: Istituto Poligrafico dello Stato, 1967.

16. Orlando, G., "Progressi e difficolta dell'agricolturà." In G. Fuà (ed.), *Lo sviluppo economico in Italia*. Milan: Franco Angeli Editore, 1969, vol. 3.

17. Orsi, A., *L'agricoltura nell'economia nazionale vista attraverso la tavola economica intersettoriale 1959*. Rome: INEA, 1965.

18. Parravicini, G., "La politica fiscale e le entrate effettive nel Regno d'Italia, 1860-1890," *Archivio Economico dell'Unificazione Italiana*, series II, vol. I, 1958.

19. Pedone, A., "Il bilancio dello Stato e lo sviluppo economico italiano, 1861-1963." *Rassegna Economica*, 2 (March-April 1967).

20. Pennacchietti, A., "Agriculture in the Italian National Economy." *Banca Nazionale del Lavoro Quarterly Review*, 75 (December 1965).

21. Romani, M., *Storia Economica d'Italia nel secolo XIX, 1815-1914*, Part I. Milan: Giuffre, 1968.

22. Romeo, R., *Risorgimento e capitalismo*. Bari: Laterza, 1959.

23. Rossi-Doria, M., *Analisi zonale dell'agricoltura italiana.* Rome: Ministero del Bilancio e della Programmazione Economica, 1969.

28. Rural
Development
in Israel

Yehuda H. Landau
and Avshalom Rokach

At the end of the nineteenth century, agriculture in Israel was based mainly on subsistence farming. In the southern region and in the plains the main agricultural branches were grain growing and the raising of livestock—mainly local breeds of goat and sheep. In the hilly regions these branches were combined with unirrigated cultivation of fruit, such as olives and figs. The peasants lived in villages, large or small according to the available cultivable area. The size of the holdings differed from region to region and from farm to farm. Some of the peasants were big landowners, others smallholders; and some were landless and worked for the landlords.

Jewish settlement first began in the 1880s with the arrival of small groups of immigrants from Eastern Europe, who aspired to live as farmers on the land. In 1881-1884 they founded six agricultural settlements, known as *moshavot,* and a few more came into being in the following years. The pattern of these settlements was similar to that of the villages in the settlers' countries of origin. The settlers had had no previous experience in agriculture; they were aided mainly by Baron Edmund de Rothschild, who offered financial support and sent experts from France to guide them in agricultural work and farm management. Agriculture in these early settlements was mainly monocultural, predominantly viticulture and almond growing. Later on, field crops, mainly cereals, were introduced. These farms made full use of the available cheap hired labor.

A second influx of immigrants from Eastern Europe, at the turn of the nineteenth century, led to the establishment of rural settlements based on cooperative principles. Besides ideological motivation, cooperation and mutual help were essential to ease the difficulties of adaptation to a new way of life, under very adverse circumstances. New farming branches were then introduced, as a step toward diversification. This settlement scheme was directed and financed by Jewish national bodies—the Zionist Organization and its various executive agencies.

By the beginning of World War I there were 43 Jewish settlements in

Yehuda H. Landau—Israel. M.Sc., Agricultural Economics, Hebrew University, Jerusalem, 1947; Director, Regional Planning Department, Ministry of Agriculture, Israel; member, Academic Council, Settlement Study Centre, Rehovot; member, Board of Directors, Institute for Planning and Development, Ltd., Israel; OECD consultant in regional planning in 1964.

Avshalom Rokach—Israel. M.Sc., Agriculture, Hebrew University, Jerusalem; assistant to the Head of the Settlement Department, the Jewish Agency, Jerusalem.

the country. The establishment of the British Mandate in Palestine opened up a new phase in Jewish immigration into that country, accelerating the rural settlement process. Most of the settlements founded from that period onward were either cooperative family farms or collective settlements. The settlements were based mainly on diversified farming, which was at that time thought to be the most suitable, for the following reasons. (1) The existence of a variety of branches reduces the risk of sudden market fluctuations and natural calamities that might affect any one of them. (2) A balanced year-round work schedule enables the farmer to make advantageous use of available family manpower and eliminates the need for hired labor. (3) Crop variation, a prerequisite of suitable crop rotation, and the keeping of livestock were expected to ensure the maintenance of a high degree of soil fertility. (4) Diversified farming provides the family with an ample food supply, including vegetables, milk, meat, eggs, and fruit.

Principles and Patterns of Settlement
Before 1948, when Israel achieved statehood, 291 Jewish rural settlements had already been founded, mainly within the framework of the principles and patterns given below, which continue to form the basis for rural development in Israel to this day.

Principles of Settlement 1. Nationally owned land. Nearly all the settlements were established on nationally owned land, which cannot be purchased. It is leased to the settler for a period of 49 years. The lease is automatically extended to one of the farmer's heirs. As the holding is indivisible, fragmentation is avoided.

2. Self-labor. The resources and means of production are allocated in such manner as to enable farming families to do nearly all the work on their farm themselves, without habitually employing hired labor.

3. Opportunity for equal income. Farm planning and allocation of the means of production are implemented according to the principle that all farmers should have the opportunity to attain a level of income that is roughly equal throughout the trade. This planned income level is equal to the nation-wide average for skilled workers.

4. Free choice of settlement pattern. Every settler is free to choose for himself the organizational and social framework within which he wishes to live. This explains the coexistence of different settlement patterns in Israel. The two prevailing settlement patterns in Israel are the moshav and the kibbutz; two others, less frequent patterns, are the moshav shitufi and the moshava.

The moshav is a cooperative of family farms, usually comprising 80 to 100 farm units. Each farming family stands as a separate economic and social unit, tilling its own fields and making its own decisions. All supplies (fertilizers, seeds, fodder, etc.) are purchased by the cooperative and made available to the farmers on a credit basis, with repayment from market returns. The produce is marketed by the cooperative, each farmer being credited according to his share in the products marketed. Certain other operations and services are also on a cooperative basis, e.g., collection, sorting, and packing of produce, storage, agricultural machinery, etc. The elected village committee also handles social services (education, health, entertainment, etc.) for the farmers.

The kibbutz is a unique form of settlement in which both production and consumption are collective. Each family has a separate housing unit, but meals are generally served in a communal dining hall, and in most kibbutzim the children live in separate nurseries or houses. Production is managed and operated as a single unit, each member working according to a centralized work-schedule. All personal services are provided for the members by the collective. Elected committees are in charge of economic planning and development, decisions on investments, etc. Matters of major importance such as decisions on the budget and the election of committees and branch managers are submitted to the general meeting of members. The profits are not distributed among the members, but are reinvested in production branches or used to raise the standard of living.

The moshav shitufi is a pattern of settlement which combines the kibbutz economic system with some of the social aspects of the moshav, i.e. collective production with private consumption. Farming operations and schedules are conducted by an elected management, as in the kibbutz. A monthly allowance is allocated to each family, which keeps its own private household.

The moshava is based on private land ownership and individual farming, as one finds in most other countries.

Settlement Activities since Independence   Statehood radically changed the political and socioeconomic set-up in the country. Trade relations with the neighboring countries ceased; the country was cut off from one of its sources of food supply. This coincided with the beginning of large-scale immigration into Israel, causing a sharp increase in the demand for agricultural produce. In 1948-51 some 650,000 immigrants entered the country, nearly doubling its population.

Development projects undertaken in the early years of statehood therefore gave priority to agriculture. The main initial aim of agricultural development was to produce fresh foodstuffs—vegetables, fruit, milk, meat, eggs, etc. After the shortage in these products had been overcome, priority was given to export crops, or to crops that replaced imports, such as sugar and cotton—a policy that helped to improve Israel's trade balance.

Another aim of rural development was that of providing productive employment for immigrants, and absorbing them in the country's social and economic structure. Furthermore, rapid rural development through the establishment of villages on a nation-wide basis was in accordance with the government's clearly defined policy of population dispersal.

From 1948 to 1967, 436 new rural settlements were founded, bringing the total number of rural settlements in the country to about 800, of which more than 700 were Jewish. In addition, many existing agricultural settlements were enlarged. Until 1948, the majority of Jewish settlements were kibbutzim—149 out of a total of 291. Since Independence, however, 284 new moshavim have been established against only 152 other settlements, most of them kibbutzim. Some 30,000 farming families live in the 436 new settlements.

The ethnic and social background of the new settlers was the main reason why they preferred the moshav. Whereas before 1948 most of the settlers had been of European origin, the new wave came mainly from traditional Afro-Asian communities; most of these settled on the land without any previous vocational or ideological preparation. The collective structure was completely alien to their social background.

The great expansion of rural settlement, the intensification of agriculture through irrigation and the improved technology, brought about a spectacular increase in agricultural production. From the first year of statehood in 1948 up to 1967 total output increased more than sevenfold.

Table 1 gives the rate of growth of agricultural output (at constant prices).[1] The average annual increase in agricultural output exceeded 10 percent. The new settlements founded since 1948 accounted for 40 percent of agricultural production in 1966-67; with total output amounting to I£1,607 million, production in the new settlements reached I£650 million.

During the last two decades, steadily growing yields, higher labor productivity, and improved farm management have led to a continuous

[1] Source: Statistical Abstracts of Israel, Jerusalem, 1968.

Table 1.
Rate of Growth of Agricultural Output.

	1948-49	1958-59	1966-67
Field Crops	100	548	1,011
Vegetables and Potatoes	100	345	451
Citrus Fruit	100	239	385
Other Fruit	100	416	1,260
Milk	100	342	522
Eggs	100	440	619
Meat	100	868	1,818
Fish	100	376	695
Miscellaneous	100	484	678
Total	100	423	743

increase in overall productivity in agriculture, which has shown an annual average rate of growth of 6 percent. (This percentage does not include growth due to increased inputs). Examples of growing yields are given in Table 2.[2] As a result of a higher degree of mechanization and improved labor productivity, the labor input per unit has gone down markedly. The average annual increase of labor productivity[3] in agriculture was 9 percent in 1952-55, 10.8 percent in 1955-59, and 11.2 percent in 1959-63. Table 3 gives some instances of the decrease in the labor input.[4]

The Organizational and Institutional Framework The planning and implementation of rural development is a complex undertaking involving many different fields: agricultural production, rural construction, irrigation systems, social services, etc. The multiple factors involved called for the coordination of all activities by a special authority. For this reason, a special rural settlement authority was entrusted in the early 1900s with responsibility for overall rural settlement and development. This authority is directly responsible to the Jewish Agency, a

[2]Source: Statistical Abstracts of Israel, Jerusalem, 1968.
[3]Output per unit of labor.
[4]R. Weitz, *Agricultural and Rural Development in Israel: Projection and Planning* (Rehovot, 1963) and *The Five-Year Plan for Israel's Agriculture: 1966-67— 1970-71,* Agriculture and Settlement, Planning and Development Center, Ministry of Agriculture (Tel-Aviv, 1968).

Table 2.
Growth Yields.

Branch	Yield in Kilograms per Hectare (national average)	
	1954-55	1965-66
Cotton Lint (irrigated)	950	1,200
Sugar Beet (irrigated)	36,000	52,000
Sorghum for Grain (irrigated)	2,700	5,600
Wheat (unirrigated)	100	155
Milk (liters per cow)	3,425	4,800

Table 3.
Decrease in Labor Input.

Crop	Man-Days per Hectare	
	1954-55	1966-67
Ground Nuts	100	32
Sugar Beets	100	56
Cotton	120	21
Potatoes	130	88
Tomatoes	370	298
Citrus	145	124

public, nongovernmental executive body of the Zionist movement, which also raises the financial means for settlement. The Settlement Authority provides settlers with long-term (35-year) development loans at 3.5 percent interest. Such loans cover investments in housing and services, as well as in the means of production.

The general principles and objectives of rural settlement are laid down by the Agriculture and Settlement Planning Board, on which the Ministry of Agriculture, the Settlement Authority, the Water Planning Authority, and various farmers' organizations are represented.

The organization of the Settlement Authority is highly decentralized. Planning and implementation are carried out in regional offices, comprising interdisciplinary teams, living in the region. The regional staff works in close cooperation with the local farmers' organizations and coordinates development activities with the various governmental departments, at the regional and local level.

Agricultural production and its regional distribution is directed by the Agricultural Planning Center (APC)[5] and by production and marketing boards for the various branches. These boards are composed of representatives of farmers' organizations and of the Ministry of Agriculture. Price policies, aimed at ensuring the implementation of production plans, include guaranteed minimum prices for certain crops, within a production quota system.

Regional Planning and Development
The comprehensive planning and development of entire regions became possible in the early years of statehood through the availability of comparatively large, sparsely settled areas, through the accelerated development of water resources for irrigation, and through mass immigration. The settlement planners had to look for new ways to meet the challenge of absorbing and integrating new settlers—mainly from underdeveloped countries and traditional societies—into the framework of modern agriculture.

The Lakhish settlement project, whose implementation, based on a comprehensive regional plan, was started in the mid-fifties, may be regarded as a turning point in Israel's rural development. The region is situated in the central part of the country, midway between Tel Aviv and Beersheba, and covers an area of about 1,000 square kilometers. In the north and west, along the Mediterranean coast, the terrain is low-lying and flat; in the east it is hilly. Climatically, it is a transition area between the rainy north and the dry, arid Negev. Being sparsely populated, it was an ideal stamping-ground for infiltrators and smugglers from Jordan and the Gaza Strip, and this dangerous gap had to be plugged by a network of settlements. The completion of a main water pipeline from the Tel Aviv area to the southern part of the country was a decisive factor in the intensive agricultural development of the region, which is so devoid of natural resources that agriculture was bound to be its main economic base.

The branches of agriculture and the type of farm best suited to the region were determined mainly by the country's changing economic needs. Whereas the existing settlements were based on diversified farming, centered round the dairy branch, these new settlements were

[5]The A.P.C. is a joint institution of the Ministry of Agriculture and the Settlement Authority, responsible to the Agriculture and Settlement Planning Board.

mainly field-crop farms, specializing in production for export, or for replacement of imports, e.g., cotton, peanuts, sugar beets, vegetables for processing, citrus—according to soil conditions. The area of these farms was usually about four hectares, all under irrigation.

The "Composite Rural Structure" In pre-state times and for a short period immediately after Independence, the moshav was planned as a compact settlement, comprising "one-plot" family farms. The labor-intensive, diversified structure of irrigation farming, prevalent at that time, called for close supervision of the different farming branches and frequent, though brief, operations on many parts of the farm. Short walking distances on the farm were therefore decisive for ensuring economic and professional efficiency. In order to achieve maximum proximity of the farmer to his fields, the family habitat, the farmyard, and all or most of the farmland were laid out as one plot, adjoining other farmers' plots, the farmyards being thirty to fifty meters wide. This layout thus determined the configuration of the plots. A centrally located communal center was maintained, although the distances between the peripheral farm units were considerable. The village center, equipped with cooperative facilities for collecting farm produce such as milk, vegetables, and eggs and providing the necessary supplies for farmwork and personal needs seemed adequate for its purpose; the same could be said of the social and cultural services (kindergarten, schools, dispensary, synagogue, etc.) located in the communal village center. From his house, the farmer could easily reach the center with a horse and cart. But such a village was necessarily limited to eighty, or at most one hundred families. Otherwise internal distances would exceed two kilometers, which would adversely affect social and cultural activities. Obviously so few families could not maintain services at an adequate standard at reasonable cost.

With gradual evolution from a diversified farm structure toward specialized farming, changes also took place in the physical layout of the village. A more intensive use of mechanical implements and their efficient application to larger land units became a precondition for lowering production costs and ensuring economic profitability. The individual holding of each separate farmer was too small for large-scale mechanization. To meet this situation, the following pattern was developed: the area adjacent to the habitat and yard was reduced to one hectare or even less. The remainder of the holding was subdivided into several plots, each block of plots representing a unit of land adapted to branch specialization, cooperative utilization of machinery, aerial spraying, and other up-to-date farming operations. Blocks of different soil types could thus also be put to appropriate cultivation.

The great importance of the multiblock layout lies in its flexibility. It allows for adjustment and adaptation to changes in the environmental and socioeconomic conditions, without disruption of the basic infrastructure. It also provides a framework which makes possible continuous improvement of agricultural methods and even changes in the size of plots, thus creating suitable conditions for "dynamic land reform."

It also became necessary to increase the farming population in the villages, in order to provide adequate services at reasonable cost. Economic considerations, however, represented only one aspect of the changed environment. The social and cultural problems of new immigrant settlers, with a highly heterogeneous cultural heritage, could not be ignored.

A new rural pattern, termed the *composite rural structure*, was therefore designed, based on the following principles: four to eight villages, each comprising about eighty families, are planned around a rural service center. The center is not more than five kilometers away from each of the settlements. Only those services which must be close to the farmer's habitat, such as grocery, kindergarten, and synagogue, are located in the villages themselves. All other services, e.g., marketing, sorting and packing, agricultural machinery, education, health, entertainment, are concentrated in the center, which includes a residential area for those employed in the regional services.

The composite rural structure helped to meet the new sociological problems, which arose as a result of the demographic changes in Israel's rural community. Experience has shown that to disperse newly arrived family clans and settle families of different origin in the same village, leads to ceaseless friction and disputes, which undermine the very existence of the community. It prevents development of leadership from within and hampers attempts to promote self-management; energies are wasted in local feuds. The most stable villages are those in which traditional ties have been preserved and in which the settlers have been united from the outset by their common origin. The feeling of closeness and unity proved to be of great assistance in adapting to new conditions and in establishing a community based on mutual aid and responsibility.

On the other hand, the development of such homogeneous communities retards the process of general modernization; it hampers the integration of groups from different countries, with different customs, cultures, outlook, and standards of training, into one society. The composite rural structure enabled each ethnic group to be settled in a separate village, while at the same time mutual influences among settlers from various backgrounds developed through contact at the center, where the merging of the different groups was accomplished. Children from all the communities attend school in common, and settlers from all the villages meet at the center for various consumer and producer services. It is here that common interests are created between the veterans and the new settlers and the different cultures intermingle at social and recreational functions.

In these rural centers socioeconomic conditions can be created to attract qualified and skilled personnel, required for the implementation of development projects. The fact that these professional workers live within the development area leads to the creation of mutual bonds between them and the farmers. The centers are also places for group-extension programs, with facilities that cannot be provided in single villages. This is obviously of special importance for training new immigrants in modern farming methods.

A number of these enlarged community structures form a settlement region. Enterprises and services on a larger scale, e.g., high schools, processing industries, and regional administration, were located in a "regional" town, set up in the center of the region.

Implementation of the Lakhish Development Plan

The planning of the region began in 1954. In 1955, twenty-six new settlements were founded; these included eighteen moshavim or kibbutzim, two big administered farms, a nursery, two training centers, two rural service centers, and a regional town, Kiryat Gat. Two additional rural centers were set up in the region in subsequent years. The town and the service centers also serve a number of additional villages in the area, which were established before the commencement of the Lakhish project. The population of the villages founded in 1955 reached 7,000 in 1968. The population of the rural centers in 1968 was 600 and that of Kiryat Gat nearly 20,000, though originally planned for 8,000 only. The main industries developed in the town are a sugar mill, a cotton gin, textile and wool processing, diamond cutting, and electronics.

The successful implementation of the Lakhish project was largely due to its organizational and administrative framework, which was based on the following principles: (a) a special interdisciplinary regional team was formed; (b) the team was given authority and budgetary means to adjust plans and their implementation to changing local conditions; (c) the team lived and worked in the region.

All the personnel for planning and implementation, such as architects, engineers, agronomists, economists, sociologists, and administrators worked together, headed by a team leader, thus ensuring full coordination among the various disciplines. The team, recruited from various departments, worked within the administrative framework of the Settlement Authority. The settlement area was given the status of an independent administrative region. From the first planning stage, the regional office was set up in the region. When a start was made with construction of the regional town, Kiryat Gat, the team moved in, to live and work there. Thus the members of the team were in close touch with the settlers, and with the problems that arose on the spot.

Members of veteran agricultural settlements volunteered to live with the new immigrants and act as instructor-advisers on agricultural, organizational, and social problems, thus helping them to overcome the initial difficulties of adaptation to the new environment. The new immigrants were brought to the region directly on arrival in the country and housed in temporary huts, prepared in advance. From the first day they were provided with full employment, mainly housing construction and work on infrastructure. Agricultural production was started soon after. In order to facilitate the training of new immigrants in agricultural work, and their adaptation to the modern structure of cooperative family farming, the new settlers initially assumed responsibility for a small part of their land only, the residual area being managed as a large "administered" farm, on which the settlers were employed as laborers. Thus the new immigrants were provided with a stable income, without assuming the risks involved in agricultural production, before they were adequately trained to do so. This system also safeguarded the large investments from the inexperienced management of new settlers. With time, through an intensive extension program, the settlers gained better farming knowledge and understanding of cooperative organization, and local leadership was developed. Centralized cultivation was then gradually reduced and the settlers' individual holdings enlarged.

The average annual family income from individual holdings thus increased from I£600 in 1955-56 to I£5,100 in 1964-65 (in 1965 prices). The increase in average yields per hectare is illustrated by Table 4.[6]

Rural Regional Cooperation
Since the late fifties, agriculture in Israel has been undergoing dynamic changes, involving transition from diversified to specialized farming. With the shortage of agricultural produce and strict food rationing turning to surpluses, and the ensuring drive for big increases in agricultural exports, arose the need for greater efficiency in production, emphasis on quality of produce, and improvement of post-harvest operations. The continuous increase in productivity, together with technological progress, brought with it an increase in the size of production units and purchased inputs, against a decrease in the labor input. This calls for mobility of rural manpower and the creation of additional employment sources in the rual areas, in order to absorb the surplus manpower locally, preventing its drift to urban centers. This again depends on the provision of adequate amenities and services in the rural areas.

These problems motivated the farmers themselves, as well as the agencies responsible for rural development, to look for new cooperative patterns on a regional scale; these new patterns were based, in part, on the experience gained in the regional settlement projects, just described. The main objectives of rural regional cooperation are

1. To develop and improve the standard of social services such as education, health, entertainment, etc. by centralizing them in rural centers serving a number of villages, on the Lakhish model. Thus the emergence of a social and cultural gap between town and countryside can be forestalled and suitable conditions maintained to prevent the rural areas from being depleted of those who have acquired education and know-how, and are capable of serving as the active, guiding element so badly needed in modern rural development.

2. To facilitate the further mechanization and modernization of agriculture. Technological progress calls for changes in the scale of operations and requires machinery and installations, the acquisition and maintenance of which are beyond the capacity of a single village. Regional cooperation enables groups of settlements to pool their resources for that purpose and also for recruiting the specially qualified personnel, skilled technicians and experts, required for large-scale operations; it

[6]R. Weitz and A. Rokach, *Agricultural Development—Planning and Implementation (Israel Case Study)* (Dordrecht: D. Reidel, 1968).

Table 4.
Average Yield in Tons per Hectare.

	1956	1965
Tomatoes	30	55
Cucumbers	15	25
Potatoes	15	25
Sugar Beets	30	50
Cotton	2	3.3
Ground Nuts	2	2.9

also facilitates the acquisition and appropriate application of know-how.

3. To increase earnings in the rural areas, by establishing in them agro-supporting and processing industries, owned cooperatively by the local farmers. Thus the added value, created by these enterprises, remains in the rural area.

4. To provide opportunities for diversification of employment in the rural areas through integration of agriculture, industry, and services, at the regional level. The expected decrease in the labor input in agricultural production need not necessarily result in a decrease in the total population living and working in the rural area. By developing industries and services in regional centers, nonfarming employment sources can be provided in order to absorb surplus manpower locally and prevent drift to the cities. Thus the social stability of the rural community can be preserved, despite inevitable structural changes.

Rural regional cooperation in Israel found its physical expression in the establishment of nearly sixty regional centers serving kibbutzim and moshavim. Although these centers differ in scope and organizational structure, all are based on the following principles: (a) The centers are located on nationally owned land, leased for that purpose to cooperative development societies. The services and enterprises set up in the centers are cooperatively owned by the settlements, managed and operated by their members. Some centers are residential. In others, the workers employed commute daily from the villages to the center and back. (b) The establishment of rural regional centers is quite new in Israel. The further development of rural regional cooperation should help the farming population to meet the social and economic problems that arise with technological progress in agriculture and call for structural changes in existing settlement patterns.

Evaluation of the Israeli Experience

The following aspects of rural development in Israel might be helpful to other countries in similar situations:

1. There was a strong ideological motivation at the root of rural development in Israel, based on the drive to create a new rural society. The motivation of the farmers and their active participation in the schemes are determinant factors in the success of rural development.

2. The provisions governing land tenure in Israel ensured that benefits arising from rural development would be channeled to the farmer, rather than to speculators, and encouraged the farmers to invest their savings in their farms. These provisions were a precondition of planned settlement.

3. The setting up of a special Settlement Authority, with a high degree of decentralization and delegation of authority to regional and local offices, made possible unified management, coordination at all levels, and continuous dialogue among policy makers, planners, and those responsible for implementation. A vital feature was the coordination of development activities with the various government departments, at regional and local levels. The regional offices, comprising interdisciplinary teams—agronomists, economists, sociologists, physical planners, engineers, and administrators, all living in the region—were provided with means for implementation and given the power to adapt programs to changing local conditions. That enabled the regional staff to win the cooperation of the local population and to develop a feeling of identification with local problems, of individual participation, and of responsibility for the success or failure of programs. Not all the staff members had academic qualifications; many relied on practical experience, and were trained on the job.

4. Israel's experience with settlers from underdeveloped countries and traditional societies stresses the importance of full cooperation on the part of those concerned in achieving the desired changes. The farmers must be trained and encouraged to take matters into their own hands and participate actively in all stages of the development process. In this, a helpful factor is cooperation with the locally accepted leaders, who should be motivated to achieve the objectives of the project, and who should be trained for their tasks.

Sociological considerations are of special importance in development projects involving traditional societies. The Israeli authorities preferred to introduce, in the initial stages, simple innovations which are easily understood, rather than drastic changes. As an example of this, they did not insist from the outset on full cooperative organization in the village or on democratic management of village institutions, but introduced transitional arrangements, better suited to the traditional background of the settlers.

5. The cooperative framework of rural settlement in Israel offered effective ways of marshaling the forces of development and of easing the difficulties encountered in building up a modern rural society, under adverse physical and environmental conditions. This was in the best interests of the settlers themselves, and the best way of achieving the national objectives. It made possible full use of the advantages of large-scale production, as well as the application of modern methods and equipment. Cooperative activity also proved to be a most effective education process in itself. It provided a communication medium, through which technical knowledge could be extended and modern methods and rational decision-making cultivated. It bred confidence in mutual help and responsibility and imbued the whole farming community with a common sense of purpose.

6. A decisive factor of rural development in Israel was the organizational and institutional measures, introduced by the public authorities as well as by the farmers themselves. An appropriate system of support, including strong local and national farmers' organizations, cooperatives for credit, marketing, and purchase of supplies, an intensified extension service, provision of adequate local social services (e.g., education, health, entertainment), development of communications, etc.—all these were at least as important as the progress of actual agricultural production.

7. The importance of providing adequate economic incentives for farmers, of reducing their risks and of assuring a minimum economic security, cannot be overemphasized. To achieve this aim, Israel developed intensive planning of agricultural production, price policies, including guaranteed minimum prices, marketing boards, and insurance against natural calamities (e.g. drought, pests)—all oriented toward a system, whereby the interests of the national economy should be reconciled with those of the individual farmer.

8. Finally, a factor worth stressing is the drive to increase farmers' earnings through the development of regional agricultural enterprises and to create additional sources of employment in the rural areas, through the integration of agriculture, industry and services in a regional cooperative framework.

Farming in Greece is both a means of earning a living and a mode of life. Present-day social and economic life on Greek farms is the product of a long history in which no significant changes occurred until the last few decades. Most of the changes have come about in a period of less than 50 years, and particularly after World War II.

The most important factors that influenced rural life during this period were (a) the extension of the rural road system, to almost all rural communities; (b) improvement of the various public communication media; (c) improvement and expansion of the services provided by the Ministry of Agriculture and the Agricultural Bank of Greece; (d) implementation of public investment programs in the rural sector; and (e) expansion and improvement of the various public services for the rural community (education, health, social security, electricity, etc.).

Furthermore, a major stimulus to favorable changes in the rural sector was provided by developments in the country's overall economy. The Greek economy has experienced a relatively fast growth rate during the postwar years. After the period of reconstruction and stabilization of the economy, and particularly in the years 1954-55 to 1966-67, the GDP grew at an average annual rate of 6 percent (in constant prices). During the same period the average growth rate of the Gross Agricultural Product was 3.5 percent, i.e., half the growth rate in the non-agricultural sector of the economy (7 percent). This caused the participation rate of agriculture in the GDP to drop from 30 to 23 percent.

Employment in Greek agriculture in the postwar period and until 1961 remained constant, or increased slightly. In 1961 more than half (56 percent) of the active population was engaged in agriculture. Since 1961, employment in this sector has declined at a rate of about 1.3 percent annually; the agricultural labor force's share of total employment was estimated at only 50 percent in 1967. This decline was due to emigration and urbanization trends, the latter having been made possi-

Abraham Rosenman—Israel. M.Sc., Agriculture and Engineering, Supreme School of Agriculture, Warsaw; Deputy Director of the Settlement Department of the Jewish Agency; leader of the team for Comprehensive Planning of the Island of Crete on behalf of the OECD, 1964, and subsequently adviser on the implementation of the Plan; member of the Israeli National Council for Planning.

G. N. Sykianakis—Greece. Dr. rer. pol., Mainz University, Germany; research economist, Center of Planning and Economic Research (CEPE), Athens.

This case study consists of two parts. The first part, by G. Sykianakis, deals with national agricultural policy and planning in Greece; the second part, by A. Rosenman, describes the Crete Development Plan.

ble by increased opportunities for more productive employment in the nonagricultural sectors. In view of former substantial labor surpluses in agriculture, this decline, matched by a parallel increase in mechanical equipment (primarily tractors) had positive effects on labor productivity. Thus from 1958-59 to 1966-67 labor productivity in Greek agriculture increased at a relatively high annual rate: 5.5 percent.

Investment in Greek agriculture has risen from 894 m.Drs.,[1] the 3-year average for 1954-1956, to 4,671 m.Drs., the 3-year average for 1964-1966. The participation of agricultural investment in total investment rose during 1954-1961 from 8 to 13 percent. Since then investment increased faster in the nonagricultural sectors of the economy, and this resulted in a drop in the share of agriculture from 13 to 11 percent. The growth of investment in agriculture is due to capital inflow for purposes of modernization and narrowing the technological gap between agriculture and the other sectors. There has been considerable growth of investment in agricultural machinery and equipment, and in irrigation and other land improvement projects. Investment in the stockbreeding sector, particularly in high-quality productive animals, has been insufficient. This explains the backwardness of the stockbreeding sector and its inability to meet the rapidly growing domestic demand for meat and dairy products. The result has been a rapid expansion, since 1960, of imports of livestock products, particularly meat.

Agriculture as a Sector of the National Economy   A major feature of the Greek economy at its present level of development is the importance of agriculture. Agriculture today contributes nearly one-quarter of the GDP and employs half the total active population, but the contribution of agriculture to the economy is measured only at the "farm gate." Moreover, agriculture creates a significant volume of other economic activities through an increased demand for services, intermediate goods, other production inputs, and finished goods, and in addition it supplies increasing quantities of raw materials for the related processing industries.

The contribution of Greek agriculture to the country's balance of payments is also significant, in view of the fact that the balance of payments problem is among the main limiting factors to Greek economic development. Greece shows a net surplus of agricultural products in its balance of trade. In 1967 the value of agricultural exports stood at 75 percent of total exports. Nevertheless the trade surplus of agricultural products relative to agricultural exports has been declining dur-

[1]$U.S. 1 approximates 30 drachmas.

ing the last few years due to a rapid increase in imports of certain agricultural products, mainly meat and dairy products. Moreover, the contribution of agricultural exports to the balance of payments has shown a relative decline, due to an increase in exports of nonagricultural goods and in invisible earnings.

Labor productivity in Greek agriculture is much lower than in other sectors of the economy; added value per person employed in agriculture is only one-third of the corresponding figure in the nonagricultural sectors.

The agricultural sector is called upon to play an important role in Greece's future economic development from several points of view. (1) The expansion of agricultural output appears necessary in order to meet the increasing demand (particularly for meat and dairy products, sugar, etc.) expected to result from economic development. (2) Prevention of an excessive increase in imports and/or facilitation of import substitution of agricultural products will economize on foreign exchange. (3) Helping to develop Greek exports by expanding the production of goods which Greece can produce advantageously, and thus improving the country's trade balance. (4) Higher labor productivity will be necessary in agriculture in order to facilitate the transfer of labor to other, more productive sectors of the economy, without a drop in agricultural production.

To achieve these goals, agriculture will have to advance in many respects. (1) The level of technology in Greek agriculture is generally low. (2) Crop and livestock yields are generally well below those in the developed European countries. (3) The existing structure of agricultural produce is characterized by excessive production of some lowpriced products, while the production of others, with good market prospects, stagnates or increases only slowly. (4) Backwardness in Greek agriculture is also combined with structural deficiencies, such as excessive fragmentation of land, small holdings and poor-quality agricultural buildings.

Besides the contribution of the agricultural sector to the economic development of Greece, the condition and development of this sector deserve closer consideration due to the weight of price support and subsidy programs in the state budget. The present cost of the agricultural income-support and subsidy policies exceeds 4,000 m.Drs.; this is about 9 percent of the gross agricultural product, or about 30 percent of the public investment budget.

In most agricultural regions, per-capita income is less than half of that in Athens. There are significant differences in living standards between Athens and the agricultural regions, as shown in Table 1.

Because of the faster growth in production and income in the non-agricultural sectors, the gap in income and living standards between rural areas and urban centers of Greece is widening and there is no significant hope of reversing this trend in the near future.

There are also sizable differences in agricultural incomes in different regions, and between areas within regions. The main reasons for these lie in differences (a) in density of farm population, (b) in climatic and soil conditions, and (c) in the distance of various areas from major consumer centers. In some cases these differences are quite significant. Mountain areas with scattered farmlands, and some of the rocky islands where production conditions are unfavorable, yield the lowest incomes, whereas the plains, where horticulture, stockbreeding, and vegetable production are pursued, have the most satisfactory agricultural incomes in the country.

Agricultural Targets of the Five-Year Plan (1968-1972)   The following basic aims have been set forth in the Plan, with a view to existing conditions in Greek agriculture, the sector's development potentialities, and the expected effects of the gradual integration of the Greek economy with that of the EEC: "A substantial increase in per-capita output of the agricultural population and maximum contribution of the agricultural sector to the country's economic development. . . . Modernization of agriculture and improvement of its competitive power, improvement of crop composition and creation of the necessary prerequisites for harmonizing Greece's agriculture with that of the E.E.C."[2]

The Plan aims to achieve a considerable growth rate of Gross Agricultural Product, i.e., 5.2 percent annually, at constant 1967 prices. This increase will be made possible by the more rapid development in stockbreeding and forestry production, the annual growth rate of which has been planned at 7.5 and 8.5 percent, respectively. The share of crop production will also be significant according to the Plan, but its annual growth rate will be lower than that of stockbreeding. As a result, stockbreeding will have an increased share of total agricultural production, rising from the present figure of 30 percent to 35 percent at the end of the Plan period.

Agricultural expansion, according to the Plan, will be achieved in parallel with improved productivity. In order to raise the farmers' incomes

[2]Ministry of Coordination, *Economic Development Plan for Greece 1968-1972* (Athens, 1968), p. 50 of the English edition.

Table 1.
Characteristic Indices Showing Inequalities in Living Standards between Athens and Some Selected Agricultural Regions.

Index	Greater Athens	Thrace	Epirus	Ionian Islands
1. Gross Per Capita Product (\$ 1965)	903	304	364	433
2. Per Capita Consumption of Electricity (1965)				
a. Total (kwh)	1,024	62	80	113
b. Household use only (kwh)	387	18	28	42
3. Private Cars (1965) per 10,000 Population	327	21	18	36
4. Bath or Shower—1961: Percent of Total Households	30	2	22	6
5. Fresh Water Supply—1961: Percent of Total Households	78	21	18	20
6. Inhabitants per				
a. Physician (1965)	307	1,835	1,740	1,377
b. Hospital bed (1965)	79	505	466	166
7. Illiterates—1961: Percent of Population	10	30	22	25

Source: Ministry of Coordination, Economic Development Plan for Greece 1968-72.

and to improve the competitiveness of Greek agriculture, the Plan aims to achieve a comparatively high growth rate in labor productivity in agriculture (6.5 percent annually). This improvement will be due partly to a decrease in the agricultural labor force, at a planned annual rate of 1.3 percent. During the Plan period, the population actively engaged in agriculture will be reduced by 110,000 and its share in the total labor force will fall from 50.1 percent in 1967 to 44.7 percent in 1972. For those 110,000 persons employment opportunities will have to be created in other sectors of the economy, where the increase in the total labor force will also have to be absorbed. The total number of new jobs to be created in the nonagricultural sectors of the economy during the five-year period of the Plan has been set at 350,000.

Ways and Means to Achieve Development Targets One may distinguish four main groups of policy measures provided in the Greek Five-Year Plan (1968-1972) for achieving the targets set for the agricultural sector: (a) measures to raise productivity and lower costs in agriculture; (b) measures to expand the marketing of agricultural produce; (c) measures to improve utilization of the labor force and increase farmers' incomes; and (d) institutional and organizational measures.

Raising labor productivity and lowering production costs in Greek agriculture will induce a substantial increase in farmers' incomes, and a significant improvement in the competitiveness of Greek agricultural produce. Taking into consideration the importance of these two targets for the future development of Greek agriculture, the plan provides for the following measures to achieve them: (a) financial support, subsidies, other incentives, and training schemes to help farmers improve their production technology through the rational use of machinery, fertilizers, improved seeds, pesticides, improved livestock, and other inputs; (b) incentives to farmers to establish large cooperative plantations of fruit trees and other crops on neighboring holdings, in order to lower production costs by procuring and using to full capacity large machines and other means of production that the small farmer cannot afford; (c) increased public investment in land reclamation projects, mainly irrigation and drainage, to improve soil productivity; (d) improvement of the regional structure of production, according to the comparative advantages of each agricultural area; (e) an improvement in the geographical pattern of Greek agriculture by concentrating investment and expenditure on the development of selected areas which have a greater potential for intensive agricultural exploitation, and the conversion of mountainous slopes and low-fertility land into pastures and forests; (f) legislative, administrative, and credit measures to accelerate land consolidation, prevent excessive fragmentation in the future, and enlarge the holdings of progressive farmers; (g) intensification of agricultural education and training schemes to assist farmers in their efforts to raise productivity and lower production costs.

Achievement of the planned rapid growth rate in Greek agriculture will not be possible unless absorption of increased production is assured. For this purpose the Plan provides the following guidelines: (a) changing the structure of agricultural production in line with prospective domestic demand, the possibilities for import substitution, and the projected export of Greek agricultural produce; (b) making full use of all opportunities offered by the association agreement with the EEC for increasing Greek exports and for financing the necessary structural changes in Greek agriculture; (c) improving the marketing and processing conditions for agricultural produce and promoting market research and advertising.

The Plan also aims at more efficient utilization of the agricultural labor force and improvement of the farmer's income through (a) increasing the occupational and geographic mobility of the rural population through creating additional employment opportunities and investment in vocational training; (b) the adoption of measures to reduce seasonal unemployment; (c) implementation of income support; (d) social measures to raise the agricultural population's standard of living.

To achieve the targets for development of the agricultural sector, the following institutional and organizational changes will be introduced: (a) modernization and extension of agricultural credit; (b) reorganization of agricultural cooperatives; (c) reorganization and expansion of the services offered by the Ministry of Agriculture (extension, research, education, and training schemes in agriculture); (d) creation of the necessary organizational preconditions for the development of stockbreeding, in view of its importance for import substitution.

The Crete Development Plan

Conscious planning for comprehensive development at the national as well as at the regional level is a relatively recent phenomenon. It was fostered mainly by the profound changes experienced after World War II in many regions of the Western world and in some of the newly developing countries. Greece, a typical country on the economic fringe of the European economy, entered the modern era of planned development after acceptance as an Associate Member of the EEC, when the development of the country's economy became a precondition for making the best use of the newly acquired membership.

The national authorities faced the well-known dilemma whether to give preference to the relatively more developed regions, with prospects of higher return to any additional drachma invested—a choice implying the broadening of the already existing gap between "Great Athens" and the other regions—or to concentrate the development effort on the most backward regions. As a compromise the policy was chosen of dividing the limited means between the more prosperous regions and those of the less developed ones, who seemed to have the best prospects to progress.

The island of Crete was chosen on these grounds, as one of the regions for planned development. A comprehensive ten-year development plan was prepared, by a team of Israeli and Greek planners, with the assistance of the Organization for Economic Cooperation and Development. Crete is the southernmost part of the European continent and its climate offers special advantages not merely for the Greek market, but also for European markets. This special feature offers a sound basis for an agricultural development program. Agriculture is the main sector of economic activity on the island. Therefore, special attention has been devoted to it in the Development Plan, considering its implications for other sectors of the economy.

One of the outstanding phenomena of Crete was the rural exodus, which, because of the proportions it might have assumed and the resulting effect on the population structure, required special attention. The Cretan population is relatively open-minded to development. The cultural and educational level is similar to that of more prosperous societies; in this respect the rural population of Greece presents a special phenomenon.

Approaches to and Methods of Planning   The planning conception began to take shape in the fact-finding and preparatory stages. The comprehensive plan includes (a) a framework plan, which laid down the main guidelines for development, related to the various economic and social activities, according to their relative importance; (b) a more detailed plan for one of the subregions; and (c) plans for selected projects chosen for immediate implementation already at the planning stage. The integration of different levels of planning (usually constituting separate stages) into one system shortens the lengthy process of planning and decision-making and creates conditions for the relatively fast realization of projects suggested by the plan.

The team was keenly aware of the time factor, especially important in the case of Crete because of the danger of emigration and loss of the most active part of the population. Within the planning framework, the trends of development for the subjects important to the development process were outlined in order to assign to each one its relative weight. The framework remained subject to reexamination in the light of implementation and was sufficiently flexible to provide guidance in the detailed planning of implementation. Its flexibility makes possible the introduction of changes that become necessary as new facts come to light during actual implementation. Since this plan aims at providing a basis for decision-making at various institutional levels it should not be overburdened with details, unless they are absolutely necessary for comprehension. It is well to recall that during the implementation of any plan, changes are so numerous that details become insignificant. Many planners tend to waste effort in gathering and collating details that later prove superfluous. The phenomenon of the artist captive of his material is not rare in this field.

At the time of preparation of the comprehensive plan, one subregion in the center of the island was chosen for detailed planning. This subregion was representative of the main Cretan development problems, and its conditions permitted almost immediate implementation of certain projects, that would also influence other parts of the island. This detailed plan had a dual purpose: (a) to examine at the microlevel the data that were used for framework planning and to benefit by the resulting feedback; and (b) as a pilot scheme for implementation.

The plan penetrated to the village level, as a planning unit, and permitted sounding of the trends and inclinations among the rural population, i.e., its reactions to and expectations of the development scheme. As a consequence of this, the planners were able to choose among the various alternatives which arose during the planning process those which would meet minimum opposition, based on habits, traditions, and customs which cannot be changed in a short time span.

After approval of the overall and the detailed plan, planning was begun for selected projects, which would also serve the purpose of experimentation and demonstration. Since irrigation is a basic condition for development of the island and its agriculture, four pilot areas were chosen for this purpose. There it was possible to carry out irrigation schemes relatively quickly, utilizing springs and by drilling. Planning at this stage reached down to the individual farm level. The local population participated in the planning work. The farmers, who were the main source of information at this stage, joined in planning the various projects.

Main Points of the Comprehensive Crete Development Plan *Basic Assumptions:* (1) The quantity of water obtainable during the period of the plan is about 400 million cubic meters annually. This estimate is based on the irrigation scheme of the Greek Ministry of Agriculture, for an area of about 770,000 stremmata.[3] (2) The consolidation of the plots to be irrigated is an essential prerequisite for the implementation of the agricultural plan. (3) The population of Crete will remain more or less stable during the period of the plan. (4) Conditions will be assured to provide the qualified manpower required for implementation of the various phases of the development plan in the different sectors. (5) The necessary public funds, amounting to 10,000 m.Drs., over a period of ten years, will be secured for the implementation of the plan.

Objectives: The aim of the comprehensive development plan for Crete

[3] 1 strema = 1000 square meters.

is to promote the economy of the island by utilizing existing possibilities to the full and developing the economic potential of the various sectors. The plan envisages (a) a considerable rise in the population's standard of living; (b) fuller and more efficient utilization of the labor force and reduction of unemployment and emigration; (c) changing the social structure by modernizing human activity patterns; and (d) adapting the pace of development of the island to that of the Greek mainland.

The target of the plan is to double the average per capita income during a period of about ten years. This target was set in accordance with the economic forecast for Greece as a whole, which envisages a doubling of the national per capita income during this period.

Principal Means of Implementation: (a) intensification of agriculture through irrigation, agrotechnical improvements, and rationalization of labor; (b) development of various industries for the absorption of surplus labor released by agriculture; (c) development of services in accordance with the expected rise in the standard of living; (d) an overall investment of 18,500 m.Drs.; (e) the transfer of about 43,000 agricultural workers to industry and services; (f) the establishment of adequate educational and vocational training facilities; and (g) provision of incentives for the implementation of the plan.

Main Proposals and Projected Results   Since agriculture at present constitutes the major sector, both as regards employment (70 percent) and total income (52 percent), special attention has been paid to this sector in order to provide it with the necessary stimulus for progress. It is this sector which is intended to serve as an impetus for all the remaining sectors. A development program has also been prepared for industry and services.

Agriculture: By increasing the area under irrigation from 236,000 to 770,000 stremmata and raising the productivity of the various branches of agriculture, the gross agricultural product is to be increased from 1.95 b.Drs. to 3.15 b.Drs. The irrigated land is to be used mainly for the traditional crops grown on the island, e.g., grapes (table grapes and raisins), olives, citrus fruit, and in-season and out-of-season vegetables, the latter mainly for export to the mainland and to other countries.

The contemplated development in livestock consists in improving sheep and goat breeding and husbandry and range betterment. While the number of heads is to be somewhat reduced, productivity is to be increased by about 60 percent. In addition, poultry rearing is to be intensified, and a dairy industry for local consumption is to be initiated.

The number of farming families is to be reduced from the present figure of 95,000 to 69,000, and the number of agricultural workers from 158,000 to 115,000. Disguised unemployment will thus be greatly cut down, while the reduction in the number of farmers and the overall increase in farm produce are expected to raise the average annual income of those engaged in agriculture from about 12,000 to 27,400 drachmas.

Industry: By expanding and rationalizing existing industrial plants and developing new industries, an increase in industrial product from 720 m.Drs. to 2.1 b.Drs. is to be attained. The main emphasis has been placed on improving, expanding, and raising the efficiency of existing industries, while new industries are to be developed in keeping with the increase in local demand, following the expected rise in the standard of living, and the progress of agriculture which will call for certain industrial accessories (building materials, irrigation equipment, etc.).

Industry will absorb a considerable portion of the surplus labor released by agriculture. The total number of industrial workers is expected to increase from 24,750 to about 43,000, and the average income of the industrial worker will rise from 29,000 to 45,000 drachmas.

Services: The development of services will run parallel to the rise in the general standard of living which will call for improved and more efficient services. Special stress has been laid on the promotion of tourism by building new hotels and improving tourist services. In order to provide adequate services even for the smaller and more remote villages, it has been suggested that they be organized on a regional basis. Service centers are to be established in selected locations to serve the inhabitants of the surrounding villages. Due to this centralization it will be possible to maintain a higher standard at an adequate scale. The gross product of the service industries is to be increased from 910 m.Drs. to 2.14 b.Drs.

The number of persons employed in the services is to be increased from about 35,000 to 55,000, with an average increase in the income of the persons employed from 26,800 to 39,000 drachmas annually.

Overall Results: It is envisaged that implementation of the development plan will bring about a doubling of the product per person employed, from 17,200 to 35,600 drachmas.

The existing labor force will be more efficiently utilized throughout the entire year so that the disguised unemployment existing at present both in agriculture and in the various urban services may be radically curtailed.

A better balance will be achieved among the principal sectors of the economy and their relative contribution to the national product will be improved.

Development Plan for the Subregion of Mires   The detailed plan deals with the development of agriculture, industry, and services, and includes also a physical plan for the subregion.

Agriculture: Natural climatic conditions and existing means of production have been taken into consideration for each village, as well as likely future means of production. The plan is based on the village unit, its means of production, and their relationship to the number of families. For each unit a program has been drawn up, taking into account land resources, the cultivable area, future irrigable areas, and existing livestock.

The coastal area, with a temperate climate and less extreme winter temperatures, is suitable for early vegetables, citrus fruits, and early grapes, whereas the inland area will sustain orchards, vegetable farms, and some dairy farms. There are also a number of upland villages; their main occupation will be dry farming and sheep raising.

The plan suggests suitable field crops and orchard areas, as well as the optimum quantity of livestock for each village according to its potential capacity. Farmers' incomes, as well as the number of workdays required for implementation of the plan, have been calculated on the basis of standardized farm types, allowing for the size of existing holdings and their location.

Industry: The industrial development plan is based on the need to absorb part of the surplus agricultural population of the subregion, while bearing in mind the necessity for an additional industrial center in Crete. Industrial development in Mires should be confined to indigenous industries, such as the processing of milk, cheese, and other dairy products; vegetable and raisin packaging; oil refining; and industries connected with local consumption of goods and services, such as building, the manufacture of building blocks, quarrying, etc. The industrial plan for Mires deals also with specific aspects of industrialization, such as vocational training and development of an industrial zone.

Services and Physical Planning: The basic assumption of the physical plan is that villages below a certain minimum size will gradually cease to exist, their population and manpower diverted to larger villages or rural centers. The underlying reason for this plan is the need to avoid fragmentation of investment through developing communications and services for units too small to justify and maintain such services.

The physical plan provides for the setting up of five settlement complexes with appropriate rural centers, and one urban center, Mires, that will serve the entire region and where various agricultural processing industries will be located. A number of villages will be linked directly to the town of Mires. Most of the economic and public services are to be concentrated in these rural centers; the establishment of separate services in the individual villages should be avoided, except for daily services, which should be near to farmers' homes.

The Planning of Four Irrigated Pilot Areas An exhaustive socioeconomic survey and a study of the demographic structure, as well as a general soil survey, were carried out in the pilot areas. The areas selected for the four projects are located in various geographical areas, each of which has a different climate and agriculture. Common to all of them was the fact that there seemed a reasonable possibility of realizing these irrigation projects in the first stage of the implementation of the development plan.

For each region, different farm types have been planned to suit different kinds of soil, climatic conditions, and size of holdings. The basic assumption was that the desire and inclination of each of the hundreds of farmers, climatic conditions, quality of land, available area, marketing conditions, etc. will lead to the crystallization of a number of farm types, representing the special features of each area. The planned farm types would enable the extension officers to guide farmers in adopting the type of farm best suited to conditions prevailing in the area. This program would also make it possible to deal with problems common to many farmers.

Analysis of the aggregate production on the basis of farm types makes it possible to examine the degree of utilization of the land, water, and labor potential in the area. This also provides data for the estimation of the potential market and enables planning of the required services and calculating the economic changes in the area.

Individual Planning of Farms in Two Villages The planning of the four selected pilot areas was extended by detailed planning at the village level, in two villages, each at a different stage of development and representing a different area and farm types.

The family farm is the basic cell in Cretan agriculture, and the family constitutes the unit for analysis. Tabulation of individual plans for each holding, with parallel analysis of the sociodemographic structure of the families operating it, permits review and improvement of the plan for the village. Planning at farm level reveals omissions and faults in decision making which do not come to light at the overall planning level, or even when planning the village as a unit.

By processing the data collected, it became possible (a) to analyze each farmer's situation, as regards means of production and available labor force; (b) to draw up a plan for every holding, including concrete suggestions for transition from the present situation to the projected one; and (c) to sum up the prospects of development for the whole village, and to adjust accordingly the plans for the area.

In Conclusion The Crete development plan took into account the physical conditions of the island as well as its social setup. Traditional Cretan society must face modern technology and its demands on the individual; the planners had to consider readiness and capability for change concerning patterns of work, education, entertainment, family and community relationships, and social status.

This complexity is reflected in the planning work—in the choice of alternatives including agricultural programs, different branches of employment, and vocational training. Planning was based on the assumption that an appropriate economic return is the precondition for change.

From the outset the planners sought to win the cooperation of the administration as well as that of the farmers who should commence implementation of the plan as soon as possible. These cooperated in fact finding, expressed their views, and contributed their know-how and experience to the planning process. By that the planners learned about the need of the people concerned, and were assisted by them to plan for their benefit.

Agricultural and General Economic Development

According to data from the Food and Agriculture Organization of the United Nations, the present agricultural product of Latin America decreased nearly 10 percent per capita, compared to the period 1934-1938. Since then, agricultural imports—mostly foodstuffs—increased more than 80 percent and seriously upset the balance of payments of most Latin American countries. In this depressing panorama of economic stagnation and regression, Mexico is the only exception.

The combined effects of land reform, road construction, irrigation, agricultural credit, and the spread of many innovations through research, extension, and training enabled the agricultural sector to grow at an average annual rate of more than 5 percent during the last thirty years and turned Mexico into the only Latin American country virtually self-sufficient in food.

While growing domestic demand has been met, exports of cotton, coffee, cattle, tomatoes, fresh vegetables, and sugar cane have increased steadily. Furthermore, until ten years ago it was customary to import corn and wheat to supplement domestic production and meet local demand. Then, quite suddenly, Mexico began to generate surpluses and became an exporter. By 1966, 684,000 tons of wheat and 800,000 tons of maize were sold below world prices, to the United Arab Republic, or to the Socialist bloc.

Table 1, compiled from data from the Food and Agriculture Organization of the United Nations, shows the course of agricultural production in eight Latin American countries. Mexico stands out as an exception not only in Latin America but in the world. To treble its agricultural product in less than three decades implies a phenomenal, sustained rate of growth. It would be difficult to find another country that has grown at such pace in modern times. This record is corroborated in a study of the development of agriculture in twenty-six nations undertaken by the U.S. Department of Agriculture, in which Mexico's rates of growth are shown to be surpassed only by Israel and Japan [9].

This does not mean, of course, that Mexico has solved all its agricultural problems and has somehow built a rural utopia. Far from it, much of farming is still done with very primitive technology which demands

Edmundo Flores—Mexico. Ph.D., Agricultural Economics, University of Wisconsin, 1948; Professor of Economics, Escuela Nacional de Economia, Universidad Nacional Autonoma de Mexico.

Table 1.
Index of Agricultural Production in 8 Latin American Countries, Based on the
Period 1934-38 = 100[a]. Final Year 1965.

Country	Index
Argentina	133
Brazil	196
Chile	166
Colombia	227
Cuba	153
Mexico	324
Peru	193
Uruguay	139

[a]Linked index.
Source: Data from FAO, taken from Folke Dovring, *Land Reform and Produc-tivity: The Mexican Case, a Preliminary Analysis,* Department of Agricultural Economics, Agricultural Experiment Station, University of Illinois, November 1966, p. 4.

strenuous efforts, is plagued by risks, and yields very little to most peasants. Average income per capita is roughly 60 percent lower than industrial and urban income. In rural areas life expectancy is much shorter than in urban areas; illiteracy is higher, unemployment and underemployment prevail, and there are fewer opportunities for personal advancement. Moreover, there are regions like Zacatecas, Yucatan, Tarahumara, and the Mixteca where many people still suffer chronic, unmitigated, outright hunger. In recent years there have been frequent newspaper reports of localized peasant uprisings and land invasions in scattered parts of the country. But, without minimizing the seriousness of these events, one should not forget that the huge industrial and urban growth attained during the last three decades has required a very high rate of capital formation, and that capital accumulation in underdeveloped countries with rural overpopulation is a cruel and painful process in which capital for overhead investment and growth comes inevitably from enforcing austerity on the bulk of the population.

The industrial backwardness of Mexico in the nineteenth century, and the turbulence of the revolution in which most of the productive plant was destroyed, made the first twenty years after 1910 a period in which agriculture was virtually the only source of capital for urban industrial growth. One must recall that between 1910 and 1941 capital, both national and foreign, fled abroad. During the armed period of the revolution, 1910-1917, there were nearly one million casualties. Thousands of Mexicans fled to Los Angeles—Mexico's second largest city—and to other parts of the United States, just as Cubans today go to Miami. In 1914, Veracruz was bombarded and occupied by U.S. military forces that stayed more than six months. On March 9, 1916, Pancho Villa raided United States territory and burned the town of Columbus, New Mexico. In reprisal, on March 13, General Pershing's punitive expeditionary forces invaded Mexico and stayed for about eleven months this time. President Calles attacked the Catholic Church, which has always opposed the revolution, and the Church fought back with all the earthly and supernatural means at its command. Land and property, of citizens and foreigners alike, were confiscated. In 1929 payment on the foreign debt was suspended. In 1937 Cardenas nationalized the railroads; in 1938 he nationalized oil. The image of the Mexican bandit and of Mexican lawlessness spread far and wide. No wonder, then, that Mexico's international financial position should have been precarious—as much as, or more so, than that of present-day Cuba.

In 1926, direct foreign investment was estimated at 3,500 million pesos. The paper value of this sum was reduced by the 1929 crash; the expropriation of oil and the railroads turned part of it into public debt, and inflation reduced its value in real terms even further. By 1939 total direct foreign investment was estimated at 2,500 million pesos; of this 50 percent went into public utilities and transport, and 40 percent into mining.

Foreign trade somewhat relieved the acute shortage of foreign currency which followed the revolution. During the decade of 1920-1930 exports of petroleum, minerals, and henequen reached record figures, and the terms of trade between 1925 and 1929 were favorable to Mexico. The 1929 depression cut down exports drastically, but by 1933 their level began to rise anew. On November 19, 1941, Mexico returned to international financial respectability after President Avila Camacho and President Roosevelt signed an agreement in which Mexico committed itself to pay foreign claims in part [2].

Between 1910 and 1941 there were two rather unusual instances of incoming capital: Jewish refugees in search of sanctuary, after Hitler took over in Germany, brought capital; and the Spanish Republicans, after their defeat by Franco, brought half of the Spanish treasury, the other half going to Russia. Because of the clandestine circumstances surrounding both transfers, it is impossible to give even rough data on their total amount. Aside from financial capital, it is well worth mentioning the inflow of "human capital" or "nonconventional capital," that is to say, the technical, scientific, or artistic ability of individuals. Most of the Jewish and Spanish refugees were indeed first-rate "human capital." Many were scientists and technicians trained in the best European universities; others were men of letters, artists, philosophers, and celebrated thinkers. This group contributed notably to the modernization of the country. Without doubt, the growth of the economy would not have been as fast or steady had it lacked the participation of European technicians and intellectuals who repaid with largesse the sanctuary offered them by helping to build modern Mexico.

But with due allowance for these exceptions, the fact remains that between 1910 and 1941 no foreign capital entered Mexico. On the contrary, wealthy Mexicans with liquid capital sent it abroad and thereby aggravated the balance of payments deficit. There were, therefore, only two ways to increase the domestic rate of capital formation: (1) the classic, painful, and expedient recourse of squeezing agriculture as much as possible; and (2) the more enterprising transfer of workers from agriculture to the emerging industrial and urban sectors, and their employment at subsistence wages in activities which would eventually increase the productive capacity of the system. This is how public works were financed and how huge government deficits were covered until 1942. This explains largely the paradox of the success and failure of Mexican agriculture: the penury of the peasants and slum dwellers and the impressive agricultural, industrial, and urban growth.

The steady drain on agriculture for capital formation purposes, begun in 1925 during the Calles administration, inevitably imposed very low levels of consumption on the peasant masses and accounts for the absence of anything resembling welfare in rural areas. The peasants tolerated this forced austerity because it came from the same government which was giving them free land and which was engaged in vigorous and unprecedented efforts to build dams, highways, and schools for themselves and their children—as shown by the budget that gave Numbers 1 and 2 priorities to public education and public works [6].

The level of agricultural development achieved thus far does not mean that Mexico has reached adequate standards of living for all members of the rural population. Instead, this development—as well as increased petroleum and tourist revenues—accounts largely for the sustained expansion and diversification of the economy.

Foreign investment entered the picture after 1942. Its importance since then has generally been overrated due to the discordant effects produced by the clash of the loud advertising of the products of foreign firms with our brand of nationalism which has many elements of xenophobia. In fact, foreign investment entered the picture only in the past three decades; it has never exceeded 15 percent of total investment; it comes from different countries and cannot take credit for the growth of the economy in any important way. Foreign investment, incidentally, seems to have acquired better manners and carefully refrains from the greed, arrogance, and paternalism of old.

Recently, some influential Mexicans have begun to think that the growth of agricultural, industrial, and service sectors has finally provided Mexico with the productive potential in terms of food, factories, equipment, and technicians required for improving rural and urban welfare. If this idea prevails, the coming phase of Mexico's development will be concerned with its entry on the stage of mass consumption under conditions approaching full employment.

The Land Reform

The key to understanding contemporary Mexico is to realize, first, that the triumph of the 1910-1917 revolution imposed a new social order, and second, that this order lacked an economic foundation. Since then, the main goal of economic policy has been to create a productive structure compatible with the new social principles, and capable of supporting and of continuing a political system in which the most important groups in society have effective representation.

It is not surprising that the people of a backward, agrarian economy, plagued by concentration of land ownership, extreme income differences, and resource waste should be obsessed with the idea of land reform. Under such conditions, what other immediate solution could be sought? Perhaps this explains why agrarian reform was the primary weapon on which the Mexican Revolution relied to achieve economic growth and social equality.

The Revolution had another effect which, in its initial stages, was perceived by few Mexicans: it opened the country to overwhelming innovational forces. Mexico shed the inertia of the colonial period to enter the cosmopolitan stream of the twentieth century. Unwittingly, the conditions for the industrial revolution had been fulfilled. The barriers to economic growth were shattered. Under the new order, technological progress became an imperative for survival. In spite of its limitations, and irrespective of the narrowness and simplicity of its initial propositions, the effects of official policy spread to some of the most remote corners of the land and prompted many second thoughts which, gradually, resulted in expanding the scope of economic policy and in giving it greater cogency.

The land reform confronted the country with a situation of the kind Toynbee calls challenge and response. The subsequent emergence of modern Mexico is the consequence of a positive reaction to this critical challenge. The break-up of the hacienda system released the multitude of complex forces to which Mexico owes its growth. The destruction of the main source of power and income of the landed oligarchy emancipated the peasants, gave the rural population horizontal and vertical mobility, eliminated the caste system, and for the first time in our history made it possible for the common Mexican to aspire to individual improvement and to a better future for his children [1].

A new power structure replaced the old. The leaders of this true, irreversible revolution—Zapata, Calles, Obregon, Cardenas—showed passionate concern for the people and the nation. These momentous changes set the stage for political stability, economic development, and an exciting cultural renaissance. They also nurtured the cohesive, petulant, and enterprising nationalism without which the great collective effort required for the success of the Revolution probably would have failed.

As land began to be redistributed massively, it became imperative to increase productivity, to diversify production, and to industrialize. First came irrigation and road construction, afterwards urban expansion. Both combined to generate a huge demand for cement, steel, and other products of the construction industry, thus setting the stage for the industrial revolution. This encouraged the growth of the rate of capital formation since, according to W. Arthur Lewis, "The expansion of capital is a function of the rate at which the building and construction industry can be expanded" [9]. That is how the Mexican economy entered the industrial revolution.

From 1915 to date, 56 million hectares (138 million acres) of all types of land—more than 50 percent of all the productive land of Mexico—have been distributed among 2.4 million peasants. These lands were freely granted to agricultural communities called ejidos. The ejido is a system of communal tenure modeled somewhat after the ancient Indian communities whose land was usurped by the hacienda. Ejido lands are held as the property of a town or village, either for collective use or for distribution among ejidatarios for cultivation in small plots to which each individual has the right of occupancy and usufruct. The average size of the ejido plot is 6.5 hectares (16 acres); but, given the tremendous regional differences peculiar to Mexico's geography, this average is meaningless. Ejido land cannot be sold or mortgaged. At present, there are 18,000 ejidos, of which approximately 4,000 are operated collectively and produce cotton, sugar cane, rice, and hemp. The remaining 14,000 are worked individually.

To compensate landlords, the government issued bonds, but only approximately 0.5 percent of the total value of expropriated land was paid for. Even in the case of land owned by foreigners (79 million acres), compensation was not paid in accordance with the rigid principle of "prompt, adequate, and effective" payment, as the United States State Department demanded. Instead, it was subject to long and protracted negotiations, culminating in an agreement between the Mexican and American governments under which payment was geared to the financial capacity of the expropriating country and extended over a long period. In that way a precedent was set which may be of great importance to the success of future land reforms in other Latin American countries [3].

The land reform also created small family farms called pequenas propiedades, which were inspired to some extent by the American family farm. Their area varies from 100 to 150 hectares (250 to 360 acres) of irrigated land or its equivalent in land of lower quality. These farms were created from lands which were exempt from expropriation when the ejidos were formed, and which remained the private property of the old hacienda owners. At present, there are approximately 40,000 pequenas propiedades, the average size of which is between 100 and 250 hectares (250 and 600 acres), and they cover an area of about 7.5 million hectares (17 million acres) of the best land. The appearance of a trend toward the concentration of land ownership in irrigated areas must be reported. Increasingly, former landlord families and members of the "new class" have begun to operate many pequenas propiedades under a unified management, particularly in the production of export crops. The landless peasants with agrarian rights—more than 1.5 million— and old agrarian reformers derisively call the owners of these huge, commercial enterprises "nylon farmers." Obviously, these new units are not comparable to the old haciendas. Yet, concentration of land ownership, even if it leads to efficient resource use and increased production, is against the land reform laws and against the spirit of the agrarian revolution.

In addition, there are approximately 1.4 million privately owned holdings of smaller size which cover an area of 170 million hectares; and, finally, there are still about 500 large haciendas of between 125,000 and 250,000 acres each. As a rule, these haciendas are located in remote, semidesert regions or in virtually inaccessible tropical jungles, or else they are owned by powerful politicians.

To sum up, in 1910 there were in Mexico 8,431 large haciendas and 48,633 ranches (between 200 and 1,000 hectares) making a total of 57,064 agricultural properties. Out of a population of 15 million, less than one percent (0.3 percent) were land owners; the rest of the people were landless! Today ejidatarios and private owners make a total of 3.8 million persons, or 8.6 percent of the total population.

The New Agricultural Structure

Since 1929, the agricultural product increased at approximately 5 percent per annum on the average, though in the period 1959-1968 it seems to have maintained a slightly higher rate of growth. However, since at the same time the gross national product increased at an average exceeding 6 percent, by 1967 the agricultural product amounted only to 15.4 percent of the gross national product (see Table 2). Index numbers of crop production for the period 1929-1965 appear in Table 3. In closer detail, Table 4 shows the behavior of the seven most important agricultural products for the more recent period 1960-1967.

The increases variously depicted in the Tables 1-4 were possible because of the combined and cumulative effects of many innovations. While the relative importance attributable to the variables involved is open to discussion, there is little argument about the main components of rural development in Mexico, namely, (a) the land reform, which, by destroying a rigid tenure structure inimical to innovation, opened the way for a policy of trial and error aimed at the modernization of the country; (b) the expansion of acreage caused by the policies of irrigation and road construction that opened up lands previously idle; (c) massive shifts in land utilization from extensive to intensive crop production and cattle breeding, which in turn were stimulated by increased demand from urban-industrial expansion as well as by modern transportation and communication and by favorable prices inside the country and abroad; and, finally and more recently, (d) increases in productivity generated by the spread of modern technology and research: high-yield seeds, fertilizers, fungicides, antibiotics, machinery, food processing and packaging, etc.

Table 2.
Mexican Economic Growth 1950-1967 (1950 Prices).

Category	1950	1960	1967
Gross Domestic Product (millions of pesos)	41,060	74,317	114,262
Agriculture and Livestock (%)	21.7	18.3	15.4
Industry (%)	30.4	33.1	36.7
Commerce, Services, and Others (%)	47.9	48.6	47.9
Per Capita Aggregate Consumption[a] (pesos)	1,303.00	3,631.00	5,224.00 (current prices)
Per Capita Gross Domestic Product (dollars)	182.00	353.00	528.00

[a]Includes changes in inventories.
Source: Bank of Mexico, S.A.

Table 3.
Index Numbers of Crop Production, 1929-1965.

	Physical Production[a]		
	Domestic use	Export	All crops
1929	100	100	100
1939	148	117	137
1949	254	210	239
1959	379	397	386
1965	523	534	527

[a]Weighted by average prices 1929-1965. Index numbers are of the 25 principal crops, 16 mainly for domestic consumption and 9 for export. These 25 crops represent close to 90 percent of total crop production.
Source: Bank of Mexico, S.A.

Quantification of the share attributable to each component is of course difficult, since all these different categories of innovation pervade the whole process, and overlap and reinforce each other cumulatively.

Table 4.
Main Crops (thousands of tons).

Years	Maize	Wheat	Cotton	Coffee	Sugar Cane	Beans	Sugar
1960	5,386	1,190	470	124	19,542	528	328
1961	5,561	1,373	450	127	19,167	723	333
1962	6,337	1,455	523	140	21,116	666	289
1963	6,070	1,703	457	142	22,150	698	329
1964	8,454	2,134	504	145	24,748	795	325
1965	8,400	1,876	552	159	28,039	812	394
1966	9,105	1,609	601	185	23,400	945	390
1967	9,264	2,096	565	165	25,800	1,008	392

Source: Nacional Financiera, S.A.

The Expansion of Acreage by Irrigation and New Roads

The National Irrigation Commission was founded in 1926. Subsequently, total government investment in irrigation through 1968 amounted to 15.7 billion pesos ($1.7 billion). Until the late 1940s irrigation works were paid by deficit financing. The area harvested in irrigation districts in 1966-67 was 2.6 million hectares, or 25 percent of the total harvested area. The construction of dams and other irrigation facilities initiated in 1926 absorbed over 90 percent of public investment in the agricultural sector since this policy went into high gear during the early forties.

Highway construction also had high priority on public expenditure. The construction of a network exceeding 60,000 kilometers made accessible lands which previously were idle or were not operated extensively. The new highways linked agricultural regions with consumption centers and ports. Thus, highways and urban-industrial expansion generated huge external economies, stimulated shifts toward more intensive land utilization patterns, and made accessible lands which were either idle or else operated merely for subsistence.

For example, a survey of the ejidos of the State of Mexico—a state adjacent to Mexico City—showed that despite fragmentation of land holdings caused by the land reform in an area of very high population density, the dairy-cattle population, even in very small ejidos, had increased considerably because of the proximity of Mexico City and the fresh milk demand of its 7.5 million population [8].

There are no estimates of the effect that the spread of urbanization and communications has had upon the expansion of acreage and the increase of productivity, but there is no doubt that such shifts contributed substantially to create a more intensive, diversified, and efficient pattern of land utilization [4].

Domestic Price Supports

Mexico began its price support policies in 1937. Initially, this policy sought to lower the prices of basic foods and favored urban consumers at the expense of farmers. In recent years, however, prices have been raised generally above the world market level, and the terms of trade have tended to favor the commercial producers in the agricultural sector. At present, the price support agency CONANSUPO (Compania Nacional de Subsistencias Populares) supports the prices of maize, wheat, beans, rice, sorghum, and chile (hot pepper). Approximately half of the wheat crop, 10 percent of the corn crop, and marginal quantities of the other products are handled through CONANSUPO.

The agricultural sector has also shown itself sensitive to world prices. Favorable prices abroad have stimulated production. In 1950-1955 cotton production increased twofold largely because of favorable competitive conditions created by the price support policies of the United States, which caused the "umbrella effect." Since then, cotton has been the leading agricultural export commodity. Likewise, the withdrawal of Cuba from the United States market acted as a powerful incentive to increase sugar cane production from about 19 million tons in 1960 to around 25 million tons in 1967. At the same time domestic consumption increased by 40 percent, while exports of sugar reached the half million mark. The limiting factor to further increases of sugar production lies, of course, in the behavior of world prices. Since 1960, agricultural exports increased more than 40 percent (Table 5).

Productivity and Extension

Gains in productivity have been mounting steadily, as exemplified by wheat. National average yields per hectare rose from 685 kilograms in 1925-29 to 1,640 kilograms in 1960-62. Afterwards, the discovery and dissemination of high-yielding varieties pushed average yields up to 2.4 tons per hectare, and yields of 8 tons per hectare are not unusual. Since 1950 average yields of potatoes increased 65 percent; cotton yields increased 85 percent; beans 50 percent; and maize 25 percent. Recent

Table 5.
Agricultural Exports (millions of dollars).

Category	1963	1964	1965	1966	1967
Cotton	199.2	173.1	214.7	221.9	143.6
Coffee	49.1	95.2	73.1	83.5	60.1
Tomatoes	24.5	33.9	35.1	62.9	49.4
Cattle and Meat	63.5	41.2	55.3	68.4	55.9
Maize	—	15.9	77.2	46.7	72.6
Wheat	5.0	35.8	41.6	3.9	12.6
Others	39.6	39.2	38.9	62.7	70.7
Total	380.9	434.3	535.9	550.0	464.9
Fish and Seafood	53.5	55.5	44.6	55.6	63.4

Source: Nacional Financiera, S.A.

breakthroughs in high-yielding hybrids will undoubtedly push up these averages in the immediate future.

Fertilizer consumption went up from 664,000 metric tons in 1960 to 1.8 million metric tons in 1969, and plans were made to double fertilizer production in the succeeding three years. Since 1960 domestic production of fertilizer increased on the average 20 percent per annum.

The National Institute for Agricultural Research of the Ministry of Agriculture, in cooperation with the Rockefeller and Ford Foundations and with FAO, has established several stations to develop and test new varieties of crops and to improve the livestock industry through breeding centers, pasture improvement, research in animal nutrition, and importation of breeding stock.

Attempts to successfully operate an extension service fashioned on the United States model have failed, and little can be said of Mexico's extension service. Before other developing countries try to copy the American experience, its careful reevaluation will be necessary. Surely, today, the transmission of technical knowhow can take advantage of the many short-cuts created by the development of mass media communications.

Population Shifts: Agriculture, Industry, and Urban Relationships
Between 1910 and 1967, the population rose from 15.1 million to 45.6 million, i.e., an absolute increase of 30.5 million and a relative increase of 202 percent. The annual rate of growth for the whole period was 2.7 percent; but considered by decades, this rate shows an accelerated

growth. In 1930-40 it was 1.7; in 1940-50, 2.8; and in 1950-60, 3 percent annually. Estimates for 1960-67 place it at 3.9 percent. The outlook for 1980 is a total population of 60 to 65 million. In all probability the rates of population growth will continue increasing during the rest of the decade and will start declining slowly in the 1970s. Such decline will come from new attitudes and behavior patterns derived from increased income, education, and urbanization. Without these prerequisites birth control policies will not be effective, assuming no radical changes in birth control techniques.

In 1910, 77.7 percent of the population was rural, that is to say, living in communities or population centers of less than 2,500 inhabitants according to the census definition. Approximately the same percentage of population was illiterate. In 1967, the percentage of rural population declined to 43 percent, and the percentage of illiteracy had dropped to around 30 percent. Urban population rose from 22.3 percent in 1910 to 57 percent in 1967. During the past decades Mexico has been exposed to an intense process of urbanization. The revolution and the land reform caused people to flee to Mexico City, to the neighboring towns of the Mesa Central, and to the United States in search of security. This was the first step in a steadily mounting exodus from country to town. Mexico City's population increased from 368,000 inhabitants in 1900 to an estimated 7.5 million today.

The original proprietors of urban real estate were the members of the old landed elite; but whereas the haciendas had been expropriated virtually without compensation, urban properties were spared, and their value multiplied at a terrific rate. Hence, when the system began its upward movement a few years after the forced capital levy of land reform, the landlord class became again the recipient of even larger rents from urban real estate holdings. Metropolitan expansion and sharply competitive land-use shifts generated high rates of capital formation. The internal economies derived from urban growth exceeded by far the partial diseconomies produced by the bottlenecks which came with the emergence of this new pattern. But, the massive migration from country to town kept wages low and depressed labor's share of total income vis-à-vis the absence of land taxes and of adequately progressive income taxes.

The huge demand for construction-industry materials generated jointly by public works and urban expansion assured high returns to investment. Conditions for the emergence of the construction industry were fulfilled, and high rates of capital formation ensured. Basic industry—

cement, iron, steel, and glass—was financed with savings from real estate fortunes complemented by credit from the public sector and from abroad.

Steel ingot output increased from 102,800 metric tons in 1930 to 3.0 million metric tons in 1967; generation of electricity went up from 1.4 million KWH in 1930 to 20.9 million KWH in 1967; cement output increased from 224,000 metric tons to 5.5 million metric tons in 1967; petroleum is up from 106,351 barrels a day in 1938—when Mexico expropriated foreign oil holdings—to 410,750 barrels a day in 1967. The final payment for expropriated oil holdings was made in the fall of 1962.

Since before the land reform until 1930, 70 percent of the labor force was employed in agriculture; this percentage declined to 54 in 1960 and to 48 percent in 1967. However encouraging, this decline does not tell the whole tale. In 1930, only 3.6 million people were in agriculture while in 1967 this number rose to 7.1 million, that is, a net increase of 3.5 million laborers.

Despite its rapid expansion, and despite the emergence of a fast-growing industrial sector, which today comprises about 25 percent of the labor force, agriculture remains congested and ridden by unemployment and underemployment. On the average, subsistence farmers, whose number exceeds one million families, work no more than 150 days a year; they live in miserable conditions and earn an estimated average family income of less than 100 dollars per year. During World War II, approximately 2 million Mexican workers migrated temporarily to the United States to work in agriculture and railroads. In spite of their large number, agricultural output increased in Mexico above average rates during their absence. This suggests that the marginal productivity of the Mexican peasant is very low. The fast-spreading improvements in farm technology will not alleviate rural unemployment because, to a large extent, they have labor-saving effects.

The remarkable development achieved thus far and the accelerated growth and diversification of production in the foreseeable future assure Mexico a growing supply of food and raw materials for domestic consumption and for export. This forecast assumes substantial increases in expenditures for research and training at different levels, and improved extension-service techniques, as well as additional irrigation, electrification, and mechanization. Since these steps are part of present-day official policy, there is ample reason to believe that the availability

of food will cease to be a limiting factor to Mexico's general development.

When so often in the field I see the many transformations going on in
Mexican agriculture, I realize that modernization, diversification, and
integration between agriculture and industrial activities are taking place
so far and successfully that anticipating annual rates of growth of
around 7 percent for the whole sector does not seem as improbable as it
would look solely from a statistical viewpoint. Since it is obvious that a
continuously expanding part of the agricultural sector is becoming increasingly sensitive to changes in domestic and foreign demand, important shifts may be predicted away from cotton, coffee, sugar cane, and
wheat into fresh vegetables, fruits, and beef, for all of which there is a
huge market in the United States, Canada, the Carribean, and even
Europe and Japan. Development of the dairy industry to satisfy growing domestic needs is also a sure bet.

To attain higher levels of employment, income, and welfare in the
rural sector, however, it is essential to reduce the size of the labor force
in agriculture to approximately 30 percent of the total within a reasonable time. This means that more than 3 million peasants will have to
leave farming, or the squalor and idiocy of rural unemployment, to
work in urban-industrial activities. Referring to the growth of the labor
force, Bruce F. Johnston notes that "Between 1950 and 1960 the nonfarm labor force in Mexico increased at nearly 4.0 percent. Apart from
Taiwan, where special circumstances existed, this is the only instance
that I have found that exceeds the 3.7 percent rate registered in Japan
between 1955 and 1964. But the "coefficient of differential growth"—
i.e., the difference between the rates of growth of nonfarm and total
employment which determines the rate of change in sector proportions—was much lower in Mexico, because the total labor force was
growing at 3.1 percent compared to the rate of 1.4 percent in Japan"
[5].

Thus, today more than ever, agricultural policy is inextricably tied to
industrial, fiscal, educational, and general development policies. Industry has become diversified and has begun to produce a torrent of lowpriced consumer goods: radios, sewing machines, bicycles, motorcycles,
medicines, cosmetics, clothing, kitchen gadgets, movies, newspapers,
books, etc. Since Mexico cannot hope realistically to find substantial
export outlets for this steadily growing, somewhat coarse flow of goods
in the immediate future, its only available outlet happens to be its own

domestic market. This means that further development of its industry depends upon creation of a vast domestic market. In turn, this market will not expand at the high rates required without full employment, or a close approximation, in agriculture and industry. But, since full employment requires higher rates of investment, Mexico will have to resort to effective, progressive income taxation and to long-term foreign credits for the import of capital goods.

Modern fiscal theory is not beyond the grasp of hard-working undergraduates. Nonetheless, its application to underdeveloped countries so far has been impossible. The difficulty, of course, is not conceptual but *instrumental*. An effective, progressive fiscal policy requires a good civil service. But a more or less efficient, more or less responsible, and more or less incorruptible public administration is itself a complex, sophisticated by-product of development. Incidentally, this elementary vicious circle escaped the attention of those who planned the Alliance for Progress.

As we have seen, five decades ago, the governments of the Revolution began to pursue many new policies. Some failed, others succeeded. Often, success was determined by good administration. Today, the highly centralized public administration of Mexico has the trained personnel and experience gathered during the implementation of our massive long-term policies of land reform, public works, industrial development, social security, and public education. Meaningful comparison with public administration in the United States or European countries is difficult because of the unavoidable and subtle intrusion of ethnocentric valuations. Mexico, however, appears to be in a better position than any other Latin American country to follow the fiscal policy required for accelerated growth at high employment levels.

With reference to long-term foreign credits for capital equipment, the international position of Mexico is excellent. Paradoxically, the very success of our early radical policies gives Mexico today the opportunity of adopting more sedate and conventional attitudes. In the turmoil and uncertainty of our times, the stability and rapid growth of Mexico provide unusual guarantees.

Clearly, the economic and social problems faced by contemporary Mexico are more complex than those of the past. Their diagnosis requires deep insight and understanding of the dynamics of Mexico's very own growth. Their solution will demand unyielding adherence to the principle of self-determination and political finesse as well as an even greater joint effort than any required in the past. But the rewards may also be unusual, for there is strong probability that Mexico will be the first indigenous society in our hemisphere to build a free and independent welfare state. However, if Mexico should fail to meet the exacting demands of modern competitive development, it could conceivably follow in Argentina's footsteps—a country that after spectacular strides toward economic development and political democracy has turned into a worrisome case of arrested growth and political deterioration.

References

1. Casanova, Pablo Gonzales, *La democracia en Mexico*. Mexico: Ediciones ERA, 1965.

2. Cline, Howard F., *The United States and Mexico*. Cambridge, Mass.: Harvard University Press, 1953.

3. Flores, Edmundo, "On Financing Land Reform: A Mexican Casebook." *Studies in Comparative International Development, III*, 6 (1967-1968), St. Louis, Mo.: Washington University, Social Science Institute.

4. ____, "The Significance of Land-Use Changes in the Economic Development of Mexico," *Land Economics, XXXV*, 2 (May 1959).

5. Johnston, Bruce F., "Agriculture and Economic Development: The Relevance of the Japanese Experience," *Food Research Institute, VI*, 3 (1966), 274-275.

6. Leopoldo, Solis M. "Hacia un analisis general a largo plazo del desarrollo economico de Mexico," *Demografia y Economia, 1*, 1, (1967), El Colegio de Mexico.

7. Lewis, W. Arthur, *The Theory of Economic Growth*. London: George Allen & Unwin, 1955, p. 208.

8. *Los Ejidos del Estado de Mexico. Catalogo*. Toluca, Mexico: Gobierno del Estado de Mexico. Direccion de Agricultural y Ganaderia, 1958.

9. United States Department of Agriculture, *Changes in Agriculture in Twenty-Six Developing Nations, 1948 to 1963*. Foreign Agricultural Economic Report No. 27, November 1965. Washington, D.C.: Government Printing Office.

Part Two
Case Studies

31. The Development
of the Gezira
in the Sudan

Arthur Gaitskell

The Relevance of the Gezira as a Case Study in Development

Gezira means "island" or "promontory" in Arabic, and the name refers
to a great plain which lies between the Blue Nile and the White Nile
south of their meeting place at Khartoum. The Gezira project was
conceived at the beginning of the twentieth century and has gradually
expanded for the last forty-five years until today it covers about two
million acres of irrigated land and serves about 75,000 farmer families.
The large number of rural people involved, the size of the irrigated area,
and the long period of its existence make the project an interesting
example in the search for improvement of the agricultural sector in
development, so critical now with all that it implies in foreign exchange
earnings, expansion of internal purchasing power, production of food,
increase in employment opportunities, and indirect stimulus to the
economy in general.

The Gezira story is also interesting because of certain principles in the
project, particularly those facilitating the adoption of modern technology and those concerned with the equitable distribution of benefits.
Irrigation is a great potential stabilizer against climatic vagaries, but its
full value as a catalyst to new high-yielding varieties, to fertilizer, and
to credit is often vitiated by unsatisfactory land tenure, irregular farm
layout, or lack of organized connection between all the links in the
chain of inputs needed to move a subsistence society to modern market
production. The Gezira project is run on a uniform rotation and is
probably the largest unit in the world conducted under centralized
management for peasant farmers. The principle adopted was a blend of
control and help: control to ensure the benefits of technology, help to
make their adoption easy. The irrigation network for instance was not
confined, as is so often the case, to major dam and canalization construction but was designed right through to the final distribution
ditches on farmers' fields, and the management's duty was to ensure for
each individual a timely water rotation. Clearing and leveling of the
land was equally an organized management operation. The same principle of fidelity to end use was adopted for all other inputs. By contrast

Arthur Gaitskell—United Kingdom. Educated Oxford University; Research Fellow
of Nuffield College, Oxford; Lecturer, EDI World Bank, Washington, 1963 to
1966; member of Board of Commonwealth Development Corporation, London;
member of International Advisory Board for the Mekong River, S.E. Asia; consultant to International Bank, UNDP, FAO, and private companies.

with the dispersal of responsibility among different ministries and agencies, so frequently an intractable problem in many countries, in the Gezira seed production, fertilizer, pest control, mechanized operations, extension, and credit were unified in the hands of the management, which was also responsible for processing at cost and marketing. Gezira is thus an example par excellence of the package-deal approach to development. Only research was left as an external responsibility, and even it was conducted on site and with very close links with the project.

But perhaps the most interesting feature of the Gezira lies in its relevance to current ideological antagonisms in today's world, and particularly in the principles adopted for a fair distribution of benefit. In the Gezira deliberate plans were made not to adopt the strategy of relying on existing landlords and potential entrepreneurs on the grounds that their initiative and resources would be the quickest generator of an economic growth rate, a strategy often advocated today by Western world advisers. These plans implied no hostility to private enterprise as such but were designed to stop the cornering of benefits by speculators, landowners, and moneylenders and the creation of a rich minority. The project was deliberately geared to improving the standard of living of the mass of the people involved. Equally, however, it eschewed the elimination of all private enterprise in a communist solution. Within a collective framework for providing the necessary inputs as economically as possible and for maximizing profit, the design was for each farmer to retain the value of his individual production. In this respect the Gezira objective was nearer to the Moshav concept in Israel or to the farmers' associations in Taiwan than to the extremes of capitalist or communist ideology. Viae mediae of their nature are today so important to world peace that the achievements, but also the shortcomings, of the Gezira project have an interest beyond the boundaries of the Sudan as a human laboratory study in development principles.

Prevalent Conditions at the Start The area of the Sudan is a million square miles, three-quarters of the size of India. It stretches from the Sahara in the north to equatorial forests in the south. For its size, but not for its natural conditions, it is still very sparsely inhabited. Nature provides only a gradual increase in rainfall from zero in the north to some 1,000 millimeters in the south, determining thereby the human usage of the land. On the edge of the Sahara only camels and goats can find sustinence. Below that, as grass increases, sheep and cattle can roam and man can catch the rain in terraces and plant a grain crop. But the rainfall is seasonal so that a natural pattern of seminomadic society emerged in the northern half of the country, and tribal units led a migratory kind of life according to available grazing and water. Only where the great Nile River flows could more settled villages be established assisted by irrigation from water wheels. In the south immense swamps from the river and its tributaries inundate the land for half the year, confining humanity to separate isolated communities and making this region one of the last in Africa to come in contact with the external world.

Historically the Sudan was conquered by the Khedives of Egypt early in the nineteenth century. The south was largely decimated by the slave trade, and toward the end of the century a rebellion in the north drove out the Egyptians. A disastrous period of local despotic rule followed, and at the very end of the century the Sudan was reconquered by an Anglo-Egyptian army and a condominium established in which the British, as senior partners, set up a paternal type of political administration.

It was in the light of the problems facing this administration that the Gezira project was conceived. There was no hurried drive for economic development such as occupies our modern world. The first objective was to bring peace, stability, and confidence in the integrity of government. But the central problem was how to do this, and particularly how to generate money for doing it, in such an immense country devoid of communications, devoid of any known mineral asset and steeped in abysmal poverty. The total annual revenue of the condominium government in its first year was £35,000. The only natural asset was the Nile, and early in the twentieth century surveys were made which indicated that the most promising means of using this resource lay on the Blue Nile branch. It was found that the Gezira plain had a gentle slope from southeast to northwest, and that if a dam and storage reservoir was constructed near the village of Sennar about 150 miles south of Khartoum large areas of the plain could be commanded by gravity irrigation.

The life of the people of the Gezira was typical of the climatic conditions of the northern Sudan. Along the river in settled villages some were accustomed to irrigating the fringes from water wheels. On the plain, villages increased as rainfall increased, and here they made terraces to catch the short seasonal rain and grow sorghum. In the rest of the year they grazed their animals. In a heavy rain year the Gezira was a granary, but for most years it was a life of extreme frugality. Famine was always a periodic visitor. The people themselves reflected the peaceful influx over some centuries of nomad Arabs who had intermingled with the earlier negroid inhabitants of the Fung kingdom and who had attracted them to the tenets of Islam. Socially, the descendants, divided into different tribal groups, traced their genealogy back to famous tribes in Arabia. Religious "fikkis" were their doctors and schoolteachers. The pace of life was tied to nature. Time was of small importance, and with long periods of leisure men's delight was in stories and in the ceremony of social occasions, and at times in strife. The universal ideal was of hospitality rather than work, which in the hot climate tended to be identified with slavery. History, environment, and religion had put a marked stamp on their character. They were tough, virile, and fatalistic, jealous of honor and indifferent to pain.

To a Western stranger the people and the land conjured up childhood impressions of the Old Testament. Various glimpses of the scene contributed: the importance of flocks, the plain or piebald sheep, the poor man's goat, the rich man's herd of camels; the endless drawing of water for the animals in skin buckets from the wells; the beautiful deportment of women in their dark blue robes carrying pitchers on their heads; the band of neighbors working in rhythmic unison to plant the precarious grain; the threshing with wooden flail and tossing with wooden spade to blow away the chaff; the patriarchal dignity of elders restraining with difficulty the violent local patriotism of the young; the quiet mysticism in people's attitudes, their respect for holy men and current belief in miracles.

It was to this extremely conservative and apparently unmaterialistic society that a new and much more demanding type of agriculture had to be applied when the Gezira project started.

The Objectives of the Development Project with Particular Reference to Agriculture   The conditions described above determined the objectives of the project. In the first place they implied a commitment to a concentration of resources in one primary area and precluded dispersal. The rest of the country would have to wait for its development. Gezira was to be the dynamo. In the second place the main purpose of the project was clear. It was to make money; to pay for the administration and the development of the rest of the country. Certain consequences followed from this purpose. Health, education, and social services came second to and dependent on economic success. More important, the state itself must have a stake in the project. This dependence on economic success affected the agriculture. There must be a cash crop and it must have predominant attention. Merely improving a subsistence crop would not pay for the capital cost, far less provide the economic dividend demanded. To obtain this the cash crop itself must be produced with maximum efficiency. These objectives differentiate the Gezira project from many colonization and settlement schemes of that time which merely provided additional land and left the farmers to use it in their own way, but they are highly relevant to today's conditions when maximum production and income have become much more important.

In the third place came the objective of making the local people the main beneficiaries, with the state, of the project. This purpose originated from the conviction in the minds of those who planned the Gezira that the benefits of the huge irrigation constructions which the British had pioneered in India and Egypt had ended up far too predominantly in the hands of landlords and moneylenders. They had made a few people very rich and left too many of the working farmers poor. The Sudan was an undeveloped country, and there was every risk that, as soon as the intention of developing the Gezira was known, speculators with resources of their own would buy the land and repeat the pattern. This third objective implied that the state required not only a financial but also a directional stake in the project.

A last objective concerned the relationship with foreign capital. It was all very fine to have these definite aims, but how was a country in abysmal poverty to get any money to carry them out? Obviously it must borrow from outside, but on what terms would outsiders risk their money on an unknown project? Would they impede the state's desire to control the destiny of the project and to obtain a substantial share from it? Could an alliance with foreign capital be made to cooperate in the state's objectives without dominating or diverting them? This also is a highly pertinent problem in today's world.

The Methodology of Planning

(N.B. This section covers the subjects of agriculture-industry relationship, the principles of physical planning, the organization of extension, research, and education, and the institutional structure of the development authority, but it does not specifically introduce them under these headings, because rather different headings seemed more appropriate to the way the Gezira project evolved.)

Planners today tend to give the impression that everything can be neatly forecast and fed into a computer so that a feasibility study can evaluate the worthwhileness of investment. Gezira planners did much the same in a less sophisticated manner, but in point of fact the Gezira story suggests that development occurs less in the form of a sectional bookcase than in the progress of a river, where chance brings different tributaries to contribute to the flow and different currents are at different stages rising to the surface. Such a simile neither invalidates the planning method nor alters the fact that very definite objectives were built into the Gezira project. It merely illustrates that development is hazardously dependent on getting the right tributary at the appropriate time.

Rural-Urban Relationships One current which did not affect Gezira planning, and hardly affects it today, was that of agriculture-industry and rural-urban relationships. In such a simple society, development began with agriculture. No nexus of protected industries was or is frantically looking for a wider home market. No swollen metropolis is burdened with the rural poor. The country is lucky for it still has plenty of land and water for irrigation, and the Gezira project, in spite of certain shortcomings, has afforded a pattern for their ordered use. Nevertheless, Gezira planners did face a jigsaw puzzle of problems concerning communications, the cash crop and its market, the crop rotation, the control of land ownership and land use, the administration of the project, and the relationship with foreign capital. The way in which they were approached makes one of the most interesting parts of the Gezira story because of their universality.

Communications The Sudan at the time had a coastline but no seaport. The Gezira is situated 600 miles inland. To send export products down the Nile to Alexandria, a distance of 1,600 miles, would involve impossibly burdensome freight charges. A railway to the coast and a local port was an infrastructure necessity, but to saddle the project from the start with the interest and redemption cost of construction would render its economic feasibility extremely doubtful. The problem was typical of those which make developing countries today clamor for soft loans, and without its solution in similar manner the Gezira project would never have survived. It was solved by a capital loan from the Egyptian treasury, free of interest, and with no fixed redemption data. The loan was repaid 30 years later when the Gezira dynamo had generated ample current to do so.

The Cash Crop and Its Market With the railway problem disposed of, investigation into the appropriate cash crop was the next necessity. In the early years of the twentieth century, long-staple cotton was rapidly increasing the wealth from the new irrigation projects in Egypt. It was natural to consider it for the Sudan, but two uncertainties had to be faced. Could it be grown with appropriate yield and quality in the soil of the Gezira, and was there a market for it? In the latter respect, providentially, a critical tributary to the river of development was available. The British textile industry at that time was disturbed at its narrow dependence on the United States and Egyptian crops and was anxious to encourage new sources of supply. Although Sudan cotton is sold in 26 or more countries in the world today, this basic market demand was invaluable at the start. To allay the former uncertainty it was essential to set up a pilot scheme in the Gezira itself.

Rotations and Pilot Schemes   At this point the objective of making local peasant farmers the main beneficiaries complicated the issue. The traditional needs were a safe food crop and ample fodder for their animals. A suitable rotation had to be found which could include these needs without any deleterious effect on the cash crop. To this end a first pilot pumping station was erected on 600 acres of rented land which was laid out in family farm units of 30 acres each, 10 acres being in cotton, 5 acres in sorghum, 5 acres in fodder, and 10 acres fallow, the fields rotating annually in that order. This size of units was selected as being sufficiently small for an individual farm family to handle without recourse to hired labor except at peak periods, and sufficiently large to ensure the family food needs and in addition a marked rise in income from the cash crop. There was some precedence for this layout from experiments conducted farther north in the Sudan.

The units were offered to local farmers on an annual tenancy, but irrigation of this nature was a novelty and there were at first no takers. Farmers from the experimental area in the north were brought down as demonstrators. The sight of the splendid irrigated crops grown by farmers like themselves compared with their own precarious rain crops, and the money paid for the new cash crop, very quickly altered the attitude of the local inhabitants, and when the pilot area was extended to 2,000 acres, there was a general clamor for tenancies. Local farmers were then interspersed with the original pioneers who helped them to understand the technical methods needed. The success of the first pilot scheme begun in 1910 was followed by a series of further pilot pumping projects on the same pattern, so that by the time the decision was made in 1923 to build the dam on the Blue Nile some 60,000 acres of the plain already had experience of what orderly irrigation could mean.

Some important principles are illustrated in this experience. One is that the productive use of the land was thought out and demonstrated before the dam was constructed. This meant that an immediate return was available to meet the interest and repayment costs of that investment, a state of affairs often neglected when dams are constructed. Another principle was that the local people were gradually conditioned to the visible benefits of innovation, which was critical to their tolerance of the extra work and discipline involved. A third principle was that this practical conditioning, and particularly the farmer to farmer demonstration pattern, was an enormous asset to the extension service far exceeding in value any theoretical advisory education to an illiterate community.

The Control of Land Ownership and Land Use   The pilot schemes had demonstrated a productive method of using the land acceptable to the local people and valuable to the country. But all along there remained the problem of how to reconcile such a pattern with the facts of land ownership in a manner which could both maintain optimum production and attain the social objective of a wide dispersal of benefit and retention of benefit by the actual farmer. To this end a number of steps were taken so that these objectives could be pursued when the whole plain came to be irrigated from the dam. An early step was to exclude external land speculators. A law was passed making all transfers of land invalid unless registered in a government land office which at the same time permitted transfers only between bonafide Gezira farmers. Another early step was a land survey to determine who did own the land and to register their title, the exact location of their holdings, and their total acreage. From the previous reference to a tribal form of society it might be thought that the land, as in many other parts of Africa, was communally owned in a tribal manner. The survey found that this was not the case, and 90 percent of the land was registered in individual private ownership ranging from fractions of an acre up to a maximum of some 3,000 acres. Ten percent was unclaimed and registered as government land. It was obvious that if water was simply supplied to this pattern, neither the economic nor the social objectives would be attained even if ownership was confined to the local community.

This dilemma was resolved by a series of what would be termed today highly socialistic decisions, although the administrators who made them were among the most conservative elements in their own British society! First of all the government announced that it intended to rent all the land required for irrigation in the Gezira for a period of 40 years[1] and that the rent would be at the highest market-rate prevailing under

[1] This period was related to the ultimate repayment date of a capital loan to build the dam.

rain conditions. Land taken up for canalization was to be bought out-right at current capital values. This decision prevented the landowners from cashing in on an increase in land values as a result of development for which the state, and not the landowners, was paying. It also enabled the state to plan the land usage in the manner it thought best for economic results and to determine who were to be the beneficiaries and under what conditions.

The government then announced that the land usage pattern would follow that to which the people had been accustomed on the pilot areas, that is to say it would be divided up into family farm units of 30 acres on a fixed rotation and allocated on a conditional tenancy. These units would be allotted in the first instance to landowners in proportion to their acreage, but no individual landowner would be granted in his own name more units than he could personally cultivate. To the rest of the units to which he was entitled he could nominate his sons, relations, and friends, but once the nomination was made they became tenants of the government and independent of the landowner. As far as possible the siting of the allocated unit would coincide with the siting of the present ownership of land. Any balance of units which remained un-claimed would be distributed to local villagers. The conditions of ten-ancy prohibited fragmentation and stipulated compliance with agricul-tural instructions and with delivery of the cash crop to the manage-ment. They also prohibited mortgage and, to strengthen the inde-pendence of the farmer from moneylenders, a law was passed making invalid the recovery of loans secured on crops produced on a tenancy except those granted by the management. Breach of the conditions of tenancy could lead to termination.

There remained the question of how the government was to recover the cost of its investment and obtain also a substantial dividend. At an early stage in the pilot projects an experimental water rate had been applied. This had turned out to be unsatisfactory. In total it was insuffi-cient to repay capital costs, and yet, while falling too lightly on those with good crops, it had fallen too heavily on those with below average crops, throwing them into debt. A precedent existed for trying an alternative method. On the fringes of the river a customary method of sharecropping distributed six-tenths of the crops to the man who sup-plied the water wheel and the land, and four-tenths to the man who worked the land and grew them. The government decided to apply this formula on the pilot areas. As the provider of the capital element in water and land it claimed the traditional 60 percent, leaving to the tenant 40 percent. The formula was, however, applied only to the cash crop, cotton. The food and fodder crops belonged to the tenant entirely, and for these, as part of the bargain, he got free water. The system had the advantage, important in a poor society, that the weight of the government's share on each tenant was proportionate to the crop he produced. This flexibility gave the government a better revenue, as long as the cash crop was good, and reduced the risk of tenant indebtedness. Like all sharecropping systems it had disadvantages which are described later. It was this formula, the government announced, which would be adopted on the main Gezira when the water flowed from the dam.

It would be reasonable to be surprised that the inhabitants of the Gezira accepted without remonstrance such socialistic proposals involving considerable restriction on freedom of individual choice. It was of course a direct paternal government, but the people were very far from "yes-men" and had already revolted against the government on other counts. Why did they accept them? Partly because the proposals were not radically different from traditional customs. The government had not said it would nationalize the land. The landowner was getting as good a rent as he had ever had. Moreover, he and his family were the main beneficiaries, albeit only as working tenants. But undoubtedly the central reason for acceptance lay in experience of the results and of the system of administration in the pilot areas. This system of administration, it was announced, would be continued in the Gezira scheme proper; in describing it in greater detail, a new tributary—that of foreign capital—comes to be mingled with the mainstream of Gezira development.

Administration and the Relationship with Foreign Capital   It was clear that if foreign loans had to be obtained for developing the Gezira there would have to be evidence that they could be repaid from the successful way in which the cash crop could be produced. There was no intention of tolerating foreign plantation concessions for this purpose as they would conflict with the social objectives of the project. For a time, therefore, it seemed that the government itself, through the Department of Agriculture, must be the administrative agency. Doubts soon developed, however, as to its capacity to perform this function, and certainly as to its efficiency in doing it in the eyes of foreign lenders. Moreover, the government itself and the Gezira beneficiaries were equally interested in maximum production at minimum cost.

To attain this goal the concept of the package deal was essential, but when sober analysis was made of all the ancillary links in the chain of inputs needed on top of just the dam and canalization, the problem appeared formidable. The terraces had to be leveled and the land cleared of trees. The water distribution network to field level, and with it an access road network, had to be laid out and constructed. The actual rotation of water had to be organized and supervised. Pure seed and other inputs had to be obtained, stored, and distributed. Machinery for cultivation and ridging had to be purchased and operated. Loans had to be advanced for each seasonal activity if moneylenders were to be defeated, and accounts for each tenant kept for this purpose and for paying him the subsequent value of his crop. Engineers, accountants, and above all extension service had to be provided, not in the manner of intermittent visiting advisers but as permanent residents, so that a tenant had someone to turn to for his day-to-day problems. Ginning factories for processing at cost had to be constructed and operated, and grading personnel obtained to ensure quality. A light railway was needed to bring the crop to the factories. For all these purposes housing, workshops, stores, and offices had to be built. Finally the crop had to be marketed, and all these costs had to be carried until it was paid for. An embryo Department of Agriculture responsible for the whole country had no resources for such a task; neither did the government. It was clear that a form of administration particular to the Gezira itself was needed, but who could provide it, and who was willing to put up the resources? It was at this point that another tributary was available, providentially, to join the mainstream.

A Sudan Experimental Plantations Syndicate had been formed early in the century by a small band of merchant adventurers from the City of London and from textile interests in Lancashire, in response to the Sudan Government's offer of unused land for development on the main Nile farther north. Among a welter of speculators this syndicate had demonstrated a genuine interest in the country. They had found that the employment of direct plantation methods was unremunerative, and on their concession in the north they had already adopted a farm tenancy system rather similar to that which the government envisaged for the Gezira. It was from this estate that the experienced farmers had been obtained who had launched the first pilot project, and it was to this syndicate that the government turned to find the resources and the management for the remaining pilot projects and ultimately the Gezira scheme itself.

But they turned to it with all the fears of being dominated or swindled that developing countries today experience in their attitude to foreign private enterprise, and the syndicate on its side had similar fears that the government would interfere with business profit objectives and might take away with one hand what they had agreed to concede with the other. After protracted negotiations these fears were allayed by agreement on specific conditions, some of which are of considerable interest. In effect, the syndicate joined the government tenant partnership and accepted its objectives. In return for providing certain needs it became entitled to 20 percent of the cash crop profits, reducing the government share thereby to 40 percent and leaving 40 percent, as before, to the tenant.

The government allayed its fears of private enterprise by enjoining common consultation on matters of significance, by providing a time limit of 25 years to the syndicate's participation, and by clauses permitting earlier termination on previously determined conditions in the event of serious disagreement. In return for this it obtained a partner who took the management and the marketing problems off its hands and had a financial interest in conducting them in a businesslike manner, a partner moreover who could find and would invest his own capital to meet all the ancillary needs. In the agreement the syndicate had to recover the costs of leveling and clearing the land and pay all the running costs for managing the project from its profits in the period.

But for those capital items which had a life beyond 25 years, such as housing, stores, factories, and workshops, a special arrangement was made. For these, annual sinking-fund charges were added to the running costs, and at the end of the period the government was to repay to the syndicate the original capital cost and to take over the sinking funds and the whole installation. These eminently sensible arrangements of an anticipated time limit obviated uncertainties about nationalization and ensured that the syndicate on its departure handed over a going concern without a wrangle. But this was not all. The fact that the government had a businesslike management agreement to start the project weighed heavily with the British government in guaranteeing a loan floated by the Sudan in London to find the much larger amount of capital required to build the dam and the canal system. Subject to these conditions the syndicate on its side obtained guarantees against increases in freight charges and taxation which might nullify its expectation of profit. It also obtained both the duty and the right to manage the project in a businesslike manner without interference.

In this now threefold partnership the government agreed to provide the land and the water and to pay for research. The syndicate agreed to find the finance for the ancillary needs and to manage the project. The tenants did not need to find capital, but through their tenancy contracts they agreed to carry out the crop production at their own expense up to the point of delivery of the cash crop at local collecting centers. From that point onward all costs, that is, of sacks, transport, ginning, storage, insurance, and marketing, were debited to a joint account, and the profit to be distributed among the partners was assessed by deducting these joint account charges from the sales of cotton lint and seed. Each partner had then to deduct his particular costs from the value of his share to arrive at his own net profit. The merit of the system was that no partner could saddle it with prior charges. All partners swam in success or sank in failure. It put a premium on endeavor. But whether the percentage shares were fair in relation to each partner's costs, only time could tell.

The tenants' share of the joint account was credited to a tenants' collective account and then allocated pro rata to each individual according to the weight and grade of the crop he produced. Because of the time lag between the end of a season and the final sale of an annual crop, initial payments of profits were made quickly to tenants on an estimated valuation, followed later by appreciation payments as the crop came to be sold. The principle in the system was to ensure that each tenant got the full value of his product. In this respect it may be contrasted with the fixed-price system adopted by marketing boards in many countries. The Gezira system obviated the temptation to raid the farmers' profits for other purposes, but although it avoided this disincentive, it meant with varying yields and prices a considerable fluctuation in annual family incomes. It is a mute point whether the complete honesty of the system outweighed the social disadvantages which these fluctuations created.

The Gezira was thus an early example of management by special authority, but certain other aspects of the situation and of the methodology of planning call for further comment. First, the project was brought to the people, not the people to the project. No resettlement upheaval was involved. Something was simply added to their existing way of life which could make this much better. Second, the huge size of the Gezira plain meant that the capital costs involved could be spread over a large contiguous productive area. Third, the decision to rent the land meant that consolidated land units could be used from the start as family farms. Fourth, the decision to concentrate on the real immediate needs, a single cash crop and improved grain and fodder crops, brought a simplicity and uniformity which enormously eased the problems of water distribution, land cultivation, extension, and credit. Diversity into more general farming certainly became a need later, but at the start these two characteristics were invaluable.

Against this background the special authority's relationship with other government departments was also simplified, and it could concentrate on the task of business management entrusted to it in its agreement. In irrigation it was the authority which determined the water that was needed, according to crop demands. The uniform cropping pattern enabled the farm units to be laid out in fields of a size, usually 90 acres, appropriate to the required water interval. Each farm unit could have its planned watering period within its field, and by rotating the fields evenly a fairly constant discharge could be maintained in the canals. The discharge could be varied according to the weather and height of the crops by a system of weekly indent days when the authority's management personnel in each locality could specify the number of cubic meters needed in each minor canal. These indents could then be totaled for each major canal and a grand total specified for discharge from the dam. It was the Sudan government's Irrigation Department which had the duty of maintaining the dam and canal system and of supplying the water, but this department had nothing to do with its use. It was the authority's duty to say how much was needed and to arrange the rotation on the land. This demarkation of responsibilities in this critical input enabled discharges of 10 million cubic meters per day to be distributed appropriately over the plain without friction.

In many countries it is the Department of the Interior which is most concerned with the lives of rural people and which might be expected to be suspicious of special authorities. In the Gezira all the administrative system of government continued as before, but the district commissioners did not become development officers. Control of the land registry was their duty, and with it the original allocation of tenancies. Thereafter the progress of a tenant's agricultural life became the duty of the authority, although if a tenancy had to be terminated, appeal lay to the district commissioner to ensure fair play. The administrative service continued to have a watching brief over the effect of the project on the people's lives, and an important consultative liaison was kept between it and the authority by the appointment of a special Gezira Commissioner; but for all business and financial questions the authority's contact was with the Department of Finance.

The Department of Agriculture was always disappointed that it had no part in the management of the country's major development project, but this fact did not impede a very close relationship between the Gezira and research, which was that department's duty. The fact that the research station was located in the center of the project enabled two-way communication. Problems which arose in the field could be quickly referred to research, and experimental work was directly related to practical needs, while technological discoveries could be tested out and demonstrated very rapidly under field, farmer, and market conditions. An annual post-mortem meeting on the season's results cemented this relationship which played a continuously important part in the checkered agricultural history of the project.

A last point for comment concerns extension. Many authorities, and especially those with a Ministry of Agriculture background, believe that extension should be deliberately divorced from credit on the grounds that an adviser should not be a debt collector, and certainly divorced from enforcement of regulations for fear of being regarded as a policeman. Gezira planners held a different view. To them the primary objective was that the farmer should succeed. To this end timely integration of all inputs in sequence was essential like rungs up a ladder, as was similarly timely execution of the right technological methods. To them the analogy in irrigation agriculture was not to the policeman but to productive industry. Moreover, in certain activities like disease control a farmer's indifference could injure all his neighbors as well as himself and the state's investment. There is no doubt that the adoption of this view played a fundamental part in establishing a successful basis for the Gezira project, but it earned a derogatory reputation for regimentation from those who still looked upon agriculture as a way of life rather than a way of livelihood.

With these principles the authority divided the Gezira into a number of estates where a central office and store could be located within donkey-riding distance by any tenant. The estates varied in size as their boundaries coincided with the irrigation canals, but on each a senior extension agent was responsible for the overall management with a varying number of assistants. These men were generalists for all the tenants' agricultural purposes. Resident in the estate and not liable to transfer outside the project, they provided for each tenant a single channel for all advice and service. Many countries are reluctant to pay for an adequate extension service or think it essential to staff it with young men with degrees, who are often themselves reluctant to serve in the rural areas. In the Gezira the field personnel were held to be the key personnel, and, although the private-enterprise authority had to pay for them from its share of the profits, it maintained a ratio of approximately 250 to 300 farm families to each extension agent.

In recruiting these extension agents, who for a long time were expensive expatriates, the authority was more concerned with character and inclinations than with formal examination records. Honesty, energy, a desire to work in the country, an equable temperament, and an ability to get on with the local people were the practical qualities looked for. Experience could be learned on the job, and the pilot schemes doubled up staff for this purpose in anticipation of the project proper. If specialist knowledge was required in agronomy, engineering, or finance, this could be backstopped from headquarters. Marketing was in any case a centralized specialty, as was pure seed production on a seed farm. Extension in the Gezira was not of course a "safe" service like a government department. A man's results could be easily judged. Unsatisfactory men could be quickly dispensed with, and good men rewarded. **The Economic Results and Their Implications on the Social Structure and Relations with the Residents** It will be clear from the preceding paragraph that a principal feature of the Gezira at the start was the progress of the individual farmer through an individual account and a direct personal link with his extension adviser.

The dam at Sennar was finished in 1925, and the first four years of the project were a phenomenal economic success. Good yields and good prices gave the government from its share a substantial surplus over its outgoings, enabled the syndicate to pay 25 percent dividends, and circulated among the tenants over £2.5 million in profits after recovery of loans. The indirect results were equally satisfying. The excellent food and fodder crops averted famine conditions in the surrounding rain lands and attracted vast numbers of humans and livestock to employment and livelihood in the project. The general money in circulation stimulated trade and import while export taxes and freight payments swelled the government's revenues. Compared with the frugal past it looked like El Dorado.

A devastating change then took place. With the world trade depression of the 1930s the price of cotton fell to one-third of its former value, from which position it did not recover until World War II. Coinciding with this for the next five years the cotton crops were ravaged by bacterial and viral diseases, and their yields fell to a third of their earlier level. The syndicate had to forgo its dividends, while to the government the Gezira became a financial burden instead of a support to the rest of the country. The tenants got no profit at all over this period, and the loans, which had to be continued to keep them going, piled up as an unpaid debt. A gradual haul out of this state of affairs as regards yield was attained by stringent and laborious disease control methods and by discovery of resistant varieties, but the low price kept all profits very meager indeed compared with the early years until demand after World War II sent them soaring up again.

By the time the syndicate's 25-year participation ended in 1950, the government had obtained a cumulative surplus of £16 million from the project, the syndicate shareholders had averaged 9 percent in dividends with a capital bonus on repayment, and the average tenancy profit was running at about £200 per annum. On a total capital investment of some £20 million in the Gezira these results demonstrated that the project had finally become a considerable economic success. They were dwarfed in 1951, the year of the Korean war, when a combination of very high yield and very high price produced a sale value of over £50 million for a single season's crop and put many tenants over a £1,000 profit level; alas to fall back steeply the following year to £200 and later to even less.

This extraordinarily varied economic history had a profound effect on local society and on the relationship of the tenants to the management and the government. The respect for patriarchal authority which had preceded the project quickly disappeared in the early years, and there was nothing to take its place. The father was no longer any better off than his sons or the landowner than his erstwhile dependents. In the years of depression, while the management was struggling to avert complete collapse, the tenants were burdened with additional drudgery in disease control on a crop from which they got no profit. Their fatalism and their irrigated grain crop saved them from deserting, but the concept that they were the main beneficiaries developing their family farms changed to that of people getting guaranteed subsistence in return for supervision of the government's crop.

When the economic basis of the project gradually became more safely reestablished, the management and the government began to pay attention to the society they had affected and concluded that certain changes were desirable. One readjustment was that emphasis on the predominance of cotton should be widened to give more attention to the creation of a class of small farmers rather than just cotton growers. Another was that the farmers should take on more of the management of the project by devolution at local level to village councils and to new elected local government councils. A third was that, essential as was the contact between extension personnel and individual tenants, there was a need in addition for a general tenants' representative body for regular consultation with management and government. A fourth was that a part of the partnership profits should be credited to a social development fund to further these objectives and improve the health, education, leisure, and general social amenities.

After 1950 the partnership was continued with a National Board replacing the syndicate as the management authority, but for a number of reasons the objective of changing to a farmer-directed project has been pursued rather slowly. For one thing it became possible to double the size of the irrigated area to nearly two million acres, thanks to a new dam farther up the Blue Nile at Roseires, itself made possible by a new international agreement with Egypt on the division of the Nile waters. This huge new development obviously required continuity of management. For another, the Sudan itself became politically independent and was for a period under a military government. These circumstances reinforced a natural fear that it might be hazardous to the country's finances to make changes in the management of its most important asset. A third reason lies in the fact that the Tenants Union, as its representative body came to be called, has been less concerned with taking on the management, although they now have representation on the management board, than with increasing their share of the proceeds and pushing many of the costs, such as seed, plowing, and harvesting, which used to be their responsibility, onto the joint account. Fertilizer and pest control were already charged there on their introduction. The image of cotton as the government crop rather than their own responsibility has thus been accentuated in tenants' minds.

It may be questioned what case the Tenants Union had to increase their share. Surely they were a privileged class compared with the rest of the country? The tenants themselves claimed that the profit figures in their accounts did not allow sufficiently for the cost of hiring labor. In fact the higher the profits the more the family reverted to the old Arab ideal of hospitality rather than work and the greater competition and the cost of hiring others. Moreover, the tenants claimed that their fortitude during the depression had saved the project and that surely they were entitled to a rising standard of living. The annual variations in tenants' incomes accentuated these feelings. Just when one had got used to a more gentlemanly way of life; when one's wife no longer fetched the water, ground the corn, or did the washing; when one's daughter no longer had to show her face among strangers in the fields; when one could pay for one's sons to have a white-collar education; and when one could get credit at the shop on the strength of the last season's profits, it was particularly galling for the whole family to face a fall in the standard of living and run into debt with a sharp drop in the next season's profits.

The call to exercise more thrift and put in more fieldwork, like a Chinese family, was no more easy to get over on the Gezira than it has been in the Mezzo Giorno in Italy or the settlement schemes in southern Spain when openings for better wages began to arise in the European Economic Community. The need for an equalization reserve to iron out the seasonal fluctuations in income and reduce the price inflation of peak profits was belatedly accepted as an addition to the tenancy contract, but this comes out of a tenants' share which has now been increased to 50 percent. The Gezira Board now has to manage with 10 percent. Of the remainder, 2 percent goes to the Social Development Fund and 2 percent to local government councils, and the government's share is 36 percent.

Meanwhile the additional water available has enabled an intensification of the farming. Wheat, ground nuts, vegetables, and fruit are grown in many holdings with free water in addition to the standard food and fodder crops. Intensive livestock production has been much slower to catch on but the opportunity is there. A temptation has naturally arisen to pay more attention to these crops which belong entirely to the tenant than to the partnership cotton crop, giving the management an increasingly difficult task in its responsibility for the country's share in the income.

In short, the principles of the project are rather at the crossroads. One might take a view that the Gezira tenant still owes it to the country to produce efficiently what is still its vital cash crop, but that pious exhortation would be more effective if all cotton over a certain yield level was deemed to be the tenant's own crop. One might take the view that the family farm concept is now unrealistic and that encouragement of a more capitalistic type of farmer on a bigger unit would be better. A few such units have existed in the Gezira, and one drawback to them is that statistics show that their average yields have been consistently below that of smaller units. Another is that there is still an unsatisfied clamor for any vacant tenancies, for alternative industrial employment has not yet developed.

One might take the view that the system of conditional tenure now deadens initiative and that a tenant would display more interest in farming his holding to the full if he owned it and had a freer choice. Finally one might take the view that it is not the conditional tenure which needs discarding (indeed this measure might be economically dangerous), but the sharecropping partnership itself. Unusual for an irrigation scheme, the Gezira has long ago repaid its original investment cost and for the future the government might obtain its revenue from water rates and taxation. This last view would place the responsibility for farming where it belongs: on the farmer, whether he operates with his family or otherwise. The whole collective organization of inputs, the system of watering, credit, and marketing is there to support him, and this system might be passed over to farmer control. This comes nearest to the successful farmers' associations solution in Japan and Taiwan and the moshav system in Israel.

There is one view that the generality of Sudanese would not support, and that is the breakup of the project and the reversion of land to its original owners. When the matter was debated in Parliament in anticipation of the expiration of the 40-year rental period, protagonists for this solution were laughed out of court. There could scarcely be a greater justification for the forethought of the original planners.

General Conclusions Drawn During the Period of Implementation
The Gezira story might be dismissed as something which was feasible in the colonial age but not applicable today. This would be a short-sighted view, for the project continues in the Sudan today and its general principles have been applied by the Sudanese to other development areas of the country. These principles have also been criticized as savoring too much of paternalism, regimentation, and socialism. In point of fact in most of the developing world today these characteristics are very difficult to avoid. With the poverty and inexperience of the rural areas and the growing population who can find no other field of employment, governments in the future may have to play the father, to insist on the right technical methods for full production, and to consider the dangers of imbalance in the distribution of benefit from development.

For many developing countries, and indeed for the trade and peace of the developed world, there is hardly a more important task than how to improve the standard of living of the rural masses, yet give the individual a worthwhile personal stake. The Gezira story, pluses and minuses, is precisely concerned with this task. Moreover, it is not a case study of some single small community which has responded to the influence of some individual. It is now a large thriving area with a very big population and with effects which radiate through a country's economic and political economy. Even, or possibly especially, countries like Mexico, Colombia, Syria, Pakistan, India, Thailand, and the Philippines, where a dynamic growth rate has been generated by emphasis on private enterprise, might find in the Gezira story some aspects which would help them to correct the imbalance which threatens to be their most formidable political and social danger. At the risk of repetition, therefore, some conclusions of a general nature might be listed here as arising from the Gezira story, when irrigation projects are under consideration:

1. the value of applying IDA type loans not merely to cover a country's balance of payments difficulties but to prevent a burden of prior charges for infrastructure from defeating the feasibility of a desirable project;

2. the importance of establishing a planned system of land usage before dam construction so that immediate production can meet the burden of loan repayments;

3. the value of securing control of land, whether by rental or otherwise, in order to direct the benefits to the actual farmer rather than to the speculator or landowner as such, and in order to plan the layout to maximum advantage;

4. the value of simplicity and uniformity at first in crop planning, and the importance of concentration on significant financial return for effort involved by the farmer, and on stabilizing a food crop;

5. the importance of locating a research station in a project area with close two-way links in the application of research to farmers' problems;

6. the value of controlled tenure to eliminate mortgage and fragmentation and to ensure compliance with technological needs;

7. the value of the timely integration of all inputs in sequence and of the package-deal concept of development, to facilitate the application of modern technology and to help the individual farmer to profit best from his own endeavor within a collective support system;

8. the value of pilot projects to test out the plan of land usage and to educate and accustom farmers and extension staff;

9. the value of farmer-to-farmer education in extension and the importance, over degree-holding, of character, inclination, residence, transport, and high density in extension staff;

10. the value of a special authority and unified management responsible to establish initially the application of the package deal;

11. the importance of transferring the management in an appropriate period to the farmers themselves;

12. the value, if private enterprise partners are desirable initially to provide capital, management, and market contacts, of agreed terms and possibly time limits, to minimize antagonisms;

13. the essential riskiness of development in spite of feasibility studies, and in this respect the virtue of family farming to take the strain of reverses, but also the value of reserve funds to cover debt;

14. the value of equalization reserve funds to minimize the social drawbacks of fluctuating incomes;

15. the short-term advantages but long-term drawbacks in using sharecropping to recover costs and obtain income;

16. the desirability of relating development planning to the circumstances confronting a period or place without any rigid concept of the permanent virtue of any system.

Part Two
Case Studies

32. Agricultural
Development
in Ceylon

Asoka B. Andarawewa

Since 1948, when political independence from Britain was achieved, Ceylon has engaged in planned economic development. Several development plans were drawn up, at different time periods, which specified strategies, magnitudes, and relative growth rates of the several sectors. These plans constitute the finest documents on coordinated programming for development in Asia. Agriculture and the rural sector received their share in the respective plans. In practice, some of the policies and targets were watered down under pressure of special circumstances, and ad hoc decisions replaced the economic logic of the plans.

Individual countries not only require different policies but also respond differently to a similar set of policies because of differences in socioeconomic, cultural, and physical conditions among them. Hence the applicability, if any, of Ceylonese policies to agricultural development in other countries is limited. However, these policies have been applied to agriculture, in some form, for nearly two decades, providing a sufficient period of time to review the efficacy of the Ceylonese approaches to development. Second, these efforts at development have been undertaken within a democratic framework. The use of rates of growth as indices of development often obscures the fundamental social and political goals attached to progress among which is the preservation of institutions for popular participation in making political decisions. In Ceylon, twice during the last two decades, political power was transferred among political parties through popular elections, without any social disruption or strife. For these reasons alone, Ceylon's experiences in development are noteworthy.

In Ceylon, the rural sector is the predominant sector, in terms of population, production, and problems. The main industry of the rural sector, as well as in the total economy, is agriculture. Hence, this paper is confined to a review of the problems of the sector and the strategies adopted for its development. The paper limits its discussions to the postindependence period, as conscious efforts at rural development were undertaken only during this period. In the first section, economic and agricultural conditions at the time Ceylon achieved independence are discussed briefly. Then, the scope of specific strategies is examined, and their effectiveness evaluated. Finally, the broad problems, arising

Asoka B. Andarawewa—Canada. Ph.D., Agricultural Economics, Michigan State University, 1964; economist, Research Division, Economics Branch, Canadian Department of Agriculture, Ottawa.

from the developments of the last two decades, and which will require greater attention in the next decade, are enumerated.

Economic and Agricultural Conditions on Independence

Ceylon covers an area of about 25,000 square miles. It is situated about 7 degrees north of the Equator, to the south of the Indian sub-continent. Physically, the island constitutes a coastal plain rising gradually in the north, and sharply in the west toward the central hills. It is located in the tropical monsoon region, and the incidence of rainfall demarcates the island into a Wet Zone and a Dry Zone. The Wet Zone receives a mean annual rainfall of over 75 inches, which is evenly distributed. In the Dry Zone, the mean annual rainfall ranges between 50 and 75 inches, but is concentrated during a short period [1]. The problems of agriculture in the Dry Zone arise from the intense seasonal drought, and their solution lies in the conservation and judicious use of water. The Dry Zone occupies about three-fourths of the total land area.

Historically, the settlement of Ceylon began in the Dry Zone. The uneven and relatively meager rainfall was utilized for agriculture by a system of lakes (artificial tanks) and connecting feeder channels. The Wet Zone was inaccessible, due to thick forests and hills, and settlement was unattractive. Successive invasions from South India, the consequent neglect of irrigation works, and the onset of diseases resulted in the gradual migration of the population to the Wet Zone.

In the sixteenth century, the Portuguese first arrived on the island. The Portuguese and the Dutch who followed and replaced them, though they controlled the western seaboard, left little or no impact on the economy of the island. The British expelled the Dutch in the late eighteenth century, and occupied the entire island from 1815 to 1948. During this period, Ceylon occupied the conventional status of a colony tied to the industrial economy of the metropolitan country. It provided both raw materials for its industries and a market for its industrial goods, and the socioeconomic, administrative, and political structure underwent fundamental changes.

The economic and social conditions prevalent on independence determined the policies of development and their implementation. These conditions, discussed below, were in part the result of colonial policies. In 1946, on the eve of independence, the population was estimated at 7.1 million persons and was increasing at an average rate of 2.7 percent per year. Incomes were low, with per capita incomes estimated at Rs.

500 in 1949-1951.[1] In 1953, 500,000 persons (about 25 percent of the work force) were estimated to be unemployed [11]. The rural sector was the largest, in 1953 having 85 percent of the total population. Rural incomes were estimated in 1950-51 at Rs. 97 per family per month [7].

Agriculture was the predominant industry in the economy, as well as in the rural sector. It consisted of two subsectors, the export-oriented plantation sector, and the traditional agricultural sector. The plantation industries were one of the most important changes introduced by the British. They introduced coffee as early as 1840, later replacing coffee with tea, and introduced rubber and organized large-scale cultivation of coconut, which up to then had been a smallholder crop [17].

Along with the development of the plantations, complementary institutions were established to facilitate the production and marketing of the products of the plantation sector. Among these were the construction of roads and railways, the growth of a banking and credit system and commercial houses, and the establishment of well-organized research stations for each of the three crops. Open immigration policies and favorable land legislation provided cheap labor and land at nominal prices.

The plantation sector contributed about 36 percent of the National Income in 1953. Tea, rubber, and coconut accounted for 95 percent of total exports in 1948-1952 [11]. Government revenue, public investment programs, and the import of consumption goods depended on the prosperity of the plantation sector. The development of the plantations had little positive effect on the economy of the traditional village, its people, or its agriculture. The legislation favoring plantations had deprived the traditional village of its communal forest, pastures, and catchment areas, and gradually confined it to the narrow river valleys of the Wet Zone. With the increases in population, the pressure on agricultural land in the village became intensified, with a growing class of agricultural families without land and acute fragmentation of agricultural holdings [6, 8].

The production factors, capital and labor, were provided from foreign sources, and the output of the sector was, to a large extent, exported. The plantations were not integrated into the village economy, but constituted an isolated, though dominant, enclave. Although export crops were successfully grown by peasants on a small scale, for example, in

[1]The official rate of exchange of the Ceylon rupee in terms of the U.S. dollar during the period 1949 to 1967 was 21 cents. Since then it has been 17 cents.

Ghana and Brazil, the possibility of such cultivation was not encouraged by either the government or plantation interests in Ceylon.

With a view to easing the pressure on land in the Wet Zone, attempts were made to settle peasants on colonization schemes in the Dry Zone. Settlements were established in the nineteenth century, as well as in the 1930s, when in the face of the economic depression facing export agriculture, the government initiated schemes to increase the production of food crops, mainly rice. These schemes were not successful because of malaria and the inadequacy of facilities. By 1947, only about 3,000 colonists had been settled under these schemes [11].

The production of the traditional agricultural sector was insufficient to meet all domestic food requirements. About one-half of the domestic requirements of rice and most of the vegetables and fruits were produced locally. The production of subsidiary food crops, such as chillies, potatoes, onions, and lentils, and of livestock was small and confined to isolated areas. The growing demand for these food items was met by imports paid for by the exports of the plantation sector.

Although in legislative matters the Ceylonese had been moving gradually toward self-government, in administration as well as in financial control, they had received less power. The chief executive was the colonial governor, who had his representative, the government agent, at the district level. Both these offices were of European origin. The efficiency of a government agent was judged by his ability to maintain peace and collect maximum revenue without making any fundamental changes in the system. It was a colonial administration, not oriented toward any kind of development.

In education, there was a high degree of literacy in the Ceylon village. A network of schools had provided elementary and some secondary education to a large proportion of the population by the early 1930s. The growth of a health service covering the island had reduced mortality rates both among adults and infants. At the end of World War II, malaria had been effectively controlled in the Dry Zone.

Certain features of Ceylon rural communities also need to be noted. In Ceylon, as in India, there exists a social stratification based on the caste system. In actual practice, the system is less rigid, and is made ineffective by the fact that, in general, in any given village, the majority of people belong to one caste. Thus, caste was not a barrier to rural development. Second, in the economic structure of a village, owner-cultivators were predominant and landlords constituted only 2 percent of all families. There were no large paddy holdings; less than 7 percent of owners of paddy lands owned more than twenty acres each [7]. Hence, redistribution of land was not a prerequisite for development of agriculture in the rural section.

Review and Evaluation of Agricultural Development Strategies
The objectives of government agricultural policies were to (a) expand the production of rice and other food items in order to feed an increasing population and reduce the need for food imports; (b) expand the production of plantation crops to maintain foreign exchange earnings; and (c) relieve population pressure on land and reduce unemployment and underemployment in the Wet Zone through colonization in the Dry Zone. The basic objective was to promote conditions conducive to rapid increases in the income and welfare of the mass of the agricultural population [9, 11].

The strategies followed included the vertical development of the plantation industries by replanting and intensive cultivation, by the opening up of the Dry Zone through government-sponsored settlement schemes and measures to raise the productivity and encourage the diversification of peasant agriculture by providing credit agencies, marketing institutions, and other organizations, and by granting incentives so that the mass of agricultural producers would receive a fair return for their endeavors.

Plantation Industries
The government followed a policy of restricting expansion of the acreage under plantations, while encouraging their replanting with selected improved varieties and use of fertilizer and other improved cultural practices, through generous subsidy programs. The response to these schemes was largely determined by the structure of each of the plantation crops.

In terms of increases in physical output, the policies followed in tea and rubber have been successful [10, 16]. As the tea industry, and, to a lesser extent, the rubber industry, is organized in a market-oriented corporate structure with large-scale holdings, there is only a short time-lag between successful research and its acceptance by the industry.[2]

However, grave problems face the plantation industries. In recent years, the slow growth in international demand for these products,

[2]For example, in 1966, 75 percent of tea and 47 percent of the rubber acreage were in holdings of 100 acres or more, respectively.

increased local production, and competition from other sources of supply and from substitutes have depressed export prices. In tea, establishment of international quotas have been frustrated, in part, by the growing tea industry in East Africa. Another problem is that of uneconomic tea and rubber holdings, which are mainly operated by smallholders, and which are located in areas marginally suitable for tea and rubber production. Hitherto, government programs have aimed at rehabilitating these lands by replanting with tea and rubber, and not on their economic use for alternative crops.

The main problem facing the coconut industry is its capacity to meet future domestic requirements. It has been estimated that Ceylon would require about 420,000 tons of oil to meet domestic requirements at the turn of the century. Total production is estimated, at that time, at 400,000 tons of oil [16]. On this basis, the industry has lagged in increasing productivity.

In spite of the large increase in output, the creation of employment opportunities by the plantation sector has been negligible, and this, too, has been supplied from the estate population itself. Through a policy of Ceylonization, the managerial staff has to some extent been replaced by local personnel. The plantations have also faced, especially in the tea and rubber districts, growing demands on their land for expansion of the densely populated villages. The traditional villages require land, not for agricultural purposes, but for living space. These demands have to be reconciled with the maintenance of productivity of the estates. Their pressure depends on the degree to which other programs relieve landlessness and unemployment in the rural districts.

In summary, after two decades of the above policies, the plantations continue to dominate the economy. They contributed 18 percent of National Income and 94 percent of foreign exchange in 1966. Foreign exchange earnings from agricultural exports (Rs. 1,601 million in 1966) are important in relation to the imports of food items (Rs. 956 million). However, in the face of declining markets and export prices, the utility of increased productivity lies in the preservation of Ceylon's competitive position *vis-à-vis* other sources of supply.

The Traditional Agricultural Sector

Policies in the traditional sector were directed at expansion of the area under cultivation, and increasing the productivity in both "new" and "old" agricultural areas. Expansion of the cultivated area was possible only in the Dry Zone. Although it contained about 75 percent of the total land area of Ceylon, in 1946 only 5.6 percent was developed compared to 60 percent in the Wet Zone.

Since independence, the government undertook the development of the Dry Zone in earnest, through construction of irrigation schemes, clearing of the jungle, land development, and the construction of roads, houses, schools and hospitals, and communal wells; and provided colonists with seed paddy and other planting material, and marketing, credit, and advisory services. In all, it has been estimated by Farmer that it cost the government about Rs. 12,000 to settle a colonist in 1951 [2]. These subsidies were reduced later, due to budget limitations.

From the beginning, land in colonization schemes was alienated to individual families. Each family was given an amount of paddy land (lowland) and highland on a perpetual lease within the schemes. Individual colonization schemes varied in size from the Gal Oya Multipurpose Scheme, which had, by 1965, developed over 54,000 acres of new land, to small schemes of about 500 acres in extent. By 1966, about 181,500 acres of paddy land and 105,300 acres of highland had been developed and alienated in major colonization schemes. About 60,000 colonists and their families were settled on these lands [16].

In both the colonization schemes and in the developed areas of the Wet Zone, the government adopted a mix of strategies aimed at increasing the productivity of the land. These strategies include utilization of all developed land, research, extension and education, development of marketing and credit institutions, price supports, and tenancy reform.

Utilization of the Developed Land   In any year, on the average, about 35 percent of the developed paddy land is not cultivated due to lack of water, flooding, salinity, poor drainage, and other factors. In the Wet Zone, two crops of paddy are grown in many areas. In other areas, where flooding and poor drainage limit greater utilization of land, deepening of channels and other minor irrigation schemes are undertaken to regulate the flow of water. In the Dry Zone, paddy land is left idle due to insufficient supply of water during the dry season. Attempts have been made not only to conserve water for this dry season, but also to encourage the cultivation of crops which are less demanding in water.

Research, Extension, and Education   In Ceylon, considerable work has been done in the adaptability of improved rice varieties. Varieties such as H-4, which was bred locally, and IR-8 of the International Rice Research Institute in the Philippines are now being used by farmers. Considerable headway has also been made on research in the use of fertilizer on paddy. To transmit these findings to farmers, the Department of Agriculture has for nearly three decades carried out limited fertilizer experiments in cultivators' fields in selected areas. Since 1963, under the Ceylon Fertilizer Project sponsored by the UN/FAO and the government of Ceylon, farm demonstrations have been carried out extensively throughout the island. These have indicated that under good management and with improved cultural practices, very high yields could be obtained. However, consumption of fertilizer is still far short of the optimum level. Since 1967, the government has been placing emphasis on expanding paddy production through increased subsidies for fertilizer use and a new agricultural credit program administered by cooperatives [10, 11, 13].

Till recently, research on the adoption of tractors and other agricultural implements had been negligible. There was no effective program for testing the suitability of different kinds of tractors and their attachments and other implements for different cultural operations, in different crops, in different areas. Early in 1969, an agricultural tractor and machinery testing station had been established in the Dry Zone.

Extension services provide the link between research organizations and farmers. In Ceylon, the agricultural advisory services were provided by agricultural instructors at a divisional level and by food production overseers at the village level. These officers are so thinly spread that their impact is less than optimal. An extension worker is estimated to serve best a maximum of 250 to 300 farmers [20]. For the 600,000 paddy cultivators in Ceylon, it would require about 2,000 qualified extension workers compared to about 400 in 1967.

Agricultural education was confined to a single School of Agriculture providing a two-year vocational course. Its medium of instruction was English, which was not the language of the farmers in Ceylon. There was no organization for training of farmers. In the late 1950s, practical farm schools were opened up, with instruction in the national languages, but very few trainees from these schools went back to farming. In recent years, some of them have been settled in special projects within the colonization schemes, where it is expected that their high management capability could be combined better with adequate land and capital resources. In-service training of extension officers has been carried out only at irregular intervals. With aid from the FAO, attempts have been made recently to set up regular training schemes for all extension officers.

Input Supply, Credit, and Marketing Traditionally, in Ceylon's villages provision of credit and the marketing of inputs and products were performed by private agencies such as the village trader and the commission agent. The village trader stocked consumption goods and a small amount of agricultural inputs such as fertilizers, small implements, and fencing material. He often supplied the consumption needs of farmers between harvests and was also an important source of rural credit. The commission agent was a city trader with adequate transport and with an outlet for the produce in urban areas. Farmers had a regular agent who advanced cash loans during cultivation periods. As in the case of the village trader, repayment was in the form of produce. Both kept the allegiance of the farmers through their economic dependence, as well as through personal contacts. Debate centered on the returns to the performance of their functions. On the whole, interest rates and price spreads reflected their strong monopsony position in rural markets. It was assumed in policy decisions that farmers were generally exploited by the village traders and other agencies that performed these functions [7, 11]. Moreover, it was evident that the typical village trader had no particular interest in persuading and assisting farmers to modernize agricultural production techniques.

Government programs aimed at the creation of agencies to provide several of the functions performed by traders. The policies for agricultural development required the supply of agricultural inputs on a scale that was considered to be far beyond that of village traders. Fertilizer, improved seed, pesticides, and implements were, in the main, inputs purchased off the farm. The import and distribution of fertilizer in respect of paddy and, to a limited extent, in plantation industries, has been handled by the government throughout the period.

Production of improved varieties of seed paddy was directed by the Department of Agriculture, and has achieved a fair degree of success. The supply of tractors, other implements, and agrichemicals was limited mainly to those received under aid programs. Tractor services provided to farmers by government-run tractor units were insufficient to meet the demand. With the emphasis on food production in recent years, requirements of these inputs are given priority in government import programs.

The lack of security, the uncertainty of agricultural production, and the small scale of individual farmer loans had made rural credit unattractive to private commercial credit institutions. Hence, the government has been using cooperatives to provide credit to the rural sector. Both short-term and medium-term loans are granted for production purposes to farmers, as well as cooperatives. Loans are given to farmers through cooperatives which are responsible for defaults of members [13].

To assure price incentives to farmers, the government guaranteed to purchase, at fixed prices, several commodities. Starting with paddy during the war, price supports have been extended to cover other important food crops, many of which were imported. Vegetables, fruits, several other food products, and rubber produced by smallholders also come under some form of price support. However, private agencies continue to dominate the marketing of all products except paddy [1,14].

In summary, the government introduced several more or less independent programs and created institutions which concentrated on the supply of inputs, provision of credit, and on marketing. However, these functions, which are complementary, were not performed in toto by these institutions. As consumption credit was not provided either in kind or in cash by the cooperative societies, farmers had to turn to the village traders for their immediate consumption needs. When loans from cooperatives were tied to the sale of products to the society at harvest time, farmers sold the cream of the crop to traders and the surplus and low quality produce to public agencies. Public agencies cannot expect farmers to transfer their allegiance to an impersonal institution which fulfills only one or two of the above functions [24].

Tenancy Reforms In Ceylon, a minority of paddy cultivators did not own the land they cultivated. They held land under several forms of tenure, the most common being *Ande* or sharecropping. The landlord's share ranged from 5 to 75 percent of total production and reflected the pressure on land and its monopoly ownership and perpetuated the inequalities in incomes between the landlords and tenants. As the demand for land increased, additional payments and services had to be made by the tenants, who had no security of tenure [23].

The Paddy Lands Acts of 1953 and 1958 were enacted to set up machinery to regulate the shares payable to landlords in each cultivation district, to provide security of tenure, and to organize the development of the paddy industry. The Department of Agrarian Services was set up to implement the legislation. At the enactment of the legislation, a mass of evictions took place, and the department became entangled not only in inquiring into evictions, but also in determining the legality of the act itself. Although cultivation committees cover all the paddy areas of the island, few of them function efficiently. However, the rents payable by tenants have been regulated, providing, in part, an incentive for them to increase production.

Administration   Many observers of the Ceylon scene have come to the obvious conclusion that there is a multiplicity of government departments, agencies, and organizations working in agricultural development at the national, district, and village level. Among government departments directly or indirectly involved in agricultural development are Agriculture, Agrarian Services, Cooperative Development, Marketing, Land Commissioner, Land Development, Rural Development, Irrigation, Public Works, and Education. All these departments have officers at the district and village level, often duplicating each other, but with no real contact or coordination.

At the district level, the vehicle of coordination of the work of these departments was the Kachcheri. The Kachcheri is a relic of the colonial era, and no fundamental changes have been made in the system. Ceylon has tried to program rural development through an administrative machinery totally unsuited to the purpose.

At the village level, the problem of coordination of public officials was not new. A committee reporting on paddy cultivation in 1930, counting among its members the Hon. D. S. Senanayake, the first Prime Minister of Ceylon, referred that they found "a lack of practical coordination between the various offices and bodies interested in agriculture, and this has been responsible for much apathy among cultivators" [5]. With the growth of government administration, in any village or group of villages, there were agricultural instructors, food production observers, cultivation officers, and many other officials, each representing a government department. Although they were expected to work through village level institutions, there was little cooperation in their efforts or coordination of their work.

Although, since independence, local officials have replaced Europeans as government agents and other higher-level officials, there was little in common in the language, culture, or aspirations between most of them and the farmers. Cynics have argued, not without justification, that the mental distance, in the early years of independence, between those who planned and implemented agricultural development at high levels and those for whom the development was planned was greater than that which existed during the colonial days. However, with the spread of education to all sections of the community, and with the establishment of the languages of the majority as national languages, the predominance of the "Brown Sahibs," as they are aptly called, has been greatly reduced in the administration as well as in politics.

Organizations   In Ceylon there were several organizations, voluntary and public, which covered one village or a group of villages. Among these were the statutory village councils, which constituted the smallest unit of local government, the cooperatives, cultivation committees, and rural development societies established to provide specific services, and the totally voluntary organizations such as the Mahila Samiti (women's societies), Shramadana (volunteer self-help), and other charitable and religious societies.

The existence of several voluntary organizations at the village level was considered to reflect not only the dynamism of village society, but also the willingness of rural people to cooperate in rural development [22]. That these organizations had not been harnessed for rural development was in part due to government vacillation and confusion in public policy vis-à-vis the role of specific organizations and partly due to deficiencies in rural organizations themselves. At various stages, some organizations have been favored and others neglected, mainly due to political changes and ministerial rivalries. At times, government interference has limited the voluntariness of organizations and subjected them to paternalistic management by a lower-rung bureaucrat.

At the same time, village-level voluntary organizations were themselves paternalistic. The management of organizations was often confined to a small group of people who constituted the village elite, and who not only did not require the services of the organizations, but also had no interest in the economic and social development of the mass of the villagers. Where the village elite was excluded from the management of these organizations, the rest of the village was unable to provide the required managers. The lack of trained managers has been the main reason for the malfunctioning of cooperatives, cultivation committees, and other organizations.

Present Status of Agriculture The results of the implementation of the above policies have been mixed. Ceylon has achieved significant increases in the production of paddy and several other food crops, and in the plantation crops. Domestic paddy production has increased both from increased yields per acre and from increases in cultivated area. This has resulted in a drastic reduction in the quantities of imported rice [11, 13, 15]. The earlier emphasis on paddy in government programs has been modified, and there have been increases in the production of onions, chillies, and other food crops, though these have yet to be grown extensively by peasants. In some products, such as eggs, potatoes, tobacco, and coffee, local production has replaced imports.

On the other hand, there has been no spectacular take-off in Ceylon's agriculture through a widespread shift in land use toward diversification and the growth of viable farms. That progress in achieving a viable peasant agriculture has been slow in spite of the generous subsidies and favorable cost-price relationships, can, as discussed in the preceding section, be found in weaknesses in the research, extension, and education systems, credit agencies, and the public and private organizations. These agencies, whose main function was to translate modern technical knowledge, a prerequisite for development, into economically attractive packages capable of being "sold" to farmers, were unable to do so, due to inadequate training of managers of organizations and lack of understanding of the process of development by government officials. Public policies were overcommitted toward investments in physical inputs and to remarkably low levels of investment in the crucial human factor. Not only was the training of farmers and all officers at all levels inadequately undertaken, but also the general education system was not in harmony with the manpower needs of development.

However, progress, though slow, has been made. Deficiencies in programs come to light only after they have been implemented for several years. With the total commitment of the national government to agricultural development, programs undergo much closer scrutiny during their formulation and implementation.

In agriculture, innovation, adoption, and growth is a cumulative process. Growth, once initiated, is compounded in the long run. The major problem is the discovery of the constituent elements of the optimal mix of policies and programs that initiate sustained growth. In Ceylon, during the last two decades, experimentation with programs has provided experiences and knowledge about them, their deficiencies, and potential, such that in the next decades sustained growth can be achieved.

Problems of Agricultural Development in Ceylon
Ceylon's problems in rural development in the next decade will relate to specific programs as well as to broad strategies and objectives, and to agriculture and the general economy. Some of these problems are common to most developing economies, while others are specific to the particular conditions in Ceylon. These problems will require reorientation of some existing programs and fundamental changes in others, as well as some completely new programs.

First, the problems posed by an increasing population on development have not received sufficient consideration. It is now an accepted tenet of economic development strategy that conscious population policies are needed so that the gains from development are not nullified through increases in population. In 1966, the population of Ceylon was estimated at 11.5 million. The average annual growth rate during 1950-1960 was 2.4 percent. Although population is projected to grow at an annual rate of 3.1 percent during 1960-1980, present trends indicate that the actual rate would be much lower due to a reduction in fertility. In developed economies, the low fertility rates are associated with increasing incomes and urbanization. In Ceylon, the reduction in fertility has been attributed to decreases in infantile mortality rates, whereby it has become unnecessary to bear a large number of children to have a normal-sized family.

Ceylon has had a few small-scale family planning projects. While no conclusive results are available on their influence, it is important for the government to adopt a conscious population policy related to development and extend family planning to serve the entire island. Related to the problem of population is that of employment. The numbers of unemployed and underemployed have been increasing rapidly. The work force in 1966 was estimated at 3.7 million, with about 100,000 persons entering the work force every year. In 1964, it was estimated that there were 566,000 persons unemployed in Ceylon. The number of registered unemployed (persons registering for employment at Labour Exchanges) was 198,704 in 1965, and 213,684 in 1966. In 1965, only 7,113 persons were placed in employment by the Exchanges [10, 12]. These figures do not represent the magnitude of rural under-employment. In 1959, surveys by the Department of Labour indicated that only about 40 percent of the rural employed had more than 20 full days of work a month; and 65 percent of paddy cultivators have, on the average, less than 15 days' work per month [10].

In addition, the number of educated unemployed has been growing. The education system has been oriented toward the teaching of the arts and humanities as against technical or vocational training. Therefore, the majority of graduates of both high schools and universities do not have the competence to direct, undertake, or manage development. Each year, the universities graduate an estimated 1,000 arts graduates, while the senior (high) schools send out about 10,000 more. Very few find permanent or satisfactory employment. While the majority of both the educated and other unemployed are from rural areas, they tend to migrate to urban areas, creating social as well as political problems.

One of the objectives of economic development was the creation of employment opportunities. However, the growth rates, the magnitude, and the orientation toward capital intensity in manufacturing industries have offered little scope for the generation of sufficient employment in the industries to absorb the growth of the work force.

On the other hand, in agriculture, the creation of employment was considered secondary to that of increasing production. Agricultural policies have largely tended to substitute capital for labor. The potential for using labor intensively in land development, village construction works, in the various improved cultural techniques, and in determining the size of a colonist's allotment was not given sufficient emphasis, especially in the light of the large number of unemployed.

For example, valuable foreign exchange has been allocated for tractor imports for cultural operations in paddy in the Dry Zone, the rationale for such imports being the shortage of labor during critical cultivation periods. No attention was paid to the fact that this apparent shortage was artificial, that it was localized, and that there was no full employment either in the rest of agriculture or in the economy. Colonists have had a practice of getting their labor supply supplemented during peak periods from their "old" villages and still continue to do so. Greater efforts could be made at increasing the mobility of labor between the various areas in Ceylon.

Agricultural development in Ceylon should include the generation of employment. As Myrdal [18] pointed out, it is illusory to believe that a large proportion of the labor force in any developing country will be productively engaged in activities outside agriculture in the next few decades. Potential employment in village cottage industries is limited as the very modernization of these industries will be labor-saving, and urban industrialization will also be confined to light industries which compete with cottage industries. Agricultural development should aim both at intensive labor use and increased agricultural production. These two objectives are mutually compatible. However, in practice, emphasis has been placed on one objective.

The policies for agriculture should aim at maximizing the employment opportunities that can be created within agriculture. During the next decade, such policies should receive emphasis. With regard to the problem of the educated unemployed, while it has to be solved within the context of overall policies to relieve total unemployment, there is an urgent need to reorient the system of education toward technical, scientific, and vocational training. Development requires more and better trained professional people.

Third, the policies for agriculture have often concentrated on setting up targets for increased production. Five-year plans for self-sufficiency, for example, in rice or a seasonal target to increase average yield by a given amount have been initiated. Often, one aspect of increasing production, such as use of fertilizer or plant protection or improved seed has been emphasized above any others. These targets were set up at a national or district level without considering how they could be translated into effective village-level projects. It was assumed, in the earlier years of planning, that once the targets were set up and the public programs introduced, paddy cultivators would respond uniformly, irrespective of their capital, land, and labor endowments, educational levels, managerial capacities, differences in location, and other factors.

Beginning with the early sixties, several strategic factors in rural planning became clear to government planners. It is now being realized that an increase in production or in yield is a joint product of a package of factors which are applied during a production period along with a given set of physical, institutional, and cultural conditions. For example, maximum returns to fertilizer or improved seed are attainable only if a regular supply of water is available. Ruttan has shown that transfer of improved methods in paddy among countries in South and Southeast Asia has been limited by lack of irrigation facilities [19]. Production increases are also the result of individual decisions taken by hundreds of farmers. Planning strategies have to maximize the opportunities for individual farmers to make production decisions consistent with the objectives of development [21].

Fourth, one factor in the diversification of peasant agriculture through cultivation of cash crops and livestock production is the growth of agricultural processing industries either in urban areas or in the rural sector. In Ceylon, policies adopted by the government regarding agricultural processing industries were contrary to the growth of a diversified and efficient commercial agriculture.

Agricultural processing is confined to tea, rubber, and coconut. Tea and rubber are virtually isolated from the production of the rural sector. The composition of the ownership, management, and the labor force of the tea and rubber industry has created this social and economic isolation. The coconut industry has been partly integrated into the village economy. Policies have to be adopted which in the long run would integrate the plantations with the rural sector and utilize their resources in rural development. This integration will also reduce and gradually eliminate the racial friction between the Indian plantation workers and the indigenous rural population, which has been mainly caused by their complete cultural, economic, and social separation.

Further, the main plan for the development of the milk industry, in the public sector, consisted of setting up a condensary and a spray drying plant. The requirements of milk for these plants were to be supplied by farms operated by the Department of Agriculture, and by large-scale producers who were to set up commercial herds. There has been little official enthusiasm to extend the animal husbandry program to the settlements in the Dry Zone, or to farmers in the Wet Zone.

Similarly, sugar cane has been successfully grown by smallholders in many countries, including India. However, in Ceylon, the requirements of raw cane for the State Sugar Factories were met by state-run plantations which were situated mainly in the colonization schemes. No attempts were made to integrate the sugar cane project into the peasant agriculture of the Dry Zone. There is no question that government should have defined objectives regarding agricultural development, and that specific policies should be geared toward the achievement of the objectives at every stage.

Fifth, the colonization schemes constitute the single largest investment in economic development undertaken by the government of Ceylon, during the last two decades. These schemes were a genuine attempt to solve some of the economic problems through agriculture. Experiences in almost every country that has attempted settlement through colonization, have indicated one common attribute—their exorbitant cost. This cost reflects the range of services provided by the government. In Ceylon, the costs were high, as the government undertook the total burden of adjustment and development. However, the success of these schemes, in terms of their net benefits and their ability to generate agricultural development has been questioned.

Few studies have been carried out on the agriculture in these schemes. In 1951, in the early years of settlement, Farmer found that there was no acceptance of improved techniques in the cultivation of paddy, that there was little diversification of farm activities, and that the highland was neglected. [2]. Studies carried out by Fonseka in 1960 and 1966 have indicated that little development has taken place since Farmer's studies [1]. Paddy yields had declined as the initial fertility of the land had diminished, and as no fertilizer was used. The highland was cultivated only during the rainy season and no permanent cropping was carried out. The organizations serving the colonists, the cooperatives and extension services, did not function efficiently. Informal fragmentation of the allotment and sharecropping were present. Pressure of population on land had led to the illegal squatting of settlers on land marked for reserves and wind belts. More and more colonists settled in new schemes were children or dependents of colonists themselves. Finally, the government received no return for its tremendous investment in the schemes. The conditions of the "old" villages in the Wet Zone seem to have been transplanted in the colonization schemes.

There are many reasons to which can be attributed the failure of these schemes to generate large-scale agricultural development. In attempting to relieve population pressure in the Wet Zone, preference was given to landless persons with large families. While the large family provided an adequate labor supply, the selected colonists did not necessarily have agricultural experience. The government compounded this deficiency by not undertaking adequate training prior to settlement. Second, the services provided did not function efficiently, reflecting the inadequacy and mismanagement of the organizations and administration involved in development. Third, the lack of a regular supply of water inhibited any permanent cropping.

The performance of the schemes looks poor when measured against the costs. But there is no doubt that the settlers in the schemes are better off in terms of incomes, housing, etc., than their brethren who remained in the "old" villages, or those who have migrated to urban areas, especially Colombo. They are much less dependent on a social elite, and, most important, they have the potential to develop economically viable farms within these schemes.

At present, the colonization schemes in particular, and the Dry Zone in general are considered to have favorable physical and other conditions, and therefore the greater potential for agricultural development in Ceylon. Measures are being taken to remedy some of the defects that have inhibited the development of these schemes. Among these are the provision of water to the highland through lift irrigation, conservation of water, rationalization of the various agencies that serve the colonists, coordination of their efforts, and training of farmers. A package approach to development has been adopted in a few selected schemes, whereby the required inputs and services are intensively supplied. While this approach is new, it could, if applied extensively, lead to integrated planning with regular feedback from the village through the district to the national level. If an area approach succeeds in increasing agricultural production, it may serve as a first step on long-run regional development with integration of agriculture and industry. However, its success depends on complementary programs that would increase the availability of trained managers and administrators who are the key elements in the package program approach.

Sixth, Ceylon's development efforts have not been evaluated in terms of social costs and benefits and alternatives. The true costs of the programs are difficult to estimate because of subsidies and price supports. As no evaluation has been undertaken of any programs, it is not possible to determine whether the program has achieved its objectives or whether it should be replaced. Programs, once introduced, become institutionalized and outlast their usefulness. While no information is available on the contribution, if any, of each program to increases in production, it is also not possible to predict the outcome of the discontinuation of a program. As the objective of the programs is to increase production, they could be discontinued once the objective is achieved. The cost of subsidies, price supports, and administration would become prohibitive with large increases in production. However, as each program has a welfare orientation in addition to its incentive aspects, the future of programs presents a political dilemma.

Ceylon has adopted, in many cases, flexible programs. The guaranteed prices are reviewed annually, and some programs, such as that for potatoes, have been eliminated after the successful development in that industry. Other programs, such as that for rice, have a strong welfare component. There is a need to differentiate between programs geared toward development and those that provide welfare. These should be applied selectively and not uniformly, providing services only to those who need them.

Finally, one of the fundamental questions of development is who pays for and who benefits from development. Today several countries have achieved remarkable rates of growth in agriculture, so that the Malthusian pessimism of the late fifties and early sixties has now been replaced by the so-called "green revolution" in agriculture [25.] Debate centers on the relative merits of the Mexican or Japanese or Pakistani model of rural development. Specific projects such as Comilla or Tanjore District are quoted as instances of the successful application of the package program approach. Less attention has been paid to the distribution of benefits and costs of such development.

Critics of the Mexican development have questioned the broadness of its base and have argued that the "miracle" in wheat resulted from research findings being quickly picked up and effectively used by a small number of farmers [4]. The tension between laborers and landlords over wages in Tanjore and the civil strife in East Pakistan have also focused attention on the distribution and use of the benefits of agricultural development within agriculture as well as among all sectors.

In terms of agriculture's contribution to overall economic development in Ceylon, there was no program of planned austerity. While the normal tax and excise revenues were collected mainly from the plantation industries and reinvested either in that sector or in other sectors, there was no extra burden placed on them to increase the contribution to economic development. During the last two decades, capital outflow in the form of dividends to plantation owners or remittances by labor to India, were continued until they were stopped by severe foreign exchange imbalances. With the increased production in agriculture, programs will be required, in the future, that will siphon capital into other sectors without destroying incentives to farmers.

Within agriculture, there is no information on the distribution of benefits. Government policies have attempted to replace the private credit and marketing agencies, mainly to ensure the availability of essential inputs to farmers at favorable prices and provide them with attractive returns. There is a danger that development efforts may be concentrated among a few farmers in a limited area. This would result in the commercialization of a few, while the vast majority would remain poor. To ensure that development has the broadest base, it is essential that the total rural community participate in the development process, not only in implementation, but also in decision-making at all levels. Their participation will ensure that farm programs are made, not for farmers by some impersonal government agency, but by farmers; that programs' benefits are fairly distributed and not confined to those who are already well off; and that the rural community has an economic as well as a social stake in rural development.

Acknowledgements

I would like to acknowledge assistance given by Rainer Schickele at every stage in the preparation of this article. I owe thanks also to Christopher Sower and officers in the Department of Information, Ceylon, who provided several essential documents and publications, and to my colleagues who commented on an earlier draft of the article. However, the responsibility for the opinions expressed is solely mine.

References

1. Ceylon Association for the Advancement of Science, *The Development of Agriculture in the Dry Zone.* Proceedings of a Symposium held July 30-31, 1967, Colombo.

2. Farmer, B. H., *Pioneer Peasant Colonization in Ceylon.* New York and London: Oxford University Press, 1957.

3. Food and Agriculture Organization, *Production Year Book 1967,* vol. 21, Rome, 1967.

4. Freebarson, D. K., "Prosperity and Poverty in Mexican Agriculture," *Land Economics,* February 1969.

5. Government of Ceylon, *Reports of District Subcommittees Appointed to Inquire into Paddy Cultivation in Ceylon.* Colombo: Board of Agriculture, 1930.

6._____, *Report of the Survey of Landlessness.* Colombo: Department of Census and Statistics, July 1952.

7._____, *A Final Report of the Economic Survey of Rural Ceylon.* Sessional Paper XI, 1954.

8._____, *Monograph on Paddy Statistics.* Colombo: Department of Census and Statistics, 1956.

9._____, *Ten Year Plan.* National Planning Council, Colombo, 1957.

10._____, *The Short Term Implementation Programme.* Department of National Planning, Colombo, 1962.

11._____, *Six-Year Programme of Investment 1954-55—1959-60.* Planning Secretariat, Colombo, 1965.

12._____, *Budget Speeches.* Minister of Finance, 1965-1967, Ceylon.

13._____, *Agricultural Development Proposals, 1966-70.* Ministry of Agriculture and Food, January 1966.

14._____, *Survey of Vegetable Production in Nuwara Eliya District, 1966,* Colombo: Department of Census and Statistics, 1966.

15._____, *Implementation Programme and Targets, 1969.* Ministry of Agriculture and Food, 1968.

16._____, *Report of the Land Utilization Committee.* Sessional Paper XI, 1968.

17. Jogaratnam, T., "Plantation Agriculture and Economic Development in Ceylon." In *International Explorations of Agricultural Economics,* a tribute to C. K. Elmhirst, Ames: Iowa State University Press, 1964.

18. Myrdal, Gunnar, *Asian Drama, An Inquiry into the Poverty of Nations.* New York: Twentieth Century Fund, 1968.

19. Ruttan, V. W., "Strategy for Increasing Rice Production in Southeast Asia." In W. W. McPherson, ed., *Economic Development of Tropical Agriculture,* Gainesville: University of Florida Press, 1968.

20. Schickele, R., "Strategy of Agricultural Development," *Journal of National Agricultural Society of Ceylon,* 5 (June 1962).

21._____, *Agrarian Revolution and Economic Progress—A Primer for Development.* New York and London: Praeger, 1968.

22. United Nations, *Report of a Rural Development Evaluation Mission in Ceylon.* D. Ghosh, C. Sower, and C. F. Ware, Department of Social and Economic Affairs, New York, 1962.

23. University of Ceylon, *The Disintegrating Village.* Economics Department, 1957.

24. Wharton, C. R., Jr., *Marketing, Merchandising, and Money Lending, A Note on Middleman Monopsony in Malaya,* Reprint, *Malayan Economic Review, VII,* 2 (October 1962).

25._____, "The Green Revolution: Cornucopia or Pandora's Box?" *Foreign Affairs, An American Quarterly Review,* April 1969.

Index